Microsoft® Official Academic Course: Microsoft Office System 2003 Edition

Microsoft Corporation

PUBLISHED BY
Microsoft Press
A Division of Microsoft Corporation
One Microsoft Way
Redmond, Washington 98052-6399

Library of Congress Cataloging-in-Publication Data pending.
    ISBN 0-7356-2097-0

Printed and bound in the United States of America.

4 5 6 7 8 9   QWE   8 7

A CIP catalogue record for this book is available from the British Library.

Microsoft Press books are available through booksellers and distributors worldwide. For further information about international
editions, contact your local Microsoft Corporation office or contact Microsoft Press International directly at fax (425) 936-7329.
Visit our Web site at www.microsoft.com/learning/. Send comments to *mspinput@microsoft.com*.

Active Directory, ActiveSync, AutoSum, Encarta, FrontPage, Hotmail, Microsoft, MSN, Outlook, PhotoDraw, PivotTable,
PowerPoint, SharePoint, Tahoma, Verdana, Visual Basic, Webdings, Windows, the Windows logo, Windows Server,
Windows Server System, and Wingdings are either registered trademarks or trademarks of Microsoft Corporation in the
United States and/or other countries. Other product and company names mentioned herein may be the trademarks of their
respective owners.

The example companies, organizations, products, domain names, e-mail addresses, logos, people, places, and events depicted
herein are fictitious. No association with any real company, organization, product, domain name, e-mail address, logo,
person, place, or event is intended or should be inferred.

This book expresses the author's views and opinions. The information contained in this book is provided without any
express, statutory, or implied warranties. Neither the authors, Microsoft Corporation, nor its resellers or distributors will be
held liable for any damages caused or alleged to be caused either directly or indirectly by this book.

Acquisitions Editor: Linda Engelman
Project Editor: Dick Brown

Body Part No. X10-35363

Contents

Starting Word 4 ■ Exploring the Word Window 6 ■ Using Menus 10 ■ Using Personalized Menus 12 ■ Entering Text 14 ■ Using Click and Type 15 ■ Saving a Document 17 ■ Closing a Document and Quitting Word 20 ■ Getting Help 22 ■ Key Points 25 ■ Quick Quiz 25 ■ On Your Own 26 ■ One Step Further 27

Opening an Existing File 30 ■ Navigating Through a Document 33 ■ Inserting Text in a Document 38 ■ Selecting Text 39 ■ Deleting and Restoring Text in a Document 42 ■ Creating a Folder 45 ■ Saving a File with a Different Name 48 ■ Saving a File in a Different Format 48 ■ Key Points 49 ■ Quick Quiz 50 ■ On Your Own 51 ■ One Step Further 52

Using the Formatting Toolbar to Format Text 54 ■ Applying Character Effects to Text 59 ■ Aligning Text in a Document 60 ■ Rearranging Text Within a Document 63 ■ Applying Styles to Text 75 ■ Creating a Paragraph Border 78 ■ Adding Shading to a Paragraph 81 ■ Previewing a Document 84 ■ Printing a Document 85 ■ Key Points 88 ■ Quick Quiz 88 ■ On Your Own 89 ■ One Step Further 89

Viewing a Document 92 ■ Changing Page Margins 99 ■ Aligning Text Vertically on a Page 103 ■ Formatting a Paragraph 104 ■ Tab Stops 110 ■ Inserting a Page Number 117 ■ Headers and Footers 119 ■ Switching Page Orientation 123 ■ Key Points 126 ■ Quick Quiz 126 ■ On Your Own 128 ■ One Step Further 129

Course Overview

Welcome to the *Microsoft Official Academic Course* series for Microsoft Office System 2003 Edition. This series facilitates classroom learning, enabling you to develop competence and confidence in using Office applications. In completing courses taught with the *Microsoft Official Academic Course* series, you learn to use the software productively and discover how to make the software work for you. This series addresses core-level and expert-level skills in Microsoft Office Word 2003, Microsoft Office Excel 2003, Microsoft Office Access 2003, Microsoft Office PowerPoint 2003, Microsoft Office Outlook 2003, Microsoft FrontPage 2002/2003, and Microsoft Project 2002/2003.

The *Microsoft Official Academic Course* series provides:

- A time-tested, integrated approach to learning.
- Task-based, results-oriented learning strategies.
- Exercises based on realistic business scenarios.
- Complete preparation for Microsoft Office Specialist (MOS) certification.
- Attractive student guides with full-featured lessons.
- Lessons with accurate, logical, and sequential instructions.
- Comprehensive coverage of skills from the basic to the expert level.
- Review of core-level skills provided in expert-level guides.
- A CD-ROM with Microsoft's e-learning tool as well as practice files.

A Task-Based Approach Using Business Scenarios

The *Microsoft Official Academic Course* uses the time-tested approach of learning by doing. By studying with a task-based approach, you learn more than just the features of the software. You learn how to accomplish real-world tasks so that you can immediately increase your productivity using the software application.

The lessons are based on tasks that you might encounter in the everyday work world. This approach allows you to quickly see the relevance of the training beyond just the classroom. The business focus is woven throughout the series, from business examples within procedures, to scenarios chosen for practice files, to examples shown in the e-learning tool.

An Integrated Approach to Training

The *Microsoft Official Academic Course* series distinguishes itself from other series on the market with its consistent delivery and completely integrated approach to learning across print and online training media.

The textbook component of the *Microsoft Official Academic Course* series uses easily digested units of learning so that you can stop and restart lessons easily.

For those who prefer online training, this series includes an e-learning tool, the Microsoft e-Learning Library Version 2 (MELL 2). MELL 2 offers highly interactive online training in a simulated work environment, complete with graphics, sound, video, and animation. Icons in the margin of the textbook direct you to related topics within the e-learning tool so that you can choose to reinforce your learning more visually. MELL 2 also includes an assessment feature that students and teachers can use to gauge preliminary knowledge about the application.

Preparation for Microsoft Office Specialist (MOS) Certification

This series has been certified as approved courseware for the Microsoft Office Specialist certification program. Students who have completed this training are prepared to take the related MOS exam. By passing the exam for a particular Office application, students demonstrate proficiency in that application to their employers or prospective employers. Exams are offered at participating test centers. For more information, see *www.microsoft.com/traincert/mcp/officespecialist/requirements.asp*.

Designed for Optimal Learning

Lessons in the *Microsoft Official Academic Course* series are presented in a logical, easy-to-follow format, helping you find information quickly and learn as efficiently as possible. The colorful and highly visual series design makes it easy for you to see what to read and what to do when practicing new skills.

Lessons break training into easily assimilated sessions. Each lesson is self-contained, and lessons can be completed in sequences other than the one presented in the table of contents. Sample files for the lessons don't depend on completion of other lessons. Sample files within a lesson assume only that you are working sequentially through a complete lesson.

Each book within the *Microsoft Official Academic Course* series features:

- **Lesson objectives.** Objectives clearly state the instructional goals for the lesson so that you understand what skills you will master. Each lesson objective is covered in its own section, and each section or topic in the lesson is covered in a consistent way. Lesson objectives preview the lesson structure, helping you grasp key information and prepare for learning skills.

- **Key terms.** Terms with which you might not be familiar are listed at the beginning of the lesson. When these terms are used later in the lesson, they appear in boldface type and are defined. The Glossary contains all of the key terms and their definitions.

- **Informational text for each topic.** For each objective, the lesson provides easy-to-read, technique-focused information.

- **The Bottom Line.** Each main topic within the lesson has a summary of what makes the topic relevant to you.

- **Hands-on practice.** Numbered steps give detailed, step-by-step instructions to help you learn skills. The steps also show results and screen images to match what you should see on your computer screen. The accompanying CD contains the sample files needed for each lesson.

- **Full-color illustrations.** Illustrated screen images give visual feedback as you work through exercises. The images reinforce key concepts, provide visual clues about the steps, and give you something to check your progress against.

- **MOS icon.** Each section or sidebar that covers a MOS certification objective has a MOS icon in the margin at the beginning of the section. The complete list of MOS objectives and the location in the text where they are covered can be found in the MOS Objectives section of this book.

- **Reader aids.** Helpful hints and alternate ways to accomplish tasks are located throughout the lesson text. Reader aids provide additional related or background information that adds value to the lesson. These also include things to watch out for or things to avoid.

- **Check This Out.** These sidebars contain parenthetical topics or additional information that you might find interesting.

- **Button images in the margin.** When the text instructs you to click a particular button, an image of the button is shown in the margin.

- **Quick Reference.** Each main section contains a condensed version of the steps used in its procedures. This section is helpful if you want only a fast reminder of how to complete a certain task.

- **Quick Check.** These questions and answers provide a chance to review material covered in that section of the lesson.

- **Quick Quiz.** You can use the true/false, multiple choice, or short-answer Quick Quiz questions to test or reinforce your understanding of key topics within each lesson.

- **On Your Own exercises.** These exercises give you another opportunity to practice skills that you learned in the lesson. Completing these exercises helps you to verify whether you understand the lesson and to reinforce your learning.

- **One Step Further exercises.** These exercises give you an opportunity to build upon what you have learned by applying that knowledge in a different way. These might also require researching on the Internet.

- **Index.** Student guides are completely indexed. All glossary terms and application features appear in the index.

- **MELL icons in the margin.** These icons direct you to related topics within the Microsoft e-Learning Library. For more information on MELL, please see the Microsoft e-Learning Library section later in this book.

Lesson Features

Lesson Objectives

Key Terms

Quick Reference

Quick Check

New for 2003

LESSON 1

Getting Started with Word

After completing this lesson, you will be able to:
- ✓ Start Word.
- ✓ Explore the Word window.
- ✓ Use menus.
- ✓ Use personalized menus.
- ✓ Enter text in a document.
- ✓ Insert text by using Click And Type.
- ✓ Save a document.
- ✓ Close a document and quit Word.
- ✓ Get help with Word.

KEY TERMS
- Ask A Question box
- button
- cascading menu
- character
- Close button
- dialog box
- document
- file
- folder
- Formatting toolbar
- icon
- insertion point
- Maximize/Restore Down button
- menu
- menu bar
- minimize
- Minimize button
- mouse pointer
- navigation buttons
- Office Assistant
- ruler
- ScreenTip
- scroll bars
- selection area
- Standard toolbar
- status bar
- taskbar
- task pane
- template
- title bar
- toggle
- toolbar
- window
- word wrap

Not too many years ago, correspondence was created with paper and pencils, pens, or typewriters. Gone are the days, however, of correction fluid, crossed-out words, and wads of crumpled papers scattered around your trash can. Today, most personal and professional correspondence is created using computers. And, in most cases, those computers are running a word-processing program to make the creation of documents easier and more accurate.

Microsoft Office Word 2003 is one such word-processing program. With the help of Microsoft Word, you can quickly and easily create memos, faxes, reports, letters, charts, and newsletters. You can also, among other

---

Lesson 3 Using Templates and Wizards   61

QUICK REFERENCE ▼

Create a template from a template

1. On the File menu, click New to display the New Document task pane.
2. Click On My Computer in the Templates section.
3. Click the desired category tab (or search for the desired template).
4. Double-click the template icon on which you want to base the new template.
5. Update the current template with changes that you want for the new template, and click the Save button.
6. In the File Name box, type the name of the new template.
7. Click the Save As Type down arrow, and click Document Template.
8. Click the Save button.

QUICK CHECK

Q. What does placeholder text do in a template?

A. Placeholder text is text that you will either delete or replace with your own text. It usually indicates what information should replace it.

Using a Wizard

THE BOTTOM LINE

A wizard is a Word tool that automatically creates a document for you after you answer a series of questions. This can save a great deal of time in creating some commonly used document types.

You can automate the creation of a document by using one of Word's many wizards. You can use wizards to create memos, letters, faxes, and many other business documents. The major difference between a wizard and a template is that a wizard walks you through text entry for many parts of a document, whereas a template simply displays placeholder text that you replace on your own. After you create a document by using a wizard, you will still need to replace some placeholder text. However, you'll notice less placeholder text than if you had created the same document by using a template.

You could also use a wizard to create a document that you would like to save as a template. For example, if you often create memos, you could use the memo wizard to enter personal information that never changes in the memos that you create. You could then save that memo as a template and simply fill in the information that varies each time you create a memo.

Create a document using a Wizard

In this exercise, you first create a document using the Memo Wizard, then modify and save the memo created by the wizard.

1. On the File menu, click New.

The New Document task pane appears.

TROUBLESHOOTING

Clicking New Blank Document on the Standard too... same as choosing New on the File menu. It will not... Document task pane.

The Bottom Line

MELL Correlation

MOS Icon

Hands-on Practice

Buttons

---

100   **Lesson 4** Formatting Text

Previewing Documents for Printing

Previewing a Document

THE BOTTOM LINE

As is the case in many situations, it is very important to check your work before sending it. In the case of a document, one of the easiest ways to do this is to look at the document in Print Preview. This allows you to take an overview of the document and to verify that it is going to print the way that you expected. You can then catch any obvious errors, thereby saving time and paper.

To see exactly how your document will look after it is printed, you can use Print Preview. The **Print Preview** window shows you exactly how the lines on the page will appear when they're printed and where page breaks will occur. If you don't like the layout, you can make adjustments before you print. Using Print Preview can help you identify desired formatting changes without wasting paper.

TIP

In Print Layout view, you can show or hide the white space between the pages. Position the pointer between the pages until the Show White Space pointer or Hide White Space pointer appears, and then click the page.

Preview a document before printing

We've made many edits to our brochure, changing the format and style as well as adding borders and shading. We are getting nearer to being ready to print the brochure. But first we must view it in Print Preview to be sure it looks the way we want it to before printing it.

1. On the Standard toolbar, click the Print Preview button.

The Print Preview screen appears with the Contoso brochure displayed.

2. If the ruler isn't visible, click the View Ruler button.

TROUBLESHOOTING

The number of pages displayed in the Print Preview depends upon the last way it was used. You may see more than one page.

3. If necessary, on the Print Preview toolbar, click the Multiple Pages button, and click the second button in the top row to view two pages at a time.

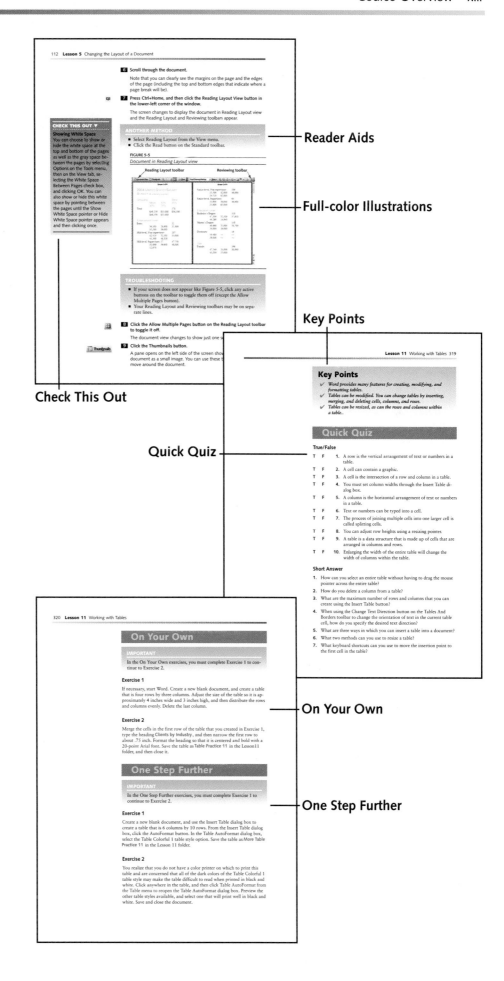

Reader Aids

Full-color Illustrations

Key Points

Check This Out

Quick Quiz

On Your Own

One Step Further

Conventions and Features Used in This Book

This book uses special fonts, symbols, and heading conventions to highlight important information or to call your attention to special steps. For more information about the features available in each lesson, refer to the "Course Overview" section.

Convention	Meaning
2003	This icon in the margin indicates a new or greatly improved feature in this version of the software.
MICROSOFT SPECIALIST OFFICE	This icon indicates that the section where it appears covers a Microsoft Office Specialist (MOS) exam objective. For a complete list of the MOS objectives, see the "MOS Objectives" section.
THE BOTTOM LINE	These paragraphs provide a brief summary of the material to be covered in the section that follows.
◆ Close the file.	Words preceded by a yellow diamond in a black box give instructions for opening, saving, or closing files or programs. They also point out items you should check or actions you should carry out.
QUICK REFERENCE ▼	These provide an "at-a-glance" summary of the steps involved to complete a given task. These differ from procedures because they're generic, not scenario-driven, and they're brief.
QUICK CHECK	This is a quick question and answer that serves to reinforce critical points and provides a chance to review the material covered.
TIP	Reader aids appear in green boxes. *Another Method* provides alternative procedures related to particular tasks, *Tip* provides helpful hints related to particular tasks or topics, and *Troubleshooting* covers common mistakes or areas in which you may have trouble. *Important* highlights warnings or cautions that are critical to performing exercises.

Convention	Meaning
CHECK THIS OUT ▼	These notes in the margin area provide pointers to information elsewhere in the book (or another book) or describe interesting features of the program that are not directly discussed in the current topic or used in the exercise.
💾	When a toolbar button is referenced in the lesson, the button's picture is shown in the margin.
Alt+Tab	A plus sign (+) between two key names means that you must press those keys at the same time. For example, "Press Alt+Tab" means that you hold down the Alt key while you press Tab.
Boldface type	Indicates a key term.
Type **Yes**.	Anything you are supposed to type appears in red bold characters.
▰▶	This icon alongside a paragraph indicates related coverage within the Microsoft e-Learning Library, (MELL)the e-learning tool. Find more information on MELL later in this book.

Using the CD-ROMs

There are two CD-ROMs included with this student guide. One contains the practice files that you'll use as you perform the exercises in the book. You can use the other CD-ROM, described below, to install a 180-day trial edition of Microsoft Office Professional Edition 2003. By using the practice files, you won't waste time creating the samples used in the lessons, and you can concentrate on learning how to use the Microsoft Office 2003 programs covered in this book. With the files and the step-by-step instructions in the lessons, you'll learn by doing, which is an easy and effective way to acquire and remember new skills.

System Requirements

Your computer system must meet the following minimum requirements for you to install the practice files from the CD-ROM and to run Microsoft Office 2003.

IMPORTANT

This course assumes that Office 2003 has already been installed on the PC you are using. Microsoft Office Professional Edition 2003— 180-Day Trial is on the second CD-ROM included with this book. Microsoft Product Support does not support these trial editions.

For information on how to install the trial edition, see "Installing or Uninstalling Microsoft Office Professional Edition 2003—180-Day Trial" later in this part of the book.

- A personal computer running Microsoft Office 2003 on a Pentium 233-megahertz (MHz) or higher processor.
- Microsoft Windows® 2000 with Service Pack 3 (SP3), Windows XP, or later.
- 128 MB of RAM or greater.
- At least 2 MB of available disk space (after installing Microsoft Office).
- A CD-ROM or DVD drive.
- A monitor with Super VGA (800 X 600) or higher resolution with 256 colors.
- A Microsoft mouse, a Microsoft IntelliMouse, or other compatible pointing device.

If You Need to Install or Uninstall the Practice Files

Your instructor might already have installed the practice files before you arrive in class. However, your instructor might ask you to install the practice files on your own at the start of class. Also, if you want to work through any of the exercises in this book on your own at home or at your place of business after class, you will need to first install the practice files.

Install the practice files

1 **Insert the CD-ROM in the CD-ROM drive of your computer.**

A menu screen appears.

IMPORTANT

If the menu screen does not appear, start Windows Explorer. In the left pane, locate the icon for your CD-ROM, and click this icon. In the right pane, double-click the file StartCD.

2 **Click Install Practice Files, and follow the instructions on the screen.**

The recommended options are preselected for you.

3 **After the files have been installed, click Exit.**

A folder called Office Practice has been created on your hard disk with five subfolders: Word Practice, Excel Practice, Outlook Practice, PowerPoint Practice, and Access Practice. The practice files have been placed in these subfolders.

4 **Remove the CD-ROM from the CD-ROM drive.**

Use the following steps when you want to delete the lesson practice files from your hard disk. Your instructor might ask you to perform these steps at the end of class. Also, you should perform these steps if you have worked through the exercises at home or at your place of business and want to work through the exercises again. Deleting the practice files and reinstalling them ensures that all files and folders are in their original condition.

Unistall the practice files from the Windows XP or later operating system

1 **On the Windows taskbar, click the Start button, then click Control Panel.**

2 **If you are in Classic View, double-click the Add Or Remove Programs icon. If you are in Category View, single-click the Add Or Remove Programs link.**

3 **In the Add Or Remove Programs dialog box, scroll down and select Word Core Practice in the list. Click the Change/Remove button.**

4 **Click Yes when the confirmation dialog box appears.**

Uninstall the practice files from the Windows 2000 operating system

1 On the Windows taskbar, click the Start button, point to Settings, and then click Control Panel.

2 Double-click the Add/Remove icon.

3 Click Office Practice in the list, and click the Remove or the Change/Remove button.

4 Click Yes when the confirmation dialog box appears.

Using the Practice Files

Each lesson in this book explains when and how to use any practice files for that lesson. The lessons are built around scenarios that simulate a real work environment, so you can easily apply the skills you learn to your own work. The scenarios in the lessons use the context of the fictitious Contoso, Ltd, a public relations firm, and its client, Adventure Works, a resort located in the mountains of California.

By default, Office programs place the Standard and Formatting toolbars on the same row below the menu bar to save space. To match the lessons and exercises in this book, the Standard and Formatting toolbars should be separated onto two rows before the start of this course. To separate the Standard and Formatting toolbars:

■ Position the mouse pointer over the move handle at the beginning of the Formatting toolbar until it turns into the move pointer (a four-headed arrow), and drag the toolbar down until it appears on its own row.

The following is a list of all files and folders used in the lessons.

File Name	Description
Part 1 Word	
Lesson02 - folder	Folder used in Lesson 2
Brochure 02	File used in Lesson 2
SkillCheck Lesson 02	File used in On Your Own
Lesson03 - folder	Folder used in Lesson 3
Brochure 03	File used in Lesson 3
Invitation 03	File used in On Your Own
Logo 03	File used in Lesson 3
Memorandum 03	File used in Lesson 3
Lesson04 - folder	Folder used in Lesson 4
Salary Survey 04	File used in Lesson 4
Lesson05 - folder	Folder used in Lesson 5
Brochure 05	File used in Lesson 5
Ruffles Article 05	File used in On Your Own

File Name	Description
Lesson06 - folder	Folder used in Lesson 6
AW Revenue_Spring 06	File used in Lesson 6
Balloon	Graphic used in Lesson 6
OrgChart	File used in Lesson 6
Tailspin Toys 06	File used in Lesson 6
Lesson07 - folder	Folder used in Lesson 7
Brochure 07	File used in Lesson 7
Industries Services 07	File used in On Your Own

Part 2 Excel

Lesson01 - folder	Folder used in Lesson 1
Employee Information	File used in Lesson 1
Lesson02 - folder	Folder used in Lesson 2
Five Years Sales02	File used in Lesson 2
Monthly Sales	File used in Lesson 2
Rentals	File used in Lesson 2
Percent Sales Increase	File used in Lesson 2
Lesson03 - folder	Folder used in Lesson 3
AW Guest Supplies	File used in Lesson 3
Lodging Analysis03	File used in Lesson 3
Lesson04 - folder	Folder used in Lesson 4
Sports Income	File used in Lesson 4
Lesson05 - folder	Folder used in Lesson 5
Filter	File used in Lesson 5
Food	File used in Lesson 5
Sports Income05	File used in Lesson 5
Lesson06 - folder	Folder used in Lesson 6
Five Year Sales	File used in Lesson 6
Member Pledges	File used in Lesson 6
Lesson07 - folder	Folder used in Lesson 7
Activity Rentals	File used in Lesson 7
Food07	File used in Lesson 7
Lodging Usage	File used in Lesson 7

Part 3 Outlook

Contact Records - folder	Folder to install before starting
E-mail Messages - folder	Folder to install before starting
Map	Image file used in Lesson 2
Syllabus	Document used in Lesson 2
Eric Lang	Image file used in Lesson 3

Part 4 PowerPoint

Lesson02 - folder	Folder used in Lesson 2
02 PPT Lesson	File used in Lesson 2
Lesson03 - folder	Folder used in Lesson 3
03 PPT Lesson	File used in Lesson 3
Lesson04 - folder	Folder used in Lesson 4
04 Marketing Outline	File used in Lesson 4
04 Holiday Outline	File used in One Step Further

File Name	Description
Lesson05 - folder	Folder used in Lesson 5
05 PPT Lesson	File used in Lesson 5
Lesson06 - folder	Folder used in Lesson 6
06 PPT Lesson	File used in Lesson 6
06 Future Picture	File used in Lesson 6
Lesson03 - folder	Folder used in Lesson 3
07 PPT Lesson	File used in Lesson 7
Ad Sales 07	File used in One Step Further
Holidays 07	File used in One Step Further
Part 5 Access	
Adventure Works 01	File used in Lesson 1
Adventure Works 03	File used in Lesson 3
Adventure Works 04	File used in Lesson 4
ImportPractice	File used in Lessons 3 and 4

Replying to Install Messages

When you work through some lessons, you might see a message indicating that the feature that you are trying to use is not installed. If you see this message, insert the application CD or Microsoft Office CD 1 in your CD-ROM drive, and click Yes to install the feature.

Locating and Opening Files

After you (or your instructor) have installed the practice files, all the files you need for this course will be stored in a folder named Office Practice (with a subfolder for each application) located on your hard disk.

Navigate to the Office Practice folder from within the application and open a file

1 On the Standard toolbar, click the Open button.

2 In the Open dialog box, click the Look In down arrow, and click the icon for your hard disk.

3 Double-click the Office Practice folder.

4 Double-click the practice folder for the part in which you are working.

5 Double-click the file that you want to open.

All the files for the lessons appear within the Office Practice subfolders.

If You Need Help with the Practice Files

Every effort has been made to ensure the accuracy of this book and the contents of the companion disc. If you have comments, questions, or ideas regarding this book or the companion disc, please send them to Microsoft Learning using either of the following methods:

E-mail: moac@microsoft.com

Postal mail: Microsoft Learning

Microsoft Official Academic Course, Editor

One Microsoft Way

Redmond, WA 98052-6399

IMPORTANT

For help using Microsoft Office programs, rather than this book, you can visit support.microsoft.com or call Microsoft Product Support at (425) 635-7070 on weekdays between 5 A.M. and 9 P.M. Pacific Standard Time or on Saturdays and Sundays between 6 A.M. and 3 P.M. Pacific Standard Time. Microsoft Product Support does not provide support for this course. Also, please note that Microsoft Product Support does not support trial editions of Office.

Installing or Uninstalling Microsoft Office Professional Edition 2003—180-Day Trial

An installation CD-ROM for Microsoft Office Professional Edition 2003—180-Day Trial is included with this book. Before you install your trial version, please read this entire section for important information on setting up and uninstalling your trial software.

CAUTION

For the best performance, the default selection during Setup is to uninstall previous versions of Office. There is also an option not to remove previous versions of Office. With all trial software, Microsoft recommends that you have your original CDs available to reinstall if necessary. If you want to return to your previous version of Office, you need to uninstall the trial software. This should be done through the Add or Remove Programs icon in Microsoft Windows Control Panel.

Installation of Microsoft Office Professional Edition 2003—180-Day Trial software will remove your existing version of Microsoft Outlook. However, your contacts, calendar, and other personal information will not be deleted. At the end of the trial, if you choose to upgrade or to reinstall your previous version of Outlook, your personal settings and information will be retained.

Setup Instructions

1 Insert the trial software CD into the CD drive on your computer. The CD will be detected, and the Setup.exe file should automatically begin to run on your computer.

2 When prompted for the Office Product Key, enter the Product Key provided with the software, and then click Next.

3 Enter your name and organization user name, and then click Next.

4 Read the End-User License Agreement, select the I Accept The Terms In The License Agreement check box, and then click Next.

NOTE

Copies of the product License Agreements are also available for review at http://www.microsoft.com/office/eula.

5 Select the install option, verify the installation location or click Browse to change the installation location, and then click Next.

The default setting is Upgrade. You will have the opportunity to specify not to remove previous versions of Office from your computer later in the installation wizard.

6 Verify the program installation preferences, and then click Next.

CAUTION

For best performance, the default selection during setup is to uninstall (remove) previous versions of Office. There is also the option not to remove previous versions of Office. With all trial software, Microsoft recommends that you have your original CDs available to reinstall if necessary.

7 To finish Setup, select the check boxes you want so that you can receive the online updates and downloads or to delete the installation files, then click Finish.

Upgrading Microsoft Office Professional Edition 2003—180-Day Trial Software to the Full Product

You can convert the software into full use without removing or reinstalling software on your computer. When you complete your trial, you can purchase a product license from any Microsoft reseller and enter a valid Product Key when prompted during Setup.

Uninstalling the Trial Software and Returning to Your Previous Office Version

If you want to return to your previous version of Office, you need to uninstall the trial software. This should be done through the Add or Remove Programs icon in Control Panel.

1 Quit any programs that are running, such as Microsoft Word or Outlook.

2 In control Panel, click Add or Remove Programs.

3 Click Microsoft Office Professional Edition 2003, and then click Remove.

NOTE

If you selected the option to remove a previous version of Office during installation of the trial software, you need to reinstall your previous version of Office. If you did not remove your previous version of Office, you can start each of your Office programs either through the Start menu or by opening files for each program, such as Microsoft Word, Microsoft Excel, and Microsoft PowerPoint files. In some cases, you may have to recreate some of your shortcuts and default settings.

MOS Objectives

Part 1 Word

Specialist	Skill	Page
WW03S-1	**Creating Content**	
WW03S-1-1	Insert and edit text, symbols and special characters	14, 38, 162
WW03S-1-2	Insert frequently used and pre-defined text	159
WW03S-1-3	Navigate to specific content	147, 148, 150
WW03S-1-4	Insert, position and size graphics	168, 171, 178, 179, 185
WW03S-1-5	Create and modify diagrams and charts	190, 193, 195, 199
WW03S-1-6	Locate, select and insert supporting information	141
WW03S-2	**Organizing Content**	
WW03S-2-1	Insert and modify tables	
WW03S-2-2	Create bulleted lists, numbered lists and outlines	
WW03S-2-3	Insert and modify hyperlinks	
WW03S-3	**Formatting Content**	
WW03S-3-1	Format text	54, 59, 75
WW03S-3-2	Format paragraphs	60, 75, 78, 81, 104, 107
WW03S-3-3	Apply and format columns	209, 214, 215, 218, 220
WW03S-3-4	Insert and modify content in headers and footers	118, 120, 121
WW03S-4	**Collaborating**	
WW03S-4-1	Circulate documents for review	
WW03S-4-2	Compare and merge document versions	
WW03S-4-3	Insert, view, and edit comments	
WW03S-4-4	Track, accept and reject proposed changes	
WW03S-5	**Formatting and Managing Documents**	
WW03S-5-1	Create new documents using templates	
WW03S-5-2	Review and modify document properties	49
WW03S-5-3	Organize documents using file folders	45
WW03S-5-4	Save documents in appropriate formats for different users	18, 47
WW03S-5-5	Print documents, envelopes and labels	87
WW03S-5-6	Preview documents and Web pages	84
WW03S-5-7	Change and organize document views and windows	92

Part 2 Excel

Part 3 Outlook

Part 4 PowerPoint

Part 5 Access

Standard	Skill	Page
AC03S-1	**Structuring Databases**	
AC03S-1-1	Create Access databases	800
AC03S-1-2	Create and modify tables	804, 810, 815, 824
AC03S-1-3	Define and create field types	841
AC03S-1-4	Modify field properties	841
AC03S-1-5	Create and modify one-to-many relationships	854
AC03S-1-6	Enforce referential integrity	854
AC03S-1-7	Create and modify queries	874, 879, 884, 889, 894
AC03S-1-8	Create forms	
AC03S-1-9	Add and modify form controls and properties	
AC03S-1-10	Create reports	
AC03S-1-11	Add and modify report control properties	
AC03S-1-12	Create a data access page	
AC03S-2	**Entering Data**	
AC03S-2-1	Enter, edit and delete records	818, 824, 827
AC03S-2-2	Find and move among records	787, 792, 849
AC03S-2-3	Import data to Access	862
AC03S-3	**Organizing Data**	
AC03S-3-1	Create and modify calculated fields and aggregate functions	889
AC03S-3-2	Modify form layout	
AC03S-3-3	Modify report layout and page setup	
AC03S-3-4	Format datasheets	834
AC03S-3-5	Sort records	847
AC03S-3-6	Filter records	851
AC03S04	**Managing Databases**	
AC03S-4-1	Identify and modify object dependencies	894
AC03S-4-2	View objects and object data in other views	783
AC03S-4-3	Print database objects and data	822, 898
AC03S-4-4	Export data from Access	839
AC03S-4-5	Back up a database	
AC03S-4-6	Compact and repair databases	

Taking a Microsoft Office Specialist Certification Test

The Microsoft Office Specialist (MOS) program is the only Microsoft-approved certification program designed to measure and validate your skills with the Microsoft Office suite of desktop productivity applications: Microsoft Word, Microsoft Excel, Microsoft PowerPoint, Microsoft Access, and Microsoft Outlook.

By becoming certified, you demonstrate to employers that you have achieved a predictable level of skill in the use of a particular Office application. Employers often require certification either as a condition of employment or as a condition of advancement within the company or other organization. The certification examinations are sponsored by Microsoft but administered through Certiport.

The MOS program typically offers certification exams at the "core" and "expert" levels. For a core-level test, you demonstrate your ability to use an application knowledgeably and without assistance in a day-to-day work environment. For an expert-level test, you demonstrate that you have a thorough knowledge of the application and can effectively apply all or most of the features of the application to solve problems and complete tasks found in business.

Preparing to Take an Exam

Unless you're a very experienced user, you'll need to use a test preparation course to prepare to complete the test correctly and within the time allowed. The *Microsoft Official Academic Course* series is designed to prepare you for either core-level or expert-level knowledge of a particular Microsoft Office application. By the end of this course, you should have a strong knowledge of all exam topics, and with some additional review and practice on your own, you should feel confident in your ability to pass the appropriate exam.

After you decide which exam to take, review the list of objectives for the exam. This list can be found in the "MOS Objectives" section at the front of the appropriate *Microsoft Official Academic Course* student guide. You can also easily identify tasks that are included in the objective list by locating the MOS symbol in the margin of the lessons in this book.

For an expert-level test, you'll need to be able to demonstrate any of the skills from the core-level objective list, too. Expect some of these core-level tasks to appear on the expert-level test.

You can also familiarize yourself with a live MOS certification test by downloading and installing a practice MOS certification test from www.microsoft.com/traincert/mcp/officespecialist/requirements.asp.

To take the MOS test, first see www.microsoft.com/traincert/mcp/ officespecialist/requirements.asp to locate your nearest testing center. Then call the testing center directly to schedule your test. The amount of advance notice you should provide will vary for different testing centers, and it typically depends on the number of computers available at the testing center, the number of other testers who have already been scheduled for the day on which you want to take the test, and the number of times per week that the testing center offers MOS testing. In general, you should call to schedule your test at least two weeks prior to the date on which you want to take the test.

When you arrive at the testing center, you might be asked for proof of identity. A driver's license or passport is an acceptable form of identification. If you do not have either of these items of documentation, call your testing center and ask what alternative forms of identification will be accepted. If you are retaking a test, bring your MOS identification number, which will have been given to you when you previously took the test. If you have not prepaid or if your organization has not already arranged to make payment for you, you will need to pay the test-taking fee when you arrive. The current test-taking fee is $75 (U.S.). Prices are subject to change and may vary depending on the testing center.

Test Format

All MOS certification tests are live, performance-based tests. There are no multiple-choice, true/false, or short-answer questions. Instructions are general: you are told the basic tasks to perform on the computer, but you aren't given any help in figuring out how to perform them. You are not permitted to use reference material other than the application's Help system.

As you complete the tasks stated in a particular test question, the testing software monitors your actions. An example question might be:

> Open the file named AW Guests and select the word Welcome in the first paragraph. Change the font to 12 point, and apply bold formatting. Select the words at your convenience in the second paragraph, move them to the end of the first paragraph using drag and drop, and then center the first paragraph.

The sample tests available from www.microsoft.com/traincert/mcp/ officespecialist/requirements.asp give you a clear idea of the type of questions that you will be asked on the actual test.

When the test administrator seats you at a computer, you'll see an online form that you use to enter information about yourself (name, address, and other information required to process your exam results). While you complete the form, the software will generate the test from a master test bank and then prompt you to continue. The first test question will appear in a window. Read the question carefully, and then perform all the tasks stated in the test question. When you have finished completing all tasks for a question, click the Next Question button.

You have 45 to 60 minutes to complete all questions, depending on the test that you are taking. The testing software assesses your results as soon as you complete the test, and the test administrator can print the results of the test so that you will have a record of any tasks that you performed incorrectly. A passing grade is 75 percent or higher. If you pass, you will receive a certificate in the mail within two to four weeks. If you do not pass, you can study and practice the skills that you missed and then schedule to retake the test at a later date.

Tips for Successfully Completing the Test

The following tips and suggestions are the result of feedback received from many individuals who have taken one or more MOS tests:

- Make sure that you are thoroughly prepared. If you have extensively used the application for which you are being tested, you might feel confident that you are prepared for the test. However, the test might include questions that involve tasks that you rarely or never perform when you use the application at your place of business, at school, or at home. You must be knowledgeable in all the MOS objectives for the test that you will take.

- Read each exam question carefully. An exam question might include several tasks that you are to perform. A partially correct response to a test question is counted as an incorrect response. In the example question on the previous page, you might apply bold formatting and move the words at your convenience to the correct location, but forget to center the first paragraph. This would count as an incorrect response and would result in a lower test score.

- You are allowed to use the application's Help system, but relying on the Help system too much will slow you down and possibly prevent you from completing the test within the allotted time. Use the Help system only when necessary.

- Keep track of your time. The test does not display the amount of time that you have left, so you need to keep track of the time yourself by monitoring your start time and the required end time on your watch or a clock in the testing center (if there is one). The test program displays the number of items that you have completed along with the total number of test items (for example, "35 of 40 items have been completed"). Use this information to gauge your pace.

- If you skip a question, you cannot return to it later. You should skip a question only if you are certain that you cannot complete the tasks correctly.

- Don't worry if the testing software crashes while you are taking the exam. The test software is set up to handle this situation. Find your test administrator and tell him or her what happened. The administrator will work through the steps required to restart the test. When the test restarts, it will allow you to continue where you left off. You will have the same amount of time remaining to complete the test as you did when the software crashed.

- As soon as you are finished reading a question and you click in the application window, a condensed version of the instruction is displayed in a corner of the screen. If you are unsure whether you have completed all tasks stated in the test question, click the Instructions button on the test information bar at the bottom of the screen and then reread the question. Close the instruction window when you are finished. Do this as often as necessary to ensure you have read the question correctly and that you have completed all the tasks stated in the question.

If You Do Not Pass the Test

If you do not pass, you can use the assessment printout as a guide to practice the items that you missed. There is no limit to the number of times that you can retake a test; however, you must pay the fee each time that you take the test. When you retake the test, expect to see some of the same test items on the subsequent test; the test software randomly generates the test items from a master test bank before you begin the test. Also expect to see several questions that did not appear on the previous test.

Microsoft e-Learning Library

Microsoft Learning is pleased to offer, in combination with our new *Microsoft Official Academic Course* for *Microsoft Office System 2003 Edition*, in-depth access to our powerful e-Learning tool, the Microsoft® e-Learning Library Version 2 (MELL 2) Desktop Edition for Office System 2003. The MELL Version 2 Desktop Edition for Office System 2003 will help instructors and students alike increase their skill and comfort level with Microsoft software and technologies—as well as help students develop the skills they need to succeed in today's competitive job market.

MELL Features

The MELL Version 2 Desktop Edition for Office System 2003 product included with this *Microsoft Official Academic Course* features:

- Fully customizable learning environments that help instructors pre-assess student's skill levels and direct them to the tasks that are appropriate to their needs.
- High-quality, browser-based training and reinforcement that offers students a familiar environment in which to acquire new skills.
- A powerful search tool that quickly scans a full library of learning materials and provides snappy answers to specific questions.
- Interactive exercises and focused lessons on specific subjects to help instructors direct their students quickly to exactly the content they need to know.
- Reliable, in-depth content, engaging simulations, automated support tools, and memorable on-screen demonstrations.
- An after hours and after class reference and reinforcement tool that students can take with them and use in their working lives.

Additionally, MELL Version 2 Desktop Edition for Office System 2003 fits easily into an existing lab and includes:

- Training solutions that are compatible with all existing software and hardware infrastructures.
- An enhanced learning environment that works without a separate learning management system (LMS) and runs in any SCORM-compliant LMS.
- The ability to send and receive shortcut links via e-mail to relevant help topics, which facilitates the learning experience in a classroom setting and encourages peer-to-peer learning.

Instructors who are preparing students for the MCSE/MCSA or MCAD credential can also use MELL 2 IT Professional Edition and MELL 2 Developer Edition to help students develop the skills they need to succeed in today's competitive job market. Both editions provide outstanding training and reference materials designed to help users achieve professional certification while learning real-world skills. Check out www.microsoft.com/mspress/business for more information on these additional MELL products.

Focused Students, Mastering Tasks

The MELL Version 2 Desktop Edition for Office System 2003 helps focus students on the tasks they need to know and helps them master those tasks through a combination of the following:

- Assessments that help determine the lessons that will require focus in the classroom or lab.
- Realistic simulations that mirror the actual software without requiring that it already be installed—making it ideal for students who may not have access to the latest Microsoft products outside of the classroom and labs.
- Within the simulation, the ability for a student to follow each step on his or her own, have the computer perform the step, or any combination of the two.

The MELL Version 2 Desktop Edition for Office System 2003 provides deep premium content that allows and encourages students to go beyond basic tasks and achieve proficiency and effectiveness—in class and eventually in the workplace. This depth is reflected in the fact that our desktop training titles are certified by the Microsoft Office Specialist Program.

The MELL Assessment Feature

MELL Version 2 Desktop Edition for Office System 2003 includes a skill assessment designed to help instructors identify topics and features that might warrant coverage during lecture or lab meetings. The skill assessment gives instructors an opportunity to see how much students already know about the topics covered in this course, which in turn allows instructors to devote meeting time to topics with which students are unfamiliar.

To use the assessment feature, follow these steps (note that the illustrations are specific to the Excel Core course, but the steps apply to all of the courses):

1 Insert the Microsoft Official Academic Course companion CD that accompanies this textbook into your CD drive.

2 From the menu, select "View e-Learning Course."

3 Click on the training course you are interested in via the left navigation pane.

4 Click on "Pre-Assessment" within any core training topic on the accompanying MELL Version 2 Desktop Edition for Office System 2003.

5 Click on "Take the Pre-Assessment."

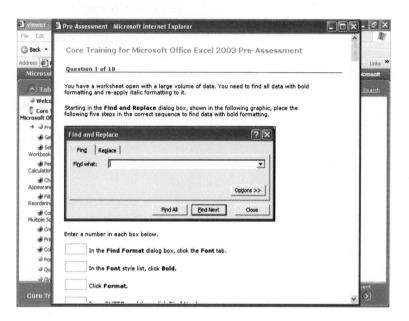

6 Input some correct answers and, if you choose, some incorrect answers as you move through the Pre-Assessment.

7 Click on "Show My Score" at the bottom of the Skills Assessment.

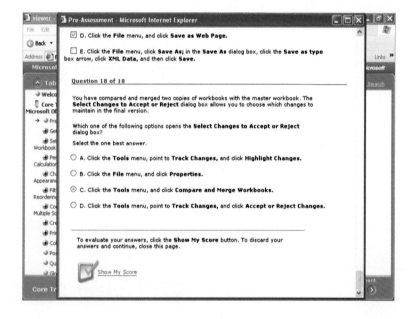

8 The "Show My Score" box details all the correct and incorrect answers and also provides correct answers for all the incorrect responses.

9 Additionally, the resultant table also provides a basic learning plan, directing you to areas you need to master while acknowledging the skills you already possess.

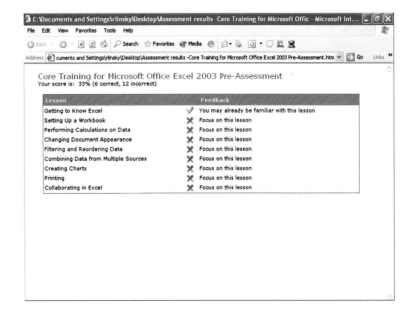

10 Click on either the "Print" or "Save" button to print or save to disk your Pre-Assessment results for future reference.

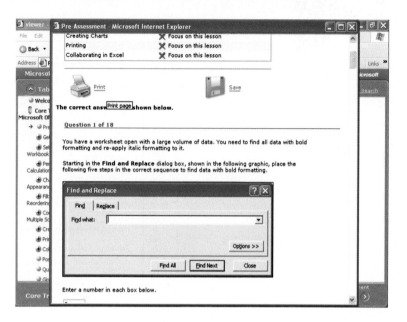

11 You are now ready to begin your interactive learning experience with MELL Version 2 Desktop Edition for Office System 2003!

Microsoft Word

LESSON

1

Getting Started with Word

After completing this lesson, you will be able to:

✔ *Start Word.*
✔ *Explore the Word window.*
✔ *Use menus.*
✔ *Use personalized menus.*
✔ *Enter text in a document.*
✔ *Insert text by using Click And Type.*
✔ *Save a document.*
✔ *Close a document and quit Word.*
✔ *Get help with Word.*

KEY TERMS

- Ask A Question box
- button
- cascading menu
- character
- Close button
- dialog box
- document
- file
- folder
- Formatting toolbar
- icon
- insertion point
- Maximize/Restore Down button
- menu
- menu bar
- minimize
- Minimize button
- mouse pointer
- navigation buttons
- Office Assistant
- ruler
- ScreenTip
- scroll bars
- selection area
- Standard toolbar
- status bar
- taskbar
- task pane
- template
- title bar
- toggle
- toolbar
- window
- word wrap

Not too many years ago, correspondence was created with paper and pencils, pens, or typewriters. Gone are the days, however, of correction fluid, crossed-out words, and wads of crumpled papers scattered around your trash can. Today, most personal and professional correspondence is created using computers. And, in most cases, those computers are running a word-processing program to make the creation of documents easier and more accurate.

Microsoft Office Word 2003 is one such word-processing program. With the help of Microsoft Word, you can quickly and easily create memos, faxes, reports, letters, charts, and newsletters. You can also, among other things, add graphics to documents and use other Microsoft Office programs to import data into a Word document. Not only is Word a convenient time-saver, but Word also allows you to check spelling, edit documents, and preview your work before printing. Reports, letters, and other documents do not have to be completely retyped just because of an error or two. Word allows you to edit quickly and leaves you with a very clean, professional-looking document (and saves you from emptying your trash can so often).

In this lesson, you will learn how to start and quit Word and how to identify the various components in the Word window, such as the menu bar and toolbars. You'll use menus to perform various actions, you'll explore the task pane, you'll practice entering text into a document, and then you'll save a document. You'll also practice using the Ask a Question and Office Assistant features of Help.

Starting Word

THE BOTTOM LINE

Learn how to open Microsoft Office Word 2003. Once it is open, you can begin using the word-processing program to create documents.

When you start Word, the program appears in its own window with a new, blank document open. A **window** is an area of the screen that displays a program or document. Every window has common components, including scroll bars and toolbars.

A **toolbar** is a group of buttons used to carry out commands. For example, the Drawing toolbar contains buttons that you can use to draw and format pictures. A **button** contains a word, a phrase, or an icon. An **icon** is a small picture that appears on the screen and represents a program or document. You'll learn more about the components of the Word window later in this lesson.

Working with Document Windows

A **document** is a self-contained piece of work created by using a program. The Word window and each open document are displayed in separate windows. You can use Word to open multiple documents (and, therefore, multiple document windows) at a time, you can resize a document window, and you can also minimize a document window. When you **minimize** a document window, the document window is reduced to a button on the Windows taskbar. The **taskbar** is the strip along the bottom or side of the screen. You use the mouse pointer to open applications on the taskbar. When a document is listed on the taskbar, it is still open; you just can't see it.

Use the Start button to open Word

Before you can begin to make use of the full features of the word-processing application, you must first get it running on your computer.

1 **Click the Start button at the left end of the Windows taskbar, which is typically located along the bottom of the screen. (You may also find it at the top or along one of the sides of the screen.)**

The Start menu appears.

2 **On the Start menu, point to All Programs.**

The All Programs submenu appears.

3 **On the All Programs submenu, point to Microsoft Office, and then click Microsoft Office Word 2003.**

Word 2003 starts with a new blank document open.

FIGURE 1-1

Word 2003 new blank document screen

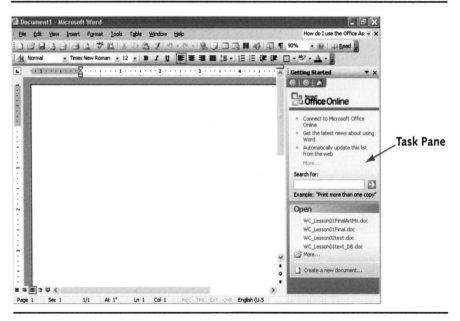

◆ **Keep this file open for the next exercise.**

ANOTHER METHOD

You can save time by opening Word from a desktop shortcut. To create a desktop shortcut, click the Start button, point to All Programs, point to Microsoft Office Word 2003, and right-click. Point to Send To and then click Desktop (Create Shortcut). A desktop shortcut is represented by an icon with a curved arrow in the left corner. Double-click the Word shortcut icon to open Word 2003.

You can start Word by double-clicking a document that was created as a Word document.

You can start Word by right-clicking a file, pointing to Open With on the pop-up menu, and then choosing Word in the list of applications that appears.

QUICK CHECK

Q. What is the name of the button you click to find programs installed on your computer?

A. Clicking the Start button enables you to find all of the programs installed on your computer.

QUICK REFERENCE ▼

Start Microsoft Office Word 2003

1 Click the Start button on the Windows taskbar.

2 On the Start menu, point to All Programs.

3 On the Programs submenu, point to Microsoft Office.

4 Click Microsoft Office Word 2003.

Exploring the Word Window

THE BOTTOM LINE

The Word window contains graphical components to help you use the application, including menus, toolbars, and buttons. Becoming familiar with the components in the Word window will save you time when you begin creating and editing documents.

Many components in the Word window are similar to those in other Windows programs. The following illustration displays the elements in the Word window, and a description of each element follows the figure.

FIGURE 1-2

Elements of the Word window

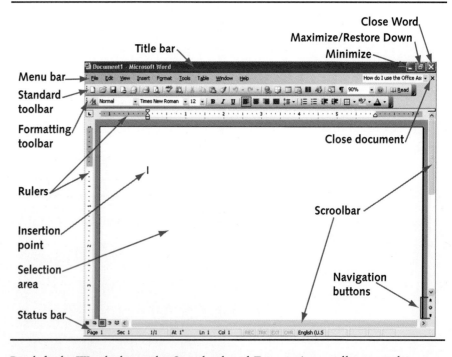

By default, Word places the Standard and Formatting toolbars on the same row below the menu bar to save window space. In the illustration above, the Standard and Formatting toolbars are separated for clarity. When the Standard and Formatting toolbars share one row, you can't see all the buttons, but you can access other buttons by clicking the Toolbar Options down arrow at the end of the toolbar. Choose Add Or Remove Buttons to see the list of available buttons.

ANOTHER METHOD

You can use the mouse to position the Standard and Formatting toolbars on two separate rows. Position the mouse pointer over the move handle (dotted vertical line) at the left end of the Formatting toolbar until it turns into the move pointer (a four-headed arrow). Drag the toolbar down a bit until it appears on its own row.

Element	Description
Title bar	The area of a window or dialog box that displays the name of the current dialog box or application and the name of the current document. It is located along the top of the window.
Menu bar	The area that lists the names of the menus available in Word. A **menu** is a collection of related commands from which you can make a selection. The menu bar is located just below the title bar.
Standard toolbar	A toolbar that provides quick access to the editing functions you use frequently. For example, on the Standard toolbar, the button that you use to save a document contains an icon of a floppy disk. The Standard toolbar is located just below the menu bar.

TIP

A button contains a word, a phrase, or an icon. An icon is a small picture that appears on the screen and represents a program or a document.

Formatting toolbar	A toolbar that provides quick access to the formatting functions that you use frequently. The names of buttons are displayed in **ScreenTips** when you position the **mouse pointer** over the buttons.
Insertion point	A blinking vertical line in the document window that indicates where the next **character** (any single letter, number, space, tab, page break, paragraph mark, or symbol that can be entered in a document) will appear.
Selection area	The area between the left edge of the window and the left edge of a line of text. You position the mouse pointer in the selection area to select an entire line of text. The pointer changes to a right-pointing arrow when it is positioned in the selection area.
Ruler	An on-screen scale marked with inches or other units of measure that can be used to change the indentation of paragraphs, reset a page margin (an area of blank space between the edge of the paper and the text), and adjust the width of columns. The rulers are located below the toolbars and along the left side of the window.
Scroll bars	Bars that are used for moving the view of the document. The vertical scroll bar is located along the right side of the window, and the horizontal scroll bar is located along the lower portion of the window, just above the status bar.

	Navigation buttons	Buttons that are used for moving the view in a long document. These buttons are located on the vertical scroll bar.
	Status bar	A bar that displays information about currently selected text at the bottom edge of the program window.
⊟	Minimize button	A button that reduces a window to a button on the Windows taskbar. It shows a horizontal line and is located in the group of three buttons at the upper-right corner of the window.
⧉	Maximize/Restore Down button	A button that switches back and forth, or **toggles** (alternately turns an option on or off each time it is selected), between displaying a window in its maximum size and restoring a window to its previous size. It is located in the group of three buttons at the upper-right corner of the window.
⊠	Close button	A button that closes the current window or application. It is located in the group of three buttons at the upper-right corner of the window.
	ScreenTip	A Help item that shows the name of a toolbar button or screen element when you rest the mouse pointer on the button or element.
	Task pane	Word organizes commands for common tasks in the task pane, a small window next to your document that opens when you need it. For example, when you start Word, you see the Getting Started task pane. You can use the Getting Started task pane to open a saved or blank document, to create a document based on an existing one, or to create a document from a **template** (a file containing structure and style settings that help you create a specific type of document, such as a memo or resume).

TIP

The Getting Started task pane opens each time you start Word and closes when you open a document. If you do not want the task pane to appear each time you start Word, click Options on the Tools menu, click the View tab, click the Startup Task Pane check box to clear it, and click OK

	Ask a Question box	A text box on the right end of the menu bar in which you can type a word, phrase, or question. This text is then used to search Word's Help topics for information. (For more information about the Ask a Question box and about the Office Assistant, read the section "Getting Help" later in this lesson.

Display ScreenTips

So far we have opened Word, looked at the window, and identified some of the components of that window. Now we are going to explore that window a little further by using the mouse to help identify a button's purpose.

1 **Position the mouse pointer over the New Blank Document button on the Standard toolbar for a few seconds, but don't click.**

A small yellow ScreenTip appears, displaying the words *New Blank Document*.

FIGURE 1-3

New Blank Document ScreenTip

2 **Position the mouse pointer over the Save button on the Standard toolbar.**

A small yellow ScreenTip appears, displaying the word *Save*.

FIGURE 1-4

Save ScreenTip

3 **Position the mouse pointer on the lower portion of the vertical scroll bar, over the Previous Page button.**

A ScreenTip appears, displaying the words *Previous Page*.

FIGURE 1-5

Previous Page ScreenTip

OVR   **4** **On the status bar, position the mouse pointer over the Overtype button.**

A small ScreenTip is shown, displaying the word *Overtype*.

FIGURE 1-6

Overtype ScreenTip

TIP

In Overtype mode, existing text is deleted and replaced by the text you type. You can learn more about the Overtype button in Lesson 2, "Editing a Document."

◆ **Keep this file open for the next exercise.**

QUICK REFERENCE ▼

Display a ScreenTip

Position the mouse pointer over a button or a screen element for a few seconds.

Using Menus

THE BOTTOM LINE

Menus display commands that you can click to perform an action in the active window or object. You can easily find most of the tools and commands that you need on the Word menus and on the Standard and Formatting toolbars..

When you display the menu, you see various commands. To display a menu, on the menu bar, click the name of the menu. Then click a command displayed on the menu to perform that command. On some menus, you might find that certain selections appear in a light, almost unreadable shade. The lighter shade indicates that those commands are not applicable to the current operation and, therefore, are not available at the time. Those same selections will be displayed in a normal shade as soon as they become relevant to the operation being performed.

When you first display a menu, you will see the commands that are most frequently used by Word users. Various menu commands might show right-pointing arrows after the command name. Position the mouse pointer over the command with a right-pointing arrow to display the cascading menu. A **cascading menu** (or submenu) is a list of commands that appears as a result of pointing to a command on the main menu that has an arrow to the right of it. The submenu's commands are related to the command from which they are linked.

Display a cascading menu

Now that we are familiar with the Word interface (another name for the Word window), we will begin to explore what happens when we click on an item on the menu bar.

1 **On the menu bar, click View.**

The View menu appears. Notice that the menu command Toolbars has an arrow to the right of it.

QUICK CHECK

Q. Does causing a ScreenTip to appear in any way activate the button or cause a change to occur?

A. **The appearance of a ScreenTip in no way causes a change to occur or a button to be activated.**

CHECK THIS OUT ▼

All Functions On Menus Every function for which you can use a button is also available somewhere within the menus. There is no feature that is not accessible in some way from the menus.

FIGURE 1-7

View menu

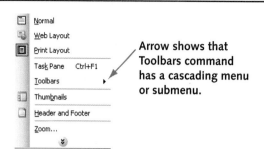

Arrow shows that Toolbars command has a cascading menu or submenu.

2 **Point to Toolbars, but don't click.**

The Toolbars cascading menu appears.

FIGURE 1-8

Toolbars cascading menu from the View menu

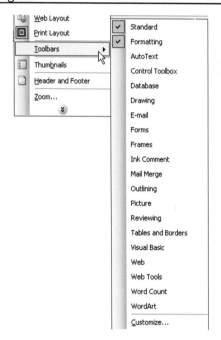

Q. Why are some menu commands hidden when you first click on the menu?

A: Some menu commands are hidden when you first open a menu because Word displays only the most frequently used commands.

3 **Click anywhere outside the menu.**

The menu closes.

◆ **Keep this file open for the next exercise.**

QUICK REFERENCE ▼

Display a menu

On the menu bar, click the name of the menu.

Using Personalized Menus

THE BOTTOM LINE

Personalized menus help you to quickly access the menu commands that you use most often. You don't have to do anything more than use the commands to add them to your personalized menu.

Word 2003 has a feature that personalizes your menus. When you click a menu name on the menu bar, the menu is displayed, but not in its entirety. A short menu appears because those are the most popular commands used by most Microsoft users. Finding a menu command on a short menu is much easier and quicker than finding a menu command on an expanded menu.

Two downward-pointing arrows are displayed on the bottom of the menu, alerting you that more menu commands are available but currently hidden. You click the double arrows to expand, or open, the entire menu. You can also view the expanded menu by holding the mouse pointer over the double arrows and waiting a few seconds for the expanded menu to appear.

After you select a command on the menu and open the menu again, Word displays your selection on the menu so you don't have to open the menu in its entirety to select that command again. Over time, Word adapts to your usage, and the commands that appear on the short menu are the commands that *you* most frequently use. If you stop using the command over time, Word returns the command to the expanded menu.

Personalize the Edit menu

So far we have explored the Word interface without causing any changes to occur. Now we are going to start using Word and observe how the program is automatically personalized to the way in which we use it.

1 **Click Edit on the menu bar to view the Edit menu.**

The Edit menu appears.

FIGURE 1-9

Unexpanded Edit menu

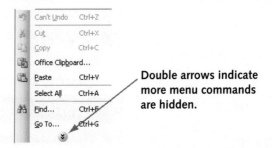

Double arrows indicate
more menu commands
are hidden.

2 **Click the arrows at the bottom of the Edit menu to view the ex-panded menu.**

The expanded Edit menu appears.

You can also view the expanded menu by holding the mouse pointer over the double arrows and waiting a few seconds for the expanded menu to appear.

3 Click Go To.

The Go To tab of the Find And Replace dialog box appears.

A **dialog box** is a screen element that appears when you need to communicate with a program. A dialog box provides a way for you to make decisions and select options.

4 Click the Close button in the Find And Replace dialog box.

5 On the menu bar, click Edit again.

Notice that Go To is now displayed on the Edit menu. Word has personalized the Edit menu for you.

FIGURE 1-10

Personalized Edit menu

You can turn off the personalized menus feature so that all commands appear all of the time on the menus. On the Tools menu, click Customize, and then click the Options tab. Select the Always Show Full Menus check box and then click the Close button.

◆ Keep this file open for the next exercise.

QUICK REFERENCE ▼

View an expanded menu

1 On the menu bar, click the name of the menu.

2 Click the double arrow at the bottom of the menu.

Or

Wait a few seconds for the expanded menu to appear on its own.

Entering Text

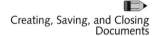

Creating, Saving, and Closing
Documents

> **THE BOTTOM LINE**
>
> You can use Word 2003 to easily begin composing and formatting documents. Features such as word wrap make creating a nice looking document easy even for someone new to word processing.

You begin creating a document by simply typing text. When you enter text into a document, Word's **word wrap** feature automatically wraps text from one line to the next each time the insertion point reaches the right margin. Word wrap breaks lines of text so that they stay within margin boundaries; you don't have to enter hard returns (pressing the Enter key). You press Enter only when you want to begin a new paragraph or insert a blank line. This is a handy feature when you are first creating a document, but it is especially advantageous in situations in which you later return to a document and make edits. If you had to manually place end-of-line hard returns, all of your lines could be thrown off if you later inserted text into the middle of a line. The word wrap feature ensures that your lines always are spaced correctly no matter how many times your revise the content of your paragraphs.

Notice in Figure 1-11 that the first four letters of the word *consultants* is on the first line. In Figure 1-12, when the rest of the word has been typed, Word wraps the word to the second line.

FIGURE 1-11

Document with text before it is wrapped to the next line

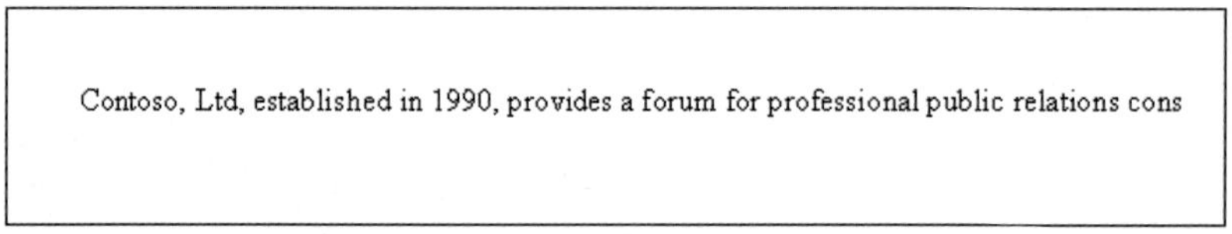

Contoso, Ltd, established in 1990, provides a forum for professional public relations cons

FIGURE 1-12

Document with text wrapped to next line

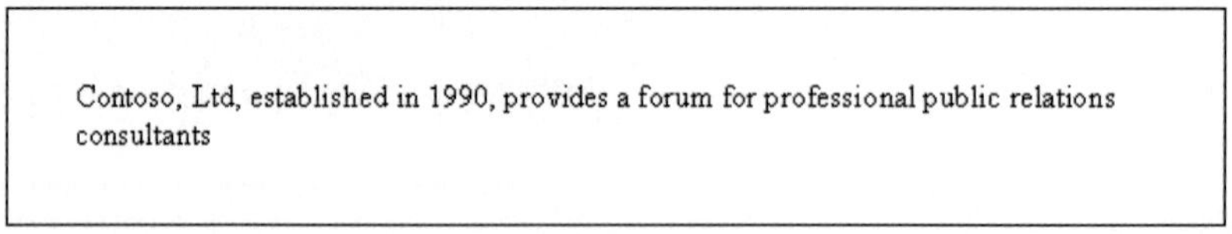

Contoso, Ltd, established in 1990, provides a forum for professional public relations consultants

As you type text, the insertion point moves, indicating the location for the next character. If you make a mistake, press Backspace to delete characters to the left of the insertion point or press Delete to delete characters to the right of the insertion point. To place the insertion point at the end of an existing line of text, click after the text that has been entered.

CHECK THIS OUT ▼

Default Page Margins
Word uses left and right page margins of 1.25 inches and top and bottom margins of 1 inch by default; however, you can reset the page margins. You'll learn more about resetting margins in Lesson 5, "Changing the Layout of a Document."

Enter text in a document

We've explored the Word interface, including menus and buttons. Now it's time to begin entering text into the document. As we do this, we will be able to observe the word wrap feature in action. The document we are creating is a brochure for Contoso, Ltd.

1 Type Founded in 1990 **into the blank document currently displayed in the window. (The blank document was displayed when you started Word.)**

2 **Type a comma, and press the Spacebar.**

3 **Continue typing the following:**

Contoso, Ltd provides a forum for professional public relations consultants throughout the state to meet, to exchange views about general business issues, and to further individual skills development.

The text is displayed in the document window as you type, wrapping to the next line when the insertion point reaches the right margin.

◆ **Keep this file open for the next exercise.**

QUICK CHECK

Q. How does word wrap determine whether a word needs to be wrapped to the next line?

A. A word is moved to the next line, regardless of its size, when there is not enough space left on the current line for the word to fit in its entirety.

TROUBLESHOOTING

Did you notice a red or green wavy line under your text? Don't worry. Word is just helping you proofread your document. Spelling and grammar checking are covered in Lesson 7, "Using Editing and Proofing Tools."

QUICK REFERENCE ▼

Enter text

1 Click to position the insertion point where you want to insert text.
2 Type the text.

Using Click And Type

THE BOTTOM LINE

When you use Click And Type, Word inserts formatting and alignment attributes at the location where you want to type. It saves you from having to select the text and choose formatting options after you have typed or having to press Enter to move down to a certain place on the page to type.

Click And Type is a feature that you can use to quickly position the insertion point in any blank area of a document. You move the mouse pointer to the desired location in the blank document, double-click, and then begin typing. As you move the mouse pointer to different areas of the page, the mouse pointer shape indicates whether the text you type will be left-aligned, centered, or right-aligned. Click And Type is an especially useful feature if you want to start text centered on a line or on a page; you don't have to use the Center button to center text on a line, nor do you have to create blank lines to center a line on a page. You simply position the pointer where you want to begin typing text, and Word creates formatting and alignment attributes based on the location where you double-click. The following table illustrates the appearance of the mouse pointer, which indicates the formatting action that will be taken by Click And Type.

Mouse Pointer	Aligns Text
≡	Left
≟	Left with the first line indented
≡	Center
≡	Right

For example, suppose you are in the middle of a multipage document. You need to insert a list of names and add more text. Double-click the center of the blank area where you want to insert the text and type your list. Word applies center alignment to the text.

After you are finished entering the list, double-click in the left area of the document and type your additional text. Word applies left alignment to the text.

IMPORTANT

Click And Type is available only in Print Layout view or Web Layout view. Your document must be displayed in Print Layout view for the next exercise. To verify that your document is in Print Layout view or to change the view to Print Layout, click Print Layout on the View menu.

Use Click And Type to insert a centered subtitle

We will continue to work in the document that we started in the last exercise. Now we will use Click And Type to insert a centered subtitle. This subtitle will be used to identify the next section of the brochure we are creating.

1 Verify that you are in Print Layout view. On the View menu, click **Print Layout.**

2 Move the pointer back and forth across the page to observe how it changes to indicate how the item will be formatted.

3 Position the pointer at the center of the page slightly below the introductory paragraph that you typed in the previous exercise.

The pointer shape indicates that the item will be centered.

FIGURE 1-13

Pointer indicating centered position

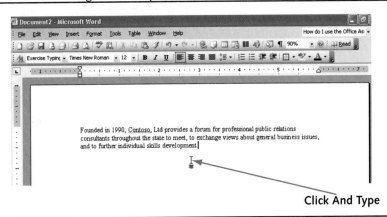

Click And Type

4 **Double-click, and type** Membership Information.

This will identify the next section of the brochure that you are creating.

◆ **Keep this file open for the next exercise.**

TROUBLESHOOTING

If you don't want to type text where you double-clicked, just double-click another area. If you've already typed text, click the Undo button on the Standard toolbar to remove the text that you inserted, and then click the Undo button again to remove the Click And Type formatting. (The Undo button appears when you show the toolbars in two rows.)

QUICK REFERENCE ▼

Use Click And Type

1 In Print Layout view, position the mouse pointer where you want to insert text.

2 Double-click, and begin typing.

Saving a Document

Save to your G:

Creating, Saving, and Closing
Documents

THE BOTTOM LINE

Saving is very important if you want to access your text again later. You can use files and folders to organize your documents and retrieve them easily and efficiently. You should save your work frequently to avoid potentially losing your document should there be a power or computer failure.

The text that you enter is stored in the computer's RAM memory, which is temporary. To keep the file for future use, you must store the document on your hard disk. A **file** is a collection of related data or information that is assigned a specific name and stored on a disk. To permanently store a document, you must save it to your hard disk. Otherwise, when you quit Word, your document is deleted. You save a document by clicking the Save button on the Standard toolbar. When you save the document, you give the document a unique file name so that you can retrieve the document for future use.

The first time you save a document, the Save As dialog box appears so that you can name the document and put it in a folder. A **folder** is a container in which to store and organize documents, programs, graphics, and files and is represented by the icon of a file folder. If you make any changes to a document and need to save it, click the Save button and the newest version of the document is saved, but the Save As dialog box does not appear.

> ## CHECK THIS OUT ▼
>
> **The Places Bar**
> The Places Bar in the Save As dialog box provides convenient access to commonly used locations for saving and storing files. For example, to save a file on a floppy disk, you click the My Computer icon on the Places Bar, then double-click 3$\frac{1}{2}$ Floppy (A:). The Places Bar also provides access to your list of Internet favorites and a list of recently opened documents (in the History folder).

A file name can contain as many as 255 characters. Word uses the first words of the document, up to the first punctuation mark or line break, as the suggested file name when you save the file for the first time. You can accept this suggested name or delete it and assign a file name yourself. Because you have up to 255 characters to work with, you should strive to make your file names as descriptive as possible. An example of a vague and cryptic file name would be *Questions*. You might not remember what the questions are or what they are for. A better file name would be *Questions for Lesson 3 Test Bank*. When you save a file, you cannot include any of the following characters in the file name: * \ / < > ? : ; "

Depending on your Windows setup, file names in the file name box might have an extension, which is a period followed by three letters. For Word, the extension is *.doc*. You do not have to type the extension after the file name in the Save As dialog box if it does not appear; Word will add it automatically.

Save a new document to your hard disk

Now that we have completed a portion of the work on our brochure, it is a good time to save it.

1 **On the Standard toolbar, click the Save button to display the Save As dialog box.**

Notice that the text *Founded in 1990* is selected in the File Name box. The selected text is deleted as you begin typing new text.

FIGURE 1-14

Save As dialog box

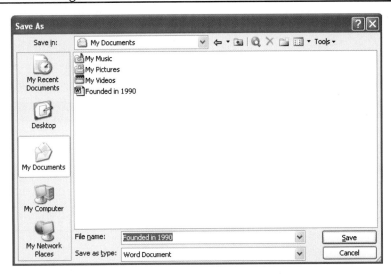

2 **In the File Name box, type** Brochure 01.

3 **Click the Save In down arrow, and click the icon for your hard disk.**

4 **Double-click the Word Practice folder.**

The Save In box displays the text *Word Practice*, and the dialog box displays the contents of the Word Practice folder.

ANOTHER METHOD

You can also click the Save In box to display a list of resources (such as your hard disk, a floppy disk, or a network drive) and available folders.

5 **Double-click the Lesson01 folder.**

The Lesson01 folder opens.

TIP

You can save a copy of the active document with a different name or in a different location. You might want to do this if you are using one document as a starting point to create another document or if you want to have a copy of the original document before you make changes to it. You will learn how to do this in Lesson 2, "Editing a Document."

6 **Click the Save button.**

The file is saved to your hard disk with the new name, which is now displayed in the Microsoft Word title bar.

7 **Click at the end of the first paragraph to position the insertion point.**

8 **Press the Spacebar, and type the following sentence:**

Meetings are held monthly, during which an expert guest speaker presents timely and pertinent information.

9 On the Standard toolbar, click the Save button.

Word saves the document.

◆ Keep this file open for the next exercise.

CHECK THIS OUT ▼

Document Recovery
Word saves documents for recovery in case the program stops responding or you lose power. The Document Recovery task pane lists all recovered documents and allows you to open the documents, view the repairs, and compare the recovered versions. Word saves the changes in a recovery file based on the amount of time indicated in the AutoRecover option. To turn on the AutoRecover option and specify a time interval in which to save, on the Tools menu, click Options, click the Save tab, select the Save AutoRecover info every check box, specify the period of time, and then click OK.

QUICK REFERENCE ▼

Save a document for the first time

1. On the Standard toolbar, click the Save button.
2. Type the file name in the File Name box.
3. Click the Save In down arrow, and select a location for the file.
4. Click the Save button.

Closing a Document and Quitting Word

THE BOTTOM LINE

It is important to close documents when you are done working on them in order to save space in the active memory of your computer as well as to ensure that no one accidentally makes changes to your document. You also need to quit Word when you are done working in it. Properly shutting down applications ensures that you will not have problems the next time you wish to use them.

Creating, Saving, and Closing Documents

After a file is stored on your hard disk, you can clear it from the screen by closing the document window or quitting Word. If the document has not been saved or if you have made changes to the file since you last saved it, Word prompts you to save the file before closing the window.

FIGURE 1-15

Save Changes message box

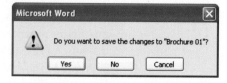

To clear a document from the document window, on the File menu, click Close, or in the upper-right corner of the screen, click the Close Window button. Closing the current document window leaves Word still running.

When you have one document open in Word, two Close buttons are displayed in the upper-right corner of the Word window. These buttons each have an X on them, and one is just above the other one. The lower Close button, called the Close Window button (a black X) is used to close the current document window. The top Close button (a larger white X on a red background) is used to close the document and to exit Word.

When you start Word, a blank document is displayed in the Word window. After you save and close this new document, Word remains open, but does not automatically display a new blank document in the window like it did when you started Word. You must click the New Blank Document button on the Standard toolbar to create a new document.

Close the current document, exit Word, and then start Word again

Since we have saved our work, it is now safe to close the current document as well as to exit Word. After we have done that, we will start Word again so that it is available to create other documents and for the next exercise in this lesson.

1 On the File menu, click Close.

The document closes, leaving Word open but no documents open.

ANOTHER METHOD

You can also close a Word document by clicking the Close Window button in the upper-right corner of the document window.

2 On the File menu, click Exit.

Word closes.

ANOTHER METHOD

You can also close Word by clicking the Close button in the upper-right corner of the Word window.

3 To restart Word, click the Start button on the Windows taskbar, point to All Programs, point to Microsoft Office, and click Microsoft Office Word 2003.

Word starts.

ANOTHER METHOD

You could also choose Microsoft Office Word 2003 from the first column of the Start menu.

You can open Microsoft Office Word 2003 from a shortcut on the desktop if one has been created.

4 Click the Close button on the Getting Started task pane.

◆ Keep this file open for the next exercise.

QUICK REFERENCE ▼

Close a document

On the File menu, click Close.

Or

Click the lower Close button in the upper-right corner of the screen.

Getting Help

THE BOTTOM LINE

If you need assistance while working with Word, you can get help through the Help menu, the Ask a Question box, or the Office Assistant. The more familiar you are with the Help features, the faster you can find answers to your word-processing questions.

Ask a Question Box

Microsoft Office Word 2003 has several Help features to assist you in answering any question you may have about using Word. If you click Microsoft Word Help on the Help menu, you can access the Table of Contents or Microsoft Office Online, if your computer is connected to the Internet. You can save time by using the **Ask a Question box** rather than searching the table of contents or index in online Help. To use the Ask a Question box, click in the text box and type a question or keyword, and then press the Enter key. Word lists Help topics so that you can choose the one that answers your question.

FIGURE 1-16

Ask A Question box on the Menu bar

Ask A Question

Office Assistant

Another way to get help is to use the Office Assistant. The **Office Assistant** offers tips for completing your task, such as creating and formatting a letter. The Office Assistant, like the Ask A Question box, helps you find answers and instructions for your Word questions. The default Office Assistant character is an animated paper clip, but it can take other forms, such as an animated cat or dog.

FIGURE 1-17

Office Assistant

To use the Office Assistant, select Show the Office Assistant from the Help menu. To change the character of the Office Assistant, right-click the Office Assistant and click Options. Click the Gallery tab, click the Next or Back buttons until you see the Office Assistant that you want, and then click OK.

TROUBLESHOOTING

If you select an assistant and receive an alert box saying that the selected assistant is not available, insert the requested Office 2003 or Word CD-ROM to install the assistant on your hard disk.

To use the Office Assistant to get help, click the Office Assistant, and then type a question or keyword in the What Would You Like To Do? box and press Enter. A variety of Help topics related to the question that you asked is displayed. Click the topic that most closely relates to your question to read more about it.

Sometimes the Office Assistant appears on its own if you're doing something that it might be able to help you with, such as writing a letter or using an advanced feature. If you already have the Office Assistant displayed, a light bulb might appear next to it to signal that the Office Assistant has a tip for you that might help you with what you're doing. Clicking the light bulb displays the tip.

TIP

You can permanently turn off the Office Assistant by right-clicking the Office Assistant, clicking Options, clicking the Options tab, clearing the Use the Office Assistant check box, and then clicking OK. You can turn on the Office Assistant again by clicking Show the Office Assistant on the Help menu.

◆ **Make sure that Word is running and that there is a new blank document open. If necessary, click the New Blank Document button to create a new document.**

Use the Ask A Question box to get help

1 Click in the Ask A Question text box.

2 Type How do I use the Office Assistant? in the box.

3 Press Enter on the keyboard.

A list of Help topics that is related to the question that you asked is displayed in the Search Results task pane. Text appearing in blue, which displays an underline when you rest the mouse on it, indicates a link to another topic.

FIGURE 1-18

Search Results task pane

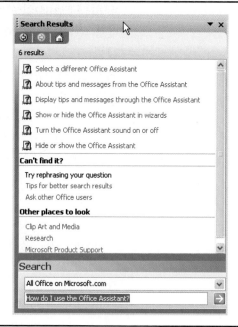

4 Click Display Tips And Messages Through The Office Assistant.

The Microsoft Word Help window displays the related Help information.

5 Click Show All in the upper-right corner of the Microsoft Word Help window.

All the Help topics related to this main topic are displayed.

6 Scroll through the information presented in this window. When you are finished using Help, in the upper-right corner of the Help dialog box, click the Close button.

7 Click the Close button in the upper right corner of the Search Results task pane.

QUICK REFERENCE ▼

Use the Office Assistant to get help

1 On the Help menu, click Show The Office Assistant if the Office Assistant isn't already displayed.

2 Click the Office Assistant.

3 Type a question in the box.

4 Click the Search button.

5 Click one of the topics to read about it.

QUICK REFERENCE ▼

Hide the Office Assistant

On the Help menu, click Hide The Office Assistant.

QUICK REFERENCE ▼

Turn off the Office Assistant

1 Right-click the Office Assistant, and click Options.

1 Click the Options tab.

1 Clear the Use the Office Assistant check box.

4 Click OK.

◆ **If you are continuing to the next lesson, close the file without saving the changes. Keep Word open for the next lesson.**

◆ **If you are not continuing to other lessons, close the file without saving the changes. Then close Word.**

Key Points

✔ *You start Word through one of several methods – the most common is by selecting it on the Start menu.*

✔ *You use menus and toolbars to access the various features and functions of Word.*

✔ *You create Word documents by entering text.*

✔ *The Click And Type feature allows you to place the insertion point directly in the desired spot within your document.*

✔ *You save a document so that you have a way of accessing it again in the future.*

✔ *Word offers two ways to obtain help: the Ask A Question box or the Office Assistant.*

Quick Quiz

True/False

T **(F)** 1. A ScreenTip appears the first time you click a button on the toolbar.

(T) F 2. When you start Word, a new blank document automatically opens.

T **(F)** 3. Minimizing a document window closes the document.

T **(F)** 4. To save a document for the first time, click the Save As button on the Standard toolbar.

T F 5. Word wrap automatically wraps text from one line to the next when it reaches the right margin.

Multiple Choice

1. Word uses default left and right margins of _____.

   (a.) 1″

   b. 1.25″

   c. 1.5″

   d. 2″

2. The area at the bottom of the program window that displays information about currently selected text is the _____.
   a. Standard toolbar
   b. Menu bar
   c. Status bar
   d. Task pane

3. What does it mean when a menu selection is displayed in a light shade?
   a. It is not available now.
   (b.) It is not applicable to the current operation.
   c. Both a and b.
   d. None of the above.

4. In order to use Click And Type, you must display your document in _____ View.
   (a.) Print Layout
   b. Normal
   c. Reading Layout
   d. Expanded Layout

5. When you position the mouse pointer over a command with a right-pointing arrow next to it, the display that appears is called a(n) _____.
   a. personalized menu
   (b.) expanded menu
   c. cascading menu
   d. menu bar

Short Answer

1. How do you save a copy of the current document without changing the original version?

2. What are two ways that you can close a document?

3. What happens when you click the red button labeled with an X in the upper-right corner of the Word window?

4. What is the difference between an expanded menu and a personalized menu?

5. How do you use Click And Type?

6. What is the Office Assistant?

7. How do you separate the Standard and Formatting toolbars?

8. What is the Start menu used for?

On Your Own

Exercise 1

If necessary, open Word by using the Start menu. In a blank document, use the Click And Type feature to insert the following heading, centered about one-quarter of the way down the page: **Expense Report Reminders**.

Use Click And Type again to position a left-aligned paragraph below the title. Type the following information:

When filing your expense reports, be sure to attach your original receipts, record beginning and ending mileage figures, and record the itemized expenses on your hotel bill separately. These are the most common reasons for expense reimbursement delays.

Save the document in the Lesson01 folder located in the Word Practice folder on your hard disk with the name Expense Reminders 01, and then close the document.

Exercise 2

Use Word's Click And Type feature to create a cover sheet for an expense report. Type the words Expense Report at the top center of the page.

Type the words Annual Report 2004 in the middle of the page.

Type your name at the bottom center of the page.

Save your document as Annual Expense Report 2004 in the Lesson01 folder located in the Word Practice folder.

Exercise 3

Open a new blank document in Word and practice using different options on the menus in order to personalize the menus to the features that you are using. Personalize several menus, and then close the document without saving any changes you have made.

One Step Further

Exercise 1

Use the Ask A Question box to find information on how to type over existing text.

Exercise 2

Use the Office Assistant to find information on the various ways to view a document. Explore using the options that you discover.

LESSON

2

Editing a Document

After completing this lesson, you will be able to:

✔ *Open a file.*
✔ *Navigate through a document.*
✔ *Scroll through text.*
✔ *Insert text in a document.*
✔ *Select text.*
✔ *Edit a document by deleting and restoring text.*
✔ *Create a folder.*
✔ *Save a file with a different name.*

KEY TERMS

- arrow keys
- backup
- file format
- Insert mode
- key combination
- network
- Overtype mode
- redo
- scroll
- undo

Before the days of computer and word-processing programs, any correspondence done by hand or on a typewriter could include crossed-out words, correction fluid, or spelling and punctuation errors. People simply couldn't edit without starting over or having flaws in their documents. Now that most personal and business correspondence is typed on a computer using a word-processing program, there is no more need for crossed-out words or correction fluid.

With Microsoft Word, you can quickly and efficiently edit letters, documents, reports, newsletters, memos, and faxes. Word displays a red wavy line if a word is misspelled or unknown and displays a green wavy line to indicate incorrect or questionable grammar usage.

In this lesson, you will learn how to open a file that you already created. Then, because the Word window often displays only a portion of a document at a time, you'll learn how to scroll to view different parts of a document. You'll move the insertion point around the document by using the mouse pointer and by pressing keys on the keyboard.

After learning how to navigate through a document, you'll begin to edit. To edit, you first need to identify the text that you want to change. Word provides shortcuts so that you can select text by the word, line, sentence, paragraph, or the entire document. After you select the desired text, you'll learn how to delete the selection. When you're finished editing the document, you'll save the file.

In this lesson, you will also learn how to create a folder in which to save the file and how to save the file with a different name. You'll also save the file in a different format so that it can be used by other word-processing programs.

> **IMPORTANT**
>
> Before you can use the practice files in this lesson, you need to install them from the companion CD for this book to their default location. For additional information on how to find and open files used in this book, see the "Using the CD-ROM" section at the beginning of this book.

Opening an Existing File

Opening and Viewing Existing Documents

> **THE BOTTOM LINE**
>
> One of the most important features of any word-processing program is the ability to open existing documents – those previously created by you as well as those created by others — and make edits to those documents.

After you save a Word document, you can reopen it later to review its contents or make changes. You'll need to navigate to the folder containing the document and then open the document itself.

Word keeps track of the last documents that you opened. Word displays the names of these files at the bottom of the File menu so that you can open them with only a few mouse clicks. To open a file that is not listed at the bottom of the File menu, you use the Open dialog box. Word also will list these files at the top of the New Document task pane so they are even more readily available when you first start Word or when you choose to open a document. In this way, you can easily continue working on a document that you were working on recently.

◆ **Be sure to start Word before beginning this exercise.**

◆ **To complete the procedures in this lesson, you will need to use the practice file Brochure 02 in the Lesson02 folder in the Word Practice folder that is located on your hard disk.**

CHECK THIS OUT ▼

Folders in the Open and Save As Dialog Boxes
Word remembers the folder in which you last saved a document. When you display the Open dialog box or the Save As dialog box, the contents of that folder are displayed so that you can easily find the files for which you are looking.

Open an existing file

In this exercise, you will open an existing file. In subsequent exercises in this lesson, you will use this file to navigate through the document, edit text, and save the file with a new name.

1 On the New Document task pane, at the bottom of the Open section, click the More link.

The Open dialog box appears.

More...

2 Click the Look In down arrow, click the icon for your local hard drive, double-click the Word Practice folder, and double-click the Lesson02 folder.

The contents of the Lesson02 folder appear in the Open dialog box.

FIGURE 2-1

Lesson02 folder in the Open dialog box

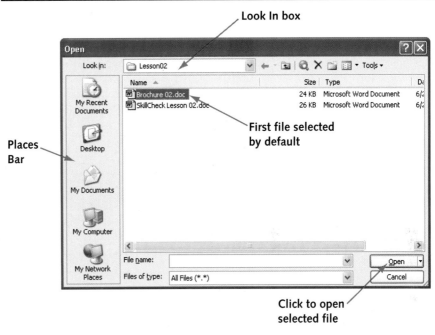

Look In box

Places Bar

First file selected by default

Click to open selected file

ANOTHER METHOD

To open a recently used document from the Open dialog box, on the Places Bar, click the History icon, and double-click the file that you want to open. The Places Bar is located along the left side of the Open dialog box.

 3 Click the file Brochure 02, and click the Open button.

The Open dialog box closes and the file Brochure 02 appears in Word.

ANOTHER METHOD

You can also open a file by double-clicking the file name in the Open dialog box.

◆ **Keep this file open for the next exercise.**

FIGURE 2-2

Brochure 02 document

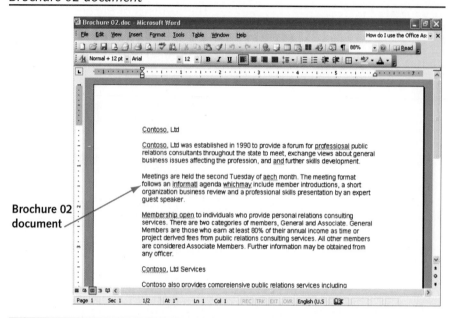

Brochure 02
document

TROUBLESHOOTING

In the illustrations used throughout this book, the Standard and Formatting toolbars are separated. For information on how to separate the toolbars, see the "Using the CD-ROM" section at the beginning of this book.

QUICK REFERENCE ▼

Open a file

1 On the Standard toolbar, click the Open button.

2 Navigate to the folder where the file is stored.

3 Click the file's name.

4 Click the Open button.

Or

1 On the New Document task pane, click the More documents option.

2 Navigate to the folder where the file is stored.

3 Click the file's name.

4 Click the Open button.

QUICK **CHECK**

Q. Can you open more than one file from the Open dialog box at one time?

A. **You can select multiple files in the Open dialog box and then click Open. This will open all of the selected files at one time.**

Navigating Through a Document

Opening and Viewing Existing Documents

THE BOTTOM LINE

Key to being able to read and edit a document is the ability to navigate through it. This can be done using the keyboard or by using the scroll bars.

Using the Keyboard

To change existing text in a document or to edit, you first move the insertion point to the location where you want to make a change. The mouse pointer, the arrow keys on the keyboard (used to move the mouse pointer or insertion point up, down, left, or right), and the scroll bars are all navigation tools that help you to move through a document.

TIP

When the mouse pointer looks like the I-beam, you can move around and make edits to the text. You can tell when the mouse pointer is in the selection area because the I-beam changes to a right-pointing arrow. The selection area is any location to the left of the left margin of your document.

To move the insertion point by using the mouse, simply move the I-beam pointer (the pointer that looks like a capital I) to the location where you want the insertion point to appear, and click.

IMPORTANT

In a new blank document, you cannot move the insertion point with the arrow keys. With the arrow keys, you can move the insertion point only to places in the document that include text, tables, or graphics. You can, however, use Click And Type to move the insertion point in a blank document.

The following table lists each keyboard key or key combination that can be used to quickly move the insertion point. A key combination is a combination of keyboard keys used to perform a function instead of using the mouse pointer to perform the same task. For example, if the key combination is Ctrl+Home, you press and hold the Ctrl button while pressing the Home button. Word moves the insertion point to the beginning of the document.

TIP

For more information about key combinations, see Lesson 3, "Formatting Text."

Press	To move the insertion point
Left arrow key	Left one character (one unit of space, such as a letter, number, punctuation mark, or other symbol)
Right arrow key	Right one character
Down arrow key	Down one line
Up arrow key	Up one line
Ctrl+Left arrow	Left one word
Ctrl+Right arrow	Right one word
Home	To the beginning of the current line
End	To the end of the current line
Ctrl+Home	To the beginning of the document
Ctrl+End	To the end of the document
Page Up	Up one full screen
Page Down	Down one full screen
Ctrl+Page Up	To the beginning of the previous page
Ctrl+Page Down	To the beginning of the next page

TROUBLESHOOTING

The key combinations of Ctrl+Page Up or Ctrl+Page Down are not always set to move forward or backward by a page. You can use the Select Browse Object button, located between the Previous and Next buttons, to select the type of item by which you want to browse, such as page, bookmark, footnote, table, graphic, or other item. This will be discussed in more depth in the next section.

Move the insertion point

Now that we have a document open, we can experiment with moving the insertion point using the keyboard and the mouse.

1 Click after the letter "M" in the word "Meetings", which is the first word in the second paragraph, and press the left arrow key to move the insertion point one character to the left.

The insertion point moves one character to the left. It is positioned in front of the letter *M* in *Meetings*.

2 Press the down arrow key.

The insertion point moves one line down. It is positioned at the beginning of the second line in the paragraph.

3 Press the up arrow key.

The insertion point moves up in front of the *M* once again.

4 Press the right arrow key.

The insertion point returns to where you started, directly after the *M*.

5 Press Ctrl+right arrow.

The insertion point moves to the beginning of the word *are*.

6 Press Ctrl+left arrow.

The insertion point moves to the beginning of the word *Meetings*.

CHECK THIS OUT ▼

Moving to Previous Location in Word
Word keeps track of the last three locations where you typed or edited text. To return to a previous editing location, press Shift+F5 until you reach the location that you want.

7 Press the End key.

The insertion point moves to the end of the line.

8 Press the Home key.

The insertion point moves to the beginning of the line.

9 Press Ctrl+Home.

The insertion point moves to the beginning of the document.

10 Press Ctrl+End.

The insertion point moves to the end of the document.

◆ **Keep this file open for the next exercise.**

QUICK REFERENCE ▼

Navigate through a document

- Use the mouse pointer.
- Use the arrow keys.
- Use the scroll bars.
- Use the key combinations.

Using the Scroll Bar

Because the document window normally displays only a portion of a page at one time, you might need to move (or scroll) the view of the document to view another section of it. If your document has more than one page, you'll need to scroll to see the other pages of the document. The vertical scroll bar, scroll arrows, and scroll box move the document up and down. The horizontal scroll bar, scroll arrows, and scroll box move the document window left and right.

FIGURE 2-3

The Word document window

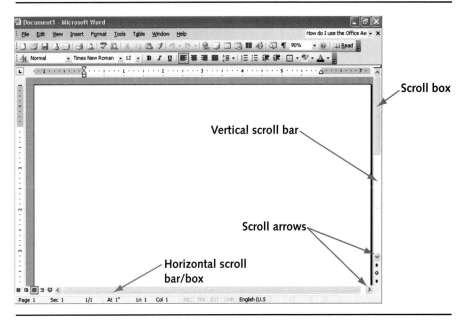

"One screen" is the amount of a document that can be displayed in the document window at one time. This amount will vary depending on your screen area settings and whether the document window is maximized.

The following table lists available scrolling tools and their functions.

Do this action	Button view	To move the document
Click the up scroll arrow	⌃	Up one line at a time
Click the down scroll arrow	⌄	Down one line at a time
Click the left scroll arrow	‹	Left a few characters at a time
Click the right scroll arrow	›	Right a few characters at a time
Click above the scroll box on the vertical scroll bar		Up one screen at a time
Click below the scroll box on the vertical scroll bar		Down one screen at a time
Click left of the scroll box on the horizontal scroll bar		Left one screen at a time
Click right of the scroll box on the horizontal scroll bar		Right one screen at a time
Drag the vertical scroll box		Continually forward or backward through the document
Drag the horizontal scroll box		Continually left or right through the document
Click the Previous Page button	⬆	To the beginning of the previous page
Click the Next Page button	⬇	To the beginning of the next page

CHECK THIS OUT ▼

Select Browse Object
The Previous and Next buttons, located below the vertical scroll bar, are not always set to move forward or backward by a page. You can use the Select Browse Object button, located between the Previous and Next buttons, to select the type of item by which you want to browse, such as page, bookmark, footnote, table, graphic, or other item. To browse by page, click the Select Browse Object button, and click the Browse By Page button.

◆ **Make sure Brochure 02 is open and on screen in Word.**

Use scroll bars and scroll arrows to move through a document

We will continue experimenting with moving through an open document. In this case, we will use the scroll bars and scroll arrows to move through the Brochure 02 document.

1 Click the Up scroll arrow once.

The document moves up one line.

The insertion point stays in the same place while the view of the document itself moves up, sliding the text down the screen.

2 **Click the Down scroll arrow.**

The insertion point stays in the same place while the document itself moves down, sliding the text up the screen.

3 **Click the scroll bar above the scroll box.**

The document moves down one screen. The first line of text on the previous screen is now the last line of text on the current screen.

TIP

The horizontal scroll bar works the same way as the vertical scroll bar.

---

4 **Click the scroll bar below the scroll box.**

The content moves down one screen.

5 **Drag the scroll box up to the top of the scroll bar.**

The text that you see in the window moves along with the scroll box, and a yellow ScreenTip tells you which page you are currently scrolling.

TROUBLESHOOTING

Scrolling does not move the insertion point. If you scroll to a new location and you want to edit at that spot, you must click that location to place the insertion point there. If you simply start typing without clicking the location, the view jumps back to where you left the insertion point, and the text will be inserted there.

---

6 **Press Ctrl+End.**

The insertion point moves to the end of the document.

7 **On the vertical scroll bar, click the Select Browse Object button.**

The Select Browse Object menu appears.

FIGURE 2-4

Select Browse Object menu

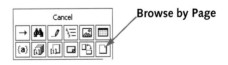

8 **Click the Browse By Page button.**

The view and the insertion point move to the beginning of the next page.

9 **Click the Previous Page button.**

The view and the insertion point move directly to the beginning of the previous page. If the insertion point is already on the first page of the document, the Previous Page button moves the insertion point to the beginning of that page.

10 **Click the Next Page button.**

Both the view and the insertion point move directly to the beginning of the next page. If the insertion point is already on the last page of the document, the Next Page button moves the insertion point to the beginning of that page.

11 **Press Ctrl+Home.**

The insertion point moves back to the beginning of the document.

◆ **Keep this file open for the next exercise.**

QUICK REFERENCE ▼

Scroll through text

- Use the vertical scroll bar, scroll arrows, and scroll box to move up and down.
- Use the horizontal scroll bar, scroll arrows, and a scroll box to move left to right.
- Use the Previous Page button to move to the beginning of the previous page.
- Use the Next Page button to move to the beginning of the next page.

Inserting Text in a Document

THE BOTTOM LINE

The main point of having a word-processing document is, obviously, to be able to insert text into a document.

One of the first steps in editing a document is learning to insert text. Word provides two modes to insert more text. For example, if the annual report for your company was typed without a current list of all the board members, the names of the board members can be inserted later. Word uses Insert mode when you start the program. In Insert mode, when you type new text, the existing text moves to the right. The alternative to Insert mode is Overtype mode. In Overtype mode, existing text is deleted and replaced by the text that you type, including spaces.

TROUBLESHOOTING

Be cautious when you use Overtype mode. When it is activated and you insert new text in the middle of a sentence or paragraph, it's easy to inadvertently lose existing text that you did not intend to remove.

Research shows that a majority of users prefer Insert mode, so Insert mode is Word's default mode. Double-clicking the Overtype button (in the Status

---

QUICK CHECK

Q. If you begin navigating through a document using the arrow keys on the keyboard, can you switch to using the scroll bars?

A. **You can use any combination of arrow keys, keystroke combinations, or scroll bars to move through the document.**

Editing Documents

OVR

bar) toggles between Insert and Overtype modes. A toggle is a button that alternately turns an option on or off each time that the option is selected.

◆ **Make sure Brochure 02 is open and on screen in Word**

Insert text

Now that we have explored the various ways of moving around within a document, we are going to move to a specific location within the document and insert text.

1 **In the last line of the first paragraph, click just before the first "s" in the word "skills" to position the insertion point.**

2 **Type individual, and press the Spacebar.**

The new text is added at the insertion point, moving the existing text to the right.

◆ **Keep this file open for the next exercise.**

QUICK REFERENCE ▼

Insert text

1 Click to position the insertion point in the document where you want to insert the text.

2 Begin typing.

Editing Documents

Selecting Text

THE BOTTOM LINE

Being able to select specific text is a critical skill in working with Word. Once you master selecting text, you can then delete the selected text—which we will do in the exercise that follows — or you can cut or copy the text or format the text, all of which will be discussed in later lessons.

To edit text in a document, you must first select the desired text. One way to select text is to hold down the mouse button and then drag the insertion point over the text that you want to select. You deselect text by clicking anywhere within the document window. You can tell when text is selected because it appears highlighted (selected text usually appears white with a black background). Any changes will affect the selected text.

TIP

When you drag the mouse pointer past the first word, Word automatically selects entire words instead of one letter at a time.

To select blocks of text quickly, Word uses the selection area. The selection area is the area in the left margin of the document. You can tell when the pointer is in the selection area because the I-beam changes to a right-pointing arrow.

To select blocks of text that are not adjacent in a document, you select the first block of text, hold down the Ctrl key, and then select the next block of text. You can also use the Shift key and the arrow keys to select adjacent words, lines, or paragraphs. You position the insertion point in the text that you want to select, hold down the Shift key, and then press an arrow key or click at the end of the text that you want to select.

The following table summarizes the methods for selecting blocks of text.

To select	Do this
A word	Double-click the word.
A line	Click the selection area to the left of the line.
A sentence	Hold down the Ctrl key and click anywhere in the sentence.
A paragraph	Double-click the selection area to the left of any line in the paragraph, or triple-click anywhere in the paragraph.
An entire document	Hold down the Ctrl key and click anywhere in the selection area, or triple-click anywhere in the selection area.

ANOTHER METHOD

You can also select text by using the keyboard. Click in front of the text that you want to select and press Shift+right arrow to select text to the right of and before the mouse pointer, or Shift+left arrow to select text to the left of the mouse pointer. Notice that if you press Shift+down arrow in the middle of a line, the selected text includes part of the next line. Likewise, if you press Shift+down arrow at the beginning of a line, the entire line is selected. You can also click at the beginning of the text that you want to select, hold down Shift, and then click at the end of the text to select a block of text.

◆ **Make sure Brochure 02 is open and on screen in Word**

Select and deselect text

We will use the open Brochure 02 document to practice selecting and deselecting text.

1 **Double-click the word "Tuesday" in the second paragraph.**

The entire word is selected.

2 **Click within the word "Tuesday" to deselect it.**

3 **Move the mouse pointer to the selection area of the first line in the second paragraph.**

4 Click once in the selection area.

The entire line of text is now selected.

5 Click anywhere within the document (other than the selection area).

The line of text is now deselected.

6 Hold down the Ctrl key.

7 Click within the sentence containing the word "Tuesday," and release the Ctrl key.

The entire sentence is now selected.

TROUBLESHOOTING

If you drag the mouse pointer to select an entire sentence, don't forget to select the ending punctuation.

8 Move the mouse to the selection area, keeping the mouse pointer level with the paragraph containing the word "Tuesday."

9 Double-click the selection area.

The entire paragraph is now selected.

10 Click anywhere within the document.

The paragraph is no longer selected.

11 Triple-click within the paragraph.

The entire paragraph is now selected.

12 Click anywhere within the document.

The paragraph is now deselected.

13 Hold down the Ctrl key.

14 Click the selection area.

The entire document is selected.

15 Click within the document.

The document is no longer selected.

16 Triple-click the selection area.

The entire document is selected.

ANOTHER METHOD

You can also select an entire document by clicking Select All on the Edit menu, or press the key combination Ctrl+A. You'll learn more about key combinations in Lesson 3, "Formatting Text."

17 Click within the document to deselect it.

◆ Keep this file open for the next exercise.

QUICK CHECK

Q. What ways can you use to select an entire document?

A. **You can select an entire document by pressing Ctrl+A, by selecting Select All from the edit menu, or by triple-clicking in the selection area (left margin) of the document.**

QUICK REFERENCE ▼

Select text

- Click and drag the mouse pointer over the text.
- Use the selection area to the left of the document.
- Use the selection area to the left of the document combined with the Ctrl key to select non-adjacent areas of text.

Deleting and Restoring Text in a Document

THE BOTTOM LINE

Being able to delete text is one of the most useful features of word processing. Being able to restore text that you have accidentally deleted runs a close second.

Now that you know how to select text, you can easily delete a selected block of text. To delete a large section of text, select the text, and press Delete or Backspace. You can save time by selecting large areas of text to be deleted, rather than deleting the text character by character.

For example, in the annual report that you prepared for your company, you typed the introduction message from your company's president; however, the president has now decided to write it himself. You don't have to delete the letter one character at a time; instead select the entire letter, and press Delete. Now the page is blank and ready for the president to add his own letter.

To delete a single character, position the insertion point to the left of the character and press Delete or to the right of the character and press Backspace. To delete whole words using the keyboard, position the insertion point to the left of the word and press Ctrl+Delete or to the right of the word and press Ctrl+Backspace.

TROUBLESHOOTING

If you use either of these key combinations while the insertion point is positioned within a word, you delete the part of the word before or after the insertion point, respectively.

OVR   Another way to delete text is to use Overtype mode. Double-click OVR on the Status bar to turn on Overtype mode. When Overtype mode is turned on, you type over the existing text.

Word keeps track of the editing changes that you make in a document so that you can easily remove a change and restore the text to the way it was prior to making the edits. If you make a mistake while editing, on the Standard toolbar, you can click the Undo and Redo buttons to change and restore text.

FIGURE 2-5

Undo and Redo from the Standard toolbar

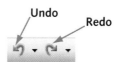

TROUBLESHOOTING

If your toolbar does not show the Undo and Redo buttons, on the Standard toolbar, click the Toolbar Options button, point to the Add or Remove command, point to Standard on the submenu, and click the Undo and Redo buttons. You can also click Undo and Redo on the Edit menu.

Editing Documents

To **undo** an action, click the Undo button. If you undo an action by mistake and need to restore or **redo** the action, you can do so by clicking the Redo button. To undo or redo multiple actions, click the down arrow to the right of the Undo or Redo button and select the action that you want to undo or redo. All actions completed after the one that you select in the list are also undone. Although most actions can be undone, actions such as saving and printing cannot.

◆ **Make sure Brochure 02 is open and on screen in Word**

CHECK THIS OUT ▼

Misspelled Words
Microsoft Word marks any word not found in its standard dictionary by placing a red wavy line beneath it. After you correct the word, the wavy line is removed. You'll learn more about the dictionary and spelling check in Lesson 5, "Creating Content and Editing Text."

Use Undo and Redo

Continuing to work with the Brochure 02 document, we will now delete and restore text to fix some of the errors in the document.

1. **Click the insertion point to the left of the last "s" in the misspelled word "professiosal" in the first paragraph.**
2. **Press the Delete key.**

   The letter *s* is deleted, and the remaining text is shifted to the left.
3. **Type n.**

   The red wavy line is removed.
4. **In the second paragraph, position the insertion point to the right of the letter "t" in the word "informatl".**
5. **Press Backspace.**

   The *t* is deleted, and the red wavy line is removed.
6. **In the second paragraph, position the insertion point in front of the "a" in the misspelled word "aech".**

OVR

7. **On the status bar, double-click the Overtype button.**

   The Overtype mode is turned on.
8. **Type ea.**

   The word is changed, and the red wavy line is removed.

9 **On the status bar, double-click OVR.**

The Overtype mode is turned off.

10 **Double-click the word "personal" in the third paragraph.**

The word *personal* is selected.

11 **Type public.**

The word *personal* is replaced with the word *public,* and the rest of the text moves to the right as you type.

12 **Double-click the selection area to the left of the first paragraph.**

The paragraph is selected.

13 **Press Delete.**

The paragraph is deleted.

14 **On the Standard toolbar, click the Undo button (displays the ScreenTip Undo Clear).**

The deleted paragraph is restored and is also selected.

15 **On the Standard toolbar, click the Redo button (displays the ScreenTip Redo Clear).**

The paragraph is deleted again.

16 **Click the Undo button again.**

The deleted paragraph is restored and is also selected.

17 **Press the down arrow key.**

The paragraph is deselected.

18 **Click after the second occurrence of the word "and" in the last sentence of the first paragraph.**

19 **Press Ctrl+Backspace.**

The word *and* is deleted.

20 **Press Ctrl+right arrow twice to move the insertion point to the word "individual."**

21 **Press Ctrl+Delete.**

The word *individual* is deleted.

◆ **Keep this file open for the next exercise.**

QUICK REFERENCE ▼

Undo an action

On the Standard toolbar, click the Undo button.

Restore an action

On the Standard toolbar, click the Redo button.

QUICK **CHECK**

Q. Is the Redo button always available on the Standard toolbar?

A. No, the Redo button only becomes available after the Undo button has been used.

Creating a Folder

Creating, Saving, and Closing Documents

THE BOTTOM LINE

Keeping the files you create organized is critical to being able to easily access them in the future. An essential component of file management is creating folders in which to store your documents. These folders allow you to group your files in a variety of ways such as by type (e.g., letters, memos, reports) or by content (e.g., gardening, baseball, vacation).

After you create a document, you might want to save the document in a folder. A folder is a storage area on your computer's hard disk or a network drive. A network is a system of computers connected by communications links. When a computer is connected via a network, you can use one computer to access the hard disk of another computer on the network. You can create folders to store files by project, author, file type, or just about any organization scheme you can imagine.

For example, you might have a folder named Memos. In this folder, you store all of the memos that you send to your boss. You might choose to have a *subfolder* (a folder within a folder) in your Memo folder named Sent Marketing. This is where you store memos that you send to the marketing department. You could even have another subfolder in your Memo folder called Sent Finance that contains the memos that you send to the finance department. Now, when you open the Memo folder, you won't have to wade through all of the memos you have sent; instead, you have sorted and saved them in subfolders so they are quick and easy to find and retrieve.

ANOTHER METHOD

You can also create folders from any other Microsoft Office application, in Windows Explorer, or in My Computer.

Word makes it easy to create folders directly from the Save As dialog box. With Word's file management features, you can easily organize, locate, and create folders to store documents and save files with different names. You can also delete files and folders from within the Open and Save As dialog boxes. To delete a file or folder, select what you want to delete, and click the Delete button or press the Delete key.

ANOTHER METHOD

You can also create new folders in Windows Explorer. You don't have to create them from within Word. To create a new folder in Windows Explorer, click the Start button, point to Programs, and then click Windows Explorer. In the Folders pane on the left side of Windows Explorer, navigate to and double-click the folder in which you want to create a new folder. On the File menu, point to New, and click Folder. A new folder appears with the name *New Folder* selected. Type the name of the new folder, and press Enter to rename it.

◆ **Make sure Brochure 02 is open and on screen in Word**

Create a folder

With all of our edits and corrections made to Brochure 02, we now need to save the document. In order to avoid overwriting the original document, we will first create a folder in which to store it as well as the results of future exercises.

1 **On the File menu, click Save As.**

The Save As dialog box appears and displays the content of the Lesson02 folder, which is the last folder that you used.

2 **Click the Create New Folder button. The New Folder dialog box appears.**

FIGURE 2-6

New Folder dialog box

3 **Type My Exercises in the Name box, and click OK.**

The New Folder dialog box closes, and the Save As dialog box appears and displays the My Exercises folder. The file Brochure 02 is listed in the File Name box because it is the file that is currently open.

4 **Click the Cancel button.**

The Save As dialog box closes and the file is not saved.

◆ **Keep this file open for the next exercise.**

QUICK REFERENCE ▼

Create a folder

1 On the File menu, click Save As.
2 Click the Create New Folder button.
3 Type a name for the folder in the Name box.
4 Click OK.

Saving a File with a Different Name

THE BOTTOM LINE

There are many situations in which you may want to save an existing file with a different name. This is easily done by selecting Save As from the File menu and then typing a new name for the file.

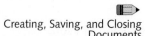

Creating, Saving, and Closing Documents

You might find it necessary to make a copy of a file. You can keep the original on hand for safekeeping or for comparison and then make changes to a new version. For example, suppose the marketing manager at an outdoor vacation resort named Adventure Works creates a revised brochure each year. When it's time to create a new brochure, she opens the previous version and saves it with a new name. Using the previous brochure helps create the new brochure quickly and efficiently with just a few updates. Saving the new brochure with a new name preserves previous versions to maintain an historical archive.

Save an existing file with a different name

In the last exercise, we created a folder in which to save documents. Now we are going to actually save our Brochure 02 document — but we will save it with a different name and in the My Exercises folder.

1 **On the File menu, click Save As.**

The Save As dialog box appears. The content of the Lesson02 folder appears.

TROUBLESHOOTING

The My Exercises folder doesn't appear in the Save In box because it isn't the last folder in which you saved a document.

2 **Double-click the My Exercises folder.**

The My Exercises folder opens.

3 **Click after "Brochure 02" in the File Name box.**

4 **Press the spacebar, and type** Edited.

5 **Click the Save button.**

The Save As dialog box closes, and the file is saved with the name Brochure 02 Edited. The file's new name appears in the title bar of your document.

◆ **Keep this file open for the next exercise.**

TIP

You should make a backup copy of important files to protect against losses from computer crashes, viruses, accidental changes, or deletions. You can save copies of files to floppy disks or to a network disk (a disk that is physically located on another computer, but is available to users on the same network), if one is available. The best way to safeguard files is to use a *tape backup system* or a writable CD. A tape backup system stores the content of hard disks on high-capacity tapes, which are typically stored in separate locations and are used to recover lost or deleted data.

QUICK CHECK

Q. If you are going to save an existing file with a different name, can you save it in the same folder as the original document?

A. An existing file can be saved with a different name in the same folder as the original document or in a different folder.

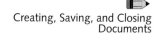
Creating, Saving, and Closing
Documents

QUICK REFERENCE ▼

Save a file with a different name

1 On the File menu, click Save As.

2 If necessary, navigate to the folder in which you want to store the file.

3 In the File Name box, type a name for the new copy of the file.

4 Click the Save button.

Saving a File in a Different Format

THE BOTTOM LINE

While Word files are transportable to the other Office applications as well as to some other programs, not all programs can open a Word document. In order to make your document accessible to these other computer applications, you need to save your document in a different format. A common word-processing format is Rich Text Format.

Your computer at work has Office 2003 installed, but you have a different word-processing program installed on your computer at home. You need to take work home with you to meet deadlines, but if you don't have the same computer software as your company, how will you be able to work at home on your computer? Luckily, Word allows you to save a document in other formats. Saving a file in a different format is useful when the document needs to be used in another word-processing program, in an earlier version of Word, or if you want to use the document as a Web page. You can save your document at work in Rich Text Format (.rtf) so you'll be able to read the document at home using other Microsoft programs such as Windows Notepad or WordPad.

A file format is the way in which information is stored in a file so that a program can open and save the file. A file's format is indicated by the three-letter extension after the file name. For example, when you save a new document in Microsoft Office Word 2003, by default, Word stores it in Word 2003 format with a .doc file extension. Files saved in Rich Text Format have the .rtf extension, and files saved in text-only format have the .txt extension.

TIP

Rich Text Format is used for transferring formatted text documents between applications.

Save a file in a different format

Now that we have saved our edited brochure as a Word document, we will also save it as an Rich Text Format file which will make it more easily transportable to applications other than Word.

1 **On the File menu, click Save As.**

2 **Click the Save As Type down arrow.**

3 **Click Rich Text Format.**

4 **Click Save.**

The file is saved in the selected format. (It will have the same name but a different extension.)

If you are not sure of the version of software in which a document was created, you can use the Properties dialog box to display file format information about the document that includes the version, type, and creator of the file. On the File menu, click Properties, and then click the General tab to display the document format information.

QUICK REFERENCE ▼

Save a file with a different format

1 On the File menu, click Save As.

2 If necessary, in the File Name box, type a new name for the document.

3 Click the Save As Type down arrow.

4 Click the file format in which you want to save the document.

5 Click Save.

◆ **If you are not continuing to other lessons, close the file and Word.**

◆ **If you are continuing to the next lesson, close the file but keep Word open.**

QUICK CHECK

Q. If you save a file in RTF format, can you then re-open it in Word?

A. Yes, a file saved in RTF can be opened in Word.

Key Points

✓ *There are several ways to open an existing file. From within Word, you can access the Open dialog box, use the Look In box to find the desired folder, and then select the desired file from within that folder.*

✓ *There are a variety of ways to navigate through a document, including using the scroll bars, arrow keys, and insertion point.*

✓ *You can edit a document by inserting, selecting, and deleting text.*

✓ *Two simple ways to manage files are to create folders to separate your work and to save a file with a different name or in a different format.*

Quick Quiz

True/False

T F 1. Word 2003 only allows you to open files that were created in Word 2003.

T F 2. The Open dialog box automatically opens to the folder in which you last saved a document.

T F 3. Once you save a Word document, you cannot save it again using a different name.

T F 4. You must use the arrow keys on the keyboard if you want to move more than one page up or down within your document.

T F 5. The Ctrl+Page Up key combination will always move you backward one page in your document.

T F 6. The Previous button performs the same action as the Ctrl+Page Up keystroke.

T F 7. Scrolling does not move the insertion point.

T F 8. In Overtype mode, existing text is deleted and replaced by text that you type.

T F 9. To select a word, you must triple-click it.

T F 10. You have the ability, from within Word, to create folders in which to store your files.

Short Answer

1. How do you delete a document in Word?

2. What are three ways that you can scroll forward through a document?

3. If you make a mistake when editing a document, what can you do to fix the problem?

4. What keys do you press to select text to the right of the insertion point?

5. What is the Select Browse Object button used for?

6. What are three ways to open a recently opened document?

7. What menu command do you use to open an existing file? What toolbar button? What task pane option?

8. What is the difference between scrolling and moving the insertion point?

9. How can you select a sentence within a paragraph?

◆ **Make sure that Word is running before you attempt to complete these exercises.**

On Your Own

IMPORTANT

In the On Your Own exercises that follow, you must complete Exercise 1 to continue to Exercise 2 and Exercise 3.

Exercise 1

Open the file SkillCheck Lesson 02 in the Lesson02 folder in the Word Practice folder that is located on your hard disk, and make the following edits.

- Type the word **provides** before the misspelled word *comprejensive* in the first sentence.
- Replace the first occurrence of the word *for* with the word *to* in the first sentence of the first paragraph.
- Delete the second occurrence of the word *has* in the sentence beginning *A full service agency.*
- Replace the Senior Vice President's name at the end of the letter with your own.
- Select the last sentence in the third paragraph, which begins with *We believe,* and delete it.
- At the end of the document, add three blank lines after *Sincerely* to allow room for the signature.
- Change the date to **January 1, 2005**.
- Make spelling corrections as needed.

The finished document should look similar to Figure 2-7.

FIGURE 2-7

Completed On Your Own Exercise 1

```
January 1, 2005

Mr. and Mrs. George Billingsley
Billingsley Inc.
5678 Elm Street
Hinesburg, VT 50265

Dear Mr. and Mrs. Billingsley,

This letter is in response to your request for information about the services provided by Contoso, Ltd. Contoso provides comprehensive public relations services including advertising and marketing communications services for a variety of diverse corporations, businesses and non-profit organizations. A full service agency, Contoso has handled public relations and advertising for everything from sewing machines and frozen foods to computer software applications and book promotions.

Contoso works with a variety of clients in the Northern New England area, Boston, New York, and New Jersey in the fields of manufacturing, healthcare, financial services, education, and computer software. Contoso also offers in-house graphic design capabilities to produce distinctive, results-oriented advertising and collateral including annual reports, brochures, corporate identity, logos and more.

With a philosophy of providing hands-on attention and personalized service for our clients, Contoso is committed to creative, high-quality work, innovative solutions and responsive service.

Please feel free to contact me for more information. I can be reached by phone at 303-555-0120, or by e-mail at someone@example.com.

Sincerely,



[Your Name]
Senior Vice President
```

Exercise 2

Create a subfolder named **On Your Own** in the Lesson02 folder, and then save the edited file from Exercise 1 in the new folder as **SkillCheck Lesson 02 Edited**.

Exercise 3

Continue to edit the SkillCheck Lesson 02 Edited document.

- Select the entire paragraph that begins *With a philosophy* and delete it.
- Select the word *Sincerely* and replace it with **Regards**.
- You realize that both of the last two edits were a mistake. Undo both of them.

◆ **Close the file without saving your changes.**

One Step Further

Exercise 1

If you have a document that is more than a page in length, what is the quickest way to move to the beginning of the document? What is the quickest way to move to the end of the document? Why would this be a useful feature in a lengthy document?

Exercise 2

Does scrolling move your insertion point? Experiment with the scroll bar if you are unsure. How can this be a useful feature?

Formatting Text

After completing this lesson, you will be able to:

✔ *Use the Formatting toolbar to format text.*
✔ *Apply character effects to text.*
✔ *Align text.*
✔ *Cut and paste text.*
✔ *Use Paste Special.*
✔ *Use drag and drop to edit text.*
✔ *Use collect and paste.*
✔ *Apply styles.*
✔ *Create a paragraph border.*
✔ *Add shading to a paragraph.*
✔ *Preview a document.*
✔ *Print a document.*

KEY TERMS

- Align Left
- Align Right
- attribute
- Center
- Clipboard
- embed
- Justify
- link

- object
- object linking and embedding (OLE)
- Office Clipboard
- Print Preview
- shading
- source file
- style

Have you ever wished that you could change the format and layout of a document to place emphasis on key words and phrases? Or have you ever read a document that you created and printed, only to find that the information on page 3 should be where the information on page 2 is located? Microsoft Office Word 2003 has numerous features to help you create and format documents in just the way you want. Word also lets you move and copy information throughout a document or even to another document.

In this lesson, you will learn how to apply formatting to make text bold, underlined, and italic, and you'll learn how to change the font size and style of text. In this lesson, you will learn different methods for cutting and copying text and objects so that you can move or copy text or other objects from one place to another. You'll practice copying and pasting text between different documents, and you'll learn how to modify the appearance of a paragraph by aligning text, creating a border, and adding shading.

IMPORTANT

Before you can use the practice files in this lesson, you need to install them from the book's companion CD to their default location. For additional information on how to find and open files used in this book, see the "Using the CD-ROM" section at the beginning of this book.

Using the Formatting Toolbar to Format Text

THE BOTTOM LINE

The Formatting toolbar, which appears near the top of the Word window by default, is the easiest way to format text. It lets you change the font, font size, font color, and style. You can make the text bold, italic, or underlined. You can also set the alignment or indentation, spacing, and borders, plus add highlighting. All of these features allow you to make the text appear exactly how you want it to appear.

Formatting Text as You Type

Although in Word you can change the appearance of text in several different ways, using the Formatting toolbar is the quickest and easiest way to make most text changes. The Formatting toolbar has several buttons and lists that you can use to change text attributes. An **attribute** is a characteristic such as bold formatting, italics, lowercasing, underlining, font (the style of the characters), font size, and even text color.

The drop-down buttons at the left end of the Formatting toolbar are, from left to right, the Style box, the Font box, and the Font Size box, as shown in Figure 3-1. These boxes tell you the name of the style, the name of the font, and the size of the font currently in use. (Styles are discussed later in this lesson.) You click the down arrows on the right sides of the boxes to open the boxes and display content lists.

TROUBLESHOOTING

In the following exercises and illustrations used throughout this lesson, the Standard and Formatting toolbars have been separated. For additional information on how to separate the toolbars, see the "Using the CD-ROM" section at the beginning of this book.

FIGURE 3-1

Components of the Formatting toolbar

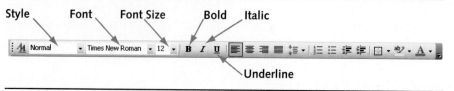

The buttons on the toolbars toggle on and off. That is, when you click a button, you turn on the attribute. When you click the button again, you turn off the attribute.

When you select formatted text, the font and font size of the selected text appear on the Formatting toolbar—in the Font and Font Size boxes—only if the font and font size of the selected text is the same. If the font, font style, or font size varies throughout the selected text, the Font, Font Size, and Font Style boxes appear blank on the Formatting toolbar. If the selected text is bold, italic, or underlined, the relevant button on the Formatting toolbar appears with a box around it and in an orange color.

You can also use the Formatting toolbar to remove formatting. For example, if you want to remove the bold formatting from a title, you simply select the title text and click the Bold button.

When you are formatting a document, you can open the Reveal Formatting task pane (from the Format menu) to display the format of the selected text, such as its font and font effects. The Reveal Formatting task pane allows you to display, change, or clear the formatting for the selected text. You also can use the Reveal Formatting task pane to select text based on formatting so that you can compare the formatting used in the selected text with formatting used in other parts of the document.

◆ **Be sure to start Word before beginning this exercise.**

◆ **Open Brochure 03 from the Lesson03 folder in the Word Practice folder that is located on your hard disk.**

Format text using the Formatting toolbar

The Brochure 03 document was created to publicize the services of the public relations firm Contoso, Ltd. We will begin experimenting with formatting text by using the Formatting toolbar buttons to make text within the brochure bold, italic, and underlined. We will also use the Formatting down arrows to open lists on the Formatting toolbar to change the font and size of a heading.

1 **Select the heading line, Contoso, Ltd Network.**

2 **On the Formatting toolbar, click the Bold button, and click the Italic button.**

The title appears bold and italic.

ANOTHER METHOD

You can also apply the Bold attribute to selected text by pressing the key combination Ctrl+B. Similarly, you can italicize selected text by pressing Ctrl+I.

B

FIGURE 3-2

Brochure 03 with format changes to the heading

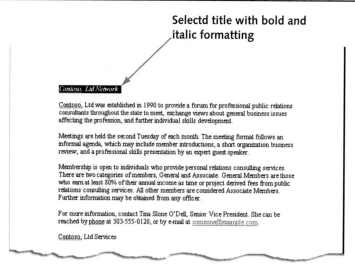

Selectd title with bold and italic formatting

3 Double-click the last word of the heading, Network, to select it.

4 On the Formatting toolbar, click the Underline button.

U

ANOTHER METHOD

You can also apply the Underline attribute to selected text by pressing Ctrl+U.

5 Click anywhere.

The text is no longer selected, and the word *Network* is underlined.

6 Triple-click the selection area (the area of the document to the left of the text).

All text in the document appears selected.

7 On the Formatting toolbar, click the Font down arrow.

A list of available fonts appears.

FIGURE 3-3

Font list

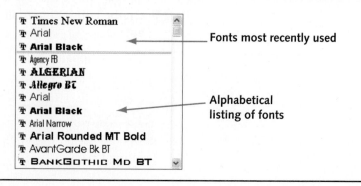

Fonts most recently used

Alphabetical listing of fonts

TIP

Note that the names listed in the Font list on your computer screen might be different from the names shown in Figure 3-3.

8 Scroll down, if necessary, and click Century Schoolbook.

The text changes to the Century Schoolbook font.

TIP

The most recently used fonts are listed first in the Font list, followed by an alphabetical listing of all available fonts.

9 On the Formatting toolbar, click the Font Size down arrow (to the right of the number 12).

A list of font sizes appears.

FIGURE 3-4

Font Size drop down list

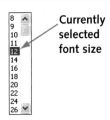

Currently selected font size

TIP

The Font Size list displays whole numbers, but you can specify font sizes in half-point increments by typing the font size (for example, *10.5*) in the Font Size box.

10 Click 10.

The selected text is displayed in a smaller, 10-point font size.

11 On the Format menu, click Reveal Formatting.

The Reveal Formatting task pane appears, displaying the format of the selected text.

FIGURE 3-5

Reveal Formatting task pane

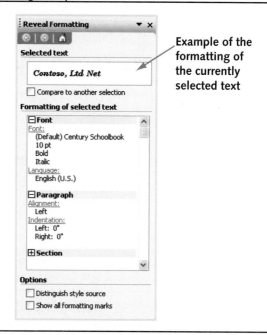

Example of the formatting of the currently selected text

TIP

Note the information that is provided in this task pane, as well as the links to other dialog boxes such as the Font dialog box and the Paragraph dialog box.

✖   **12** **In the Reveal Formatting task pane, click the Close button.**

The Reveal Formatting task pane closes.

◆ **Save the document as Brochure 03 Edited.**

◆ **Keep this file open for the next exercise.**

QUICK REFERENCE ▼

Format text

1 Select the text.

2 On the Formatting toolbar, click the Style down arrow.

Or

Click the Font down arrow.

Or

Click the Font Size down arrow.

Format text using the Font dialog box

1 Select the text.

2 On the Format menu, click Font.

3 Make selections as desired.

Apply a bold attribute

1 Select the text.

2 On the Formatting toolbar, click the Bold button.

Or

Press Ctrl+B.

Apply the italics attribute

1 Select the text.

2 On the Formatting toolbar, click the Italic button.

Or

Press Ctrl+I.

Apply the underline attribute

1 Select the text.

2 On the Formatting toolbar, click the Underline button.

Or

Press Ctrl+U.

QUICK CHECK

Q. What are two ways to format text as bold?

A. **You can either click the Bold button on the Formatting toolbar or you can type Ctrl+B on the keyboard.**

Changing the Look of Characters

Applying Character Effects to Text

THE BOTTOM LINE

In addition to the formatting options that are readily available from the Formatting toolbar, there are also a number of formatting attributes and effects that can be accessed from the Font dialog box. These special, and less-often used, formatting attributes allow you to apply unique effects to your text, such as shadow and emboss.

You can apply formatting attributes and effects that are not available on the Formatting toolbar, such as superscript, subscript, strikethrough, and small caps character effects, from the Font dialog box. When you use the Font dialog box, you can also change multiple attributes at once and display a sample of the selected attributes before you apply them to the text. Other attributes that are available only from the Font dialog box include special effects such as shadowed or embossed text and the color of the line for underlined text.

To use the Font dialog box, you select the text that you want to format, and on the Format menu, click Font. Or before you begin typing text, on the Format menu, click Font. All text that you type will then appear in the format that you selected in the Font dialog box until you change the formatting again.

FIGURE 3-6

Font dialog box

QUICK CHECK

Q. If you select a font attribute before you begin
typing, can you then
change that attribute
after the text is typed?

**A. You can always change
the attributes of text—
either before it is typed,
after it is typed, or both
before and after. There
is no limit to the number
of times you can change
text format.**

TIP

Since all of the font attributes are visible in the Font dialog box,
modifications can be made quite easily. You can use the Preview box
to see how the modifications will look in the document.

Aligning Text in a Document

THE BOTTOM LINE

Depending upon the text you are typing, the desired layout of the
document you are creating, or the way in which one paragraph needs
to stand apart from others, you will need to set the alignment of the
text on the page. Align Left is the default alignment setting, but you
can also choose Center, Align Right, or Justify.

Changing the Look of Characters

By default, text that you type has the **Align Left** alignment attribute applied.
That is, text is aligned with the left margin. However, you can use the
Center, Align Right, or **Justify** attributes to align text. Centered text is placed
equally between the left and right margins, right-aligned text is placed at the
right margin, and justified text fills out all the space between the right and
left margins. To align an existing paragraph, click anywhere in the paragraph
and click one of the following buttons on the Formatting toolbar.

FIGURE 3-7

Alignment buttons on the Formatting toolbar

TIP

As is true with text attributes, when an alignment attribute is turned on, all text typed from that point on is affected until you turn off the attribute.

Use the alignment buttons on complete paragraphs rather than on characters or phrases. You do not need to select all of the text in a paragraph before you apply an alignment. You only need to click to place the insertion point somewhere in the paragraph.

Figure 3-8 shows the four different types of alignment attributes.

FIGURE 3-8

Alignment attributes illustrated

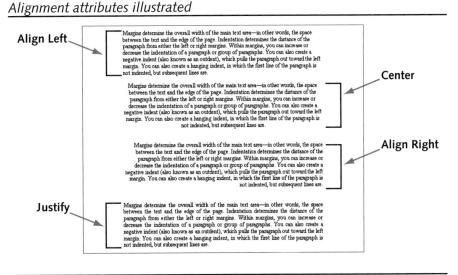

Aligning text

Continuing working in the Brochure 03 Edited document, we will now practice making adjustments to the alignment of text. You will center, right-align, left-align, and justify text.

1 Select the first heading line, Contoso, Ltd Network.

2 On the Formatting toolbar, click the Center button.

The heading line moves to the center of the document.

3 Click anywhere in the first paragraph.

4 On the Formatting toolbar, click the Align Right button.

The paragraph moves to the right margin.

FIGURE 3-9

Brochure with first paragraph aligned right

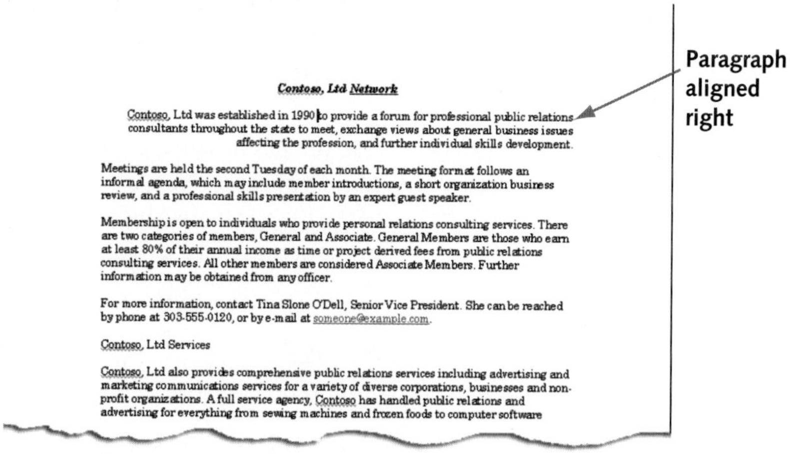

Paragraph
aligned
right

5 **On the Formatting toolbar, click the Align Left button.**

The paragraph moves back to the left margin.

6 **On the Formatting toolbar, click the Justify button.**

The lines in the paragraph now extend to both the left and right margins, except for the last line of the paragraph, which doesn't extend all the way to the right margin because it is shorter than the other lines.

7 **On the Formatting toolbar, click the Align Left button to return the text to its original alignment.**

◆ **Keep this file open for the next exercise.**

QUICK REFERENCE ▼

Align text

1 Click the paragraph that you want to align.
Or
Select all or part of the multiple paragraphs that you want to align.

2 On the Formatting toolbar, click the appropriate alignment button.

QUICK CHECK

Q. What alignment would you typically use for a title or heading of a document?

A. **Center alignment is typically used for headings or titles.**

Rearranging Text Within a Document

Editing Documents

> **THE BOTTOM LINE**
>
> One of the great advantages of word-processing applications over handwritten documents is the ease with which existing text can be moved around within the document. This is done using the Cut, Copy, and Paste tools or by dragging and dropping text.

Cutting and Pasting Text

When you cut and paste text, you are removing text from one location in a document and placing it in another location in the same document or in a different document. Copying and pasting duplicates the original information in another location or document. There are various methods for cutting and pasting text: you can click Cut and Paste on the Edit menu, use the mouse pointer to drag and drop text, or click the Cut and Paste buttons on the Standard toolbar. For example, the marketing manager at Contoso, Ltd is updating the company brochure. The new brochure will contain information from an internal memorandum that was distributed to company employees. To save time, she will copy the information in the memo rather than retyping it and will paste the information into the brochure that she is updating.

When you use the Copy command, text that you select is duplicated in a new location while also remaining in the original spot. When you use the Cut command, the text that you select is taken from its original position and moved to another location.

When you paste something from the Clipboard, the Paste Options button appears next to the item you have pasted. Clicking the Paste Options button displays a list of actions that Word can initiate regarding the pasted item. This list will vary depending upon the content of the pasted item, but generally (for text items) will include Keep Source Formatting, Use Destination Styles, Match Destination Formatting, and Keep Text Only. These options allow you a quick and easy way to format pasted text to match an existing document—or not, depending upon your needs.

> **TIP**
>
> The **Clipboard** is a temporary storage area designed to hold text and/or pictures that have been cut or copied.

Open Memorandum 03 from the Lesson03 folder in the Word Practice folder that is located on your hard disk.

Copy and paste text

You now have two files open: Brochure 03 Edited – the document you have been working in – and Memorandum 03. Memorandum 03 contains some text that you need in the Brochure 03 Edited document. You will copy selected text from one document to the other.

1 Select the main paragraph of the memo.

2 On the Standard toolbar, click the Copy button.

Nothing changes on the screen, but the text is copied to the Clipboard. The main paragraph remains selected.

ANOTHER METHOD

- To use a shortcut menu to copy text, right-click the selected text, and on the shortcut menu, click Copy.
- To copy text with keystrokes, type Ctrl+C.
- To use a menu to copy text, choose Copy from the Edit menu.

3 On the File menu, click Close to close the memorandum document.

The brochure is now visible.

ANOTHER METHOD

You can also close a document, without closing the entire application or other documents that are currently open, by clicking the Close Window button at the far right of the Menu bar.

4 Scroll down and click at the end of the document after the word "Photography".

5 Press Enter twice.

The insertion point moves two lines below the word *Photography*.

6 On the Standard toolbar, click the Paste button.

The paragraph remains in the original document, and a copy of the paragraph is inserted at the new location in the brochure.

FIGURE 3-10

Brochure with pasted paragraph

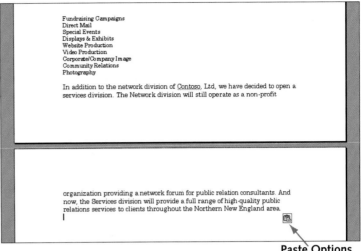

Paste Options

ANOTHER METHOD

- To use a shortcut menu to paste text, right-click the location where you want to paste the text, and on the shortcut menu, click Paste.
- To paste text with keystrokes, place the insertion point in the desired location, and type Ctrl+V.
- To use the menus to paste text, click in the location where you want to paste the text, and then select Paste from the Edit menu.

7 **Click the Paste Options button.**

The menu of options for pasting opens.

FIGURE 3-11

Paste Options menu

8 **Click Match Destination Formatting.**

The font size changes to 10.

◆ **Save the Brochure 03 Edited document and keep it open for the next exercise.**

Cut and paste text

Now you will cut and paste selected text within the Brochure 03 Edited document.

1 **Select the fourth paragraph, which begins "For more information."**

2 On the Standard toolbar, click the Cut button, and press Delete to remove the extra blank line.

The paragraph is removed from its location in the document and is placed on the Clipboard. (The Clipboard is not visible.)

ANOTHER METHOD

- To use a shortcut menu to cut text, right-click the selected text, and on the shortcut menu, click Cut.
- To cut text with keystrokes, type Ctrl+X.
- To use a menu to cut text, choose Cut from the Edit menu.

---

3 Click the blank line below the word "Photography" (the last item in the list of services).

4 Press Enter to separate the paragraph with a blank line, and on the Standard toolbar, click the Paste button.

The paragraph appears at the new location after the list of services.

FIGURE 3-12

Brochure with paragraph that has been cut and pasted

Contoso, Ltd works with a variety of clients in the Northern New England area, Boston, New York, and New Jersey in the fields of manufacturing, healthcare, financial services, education, and computer software. Contoso also offers in-house graphic design capabilities to produce distinctive, results-oriented advertising and collateral including annual reports, brochures, corporate identity, logos and more.

With a philosophy of providing hands-on attention and personalized service for our clients, Contoso is committed to creative, high-quality work, innovative solutions and responsive service. We believe dedicated teamwork is the key to helping our clients achieve success.

Following is a list of services provided by Contoso, Ltd:

News Releases
Public Information Campaigns
Fundraising Campaigns
Direct Mail
Special Events
Displays & Exhibits
Website Production
Video Production
Corporate/Company Image
Community Relations
Photography

For more information, contact Tina Slone O'Dell, Senior Vice President. She can be reached by phone at 303-555-0120, or by e-mail at someone@example.com.

In addition to the network division of Contoso, Ltd, we have decided to open a services division. The Network division will still operate as a non-profit organization providing a

Cut and pasted paragraph

◆ Keep this file open for the next exercise.

QUICK REFERENCE ▼

Cut or copy and then paste text

1 Select the text that you want to move or copy.

2 On the Standard toolbar, click the Cut or Copy button.

3 Click the insertion point in the location where the text is to appear or be duplicated.

4 On the Standard toolbar, click the Paste button.

QUICK CHECK

Q. What are four ways to paste text that has already been cut or copied to the Clipboard?

A. To paste text, you can use the Paste button on the toolbar, use the Ctrl+V keys, choose Paste from the Edit menu, or right-click and choose Paste from the shortcut menu.

Using Paste Special

The Paste Special command extends the capabilities of the Paste command. In Microsoft Word, the Paste Special command uses Microsoft's **object linking and embedding (OLE)** technology to integrate data created by other Microsoft Office programs. To understand the difference between Paste and Paste Special, consider what happens when you paste part of a Microsoft Excel worksheet into a Word document by using the Paste command on the Edit menu or the Paste button on the Standard toolbar. You begin by copying a range of cells from the worksheet to the Windows Clipboard. You then switch to your Word document, position the insertion point where you want to paste the data, and then use the Paste command or Paste button to insert the data into the Word document. The data from the worksheet appears in the Word document as a Word table, and you can format and edit the table text just as you would edit any other table.

When you paste data that originated from a different program into a Word document, as in the example just mentioned, the pasted data is no longer associated with the original program. If you want to maintain an association between the pasted content and the original application, you use the Paste Special command. You can use two basic approaches: you can either **embed** or **link** the Clipboard contents.

If you use Paste Special to embed the pasted contents, Word converts the pasted contents to an object and retains its association with the program in which the contents originated. In the Excel example, if you paste and embed the contents of an Excel worksheet into a Word document, the contents are converted to an Excel object that can be edited in Excel but not in Word. If you double-click the object, Word launches Excel, which you can then use to make changes to the data. The pasted contents are no longer associated with the original workbook file, but they are associated with the Excel program.

> **TIP**
>
> An **object** is a collection of data that is treated as a single element within a document.

Why is this useful? Suppose the cells that you copied from the Excel worksheet contained several formulas that make calculations on other cells. If you simply paste the data into Word, you lose all of these formulas. If you paste and embed the worksheet data as an Excel object, you can double-click the object, change formulas or other values, and then have Excel re-calculate the formulas. When you exit Excel and return to your Word document, the changes you made in Excel appear in the Excel object.

If you use Paste Special to link your pasted contents, Word creates a connection, or link, between the pasted data and the file (called the source file) in the originating application. In the Excel example, if you copy a range of cells from an Excel workbook and then paste and link the data in a Word document, Word converts the data to an Excel object and links it to the original workbook. If you double-click the Excel object, Excel launches and opens the workbook that contains the pasted data. You can make changes to the workbook and save your changes. Then, in the Word document, you can update the Excel object to reflect the changes that have been made in the Excel workbook.

So how is linking different than embedding? When you embed an object in Word, the object becomes part of the Word document. A connection is made to the program in which the object originated, but not to the source file where the data originated. In other words, there is no longer any relationship between the Excel object in Word and the contents of the original workbook (source file). However, if you link pasted contents, the data are not truly part of the Word document—they remain part of the source file. Suppose that you save and close your Word document after pasting and linking an Excel object. Now suppose that you or someone else opens the Excel workbook, makes changes to values or formulas in the workbook, and then saves the workbook. When you reopen the Word document, you can click the Excel object and then use the Link dialog box in Word to update the Excel object to reflect the changes you have made in the Excel workbook.

QUICK REFERENCE ▼

Paste from a file created in another program

1 Open the file and select the text or object that you want to paste into Word.

2 Copy the selected text or object.

3 Switch to Word, and on the Edit menu, click Paste Special.

4 In the Paste Special dialog box, select the format that you want inserted into the text or object.

5 Select Paste.

Or

Select Paste link.

6 Click OK.

Using Drag and Drop to Edit Text

To cut and paste without using buttons, you can use the drag-and-drop technique. As is true with other editing techniques, you begin by selecting the desired text. To drag and drop, select the text, position the mouse pointer over the selected text, hold down the left mouse button, and then drag the selection to a new location.

Use drag and drop

We are now going to make some additional edits to the Brochure 03 Edited document. This time, however, you will use drag and drop to move text within the document.

1 Click the selection area to the left of the word "Photography" to select the entire line.

2 Position the mouse pointer over the selected text, and press and hold down the left mouse button.

A dotted rectangle appears near the mouse pointer as well as a dotted vertical line wherever the mouse is pointing.

FIGURE 3-13

Text ready to be dragged and dropped

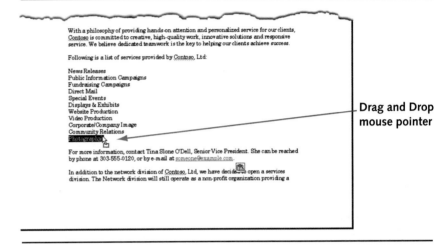

Drag and Drop mouse pointer

ANOTHER METHOD

To copy text using drag and drop, position the mouse pointer over the selected text, hold down the mouse button, hold down Ctrl, and then drag to the new location.

3 Drag the text, by moving the mouse, until the vertical dotted line is directly in front of the "N" in "News Releases" (the top line in the list of services).

4 Release the mouse button.

The text moves to the new location.

◆ Save the Brochure 03 Edited document.

◆ Keep this file open for the next exercise.

QUICK CHECK

Q. Which requires fewer keystrokes or mouse clicks: cutting and pasting text or dragging and dropping text?

A. Dragging and dropping requires fewer keystrokes and mouse clicks.

QUICK REFERENCE ▼

Move text using the mouse pointer

1 Select the text that you want to move or copy.

2 Position the mouse pointer over the selected text, and hold down the left mouse button.

3 Drag the mouse pointer to the new location.

Using Collect and Paste

Editing Documents

Microsoft Office actually uses two clipboards—the Windows Clipboard (which you have already used in this lesson) and the Office Clipboard. The Windows Clipboard can store only one selection at a time. However, the **Office Clipboard** can hold up to 24 items at a time, and you can paste any of these items into documents—not just the item that you most recently copied or cut to the Clipboard. You need to view the Office Clipboard's task pane so that you can see its contents.

FIGURE 3-14

Office Clipboard task pane

Last item that was cut or copied

TIP

The Office Clipboard is available in Microsoft Word, Excel, PowerPoint, and Outlook 2003. However, it is not available in Microsoft FrontPage 2003 or any non-Microsoft Office programs.

The Clipboard displays the first 50 characters of text or, if it is a graphic or some other form of data, as much of the item as is possible. Each item also has an icon next to it that indicates the program from which it came.

The Clipboard task pane can appear automatically when you copy or cut two items consecutively if you have it set up to do so. If this option is turned off, you can manually open the Clipboard task pane by clicking Office Clipboard on the Edit menu.

The Office Clipboard can hold up to 24 items. If you try to copy a twenty-fifth item, a message asks whether you want to discard the first item on the Office Clipboard and add the new item to the end of the Clipboard. If you click OK, the next time that you copy an item from any program, the Office Clipboard automatically discards the first item and adds the new item. If you click Cancel, any new items that you copy won't be added to the Office Clipboard until you make space on the Office Clipboard by pasting or cutting items already stored there. You won't see the message again until the Office Clipboard is full. Note that the collected items remain on the Office Clipboard until you quit all open Microsoft Office programs on your computer.

To adjust the way in which the Office Clipboard works, click the Options button at the bottom of the Clipboard. From the menu choices that appear, you can choose to *Show Office Clipboard Automatically* when you cut or copy two items consecutively, *Show Office Clipboard When Ctrl+C Pressed Twice*, or *Collect Without Showing Office Clipboard*. If you choose to *Show Status Near Taskbar When Copying*, you'll see a ScreenTip near the Windows taskbar each time you cut or copy an item. You can also choose *Show Office Clipboard Icon on Taskbar*, which places an icon on the Windows taskbar. This icon will be displayed any time that the Clipboard is open in one of the Microsoft Office applications. You can then double-click this icon to display the Office Clipboard.

FIGURE 3-15

Office Clipboard Options

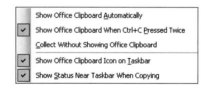

◆ **Make sure you have access to Logo 03 from the Lesson03 folder in the Word Practice folder that is located on your hard disk.**

Use the Office Clipboard

In this exercise, you continue making edits to the brochure – this time using the Office Clipboard. First, you will open the Clipboard task pane to see how the Office Clipboard handles multiple items. You will then paste from the Office Clipboard and, lastly, clear it.

1 **On the Edit menu, click Office Clipboard.**

The Clipboard task pane opens.

2 **Click the Clear All button.**

If there were any cut or copied items in the Clipboard, they are cleared.

FIGURE 3-16

Empty Office Clipboard

Clipboard cleared - no items stored in it

 3 On the Standard toolbar, click the Open button. In the Open dialog box, select the file named Logo 03, and click Open.

Word opens the file.

ANOTHER METHOD

You can also double-click the file name (Logo 03) to open it.

4 Click the text "Contoso, Ltd."

Little boxes appear around the logo, indicating that the logo is selected.

 5 On the Standard toolbar, click the Copy button.

The logo is copied from the document and placed in the Clipboard. A ScreenTip appears briefly on the taskbar indicating that the item has been collected. There is one item available in the Clipboard.

FIGURE 3-17

Office Clipboard ScreenTip

6 Close the logo document.

The logo document closes, and the brochure document appears.

FIGURE 3-18

Copied item in the Office Clipboard

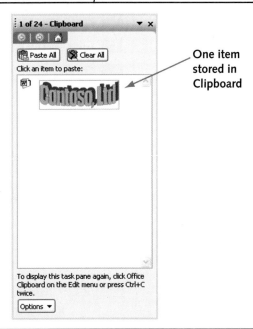

One item
stored in
Clipboard

7 Double-click in the selection area next to the last paragraph of the brochure document that begins "In addition to the network."

 8 On the Standard toolbar, click the Cut button.

The paragraph is removed from the document and placed on the Office Clipboard. The Clipboard task pane now contains two items.

FIGURE 3-19

Two items in the Office Clipboard

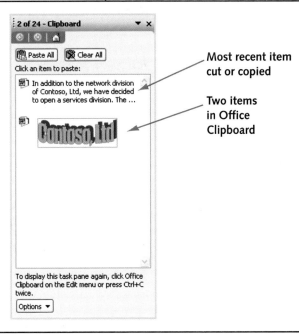

Most recent item
cut or copied

Two items
in Office
Clipboard

9 Scroll up to the top of the document, and click in front of the letter "C" in the heading "Contoso, Ltd Network."

10 Press Enter ten times to move the title down.

11 Click at the top of the document to position the insertion point.

12 On the Clipboard task pane, click the logo item.

The logo *Contoso, Ltd* now appears at the top of the brochure. (Click and drag, if necessary, to position the logo in the center of the page.)

13 Scroll down and click the blank line above the second heading, "Contoso, Ltd Services," and then press Enter to insert another blank line.

14 On the Clipboard task pane, click the copied paragraph.

The paragraph is inserted at the bottom of the first section in the document.

FIGURE 3-20

Brochure with items pasted from the Clipboard

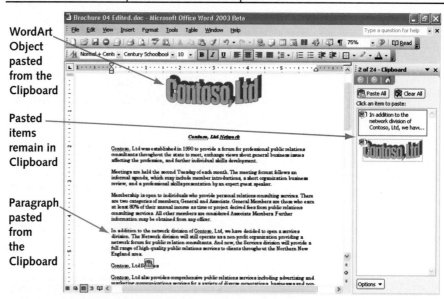

WordArt Object pasted from the Clipboard

Pasted items remain in Clipboard

Paragraph pasted from the Clipboard

 Clear All

15 On the Clipboard task pane, click the Clear All button.

16 In the upper-right corner of the Clipboard task pane, click the Close button.

The Clipboard task pane closes.

◆ Save the Brochure 03 Edited document.

◆ Keep this file open for the next exercise.

QUICK REFERENCE ▼

Paste from among multiple selections in the Office Clipboard

1 Select the text that you want to move or copy.

2 On the Standard toolbar, click the Cut or Copy button.

3 Repeat steps 1 and 2 for every selection that you want to move or copy.

4 Click where the item is to appear.

5 On the Edit menu, click Office Clipboard.

6 On the Clipboard task pane, click the item that you want to paste.

7 Repeat step 6 for every item that you want to paste.

Applying Styles to Text

THE BOTTOM LINE

A style is a set of formatting characteristics that you can apply to text (including tables and lists) in your document. With a style, you can quickly change the appearance of text, allowing you to apply numerous formats in one simple step.

Styles save you time when formatting a document and help you maintain a consistent format within the same document and from document to document. For example, suppose that you are creating a document that contains several subheadings. You want these subheadings to be green and a different font than your text. Instead of using the formatting options on the Formatting toolbar every time that you type a subheading in the document, you can create a style.

After you create the style, simply place the insertion point anywhere in the existing text or in the document where you want the style to start, and click the Style down arrow. Select the style that you want, and the text is modified with the chosen style.

Whenever you open a new, blank document, Word automatically attaches a standard template to the document. A template is a preformatted document that has its own set of styles. When you type in a new, blank document, the characters are set in a default style that is called Normal. The words that you type are automatically formatted in the font Times New Roman, at 12 points in size, and aligned against the left margin. The Normal template has five styles, three of which are designed for use as headings. The names of styles are located on the Formatting toolbar, in the Style list, as shown in Figure 3-21.

FIGURE 3-21

Style list

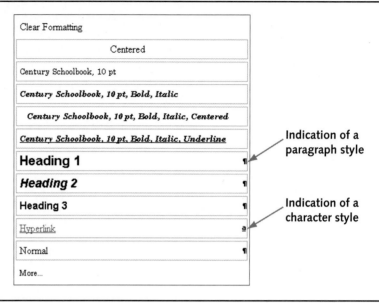

You can use styles to quickly apply multiple formatting attributes to text. For example, you could specify attributes such as bold, left align, italicize, and even font color, and then apply all of those attributes at the same time by applying a style. Simply select or click the text, and on the Formatting toolbar, click the Style down arrow, and click the style that you want to apply. If you want to apply a style to an entire paragraph, you need only click anywhere in that paragraph and click the style name in the Style list. You can also apply a style by clicking a blank line, selecting a style from the Style list, and typing. The text that you type from then on appears in the style that you selected.

Apply styles to paragraphs

Now that all of the content of our brochure is arranged the way we want it, we can begin to think about how the brochure looks. We've made some edits to the format of the text, but much more can be done through the use of styles.

1 **Scroll down in the document, and click anywhere in the word "Photography," which is the first item in the list of services near the end of the document.**

2 **On the Formatting toolbar, click the Style down arrow, and click Heading 3.**

The style is applied to the current paragraph—in this case, the single line *Photography*.

3 **Select the remaining list items, click the Style down arrow, and click Heading 3.**

The Heading 3 style is applied to all the paragraphs in the list.

ANOTHER METHOD

On the Edit menu, click the Repeat command to apply styles to multiple paragraphs that are scattered throughout the document. Apply the style that you want to use in the first paragraph, click or select the next paragraph, and press Ctrl+Y or F4. Use this method until you are finished applying the style.

4 Click outside of the list to deselect the paragraphs.

The list should look like the one in Figure 3-22.

FIGURE 3-22

The list in the brochure with the Heading 3 style applied

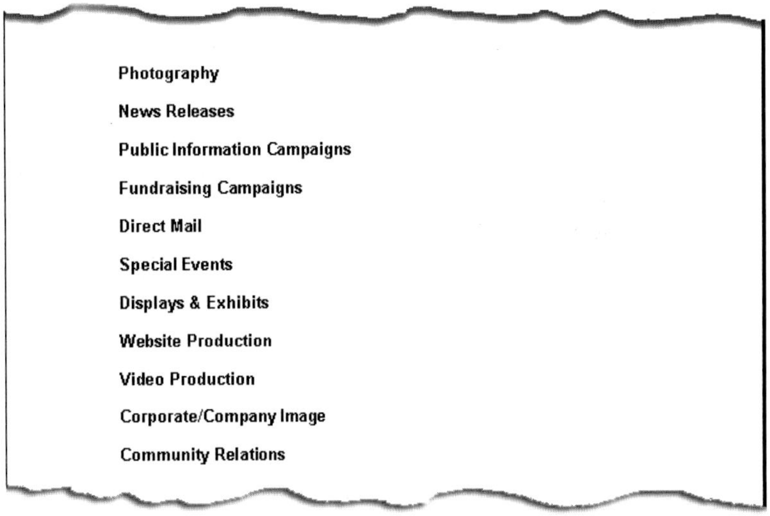

Photography

News Releases

Public Information Campaigns

Fundraising Campaigns

Direct Mail

Special Events

Displays & Exhibits

Website Production

Video Production

Corporate/Company Image

Community Relations

5 Click in front of the first line in the last paragraph of the document.

6 On the Formatting toolbar, click the Style down arrow, and click Heading 1.

The style is applied to the entire paragraph except for the Web address, which retains its Hyperlink style.

7 On the Standard toolbar, click the Undo button to remove the formatting that you just applied.

8 In the last paragraph of the document, select the words "For more information."

9 On the Formatting toolbar, click the Style down arrow, and click Heading 3.

The style is applied only to the selected text and not to the entire paragraph.

10 Select the "P" in the word "Photography," which is the first item in the list of services.

11 Click the Style down arrow, and click Heading 1.

The character becomes larger.

12 On the Standard toolbar, click the Undo button to remove the formatting that you just applied.

◆ Save Brochure 03 Edited.

◆ Keep this file open for the next exercise.

QUICK REFERENCE ▼

Apply a style to text

1 Select the text to be formatted.

2 On the Formatting toolbar, click the Style down arrow.

3 Click the style that you want to apply.

Changing the Look of Paragraphs

Creating a Paragraph Border

THE BOTTOM LINE

Placing a border around sections of text is a simple way to make part of your document stand out or to separate it from the rest of the text.

You can use borders to enhance the appearance of the documents that you create and help distinguish blocks of text. Borders are a great way to catch a person's eye. Suppose that you are creating a corporate memo reminding your coworkers about the upcoming company picnic. The information in the memo includes the date, time, location, menu, and activities planned. You need to remind your coworkers to bring $5 with them to the picnic. Important information like this can get lost in a document, so you add a border around this sentence so that they'll be sure not to miss the message.

You can create a border around entire pages in a document or around only selected paragraphs. Word provides a variety of preset borders to choose from, and all borders are customizable.

A border is based on a rectangular design, used to frame text in a document. Borders do not have to surround the text on all four sides of a document; you can display or hide any combination of the four lines that form the rectangle. For example, you could display only a bottom border for a paragraph. The marketing manager at Contoso, Ltd likes to create a two-line border (one line along the bottom and the other to the right) for the introductory paragraphs in her brochures. You can apply a border to a single paragraph or to multiple paragraphs.

One way to customize a border is to alter its line weight, which is the width of the lines that make up the border. To change the line weight, on the Tables And Borders toolbar, click the Line Weight down arrow, and click a point size for the border width. You can also click the Border Color button to choose a color for the lines.

Another option is to apply the border to a particular side of the paragraph. For example, if you want the border to appear below the paragraph rather than surrounding it on all four sides, click the Border down arrow to specify the side of the paragraph on which the border should appear.

ANOTHER METHOD

You can also create and format paragraph borders by clicking Borders and Shading on the Format menu, clicking the Borders tab, and then setting border characteristics.

Create and apply a border to a paragraph

In addition to formatting and styles, you can also alter the look of your document by applying borders. We will you use the Tables And Borders toolbar to create and apply a border to a paragraph within our brochure.

1 Click anywhere in the paragraph that begins with the words "With a philosophy" (the eighth paragraph, located above the list of services).

2 On the Standard toolbar, click the Tables And Borders button.

The Tables And Borders toolbar appears on your screen, and the

mouse pointer looks like a pencil.

FIGURE 3-23

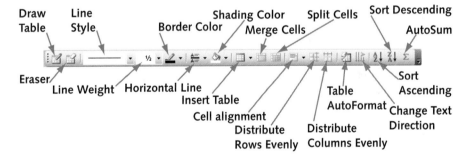

TROUBLESHOOTING

The Tables And Borders toolbar may appear as a floating toolbar or as a toolbar at the top of the document (with the Standard and Formatting toolbars). The way that the toolbar was last used dictates how it will be set the next time you open it.

3 On the Tables And Borders toolbar, click the Line Style down arrow.

A list of line styles appears.

4 Scroll down until you see a double squiggly line, and click it.

FIGURE 3-24

Line Style list

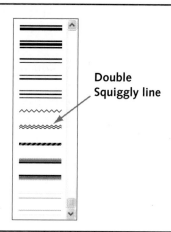

Double
Squiggly line

5 On the Tables And Borders toolbar, click the Border Color button.

A color palette appears.

6 Click the Gold square (fourth row, second square).

7 Click the down arrow on the Border button.

A list of border buttons appears, each button displaying a type of border.

TROUBLESHOOTING

What actually appears on the Border button depends upon the border that was last applied. The Horizontal Line is the option (shown next to step 7 above) appears by default, but the graphic on the button will change as the button is used. If you want to apply the same border you can simply click the button. If you want to choose a different button, you select it from the drop-down menu.

FIGURE 3-25

Border options menu

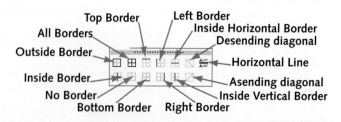

TROUBLESHOOTING

You can remove a border by clicking the affected text and then clicking the Border down arrow. When the border choices are displayed, click the No Border button. You can also display the Borders and Shading dialog box, and in the Setting section, click None to remove a border.

8 **On the Tables And Borders toolbar, click the Outside Border button.**

The line style, color, and border type that you specified are applied to the paragraph. The paragraph should look similar to the one shown here.

FIGURE 3-26

Paragraph with border

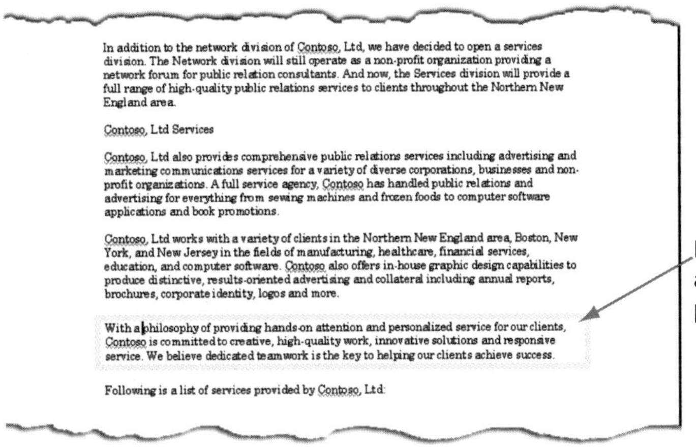

In addition to the network division of Contoso, Ltd, we have decided to open a services division. The Network division will still operate as a non-profit organization providing a network forum for public relation consultants. And now, the Services division will provide a full range of high-quality public relations services to clients throughout the Northern New England area.

Contoso, Ltd Services

Contoso, Ltd also provides comprehensive public relations services including advertising and marketing communications services for a variety of diverse corporations, businesses and non-profit organizations. A full service agency, Contoso has handled public relations and advertising for everything from sewing machines and frozen foods to computer software applications and book promotions.

Contoso, Ltd works with a variety of clients in the Northern New England area, Boston, New York, and New Jersey in the fields of manufacturing, healthcare, financial services, education, and computer software. Contoso also offers in-house graphic design capabilities to produce distinctive, results-oriented advertising and collateral including annual reports, brochures, corporate identity, logos and more.

With a philosophy of providing hands-on attention and personalized service for our clients, Contoso is committed to creative, high-quality work, innovative solutions and responsive service. We believe dedicated teamwork is the key to helping our clients achieve success.

Following is a list of services provided by Contoso, Ltd:

Border applied to paragraph

◆ **Save the Brochure 03 Edited document.**

◆ **Keep this file open for the next exercise.**

QUICK REFERENCE ▼

Create a paragraph border

1 Click in the paragraph to be formatted.

2 On the Standard toolbar, click the Tables And Borders button.

3 On the Tables And Borders toolbar, click the Line Style down arrow, and click a border style.

4 Click the Border down arrow, and click the Border button to apply the border.

Changing the Look of Paragraphs

Adding Shading to a Paragraph

THE BOTTOM LINE

Much like adding a border, adding shading allows you to emphasize certain areas of text. This is just one more way in which you can customize a document to appear exactly how you would like it to appear.

You can call attention to selected paragraphs by adding **shading**—either as a shade of gray or in color. If you apply color shading to a paragraph but print the document on a black-and-white printer, the color shading will be printed as a shade of gray.

If the Tables And Borders toolbar is not displayed, on the Standard toolbar, click the Tables And Borders button.

To expand the shading color list, on the Tables And Borders toolbar, click the Shading Color down arrow, and click the desired color square to add shading to selected text.

Add shading color to a paragraph

Just as we added a border to our brochure to add visual interest, we will now add a shading color to the last paragraph of the document.

1 **Click anywhere in the last paragraph (the one beginning with the words "For more information").**

2 **On the Tables And Borders toolbar, click the Shading Color down arrow.**

A color palette is displayed.

FIGURE 3-27

Color palette

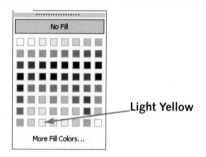

3 **Click the Light Yellow square (eighth row, third square).**

The paragraph is now shaded in light yellow. Notice that the color on the Shading Color button is also light yellow.

TIP

The light yellow color on the Shading Color button indicates that this is the color that you most recently used. If you select another paragraph and click the Shading Color button, the paragraph changes to light yellow. If you change the color to sea green, the Shading Color button turns sea green, and any text or paragraph that you select before clicking the button again will also turn sea green.

4 **Scroll up to the paragraph that has a border surrounding it, and click the paragraph.**

5 **Click the Shading Color button.**

The bordered paragraph is now shaded in light yellow, too.

FIGURE 3-28

Paragraph with border and shading

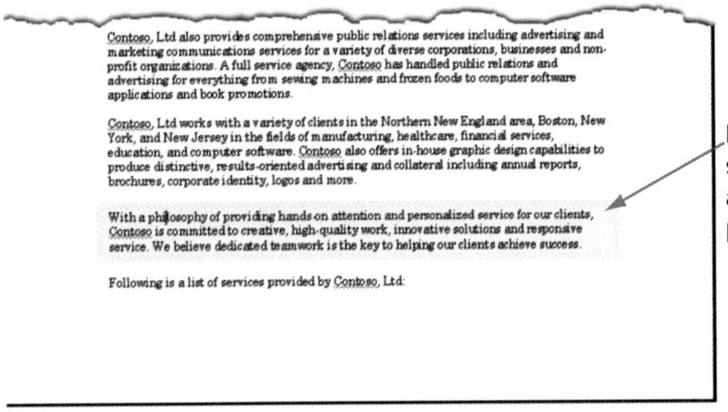

Border and shading applied to paragraph

TROUBLESHOOTING

If the shade that you pick is dark, Word automatically converts the text to white for readability. To remove shading, first select the shaded text. On the Tables And Borders toolbar, click the Shading Color down arrow, and click No Fill.

6 On the Standard toolbar, click the Undo button.

Word removes the shading from the paragraph.

7 In the upper-right corner of the Tables And Borders floating toolbar, click the Close button or, to close the docked toolbar, open the View menu, point to Toolbars, and click Tables And Borders.

◆ Save the brochure.

◆ Keep this file open for the next exercise.

QUICK CHECK

Q. What would happen if you selected the same color for the text as for the shading color?

A. If the shading color and the text color are the same, the text will not be visible.

QUICK REFERENCE ▼

Add shading to a paragraph

1 Click in the paragraph to be shaded.

2 On the Standard toolbar, click the Tables And Borders button.

3 Click the Shading Color down arrow, and click a color.

Previewing a Document

Previewing Documents for Printing

THE BOTTOM LINE

As is the case in many situations, it is very important to check your work before sending it. In the case of a document, one of the easiest ways to do this is to look at the document in Print Preview. This allows you to take an overview of the document and to verify that it is going to print the way that you expected. You can then catch any obvious errors, thereby saving time and paper.

To see exactly how your document will look after it is printed, you can use Print Preview. The **Print Preview** window shows you exactly how the lines on the page will appear when they're printed and where page breaks will occur. If you don't like the layout, you can make adjustments before you print. Using Print Preview can help you identify desired formatting changes without wasting paper.

TIP

In Print Layout view, you can show or hide the white space between the pages. Position the pointer between the pages until the Show White Space pointer or Hide White Space pointer appears, and then click the page.

Preview a document before printing

We've made many edits to our brochure, changing the format and style as well as adding borders and shading. We are getting nearer to being ready to print the brochure. But first we must view it in Print Preview to be sure it looks the way we want it to before printing it.

 1 On the Standard toolbar, click the Print Preview button.

The Print Preview screen appears with the Contoso brochure displayed.

 2 If the ruler isn't visible, click the View Ruler button.

TROUBLESHOOTING

The number of pages displayed in the Print Preview depends upon the last way it was used. You may see more than one page.

 3 If necessary, on the Print Preview toolbar, click the Multiple Pages button, and click the second button in the top row to view two pages at a time.

FIGURE 3-29

Print preview of the Contoso brochure

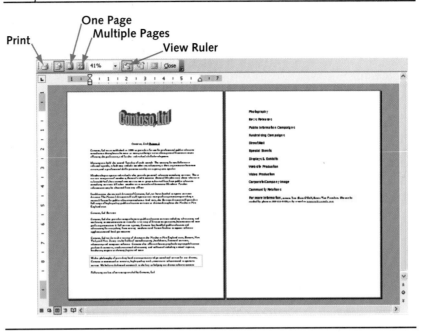

4 Click the One Page button to return to the single-page view.

5 On the Print Preview toolbar, click Close.

Close

The Print Preview closes, and Word returns to the previous view of the document.

ANOTHER METHOD

To print a document in Print Preview, on the Print Preview toolbar, click the Print button.

◆ Keep this file open for the next exercise.

QUICK REFERENCE ▼

Preview a document

On the Standard toolbar, click the Print Preview button.

Printing a Document

THE BOTTOM LINE

While many documents today travel electronically and are never actually printed and distributed in "hard copy," there are still many instances in which you will need to print out the document that you have created. Word makes printing a document a very easy activity by using the Print button or the Print dialog box.

Printing Documents

You can use two methods to print a document in Word. One way is to use the Print button to print one copy of all pages in the current document using the default printer. The default printer is the specific printer that is selected automatically as the location where documents will be printed from your computer. This method is convenient when you want to print the entire document.

The other method is to use the menu to display the Print dialog box. If you want to print multiple copies of the document, print from a different printer, print selected text, or print a range of pages, you use the Print dialog box to specify any of these options. For example, instead of printing the entire document simply to review and edit page 6, you can use the Print dialog box to print page 6 only.

IMPORTANT

You must have a printer to complete the following exercise.

Print a document

Finally, after completing all of the edits and then previewing the brochure, we are ready to print it. We will practice printing the brochure by using both the Print button and the Print dialog box, and then we will print only a selected block of text.

1 **On the Standard toolbar, click the Print button.**

One copy of the current document is printed on the default printer.

2 **Click anywhere on the first page of the document.**

3 **On the File menu, click Print.**

The Print dialog box appears.

FIGURE 3-30

Print dialog box

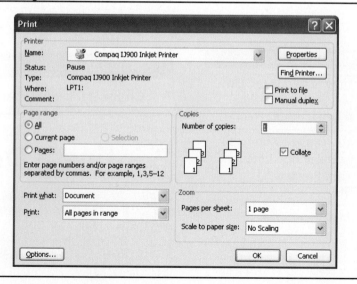

4 In the Page Range section, click the Current Page option, and click OK.

The first page of the document is printed.

ANOTHER METHOD

You can also print a specific page other than the current page by typing the number of the page that you want to print in the Pages box in the Print dialog box. To print multiple pages, but not the entire document, you can type the page numbers, inserting a comma between page numbers for non-sequential pages or using a dash to indicate a continuous range of sequential pages. For example: 1, 3, 5 or 4-6.

5 Select the first paragraph, which begins "Contoso, Ltd."

6 On the File menu, click Print.

The Print dialog box appears.

7 In the Page Range section, click the Selection option, and click OK.

The selected text is printed.

◆ Save and close Brochure 03 Edited.

◆ If you are continuing to the next lesson, leave Word open.

◆ If you are not continuing to the next lesson, close Word.

QUICK REFERENCE ▼

Print a document

On the Standard toolbar, click the Print button.

Print a document using special printer settings

1 On the File menu, click Print.

2 In the Copies section, type the desired number of copies in the Number of copies box.

3 In the Page range section, click Current page to print the current page; click All to print all the pages; click Pages to print specific pages, and then type the desired page numbers in the Pages box.

4 Click OK.

Print selected text

1 Select the text that you want to print.

2 On the File menu, click Print.

3 In the Page range section, click Selection.

4 Click OK.

QUICK CHECK

Q. What does the Collate option on the Print dialog box do?

A. When you are printing multiple pages of a document and printing them multiple times, you can keep them in the order in which they appear in the document by selecting Collate. If you do not have Collate selected, the document will print the selected number of copies of each page. (for example, two copies of the first page, then two copies of the second page, etc.).

Key Points

- ✔ *You can format text using a variety of tools and methods, including the Formatting toolbar and the Format dialog box.*
- ✔ *You can use various text attributes to make certain words or phrases stand out in a document.*
- ✔ *Being able to cut or copy and then paste text allows you to re-purpose existing text without having to retype every time you decide you would like text placed in a different location within the document.*
- ✔ *Using the Office Clipboard allows you to paste multiple selections.*
- ✔ *When you apply styles, paragraph borders, and shading, you can accent and highlight certain elements of your document.*
- ✔ *Before you print a document, you can preview it to make sure it will appear exactly how you would like it to appear.*

Quick Quiz

True/False

T   F   **1.** Embedding is the act of placing an object in a document while maintaining a connection to the source file.

T   F   **2.** An attribute is a characteristic that is applied to text in a Word document.

T   F   **3.** An object is a collection of data that is treated as a single element within a document.

T   F   **4.** Linking connects an embedded object with the original program and source file.

T   F   **5.** OLE is a technology for transferring and sharing information among programs.

T   F   **6.** Print Preview automatically sends your document to the printer.

T   F   **7.** When you center a paragraph, the block of text is flush with both the left and right margins.

T   F   **8.** When you justify a paragraph, each line of a block of text is an equal distance from the left and right margins.

T   F   **9.** A rectangle of color surrounding and behind a block of text is called shading.

T   F   **10.** A rectangle of color surrounding a block of text, but not behind it, is called a border.

Short Answer

1. What key combination and shortcut key allow you to apply styles to multiple non-consecutive paragraphs?

2. What are four methods to cut and paste a selection of text?

3. Before you print a document, how can you be sure that the margins will look right?

4. What is a style?

5. What are two ways that you can apply bold formatting to a selection of text?

6. How can you view multiple selections of text in the Office Clipboard?

7. What is the difference between cutting and copying text?

8. How do you change the line style of an existing border?

9. How can you edit a linked object in a Word document?

On Your Own

IMPORTANT

In the On Your Own exercises, you must complete Exercise 1 to continue to Exercise 2

Exercise 1

If necessary, start Word. Open the document named Invitation 03 from the Lesson03 folder. Center all of the text in the document. Change the second paragraph from the bottom to a 20-point font size, in small caps, blue, and bold. Select the lines of text *You're invited to...*, *When*, and *Where*, and change them to 16 points and bold. Change all text to the font Garamond. Finally, move the last three paragraphs to the top of the document. Print two copies of the document. Save the document as Invitation 03 Edited in the Lesson03 folder.

Exercise 2

Select all of the text in the invitation and create a blue border. Add light turquoise shading inside the border. Save the document and close it.

One Step Further

Exercise 1

Open one of the documents that you have worked with in this lesson and view it in Print Preview. Adjust the margins using the Ruler. Zoom in and out of the document using the Magnifier. Zoom in and out of the document using the drop-down list. View the print preview in full screen, and then return to the normal print preview screen. Use Word's Help files to determine the purpose of the Shrink to Fit button. Would that feature be useful in the document that you opened? If so, use the Shrink to Fit button. Leave the document open for the next Exercise.

Exercise 2

Select and copy several paragraphs in your document. (If necessary, manually open the Office Clipboard.) As you are copying text, note the order in which the paragraphs are placed on the Clipboard. Which item is at the top of the list? If you click on the down arrow next to an item, what options are available? When would it be useful to use the Paste All option on the Office Clipboard?

Exercise 3

In this lesson, we briefly explored the Reveal Formatting task pane. Open the task pane again, and click on the links to determine what other dialog boxes are accessible through this task pane. Think of ways in which this task pane could be useful in your work with Word. Use Word's Help files to learn more about Reveal Formatting. Write a brief explanation of the features available through this task pane and how you would use them. Close the document that you opened for these Exercises without saving any changes.

LESSON

4

Changing the Layout of a Document

After completing this lesson, you will be able to:

✔ *View the document in different ways.*
✔ *Adjust page margin settings.*
✔ *Set paragraph alignment, indentation, and spacing.*
✔ *Change indents and tab settings.*
✔ *Insert and clear tabs.*
✔ *Add page numbers to a document.*
✔ *Create and customize headers and footers.*
✔ *Change page orientation.*

KEY TERMS

- alignment
- first line indent
- footer
- hanging indent
- header
- horizontal ruler
- indents
- landscape
- leader tab
- Normal view

- page margin
- paragraph
- paragraph mark
- portrait
- Print Layout view
- ruler
- spacing
- tab (tab stop)
- vertical alignment
- vertical ruler

Rather than using the default settings that Microsoft Word 2003 provides, you can use other settings and tools to change how your letters, lists, proposals, and general correspondence look, as well as how you view the document while you are working with it. One way to quickly customize a document is by changing the way the text appears on the page by altering page margins, resetting paragraph alignments, changing tab settings, and customizing headers and footers. When you create a document, you are doing more than just formatting text. You have the capability to change the page layout of the document by altering how text appears on the page.

You start this lesson by learning to work with your documents in a view that suits your current needs. Depending upon what you are trying to accomplish, there are times when one view of the document is preferred over another.

You will then learn how to change a page margin. A **page margin** is the amount of space at the top, bottom, or sides surrounding the text on a page. You can also use a header or a footer on a document with multiple pages. A **header** is the text that appears at the top of a page that typically includes the title of the work, the date, and page numbers. A **footer** is text printed at the bottom of the page that might include the date, author's name, and the title of the document.

You'll also set tab stops for a particular paragraph within the document. A **tab stop** or **tab** is used to indent the first line of a paragraph or to align text or numbers in columns. You can also use Tabs to align columns of text within a paragraph. Other settings include indents and spacing. **Indents** determine the alignment of the paragraph in relation to the page margin setting, and **spacing** indicates the area above and below the paragraph as well as the space between the lines.

IMPORTANT

Before you can use the practice file for this lesson, you need to install it from the book's companion CD to its default location. For additional information on how to find and open files used in this book, see the "Using the CD-ROM" section at the beginning of this book.

Viewing a Document

THE BOTTOM LINE

An important part of working with a Word document is knowing how to change the way in which you view your document. The document view is another tool that allows you to quickly and easily work with your document in the most efficient manner.

Microsoft Word offers various ways to look at a document. Depending upon the purpose of your document, you may want or need to change the view that you are using. You should think of the document view as another tool that you can use. These tools are customized to meet specific needs for certain types of documents. The table below outlines the different views available and gives a brief description of each.

Deciding Which View to Use When

View	Description
Normal	Displays a document in a simplified manner so you can type and edit quickly and easily. In this view, page breaks are indicated by a dotted line and you cannot see some layout elements, such as headers and footers.
Web Layout	Displays a document the way that it will appear when viewed in a Web browser. This allows you to see backgrounds, AutoShapes, and all text effects; how the text will wrap to fit the window size; and how graphics will be placed.
Print Layout	Displays a document as it will appear when it is printed. You see the edges of the page, margins, page breaks, text effects, shapes, graphics, headers and footers—among other things—exactly as they will appear on the printed page.

Reading Layout	Displays as much of the content of the document as will fit on your screen in a size that is comfortable for viewing. (You can adjust the viewing size to one that suits you.) Selecting this view automatically opens the Reading Layout toolbar as well as the Reviewing toolbar. You can use these toolbars to adjust the view (display the Document Map, Thumbnails, etc.), search the document, and make changes to the document. Text formatting and effects are visible in this view, but pagination is not displayed.
Outline	Displays the document as nested levels of headings and body text. This view provides the tools for viewing and changing the hierarchy of text.
Document Map	This view can be used in conjunction with any one of the document layout views. Document Map displays a list of your document's headings in a pane to the left of the document pane. In this pane, you can see the structure of the document while viewing and editing its text.
Thumbnails	This view can be used in conjunction with any one of the document layout views. When you select Thumbnails, a pane opens to the left of the document that shows miniature pictures of either the pages or screens. You can use these thumbnails to move quickly through your document.

Using Outline to Rearrange
Paragraphs

The page layout views can be selected from the View menu or from the buttons in the lower-left corner of the document window, shown in Figure 4-1.

FIGURE 4-1

Page Layout view buttons

Web Layout View
Normal View
Print Layout View
Outline View
Reading Layout View

Some page layout views can also be selected from within toolbars in other views. For example, you can switch to the Reading Layout view by selecting the Read button on the Standard toolbar while you are in any of the other views. You can then select Close on the Reading Layout toolbar to return to your former view.

The Document Map and Thumbnails panes can be opened and closed from the View menu. You can only select one of these at a time; selecting one automatically deselects the other. You can also open either of these panes with buttons on the Reviewing Layout toolbar.

TROUBLESHOOTING

In the following exercises and in the illustrations used throughout this lesson, the Standard and Formatting toolbars have been separated. For additional information on how to separate the toolbars, see the "Using the CD-ROM" section at the beginning of this book.

◆ **Be sure to start Word before beginning this exercise.**

◆ **Open Salary Survey 04 from the Lesson04 folder in the Word Practice folder that is located on your hard disk.**

Change document views

The Salary Survey 04 document was created to publicize the results of a salary and benefits survey administered to a random sampling of the members of Contoso, Ltd's public relations networking group. In this exercise, we will explore Word's views so that you can become acquainted with which one would be most appropriate for various tasks that you will encounter in using Word.

1 **Click the Normal View button in the lower-left corner of the window.**

The document is displayed in Normal View.

ANOTHER METHOD

Select Normal from the View menu.

FIGURE 4-2

Document in Normal view

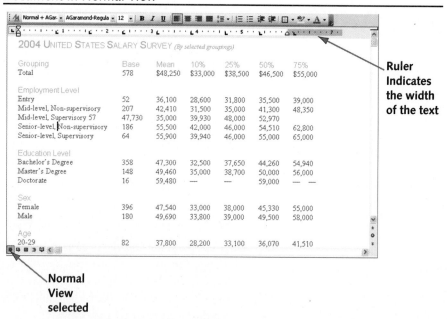

Ruler
Indicates
the width
of the text

Normal
View
selected

2 **Scroll through the document.**

Note that you can view the content of the document, but you cannot see any of the elements such as the page edges and margins. You must rely on the ruler to see the width of the text, and dotted lines indicate page breaks. You can see large portions of the document at one time, and scrolling is quick and easy.

3 **Press Ctrl+Home, and then click the Web Layout View button in the lower-left corner of the window.**

ANOTHER METHOD

Select Web Layout from the View menu.

FIGURE 4-3

Document in Web Layout view

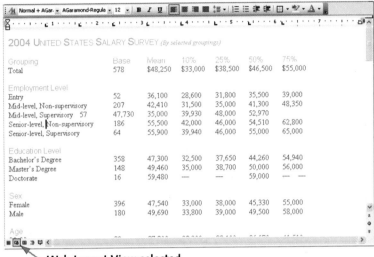

Web Layout View selected

4 Scroll through the document.

Note that, in this view, the text column fills the window and no page breaks are shown.

5 Press Ctrl+Home, and then click the Print Layout View button in the lower-left corner of the window.

ANOTHER METHOD

Select Print Layout from the View menu.

FIGURE 4-4

Document in Print Layout view

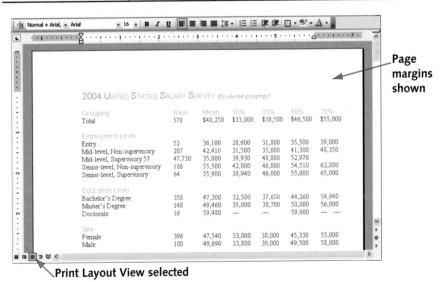

Page margins shown

Print Layout View selected

6 **Scroll through the document.**

Note that you can clearly see the margins on the page and the edges of the page (including the top and bottom edges that indicate where a page break will be).

7 **Press Ctrl+Home, and then click the Reading Layout View button in the lower-left corner of the window.**

The screen changes to display the document in Reading Layout view and the Reading Layout and Reviewing toolbars appear.

ANOTHER METHOD

- Select Reading Layout from the View menu.
- Click the Read button on the Standard toolbar.

FIGURE 4-5

Document in Reading Layout view

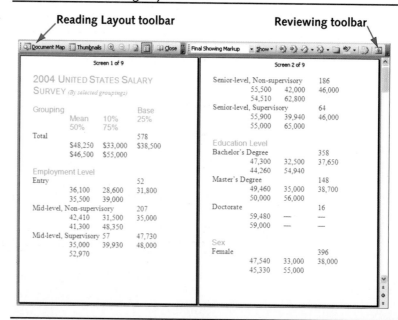

TROUBLESHOOTING

- If your screen does not appear like Figure 4-5, click any active buttons on the toolbar to toggle them off (except the Allow Multiple Pages button).
- Your Reading Layout and Reviewing toolbars may be on separate lines.

8 **Click the Allow Multiple Pages button on the Reading Layout toolbar to toggle it off.**

The document view changes to show just one screen.

 Thumbnails

9 **Click the Thumbnails button.**

A pane opens on the left side of the screen showing each screen of the document as a small image. You can use these thumbnails to quickly move around the document.

FIGURE 4-6

Thumbnails in Reading Layout view

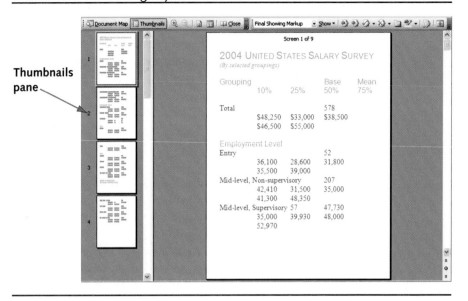

Thumbnails pane

10 **In the Thumbnails pane, use the scroll bar to move down, and click Thumbnail 6.**

The sixth screen appears on the screen. (Note that this is not the sixth page, but rather the sixth screen in the Reading Layout view.)

11 **On the Reading Layout toolbar, click the Document Map button.**

An outline of headings appears in the left pane instead of the thumbnails. The first heading of the active page is highlighted (even though it does not appear on the current screen).

FIGURE 4-7

Document Map in Reading Layout view

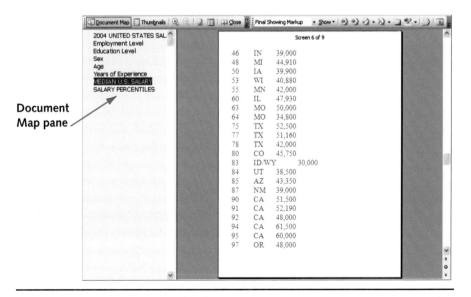

Document Map pane

12 **Click the Close button in the Reading Layout toolbar.**

The Reading Layout view is closed, and you are returned to the previous layout – in this case, the Print Layout view.

13 **Press Ctrl+Home and then click the Outline View button in the lower-left corner of the window.**

The screen changes to show the document in its hierarchical structure. The Outlining toolbar also appears.

ANOTHER METHOD

Select Outline from the View menu.

FIGURE 4-8

Document in Outline view

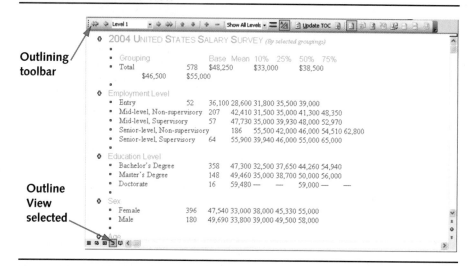

14 **Scroll through the document.**

Notice that each level can be collapsed and expanded. Margins and page edges are not visible, nor are page breaks.

15 **Click the Print Preview button in the lower-left corner of the window.**

TIP

To learn more about using the Outline view or any of the other page layouts, search Word's Help files or experiment with the open document.

◆ **Keep this file open for the next exercise.**

QUICK REFERENCE ▼

Change document view

1 On the View menu, click Normal, Web Layout, Print Layout, Reading Layout, or Outline.

2 You can also select Document Map or Thumbnails.

QUICK CHECK

Q. If you have multiple documents open, can you view each in a different layout? If you change the layout in one document, will it change in others?

A. You can choose different views for different documents, including whether the Document Map or Thumbnails are displayed.

Changing Page Margins

THE BOTTOM LINE

You can change the margins of a document to fit more or less information on a page or to control where the information appears.

Controlling What Appears on Each Page

By default, Word includes left and right page margins of 1.25 inches and top and bottom page margins of 1 inch. Page margins affect the entire document because, after page margins are changed, the number of pages in the document might increase or decrease depending on how much text the page margin allows per page. To change page margins in a document, you can use the ruler at the top of the document or the Page Setup dialog box, which is accessed by clicking Page Setup on the File menu.

Changing Page Margins Using the Page Setup Dialog Box

The Page Setup dialog box is most commonly used for setting page margins. When you use the Page Setup dialog box, you determine how the document appears on the printed page. You can use the Page Setup dialog box to adjust top, bottom, left, and right page margin settings, determine the placement of headers and footers, and select the amount of text that you want the settings to affect.

FIGURE 4-9

Page Setup dialog box

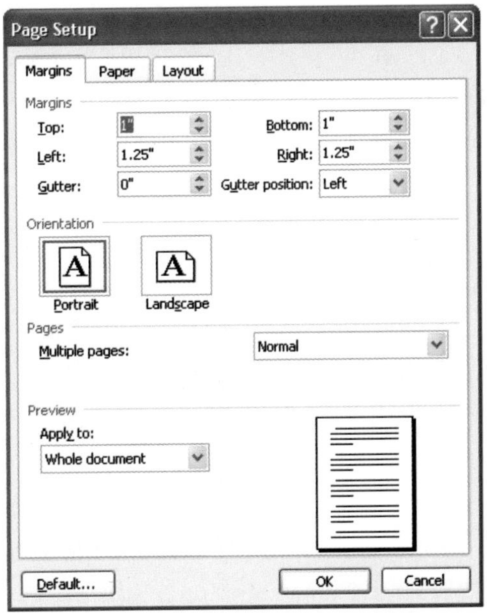

TIP

You can click the Apply To down arrow to define whether you want the setup changes to apply to the whole document, the selected text only, or from the position of the insertion point forward.

Change page margins using the Page Setup dialog box

In the first exercise, we opened Salary Survey 04 and viewed it in a variety of layouts. In the course of viewing the document in Print Layout view, you may have noticed that the margins on the right side of the document were smaller than those on the left, leaving the page looking unbalanced. We will change the page margins in the Salary Survey document by using the Page Setup dialog box.

1 **On the File menu, click Page Setup.**

The Page Setup dialog box appears. The current top margin setting (1") is selected.

TROUBLESHOOTING

You may need to click the Margins tab in the Page Setup dialog box in order to adjust the margins.

2 **In the Top box, type 1.5, and press Tab.**

In the Preview section at the bottom of the dialog box, the top page margin shifts down to show what the text will look like.

ANOTHER METHOD

You can also use the up and down arrows to the right of the settings to select preset sizes. The up arrow increases the page margin size, and the down arrow decreases the page margin size.

3 **In the Bottom box, type 1.5, and press Tab.**

In the Preview section, the bottom page margin shifts up.

4 **Click OK.**

The top and bottom page margins are now 1.5 inches instead of 1 inch.

TIP

There is no visible change to the text in Normal view, which is the currently selected view for the document.

◆ **Save the file as** Salary Survey 04 Edited **in the Lesson04 folder.**

◆ **Keep this file open for the next exercise.**

QUICK REFERENCE ▼

Change the page margins using the Page Setup dialog box

1 On the File menu, click Page Setup.

2 If necessary, click the Margins tab.

3 Type the new page margin settings in the appropriate boxes.

4 Click OK.

Changing Page Margins Using the Ruler

You can also change page margins using the ruler. The **ruler** is a scale shown in the document window that is marked in inches or other units of measurement. A horizontal ruler in Normal view and both horizontal and vertical rulers in Print Layout view are provided in Word.

> **TIP**
>
> To turn the rulers on or off in Normal view and Print Layout view, on the View menu, click Ruler.

To use the ruler, you should use **Print Layout view**, not the default setting of Normal view, so that you can see the page margin settings relative to the page borders. You use **Normal View** to edit and format the document, but Normal view doesn't show the page margins relative to the page borders. You can also use Print Preview to view your document as it will be printed, and you can make changes to the margins in this view.

The **horizontal ruler** along the top of the document window shows the left and right page margins as well as the left and right paragraph indents, such as first line and hanging indents (you'll learn more about these indents later in this lesson). Often, paragraph indents and page margins are the same; however, it's important to recognize that you can adjust the page margins or indents of paragraphs independent of the page margins. The **vertical ruler** along the left edge of the document shows the top and bottom page margin boundaries.

To change page margins using the ruler, you use Print Layout view, which is shown below. This view allows you to see the page margins on the vertical and horizontal rulers. When you position the mouse pointer over the page margin, the mouse pointer appears as a horizontal double arrow. You can then drag the first line indent, hanging indent, left indent, or right indent marker to a new location to reset the page margin. You'll learn more about these indents in this lesson.

FIGURE 4-10

Margins and indentations shown on the ruler

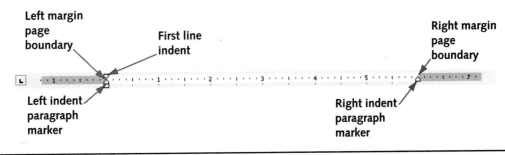

TIP

To display the page margin measurements as you adjust them, hold down the Alt key as you drag a marker. This technique also allows you to adjust the page margin in smaller increments.

Change page margins using the ruler

In this exercise, you change the page margins of the document using the ruler.

1 Position the mouse pointer above the Left Margin marker on the horizontal ruler until the pointer is displayed as a double arrow.

FIGURE 4-11

Left Margin marker

2 Hold down the Alt key.

3 Click and drag the marker to the left until the measurement of 6.5" is displayed in the white portion of the ruler.

FIGURE 4-12

Margin measurements

The left page margin shifts to the left, and all of the text in the document is adjusted. Notice that the tabs and columns in the document are disrupted.

4 Release the mouse button and the Alt key.

5 Position the mouse pointer over the Right Margin marker until the pointer is displayed as a double arrow.

6 Hold down the Alt key, and drag the marker to the right until the measurement of 7" is displayed in the white portion of the ruler.

The right page margin shifts to the right, and the text is adjusted. Both the left and right page margins are now set at .75 inch.

7 Release the mouse button and the Alt key when the page margin is set.

◆ Save Salary Survey 04 Edited.

◆ Keep this file open for the next exercise.

Q. If you need to adjust all of the margins of a document, what would be the quickest way to do so?

A. If you need to adjust all of the margins within a document, it would be quickest to open the Page Setup dialog box where you can alter all margins in one step.

Changing the Look of Paragraphs

Q. Can text be centered both vertically and horizontally at the same time?

A. Text can be aligned to any desired position, both vertically and horizontally, at the same time if desired.

Change page margins using the ruler

1 On the View menu, click Print Layout.

2 Position the insertion point over the page margin marker until the insertion point becomes a double-headed arrow.

3 Drag the marker to the new location.

Aligning Text Vertically on a Page

THE BOTTOM LINE

In most cases, you want text to align with the top margin, but in certain situations, you may choose to align text with the bottom of the page or to center text on the page.

You can change the vertical alignment of text using the Layout tab of the Page Setup dialog box. **Vertical alignment** is the way that text lines up between the top and bottom page margins. (Horizontal alignment can be adjusted by using the Left, Center, Right, or Justify buttons on the Formatting toolbar; vertical alignment of text can be set only from the Page Layout dialog box.) Typically, you want text to align with the top margin. That is, when you begin typing text on a new page, the text appears at the top of the page and new lines of text are added below. However, you can change the text alignment on a page so that it aligns with the bottom of the page (the first line starts at the bottom, and each new line appears at the bottom of the page, causing previously typed lines to be "pushed" upward) or is centered vertically on the page (the first line of text appears at the midpoint on the page, and new lines are positioned so that an even amount of space is maintained between the top and bottom page margins).

To change vertical text alignment, on the File menu, click Page Setup, and click the Layout tab. In the Vertical Alignment box, click the down arrow, and click Top, Center, Justified, or Bottom to define how the text is aligned vertically on the page. The default vertical alignment is the Top setting. The Justified setting fills in paragraphs (rather than individual lines, which is the case with the Center alignment setting) evenly between the top and bottom margins. For example, when you type the first paragraph on a page, the text appears at the top of the page. When you press Enter to begin a new paragraph, the next paragraph begins at the bottom of the page. When you press Enter and begin a third paragraph, the second paragraph moves to the middle of the page, and the new paragraph is entered near the bottom of the page.

Formatting a Paragraph

Changing the Look of Paragraphs

THE BOTTOM LINE

In addition to formatting specific text, you can also apply formatting options to paragraphs or to the entire document. These formatting options can be set through the Paragraph dialog box. Additionally, some of the paragraph format settings can be applied by using the ruler in the document window.

Word defines a **paragraph** as any amount of text that ends with a hard return. Each time you press Enter, a **paragraph mark** (a hidden formatting character that designates the end of a paragraph) is inserted into the document. Although you see the actual paragraph mark only if the display of nonprinting characters (or formatting marks) is turned on, the paragraph mark is still present. Even a blank line is considered to be a paragraph because it ends with a hard return.

The formatting that you select for a paragraph is applied to the next paragraph that you type. This process occurs because all formatting associated with a paragraph is stored in the paragraph mark. When you begin a new paragraph, the paragraph takes on the formatting characteristics of the previous paragraph. Alternatively, when you delete a paragraph mark, the preceding paragraph takes on the formatting characteristics of the next paragraph.

Paragraphs are set by default to be single-spaced and left-aligned with no indentation. You change the default paragraph settings for single paragraphs or groups of paragraphs by using the Paragraph dialog box. To access the Paragraph dialog box, on the Format menu, click Paragraph.

CHECK THIS OUT ▼

Showing Formatting Marks
As you enter and edit text, Word inserts special characters or formatting characters—such as spaces, tabs, and paragraph marks—into your document. These characters are not printed and do not appear on the screen unless you click the Tools menu, click Options, and select the Formatting Marks check box on the View tab or the Show/Hide ¶ button on the Standard toolbar.

FIGURE 4-13

Paragraph dialog box

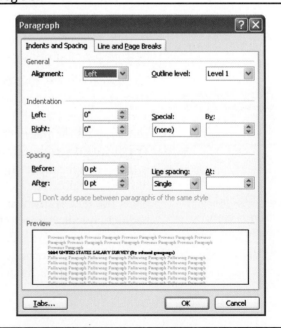

As with most Word formatting commands, you either select the paragraphs that you want changed and then apply formatting, or apply the formatting first and then type the desired text.

Indenting Text Using the Paragraph Dialog Box

You can use the Indents and Spacing tab of the Paragraph dialog box to use and modify **alignment** and indentation:

Alignment	The arrangement of text in fixed or predetermined positions. If the paragraph is left-aligned, all of the text in the paragraph will begin on the left side of the document.
Indentation	Determines the position that text is moved inward from the page margin. You can also specify positions for **hanging indents** (indenting all but the first line of a paragraph to the same point) and **first line indents** (only indenting the first line of a paragraph) by clicking the Special down arrow and then selecting the desired indent type.

TIP

To format only one paragraph, click anywhere in that paragraph. To format multiple paragraphs, first select the paragraphs that will be affected.

Format a paragraph

In the first part of our survey, the text alignment and paragraph formats seem fine, but if you scroll to the last page of the document, you will see that some of the text is not correctly aligned and is, therefore, difficult to read. We will need to change the paragraph spacing and create hanging indents to arrange the information in this section of the document into a readable format. We will make these changes using the Paragraph dialog box.

1 Scroll to the heading Salary Percentiles, and select the heading and all of the text under the heading.

2 On the Format menu, click Paragraph.

The Paragraph dialog box appears.

3 Click the Indents And Spacing tab, if necessary.

4 In the Spacing section, in the After box, click the up arrow twice.

The paragraph spacing is changed to 12 points, and a preview of the change is shown in the Preview section.

FIGURE 4-14

Paragraph dialog box with spacing adjustment

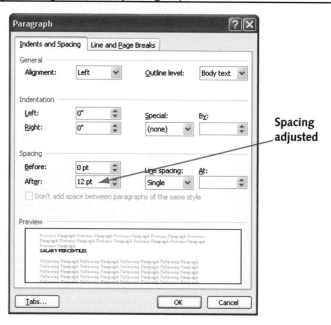

5 **Click OK, and click anywhere to deselect the text.**

The Paragraph dialog box closes, and 12 points of space are added after each paragraph in the document.

FIGURE 4-15

Result of changing the paragraph spacing

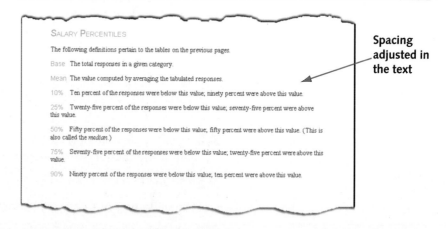

TIP

You don't have to select all text in every paragraph before you apply a paragraph format. You need to include only part of the first and last paragraphs in the selection. The formatting that you apply still affects all the partially selected paragraphs.

6 **In the same section of the Word document, select the definitions under the text "The following definitions pertain to...".**

7 On the Format menu, click Paragraph.

The Paragraph dialog box appears.

8 Click the Special down arrow in the Indentation section, click Hanging, and then click OK.

Word creates a hanging indent for the definition paragraphs, where the first line *hangs* farther out from the following lines. The default value for a hanging indent is 0.5 inch, which is what you use for this exercise.

9 Click anywhere in the document to deselect the text.

FIGURE 4-16

Result of adding a hanging indent

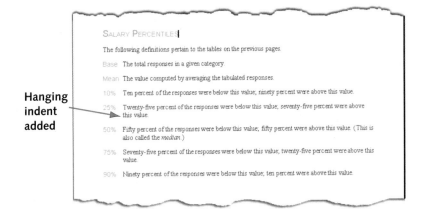

◆ Save Salary Survey 04 Edited.

◆ Keep this file open for the next exercise.

QUICK REFERENCE ▼

Apply paragraph formatting

1 Select the appropriate paragraph(s).

2 On the Format menu, click Paragraph.

3 Change the settings as necessary.

4 Click OK.

Indenting Text Using the Ruler

To quickly create a hanging or first line indent, you can use the ruler. The ruler contains markers for both of these indents, as well as a right indent, as displayed here.

FIGURE 4-17

Ruler for changing paragraph formatting

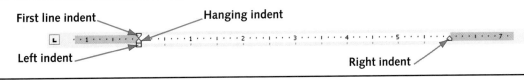

You begin indenting paragraphs by selecting the text and dragging the appropriate marker to the desired position on the ruler.

To	Do this
Fully indent a section	Drag the Left Indent marker. All three formatting markers move.
Indent only the first line	Drag the First Line Indent marker only.
Create a hanging indent	Drag the Hanging Indent marker only.

Change indent settings using the ruler

In the previous exercise, we made changes to the paragraph spacing as well as the hanging indent through the Paragraph dialog box. Sometimes, however, it's easier to make changes when you can see the result of those changes immediately. This can be done using the ruler.

1 Under the sentence, "The following definitions pertain to...", select the seven definition paragraphs.

2 Position the mouse pointer over the Hanging Indent marker on the ruler (the bottom triangle).

The ScreenTip *Hanging Indent* appears.

FIGURE 4-18

ScreenTip for making ruler selections

TROUBLESHOOTING

Be precise with the mouse while working with the ruler because it is easy to click and drag the wrong marker. Take your time and make sure that you grab the right marker by checking the ScreenTip. If you find that you dragged the wrong marker and your text is indented incorrectly, press Ctrl+Z to undo the change before you try again.

3 Hold down the Alt key, and drag the Hanging Indent marker to the right until a measurement of .75" appears to the left of the marker. Release the mouse button and the Alt key, but do not deselect the text.

The paragraphs are indented 0.75 inch from the first line of each paragraph.

TIP

Although you don't need to hold down the Alt key when you drag one of the paragraph markers, doing so allows you to see the measurement that you want to set.

4 With the definition paragraphs still selected, drag the Left Indent marker (the square) to the 2-inch mark on the ruler.

Notice that all three formatting markers move and the paragraphs are fully indented.

5 With the definition paragraphs still selected, drag the Right Indent marker (the triangle on the lower-right side of the ruler) to the 5.5-inch mark on the ruler.

The right margin of the selected text moves to the left.

6 Click anywhere to deselect the text.

FIGURE 4-19

Result of adjusting the indents with the ruler

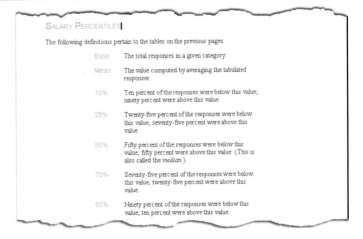

7 Scroll through the document to view the various paragraph formats.

◆ Save Salary Survey 04 Edited.

◆ Keep this file open for the next exercise.

QUICK REFERENCE ▼

Indent a paragraph using the ruler

1 Select the paragraph.

2 Drag the First Line Indent, Hanging Indent, and the Left Indent markers to fully indent the paragraph.

Or

Drag only the First Line Indent marker to indent the first line.

Or

Drag only the Hanging Indent marker to create a hanging indent.

Or

Click and drag the Left Indent marker.

3 Deselect the text.

QUICK CHECK

Q. What is the quickest way to adjust the hanging indent for a paragraph or a selected section of text?

A. The quickest way to adjust a hanging indent for a paragraph or selected paragraphs is to drag the Hanging Indent marker on the ruler.

Tab Stops

Changing the Look of Paragraphs

THE BOTTOM LINE

Tab stops are locations across the page that you can use to align text. By default, there are left-aligned tab stops set at every half-inch across the page. However, these can be changed or deleted through the Tabs dialog box or from the ruler.

Word automatically left-aligns tab stops and spaces them at every half-inch. Each time that you press the Tab key, the insertion point moves to the next tab stop on the current line. Unless you specify otherwise, Word inserts a left tab stop each time that you press Tab. A left tab aligns text at a specific distance from the left page margin. The following table explains the types of tabs that are available. You can change the tab alignment by clicking the Tab button to the left of the horizontal ruler or by clicking Tabs on the Format menu and clicking the desired alignment option in the Tabs dialog box.

Tab Type	Button	Effect
Left	L	Aligns text to the right of the tab
Right	⌐	Aligns text to the left of the tab
Center	⊥	Centers text on either side of the tab
Decimal	⊥.	Aligns numbers along a common decimal position
Bar	I	Inserts a vertical bar at the tab stop

Changing Tab Settings

While automatic spacing between tab stops might be acceptable for most documents that you create, you have the option of changing the spacing. For example, if you are working on a document that has several columns of data, you can change the tab settings so that the data is spaced evenly and is legible on the page. When you use tabs, you might find that the columns created are not always wide enough to accommodate your text.

Change tab settings

Now that we have the last section of our survey formatted the way we want, we need to work on the second section to improve its readability. We will widen columns using the Tabs dialog box to change tab settings.

1 Scroll to the heading Median U.S. Salary By Two-Digit Zip Codes, and select all the zip code lines below the heading (from 01 through 98).

2 On the Format menu, click Tabs.

The Tabs dialog box appears.

3 In the Tab Stop Position box, type 1.

4 **Click the Set button.**

The tab is set, and the tab position number appears in the Tab stop position list.

FIGURE 4-20

Tabs dialog box with one tab set

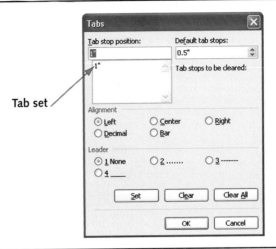

Tab set

5 **Type 2.5, and click the Set button.**

The second tab is set, and the tab position number appears in the Tab stop position list.

6 **Click OK to close the Tabs dialog box.**

The columns of information are neatly spaced and aligned according to the tab stops that you just inserted.

7 **Click anywhere on the page to deselect the text.**

FIGURE 4-21

Result of tab stop settings

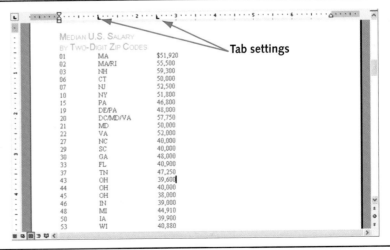

Tab settings

◆ **Keep this file open for the next exercise.**

Set one tab stop

1 On the Format menu, click Tabs.

2 Type the new tab stop in the Tab Stop Position box.

3 If desired, in the Alignment section or Leader section, select the desired option.

4 Click the Set button.

5 Click OK.

Set multiple tab stops

1 On the Format menu, click Tabs.

2 In the Tab Stop Position box, type the position for the first tab stop.

3 In the Alignment section, select the desired tab alignment.

4 If desired, in the Leader section, select the desired leader option.

5 Click the Set button.

6 In the Tab Stop Position box, type the position for the second tab stop.

7 If necessary, in the Alignment or Leader sections, select the desired option.

8 Click the Set button.

9 Repeat the process for additional tab stops that you want to set.

10 Click OK when all the tabs are set.

Setting and Clearing Specific Tab Stops

When making lists, charts, or other highly formatted sections of text, it can be helpful to create tabs at special intervals to break up information in a visually appealing way. The type of tab alignment that you select in the Alignment section of the Tabs dialog box determines how the text is aligned at that tab stop. There are five types of tab stops available in Word.

ANOTHER METHOD

You can also select the type of tab and insert tab stops using the horizontal ruler, which is explained later in this lesson.

You can also create a **leader tab,** which is displayed as a row of dots from the insertion point to the next tab stop. Leader tabs can be left-aligned, right-aligned, centered, or decimal-aligned as well. You might have seen a leader tab before in a ledger or on a bill, where the *total* line has a row of dots leading to the total of the bill to distinguish it from other entries that are above the leader tab.

You set and clear tabs using the Tabs dialog box. Here you can set one or multiple tabs, determine the alignment of the text to the tab stop, or clear all existing tabs.

Set and clear tab stops

Now that we are happy with the formatting changes made to our survey, we want to create a new section at the end of our document. We will set tabs using the Tabs dialog box and then enter text to see the results of the tabs that we add. We will also clear a tab setting.

1 **Press Ctrl+End to move the insertion point to the end of the document.**

2 **On the Format menu, click Tabs.**

The Tabs dialog box appears.

> **TIP**
>
> If you intend to set a lot of custom tabs, it is best to clear the defaults first. To clear the defaults, in the Tabs dialog box, click the Clear All button before setting the custom tabs. If you leave the default tabs selected, you have to press the Tab key more often.

3 **In the Tab Stop Position box, type 1, and click the Set button.**

4 **In the Tab Stop Position box, type 3, and click the Set button.**

5 **In the Tab Stop Position box, type 4.**

6 **In the Alignment section, click the Decimal option, click the Set button, and then click OK.**

Two left-aligned tabs and a decimal tab are displayed on the ruler, and the Tabs dialog box closes.

FIGURE 4-22

Tab settings indicated on the ruler

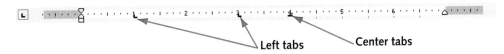

Left tabs   Center tabs

7 **Press Tab, type Employment Level, and press Tab again.**

8 **Type Base, and press Tab.**

9 **Type Mean, and press Enter.**

The headings appear as you type.

10 **To enter the first line of information, press Tab, and type the following, pressing Tab between each entry and Enter after the last entry.**

Entry
52
$36,100.00

The information for the first line in the table is entered.

11 Press Tab, and type the following, pressing Tab between each entry and Enter after the last entry.

Mid Level
207
$42,410.00

The information for the second line in the table is entered. Notice that the number is aligned at the decimal point rather than at the default left.

12 Press Tab, and type the following, pressing Tab between each entry and Enter after the last entry.

Senior Level
186
$55,500

Notice that, even though you didn't type a decimal point in the number, it is still aligned properly with the other numbers.

FIGURE 4-23

Text entered using preset tab stops

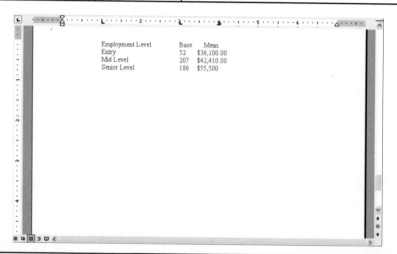

13 On the Format menu, click Tabs.

14 Click the 3" setting in the Tab Stop Position list, and click the Clear button.

The 3" tab setting is cleared. Notice that Word automatically selected the 4" setting in the Tab Stop Position list.

15 With the 4" setting selected, click the 2 option in the Leader section.

16 Click the Set button, and click OK.

17 Press Tab, and type Average.

18 Press Tab, and type $44,670.

The space before the second tab is filled with leader dots.

FIGURE 4-24

Text entered using preset tab stops

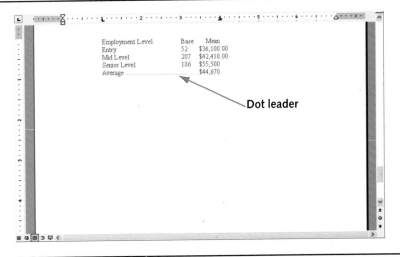

◆ Save the Salary Survey 04 Edited document.

◆ Keep this file open for the next exercise.

Using the Ruler to Set and Clear Tab Stops

You can also quickly set and clear tab stops using the ruler. This tactic works well when you want to set tab stops visually by lining them up with the text below rather than specifying a set number at which to place the stops.

To set a tab stop using the ruler, you select the paragraph(s) to be affected, then click the Tab Align button at the far left side of the ruler to specify the tab alignment type. Click the ruler at the desired position to place the tab stop marker. A tab stop marker appears at that position.

ANOTHER METHOD

You can also use the Tab Align button to set the first line indent and the hanging indent. Click the Tab Align button until the First Line Indent or Hanging Indent symbol appears. Then, on the ruler, click the position where you want to set the indent.

Set and clear tabs using the ruler

We will continue to add information to our survey document. This time, however, we will set the tab stops using the ruler instead of the tab dialog box. We will also clear tabs from the ruler.

1 Click to position the insertion point after the last "0" in the number "$55,500" and press Enter two times.

2 Type the following four lines of information, using the Tab key to move to each tab setting, and press Enter after each line. Press Tab and type:

Age	Base	Mean
20-29	82	$37,800
30-44	178	$47,290
45 and over	200	$50,440

Now that there is more text on your screen, the results of the alignment settings are more apparent.

FIGURE 4-25

Text entered using preset tabs

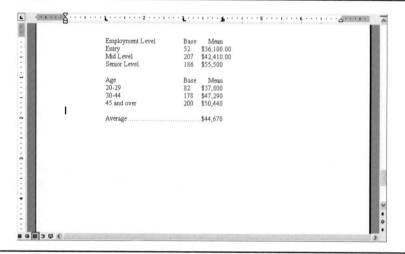

3 Select all the rows of text on this page, except for the row labeled Average, which is the last row.

4 Drag the second tab marker (located on the 3-inch mark) off the ruler.

The tab is cleared and the text shifts.

5 On the left side of the ruler, click the Tab Align button, which now appears as the Left Tab button.

The Tab Align button changes to a Center Align button.

6 Click the ruler at the 3-inch mark.

A centered tab is set, and the text is realigned.

7 Click anywhere to deselect the text.

FIGURE 4-26

Text adjusted by changing tab stops on ruler

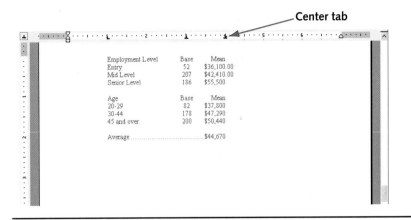

Center tab

❖ **Save the Salary Survey 04 Edited document.**

❖ **Keep this file open for the next exercise.**

QUICK REFERENCE ▼

Set a tab stop using the ruler

1 Select the paragraph(s) for which you want to set tabs.

2 Click the Tab Align button at the far left side of the ruler to specify tab alignment type.

2 Click the ruler at the location where you want the new tab.

3 Deselect the text.

Clear a tab stop

Drag the tab stop marker off the ruler.

Or

1 Click Tabs on the Format menu.

2 In the Tab stop position list, select the tab stop to be removed.

3 Click Clear.

4 Click OK.

Inserting a Page Number

THE BOTTOM LINE

If you create a document containing more than a page or two, it is always useful to have page numbers on your pages so that anyone reading the document can easily keep it in order. Word makes inserting page numbers easy through an option on the Insert menu.

Changing the Look of Paragraphs

When you create a document that has more than one page, you might consider using page numbers to mark each page. Using page numbers comes in handy when you are presenting the document to other people. The people reading your document do not know the information thoroughly, like you do. Instead of telling them to find the paragraph "under the picture toward the middle of the document," simply tell them to "turn to page six and read the paragraph under the picture." Page numbers also come in handy when you are creating a lengthy document. Page numbers allow you to keep the document in order, especially if you print random pages from the document or make edits. Page numbers remind you of where you are in the document.

You can add page numbers to a document using the Page Numbers command on the Insert menu. By default, page numbers are displayed at the lower-right corner of each page. You can change the page number position to either the top or bottom of the page, and then you can specify the left, right, or middle of the page. You also have the option to show a page number only on the first page.

TROUBLESHOOTING

If you are using Normal view, you won't be able to view any page numbers that you insert. You can, however, view page numbers in Print Preview or Print Layout view.

Insert page numbers

Now it is time to put the finishing touches on the survey. The first thing we will do is add page numbers.

1 Press Ctrl+Home to move the insertion point to the top of the document.

2 On the Insert menu, click Page Numbers.

The Page Numbers dialog box appears, and the page number's current position is displayed in the Preview section.

FIGURE 4-27

Page Numbers dialog box

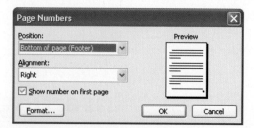

TIP

If you want to change the position of the page number, click the Position down arrow, and select either the top or the bottom of the page.

3 **Click the Alignment down arrow, and click Center.**

The page number is centered in the sample in the Preview section.

4 **Click OK, and scroll down to the bottom of the page to view the page number.**

If you are not already in the Print Layout view, the document is switched to Page Layout view automatically so that you can see the page number you have added to the footer.

FIGURE 4-28

Page number added to document

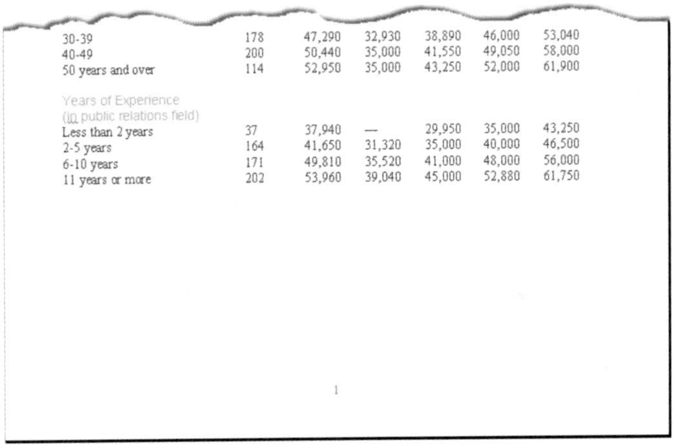

30-39	178	47,290	32,930	38,890	46,000	53,040
40-49	200	50,440	35,000	41,550	49,050	58,000
50 years and over	114	52,950	35,000	43,250	52,000	61,900
Years of Experience (in public relations field)						
Less than 2 years	37	37,940	—	29,950	35,000	43,250
2-5 years	164	41,650	31,320	35,000	40,000	46,500
6-10 years	171	49,810	35,520	41,000	48,000	56,000
11 years or more	202	53,960	39,040	45,000	52,880	61,750

1

◆ **Keep this file open for the next exercise.**

QUICK CHECK

Q. If you insert a page number, is a footer created?

A. **Whenever you insert a page number, a footer or a header is automatically created.**

QUICK REFERENCE ▼

Add page numbers

1. On the Insert menu, click Page Numbers.
2. Click the Position down arrow, and then select the page number position.
3. Click the Alignment down arrow, and then select the desired alignment.
4. Click OK.

Headers and Footers

Controlling What Appears on Each Page

THE BOTTOM LINE

Headers and footers are used in a document to convey useful information such as the name of the document, the page number, the location of the file, the author of the document, etc. These can easily be added by using the Header and Footer toolbar. While there are standard elements that you will find in headers and footers, there are also times when you will want to create a unique header. For those situations, Word lets you customize the headers and footers of a document.

Along with page numbers, headers and footers are useful for documents that contain more than one page. Headers and footers work well in documents containing chapters or sections because you can let readers know where they are in the document by using the header or footer to show them what section they are reading.

While creating the header or footer, you have access to both the Formatting toolbar and the Header And Footer toolbar. The Header And Footer toolbar offers a variety of tools specifically used for customizing headers or footers.

FIGURE 4-29

Header And Footer toolbar

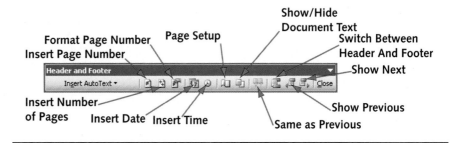

TROUBLESHOOTING

You cannot see the header and footer in Normal view, but you can see them in Print Layout view.

Creating Headers and Footers

You can add header or footer text to a document in the upper- or lower-page margins. This text can be a document identifier, such as a file name, or perhaps a page number or information about the author.

TROUBLESHOOTING

If the Header And Footer toolbar is in your way, drag the toolbar to move it.

Create a header

We will now add a header that contains your name to the document. This header shows, at a glance, who created this document.

1 On the View menu, click Header And Footer.

The Header And Footer toolbar and Header and Footer boxes appear, and you now have access to the header. Notice that the Header box is at the top of the page and the Footer box is at the bottom of the page.

2 On the Header And Footer toolbar, click the Switch Between Header And Footer button.

The insertion point moves from the header to the footer.

3 Click the Switch Between Header And Footer button again.

The insertion point is back in the header.

4 Type your name.

Your name appears in the upper-left corner of the header.

5 Scroll to the second page and look at the header.

Your name also appears there.

Close

6 On the Header And Footer toolbar, click the Close button.

The Header and Footer toolbar closes. You can see the header and the page number that you entered in the footer.

FIGURE 4-30

Header and page number footer in the document

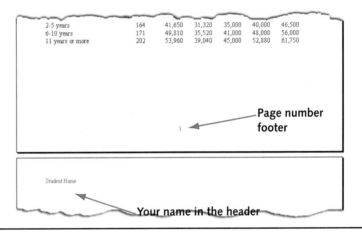

2-5 years	164	41,650	31,320	35,000	40,000	46,500
6-10 years	171	49,810	35,520	41,000	48,000	56,000
11 years or more	202	53,960	39,040	45,000	52,880	61,750

Page number footer

Student Name

Your name in the header

◆ Keep this file open for the next exercise.

Customizing Headers and Footers

As mentioned above, you can customize headers and footers through the Header And Footer toolbar. You might customize a header or footer for the company's annual report. The report is divided into several sections (or chapters), and you can use a footer to insert the page number and the title of the section on each page. You can create a header to go on each page with the title of the annual report, and you can include your company name on the header, too.

You can use the Formatting toolbar while editing headers and footers to make the text as plain or ornate as you want.

Customize a header and footer

Now that we've created a basic header and footer, we will use the Header And Footer toolbar to make edits to these.

1 On the View menu, click Header And Footer.

The Header And Footer toolbar appears, and the headers and footers are available for editing.

ANOTHER METHOD

You can also open an existing header or footer by double-clicking the header or footer in Print Layout view.

2 Scroll to any footer within the document.

3 Click the page number.

A box made up of short diagonal lines now surrounds the page number.

FIGURE 4-31

Page number selected

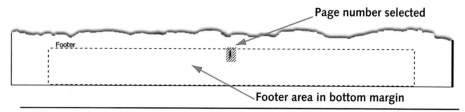
Page number selected
Footer
Footer area in bottom margin

4 Move the mouse pointer over the box until it changes from the I-beam to a four-headed arrow, and click the box surrounding the page number.

A group of smaller black boxes forms within the dashed box.

5 Press Delete.

The page number disappears, and the insertion point moves to the left side of the footer.

6 Type Page, and press the spacebar.

The text appears on the left of the footer box. As you type the *e*, a ScreenTip appears with the text *Page X of Y*.

FIGURE 4-32

Page number footer with ScreenTip

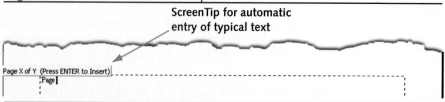
ScreenTip for automatic entry of typical text
Page X of Y (Press ENTER to Insert)
Page

7 On the Header And Footer toolbar, click the Insert Page Number button.

The current page number appears.

8 Press the spacebar, type *of*, and press the spacebar again.

9 On the Header And Footer toolbar, click the Insert Number of Pages button.

The total number of pages in the document appears.

 10 On the Formatting toolbar, click the Center button.

The custom page number is centered in the Footer box.

FIGURE 4-33

Centered, custom page number footer

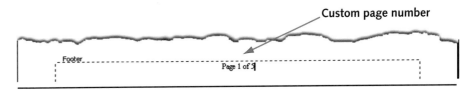

Custom page number

11 On the Header And Footer toolbar, click the Switch Between Header And Footer button.

The view of the document moves up to the header on the same page.

12 On the Formatting toolbar, click the Align Right button.

Your name moves to the right of the header box.

13 Close the Header And Footer toolbar.

◆ Save the Salary Survey 04 Edited document.

◆ Keep this file open for the next exercise.

Edit a header or footer

1 On the View menu, click Header And Footer.

2 Switch to or use the Show Next and Show Previous buttons to get to the header or footer that you want to change.

3 Click the toolbar buttons that you want to use.

4 Type or edit the text as necessary.

Switching Page Orientation

THE BOTTOM LINE

Because the width and length of your content may vary, you can choose to orient your pages in two different ways: portrait orientation (pages are oriented as they are in this book) or landscape orientation. These options allow you another way to set up your pages exactly in the manner you need to best display the content of your document.

CHECK THIS OUT ▼

Different First Page Footer
You can create a different header and footer for the first page of the document than for the other pages. To vary the header and footer on the first page, on the Header And Footer toolbar, click the Page Setup button. In the Headers And Footers section of the Layout tab in the Page Setup dialog box, select the Different First Page check box.

QUICK CHECK

Q. Can a page number be placed in a header?

A. A page number can be placed in a header, a footer, or both.

Previewing Documents for Printing

You can lay out the text on a page in two ways: portrait orientation and landscape orientation. Text placed in **portrait** orientation appears horizontally on a vertical page and is the default page orientation in Word. Text placed in **landscape** orientation appears horizontally on a page that is turned on its side. Diplomas and awards are usually oriented in this manner.

The following figures illustrate portrait and landscape orientation.

FIGURE 4-34

Portrait and landscape orientation

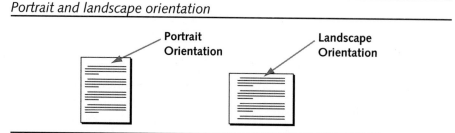

You can change orientation even after you've started creating a document.

Switch page orientation

Since the Salary Survey 04 Edited has so many columns of information, it would look better if we change the page orientation from portrait to landscape.

1 **On the File menu, click Page Setup.**

The Page Setup dialog box appears.

2 **Click the Margins tab, if necessary.**

FIGURE 4-35

Page Setup dialog box

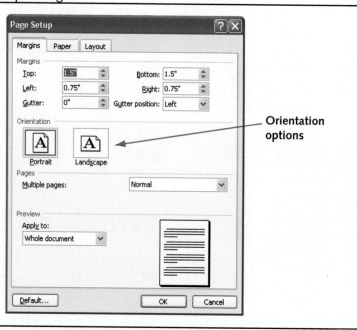

> **TIP**
>
> Notice in the Preview box that the page orientation changed from portrait (8.5" x 11") to landscape (11" x 8.5").

3 **Click the Landscape option, view the Preview box, and click OK.**

The text appears in landscape orientation.

87% ▾

4 **On the Standard toolbar, click the Zoom down arrow, and click Whole Page.**

FIGURE 4-36

Zoom list with Whole Page selected

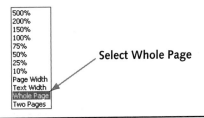

The first page of the document should now look similar to Figure 4-37.

FIGURE 4-37

Result of changing document orientation

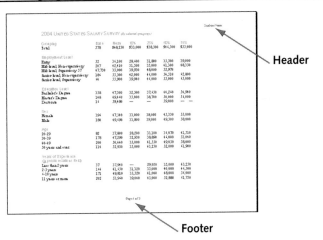

◆ If you are continuing to other lessons, save and close the Salary Survey 04 Edited document. Keep Word open.

◆ If you are not continuing to other lessons, save and close the Salary Survey 04 Edited document and then close Word.

Q. What is the default page orientation in Word?

A. Portrait orientation is the default page orientation in Word.

QUICK REFERENCE ▼

Change page orientation

1 On the File menu, click Page Setup.

2 If necessary, click the Margins tab.

3 In the Orientation section, click the Portrait or Landscape option.

4 Click OK.

Key Points

✔ *You can view a document in a variety of ways depending on your needs as you create a document and on the purpose for which you are creating it.*

✔ *Page margins within a document can be set to your exact specifications through the Page Setup dialog box (available from the File menu) or by using the ruler.*

✔ *Paragraphs are formatted through the Paragraph dialog box (available from the Format menu). Indentations can also be set by using the ruler.*

✔ *Tab stops can be set and changed by using the Tabs dialog box (available from the Format menu) or by using the ruler. Tabs with leaders must be set in the Tabs dialog box.*

✔ *Headers and footers can be added to your document as a means of displaying important information that you want to be repeated on each page. You can also choose to simply insert page numbers (from the Insert menu) that actually creates a header or a footer with just the page number.*

✔ *The orientation of a document can be set to either portrait or landscape in order to best display the contents of your document and make the best use of the space available on a sheet of paper.*

Quick Quiz

Multiple Choice

1. A paragraph setting that specifies the indent for the first line of a paragraph is called _____ indent.
   a. hanging
   b. first line
   c. left
   d. right

2. A document view that displays the document on the screen in the manner that it will appear when printed is called _____ view.
   a. Normal
   b. Web Layout
   c. Print Layout
   d. Reading Layout

3. A paragraph setting that specifies the indentation of the entire paragraph from the right margin of the page is called _____ indent.
   a. hanging
   b. first line
   c. left
   d. right

4. A document view that displays the document on the screen in the manner that it will appear when viewed in a Web browser is called _____ view.
   a. Document Map
   b. Web Layout
   c. Print Layout
   d. Reading Layout

5. A paragraph setting that aligns the first line of a paragraph flush with the left page margin and indents all subsequent lines a specified distance to the right is called _____ indent.
   a. hanging
   b. first line
   c. left
   d. right

6. A document view that displays as much of the content of the document as will fit in the screen at a size that is comfortable for viewing is called _____ view.
   a. Normal
   b. Web Layout
   c. Print Layout
   d. Reading Layout

7. A paragraph setting that specifies the indent of the entire paragraph from the left margin of the page is called _____ indent.
   a. hanging
   b. first line
   c. left
   d. right

8. A document view that displays a list of your document's headings in a separate pane so that you can see the structure of the document is called _____ view.
   a. Outline
   b. Document Map
   c. Thumbnails
   d. Reading Layout

9. A tab that aligns text to the left of the tab is called a _____ tab.
   a. left
   b. right
   c. center
   d. decimal

10. A tab that aligns text to the right of the tab is called a _____ tab.
    a. left
    b. right
    c. center
    d. decimal

Short Answer

1. Name three ways in which you can change the page margins in Word.

2. How is vertical alignment similar to and different from horizontal alignment?

3. How do you display the measurements of the page margins?

4. How do you display the Headers And Footers toolbar?

5. What's the difference between the Left Indent marker and the Left Page Margin marker on the ruler?

6. How do you clear a tab stop?

7. How do you specify that you want to insert a page number in the upper-right corner of the document?

8. When the headers and footers boxes are displayed, what are two ways that you can switch between the header and the footer?

9. When you delete a paragraph mark, what formatting characteristics does that paragraph take on?

On Your Own

IMPORTANT

In the On Your Own exercises that follow, you must complete Exercise 1 to continue to Exercise 2.

Exercise 1

If necessary, open a new blank Word document. Adjust the left and right page margins to 2 inches and change the orientation to landscape. Insert tab stops at 2 inches, 4 inches, 6 inches, and 8 inches. The 6-inch tab stop should be a decimal tab, and the 8-inch tab stop should be a right tab. Type the following headings in the first line:

Years Experience, Base, Mean, 90%.

Insert a new line, make heading text bold, and then save the document as **Practice 04**.

You will use Exercise 1 to complete the following exercise.

Exercise 2

Type the following information on the next two lines, pressing Tab between the entries.

| Less than 2 years | 37 | $37,940 | $43,250 |
| 2–5 years | 164 | $41,650 | $55,000 |

Create a centered heading with the title *Survey Results* and a footer with the current date on the left and Page *X* of *Y* on the right (where *X* is the current page and *Y* is the number of pages). Save the file in the Lesson04 folder, and close the document.

One Step Further

Exercise 1

In the Header And Footer toolbar, there is an Insert AutoText button. Open a new blank document and experiment with the various options available through this feature. Save the file in the Lesson04 folder, and close the document.

Exercise 2

In your open document, create a list of your favorite musical artists. Set a Left tab at 1", and enter the name of the group or musician. Set another Left tab, and enter the name of a CD that you own by this artist. If you own multiple CDs, press Enter, and press Tab twice to enter each of the CDs that you own in a separate line of text. Next to this information, set a Right tab at 5", and rank each CD on a scale of 1 to 10 (least favorite to favorite). Fill in the information for several artists. Save the file in the Lesson04 folder, and close the document.

Exercise 3

In this lesson, we adjusted the spacing after a paragraph. What other Spacing options are available for paragraphs and for lines? Explore the Paragraph dialog box or use Word's Help files to find out more information about paragraph and line spacing.

5

Creating Content and Editing Text

After completing this lesson, you will be able to:

✔ *Check spelling in a document.*
✔ *Check for grammatical errors.*
✔ *Translate text to and from other languages.*
✔ *Use the thesaurus.*
✔ *Find specific text.*
✔ *Replace specific text.*
✔ *Create AutoCorrect entries and exceptions.*
✔ *Highlight text.*
✔ *Insert the date and time as text or as a field.*
✔ *Insert special characters.*

KEY TERMS

- AutoCorrect
- comments
- exception
- field
- grammar checking
- readability statistics
- research services
- search string
- Sounds like
- special characters
- spelling checking
- wildcard
- writing style
- variable-width

Before you deliver a Microsoft Office Word 2003 document to others, you should always proofread it carefully. Proofreading involves correcting all spelling and grammar errors and making any other final changes to the document. Fortunately, Word's spelling and grammar capabilities can do some of this work for you.

The dictionary contains all words that Microsoft identifies as correct when you check the spelling of a document, including many proper nouns and acronyms. If you type *Our plans is to send the document after it has been proofread*, Microsoft will mark *plans is* as a grammatical error. On the other hand, if you type *Too whom it may concern*, Word will not mark the word *Too* as being a grammatical error. The bottom line: even after you use Word's spelling and grammar-checking features to make corrections in a document, you still need to read through the document carefully to look for any additional errors.

You can also customize the spelling and grammar-checking feature by defining which grammar rules apply. For instance, you might want to use casual language (including contractions) when you compose a letter to a friend. When you compose letters to business associates, you might want to use more formal language. You can change the language style to suit your audience. Word will then mark grammatical errors based on the rules for the style of language that you have chosen. If you specify that you want to use the Formal language style, and you type *I don't think this is an acceptable solution*, Word will mark *don't* as a grammatical error because contractions generally aren't permitted in formal English.

Word can also automatically correct common grammatical errors as you type them. For instance, if you type *Your my top candidate*, Word will change *Your* to *You're* as soon as it identifies the grammatical error.

You might also want to find a synonym for a particular word to give your document a more forceful or professional tone. Word has a thesaurus that you can use to improve the word choices in your document. In this exercise, you will use these and other proofing and editing tools to correct and improve documents.

In this lesson, you will check spelling and grammar in a document, use the thesaurus, and find and replace specific text. You will create AutoCorrect entries, highlight text, and insert date and time fields and special characters.

IMPORTANT

Before you can use the practice files for this lesson, you need to install them from the book's companion CD to its default location. For additional information on how to find and open files used in this book, see the "Using the CD-ROM" section at the beginning of this book.

Spelling and Grammar Checking

THE BOTTOM LINE

Word's built-in spelling and grammar checkers can help you quickly identify many kinds of mistakes in your document, although you still need to proofread your document.

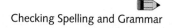
Checking Spelling and Grammar

As you type the contents of a document, you might notice that some words or phrases are underlined with red or green wavy lines. These symbols are part of the **spelling checking** and **grammar checking** features in Word. A red wavy underline identifies words that are not found in the dictionary, and a green wavy underline indicates phrases and grammatical constructions that Word detects as being potentially grammatically incorrect. To correct the error, you can manually edit the word or phrase, or you can use the Spelling And Grammar dialog box to view and select from suggested changes. After the word or phrase has been corrected, the red or green wavy line no longer appears.

You can check the spelling of a single word, or you can use the Spelling And Grammar dialog box to check the spelling and grammar in an entire document. This feature marks incorrectly spelled words, locates repeated words, and identifies capitalization and grammatical errors. To access the Spelling

And Grammar dialog box, on the Standard toolbar click the Spelling And Grammar button, or on the Tools menu, click Spelling And Grammar.

If you are correcting an individual spelling error, Word can display a list of possible corrections for a misspelled word. To check a single spelling error, simply right-click the text that is underlined in red to display a shortcut menu, and select the correct spelling from the list of possible corrections.

FIGURE 5-1

Shortcut menu with spelling correction options

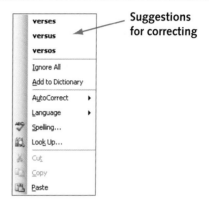

Suggestions for correcting

When you check the spelling for a complete document, Word compares each word in the document with words in its standard dictionary. If an error is found, the word is selected in the document window, and alternative selections are listed in the Suggestions list. After a possible misspelled word has been located, the following options are available, which appear as buttons in the Spelling And Grammar dialog box.

Button	Function
Ignore Once	Ignores only that occurrence of the selected word
Ignore All	Ignores all occurrences of the word
Add To Dictionary	Adds the word to the custom dictionary
Change	Replaces the selected word with the word selected in the Suggestions list
Change All	Replaces all occurrences of the word with the selected word in the Suggestions list
AutoCorrect	Adds the word to a list that Word uses to automatically correct spellings of the word as you type it
Undo	Returns a spelling correction to its previous state
Delete	Appears if a double occurrence of a word is detected (such as *to to modify the document*) and can be used to delete the second occurrence of a word
Delete All	Appears if a double occurrence of a word is detected in more than one location. Can be used to delete all of the second occurrence of a specific word.
Options	Customizes spelling and grammar checking. For example, you can specify whether you want Word to ignore certain words with uppercase characters or words with numbers when Word checks spelling.

Using the Shortcut Menu for Words and Phrases

To identify the cause of a single grammatical error, you can right-click any word marked with a green wavy line to display a shortcut menu and then make a selection from the shortcut menu as desired.

FIGURE 5-2

Shortcut menu with grammar correction options

The first item on the menu is a brief description of the error. If you click the About This Sentence item on the shortcut menu, Word displays a more thorough explanation of the grammatical problem and suggests ways to correct it.

If a red wavy line appears under a word that you know is spelled correctly (such as a proper name), you can add that word to the dictionary. To add a word to the dictionary and remove the red wavy line from all instances of that particular spelling, right-click the word to display a shortcut menu, and click Add To Dictionary.

Checking Spelling in a Document

There are three basic ways to check spelling in a document, depending on whether you want to correct errors as soon as Word identifies them or whether you want to wait and check spelling for the entire document after you have created it:

- Right-click a word that has a red wavy underline, and then select a suggested correction from the list.
- On the Standard toolbar, click the Spelling And Grammar button to check spelling and grammar in the entire document.
- On the Tools menu, click Spelling And Grammar to check spelling and grammar in the entire document.

TROUBLESHOOTING

In the following exercises and in the illustrations used throughout this lesson, the Standard and Formatting toolbars have been separated. For additional information on how to separate the toolbars, see the "Using the CD-ROM" section at the beginning of this book.

◆ Be sure to start Word before beginning this exercise.

◆ Open Brochure 05 from the Lesson05 folder in the Word Practice folder that is located on your hard disk

Check spelling in a document

The Brochure 05 document explains the services provided by the public relations firm Contoso, Ltd, but it is a first draft that needs some work before it will be ready to send to potential clients. We will begin by correcting spelling errors that Word identifies.

1 **In the first line of the second paragraph, right-click the misspelled word "aech," and click "each" in the list of possible corrections that appears.**

The word is corrected in the document.

2 **On the Standard toolbar, click the Spelling And Grammar button.**

The Spelling And Grammar dialog box appears with the word *CLnetworks* selected in the document window. Word has only one suggestion for this term and it is obviously not the correct substitution.

FIGURE 5-3

Spelling And Grammar dialog box

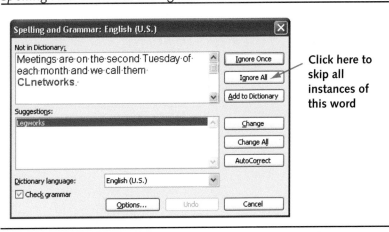

3 **Clear the Check Grammar check box if it is currently selected.**

4 **Click the Ignore All button.**

The word and all future instances of it in the document are ignored, and the word *an* is selected. Because this is an occurrence of a double word and not a misspelling, no alternative spellings are offered.

5 Click the Delete button.

The second occurrence of the word *an* is deleted, and the capitalization error *MEmbership* is selected. The correct usage of the capitalized word is displayed and selected in the Suggestions list.

6 Click the Change button to change the capitalization to Membership.

The capitalization is changed, and the word Contoso is selected.

7 Choose Ignore All.

8 Word continues to check the document for spelling errors. When an error occurs, choose the best choice in the Suggestions list and click the Change button. Continue making the necessary corrections in the document.

When Word has finished locating all potential spelling errors, the Spelling And Grammar dialog box closes, and the following message box appears.

FIGURE 5-4

Spelling check completed message box

9 Click OK.

The message box closes.

TIP

You can undo spelling corrections one by one immediately after closing the Spelling And Grammar dialog box. On the Standard toolbar, click the Undo button to undo the most recently corrected word. Click the Undo button again to undo the next corrected word. Repeat this procedure to undo any other spelling corrections.

◆ Save the document as Brochure 05 Edited.

◆ Keep this file open for the next exercise.

QUICK REFERENCE ▼

Customize the spell check operations

1 On the Tools menu, click Options.

2 Click the Spelling & Grammar tab, and make selections as desired.

3 Click OK.

Q. Can you edit the text in a document when the Spelling And Grammar dialog box is open?

A. You can edit a document while the Spelling And Grammar dialog box is open. This allows you to make corrections to your document when the suggestions in the Spelling And Grammar dialog box are not sufficient.

Check the spelling of an entire document

1 On the Standard toolbar, click the Spelling And Grammar button.

2 Click an option in the Suggestions box, and click the Change or Change All button.

Or

Click the Ignore Once button to ignore the word; click the Ignore All button to ignore the word throughout the document.

Or

To add the word to the dictionary, click Add To Dictionary.

3 Click OK.

Checking for Grammatical Errors

After you have typed your document, you can use Word to check the entire document for grammar and spelling errors. If an error is found, the word or phrase is selected in the Sentence box, and alternative words or phrases appear in the Suggestions list. You can ignore the error, check the grammar rule, or make changes to the existing document.

Normally, Word checks for spelling and grammatical errors at the same time—with one exception. If you clear the Check Grammar With Spelling check box, Word checks only for spelling errors. You cleared this check box in the previous exercise to check for spelling errors only, so grammatical errors might still occur in your document. You can still check for grammatical errors at a later time.

FIGURE 5-5

Spelling & Grammar tab on the Options dialog box

With this cleared, only spelling will be checked

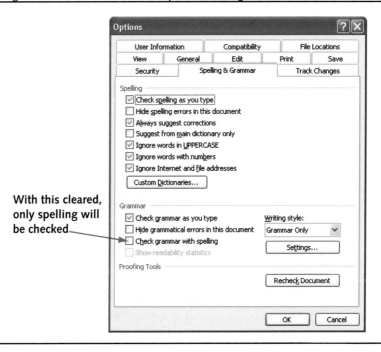

To check grammar in a document (after you've turned on grammar checking), on the Standard toolbar, click the Spelling And Grammar button to display the Spelling And Grammar dialog box. Click the Ignore Once button to ignore an error, click the Ignore All button to ignore the error wherever it occurs, or click the Change button to make the suggested replacement that appears in the Suggestions list. Change All will review the document, find any other words that are the same, and replace them with the text chosen in the Suggestions list.

If Word identifies a grammatical problem that can't be corrected with a simple replacement (such as a sentence fragment or words that appear to be out of order), the Change button will be grayed out (made unavailable). However, the dialog box will suggest that you consider revising the sentence.

FIGURE 5-6

Grammar error in the Spelling And Grammar dialog box

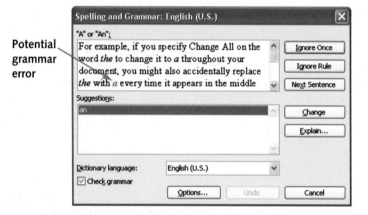

Check grammar in a document

With the spelling corrected in our brochure, we will now check the grammar in the document.

1 Press Ctrl+Home to position the insertion point at the beginning of the document.

2 On the Tools menu, click Options.

The Options dialog box appears.

3 In the Options dialog box, click the Spelling & Grammar tab, if necessary.

4 In the Grammar section, select the Check Grammar With Spelling check box, verify that the Check Grammar As You Type option is selected, and click OK.

5 Scroll down until you see the words that are underlined with a green wavy line (the sentence begins "Membership open to individuals").

6 **Right-click anywhere in the underlined area.**

Word displays a shortcut menu that shows suggested corrections as well as providing access to further information.

FIGURE 5-7

Grammar Error shortcut menu

Suggestions for correcting error

TIP

If you want to learn more about what Word has identified as an error, you can click Grammar to open the Spelling And Grammar dialog box, and then click the Explain button. The Office Assistant appears and explains, in this case, the meaning of subject-verb agreement and suggests ways to correct the grammatical error.

---

7 **Click after the space following the word "Membership," type is, and then press the spacebar.**

The error is corrected by adding a verb to the sentence, and the green wavy line no longer appears.

◆ **Keep this file open for the next exercise.**

QUICK REFERENCE ▼

Turn on grammar check for a document

1 On the Tools menu, click Options.

2 Click the Spelling & Grammar tab, if necessary.

3 Click the Check Grammar With Spelling check box to turn this feature on, and click OK.

Check the grammar of a document

1 On the Standard toolbar, click the Spelling And Grammar button.

2 Click the Change button to make the suggested replacement displayed in the Suggestions text box.

Or

Click the Ignore Once button to ignore an error; click the Ignore All button to ignore the error throughout the document.

QUICK CHECK

Q. Can you select Ignore All from the shortcut menu?

A. You can choose to Ignore Once from the shortcut menu that appears when you right-click on a grammar error, but Ignore All is not an option on the shortcut menu.

Specifying a Writing Style and Using Readability Statistics

THE BOTTOM LINE

An extension of grammar checking is the ability to set the writing style for your document. This allows you to choose to be more or less "grammatically correct" based upon your intended audience.

Word checks the grammar of a document based on writing styles. A **writing style** is a set of grammatical rules and conventions that determine whether a particular phrase or sentence structure is appropriate for your intended audience.

For example, different departments at Contoso, Ltd use different writing styles for their grammar checks. The marketing manager likes to set the grammar checker to use a casual writing style because most of her documents are about upcoming events and are sent to previous and prospective clients. The operations manager, on the other hand, prefers to set the grammar checker style to be more formal because he sends most of his documents to contractors and business partners.

By default, the grammar checker uses a set of standard writing style rules. To change the writing style, on the Tools menu, click Options to display the Options dialog box, and then click the Spelling & Grammar tab, if necessary. In the Writing style box, click the down arrow, and select the desired style: Grammar & Style or Grammar Only. To change the style rules that are applied, click the Settings button. The Grammar Settings dialog box opens, in which you can pick and choose the grammar or style rules that you want to use.

You can also use the Spelling And Grammar dialog box to display your document's readability statistics. *Readability statistics* show useful information about the document, such as the average number of words per sentence and the average number of characters per word. For instance, if the readability statistics show that the average number of words per sentence is more than 20, you might want to consider breaking some sentences into two sentences to enhance readability. If you have selected the Show Readability Statistics check box prior to checking a document for grammatical errors, the Readability Statistics window appears after the spelling and grammar check is completed.

FIGURE 5-8

Readability Statistics dialog box

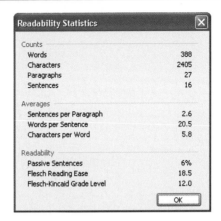

Q. What can the Readability Statistics tell you about whether your document will be understood by your intended audience?

A. **The Readability Statistics include information on the approximate grade level required to read a document. If you are writing for people who are not reading at or above that level, they may have trouble understanding what you have written.**

QUICK REFERENCE ▼

Change writing style options

1 On the Tools menu, click Options.

2 Click the Spelling & Grammar tab, if necessary.

3 Click the Writing Style down arrow and select the desired rule guidelines.

4 Click the Settings button for more control over the writing style.

5 Click OK.

Using the Research Task Pane

THE BOTTOM LINE

With Microsoft Office Word 2003, you can quickly reference information online and on your computer without leaving your Microsoft Office program. You can easily insert definitions, synonyms, language translations, stock quotes, and other research information into your document, as well as customize settings to suit your research needs.

Researching Information

The Research task pane is a new feature in Microsoft Office Word 2003. It is available from the Research command on the Tools menu, from the Research button on the Standard toolbar, and by pressing the Alt key as you click on any word or phrase.

From the Research task pane, you can search multiple sources or select a specific source. If your browser is Internet Explorer and you click a link, the Research task pane travels with you and is displayed on the left side of your screen as you view Web pages.

The following *research services* are available from the Research task pane.

Service	Description of Service
Dictionary	Look up words or phrases in the Microsoft Encarta English dictionary easily while you work. The Encarta dictionary contains approximately 400,000 entries and, in addition to definitions, includes pronunciation keys, word histories, and word usage notes. You can also add other dictionaries, which are then compared against Encarta standards to ensure that you receive the best results.
Thesaurus	Look up synonyms while you work, and insert them into your document directly from the Research task pane. You can also click a result to look up additional words, and you can look up words in the thesaurus of another language.
Encyclopedia	Research your subject in Microsoft Encarta Encyclopedia, which contains more than 42,000 articles. Ask a question and review the results. In the list of results, you can view summaries and click related links that take you to additional information.
Translation	Get translations quickly using bilingual dictionaries on your computer and online, or use machine translation on the Web. You can use the bilingual dictionaries to translate single words or short phrases. Machine translation services can translate phrases, paragraphs, or your entire document.
Stock quotes and company information	Look up stock quotes and company information while you work. If you aren't sure of a stock symbol or company name, type a few words. Search will find the symbol or name. You can also insert company information into your document and perform custom actions.

TIP

Custom actions come from the smart tags that reside on your computer. Not all languages support this feature. Comprehensive company information is provided by Gale, a company profile service provider. From the Research task pane, you can reference industry information, company fundamentals, contact information, and other company details.

Third-party services	Add third-party premium content to your list of research services, and the Microsoft Office System will present the most relevant information to you based on your search scope and question. Examples of third-party services include Factiva (news), eLibrary (news and periodicals), Gale (company profiles), and WorldLingo (translation provider).
Intranet sites	If your company has an intranet site, you can add it to the Research task pane for easy access. Microsoft Office SharePoint Portal Server 2003 sites are supported. To add a SharePoint Portal Server site to the

	list of All Intranet Sites and Portals, in the Add Services dialog box, type *http://your root directory/_vti_bin/search.asmx*.
Web search	Search the Web alongside your document by using MSN Search. To read more, click a link to view more information on the Web.

We will use the thesaurus and the translation service in the next sections.

Using the Thesaurus

THE BOTTOM LINE

As you are creating or editing a document, you will occasionally come across a word for which you know there is another word that would sound better—but you just cannot think of it. For these situations, Word has a built-in Thesaurus to help you determine the right synonym.

Word's thesaurus helps you look up alternatives, or synonyms, for a particular word. To use the thesaurus, click the word that you want to look up. On the Tools menu, point to Language, and click Thesaurus to display the Thesaurus panel in the Research task pane.

ANOTHER METHOD

You can also press Shift+F7 to display the Thesaurus dialog box.

FIGURE 5-9

Thesaurus panel in the Research task pane

Word for which you are searching for a synonym

List of possible synonyms

In the Thesaurus panel, if you see a word that you would rather use, point to the word, click the down arrow that appears next to it, and then click Insert to replace your original word with the synonym. To look up additional synonyms, point to a new word in the list of synonyms, click the down arrow, and click Look Up to view a new list of words in the Thesaurus panel.

You can also use the shortcut menu to look up synonyms. To do so, right-click a word, and point to Synonyms on the shortcut menu. Words with similar meanings are listed. The word that appears first in the list is the term that Word suggests as being the closest in meaning to the word selected. Click the desired word in the list, or click Thesaurus at the bottom of the list to access the Research task pane.

FIGURE 5-10

Shortcut menu of synonyms

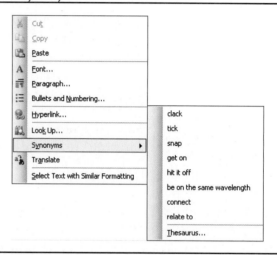

Use the thesaurus

In reading our letter, we notice a word for which we think there is a better word. We will use the thesaurus to replace a word with a more appropriate synonym.

1. **Scroll down until you see the paragraph that begins "Contoso also provides."**

2. **In the second line, right-click the word "variety," and point to Synonyms on the shortcut menu that appears.**

A list of synonyms for *variety* appears.

FIGURE 5-11

Shortcut list of synonyms for variety

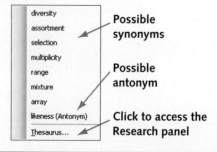

3 In the list of synonyms, click "range."

3 In the list of synonyms, click "range."

Word replaces the word *variety* with *range*.

◆ **Keep this file open for the next exercise.**

QUICK REFERENCE ▼

Use the thesaurus

1 Right-click the word in question.

2 Point to Synonyms on the short-cut menu.

3 Click the synonym you want to use.

Or

On the Tools menu, click Language, and point to Thesaurus.

Translating Text in Another Language

THE BOTTOM LINE

In our global community, it is not uncommon to have correspondence with someone who speaks, as their first language, a different language from us. When you encounter words in a language that you do not speak or read or when you want to write words in another language, you can use Word's text translator.

Word provides a basic multi-language dictionary and translation feature so that you can look up text in the dictionary of a different language and translate simple, short phrases. You can often use these translations to determine the main ideas in a document written in a foreign language. If you need to translate longer sections of text, you can connect to translation services on the World Wide Web directly from the Research task pane. For important or sensitive documents, you might want to have a trained person do the translation, since computer translation might not preserve the text's full meaning, detail, or tone. You can also look up words or phrases in the dictionary of a different language, provided that the language dictionary is installed on your computer and enabled through Microsoft Office 2003 Language Settings. To enable a language, click the Start button on the taskbar, point to All Programs, point to Microsoft Office Tools, click Microsoft Office 2003 Language Settings, click the Enabled Languages tab, select a language, and then click Add. You will need to shut down your Microsoft Office 2003 applications and restart them for the chosen language to be enabled.

QUICK CHECK

Q. Can you open the thesaurus if the Research task pane is already open with a different panel displayed?

A. If the Research task pane is already open, you can click the down arrow next to the box below the Search For text box. Here you will see a list of research services available to you. Click Thesaurus in this list to switch to the Thesaurus panel. You are also automatically switched to the Thesaurus if you select the Thesaurus service through the Tools menu or a pop-up menu.

To translate text in another language:

1. Select the text in your document that you want to translate.
2. On the Tools menu, point to Language, and then click Translate.

   The Research task pane appears with the Translation panel open and the selected text in the Search For text box.

ANOTHER METHOD

You can also access the Translation panel on the Research task pane by right-clicking on any word or selection and choosing Translate from the shortcut menu.

FIGURE 5-12

Translation panel in the Research task pane

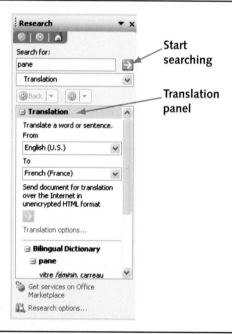

3. In the Translation panel, select the languages that you want to translate From and To, and then click the Start Searching button.

   The translated text appears in the Bilingual Dictionary section of the task pane.

QUICK CHECK

Q. Can you translate a phrase or only one word at a time?

A. **You can translate phrases, but you may need to use online translators that are also accessible from the Research task pane.**

QUICK REFERENCE ▼

Translate text in another language

1 Select the text that you want to translate.

2 On the Tools menu, point to Language, and then click Translate.

3 In the Dictionary box, select the languages that you want to translate from and to, and then click Start Searching.

Navigating to Specific Content

Finding and Replacing Text

THE BOTTOM LINE

Being able to quickly locate a specific word or phrase in a document or being able to go to a certain page or section is one of the many advantages of an electronic document over a hard copy. Word allows you to access these navigation features through the Find And Replace dialog box and the Select Browse Object button.

When you edit long documents, you might want to move quickly to a particular location in the document so that you can review or edit text at this location. If you know that the location of the document contains a unique word or phrase, you can use Word's Find And Replace dialog box to locate the word or phrase. You can also use the Go To tab in the Find And Replace dialog box to move the insertion point to specific text in the document, such as a specific page, section, or heading.

The Select Browse Object button lets you access the Find feature and the Go To feature. Additionally, it lets you search for a specific item in the text by allowing searches for headings, graphics, tables, **comments**, sections, page numbers, footnotes, endnotes, fields, or edits.

Finding Specific Text

Word's Find And Replace dialog box allows you to look for specific content within your document. You can display the Find tab of the Find And Replace dialog box by clicking Find on the Edit menu.

FIGURE 5-13

Find tab of the Find And Replace dialog box

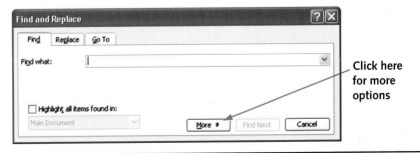

Click here for more options

ANOTHER METHOD

You can also display the Find tab of the Find And Replace dialog box by pressing Ctrl+F or by clicking the Select Browse Object button (lower-right corner of the Word window) and then clicking Find.

In the Find And Replace dialog box, you can click the More button to display additional search options. These search options allow you to define settings such as whether you are using wildcards or the Sounds like feature.

FIGURE 5-14

More options shown in the Find And Replace dialog box

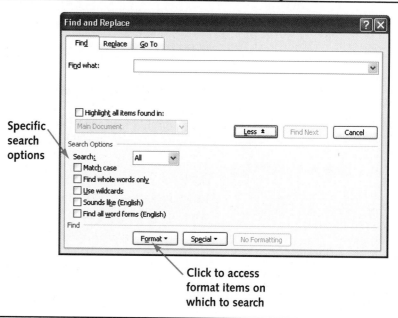

A **wildcard** character stands for any character that appears in one or more positions within a word or string of text. To use wildcards, in the Find And Replace dialog box, click the More button, and select the Use Wildcards check box. Use the question mark (?) wildcard symbol in a search string to represent any character in a single position within the word or text string. For example, the string *h?t* finds *hat, hit, hot,* and *hut.* Use the asterisk (*) wildcard symbol to represent any string of characters. For example, the string *h*t* finds *hat, hurt,* and even *had sent.*

TIP

A **search string** is a group or string of characters to be matched in the document when a search is performed.

You can use the **Sounds like** feature to find words that sound similar to the text string you are searching for, but which might be spelled differently. For example, when you use the Sounds Like feature for the word *meet,* Word identifies *meet, meat,* and *mete* as matching the Sounds like rule.

Use Find And Replace

We will now experiment with using the Find And Replace dialog box. We will find a string of text within the current document and expand the Find And Replace dialog box to display additional search options.

1 **Press Ctrl+Home to position the insertion point at the beginning of the document.**

2 **On the Edit menu, click Find.**

The Find And Replace dialog box appears.

3 **In the Find What box, type meetings, and click the Find Next button.**

The word *meetings* at the beginning of the second paragraph is now selected. The Find And Replace dialog box remains unchanged.

ANOTHER METHOD

You don't have to search for full words. You can also search for parts of words or phrases. For example, if you want to find the word *envelope*, you could shorten the search string by just searching for *envel* to find all words that have that set of characters in the text.

4 **In the Find And Replace dialog box, click the Find Next button to display the next occurrence of the word meetings.**

The word *meetings* at the end of the second paragraph is now selected. The Find And Replace dialog box still remains unchanged.

TROUBLESHOOTING

You may need to drag the Find And Replace dialog box out of the way so that you can see the selections within the document.

5 **Click the Find Next button again.**

Word searches again for the word *meetings* and displays a message box indicating that Word has finished searching the document.

6 **Click OK.**

The message box closes.

7 **In the Find And Replace dialog box, click the More button.**

The dialog box expands to show the Search Options section.

8 **In the Find And Replace dialog box, click the Cancel button.**

The dialog box closes.

◆ **Keep this file open for the next exercise.**

QUICK CHECK

Q. Can you search for text in a particular font?

A. Yes, you can search for text that is in a particular font by clicking the Format button in the Find And Replace dialog box and selecting the Font option in the pop-up menu.

QUICK REFERENCE ▼

Perform a Find operation

1 On the Edit menu, click Find.

2 To increase Find criteria and narrow the search, click the More button to display the search options.

3 In the Find What box, type the find search string.

4 Click the Find Next button until you're finished searching or there are no more occurrences.

5 Click the Cancel button to return to the document window.

Using Go To

To access the Go To tab, on the Edit menu, click Go To.

FIGURE 5-15

Go To tab of the Find And Replace dialog box

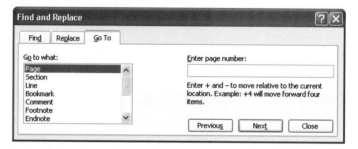

ANOTHER METHOD

To quickly display the Go To section of the Find And Replace dialog box, you can also press F5, press Ctrl+G, or click the Select Browse Object button (lower-right corner of the Word window) and then click the Go To button.

In the Go To What list, select the option with which you want to search your document. For example, if you choose Footnote, Word narrows the search to the Footnotes in your document. You can type a plus sign (+) followed by a number and click the Go To button to move forward the designated number of items relative to the current position of the insertion point. For example, if you type a plus sign (+) followed by the number 2 and click the Go To button, the insertion point would move forward two items from where the insertion point was located in the document before you used the Go To button. You can also type a minus sign (-) to move backward the specified number of items.

To go to a specific page in a document, on the Edit menu, click Go To to display the Go To tab in the Find And Replace dialog box. Select Page in the Go To What list, type the desired page number in the Enter Page Number box, and then click the Go To button.

CHECK THIS OUT ▼

Variable-Width Fonts and Double-Spacing After a Period

Most fonts are called **variable-width** fonts because the spaces between characters (kerning) can be adjusted to accommodate adjoining characters of different widths. For instance, in the word *Wide*, the width of the letter *W* is much greater than the width of the letter *i*. With most fonts, the space before the letter *i* is reduced so that the letter is "tucked in" closer to the letter *W*. When you use variable-width fonts, sentences look more professional when only one space follows a period. (The convention of typing two spaces after a period stems from the use of typewriters to create documents; most typewriters cannot adjust the widths between characters and words.) To make sure that only one space is used at the end of all sentences in a document, you can use Find And Replace. In the Find box, type a period (.) followed by two spaces. In the Replace box, type a period (.) followed by one space. Word searches for all the periods followed by a double space and replaces them with a period followed by a single space.

QUICK REFERENCE ▼

Use Go To operation

1 On the Edit menu, click Go To.

2 Select item in the Go To What list.

3 Type the desired page number in the Enter Page Number box.

4 Click the Go To button.

Replacing Specific Text

The Replace command allows you to quickly locate any string of characters, such as a word or phrase. The string of text, when found, can be replaced by a different string using the Find And Replace dialog box.

For example, the marketing department is revising a brochure about the organization and services provided by Contoso, Ltd. The company used to be commonly referred to as *Contoso*; however, the company now wants to use the full company name *Contoso, Ltd* in all communications. The marketing manager must find every instance of *Contoso* in the brochure and change it to *Contoso, Ltd*.

TIP

You can use Find And Replace in only a portion of a document by selecting text before you begin the replacement.

The marketing manager could scroll through the brochure to visually search for text and replace each instance of *Contoso* with *Contoso, Ltd*, but this task is time consuming and is not a foolproof way to guarantee that all corrections will be made. A better approach is to use Word's feature for replacing specific text.

Replace specific text

Now that we have explored the Find And Replace dialog box and are comfortable with it, we will find and replace each instance of *Contoso* with *Contoso, Ltd* in our brochure.

1 **On the Edit menu, click Replace.**

The Find And Replace dialog box opens with the Replace tab selected.

ANOTHER METHOD

You can also display the Replace tab of the Find And Replace dialog box by pressing Ctrl+H.

FIGURE 5-16

Replace tab of the Find And Replace dialog box

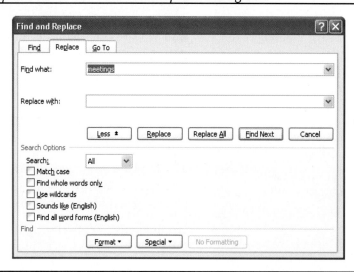

TIP

Word keeps track of the previous word or phrase that you searched for in case you want to perform the search again. Notice that the Find What box contains the word *meetings*, which you searched for in the previous exercise.

2 **Press Delete.**

The word *meetings* is removed from the Find What box.

3 **In the Find What box, type Contoso.**

4 **Press the Tab key, or click in the Replace With box, and type Contoso, Ltd.**

5 **Click the Find Next button.**

The first occurrence of *Contoso* is selected.

6 **This first instance of Contoso already has "Ltd" following it, so click Find Next.**

The next occurrence of Contoso is selected. This, too, already has *Ltd* following it.

7 **Click the Find Next button.**

The next occurrence of Contoso is selected. This does not have *Ltd* following it.

8 **Click the Replace button.**

The abbreviated company name is replaced with the full company name, and the next occurrence of *Contoso* is selected.

TIP

You can use the Undo command to reverse the previous replacement (when confirming replacements) or to reverse all replacements (if you specified Replace All).

9 **Continue clicking Replace or Find Next as appropriate.**

All additional occurrences of *Contoso* are replaced with *Contoso, Ltd.* After the last replacement, Word displays a message box indicating that it has completed the search and asks whether you want to continue the search at the beginning of the document.

TROUBLESHOOTING

Be careful when you use Replace All because you can accidentally replace things that you didn't intend to. For example, if you are replacing *the* with *a* and you click Replace All, you might also accidentally replace *the* with *a* every time it appears in the middle of a word. For example, *lithe* becomes *lia* and *weather* becomes *weaar*.

10 **In the message box, click No.**

The message box closes

11 **In the Find And Replace dialog box, click Close.**

The Find And Replace dialog box closes.

◆ **Save Brochure 05 Edited.**

◆ **Keep this file open for the next exercise.**

QUICK REFERENCE ▼

Perform a Replace operation

1 On the Edit menu, click Replace.

2 To increase the Find criteria and narrow the search, click the More button to display the search options.

3 Type the search string in the Find What box.

4 Type the replacement string in the Replace With box.

5 Click the Replace button to make the replacement; click the Replace All button to make all replacements throughout the document without confirmation.

6 Click OK.

Creating AutoCorrect Entries and Exceptions

THE BOTTOM LINE

Word's AutoCorrect feature helps eliminate typographical errors in documents.

Using Text-Entry Shortcuts

Word uses **AutoCorrect** to automatically make certain sentence corrections as you type, such as irregular capitalization or commonly mistyped words. AutoCorrect also substitutes certain words or characters when you type. For example, in words like *1st* and *2nd*, AutoCorrect automatically makes the *st* and *nd* superscript (*1st , 2nd*). When you type fractions by typing a number, typing the slash (/) key, and then typing another number, AutoCorrect "shrinks" the fraction into one character (called a stacked fraction) rather than three characters.

FIGURE 5-17

Stacked fraction versus three characters

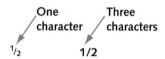

To open the AutoCorrect dialog box, on the Tools menu, click AutoCorrect Options. In the AutoCorrect dialog box, you can view the words and symbols that are automatically replaced. On the AutoCorrect tab of the AutoCorrect dialog box, scroll through the list in the dialog box to display the symbols and words that are automatically replaced.

FIGURE 5-18

AutoCorrect dialog box

TIP

If you do not want the AutoCorrect Options button to appear next to pasted items, you can choose to turn off that option by deselecting Show AutoCorrect Options Buttons in the AutoCorrect dialog box.

You can also use the AutoCorrect dialog box to create your own AutoCorrect entries, typically to correct an error that you frequently make that isn't already defined in Word. For example, suppose that you have a habit of inverting the *th* in the word *then* and typing *hten* instead. You could create an AutoCorrect entry to correct this error whenever you type it in a document.

You can use AutoCorrect to create replacement text for a shorthand version that you type. For instance, you can specify that Word replace *CL* with *Contoso, Ltd* whenever you type *CL*. This approach is similar to AutoText, except you don't need to press F3 to make the replacement. Use AutoCorrect in this way if you're sure that you *always* want to replace a shorthand version of a text string with a lengthier string. If you want *CL* to remain an acronym in some locations in a document, but want to replace it with *Contoso, Ltd* in other locations, create an AutoText entry instead of an AutoCorrect entry.

For words that you want uncorrected, such as names, you can use AutoCorrect to create exceptions. AutoCorrect corrects initial caps in words and capitalizes the first letter of sentences. For example, even though Word capitalizes the first letter of sentences, you do not want Word to capitalize the word following an abbreviation when you use the abbreviation within the middle of a sentence. This is considered an **exception**, or an item that Word treats differently than its core rule. Most common abbreviations (such as *dept., Sr., Jr., Assoc., pt., in.*) are already in Word's list of exceptions, but occasionally you might need to specify other exceptions. You might also find that certain acronyms or names require two capital letters at the beginning, such as ULimports. These words can also be added as exceptions to Word's initial capitals AutoCorrect rule.

FIGURE 5-19

AutoCorrect Exceptions dialog box

CHECK THIS OUT ▼

Changing Case with Shift+F3
You can press Shift+F3 repeatedly to change the case of a word to title case (the first letter of every word is capitalized, except for prepositions or articles), all caps, and then all lowercase, in that order. You don't need to select the entire word; just click anywhere in the word.

You can also create exceptions by example. For instance, if you type *Our sister organization in San Anselmo, Calif. can also be of service*, Word corrects this as *Our sister organization in San Anselmo, Calif. Can also be of service*, which is not what you want. However, if you correct the sentence by changing *Can* to *can*, Word detects the correction and adds *Calif.* to the list of exceptions. The next time you use the abbreviation *Calif.*, Word does not capitalize the word that follows it.

Create an AutoCorrect entry and an exception

In this exercise, we will create an AutoCorrect entry to replace *htat* with *that*. Then we will create an AutoCorrect exception so that Word will not change *ICorrect* to *Icorrect* when you type this text string.

1 **Press Ctrl+End, and press Enter twice.**

Word positions the insertion point at the end of the document and then inserts two blank lines.

2 **Type We hope htat you too will take full advantage of these services.**

Word marks *htat* as a potential misspelling but does not correct it.

3 **Select the sentence that you just typed, and press Delete.**

The sentence is deleted.

4 **On the Tools menu, click AutoCorrect Options.**

The AutoCorrect dialog box appears.

5 **In the Replace box, type htat, and press Tab.**

6 **In the With box, type that.**

Word will replace all occurrences of *htat* with *that*.

7 **Click the Add button, and click OK.**

The AutoCorrect dialog box closes.

TROUBLESHOOTING

If Word uses AutoCorrect for a word that you don't want corrected, you can select the corrected word and then type the original word. Word will not make an auto correction when you select the corrected word and type the original word or letter.

8 **Type We hope htat you too will take full advantage of these services.**

Word replaces *htat* with *that*.

9 **Press Enter twice, type ICorrect, and press the spacebar.**

Word makes an auto correction by converting the C in ICorrect to lowercase.

10 **On the Tools menu, click AutoCorrect Options.**

The AutoCorrect dialog box appears.

11 **Click the Exceptions button, and click the INitial CAps tab.**

FIGURE 5-20

INitial CAps tab in the AutoCorrect Exceptions dialog box

12 **In the Don't Correct box, type ICorrect, and click the Add button.**

The exception is added.

13 **Click OK to close the AutoCorrect Exceptions dialog box, and click OK again to close the AutoCorrect dialog box.**

Both dialog boxes close.

14 **Select the word "Icorrect," and type the following:**
We also provide a new service called ICorrect. Customers can send their Word documents to us via e-mail, and our expert editors can correct errors and suggest changes.

This time, Word does not change *ICorrect* to *Icorrect*.

> **TIP**
>
> Notice that *ICorrect* is still underlined in red, even though AutoCorrect did not change the two capitalized letters. The word ICorrect is underlined because it has not been added to Word's dictionary and is unrecognized when Word checks the spelling of the document.

◆ **Save Brochure 05 Edited.**

◆ **Keep this file open for the next exercise.**

QUICK REFERENCE ▼

View AutoCorrect entries

1 On the Tools menu, click AutoCorrect Options.

2 Click the AutoCorrect tab, if necessary.

3 Scroll through the list at the bottom of the dialog box.

Add an exception to AutoCorrect

1 On the Tools menu, click AutoCorrect Options.

2 Click the AutoCorrect tab, if necessary.

QUICK CHECK

Q. If you have a unique company name, how could you make sure that it is always spelled correctly?

A. To make sure that your company name is always spelled correctly, you could enter all of the potential misspellings of the name into the AutoCorrect list.

3 Click the Exceptions button.

4 Click the desired tab, and type the exception.

5 Click the Add button.

6 Click OK.

Highlighting Text

THE BOTTOM LINE

Just as you would highlight important text on a printed page, you can highlight important text within a Word document as well.

You can use Word to highlight text in your document. The Highlight feature works like a highlight color marker that you use on paper. Highlighting text comes in handy when you want to mark text that you are unsure about or you want to call attention to a particular word or phrase. If you highlight text and later determine that the text needs to be changed, highlighting can help you remember to make the change before you print or e-mail the document.

 You can always tell what color the highlighting will be by looking at the Highlight button. The colored line in the button indicates the currently selected color. If the colored line is white, no highlight color has been selected. If you click the Highlight button before you select text, the pointer changes to a highlight marker, indicating that text you select will be highlighted in the designated color. You can then select the text that you want to highlight. To turn off highlighting, click the Highlight button again.

The marketing manager at Contoso, Ltd is sending out a company memo reminding the staff to straighten up their offices because the shareholders will be touring the facilities at the end of the week. She uses the highlighter to highlight the words *"mandatory request per the president"* so that all of the staff will recognize the importance of the message.

Highlight text

We will work with our existing document to experiment with highlighting text and removing highlighting.

1 Double-click the word "ICorrect," which you created when you typed the final paragraph in the previous exercise.

The word is selected.

 2 On the Formatting toolbar, click the Highlight down arrow, and click the Yellow square.

The selected text appears highlighted in yellow.

3 **Double-click the word "ICorrect."**

The word is selected.

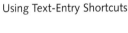

4 **Click the Highlight down arrow, and click None.**

The highlighting is removed from the selected text.

◆ **Keep this file open for the next exercise.**

QUICK REFERENCE ▼

Highlight text

1 Select the text that you want highlighted.

2 On the Formatting toolbar, click the Highlight down arrow.

3 Click a color.

Remove highlighted text

1 Select the highlighted text.

2 On the Formatting toolbar, click the Highlight down arrow.

3 Click None.

Inserting the Date and Time

THE BOTTOM LINE

You can also use Word to insert the current date and time into a document. This information can be inserted as text or as a field that can be automatically updated to the correct date and time each time that the document is opened.

Using Text-Entry Shortcuts

Occasionally, the Human Resources department of Contoso, Ltd sends a document containing amended company policies to all employees. The date and time is inserted within the footers of the document so that the employees know that they are reading the most current version of the policies.

Date and time information is available in many different formats and can be inserted as text or as a field. A **field** is a formula that generates specific results within your document. You add the field where you want the information to appear, and the field inserts information when you open the document. For example, if the date or time is inserted as a field, it is updated automatically when a particular action is performed such as opening, saving, or printing the document.

Insert the current date

We have nearly completed our brochure letter, but we want to add the current date to the document as text. We also want to add a field with the date and time that our document was last saved so that we can use this document in the future and be assured that the date shown will always be accurate.

1 **Press Ctrl+Home to position the insertion point at the beginning of the document.**

2 **On the View menu, click Header And Footer.**

The Header And Footer toolbar is displayed.

3 **On the Header And Footer toolbar, click the Switch Between Header And Footer button.**

The view of the document moves to the Footer box on the bottom of the first page.

4 **On the Insert menu, click Date And Time.**

The Date And Time dialog box appears, showing all of the possible date and time formats in the Available Formats list.

FIGURE 5-21

Date And Time dialog box

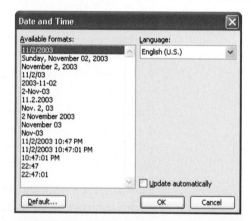

5 **Click the third available format (the month that is spelled out, date, and the year), and click OK.**

The current date is inserted, and the dialog box closes.

6 Press Tab twice to move to the right edge of the footer, type Last update on, and then press the spacebar.

7 On the Insert menu, click Field.

The Field dialog box appears.

8 Click Date And Time in the Categories list.

The Field Names list displays the options that are available for the Date And Time category.

FIGURE 5-22

Field dialog box

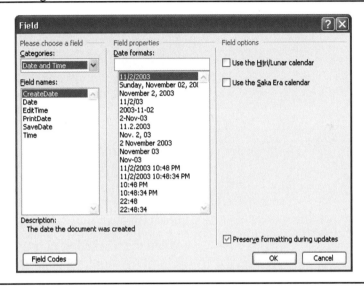

9 In the Field Names list, click SaveDate, and click OK.

The date and time that the document was last saved are inserted on the right side of the footer. Every time this document is saved, the date field is automatically updated.

TIP

The dates that you insert in steps 5 and 9 show the current date, but only the date field in step 9 is automatically updated each time the document is saved.

---

10 Click the Close button on the Header And Footer toolbar. Save Brochure 05 Edited.

◆ Keep this file open for the next exercise.

QUICK REFERENCE ▼

Insert the date and/or time

1 On the Insert menu, click Date And Time.

2 Click the desired format.

3 Click OK.

QUICK CHECK

Q. How do you set a date
or time to be updated
automatically?

**A. In the Date And Time di-
alog box, select the
Update Automatically
check box so that the
date or time will always
be updated whenever
the document is opened.**

Insert a field

1 On the Insert menu, click Field.

2 Select the desired category.

3 Select the desired field name.

4 Click OK.

Inserting Special Characters

THE BOTTOM LINE

There are some characters that you may want to put into your document that do not appear anywhere on the standard keyboard. These "special characters," however, can be inserted through the Insert menu.

Special characters are symbols and punctuation marks that do not have a key on most keyboards, such as an em dash (—), an ellipsis (...), a copyright symbol (©), or a trademark (™) symbol. You can insert these special characters by using the Symbol command on the Insert menu. Many symbols also have shortcut keys listed next to them in the dialog box.

When the marketing manager at Contoso, Ltd puts together a brochure for a local toy store, throughout the brochure are listings of various toys. The marketing manager uses Word's special characters to insert the trademark symbol after the product name.

Insert a symbol

Contoso, Ltd has trademarked ICorrect. As the last step to editing our brochure, we will insert the trademark symbol next to the term ICorrect.

1 Press Ctrl+End to ensure that the insertion point is at the end of the document.

2 Click to position the insertion point between the "t" and the period in "ICorrect."

3 On the Insert menu, click Symbol.

The Symbol dialog box appears.

4 Click the Special Characters tab.

The contents of the Special Characters tab appear.

FIGURE 5-23

Special Characters tab in the Symbol dialog box

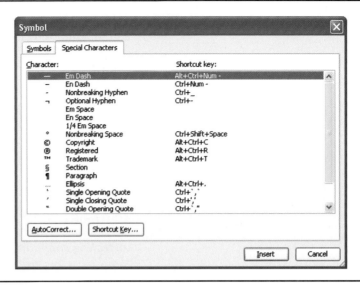

TIP

You can also find many common symbols on the Symbols tab. Click to position the insertion point in the document where you want to insert the symbol, click on the Symbol tab, click the symbol, and click Insert. Word inserts the symbol in the document. Click Close to close the Symbol dialog box.

5 **Click Trademark, and click the Insert button.**

The trademark symbol is inserted in the document at the current position of the insertion point.

6 **Click the Close button.**

QUICK REFERENCE ▼

Insert a special character

1 On the Insert menu, click Symbol.

2 Click the Special Characters tab.

3 Select the desired character.

4 Click the Insert button.

5 Click Close.

◆ To return the AutoCorrect features to their state before this lesson: On the Tools menu, click AutoCorrect. Click the Exceptions button, and make sure that the INitial CAps tab is selected. In the list of exceptions, click ICorrect, and click the Delete button. Click OK to close the AutoCorrect Exceptions dialog box. In the list of replacements, scroll down until you see the replacement for htat, click this line in the list, and click the Delete button. Click OK to close the AutoCorrect dialog box.

QUICK CHECK

Q. Are there any shortcut keys for inserting the Trademark symbol or any other symbol?

A. You can insert the trademark symbol by clicking Ctrl+Alt+T. Many of the other symbols have shortcut keys as well. The shortcut keys are listed in the Symbol dialog box.

◆ If you are continuing to the next lesson, save and close Brochure 05 Edited, but leave Word open.

◆ If you are not continuing to other lessons, save and close Brochure 05 Edited, and then close Word.

Key Points

✔ *You can use Word's editing and proofing tools, such as spelling and grammar checking, to improve the accuracy of your document.*

✔ *You can search for specific text as well as replace specific text.*

✔ *The Go To feature can be used to seek out specific locations within your document.*

✔ *AutoCorrect allows you to take advantage of automatically correcting common mistakes as well as adding your own common errors to the list of errors that will be corrected.*

✔ *In addition to text that you type into your document, you can insert dates, times, and special characters.*

Quick Quiz

True/False

T F 1. You can search for spelling errors and not search for grammatical errors.

T F 2. You can search for grammatical errors and not search for spelling errors.

T F 3. All grammatical errors are marked regardless of the writing style you are using.

T F 4. Symbols and punctuation marks that do not have a key on most keyboards are referred to as special characters.

T F 5. An exception is an item that Word treats differently than its core rule.

T F 6. A wildcard is a formula that generates specific results within your document.

T F 7. A search string is a group or string of characters to be matched in the document.

T F 8. Similar To is a search feature available in the Find dialog box that allows you to find words that sound similar to the text string for which you are searching.

T F 9. AutoCorrect is a feature that automatically corrects errors and replaces words or characters as text is typed.

T F 10. Common misspellings or capitalization errors are automatically corrected with Spelling Checking.

Short Answer

1. How do you specify a date format when you insert the current date into a document?

2. How do you add an AutoCorrect exception?

3. When searching for a string of text, how can you specify that you want to search for a word that sounds like the one for which you are searching?

4. If you commonly use a word that is interpreted as a spelling error, what command on the shortcut menu allows you to enter this word in the custom dictionary?

5. In a document, what do red and green wavy underlines indicate?

6. How do you replace a text string throughout a document without having to confirm it each time?

7. How can you use the Find And Replace dialog box to display a specific page in the current document?

8. How do you view readability statistics when you check spelling and grammar in a document?

9. How can you view a list of synonyms for a particular word?

10. How would you insert the registered trademark symbol (®) in a document?

IMPORTANT

In the On Your Own and One Step Further sections that follow, each exercise builds upon the previous one. The exercises work best if they are completed consecutively.

On Your Own

Exercise 1

Contoso, Ltd has a client who sells fabric and wants to publish an article to help promote sewing. The operations manager at Contoso, Ltd has agreed to edit the article.

Open the Ruffles Article 05 document located in the Lesson05 folder in the Word Practice folder on your hard disk. Change the writing style of the grammar checker to Formal, check the spelling and grammar, and correct any errors. Use your judgment about which errors you want to ignore and which you want to change. Then search for the word *material* and replace all instances of the word with *fabric*.

Exercise 2

Add an AutoCorrect entry so that whenever you type *hwen*, it is replaced with the text *when*. To the last sentence in the second paragraph that ends *purchasing your fabric*, add the following text: **Then hwen you place an order, you'll be sure to purchase the correct amount.** Verify that the AutoCorrect entry was added correctly. Insert the date in the bottom footer and align it with the right margin. Save the document as **Ruffles Article 05 Edited.**

Exercise 3

Search for any instances where there is a period with two spaces after it and replace it with a period and only one space. (*Hint:* You may need to search the document more than once if there are any instances where more than two spaces were inserted.) Save the document.

One Step Further

Exercise 1

The client thinks that the article will have more of an appeal if the French word for *ruffles* is used. Use Word's translate feature to determine the French word for *ruffles*. Use Find And Replace to replace all instances of *ruffles* with its French translation. Save and close the document.

Exercise 2

Explore the Research task pane that we introduced in this lesson. What other features are available from this task pane? What other panels can you open? Can you access the Internet for assistance with any other translation features?

6

Working with Graphics

After completing this lesson, you will be able to:

✔ *Insert pictures from files.*
✔ *Insert pictures from the Microsoft Clip Gallery.*
✔ *Resize and reposition a picture.*
✔ *Create and modify WordArt.*
✔ *Create and modify AutoShapes.*
✔ *Create and modify diagrams.*
✔ *Create and modify charts.*

KEY TERMS

- AutoShape
- axes
- category axis
- cell
- chart
- clip art
- Clip Gallery
- column heading
- columns
- datasheet
- diagram
- digital camera
- legend
- object
- picture
- row heading
- rows
- series
- shape
- sizing handles
- ungroup
- value axis
- WordArt

Documents that contain only text can certainly provide a wealth of information to readers, but they usually aren't visually interesting. Fortunately, Microsoft Word 2003 makes it easy to insert pictures and other graphics into your text documents. A **picture** is any graphical image that is created by another program, captured from a scanner or digital camera, or downloaded from the Web. Pictures include drawings, photographs, and all of the clip art stored in the Microsoft Clip Gallery.

In addition to inserting pictures, you can also create shapes and other graphical objects by using the Drawing toolbar. An **object** can be a curve, a line, an AutoShape, WordArt, or a combination of any graphics that you group together so that they can be manipulated as a single unit. An **AutoShape** is a ready-made shape—such as an arrow, banner, starburst, or flowchart symbol—that you select from the AutoShapes menu on the Drawing toolbar. **WordArt** is decorative text that you can insert into a Word document. You can also use the Drawing toolbar to change and enhance objects with colors, patterns, borders, and other effects.

In addition to pictures, clip art, and things you have drawn, Word also provides you with the tools to easily create both diagrams and charts, which are also graphical objects.

Although tables and lists are useful in organizing data, you might find that you need to do more with data than just organize it. Data is often easier to interpret when it's in a graphical format (such as a bar chart or line graph) rather than a table format. Traditionally, the terms *chart* and *graph* were used to differentiate certain kinds of graphical data. For example, a graphic that represented data as trend lines was called a line graph, while a graphic that represented data as bars was called a bar chart. In Microsoft Word, the word **chart** refers to all types of graphical data.

To create a chart in a Word document, you use Microsoft Graph Chart. Microsoft Graph Chart is a supplementary application available in Word and other Microsoft Office applications. Microsoft Graph Chart makes it easy to create and modify charts to suit different presentations. For example, you could use a chart to present income and expense data in a visual format or compare sales from month to month. You can change the shape, size, and color of charts.

In this lesson, you will learn how to insert and edit pictures and graphical objects in a document. You will also learn how to create and modify diagrams and charts.

IMPORTANT

Before you can use the practice files for this lesson, you need to install them from the book's companion CD to its default location. For additional information on how to find and open files used in this book, see the "Using the CD-ROM" section at the beginning of this book.

Inserting and Positioning Pictures

Inserting and Modifying Pictures

THE BOTTOM LINE

Pictures and graphics can greatly enhance a document. You can insert pictures from files or select graphics from a vast array of clip art. Once you have inserted a graphic object into a document, you can size and position it exactly the way you want it to be. You can also control the way that the text in your document flows around it.

Inserting a Picture from a File

You can choose from dozens of programs for creating and editing pictures on your computer. A few examples are Adobe Photoshop, Adobe Illustrator, Microsoft Paint, Paint Shop Pro, and Microsoft PhotoDraw. These and other programs allow you to create, edit, and save pictures. A scanner or **digital camera** is also useful when you want to capture and then store pictures as files on disk. And, of course, millions of picture files are available for downloading on the Web.

Contoso, Ltd has a client who owns a chain of recreational sporting goods stores. The president of the company wants a brochure with picturesque views of mountains, rivers, trails, forests, and so on. The marketing manager, armed with her digital camera, went into the wilderness and took several scenic pictures. She can store the pictures on a disk and later insert them into the brochure.

If you have picture files available on your hard disk, on a floppy disk, or on a CD-ROM, you can insert them easily into your Word documents. A picture is inserted at the location of the insertion point. To work with pictures, you must use Word's Print Layout, Web Layout, or Reading Layout views; pictures do not appear in Normal view.

TIP

You can switch to Print Layout view from the status bar in the bottom of the Word window by clicking the Print Layout View button.

TROUBLESHOOTING

In the following exercises and in the illustrations used throughout this lesson, the Standard and Formatting toolbars have been separated. For additional information on how to separate the toolbars, see the "Using the CD-ROM" section at the beginning of this book.

◆ **Be sure to start Word before beginning this exercise.**

◆ **Open Tailspin Toys 06 from the Lesson06 folder in the Word Practice folder that is located on your hard disk.**

Insert a picture from a file

Tailspin Toys 06 contains all of the text for a promotional flyer, but no pictures. We will insert a picture into a Word document from a file stored on your hard disk.

1 **Click the blank line above the line that reads "Fly up, up, and away."**

2 **On the Insert menu, point to Picture, and click From File.**

The Insert Picture dialog box appears.

Insert Picture dialog box

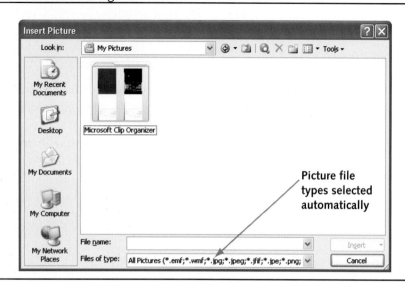

3 Click the Look In down arrow, and navigate to the Lesson06 folder in the Word Practice folder.

Picture files in the folder appear in the Insert Picture dialog box.

4 Select Balloon, if necessary, and click the Insert button.

The picture is inserted where the insertion point was positioned. The blank line that you clicked prior to inserting the picture has already been formatted as a centered paragraph. If the insertion point had been in a paragraph that was left-aligned, the picture would have been inserted along the left margin of the page.

ANOTHER METHOD

Rather than clicking the Insert button, you can double-click the file name in the list to insert the picture.

FIGURE 6-2

Balloon picture inserted into flyer

◆ **Save the document as Tailspin Toys 06 Edited.**

◆ **Keep this file open for the next exercise.**

Insert a picture into a document

1 If necessary, click the Print Layout View button on the status bar.

2 Click to position the insertion point where you want to insert the picture.

3 On the Insert menu, point to Picture, and click From File.

4 In the Insert Picture dialog box, click the Look In down arrow, and select the appropriate drive and folder.

5 In the file list, click the file that you want to insert.

6 Click the Insert button.

Inserting a Picture from the Clip Gallery

Microsoft Office includes hundreds of ready-made pictures that are available from the Microsoft Clip Gallery. Word refers to these pictures as **clip art**. The **Clip Gallery** includes a wide variety of pictures, from scenic backgrounds to maps, buildings, people, and some photographs that you can insert into any Word document. Depending on how Word was installed on your computer, as many as several hundred or as few as 144 pictures might be installed on your hard disk. Use clip art pictures to add visual excitement to a document, break up document text, or help illustrate key points within a document.

The marketing manager at Contoso, Ltd created a company memo reminding coworkers of the upcoming holiday office party. She used a picture of snowflakes and a picture of a snowman in the memo to make the appearance of the document more fun. She found these pictures in the Clip Gallery.

Many clip art pictures are stored in the WMF (Windows Metafile) graphic format, which means that you can ungroup the image. When you **ungroup** a clip art picture, each component (or individual part) of the picture is defined as a separate drawing object and can be modified independently. Suppose that you insert a WMF picture showing several balloons and streamers. If you right-click the picture and then click Edit Picture, you can edit different parts of the picture individually. For example, you could delete or move a streamer or change the color of a balloon.

Insert a picture from the Clip Gallery

We want to continue to enhance the Tailspin Toys promotional flyer. In this exercise, we preview clip art pictures in the Clip Gallery's Clip Art task pane and then insert a clip art picture.

1 Press Ctrl+Home.

The insertion point moves to the top of the document.

2 On the Insert menu, point to Picture, and click Clip Art.

The Clip Art task pane appears.

ANOTHER METHOD

You can also access the Clip Art task pane by clicking the Insert Clip Art button on the Drawing toolbar.

TROUBLESHOOTING

Before the Insert Clip Art task pane opens, you may see a message box asking whether you want to add clips to the organizer. If you see this dialog box, click Later.

FIGURE 6-3

Clip Art task pane

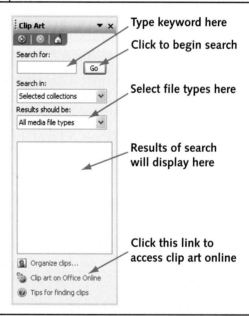

Type keyword here

Click to begin search

Select file types here

Results of search will display here

Click this link to access clip art online

3 Click the down arrow in the Results Should Be box, and deselect all media types except for Clip Art.

4 In the Search For text box, type fireworks, and click the Go button.

The Clip Art task pane displays small versions of the available pictures that match this keyword search.

TROUBLESHOOTING

Depending on how Word was installed on your computer, your Insert Clip Art window might display more or fewer pictures than the illustration shown. If your search on *fireworks* does not find any clip art, try searching for *balloon*.

FIGURE 6-4

Search results in Clip Art task pane

Keyword
searched for

Results of
keyword search

TIP

To see more pictures at once, resize the task pane by dragging the dividing bar between the task pane and the document window.

5 Point to an image of a firework, and then click the down arrow that appears to the right of the picture.

A menu of options appears.

FIGURE 6-5

Clip Art options menu

ANOTHER METHOD

You can also drag a picture from the Clip Gallery into your document, or simply click on the picture to insert it.

6 Click the Insert option on the menu.

The picture is inserted in the upper-left corner of the document

7 **In the upper-right corner of the Clip Art task pane, click the Close button.**

The task pane closes.

◆ **Save the document.**

◆ **Keep this file open for the next exercise.**

QUICK REFERENCE ▼

Insert a Clip Art picture into a document

1 If necessary, click the Print Layout View button on the status bar.

2 Click to position the insertion point where you want to insert the picture.

3 On the Insert menu, point to Picture, and click Clip Art.

4 If necessary, in the Clip Art task pane, click the Clip Art option in the Results Should Be drop-down list.

5 In the Search text box, type in a keyword to be used in searching for a clip art.

6 Click Search.

7 Click the picture that you want to insert.

Resizing a Picture

After inserting a picture into a Word document, you can easily increase or decrease the size of the picture. You begin by selecting the picture. When selected, a picture displays eight **sizing handles** (small white or black boxes) around its perimeter.

To resize a picture using the sizing handles, click the picture to select it. You can drag the left or right sizing handles to change the horizontal width of the picture, the top or bottom sizing handles to change the vertical height of the picture, or a corner handle to simultaneously change the width and height.

You can also use the Format Picture dialog box to size a picture to a specific height and width. To size a picture using the Format Picture dialog box, double-click the picture that you want to resize, and click the Size tab, if necessary. Click the Height and Width arrows in the Scale section to the desired percentage.

When you insert a picture, you'll often discover that text wraps around (or surrounds) the picture in a way that you didn't intend. You can change the text-wrapping style by using either the Picture or Drawing toolbar. The Picture toolbar appears whenever you select a picture.

FIGURE 6-6

Picture toolbar

Text Wrapping

TIP

You can learn more about Text Wrapping in Lesson 1, "Using Advanced Paragraph and Picture Formatting," in the Microsoft Word 2003 Microsoft Official Academic Courseware Expert Skills Student Guide.

To display the Drawing toolbar, point to Toolbars on the View menu and click Drawing, or click the Drawing button on the Standard toolbar. To change the text-wrapping style, click the Text Wrapping button on the Picture toolbar and select the desired wrapping style, or click the Draw button on the Drawing toolbar, point to Text Wrapping, and then click the desired wrapping style on the menu.

FIGURE 6-7

Text Wrapping options

The following text-wrapping styles are available on the Drawing and Picture toolbars.

Text Wrapping Style	Button	Effect
In Line With Text		Places the object at the insertion point in a line of text in the document
Square		Wraps text around all four borders of the picture
Tight		Wraps text around the picture itself, often within the borders of the picture

Text Wrapping Style	Button	Effect
Behind Text		Allows text to be displayed on top of the picture
In Front Of Text		Allows the picture to be displayed on top of text
Top And Bottom		Allows text to wrap above and below the picture, but not around the left and right borders of the picture
Through		Wraps text in the same way as the Tight text-wrapping style, but also wraps text into any open areas of the graphic
Edit Wrap Points		Allows access to adjusting the specific wrap points of the object

ANOTHER METHOD

You can also change text wrapping by double-clicking the picture and clicking the Layout tab in the Format Picture dialog box. Additional text-wrapping styles are available in this dialog box by clicking the Advanced button.

Resize a picture and change text wrapping

Now that we have the pictures we want in our flyer, we need to make adjustments to their size and how the text flows around them.

1 **Click the firework picture in the upper-left corner of the document.**

The picture is selected, and eight black sizing handles appear around the perimeter of the picture.

2 **Position the mouse pointer over the lower-right sizing handle until it becomes a diagonal two-headed resizing arrow, and drag up and to the left until the firework is about half its original size, as shown in Figure 6-8.**

FIGURE 6-8

Flyer with clip art inserted

Pictures often look better if you shrink them rather than enlarge them. For example, just as photographs will become grainy if they are enlarged, pictures can become blurry if you enlarge them too much beyond their original size.

3 On the Picture toolbar, click the Text Wrapping button.

A menu of text-wrapping styles appears.

4 Click the In Front Of Text button.

The text returns to the top of the document, and the firework picture remains in the same position. Notice that the selection handles become clear circles.

5 Click anywhere outside the picture to deselect it.

The top portion of your document should look similar to Figure 6-9.

FIGURE 6-9

Clip Art with text wrapping adjusted

Text Effects
You can create the sparkle text effect, as well as other text effects, by selecting the text, clicking Font on the Format menu, clicking the Text Effects tab, and selecting one of the animation effects that appear in the list. These text effects do not appear in a printed document.

6 On the Standard toolbar, click the Print Preview button.

The document appears in the Print Preview window, showing how the document will look when it is printed.

7 On the Print Preview toolbar, click the Close button.

The document returns to Print Layout view.

◆ Save the document.

◆ Keep this file open for the next exercise.

QUICK REFERENCE ▼

Size a picture using the sizing handles

1 Select the picture.

2 Drag the left or right sizing handles to change the horizontal width of the picture.

Or

Drag the top or bottom sizing handles to change the vertical height of the picture.

Or

Drag a corner handle to simultaneously change both the horizontal and vertical dimensions.

Change the text wrap style

1 Select the picture

2 On the Picture toolbar, click the Text Wrapping button.

3 Select the desired text wrap style from the drop down menu, and then click anywhere outside the picture to deselect it.

Repositioning a Picture

The marketing manager at Contoso, Ltd is reviewing a brochure layout created by one of her assistants. Inadvertently, the assistant has transposed several pictures. Rather than deleting the current pictures and reinserting them in the appropriate spots, the marketing manager can save time and just drag the pictures to the new locations. You can also attach, or anchor, a picture to a paragraph mark so that, if you move the paragraph, the picture automatically moves with it. Additionally, you can move or "nudge" pictures in small increments by selecting the picture and pressing the arrow keys. If you want to move an item only horizontally or vertically, press Shift as you drag.

You can select multiple drawing objects or pictures at once and then reposition or resize them at the same time. To select multiple items, click the Select Objects button on the Drawing toolbar. The mouse pointer changes to a left-pointing arrow. Drag the pointer to draw a box around all of the items that you want to select.

The Layout tab of the Format Picture dialog box includes several options for adjusting the placement of a picture on a page and controlling the way text wraps around a picture. (Some of these options are available only by clicking the Advanced button on the Layout tab.) To position a picture in relation to the page, a paragraph, or another anchor, select the item that you want to reposition. On the Format menu, click Picture. In the Format dialog box, click the Layout tab, and click the Advanced button. You can use this method to position other objects, including WordArt and AutoShapes. To ensure that a picture moves up or down with the paragraph to which it is anchored, in the Advanced Layout dialog box, select the Move Object With Text check box. To ensure that a picture remains anchored to the same paragraph when you move the paragraph, in the Advanced Layout dialog box, select the Lock Anchor check box.

In the Advanced Layout dialog box, click the Picture Position tab, and select the options that you want for the horizontal and vertical positioning. For example, you can align the picture horizontally relative to the margin, the page, the column, or a character. You can also specify a precise numeric position for the picture relative to the page, the paragraph, and so on.

Creating WordArt

THE BOTTOM LINE

You can customize the look of text in a document through the formatting options within the Font dialog box. Sometimes, however, you might want to do something more graphically interesting with text. For these situations, you can use WordArt text.

You can create decorative text effects with WordArt, a ready-made collection of text designs called WordArt styles. To create WordArt, you first select one of the text styles, and then type the text that you want to appear in that style. When you create WordArt text, the text is inserted into your document as an object. The following figure shows a WordArt object that was created for the text *Welcome to AW*.

FIGURE 6-10

WordArt text

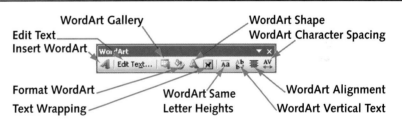

When you click a WordArt object, the WordArt toolbar appears.

FIGURE 6-11

WordArt toolbar

You can use the WordArt toolbar to modify the appearance of the WordArt object. The following table explains the buttons that appear on the WordArt toolbar.

Description	Button	Used to
Insert WordArt		Insert a new WordArt object into a document
Edit Text	Edit Text...	Change the font, font size, and font style for the WordArt text, or enter different text
WordArt Gallery		Change the text to a different ready-made WordArt style

Description	Button	Used to
Format WordArt		Change the fill colors, wrapping style, object size, and other formatting attributes. When you click the Format WordArt button, a dialog box appears and provides different formatting tabs. Most of the formatting changes you can make in this dialog box can be made more easily by using the Drawing toolbar or by resizing the object using the sizing handles around the WordArt object.
WordArt Shape		Change the shape that the WordArt text forms. For example, you can change the shape to form a ring or a wave or to slant the text up or down.
Text Wrapping		Change the way text wraps around the WordArt object
WordArt Same Letter Heights		Convert all text to the same height. For example, if you typed the WordArt text with mixed uppercase and lowercase letters, the WordArt Same Letter Heights button, when clicked, would convert all letters to the same height as the uppercase letters.
WordArt Vertical Text		Display the text vertically instead of horizontally
WordArt Alignment		Change the text alignment (right, left, center, etc.) when the WordArt text is on multiple lines
WordArt Character Spacing		Change (expand or condense) the spacing between text characters

You can also use the Drawing toolbar to change WordArt text effects. For example, you can change the fill colors that appear in the text characters, create a text shadow, or change the text to appear with a 3-D effect.

Create and modify a WordArt object

The Tailspin Toys flyer is looking better with the graphics that have been added, but the title lines could be improved. We will create a WordArt object to replace the title lines in the Tailspin Toys Edited document. We will also change several WordArt settings to enhance the appearance of the WordArt object.

1 **Select the three heading lines (Come Celebrate the Grand Opening of Tailspin Toys) at the top of the document, and press Delete.**

The header lines are removed.

2 **On the View menu, point to Toolbars, and click Drawing, if necessary.**

The Drawing toolbar appears along the bottom of the window.

FIGURE 6-12

Drawing toolbar

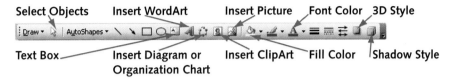

ANOTHER METHOD

You can also open the Drawing toolbar by clicking the Drawing toolbar on the Standard toolbar.

3 **On the Drawing toolbar, click the Insert WordArt button.**

The WordArt Gallery dialog box appears.

FIGURE 6-13

WordArt Gallery dialog box

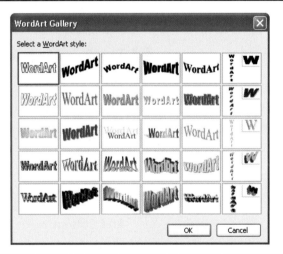

TIP

The WordArt object you choose is displayed in your document in the colors shown in the WordArt Gallery dialog box. You'll learn how to change the colors of a WordArt object later in this exercise.

4 **Click the gold-colored WordArt style in the first column of the third row, and click OK.**

The Edit WordArt Text dialog box appears.

FIGURE 6-14

Edit WordArt Text dialog box

TIP

Notice that the toolbar includes the buttons to change the formatting of the WordArt text to bold or italics.

5 Type **Come Celebrate the, and press Enter.**

The first line of WordArt text is entered.

6 Type **Grand Opening of, and press Enter.**

The second line of WordArt text is entered.

7 Type **Tailspin Toys, click the Size down arrow, click 24, and then click OK.**

The WordArt object is inserted in the document with text sized at 24 points, and the WordArt toolbar disappears.

8 Click the WordArt object to display the WordArt toolbar. On the Word Art toolbar, click the Text Wrapping button, and click Top And Bottom.

Word wraps text and objects above and below the WordArt object.

9 Position the mouse pointer over the WordArt object until the move pointer appears, and then drag the WordArt object so that it is in the position shown in the following illustration.

FIGURE 6-15

WordArt inserted into flyer

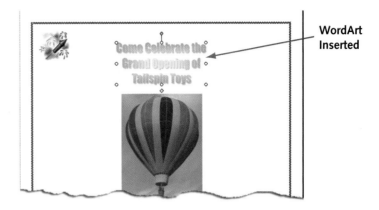

WordArt
Inserted

 10 On the WordArt toolbar, click the WordArt Shape button.

A menu of WordArt shapes appears.

FIGURE 6-16

WordArt shape menu

Wave1

TIP

Position the mouse pointer over a WordArt shape to view its name.

 11 Click the Wave1 shape (the fifth shape in the third row).

The WordArt object appears in the wave shape.

 12 On the Drawing toolbar, click the Fill Color down arrow.

A color palette appears.

FIGURE 6-17

Color palette

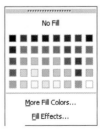

13 On the color palette, click Fill Effects.

The Fill Effects dialog box appears.

FIGURE 6-18

Fill Effects dialog box

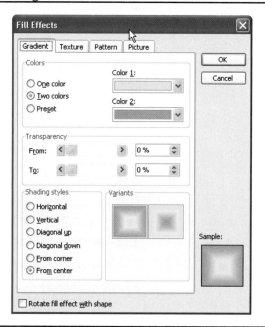

Notice that the current fill effect is a two-color gradient.

14 Click the Color 2 down arrow, and click the Blue square (second row, sixth square).

15 Click OK.

The WordArt text appears with the new gradient colors.

16 Click an empty area of the document.

The WordArt object is deselected, and the WordArt toolbar is removed from view. The top portion of your document should look similar to Figure 6-19.

FIGURE 6-19

WordArt in wave shape and with gradient color

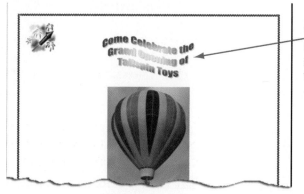

WordArt with custom color gradient and wave shape

◆ Save the document.

◆ Keep this file open for the next exercise.

QUICK REFERENCE ▼

Create WordArt

1 If necessary, on the View menu, point to Toolbars, and click Drawing.
Or
Click the Drawing button on the Standard toolbar.

2 On the Drawing toolbar, click the Insert WordArt button.

3 Click the desired style and click OK.

4 Type the desired text, select font and size, and then click OK.

QUICK CHECK

Q. Can a WordArt object be moved or resized once it has been placed in a document?

A. A WordArt object, like any other graphic object, can be moved and re-sized at any time after it has been placed in a document.

Drawing and Modifying Shapes

Drawing a Shape

THE BOTTOM LINE

Word comes with a set of ready-made AutoShapes that you can insert into a document.

AutoShapes include complex shapes, block arrows, flowchart symbols, stars and banners, and callout balloons (much like the text balloons that appear in comic strips) that you can select to insert in a document. When you select an AutoShape, Word inserts the shape into your document, saving you the time and effort of creating the shape on your own.

You can also use the Drawing toolbar to draw basic **shapes**, such as rectangles, circles, and lines. After you've inserted an AutoShape or drawn a shape in a document, you can use the Drawing toolbar to change the characteristics of the shape, such as resizing, rotating, or flipping the shape, or changing its fill color. In addition, you can combine and group different shapes to make a more complex design.

TIP

AutoShapes are inserted with the In Front Of Text wrapping style applied. To change the text- wrapping style, on the Drawing toolbar, click the Draw button, point to Text Wrapping, and then click the desired option.

After you've created an AutoShape, you can resize the object using the sizing handles. Additionally, some AutoShape objects appear with yellow diamonds on the drawing that allow you to change the internal shape of the object.

For example, if you choose the AutoShape Up Ribbon banner, yellow diamonds appear above and below the ribbon. You can click the yellow diamond to change the dimensions of the banner.

Word uses a drawing canvas to simplify inserting, changing, and manipulating drawing shapes and pictures. A drawing canvas is an area that contains drawing shapes and pictures. You can create a drawing canvas by selecting a drawing tool from the Drawing toolbar or AutoShapes menu on the Drawing toolbar. When you draw within the drawing canvas, you can resize and move the drawing canvas and the objects that it contains as a unit. This allows you to make design decisions once and then apply them to all related objects.

TROUBLESHOOTING

Word inserts a drawing canvas by default when you select a drawing tool. If you find that the feature has been turned off in Word, click Options on the Tools menu, and then click the General tab. Select the Automatically Create Drawing Canvas When Inserting AutoShapes check box, and then click OK.

When you first insert a drawing canvas into your document, you see no border or shading around the canvas. However, because the drawing canvas is an object, you can apply borders and shading to it just as you would to any other object in Word.

When you work with a drawing canvas, you can use the tools on the Drawing toolbar. These tools let you fit a drawing canvas to its contents, expand a drawing canvas on the document, scale the drawing canvas, or apply text-wrapping features. You can also fit the drawing canvas to the document environment so that you use only as much space in your document as you need.

TIP

If you find that you do not want to use the drawing canvas, you can press Esc to remove the canvas from your document.

You can move drawing objects or pictures on the drawing canvas by dragging them. You can also move them by selecting them within the drawing canvas, clicking the Draw button on the Drawing toolbar, and then selecting an option from the menu. Options include nudging the objects up or down by small increments, rotating or flipping them, or applying text-wrapping features to them.

Work with AutoShapes

The Tailspin Toys flyer is looking better all the time, but there are still a few additional items needed. To complete the flyer, we need to insert two AutoShapes into the flyer, add fill colors to both shapes, and rotate one of the shapes.

1 Scroll down until you can see the lines "Entertainment," "Prizes," and "Great Food."

AutoShapes ▾

2 On the Drawing toolbar, click the AutoShapes button.

The AutoShapes menu appears.

FIGURE 6-20

AutoShapes menu

3 Point to Stars And Banners.

The Stars And Banners menu appears.

FIGURE 6-21

Stars And Banners menu

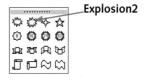

Explosion2

TIP

Position the mouse pointer over an AutoShape to view its name.

4 Click the Explosion 2 button (the second AutoShape in the first row).

The drawing canvas appears and shifts the existing text around it, and the mouse pointer changes to a crosshair pointer.

FIGURE 6-22

Empty drawing canvas

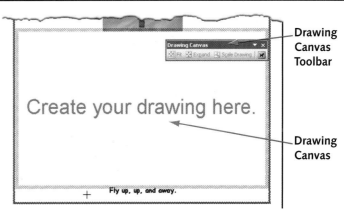

Drawing Canvas Toolbar

Drawing Canvas

5 **Press Esc.**

The drawing canvas is closed, and the page reappears.

6 **Drag the mouse pointer so that the Explosion 2 AutoShape is drawn at the approximate size and location as the one shown here.**

FIGURE 6-23

Explosion 2 AutoShape inserted in document

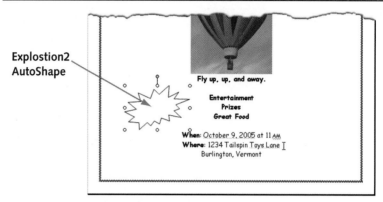

7 **Make sure that the shape is still selected, and on the Drawing toolbar, click the Fill Color down arrow.**

A color palette appears.

8 **In the color palette, click the Light Orange square (third row, second square).**

The AutoShape is filled with the selected color.

> **TIP**
>
> You don't need to deselect a shape in order to select another shape on the Drawing toolbar. Word will automatically deselect the current shape when you select and insert another shape.

AutoShapes ▾

9 **On the Drawing toolbar, click the AutoShapes button.**

The AutoShapes menu appears.

10 **Point to Stars And Banners.**

The Stars And Banners menu appears.

 11 **Click the Curved Down Ribbon button (the fourth AutoShape in the third row).**

The mouse pointer changes to a crosshair.

12 **Drag the mouse pointer so that the ribbon is drawn at the approximate size and location as the one shown here.**

FIGURE 6-24

Curved Down Ribbon banner inserted in document

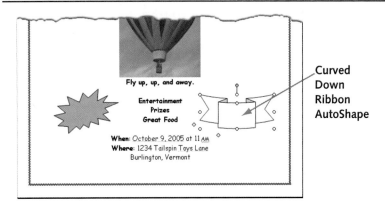

Curved
Down
Ribbon
AutoShape

13 Make sure that the ribbon shape is still selected, and on the Drawing toolbar, click the Fill Color down arrow.

A color palette appears.

14 On the color palette, click the Dark Blue square (first row, sixth square).

15 Point to the green circle above the selected shape until the pointer changes to the free rotate pointer.

FIGURE 6-25

Curved Down Ribbon banner

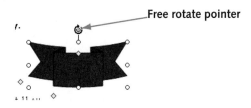

Free rotate pointer

16 Click the free rotate handle, and drag it to the right and down until the ribbon is at the approximate angle of the one shown here.

FIGURE 6-26

Banner rotated in document

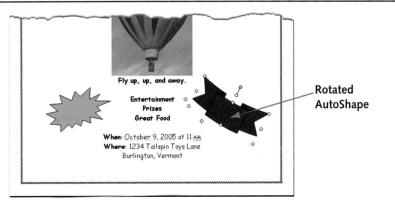

Rotated
AutoShape

17 **Click anywhere outside the shape.**

The sizing handles no longer appear around the shape.

◆ **Save and close the document.**

◆ **Keep this file open for the next exercise.**

QUICK REFERENCE ▼

Create an AutoShape

1 On the Drawing toolbar, click the AutoShapes button to display the AutoShapes menu.

2 On the AutoShapes menu, point to the category of shape that you want to create, and click the desired shape.

3 In the area where you want to insert the AutoShape, drag to draw the AutoShape.

Fill a shape with color

1 Click the shape.

2 On the Drawing toolbar, click the Fill Color button's down arrow.

3 Click the desired fill color.

Creating a Diagram

THE BOTTOM LINE

To help you organize personnel data or other types of information, you can insert and modify diagrams in your documents.

Inserting and Modifying Diagrams

A **diagram** is a visual and relational representation of information. A common diagram is an organization chart. You can also create cycle diagrams, radial diagrams, pyramid diagrams, Venn diagrams, and target diagrams.

When you insert an organization chart into a document, the chart has placeholder text that you click and replace with your own. The boxes and lines of the organization chart are objects that you can move and change.

◆ **Open OrgChart from the Lesson06 folder in the Word Practice folder that is located on your hard disk.**

Create a diagram

The OrgChart document is the beginning of a memo regarding a new organization chart. We will add an example organization chart to this memo.

1 Press Ctrl+End to place the insertion point at the end of the document.

 2 On the Drawing toolbar, click the Insert Diagram Or Organization Chart button.

The Diagram Gallery dialog box appears, with the Organization Chart selected by default.

TROUBLESHOOTING

If the Drawing toolbar is not open on your screen, on the View menu, point to Toolbars, and then click Drawing.

FIGURE 6-27

Diagram Gallery dialog box

3 Click OK.

An organization chart is inserted into the document, and the Organization Chart toolbar appears.

FIGURE 6-28

Organization chart inserted in document

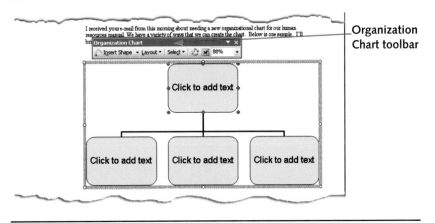

Organization Chart toolbar

4 In the organization chart, click the top box to place the insertion point, and then type Contoso Board of Directors.

5 Click the first box in the second row, type Tai Yee, click the second box in the second row, type Marc Faeber, click the third box in the second row, and then type David Campbell.

All boxes contain names. The last box is still selected.

FIGURE 6-29

Completed organization chart

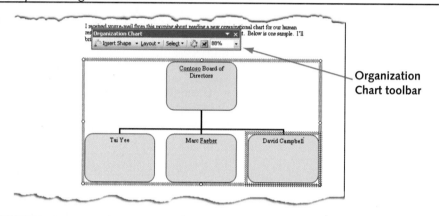

Organization Chart toolbar

6 On the Organization Chart toolbar, click the Select button, and then click All Connecting Lines.

All connecting lines in the organization chart are selected.

7 On the Format menu, click AutoShape.

8 The Format AutoShape dialog box appears.

9 Select the Colors and Lines tab, if necessary, and in the Line section, click the Color down arrow, and then click the Red color box (row 3, column 1).

The line color selection is now red.

10 In the Arrows section, click the Begin Style down arrow, click the second option in the first row, and then click OK.

The lines in the organization chart are now red with arrows attached.

TIP

You can quickly format an organization chart using a predefined style by clicking the AutoFormat button on the Organization Chart toolbar.

---

11 Click a blank area of the document to deselect the organization chart.

◆ Save the document as OrgChart Edited, and close it.

◆ Keep this file open for the next exercise.

QUICK REFERENCE ▼

Create a diagram

1 Click the mouse pointer in the Word document where you want the diagram to appear.

2 On the Insert menu, click Diagram to display the Diagram Gallery dialog box.

3 Choose the type of diagram that you want to insert, and then click OK.

4 Fill in the text areas of the diagram with the desired information.

5 Add additional diagram components as needed or remove unwanted components.

Creating and Modifying a Chart

Inserting and Modifying Charts

THE BOTTOM LINE

A chart is another way to display information. With a chart, you can take a table of numbers and display them in a way that is visually more interesting and easier to interpret. Word lets you create a chart directly within your document by filling in a datasheet with the appropriate information.

Charts that you create with Microsoft Graph Chart are embedded as objects in Word documents. When you start Microsoft Graph, a sample chart and datasheet are displayed in the Word document. A **datasheet** is a table that contains the data presented in the chart. When you make changes to the datasheet, the changes are reflected in the chart.

You can create several different chart types using Microsoft Graph Chart. The following table lists the available standard chart types and their icons and descriptions.

Chart Type	Icon	Description
Area		Displays the trend of values over time or categories
3-D Area		Displays the trend of values over time or categories
3-D Surface		Displays data across two dimensions in a continuous curve
Bar		Presents data in horizontal bars and compares values across categories
3-D Bar		Presents data in horizontal bars and compares values across categories

Chart Type	Icon	Description
Radar		Displays changes in values relative to a center point
Column		Presents data in vertical columns and compares values across categories
3-D Column		Presents data in vertical columns and compares values across categories
Bubble		Describes connections between concepts without emphasizing a structural sequence
Line		Presents data in lines and displays trends over time or across categories
3-D Line		Presents data in lines and displays trends over time or across categories
(XY) Scatter		Compares pairs of values and displays values as single data points optionally connected by lines
Pie		Displays the relationship of each value to a total as a fractional slice
3-D Pie		Displays the relationship of each value to a total as a fractional slice
Doughnut		Displays data in the same way as a pie chart, but can contain multiple series
3-D Cylinder		Displays data in columns with a cylindrical shape
3-D Cone		Displays data in columns with a conical shape
3-D Pyramid		Displays data in columns with a pyramidal shape

A datasheet resembles a table. Like a table, a datasheet is made up of a series of columns and rows. **Columns** are identified by letters, and **rows** are identified by numbers. A **cell** is the box that is the intersection of a column and a row. You use cells to type data that you want to include in a chart into the datasheet. A datasheet reserves a row and column for headings that you supply.

A **row heading** is the numbered grey area to the left of a row. To select an entire row, you click the row heading. A **column heading** is the lettered or numbered area at the top of each column. To select an entire column, you click the column heading. To select the entire datasheet, you click the Select All button, which is located in the upper-left corner of the datasheet. After you create a chart, you click a blank area of the Word document to hide the related datasheet and show just the chart. To display the datasheet so that you can modify the chart, you double-click the chart.

FIGURE 6-30

Example datasheet and chart

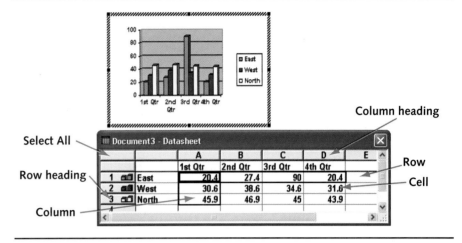

Column heading

Select All

Row heading

Row

Cell

Column

Creating a Chart

When you insert a new chart in a Word document, Word displays a column chart along with sample data in the datasheet, including sample row and column headings. The sample data is intended to help guide you in entering your own data. After you insert a chart, the first step is to change the datasheet contents. When you change the values in the datasheet, the chart changes to reflect the new values.

The accountant at Adventure Works is preparing to meet with the owners of the resort, who want to know how the resort's various departments performed during the second quarter. The accountant created a Word document that shows this information in a table, but she also wants to make a chart to present the data to the owners.

◆ **Open AW Revenue_Spring 06 from the Lesson06 folder in the Word Practice folder that is located on your hard disk.**

Create a chart

The AW Revenue_Spring 06 document is the beginning of a document that will contain a chart for the Adventure Works accountant to use in her presentation.

1 **Press Ctrl+End.**

The insertion point moves to the end of the document.

2 **On the Insert menu, click Object.**

The Object dialog box appears, with the Create New tab displayed.

FIGURE 6-31

Object dialog box

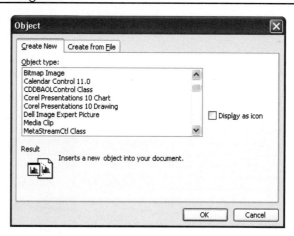

Depending on the programs installed on your computer, your list of object types might differ from the illustration.

3 **Scroll down the Object Type list, click Microsoft Graph Chart, and then click OK.**

A sample chart and datasheet appear.

FIGURE 6-32

Default datasheet and chart

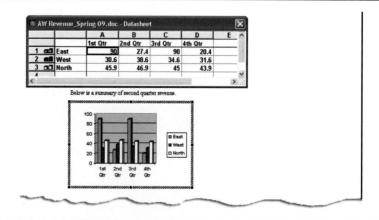

4 **Click the Select All button on the datasheet, and press Delete.**

The sample data is deleted.

5 **Click the cell in row 1 in the column before column A, type LODGING, and press Enter.**

The heading is entered and appears in the legend in the chart. The insertion point moves to the cell below *LODGING*.

TROUBLESHOOTING

Notice that the words *RESTAURANT* and *RECREATION* don't fit completely in the cells in the datasheet.

6 Type RESTAURANT, **and press Enter.**

The heading is entered and appears in the legend in the chart. The insertion point moves to the cell below *RESTAURANT*.

7 Type RECREATION, **and press Enter.**

The heading is entered and appears in the legend in the chart. The insertion point moves to the cell below *RECREATION*.

TROUBLESHOOTING

Notice that the words *RESTAURANT* and *RECREATION* don't fit completely in the cells in the datasheet.

FIGURE 6-33

Edits made to datasheet and chart

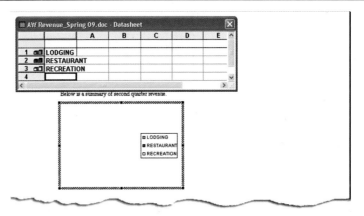

 8 In the datasheet, position the mouse pointer over the vertical line between the blank column heading and the column A heading until the mouse pointer turns into a double-headed resize pointer, and drag the vertical line to the right until the words fit within the column.

FIGURE 6-34

Column width in datasheet adjusted

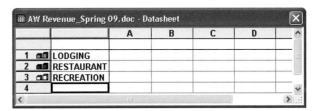

9 Click the cell in column A in the row above row 1, type April, and then press Tab.

April is added to the chart, and the insertion point moves one cell to the right.

10 Type May, and press Tab.

May is added to the chart, and the insertion point moves one cell to the right.

11 Type June, and press Enter.

June is added to the chart, and the insertion point moves down one cell.

12 Click the first empty cell: row 1, column A. Type the data in the table shown here into the chart's datasheet. (Be sure to include the dollar signs and commas.)

	April	May	June
LODGING	$297,830	$426,255	$525,165
RESTAURANT	$165,005	$224,650	$323,500
RECREATION	$76,910	$95,765	$124,565

ANOTHER METHOD

Move the insertion point from row to row by pressing Enter. Move the insertion point from column to column by pressing Tab. (Use Shift+Tab to move backward, or Shift+Enter to move up a row.) You can also use the arrow keys to move up, down, left, and right in the datasheet.

FIGURE 6-35

Completed datasheet and chart

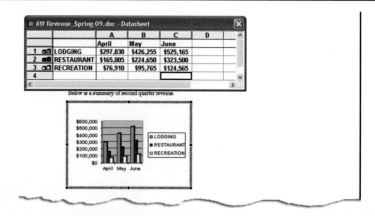

TIP

Notice that when you click outside the chart, the datasheet no longer appears, but the chart remains displayed. To activate the datasheet, you just double-click the chart.

13 Click outside the datasheet.

The datasheet closes, and the completed chart remains in the document.

◆ Save the document as AW_Revenue_Spring 06 Edited.

◆ Keep this file open for the next exercise.

QUICK REFERENCE ▼

Create a chart using Microsoft Graph

1 Click the mouse pointer in the Word document where you want the chart to appear.

2 On the Insert menu, click Object to display the Object dialog box.

3 Scroll down the Object Type list, and click Microsoft Graph Chart.

4 Click OK.

5 Click the Select All button in the data sheet, and press Delete to remove the sample data.

6 In the datasheet, click the cell where you want to begin typing data.

7 When you have finished entering data in the datasheet, click a blank area of the document to close the datasheet. The chart will still be displayed in the Word document.

Modifying Charts

You aren't limited to the chart type that Word provides when you insert a chart object, nor are you limited to the default formatting for the chart. You can change to a different, more suitable type of chart if you want, and you can change other elements in the chart including fill colors and patterns, fonts and font sizes, and more. The following table explains several modifications that you can make to a chart, and the illustration that follows shows the various parts of the chart.

Select	To
Chart Type	Display the same data in a different chart format. For example, the same data can be displayed as a bar chart, bubble chart, or pie chart.
Color, pattern, lines, fills, and borders	Modify the format of the chart. For example, you can add a border around the chart, change a border's fill color (the color inside a closed area) or pattern, or change the color of the data (series) in a chart.
Font	Change the appearance of text in a chart by changing the font style and font size
Gridlines	Add or remove vertical and horizontal gridlines on several chart types. By default, a chart shows horizontal gridlines only.

Select	To
Title	Add and modify chart titles, as well as titles of the axes within charts. **Axes** are lines that provide a frame of reference or comparison in a chart by identifying incremental values on the chart. For example, when you first insert a chart object, the sample column chart displays horizontal gridlines in increments of 20. The vertical or **value axis** is typically called the y-axis. The horizontal or **category axis** is known as the x-axis. In a three-dimensional system, a z-axis is also used to show depth.
Legend	Modify the text and formatting of the legend. The **legend** is text that describes or explains the graphic. On a graph or map, the legend is the key to the patterns, colors, or symbols used in bars, lines, slices of a pie, and other representations of chart values.

TIP

You can change gridlines so that they appear in more frequent increments, or you can remove gridlines completely.

FIGURE 6-36

Example chart

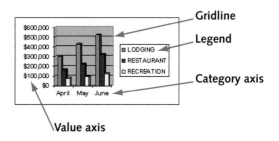

FIGURE 6-37

Chart tools on the Standard toolbar

To change the formatting for a chart, you first click the part of the chart that you want to modify. You then make changes by clicking buttons that appear on the Standard toolbar when a chart is activated and the datasheet is displayed or by clicking the appropriate menu commands.

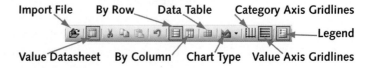

When you work with a chart, the Standard toolbar remains in the Word window, but includes additional buttons for modifying the chart, as shown in the following table. The table also explains the purpose of each button.

Button	Button Name	Purpose
	Import File	Allows you to import data from text files and other programs

Button	Button Name	Purpose
	View Datasheet	Displays or hides the view of the datasheet
	By Row	Charts values according to the data entered in rows of the datasheet (the default)
	By Column	Charts values according to the data entered in columns of the datasheet. For example, if you click the By Column button for the chart you created in the previous exercise, Word would display columns for LODGING, RESTAURANT, and RECREATION rather than for April, May, and June.
	Data Table	Displays a row-and-column table of the data used to create the chart. Although this table is similar to the datasheet, it is a component of the chart itself, whereas the datasheet is used to create data values for the chart.
	Chart Type	Changes the current chart to a different type of chart, such as a line to a pie chart
	Category Axis	Displays vertical gridlines for the Gridlines category axis
	Value Axis	Displays horizontal gridlines for the Gridlines value axis. This option is turned on by default.
	Legend	Turns on or off the display of the legend. The legend is turned on by default.
	Fill Color	Changes the fill color of a selected area of the chart, such as the wall (background) or a series.

Modify a chart

In this exercise, you change the chart type and several colors in the
AW Revenue Chart.

IMPORTANT

If you dragged the datasheet out of the way, you'll need to double-
click the chart before you can proceed with the steps in this exercise.

1 **If necessary, double-click the chart to activate it.**

 2 **On the Standard toolbar, click the View Datasheet button.**

The datasheet is closed.

ANOTHER METHOD

You can also close the datasheet by clicking the Close button in the
upper-right corner of the datasheet.

 3 **On the Standard toolbar, click the Chart Type down arrow.**

The list of chart types appears.

FIGURE 6-38

Chart Type menu

 4 **Click the 3-D Bar Chart button (the second button in the second row
of the list).**

The chart type changes to a 3-D bar chart.

FIGURE 6-39

A 3-D Bar chart

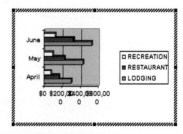

Note that the Value Axis labels that appear along the bottom of the chart are not readable. You can easily correct this by resizing the chart.

5 On the right border of the chart, drag the middle sizing handle to the right until you can easily read the numbers at the bottom of the chart.

FIGURE 6-40

Completed revenue chart

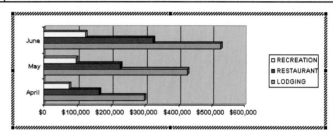

6 Click the gray background (Walls) of the chart.

 7 Click the Fill Color down arrow.

The Fill Color palette appears.

8 Click the Sea Green square (third row, fourth column).

The background of the chart changes to sea green.

9 Click any of the yellow bars that represent Recreation revenue on the chart.

All of the yellow bars that represent Recreation revenue are selected.

10 On the Standard toolbar, click the Fill Color down arrow.

The Fill Color palette appears.

11 Click the Light Green square (bottom row, fourth column).

The series bars for Recreation revenue change to light green.

You can double-click different areas of the chart to select the part of the chart that you want to modify. When you double-click an area of the chart, the Format dialog box, with which you can edit the chart, is displayed. Where you double-click in the chart determines what kind of Format dialog box appears. For example, if you double-click a bar in the chart, the Format Data Series dialog box is displayed with multiple tabs, letting you decide how to modify the bars in the chart. If you double-click the background of the chart, the Format Walls dialog box appears, and you can choose from the Patterns tab to change the background color or modify the chart border.

QUICK REFERENCE ▼

Modify the chart type

1 Double-click the chart to activate it.

2 On the Standard toolbar, click the Chart Type down arrow.

3 Click the desired Chart Type button.

4 Drag the sizing handles of the chart to make sure the numbers and text fit into the chart.

Change the background color of a chart

1 Double-click the chart to activate it.

2 Click the background that you want to modify.

3 On the Standard toolbar, click the Fill Color down arrow.

4 Click the square with the desired color.

Change the bar colors in a bar chart

1 Double-click the chart to activate it.

2 Click the bar that you want to modify.

3 On the Standard toolbar, click the Fill Color down arrow.

4 Click the square with the desired color.

◆ **If you are continuing to other lessons, save and close the document, but leave Word open.**

◆ **If you are not continuing to other lessons, save and close the document, and close Word.**

Key Points

✔ *You can insert and resize pictures from a file and from the Clip Gallery.*

✔ *With WordArt and AutoShapes, you can insert graphical objects into documents.*

✔ *Many graphical objects, including AutoShapes and WordArt, can be altered by changing the fill color or rotating the shape.*

✔ *Diagrams and charts can be created and modified directly in a Word document.*

Quick Quiz

True/False

T   F   **1.** An AutoShape is a ready-made design that you can use to create decorative and colorful text.

T   F   **2.** WordArt is a preset shape that comes with Word.

T   F   **3.** The value axis is the vertical axis used to plot data on a bar, column, or line chart.

T   F   **4.** The category axis is the horizontal axis used to plot data on a bar, column, or line chart.

T   F   **5.** An axis is the horizontal arrangement of a series of text or numbers in a datasheet.

T   F   **6.** The values in a chart that are represented pictorially as bars, lines, pie slices, or other pictorial representations are called series.

T   F   **7.** Sizing handles are small white or black squares located in the corners and on the sides of a picture or object.

T   F   **8.** Sizing handles are used to separate a graphic into its individual graphical elements, which can then be edited independently.

T   F   **9.** A datasheet is a table that contains the data displayed in a chart.

T   F   **10.** Clip art are picture files that can be inserted into Word documents.

Short Answer

1. How do you access the AutoShapes menu?

2. How do you rotate an AutoShape?

3. Identify two methods that you can use to resize a picture.

4. From the Insert Clip Art dialog box, what two ways can you use to insert a picture?

5. How do you change the shape of WordArt text?

6. How do you change the text size in a WordArt object?

7. When you select a picture, small boxes surround the perimeter. What are these boxes used for?

8. What menu command do you use to insert a picture that exists in another file and isn't a clip art picture?

9. Which command do you use to insert a clip art picture?

10. Why would you want to put information or data into a chart format?

IMPORTANT

In the On Your Own section that follows, you must complete Exercise 1 before continuing to Exercise 2.

On Your Own

Exercise 1

Open a new blank document, and create an invitation for the grand opening of a coffee house. Type the following text in the invitation, except insert a WordArt object for the first three lines. Format the WordArt object as desired, and position it near the center at the top of the document, with the address and other invitation information below the WordArt object. Use the Clip Gallery to add a clip art picture related to coffee or a bakery, and place the picture below the invitation.

You're invited to celebrate
The grand opening of
Fourth Coffee
5678 Main Street, Burlington, Vermont
On Saturday, November 06, 2004, beginning at 6:30 p.m.
Entertainment and dinner provided.

Exercise 2

Insert two five-point stars (AutoShapes) to the right and left of the address, and fill both stars with a two-color gradient. Rotate both stars about 30 degrees. Add a shadow effect to both stars (*Hint*: use the Drawing toolbar). Save the document as **Coffee House Opening**.

> **IMPORTANT**
>
> In the One Step Further section that follows, you must complete Exercise 1 before continuing to Exercise 2.

One Step Further

Exercise 1

Open a new blank document, and create a chart to display the second-quarter expenses for the retail stores at Adventure Works. Use the following information:

	April	May	June
Gift Shop	$9,310	$7,940	$8,457
Restaurant	$10,874	$9,986	$10,045
Rentals	$4,000	$3,967	$5,870

Save the document as **AW Retail Expense**.

Exercise 2

Change the chart that you created in Exercise 1 to a 3-D bar chart. Change the color of the Gift Shop bars to red, change the Restaurant bars to indigo, and change the Rentals bars to light blue. The background of the chart should be green, and the chart area should be orange. Add minor, vertical gridlines to the chart. Save the document.

Exercise 3

In a new blank document, create an organization chart that shows the management structure of an organization with which you are familiar. This could be your place of employment, your school, or even your family.

Working with Columns

After completing this lesson, you will be able to:

✔ *Create columns.*
✔ *Adjust column width.*
✔ *Adjust column spacing.*
✔ *Insert a column break.*
✔ *Insert a vertical line between columns.*

KEY TERMS

- column break
- columns
- section break

Open a dictionary, newspaper, or issue of your favorite magazine, and you'll usually see text displayed in columns. In word processing, **columns** are two or more blocks of text on a page in which text flows to the top of the next column when the first column is filled. (Columns can also contain pictures and objects.) Numerous readability studies show that people are more likely to read text carefully when the widths of lines are short. That's why most newspapers and magazines format text into columns that are usually no more than three inches wide.

You can use Microsoft Office Word 2003 to easily format text into columns. Although columns aren't always appropriate (you probably wouldn't use them in letters, memos, or many business reports), they work well for newsletters, brochures, indexes, and lists. At times, columns can even help make a document shorter, typically when most lines of text are short. For example, if you typed the names of all the glossary terms in this book and pressed Enter after each entry, you would have dozens of pages of text, but a great deal of empty space on the right side of the document. If you typed the terms using two or three columns per page, the glossary would occupy far fewer pages.

Depending on how margins are set in a Word document, you can create up to 12 columns per page, although you'll rarely need more than four or five columns per page. After you define columns in a document and type text so that it flows into the columns, you'll often discover that you can improve formatting by manually changing where some columns break at the bottom, especially when a column ends in the middle of a sentence. You might also want to customize columns by changing the width, length, or spacing between them. You can perform all of these column-formatting tasks in Word. You can even add a vertical line between columns to enhance your document's appearance.

In this lesson, you will learn how to convert the text in a brochure to columns and adjust the formatting for different sections of the brochure.

IMPORTANT

Before you can use the practice files for this lesson, you need to install them from the book's companion CD to its default location. For additional information on how to find and open files used in this book, see the "Using the CD-ROM" section at the beginning of this book.

Creating and Modifying Columns

Presenting Text in Columns

THE BOTTOM LINE

Columns are a useful tool for adjusting the flow of text on the pages of your document. You can use from two to twelve columns of varying widths in your document, and you can apply columns to the entire document or just portions of it.

Before you begin modifying a document to create columns, it's important to think about how you want the columns to look on the page, how many columns you want, and how you want them to be formatted. The following is a list of items that you should consider when using columns.

- The width of the page minus the left and right margins

    If the right and left page margins are two inches each, the width of the document becomes much smaller. Remember that you'll also have to include space between the columns. The wider you want the page to be, the smaller the page margins should become to accommodate the text and columns.

- The number of columns that you want to appear across the page

    Most documents that use columns have either two or three columns per page. The more columns that you have on one page, the narrower the columns become. Narrower columns increase the number of hyphenated words and make the document harder to read.

- The length of each column

    The length of each column determines how far the text extends to the bottom of the page.

- The amount of space between columns

    Standard space between columns is .5 inch. If you have less space between the columns, the page becomes difficult to read. The greater the space between the columns, the smaller the columns become and the harder the document is to read.

Creating Columns

You can quickly create columns of equal width by using the Columns button on the Standard toolbar. When you click the Columns button, Word displays a graphical menu that you can use to specify the number of columns that you want. You can also use the Columns dialog box to create columns of equal or unequal width, or you can customize each column with a specific column measurement. After you define the column formatting, you can modify the columns using either the Columns dialog box or the ruler. If you define columns in an existing document but don't select any text, Word flows the entire document into columns using the formatting that you've specified.

> **TIP**
>
> To arrange text into more than six columns, you must use the Columns dialog box. On the Format menu, click Columns, and type the number of columns that you want.

If you want only certain sections of a document to be formatted into columns, you first select the text that you want formatted into columns and then apply column formatting to the selection. Word automatically inserts section breaks at the beginning and end of the selected text and flows the text into columns. In Word, a **section break** is a portion of a document that can have its own page formatting, independent of the formatting in other sections of the same document.

To create columns of equal width, select the text that is to be formatted into columns. On the Standard toolbar, click the Columns button to display the Columns menu, and click the number of columns that you want.

You can also use Word to create columns of unequal width. You might want to do this to create a unique appearance or to accommodate different types of text (for example, a list of topics in a narrow column and topic descriptions in a wider column).

To create columns of unequal width, select the text to be formatted, and on the Format menu, click Columns to display the Columns dialog box. To create two columns of unequal width, in the Presets section, click Left to make the left column narrower or click Right to make the right column narrower.

To create customized columns using the Columns dialog box, type the desired number of columns in the Number Of Columns box, clear the Equal Column Width check box, and then type the desired measurements in the Width boxes. (You'll customize column widths in a later exercise.)

The marketing manager at Contoso, Ltd decided that she wants to reformat a brochure that describes the services that the company provides. Specifically, she wants the text to appear in columns.

TROUBLESHOOTING

In the following exercises and in the illustrations used throughout this lesson, the Standard and Formatting toolbars have been separated. For additional information on how to separate the toolbars, see the "Using the CD-ROM" section at the beginning of this book.

◆ Be sure to start Word before beginning this exercise.

◆ Open Brochure 07 from the Lesson07 folder in the Word Practice folder that is located on your hard disk

Create columns

Brochure 07 was created to explain the public relations services provided by Contoso, Ltd. We will format the entire Contoso, Ltd brochure into columns by using the Columns button, and then you format a selection of text into uneven columns by using the Columns dialog box.

¶

1 On the Standard toolbar, click the Show/Hide ¶ button, if necessary, to show the formatting characters.

Formatting characters appear in the document.

TIP

To learn more about formatting marks see Lesson 4, "Changing the Layout of a Document."

2 On the Standard toolbar, click the Columns button.

The Columns menu appears. Unlike most menus, the Columns menu is a graphical representation that you can use to specify the number of columns for a document or section of a document.

FIGURE 7-1

Columns menu

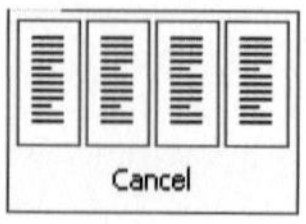

Cancel

CHECK THIS OUT ▼

Number of Columns
You aren't limited to four columns, as the Columns menu seems to indicate. To create more than four columns, drag to the right on the Columns menu to expand the menu up to six columns, and select the desired number of columns that you want.

3 Click the third column in the menu.

The text in the entire document is arranged into three columns. The WordArt object appears over some of the text at the top of the page.

FIGURE 7-2

Brochure 07 set in three columns

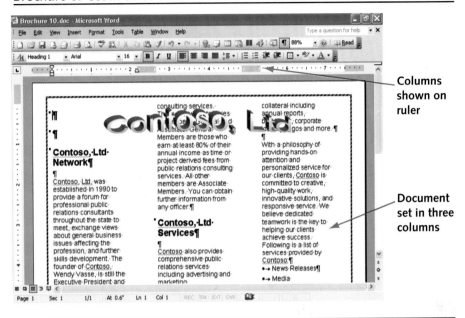

Columns shown on ruler

Document set in three columns

 4 On the Standard toolbar, click the Undo button.

The document returns to its original layout.

5 Position the insertion point to the left of the paragraph mark under the subheading Contoso, Ltd Network.

6 Select the paragraph mark and all of the text under the Contoso, Ltd Network subheading. Be sure to select the last paragraph mark in this section, but do not select the subheading Contoso, Ltd Services or any text under this heading.

TIP

To select large blocks of text, click to position the insertion point at the beginning of the text, hold down the Shift key, and then click to the right of the last word that you want to select.

 7 On the Standard toolbar, click the Columns button, and in the Columns menu, click the second column.

The selected text is formatted into two columns.

8 Click anywhere in the document to deselect the text.

FIGURE 7-3

Section of Brochure 07 set in two columns

Section of document in two columns

Automatic section break

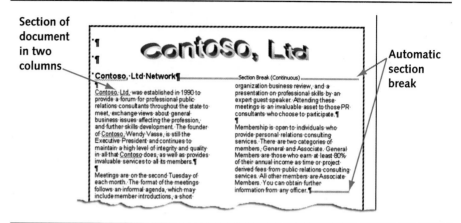

9 **On the Standard toolbar, click the Zoom down arrow, and click Whole Page.**

10 **Select all of the text under the subheading Contoso, Ltd Services (including the bulleted list), but do not select the subheading.**

TROUBLESHOOTING

Make sure that you select text to the end of the document on the second page, *not* just to the end of the first page.

11 **On the Format menu, click Columns.**

The Columns dialog box appears.

FIGURE 7-4

Columns dialog box

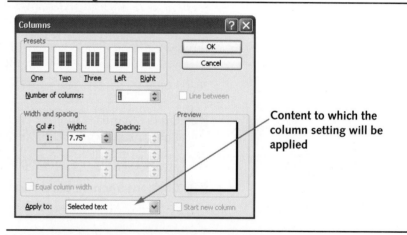

Content to which the column setting will be applied

12 **In the Presets section, click Right, and click OK.**

The selection of text is formatted into two columns, and the left column is wider than the right column.

13 **Click anywhere in the document to deselect the text.**

The document should look similar to the following illustration.

FIGURE 7-5

Two sections in Brochure 07 with varied column widths

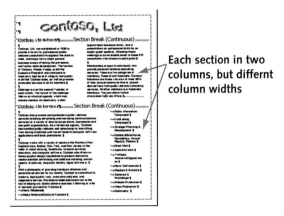

Each section in two columns, but differnt column widths

39%

14 **On the Standard toolbar, click the Zoom down arrow, and click 75%.**

The document layout appears at 75 percent of its actual size.

TROUBLESHOOTING

The zoom percentage that appears in the Zoom box can vary depending on the size of your monitor and the number and arrangement of toolbars that are open.

◆ **Save the document as Brochure 07 Edited in the Lesson07 folder.**

◆ **Keep this file open for the next exercise.**

QUICK REFERENCE ▼

Create columns of equal width

1 Select the text that is to be formatted into columns. (Skip this step if you want the entire document formatted into columns.)

2 On the Standard toolbar, click the Columns button.

3 Click the number of columns that you want.

Create columns of unequal width using the Columns dialog box

1 Select the text to be formatted into columns.

2 On the Format menu, click Columns.

3 To create two columns of unequal width, in the Presets section, click Left to make the left column narrower or click Right to make the right column narrower.

Or

To create customized columns, in the Number Of Columns box, type the desired number of columns, clear the Equal Column Width option, and then type the desired measurements in the Width boxes.

4 Click OK.

QUICK CHECK

Q. If you want your document to have seven columns, what is the quickest way to set up the columns?

A. **If you want your document to have seven columns, it must be set up through the Columns dialog box.**

Specifying Column Width

In the previous exercise, you learned how to use the Presets section of the Columns dialog box to create columns of unequal widths. You can also modify the widths of columns using either the ruler or width settings in the Columns dialog box. Depending on how wide or narrow you make the columns, the space between the columns might automatically become wider or narrower.

For example, if you specify in the Columns dialog box that you want five columns, Word automatically formats the columns with equal width and spacing. If you make one of the columns wider in the Width box, all subsequent column widths become narrower to accommodate the wider column. If you want to customize column widths, you should check the Preview area in the Columns dialog box as you change the settings to see how the other columns are affected by the modifications.

ANOTHER METHOD

You can also use the up and down arrows to the right of the Width box to change the column width in increments of .5 inch.

FIGURE 7-6

Column markers on the ruler

Move Column Marker

Change column width

The Brochure 07 Edited document looks better now that it is set in columns, but it is not exactly what the marketing manager had in mind. We will now customize the column widths using both the Columns dialog box and the ruler.

1 **Click anywhere under the subheading Contoso, Ltd Services.**

2 **On the Format menu, click Columns.**

The Columns dialog box appears.

3 **In the Width box for the first column, select the contents, type 4.5, and press Tab.**

The width for column 2 automatically changes to 2.5 inches to accommodate the available space for this column after the left and right margin widths, the column width for column 1, and the space between columns have been calculated.

4 **Click OK.**

The column widths are adjusted based on the measurement that you enter.

5 On the ruler, position the mouse pointer on the Move Column marker until the pointer turns to a double-headed arrow. Hold down the Alt key, and drag the marker to the left so that the left column is 4.25 inches wide (at which point the right column will be 2.75 inches wide).

> **TIP**
>
> It isn't necessary to hold down the Alt key when you drag the Move Column marker; however, doing so allows you to view the measurements for the column widths so that you can be more precise.

6 Release the Alt key.

The column widths are adjusted.

◆ Save the document.

◆ Keep this file open for the next exercise.

QUICK REFERENCE ▼

Adjust column widths using the Columns dialog box

1 Click the column text to be modified.

2 On the Format menu, click Columns.

3 To convert the text to two columns of unequal width, in the Presets section, click Left to make the left column narrower or click Right to make the right column narrower.

Or

To customize the column widths, clear the Equal column width box, and type the desired measurements in the Width boxes.

4 Click OK.

Adjust column widths using the ruler

1 Click or select the column(s) to be modified to display the ruler.

2 Position the mouse pointer on the Move Column marker.

3 Hold down the Alt key, and drag the marker to adjust the column widths.

4 When the columns are adjusted to the desired measurements, release the Alt key.

QUICK CHECK

Q. If you have set column widths through the Columns dialog box, can they be altered using the ruler?

A. **Column widths can be adjusted through either the ruler or the Columns dialog box, regardless of which way they were originally set.**

Adjusting Column Spacing

If you want to change the spacing between columns, you can use the ruler or the Columns dialog box to adjust the spacing. If you use the Columns dialog box, be sure to preview how the changes affect the columns.

> **TIP**
>
> The measurements in the Spacing boxes identify the blank space that appears *after* each column. Be sure to look in the Preview area to see how the modifications affect other columns.

To change column spacing using the ruler, click anywhere in the section that contains the columns that you want to modify. The ruler displays the Move Column markers. Position the mouse pointer on the right edge of the Move Column marker until you see the ScreenTip *Left Margin*, and drag the marker to the new position.

For example, while creating the brochure, the marketing manager specifies in the Columns dialog box that she wants two columns. Word displays a preview of the columns, both set to 3.5 inches wide. The spacing between columns is set to .5 inch. The marketing manager decides to do some experimenting and sets the spacing to 2.5 inches; however, when she does this, the first column's width automatically changes to 1.5 inches, and the second column's width remains at 3.5 inches. Dissatisfied with the results, the manager sets the second column's width to 1.5 inches, which automatically changes the first column's width to 2.5 inches. She likes the preview, so she applies the settings to the brochure.

Adjust column spacing

In the previous exercise, we adjusted the column widths in Brochure 07 Edited. Now we will change the spacing between columns by using the Columns dialog box.

1 Click anywhere in the section under the subheading Contoso, Ltd Network.

2 On the Format menu, click Columns.

The Columns dialog box appears.

3 Clear the Equal Column Width check box, if necessary.

4 Select the measurement in the Spacing box for column 1, type .1, and press Tab.

The width of the second column changes to 3.9 inches.

5 Select the measurement in the Width box for the first column, type 3.7, and press Tab.

The width of both columns is adjusted to 3.7 inches.

6 Click OK.

The Columns dialog box closes, and the spacing between the columns changes.

7 On the Standard toolbar, click the Zoom down arrow, and click Whole Page.

The document layout is displayed as an entire page on your screen.

8 Click anywhere in the two-column section under the subheading Contoso, Ltd Services.

9 On the Format menu, click Columns.

The Columns dialog box appears.

10 Select the measurement in the Spacing box, type .1, and press Tab.

The width of the second column changes to 3.15 inches.

11 Click OK.

The Columns dialog box closes, and the spacing between the columns changes.

FIGURE 7-7

Brochure 07 Edited with column spacing adjusted

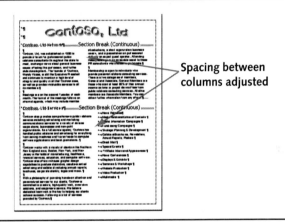

Spacing between columns adjusted

12 Click the Zoom down arrow, and click 75%.

The document appears at 75 percent of its actual size.

◆ Save the document.

◆ Keep this file open for the next exercise.

QUICK REFERENCE ▼

Change the spacing between columns using the Columns dialog box

1 Click the column text to be modified.

2 On the Format menu, click Columns.

3 If necessary, in the Columns dialog box, clear the Equal Column Width check box.

4 In the Spacing boxes, type the desired measurements.

5 Make adjustments to the Width boxes as desired.

6 Click OK.

Change the spacing between columns using the ruler

1 Click or select the column(s) to be modified to display the ruler.

2 On the ruler, drag the desired column marker to adjust the column spacing as desired.

Inserting a Column Break

THE BOTTOM LINE

Once you have set your text into columns, you may find places where the text break between one column and the next is awkward or doesn't look right. You can insert a column break at any location with the columns to dictate exactly where the text will flow into the next column.

When text in a column reaches either the bottom margin of a page or the next section break, the text flows into the next column on that page or section. When the text reaches the bottom of the last column on a page, the text flows into the first column on the next page. You can override an automatic **column break** that Word creates by inserting a manual column break.

To insert a manual column break, position the insertion point at the location where you want to insert the break. On the Insert menu, click Break. In the Break dialog box, click the Column break option, and click OK.

ANOTHER METHOD

You can also insert a manual column break by pressing Ctrl+Shift+Enter.

To delete a column break, make sure the Show/Hide ¶ button is selected on the Standard toolbar, click the Column Break marker, and press Delete.

Insert and delete a column break

The marketing manager wants to see whether inserting a column break will improve the flow of the text. In this exercise, we create a column break in the second column and view the results. We then delete the column break.

1 In the last section, click to position the insertion point at the beginning of the third paragraph (which begins "With a philosophy...").

2 On the Insert menu, click Break.

The Break dialog box appears.

FIGURE 7-8

Break dialog box

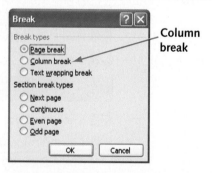

Column break

3 Click the Column Break option, and click OK.

The first column ends at the location of the column break.

FIGURE 7-9

Brochure 07 Edited with manual column break

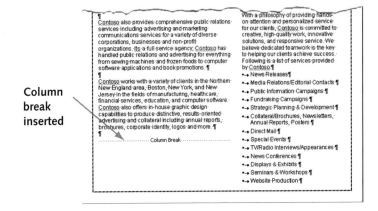

TIP

Notice that the column break moves two of the bulleted items to the second page, which is an undesirable result.

4 Click the Column Break marker, and press Delete.

The column break is removed, and the columns are formatted the way they were before you inserted the column break.

◆ Save the document.

◆ Keep this file open for the next exercise.

QUICK REFERENCE ▼

Insert a manual column break using a keystroke combination

1 Move the insertion point to the location where you want to insert the break.

2 Press Ctrl+Shift+Enter.

Insert a manual column break

1 Move the insertion point to the location where you want to insert the break.

2 On the Insert menu, click Break.

3 In the Break dialog box, click the Column Break option.

4 Click OK.

Q. How is a column break different from a page break?

A. A page break forces all text after it to the next page of the document. A column break forces all text after it to the next column, which may be on the next page or the same page.

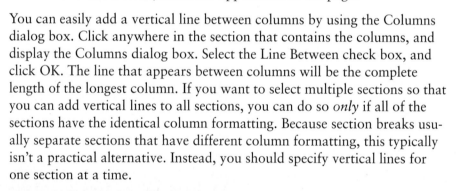

Delete a manual column break

1 Click the Show/Hide ¶ button to show the paragraph marks.

2 Position the insertion point on or to the right of the column break marker.

3 Press Delete or Backspace.

Inserting Vertical Lines Between Columns

THE BOTTOM LINE

Sometimes it is easier to follow text that has been formatted in columns if there is a vertical line separating the columns. This can also add visual appeal. With Word, you can easily add these vertical lines through the Columns dialog box.

If you review the column formatting in magazines and newspapers, you'll often notice that columns are separated with a vertical line as well as column spacing. The vertical lines help the reader to distinguish between columns and add a clean, attractive appearance to the page.

You can easily add a vertical line between columns by using the Columns dialog box. Click anywhere in the section that contains the columns, and display the Columns dialog box. Select the Line Between check box, and click OK. The line that appears between columns will be the complete length of the longest column. If you want to select multiple sections so that you can add vertical lines to all sections, you can do so *only* if all of the sections have the identical column formatting. Because section breaks usually separate sections that have different column formatting, this typically isn't a practical alternative. Instead, you should specify vertical lines for one section at a time.

If you want to control the length and width of the vertical lines that appear between columns, you can use the Drawing toolbar to manually draw lines between columns. However, if you change the widths or lengths of any columns, the manually drawn lines do not change their positions. By contrast, when you use the Columns dialog box to insert vertical lines between columns, the location and length of the lines are automatically adjusted whenever you change column widths or add column breaks.

TIP

To activate the Drawing toolbar, on the View menu, click Toolbars, and click Drawing, or click the Drawing button on the Standard toolbar.

Insert lines between columns

Now that the columns are arranged the way we want in Brochure 07 Edited, we want to improve the appearance by adding vertical lines between the columns in the brochure.

1 **Click anywhere in the section under the subheading Contoso, Ltd Network.**

2 **On the Format menu, click Columns.**

The Columns dialog box appears.

3 **Select the Line Between check box, and click OK.**

A vertical line now separates the columns in the section.

FIGURE 7-10

Vertical line added in the first section

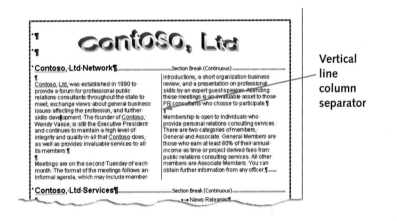

4 **Click anywhere in the section under the subheading Contoso, Ltd Services.**

5 **On the Format menu, click Columns.**

The Columns dialog box appears.

6 **Select the Line Between check box, and click OK.**

A vertical line now separates the columns in both sections.

7 **On the Standard toolbar, click the Show/Hide ¶ button.**

The formatting characters are hidden. Your document should appear similar to Figure 7-11.

FIGURE 7-11

Completed brochure

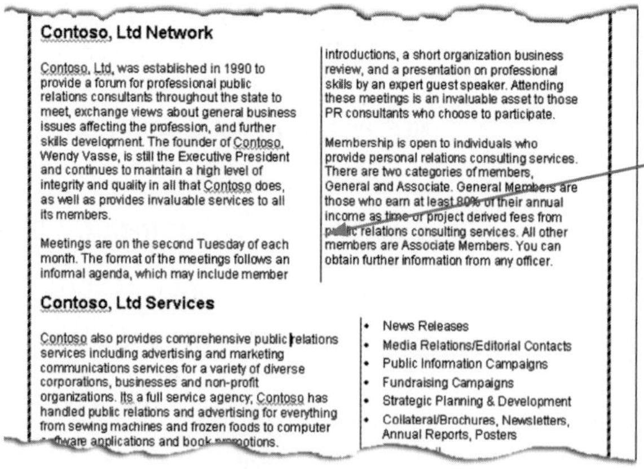

Vertical line separating columns in both sections

TIP

By default, Word centers a vertical line between columns. In this figure, the vertical line appears against the left edge of the second column because you specified a column spacing of .1 inch in the previous exercise.

QUICK CHECK

Q. Where is the vertical line between columns placed?

A. The vertical line between columns is centered between the columns unless the spacing between columns is adjusted.

QUICK REFERENCE ▼

Insert a vertical line between columns

1 Click anywhere in the section that contains the columns that you want to separate with a vertical line.

2 On the Format menu, click Columns.

3 Select the Line Between check box, and click OK.

◆ If you are continuing to other lessons, save and close the document, but keep Word open.

◆ If you are not continuing to other lessons, save and close the document, and close Word.

Key Points

✔ *You can use Word's column-formatting features to establish columns in your document.*

✔ *Once columns are created, you can adjust column width and spacing so that your text is displayed in the exact manner that you want.*

✔ *You can insert manual column breaks within your columns to cause the text to move from one column to the next.*

Quick Quiz

Multiple Choice

1. A _____ break is a demarcation that designates where text from one column ends.
    a. page
    b. column
    c. section
    d. manual

2. A _____ can have its own page formatting independent of the formatting in other sections of the same document.
    a. page
    b. column
    c. section
    d. manual

3. Columns of varying widths can only be created if the _____ check box in the Columns dialog box is deselected.
    a. Line Between
    b. Start New Column
    c. Apply To
    d. Equal Column Widths

4. _____ are vertical blocks of text that are separated by a blank space.
    a. Cells
    b. Columns
    c. Rows
    d. Fields

5. The maximum number of columns that you can have in a document is _____.
    a. two
    b. four
    c. six
    d. twelve

6. The minimum number of columns that you can have in a document is _____.
    a. one
    b. two
    c. four
    d. six

7. The standard amount of space between columns is _____.
    a. 0.25 inch
    b. 0.5 inch
    c. 0.75 inch
    d. 1.0 inch

8. You adjust the _____ on the ruler in order to change the width of the columns.
   a. tabs
   b. indents
   c. Move Column marker
   d. Ruler marker

9. The _____ box in the Columns dialog box adjusts the spacing between columns.
   a. Spacing
   b. Space Between
   c. Width
   d. Number Of Columns

10. The _____ box in the Columns dialog box adjusts the width of columns.
   a. Spacing
   b. Column Width
   c. Width
   d. Number Of Columns

Short Answer

1. What is the fastest way to create columns of equal width?

2. If you want to define columns of varying widths, what check box do you need to clear in the Columns dialog box?

3. What two ways can you use to customize column widths in a document?

4. If you format a document into columns and later decide that you don't want the columns, how could you remove the column formatting?

5. How do the left and right page margins affect how you define the columns in a document?

6. When you change the spacing between two columns, how are the columns affected?

7. What steps do you perform to insert a vertical line between columns?

8. What happens if you define columns in an existing document, but don't select any text?

On Your Own

IMPORTANT

In the On Your Own exercises that follow, you must complete Exercise 1 to continue to Exercise 2.

Exercise 1

Open the Industries Services 07 document in the Lesson07 folder in the Word Practice folder. Format the first portion of the document to two columns of equal width, excluding the title at the beginning and the last section (the part under the subheading *We Know Your Message*). Save the document as **Industries Services 07 Edited**.

Exercise 2

Using the file Industries Services 07 Edited, adjust the widths of the columns that you just created so that the left column is about twice as wide as the right column (4 inches for the first column and 2 inches for the second), and change the spacing between the two columns to .1 inch. Format the final section of the document into four columns excluding the subtitle from the columns, and change the spacing between the four columns to .1 inch. Insert vertical lines between all columns. Save and close the document.

One Step Further

Exercise 1

Open a new blank document, and create a newsletter for an organization in which you are involved. This newsletter should tell about upcoming events, important dates, and perhaps contain an article recapping a past event. Use the tools that you have learned about in this lesson as well as in other lessons (i.e., WordArt and inserting pictures or graphics) to enhance your newsletter. Save and close the newsletter.

Exercise 2

Create a brochure to advertise your lawn maintenance services. This brochure should be set to print in landscape and should have three equal-width columns (so that the brochure can easily be folded in thirds). Place lines between each column, and make sure that there is plenty of space between each column so that it is very easy to read. Content should include, among other things, the name of your company, areas in which your service is available, range of prices for your services, and a number where you can be reached. Enhance the brochure with graphics and WordArt. Save, print, and close the brochure.

Exercise 3

Word offers another feature to assist with the layout of text on a page. This feature is called column boundaries. Type Column in the Ask A Question box, and then select Display or hide newsletter-style column boundaries. Read the information provided by Word's Help file to learn how to turn on/off this feature. Open one of the documents that you have created in these Exercises, turn on the boundaries feature, and explore using these text boundaries. Observe how they can assist with the placement of text, graphics, and objects (such as WordArt). When you have finished, close your document without saving.

Microsoft Excel

LESSON

Learning Worksheet Fundamentals

After completing this lesson, you will be able to:

✔ *Create a workbook.*
✔ *Understand Microsoft Excel window elements.*
✔ *Select cells.*
✔ *Enter text, numbers, and dates in a worksheet.*
✔ *Enter a range of data.*
✔ *Edit cell contents.*
✔ *Move between worksheets.*
✔ *Name and save a workbook.*
✔ *Open a workbook.*
✔ *Rename a worksheet.*
✔ *Preview and print a worksheet.*
✔ *Close a workbook and quit Excel.*

KEY TERMS

- active cell
- cell
- Print Preview
- range
- selecting
- task pane
- templates
- workbook
- worksheets

Introducing Excel

Microsoft Office Excel 2003 is a powerful spreadsheet program designed for organizing, formatting, and calculating numeric data. Excel displays data in a row-and-column format, with gridlines between the rows and columns, similar to accounting ledger books or graph paper. Consequently, Excel is well suited for working with numeric data for accounting, scientific research, statistical recording, and any other situation that can benefit from organizing data in a table-like format. Teachers often record student grade information in Excel, and managers often store lists of data—such as inventory records or personnel records—in Excel. As you work through this course, you'll learn how Excel makes it easy to perform calculations on numeric data and provides dozens of ways to format data for presentation purposes, including charts and reports.

IMPORTANT

Before you can use the practice files in this lesson, you must install them from the book's companion CD to their default location. For additional information on how to find and open files used in this book, see the "Using the CD-ROM" section at the beginning of this book.

Creating a Workbook

Creating a Workbook

When you start Excel, a new blank workbook opens automatically. The workbook contains three worksheets by default. Each workbook should contain information about a unique subject, such as inventory, employees, or sales. Each worksheet should hold a subset of information regarding that subject, such as inventory levels by location, salaried versus commissioned employees, or sales information for a given month.

You start Excel by using any of the methods that you use to start other Microsoft Windows programs. One common method is clicking the Start button, pointing to All Programs, pointing to Microsoft Office, and then choosing Microsoft Office Excel 2003 on the submenu. You can also click a shortcut icon, if one exists, on the desktop or on the Quick Launch bar.

TIP

Each open workbook is represented on the Excel button on the taskbar. It's easy to click a button to display a different workbook. When you have many open applications, each application has a button on which can be found a list of open files.

When you start Excel, a blank **workbook,** titled Book1, opens by default. A workbook is a file that can contain multiple **worksheets.** In turn, a worksheet is a grid of rows and columns in which you can enter data. For example, you might create four budget worksheets in a single workbook, with each worksheet containing a budget for one quarter of the upcoming fiscal year. If you're a teacher using Excel, you might create grading worksheets in the same workbook, with each worksheet storing grade records for a semester of the same class. As you can see, a workbook allows you to assemble worksheets that contain related data. After you create a workbook, you can save it as a single file on your hard disk.

◆ To complete the procedures in this lesson, you must use the practice file Employee Information in the Lesson01 folder in the Excel Practice folder that is located on your hard disk.

Start Excel, create a standard workbook, and close the workbook

In this exercise, you start Excel, create a standard workbook, and close the workbook.

1 On the Windows taskbar, click the Start button, point to All Programs, point to Microsoft Office, and click Microsoft Office Excel 2003.

Excel opens with Book1 ready for you to use.

FIGURE 1-1

Creating a new workbook

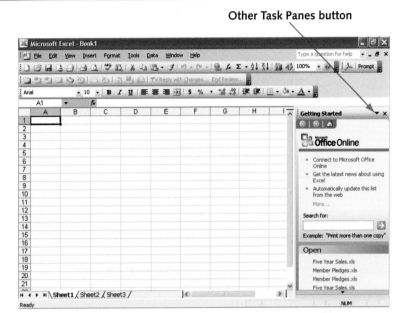

Other Task Panes button

If the task pane is not displayed, open the View menu and click Task Pane.

2 Display the New Workbook task pane by clicking the Other Task Panes button and clicking New Workbook.

3 In the New section of the New Workbook task pane, click Blank Workbook.

Excel creates a workbook called Book2, and the task pane disappears.

ANOTHER METHOD

Click Create A New Workbook at the bottom of the Getting Started task pane, and then choose Blank Workbook in the New Workbook task pane.

4 On the File menu, click Close.

Excel closes Book2, and Book1 reappears.

ANOTHER METHOD

Click the workbook's Close Window button.

◆ Keep this file open for the next exercise.

QUICK REFERENCE ▼

Start Excel, and create a new workbook

1 Click the Start button, point to All Programs, point to Microsoft Office, and click Microsoft Office Excel 2003.

2 On the New Workbook task pane, click Blank Workbook.

Creating a Workbook from a Template

Excel also provides **templates** that let you create workbooks already set up to track certain kinds of data, such as invoice and purchase order information. Templates are timesaving tools—they eliminate the need for you to spend time setting up the structure of a worksheet and applying complex formatting and formulas. All you need to do is enter the raw data. To create a workbook based on a template, click New on the File menu, which opens the New Workbook task pane. Under the Templates section, choose On My Computer.

FIGURE 1-2

Templates dialog box

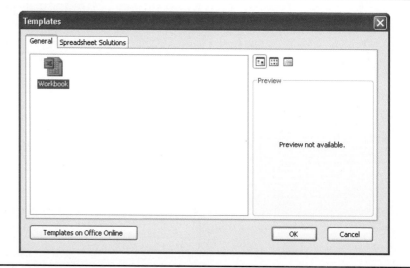

TROUBLESHOOTING

The templates you see in the Templates dialog box may be different than what is shown in Figure 1-2.

From the Templates dialog box, you can choose the General tab or the Spreadsheet Solutions tab and then select one of the templates shown.

Understanding Microsoft Excel Window Elements

THE BOTTOM LINE

The workbook window contains many of the same components that you use in other Windows applications. Being able to identify the main components of the Excel window will help you work more efficiently.

Many elements in the Excel window are similar to those in windows of other Windows programs. In Figure 1-3, the main components of the Excel window are identified.

FIGURE 1-3

Elements of the workbook window

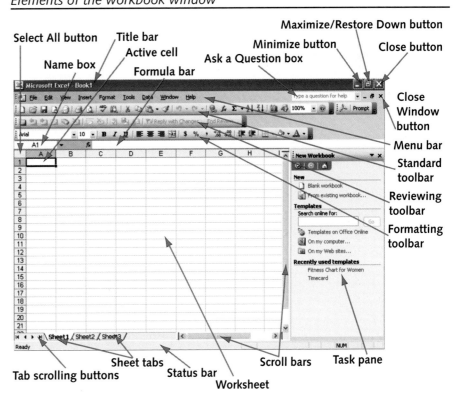

The following table describes the elements in the Excel window.

Element	Description
Title bar	Identifies the current program and the name of the current workbook
Menu bar	Lists the names of the menus in Excel
Toolbars	Give you quick access to functions that you use frequently, such as formatting, aligning, and totaling cell entries; the Standard and Formatting toolbars appear by default
Name Box	Displays the address of the active cell
Formula bar	Displays the contents of the active cell
Task pane	Lets you open files, paste data from the Clipboard, create blank workbooks, and create Excel workbooks based on existing files
Ask A Question box	Allows you to query the Help system; help topics that match your request are displayed in the task pane
Status bar	Displays information about a selected command; it also indicates the status (on or off) of the Caps Lock and Num Lock keys
Scroll bars	Include a vertical and a horizontal scroll bar and four scroll arrows, each used to display different areas of the worksheet
Select All button	Selects every cell in a worksheet
Sheet tabs	Identify the worksheets in the open workbook; click a tab to display a worksheet
Tab scrolling buttons	Let you display and navigate sheet tabs
Worksheet	A grid of vertical columns (identified by alphabetic characters) and horizontal rows (identified by numeric digits); columns and rows intersect to form cells; each cell can be identified by a full-cell reference, or address, consisting of the column and row coordinates of that cell—for example, B3
Active cell	The cell, designated by a thick border, that will be affected when you type or edit data
Minimize button	Minimizes the window to a button on the taskbar
Maximize/Restore Down	Toggles (switches back and forth) between maximizing a window and restoring a window to its previous size
Close Window button	Closes the current workbook window
ScreenTip	A small pop-up box that displays the name of an object or a toolbar button when you point to it with the mouse pointer

A great advantage of the **task pane** is that it groups many common actions, such as opening or creating new files, in one place and lets you perform them with a single mouse click. The only drawback of the task pane is that it takes up valuable screen space. Fortunately, you can show or hide the task pane easily. On the View menu, click Task Pane; Excel hides the task pane if it is currently displayed or shows it if it is currently hidden.

The benefit of placing the Ask A Question box in the main Excel window is that you can quickly and easily get help while your question is fresh in your mind, without adding any steps that might distract you from your question. With this feature, you no longer have to go to the Help menu or Office Assistant when you need help.

Become familiar with Excel window elements

In this exercise, you work with Excel window elements.

1 **Point to the Chart Wizard button on the Standard toolbar for a few seconds.**

A ScreenTip appears, displaying the words *Chart Wizard.*

2 **Point to the Name Box, which contains the cell address A1.**

A ScreenTip appears, displaying the title *Name Box*.

FIGURE 1-4

Displaying ScreenTips

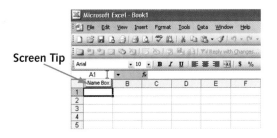

3 **Click the Toolbar Options button at the end of the Formatting toolbar.**

A menu with options appears.

FIGURE 1-5

Displaying Toolbar Options

4 **Point to the Add Or Remove Buttons command.**

A menu with additional commands appears.

5 **Point to Formatting on the submenu.**

A menu with the formatting button options appears.

FIGURE 1-6

Formatting button options

6 **Review the names of buttons on the menu.**

7 **When you are done, click somewhere outside of the open menus to close the menus.**

◆ **Keep this file open for the next exercise.**

Selecting Cells

THE BOTTOM LINE

Once you have opened a workbook, you can examine and modify its contents. To change specific data, you must first select the cell containing the data.

Before you can enter data in a worksheet, you must identify the **cell** (the intersection of a row and a column) in which you want to put the data. This is known as **selecting** the cell. You can select a single cell, a row, a column, and groups of adjacent and nonadjacent cells. You might select more than one cell in order to perform the same operation on all of them; for example, you might want to delete all of the data in a selected row.

To select a single cell, simply click that cell. When a cell is selected, a black border surrounds it, and that cell becomes the **active cell**, as shown in Figure 1-7.

FIGURE 1-7

Selecting a cell

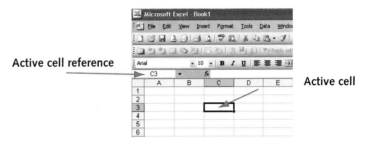

You can select all of the cells in a worksheet by clicking the Select All button at the top left corner of the worksheet.

FIGURE 1-8

Selecting all cells in a worksheet

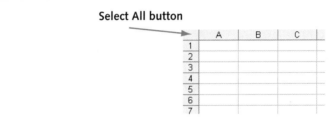

You can select a single row or column in a worksheet by clicking the corresponding row or column selector. For example, you might want to move an entire row of data to a new location in the worksheet, or you might want to apply a currency format to all of the data in a column.

FIGURE 1-9

Selecting a row or column

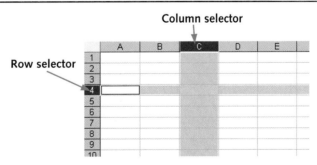

TIP

When you select a cell, the text on its row selector and its column selector appear shaded in orange instead of gray like the rest of the row and column selectors. That feature makes it easier to see the row and column "coordinates" of the selected cell. In addition, the cell address appears in the Name Box.

Select an entire row and an entire column in a worksheet

In this exercise, you select an entire row and an entire column in the current worksheet.

1 **Click the column selector for column D.**

Column D is selected.

2 **Click the row selector for row 1.**

Row 1 is selected.

3 **Click the column selector for column B, and drag the mouse pointer to the column selector for column E.**

The columns are selected.

4 **Click any cell in column G.**

Columns B, C, D, and E are deselected.

◆ **Keep this file open for the next exercise.**

ANOTHER METHOD

Another way to select a range of columns is to click the first column selector in the range, hold down the Shift key, and click the last column selector in the range. The same method works for selecting a range of rows.

QUICK REFERENCE ▼

Select a row or a column in a worksheet

Click the row or column selector.

QUICK **CHECK**

Q. What does a black border around a cell indicate?

A: A black border indicates that the cell is active.

Selecting a Range of Cells

THE BOTTOM LINE

Just as you can change the data in a single cell, you can also make changes to the data in a range, or contiguous group, of cells by selecting the range. Working with a range of cells saves you the time of performing the same operations, such as cutting, copying, or formatting, repeatedly on individual cells.

A **range** is normally identified by the references for its first and last cells, with a colon between them. For example, the vertical range extending from cell A1 to cell A9 is identified as A1:A9. Likewise, the horizontal range extending from cell C3 to cell G3 is identified as C3:G3. Ranges that extend across a block of columns and rows are identified by the addresses for the cells in the top left and bottom right corners of that block (B5:F9), as shown in Figure 1-10.

FIGURE 1-10

Selecting the range B5:F9

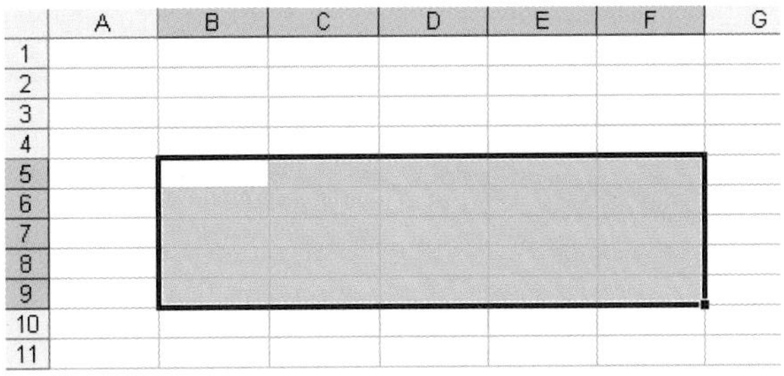

You select a range of cells by dragging the mouse pointer over the cells. When you select a range of cells, the first cell chosen becomes the active cell. The active cell is white, and the range of cells is blue. As you have learned, when you select more than one cell, you can perform the same operation on all of the cells at once.

Select a group of adjacent cells in the current worksheet

You've learned how to select a cell, a column, and a row. Now you will learn how to select a group of adjacent cells.

1 **Click cell E3, hold down the mouse button, drag the mouse pointer down to cell E12, and release the mouse button.**

The range E3:E12 is selected, and E3 remains the active cell.

2 **Click cell A5, hold down the Shift key, and click cell H16.**

The range is selected, and A5 remains the active cell.

FIGURE 1-11

Selecting the range A5:H16

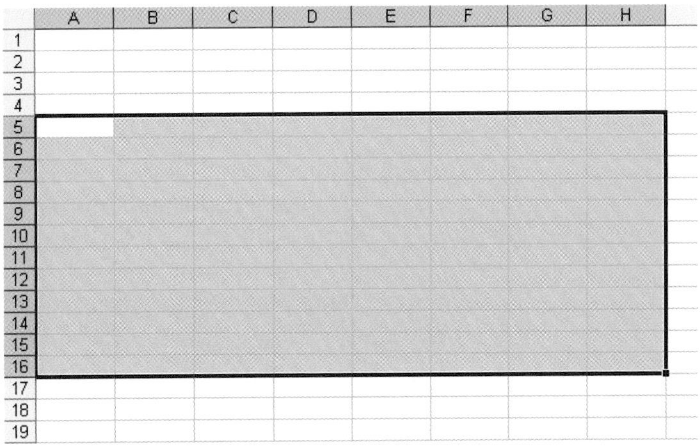

TIP

To select multiple nonadjacent cell ranges, select the first range, hold down the Ctrl key, and select any additional ranges.

3 **Click cell F17, hold down the Shift key, and press the Down arrow key four times.**

The range of cells from F17 to F21 (referred to as F17:F21) is selected.

QUICK REFERENCE ▼

Select a range of cells

1 Click the top left cell of the range of cells.

2 Drag the mouse to the bottom right cell in the range of cells.

Entering Text in a Worksheet

THE BOTTOM LINE

Worksheets contain three types of data: text, numbers, and formulas. Text values are sometimes referred to as "labels." These values can be the names of employees or a list of products. They are often used to help identify the numeric data contained in the worksheet, but they can also be used for other tasks, such as sorting and grouping data.

You can enter three basic categories of data in an Excel worksheet: text, numbers, and formulas. To enter text or numbers in a cell, you select the cell and type the information. As you type, each character appears in the Formula bar and in the active cell, along with the insertion point. The insertion point indicates where the next character will be inserted.

A text entry, which is sometimes called a label, is one that contains the characters *A* through *Z* or any other character that doesn't have a purely numeric value. Sometimes a text entry includes numbers, such as in a street address.

By default, a text entry appears left-justified in a cell. When the entry is longer than the defined width of the cell, it either "spills over" into the adjacent cell (if that cell is empty) or it appears in truncated form (if the adjacent cell is not empty). Internally, however, the text is stored in only one cell and includes each character originally entered.

Enter text in a worksheet

In this exercise, you enter text in a worksheet.

1 **Click cell A1, type Sales, and press Enter.**

The text is entered in cell A1, and A2 becomes the active cell.

ANOTHER METHOD

Press Tab or an arrow key to enter data and move to another cell.

2 Click cell A3, type **Cabins**, and press Enter.

Cell A3 contains the word *Cabins,* and the active cell moves to A4.

3 Type **Condos**, and press Enter.

The word *Condos* is entered in cell A4.

FIGURE 1-12

Entering text in a cell

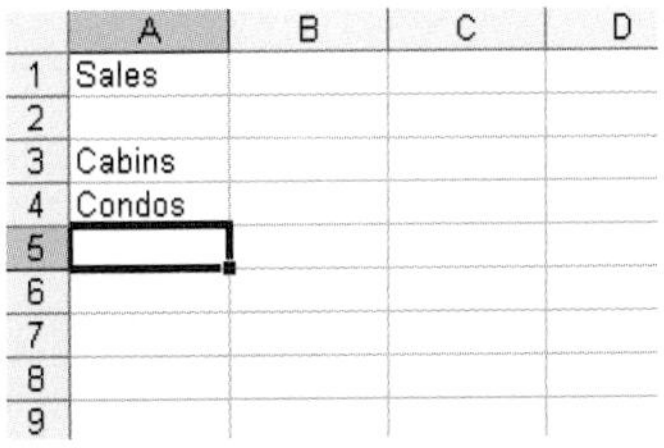

	A	B	C	D
1	Sales			
2				
3	Cabins			
4	Condos			
5				
6				
7				
8				
9				

◆ Keep this file open for the next exercise.

Entering Numbers in a Worksheet

THE BOTTOM LINE

Once you enter numeric values in a worksheet, you can perform all kinds of calculations and analyses on them. Numbers can be formatted as currency, percentages, decimals, and fractions. Numeric values are also used to develop complex charts and graphs in Excel, which are useful tools for doing comparisons and making projections.

A numeric entry contains some combination of the digits 0 through 9 and, optionally, the following special characters.

Character	Used To
+	Indicate a positive value
- or ( )	Indicate a negative value
$	Indicate a currency value
%	Indicate a percentage
/	Indicate a fraction
.	Indicate a decimal value
,	Separate the digits of the entry
E or e	Display the entry in scientific (exponential) notation

When you start an entry with a plus sign to indicate a positive number, Excel ignores the sign. When you type parentheses to indicate a negative number, the number appears with a minus sign. When you include a dollar sign, a percent sign, a forward slash, a comma, or an exponential symbol, the program automatically assigns a numeric format to the entry.

By default, a numeric entry appears right-justified in a cell. When the entry is longer than the defined width of the cell, it appears in scientific notation, as pound signs (####), or rounded. Internally, however, Excel stores all numbers as originally entered.

ANOTHER METHOD

You can enter numbers by using the number keys above the letters on your keyboard or by pressing the Num Lock key and using the numeric keypad. Num Lock is a toggle key. An indicator light on your keyboard shines when Num Lock is on.

Enter sales figures in your worksheet

In this exercise, you enter numeric data in the worksheet.

1 Click cell B3, type 42848, and press Enter.

The number is entered in cell B3, and B4 becomes the active cell.

2 Type 92346, and press Enter.

The number is entered in cell B4, and B5 becomes the active cell.

◆ Keep this file open for the next exercise.

Entering Dates in a Worksheet

THE BOTTOM LINE

Dates are commonly used in worksheets to track data over a specified time period. Like other numeric values, they can be used in formulas and in developing charts and graphs.

Dates in Excel worksheets can be represented using only numbers or a combination of text and numbers. For example, *January 22, 2004*, and *1/22/04* are two ways of entering the same date. Like text, dates are often used as row and column labels. But unlike text, dates are considered *serial numbers*; they are sequential and can be added, subtracted, and used in calculations.

Be careful when representing a year with just the last two digits of the year. Excel interprets two-digit years from 00 to 29 to represent the years 2000 to 2029; two-digit years from 30 to 99 are interpreted as 1930 to 1999. The default year format uses two digits; however, it is a good idea to type four-digit years to avoid ambiguity.

By default, a date entry appears right-justified in a cell. After you type and enter a date in a cell, Excel might reformat the date and express it in a different way. The way in which a date is represented in a cell is initially based on your computer's default date setting. You will learn how to choose date formats, including the four-digit year options, in the next lesson.

Enter dates in a worksheet

You have learned how to enter text and numbers in a worksheet. Now you will enter dates in the worksheet.

1 Click cell B1, type January 2005, and press Tab.

Excel abbreviates the date to *Jan-05*, and C1 becomes the active cell.

2 Type Feb 2005, and press Tab.

Excel uses the same date formatting as above, and *Feb-05* is entered in cell C1. D1 is now the active cell.

◆ Keep this file open for the next exercise.

QUICK REFERENCE ▼

Enter data in a cell

1 Select a cell.

2 Type the data in the cell.

3 Press Enter.

Entering a Range of Data

THE BOTTOM LINE

When you select a range of cells first, the next cell in which you want to enter data automatically becomes active when you press the Enter key. This saves you the time of going to specific cells, such as the top of the next column in the range or the beginning of the next row in the range.

To enter data in an individual cell, you type the data and then press Enter. When you have several consecutive entries to make, you can select the range first to enter the data more quickly. For example, you might have several rows listing expenses and columns that label the expenses by day of the week. When you select the range first, you simply type the raw expense figures and press Enter. When you get to the bottom cell of a column in the range and press Enter, the insertion point automatically jumps to the first cell in the next column of the range.

Enter more sales figures in your worksheet

You have learned how to enter data by navigating to a selected cell and typing the data. In this exercise, you will learn how to enter a range of data.

1 Click cell C3, drag to cell D4, and release the mouse button.

Cells C3, C4, D3, and D4 are selected.

2 Type **39768**, and press Enter.

The number is entered in cell C3, and C4 becomes the active cell.

3 Type **90426**, and press Enter.

The number is entered in cell C4, and D3 becomes the active cell.

> **TIP**
>
> When entering text in a range of cells, you can press Tab to move from cell to cell horizontally and Enter to move from cell to cell vertically. When you reach the end of a column within a range, pressing Enter will take you to the cell at the top of the next column in the range.

4 Type **45122**, and press Enter.

The number is entered in cell D3, and D4 becomes the active cell.

FIGURE 1-13

Entering a range of data

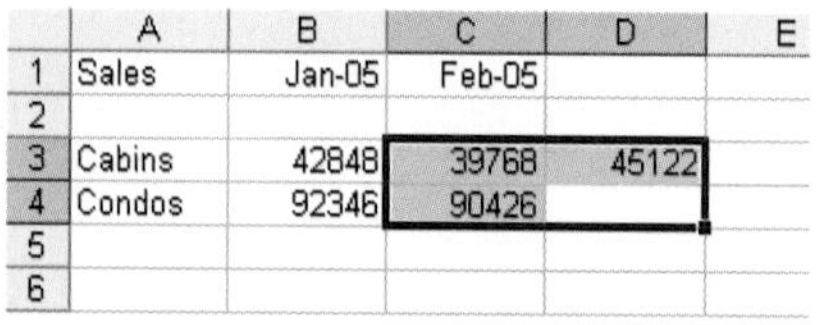

	A	B	C	D	E
1	Sales	Jan-05	Feb-05		
2					
3	Cabins	42848	39768	45122	
4	Condos	92346	90426		
5					
6					

5 Type **87409**, and press Enter.

The number is entered, and cell C3 becomes the active cell.

◆ **Keep this file open for the next exercise.**

QUICK REFERENCE ▼

Enter data in a range of cells

1 Select the range of cells.

2 Type the data in one of the cells, and press Enter.

3 Continue typing data and pressing Enter until the range of cells is filled.

QUICK CHECK

Q. Which key do you press to move from cell to cell horizontally when entering data in a range of cells?

A: You press the Tab key.

Editing Cell Contents

THE BOTTOM LINE

Once you've entered values in a worksheet, you might want to delete them, add to them, or change them completely. Worksheets are not static, which makes it easy to correct a mistake or edit cell contents.

Checking and Correcting Data

After you have entered data in a cell, you can easily change the contents of the cell. However, you must first double-click the cell or click the cell and click in the Formula bar. Either of these actions puts Excel in Edit mode, which you can verify by checking that the word *Edit* appears in the status bar. After that, you type and press the Delete or Backspace key to edit the data in the cell. When Excel is in Edit mode, two buttons appear to the left of the Formula bar: Cancel and Enter.

FIGURE 1-14

Edit mode buttons on the Formula bar

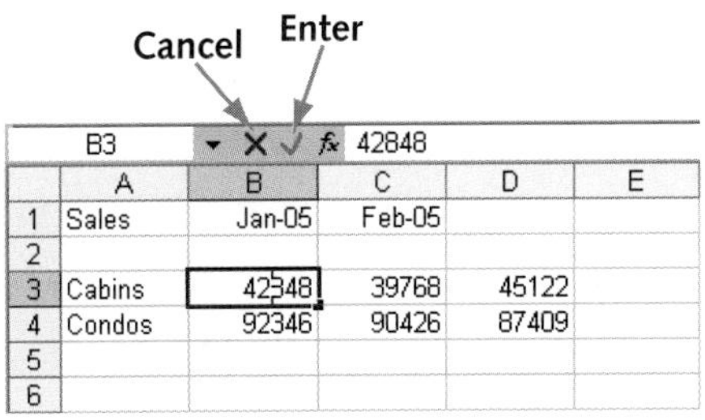

Cancel   Enter

B3	▾ ✗ ✓	*fx* 42848		
	A	B	C	D	E
1	Sales	Jan-05	Feb-05		
2					
3	Cabins	42848	39768	45122	
4	Condos	92346	90426	87409	
5					
6					

You can click the Cancel button or press the Esc key to cancel an entry before it is actually entered in the worksheet. Doing either of these deletes anything you have typed and brings Excel out of Edit mode. It also restores the previous contents of the active cell if that cell contained data. You can click the Enter button to complete an entry.

Revise entries in the current worksheet

In this exercise, you make changes to some of the entries in the current worksheet.

1 **Click cell B3, position the mouse pointer between 2 and 8 in the Formula bar, and click.**

Edit mode is activated, and the insertion point appears as an I-beam.

2 **Press Backspace, type 6, and press Enter.**

Cell B3 now contains the entry 46848.

ANOTHER METHOD

When you click a cell and then press F2, Edit mode is activated and the insertion point is placed at the end of the cell, allowing you to edit the current contents.

3 **Click cell C4, type 92313, and press Enter.**

Cell C4 now contains the entry 92313.

4 **Click cell C3, type 65452, and click the Cancel button on the Formula bar.**

The data entry is canceled, and the original value is restored.

◆ **Keep this file open for the next exercise.**

QUICK CHECK

Q. List three methods for editing the value in a cell.

A: **You can click the cell and type the new value, you can double-click the cell and edit directly in the cell, or you can click the cell and edit the value in the Formula bar.**

QUICK REFERENCE ▼

Edit the contents of a cell

1 Double-click the cell.

2 Edit the data by deleting, inserting, and replacing characters.

Moving between Worksheets

THE BOTTOM LINE

Often the workbooks you create will contain a number of worksheets. You can easily move between worksheets by clicking their sheet tabs at the bottom of the worksheet window.

As explained at the beginning of this lesson, each Excel workbook is made up of individual worksheets. This gives you the flexibility to group worksheets with similar subject matter together in one workbook. By default, a new workbook contains three blank worksheets. More worksheets can be added as needed, and unused worksheets can be deleted if desired. The names of the sheets appear in tabs along the bottom of the workbook window.

FIGURE 1-15

Sheet tabs

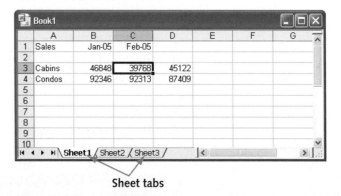

Sheet tabs

View two worksheets within the same workbook

You have learned how to move around in a worksheet. Now you will learn how to move between different worksheets within the same workbook.

1 **Click the Sheet2 tab at the bottom of the workbook window.**

Sheet2 and its contents appear. The worksheet is blank.

2 **Click the Sheet1 tab at the bottom of the workbook window.**

Sheet1 and its contents reappear.

◆ **Keep this file open for the next exercise.**

TIP

Right-click a sheet tab to display a shortcut menu that allows you to, among other options, insert or delete worksheets.

QUICK REFERENCE ▼

Move to another worksheet in the same workbook

Click the sheet tab for the worksheet.

QUICK CHECK

Q. What is the default name of the first work-sheet in a workbook?

A: The default name is Sheet1.

Naming and Saving a Workbook

THE BOTTOM LINE

Like any data you enter in a computer file, you'll want to save your workbook files so that you can work with them later. Excel allows you to save workbooks in a variety of formats so that they can be opened and used in different spreadsheet programs and even in non-spreadsheet programs, such as in Microsoft Word and Access and on the Web.

Saving Changes to an Existing Workbook

When you finish entering and editing data in a workbook, you need to name and save the workbook on your hard disk so that the information will be available the next time you start your computer. Saving workbook files is similar to saving other types of files in Windows programs. The first time you save a workbook, you need to name it and specify in which folder you want to save it. You can save it in a folder on your computer's hard disk or, if your computer is connected to a network, on a hard disk in a different computer. You can even create a folder in which to save the workbook by using tools within Excel. After you've saved a workbook, you just click the Save button on the Standard toolbar to save any changes you made after the last time you saved. The workbook will be saved with the same name and in the same place.

When you want to save the workbook with a different name or in a different folder, you make those changes by performing the same steps that you performed when you saved the workbook for the first time. As with any other Windows file, a workbook's name can be up to 255 characters long, but it can't contain any of the following characters:

/ \ > < * ? " | : ;

You can also use the controls in the Save As dialog box to specify a different format for the new file. For example, you might need to save an Excel file in a different format so that you can share the file with another person who uses a different spreadsheet program, such as Lotus, or even for use in a non-spreadsheet program.

TIP

The Places bar in the Open and Save As dialog boxes gives you convenient access to files stored in your My Documents folder, in your Favorites folder, and on your desktop. The History folder on the Places bar also provides easy access to recently opened workbooks.

Save a workbook to a folder, and save a workbook as a Lotus file

In this exercise, you save your workbook into a folder you create within Excel. You also save the workbook as a Lotus file.

1 **On the File menu, click Save As.**

Excel displays the Save As dialog box. The files and folders that appear in this dialog box will depend on the folder that was last used to save a workbook on your computer.

FIGURE 1-16

Save As dialog box

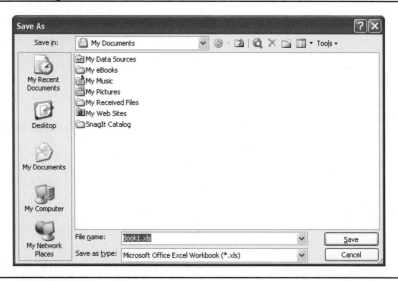

2 **Click the Save In down arrow, and click the icon for your local hard disk (probably drive C).**

3 **Double-click the Excel Practice folder.**

 4 **Click the Create New Folder button in the dialog box.**

The New Folder dialog box appears.

5 **Type 2005 Sales, and click OK.**

The New Folder dialog box closes, and the Save As dialog box displays the 2005 Sales folder. The name Book1 appears in the File Name text box because Book1 is the open file.

ANOTHER METHOD

You can also create folders using Windows Explorer. You don't need to create them within Excel.

6 Select the text in the File Name text box, type Lodging Sales, and then click Save.

The file is named and saved.

7 On the File menu, click Save As.

8 In the Save As dialog box, click the down arrow in the Save As Type text box.

9 Scroll and select the WK4(1-2-3)(*.wk4) option.

10 Click Save.

A message box appears explaining that there may be some features in your file that are not supported in the format you have chosen.

11 Click Yes in the message box.

Your file is now saved with the same name but as a Lotus spreadsheet, so it has a different file name extension.

◆ Close Lodging Sales.wk4. Leave Excel open for the next exercise.

QUICK REFERENCE ▼

Create a folder

1 On the File menu, click Save As.

2 Navigate to the location where you want to create the folder.

3 Click the Create New Folder button in the Save As dialog box.

4 In the New Folder dialog box, type a name for the folder in the Name Box and click OK.

QUICK CHECK

Q. How many characters can be in the file name for a workbook?

A: A file name can have up to 255 characters.

Opening a Workbook

THE BOTTOM LINE

After you save an Excel workbook, you can reopen it at any time to review its contents and make changes.

Once you've saved a workbook to disk, you can open it in a number of ways. You can click the Open button or select Open on the File menu and then select the file from the Open dialog box. Or you can open it from the Getting Started task pane. If the workbook is one of the last four you've worked on, it will be listed at the bottom of the File menu, and all you need to do is click it to open it.

Open an existing workbook

You have learned how to create a new blank workbook. Now you will learn how to open an existing workbook.

1 **On the Standard toolbar, click the Open button.**

The Open dialog box appears.

ANOTHER METHOD

- Click Open on the File menu.
- Press Ctrl+O.

2 **Click the Look In down arrow, click the icon for your hard disk, and double-click the Excel Practice folder.**

The contents of the Excel Practice folder appear in the Open dialog box.

FIGURE 1-17

Opening an existing workbook

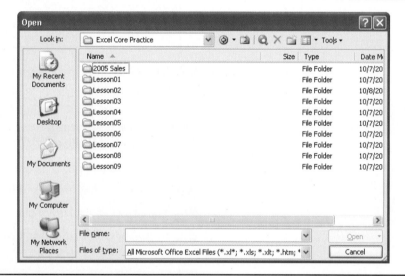

3 **Double-click the Lesson01 folder.**

The names of the files stored in the Lesson01 folder appear.

TIP

If you open an existing workbook, Excel closes the blank Book1 workbook that appeared when you started the program.

4 **Click the Employee Information file, and click Open.**

The Open dialog box closes, and the Employee Information file appears.

Double-click the Excel icon next to the file name in the Open dialog box.

5 **On the File menu, click Close.**

Excel closes the Employee Information workbook.

Click the workbook's Close Window button.

6 **Click File on the menu bar.**

Excel displays a list of recently opened workbooks at the bottom of the File menu.

7 **On the File menu, click Employee Information.**

The file opens.

◆ **Keep this file open for the next exercise.**

QUICK REFERENCE ▼

Open a previously created workbook

1 On the File menu, click Open.

Or

Click More on the Getting Started task pane.

2 Browse to the location of the file.

3 Click the file name.

4 Click Open.

QUICK CHECK

Q. What methods can you use to open an existing workbook?

A: You can click the Open button, select Open on the File menu, click More in the Getting Started task pane, or press Ctrl+O to display the Open dialog box (where you can navigate to and open the desired workbook). If the workbook is one of the four most recent that you worked on, it will be listed at the bottom of the File menu and in the Open section of the Getting Started task pane. All you need to do is click it to open it.

Renaming a Worksheet

THE BOTTOM LINE

In workbooks that contain more than one worksheet with data, you'll probably want to assign names to the sheets that help identify the data that's on them.

Making Workbooks Easier to Work With

By default, the worksheets in each Excel workbook are named Sheet1, Sheet2, and Sheet3. Just as giving a unique name to your workbook helps you remember what is in it, renaming a worksheet can remind you of its contents. For example, a chain of restaurants might have a budget workbook that contains a worksheet for each restaurant location. The sheets are named according to location.

Rename a worksheet

In this exercise, you give a worksheet a different name.

1 **Double-click the Sheet1 sheet tab.**

Sheet1 is selected within the tab.

2 **Type Directory, and press Enter.**

Directory appears on the sheet tab.

◆ **Keep this file open for the next exercise.**

Right-click a sheet tab, and then click Rename.

QUICK REFERENCE ▼

Rename a worksheet within a workbook

1 Double-click the sheet tab at the bottom of the worksheet.

2 Type a new name, and press Enter.

Q. Why would you want to rename a worksheet?

A: You would rename a worksheet to more easily identify the data that it contains.

Previewing and Printing a Worksheet

THE BOTTOM LINE

You can see how a worksheet looks before printing it by displaying it in the Print Preview window. Previewing the worksheet can help you spot formatting inconsistencies and irregular page breaks, which you can then correct before printing. Having a printout of a worksheet can also help you identify errors or formatting problems, but it's also useful when you want to distribute copies to people who don't have access to the electronic file.

After a worksheet is complete, you can preview and print its contents. To print a worksheet, you begin by displaying the Print dialog box. In this dialog box, you can change most print settings, preview the data, and print the worksheet.

You should check the spelling in a worksheet before printing it. Click the Spelling button on the Standard toolbar to begin checking the worksheet.

Also, before printing a worksheet, you can preview it. The **Print Preview** window, shown in Figure 1-18, displays a full-page view of the file just as it will be printed so that you can check the format and overall layout before actually printing.

FIGURE 1-18

Print Preview window

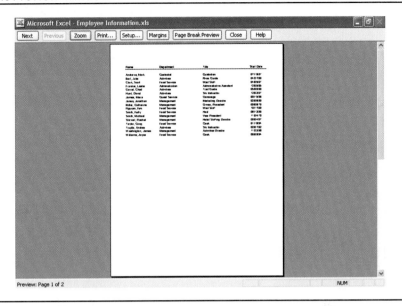

Commands available in the Print Preview window appear as buttons across the top of the window. The current page number and total number of pages in the worksheet appear in the bottom left corner of the window.

Printing Worksheets

When you're ready to print, you can decide to print the entire workbook, a single sheet in a workbook, or just a selected range of data. You can select the range of cells you want to print before displaying the Print dialog box, or you can specify the range you want to print in the Print dialog box.

Preview and print the current worksheet

Now that you've entered data in a worksheet and saved it, you'll preview and print it.

1 Click the Print Preview button on the Standard toolbar.

The file appears in the Print Preview window.

ANOTHER METHOD

Click Print Preview on the File menu.

2 Click anywhere in the worksheet.

The zoom factor is increased, and the preview is enlarged.

3 Click anywhere in the worksheet again.

The zoom factor is decreased, and the preview is reduced.

TIP

To print a file from the Print Preview window, click Print on the Print Preview toolbar to display the Print dialog box.

4 **Click the Close button on the Print Preview toolbar.**

The Print Preview window closes.

5 **On the File menu, click Print.**

The Print dialog box appears.

ANOTHER METHOD

Press Ctrl+P.

6 **Click OK.**

The current worksheet is printed.

7 **Click the Save button on the Standard toolbar.**

The worksheet is saved using the current name.

ANOTHER METHOD

Click Save on the File menu.

◆ **Keep this file open for the next exercise.**

IMPORTANT

The Close button above the Close Window button is used to quit Excel. Be careful not to click Close instead of Close Window. When you're not sure which button to click, position the mouse pointer over the button for a moment. A ScreenTip will appear, telling you the name of the button on which the mouse pointer is positioned.

QUICK REFERENCE ▼

Preview and print a worksheet

1 Click the Print Preview button on the Standard toolbar.

2 On the File menu, click Print.

Or

Press Ctrl+P to open the Print dialog box.

3 Make selections as desired, and click OK.

QUICK CHECK

Q. When you are in the Print Preview window, which button do you click to return to Normal view?

A: You click the Close button.

Closing a Workbook and Quitting Excel

THE BOTTOM LINE

When you are done working in a file, you should close it to keep your taskbar and desktop uncluttered. This also helps eliminate the possibility of someone else making unwanted changes to the file.

You can remove a workbook from the window by closing the workbook or by quitting Excel. Closing the current workbook leaves Excel running, while closing quits the Excel program.

After a workbook is saved on your hard disk, you can clear it from the screen by closing the workbook window. If the workbook has not been saved, Excel will prompt you to save it before closing the window. When you have finished using Excel, you need to close it using Excel commands. Do not turn off your computer while a program is running.

QUICK CHECK

Q: Which command on the File menu would you use if you wanted to close multiple workbooks at the same time?

A: **You would use the Close All command.**

TIP

To close all open workbooks at once, hold down the Shift key and then click Close All on the File menu.

Close a workbook, and quit Excel

In this exercise, you close a workbook and quit Excel.

1 **Click the Close Window button in the top right corner of the workbook window.**

The workbook closes.

2 **Click the Close button in the top right corner of the Excel window.**

Excel closes.

ANOTHER METHOD

Click Exit on the File menu.

◆ **If you are continuing to other lessons, restart Excel.**

Key Points

✔ *Excel is a powerful spreadsheet program you use to organize and calculate data.*

✔ *Before you can enter data or make modifications to it, you must first select the cell or range containing the data.*

✔ *You enter data in a worksheet by simply typing in the selected cell. Often you will want to make changes to the data you enter. All you need to do is select the cell and type your changes directly in the cell or in the Formula bar.*

✔ *You will likely enter data on a number of worksheets within a workbook. You can switch to a different sheet by clicking its sheet tab.*

✔ *As with just about any computer file, you will want to save a workbook to disk so that you can open it and work with it again.*

✔ *In workbooks that have more than one worksheet containing data, you should name the worksheets so that you can easily identify the data that they contain. You also might want to print individual worksheets so that you can review a hard-copy printout of data or distribute them to others to review.*

Quick Quiz

True/False

T F **1.** You can move between worksheets by clicking the scroll arrows.

T F **2.** You can create a workbook from templates that are stored on your computer or from templates you find online.

T F **3.** By default, a new workbook contains three worksheets.

T F **4.** The title bar contains the names of Excel's menus.

T F **5.** The columns in a worksheet are identified by numbers.

T F **6.** You cannot print a worksheet while in the Print Preview window.

Multiple Choice

1. Which key can you press to put Excel in Edit mode?
   a. Esc
   b. F1
   c. F2
   d. F3

2. How is the active cell in a worksheet identified?
   a. It has a black border surrounding it.
   b. It is white, while the rest of the cells are gray.
   c. It is shaded in orange.
   d. It is shaded in black.

3. Which element in the Excel window displays information about a selected command?
   a. Formula bar
   b. horizontal scroll bar
   c. Name Box
   d. status bar

4. Which element in the Excel window displays the contents of the active cell?
   a. Formula bar
   b. horizontal scroll bar
   c. Name Box
   d. status bar

Short Answer

1. How can you select all cells in a worksheet simultaneously?

2. How can you open an existing workbook?

3. What is the easiest way to enter data in a range of cells?

4. How can you rename a worksheet?

5. How can you close all open workbooks at once?

6. What are two ways to select a range of cells?

7. How can you select nonadjacent ranges of cells?

8. What's the difference between clicking New on the File menu and clicking the New button?

9. What are three characters that can't be used in the name of a workbook?

10. What information does the Name Box display?

IMPORTANT

In the On Your Own section below, you must complete Exercise 1 before continuing to Exercise 2.

On Your Own

Exercise 1

Create a workbook named **MyFirst**. In cells B1, C1, and D1, type the names and years of the next three months, such as **July 2004, August 2005**, and **September 2005**. Select the range B2:D3, and enter numbers in the cells.

Exercise 2

Click cell C3, and use the Formula bar to change the number in the cell. Rename Sheet1 **MyFirstSheet**. Select column B, and then select row 5. Simultaneously select the ranges B1:D2 and B5:D7. Preview your worksheet, print it, and save it.

One Step Further

Exercise 1

This lesson discussed the fact that Excel provides a number of predesigned templates for your use. Open the Loan Amortization template (in the Spreadsheet Solutions templates), and give a brief description of its purpose. If you don't have the Loan Amortization template, open another one. Enter data in the worksheet to explore how the spreadsheet works. How would a template like this be useful to you?

Exercise 2

You may have noticed in the Templates section of the New Worksheet task pane that there are two other sources of templates besides those that were installed on your computer with the Excel application. One is Web sites that you may learn of, and the other is Microsoft's Web site. If you have Internet access, click the Templates on Office Online option and explore the templates available there. (*Hint:* You may wish to explore the templates that deal with your personal interests and hobbies.)

Exercise 3

In this lesson, you learned how to select a range of cells. Use the Ask A Question box to find out how to deselect some portion in a range without deselecting the entire range and reselecting the desired cells.

LESSON 2

Editing and Formatting Worksheets

After completing this lesson, you will be able to:

✔ Format numeric data.
✔ Adjust the size of rows and columns.
✔ Align cell contents.
✔ Find and replace cell contents.
✔ Insert and delete cells, rows, and columns.
✔ Cut, copy, paste, and clear cells.
✔ Use additional paste techniques.

KEY TERMS

- clear
- collect and paste
- column width
- copy
- cut
- Office Clipboard
- paste
- Paste Special
- points
- row height
- string

Microsoft Excel provides tools that give you great flexibility in changing the appearance of your data and the structure of your worksheets. With a little effort, you can adjust spacing, alignment, and the look of type to make a worksheet easier to view, follow, and update; they're easier for others to use, too.

You can change the way numbers are displayed so that their appearance corresponds with the type of numbers you are using. For instance, if you enter sales amounts in a worksheet, you can format them so that they look like monetary values. That is, if you enter *1455* in a worksheet, you can format this number so that it appears as *$1,455*.

You can also change the width of columns so that the data in the column fits appropriately, and you can increase the height of a particular row to call attention to the data in the row. As you work with worksheets, you'll often find that you must move or copy data to other locations—a feature that is easy to perform in Excel. In fact, Excel provides numerous techniques you can use to copy or move data to a different location in a worksheet or even to a different worksheet.

You can also use Excel to look for specific data in a worksheet and then display the cell where the data appears. When you want to replace data with different data, Excel provides a way to automate this process as well.

Formatting Numbers

Making Numbers
Easier to Read

THE BOTTOM LINE

Numeric values can be used for various types of data—currency, percentages, decimals, and more. Applying accurate formatting to numeric data makes it more useful and easier to interpret and analyze.

Most of the data that you use in Excel is numeric. This data includes financial figures, dates, fractions, percentages, and other information that usually appears with a mix of numerals and symbols. To be more meaningful, most numeric data needs some special touches—a dollar sign, a certain number of decimal places, or a percent sign, for example.

At a resort hotel, for example, the bookkeeper tracks room sales collected per week. She wants the sales amounts to look like monetary amounts; for example, $53.00, not just 53. In entering the sales amounts, she could type a dollar sign, followed by the number of dollars, followed by a decimal point, followed by the number of cents. But she knows that it's much easier to enter the raw sales amounts and let Excel add these currency formats.

To quickly change how your numeric data appears, you can select one of Excel's options for formatting numbers, either before or after you enter the number in the cell. These options automatically insert and delete symbols and digits to reflect the format you choose. By default, all data you enter is formatted with the General option, which shows the data exactly as you enter it. If you include a date or a special character ($ % / , E e) when entering a number, Excel automatically formats it with the appropriate option. When you want entries to appear differently, you can choose from the following formats, organized by category.

Category	Appearance	If You Type	It Looks Like
General	Displays data exactly as you enter it	1234	1234
Number	Displays two decimal places by default	1234	1234.00
Currency	Displays currency and other symbols appropriate for various regions of the world (including the euro)	1234	$1,234.00
Accounting	Displays currency symbols and aligns decimal points of entries in a column	1234 12	$1,234.00 $12.00
Date	Displays days, months, and years in various formats, such as *May 18, 2005, 18-May,* and *3/14/2001*	1234	May 18, 1903 18-May 5/18/1903
Time	Displays hours, minutes, and seconds in various formats, such as *8:47 PM, 20:47,* and *8:47:56*	12:34	12:34 AM 12:34 12:34:00
Percentage	Multiplies cell values by 100 and displays the result with a percent sign	1234	123400.00%
Fraction	Displays entries as fractions in various denominations and to various degrees of accuracy	12.34	12 1/3
Scientific	Displays entries in scientific or exponential notation	1234	1.23E+03
Text	Displays entries exactly as they were entered, even if the entry is a number	1234	1234
Special	Displays and formats list and database values, such as Zip Codes, phone numbers, and U.S. Social Security numbers	12345 123-555-1234 000-00-0000	12345 123-555-1234 000-00-0000
Custom	Allows you to create formats that aren't available in any of the other categories		Appearance varies based on format you create

After you choose an option, you might need to further specify how you want the numbers to appear; for example, you can choose how many decimal places to use, select international currency symbols, and set the format for negative numbers.

◆ To complete the procedures in this lesson, you must use the practice files Percent Sales Increase, Five Years Sales02, Rentals, and Monthly Sales in the Lesson02 folder in the Excel Practice folder that is located on your hard disk.

◆ Open Percent Sales Increase from the Excel Practice/Lesson02 folder.

Format several numeric entries in a worksheet

In this exercise, you apply formats to raw numeric data that's already been entered.

1 **Make sure that cell A1 is currently selected, and on the Format menu, click Cells.**

The Format Cells dialog box appears.

ANOTHER METHOD

- Press Ctrl+1.
- Right-click a cell, and choose Format Cells on the shortcut menu.

2 **Click the Number tab, if necessary, and in the Category list, click Date.**

The Number tab is displayed, and the Type list is filled with options for formatting dates.

FIGURE 2-1

Number tab in the Format Cells dialog box

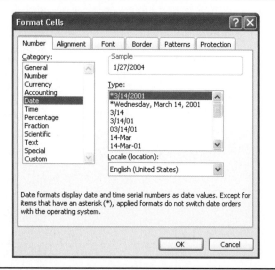

3 **In the Type list, click 3/14/01, and click OK.**

The date in cell A1 changes to match the date format that you selected.

4 **Select the range B3:F8.**

5 **On the Format menu, click Cells, and then click Currency in the Category list.**

The Format Cells dialog box appears with formatting options for Currency (monetary values) shown. Notice that the default format for currency includes the dollar sign ($), a thousands comma separator, and two decimal places.

FIGURE 2-2

Currency formats

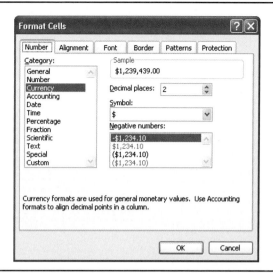

IMPORTANT

Make sure that you type a zero at step 6, *not* the letter O.

6 **Double-click in the Decimal places box, type 0, and press Enter.**

The selected cells are now in currency format, with no decimal places.

7 **Select the range C10:F10.**

8 **On the Format menu, click Cells, and then click Percentage in the Category list.**

The Format Cells dialog box appears with Percentage selected, and the dialog box shows the sample format for the first cell in the selected range. The only option you can change for the percentage format is the number of decimal places.

FIGURE 2-3

Applying the Percentage format

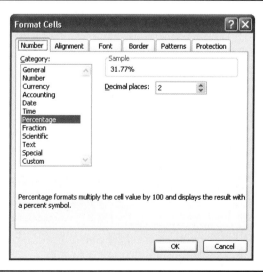

9 Click OK.

The selected cells appear in percentage format, with two decimal places.

10 Click any blank cell in the worksheet.

The selected range is deselected. The worksheet looks similar to that shown in Figure 2-4.

FIGURE 2-4

Applying number formats to data

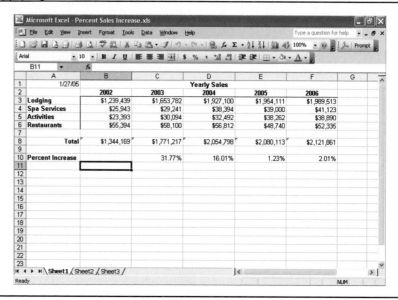

ANOTHER METHOD

You can also use the Formatting toolbar to specify some of the more widely used number formats. Lesson 3, "Formatting Cells," explains how to use the Formatting toolbar to format numbers.

11 On the File menu, click Save.

ANOTHER METHOD

- Click the Save button on the Standard toolbar.
- Press Ctrl+S.

◆ Close Percent Sales Increase, and leave Excel open for the next exercise.

QUICK REFERENCE ▼

Format numeric entries in a worksheet

1 Select the cell or cells to be formatted.

2 On the Format menu, click Cells; or right-click the selection and click Format Cells on the shortcut menu.

3 Click the Number tab, if necessary.

4 Select the formatting options you want.

5 Click OK.

Adjusting the Size of Rows and Columns

Making Data Easier to Read

THE BOTTOM LINE

Modifying column width and row height can make a worksheet's contents easier to read and work with.

Although a cell entry can include up to 32,000 characters, the default **column width** is only 8.43 characters. For some number formats, when you enter a value that won't fit within the default column width, the number "spills over" into the next column. For other number formats, a number that won't fit within a column is displayed as a series of pound signs (######), indicating that the number is too long for the current column width. For example, as shown in Figure 2-5, when the bookkeeper for Adventure Works enters a sales amount for *Lodging* in currency format, the number appears in the cell as a series of pound signs because the total, $1,239,439, is 10 characters wide—too large to fit within the default column width of 8.43 characters.

FIGURE 2-5

Entries that are too long for the column width

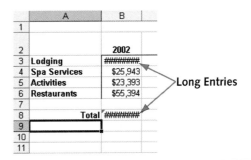

When a number appears as a series of pound symbols, it doesn't affect the value that is stored internally; you can view any of these entries by selecting the cell and looking at the value displayed in the Formula bar or by simply widening the column so that entries appear in full and as entered.

On the other hand, at times, the default column width will be wider than you need it to be. For instance, the bookkeeper at Adventure Works creates a column that stores only Yes or No entries for each sales amount, indicating whether the actual sales amount met or exceeded the projected amount. In this case, the column width doesn't need to be 8.43 characters—three or four characters would probably be wide enough. By reducing the width of the column, you can view more columns on your screen at a time.

Excel provides three methods for adjusting column width:

- You can use the Column Width dialog box (available on the Format menu) to enter the character width that you want.
- You can drag the right edge of the column selector to the right or to the left to increase or decrease the column width. When you position the mouse pointer on the right edge of a column selector, a resize pointer appears, indicating that you can resize the column. For instance, when you click the right edge of the column selector for column G and drag the selector to the right, the column is widened as you drag, as shown in Figure 2-6. As you drag, the width of the column in characters and pixels appears in a yellow ScreenTip above the column selector. Similarly, when you drag the column selector to the left, the column is narrowed as you drag.

FIGURE 2-6

Resizing a column

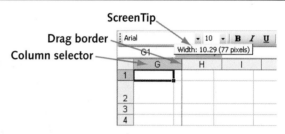

- You can automatically adjust a column to fit the longest entry in the column by double-clicking the right edge of a column selector.

ANOTHER METHOD

You can also click AutoFit Selection (on the Column submenu on the Format menu) to adjust the column width to accommodate the entry in the active cell or the longest entry in a selected range.

You can also adjust the **row height** for a particular row by using the same basic methods. That is, you can use the Row Height dialog box (also available from the Format menu) to specify the height of a row in **points.** One point is equal to 1/72 inch. So a row height of 12 points is equal to 1/6 inch. You can also change the height of a row by clicking the bottom of the row selector and dragging it up or down.

FIGURE 2-7

Resizing a row

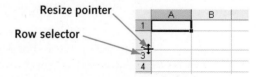

You might want to adjust row height to accommodate larger characters, such as a worksheet title or row headings that appear in larger type. However, it is more common to adjust column width to account for lengthy or short labels or numbers.

◆ **Open Five Year Sales02 from the Excel Practice/Lesson02 folder.**

Resize columns and rows

In this exercise, you resize columns and rows. For this exercise, the width of columns in the practice file has been preset to 15 characters.

1 **Select the range B4:F4. On the Format menu, point to Column, and then click Width.**

The Column Width dialog box appears, showing the current column width.

FIGURE 2-8

Column Width dialog box

ANOTHER METHOD

Drag the right border of one of the column selectors in the selected range to the desired width.

TIP

To specify a standard width for all columns in a workbook, on the Format menu, point to Column, and click Standard Width. Type the desired width, and click OK.

2 **Type 13 in the Column Width text box, and click OK.**

The width of columns B through F decreases from 15 characters to 13 characters.

3 **Click any cell.**

The range B4:F4 is no longer selected.

4 **Point to the bottom of the row selector for row 2.**

The mouse pointer changes to a double-headed arrow—the resize pointer—as shown below.

5 **Drag the row selector down until the row has a height of about 20.25 points (27 pixels, or screen picture elements). Use the ScreenTip to achieve the exact height.**

The height of row 2 increases.

FIGURE 2-9

Increasing the height of a row

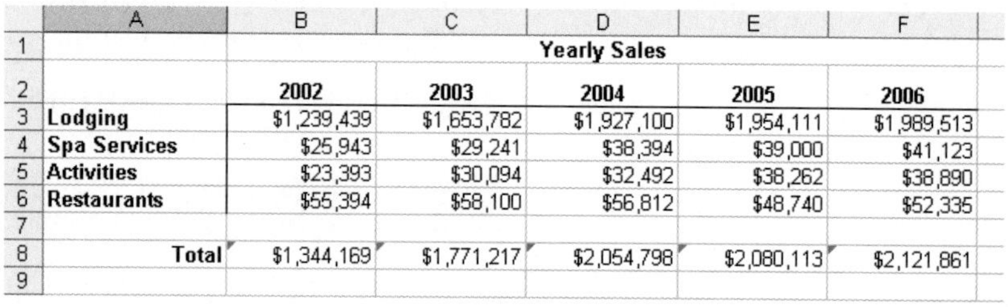

	A	B	C	D	E	F
1				Yearly Sales		
2		2002	2003	2004	2005	2006
3	Lodging	$1,239,439	$1,653,782	$1,927,100	$1,954,111	$1,989,513
4	Spa Services	$25,943	$29,241	$38,394	$39,000	$41,123
5	Activities	$23,393	$30,094	$32,492	$38,262	$38,890
6	Restaurants	$55,394	$58,100	$56,812	$48,740	$52,335
7						
8	Total	$1,344,169	$1,771,217	$2,054,798	$2,080,113	$2,121,861
9						

ANOTHER METHOD

Select the row, open the Format menu, click Row, click Height, and enter the desired height in the Row Height dialog box.

6 **Point to the right edge of the column selector for column D.**

The mouse pointer changes to a double-headed arrow.

7 **Double-click the right edge of the column selector for column D.**

The width of column D decreases to better fit the column contents.

FIGURE 2-10

Decreasing the width of a column

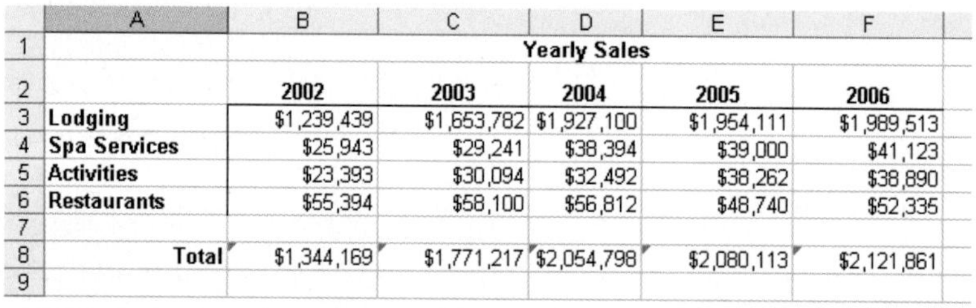

	A	B	C	D	E	F
1				Yearly Sales		
2		2002	2003	2004	2005	2006
3	Lodging	$1,239,439	$1,653,782	$1,927,100	$1,954,111	$1,989,513
4	Spa Services	$25,943	$29,241	$38,394	$39,000	$41,123
5	Activities	$23,393	$30,094	$32,492	$38,262	$38,890
6	Restaurants	$55,394	$58,100	$56,812	$48,740	$52,335
7						
8	Total	$1,344,169	$1,771,217	$2,054,798	$2,080,113	$2,121,861
9						

◆ **Keep this file open for the next exercise.**

QUICK REFERENCE ▼

Adjust the size of a column or row

1 Position the mouse pointer on the right border of the column selector or on the bottom border of the row selector.

2 Drag the border to the desired width.

Or

Double-click the right border of the column selector or the bottom border of the row selector to adjust the size to match the longest or largest entry.

Adjust the size of multiple columns or multiple rows

1 Select at least one cell from each column or at least one cell from each row.

2 On the Format menu, point to Column, and click Width, or point to Row, and click Height.

3 Type the new width in the Column Width box or the new height in the Row Height box.

4 Click OK.

Aligning Cell Contents

THE BOTTOM LINE

Text entries are normally aligned to the left, and numeric entries are normally aligned to the right. Proper alignment of data enhances readability and ensures that the data conforms to customary standards of displaying data (i.e., aligning decimal points in entries that are used for accounting purposes).

In addition to formatting numbers, you can also change the way they align relative to the edges of cells. You can change the horizontal alignment of selected cells to the left, right, or center. Text entries are normally left-aligned horizontally in a cell, meaning the first character in the cell appears next to the left edge of the cell. Numeric entries are normally right-aligned, meaning the last character in the cell appears next to the right edge of the cell. In a center-aligned cell, the characters in the cell are centered evenly between the left and right edges of the cell. Normally right alignment works best for numbers because all of the numbers in a column are aligned under the same digit positions, as shown in Figure 2-11.

FIGURE 2-11

Numbers aligned right

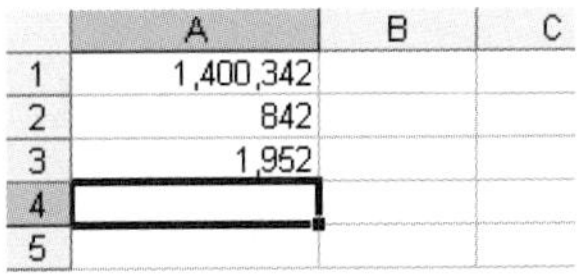

	A	B	C
1	1,400,342		
2	842		
3	1,952		
4			
5			

However, you might want to left-align or center-align numbers to achieve a different effect. For instance, you might want to left-align dates because the digit position of dates is generally not important. Or you might want to center-align numbers to achieve a stylized look. For example, the sales manager at Adventure Works tracks sales for different categories (room charges, gift shop sales, horse stable rentals, kennel charges, and so on) and creates a column that provides a ranking (based on which category has the most sales) for each category. A center-aligned effect can enhance the appearance of the column, as shown in Figure 2-12.

FIGURE 2-12

Centering numeric data

	A	B	C
1		**Ranking**	
2	Kennel	12	
3	Lodging	4	
4	Weight Room	32	
5	Jukebox	101	
6			
7			

You also can change the vertical alignment of cell contents; that is, the way in which a cell entry is positioned between the top and bottom edges of the cell. The default alignment for text and numbers is bottom, which means characters are placed just above the bottom edge of the cell. You can also change the vertical alignment of cells to the top or center. Center alignment often looks good when you want to increase the height of a row to call attention to labels or values stored in the row, but keep the entries centered between the top and bottom of the row.

Align cell contents horizontally and vertically

In this exercise, you set the vertical and horizontal alignment of cell contents. You also use the Undo and Redo buttons to see how changes can be undone and reapplied as desired.

1 **Select the range B3:B6.**

2 **On the Format menu, click Cells.**

The Format Cells dialog box appears.

3 **Click the Alignment tab.**

The Alignment tab appears.

FIGURE 2-13

Alignment tab in the Format Cells dialog box

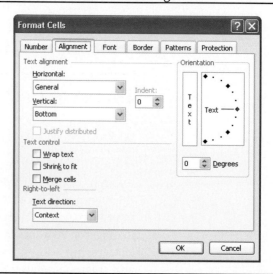

4 **Click the Horizontal down arrow, and click Left (Indent) in the list.**

5 **Click the Vertical down arrow, and view the list choices.**

Choices on the Vertical list let you align the data up and down inside the cell. Vertical alignment becomes more apparent when your rows are significantly taller than the data they contain.

6 **Click the Vertical down arrow again to close the list without changing the vertical alignment.**

7 **Click OK.**

The contents of the selected cells are aligned to the left.

8 **On the Standard toolbar, click the Undo button.**

Excel returns the cells to their previous formatting.

> **ANOTHER METHOD**
>
> - Select Undo on the Edit menu.
> - Press Ctrl+Z.

9 **On the Standard toolbar, click the Redo button.**

Excel reapplies the cell formatting.

> **ANOTHER METHOD**
>
> - Select Redo on the Edit menu.
> - Press Ctrl+Y.

10 **On the Standard toolbar, click the Undo button.**

Excel undoes the cell formatting again.

11 **Click the Save button on the Standard toolbar.**

> **ANOTHER METHOD**
>
> - Click Save on the File menu.
> - Press Ctrl+S.

◆ **Close Five Year Sales02. Leave Excel open for the next exercise.**

> **IMPORTANT**
>
> Once you save a workbook, you can no longer undo or redo changes. If you think you might want to undo or redo a particular action, don't save changes to the workbook until you are satisfied with the results.

QUICK CHECK

Q: In what three ways can data be horizontally aligned within a cell?

A: **Data can be left-, right-, or center-aligned.**

QUICK REFERENCE ▼

Align one or more cell entries

1 Select the cell or cells to be aligned.

2 On the Format menu, click Cells.

3 Click the Alignment tab.

4 Click the Horizontal or Vertical down arrow, and choose options from the lists.

5 Click OK.

Finding and Replacing Cell Contents

THE BOTTOM LINE

The Find and Replace options let you locate specified data quickly and, if necessary, replace it with different data. These features are most effective in large worksheets in which all of the data is not visible on the screen, thus saving you the time of scanning through vast amounts of data to find what you're looking for.

A single worksheet can contain more than 65,000 rows and 256 columns. You probably won't work with too many worksheets that have data in all of the rows and columns, but you likely will use worksheets in which the content of some rows or columns do not fit on one screen. You can use Excel's Find and Replace features to find data and, if desired, replace it with different data.

Finding Data

If you want to locate a particular item of data that isn't immediately visible—for example, you might want to search a list of several hundred employees to find those who are in the Accounting Department—you can scan the worksheet visually to look for the item. A much easier and quicker way, though, is to use the Find tab of the Find And Replace dialog box. When you enter the text or number that you want to find, Excel locates the first occurrence of this search **string**. A string is any sequence of letters or numbers that you type. When the first entry found isn't the one you want, you can continue to the next entry.

◆ **Open Rentals from the Excel Practice/Lesson02 folder.**

Find text

In this exercise, you find a word in a worksheet.

1 On the Edit menu, click Find.

The Find And Replace dialog box appears.

ANOTHER METHOD

Press Ctrl+F.

2 Click the Options button, if necessary, to expand the dialog box.

FIGURE 2-14

Find And Replace dialog box

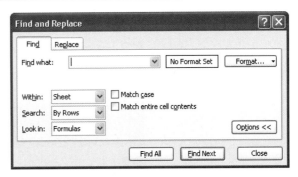

3 In the Find What text box, type Ski.

TIP

It does not matter which cell is currently the active cell. If you don't select a range of cells, Excel will search the entire worksheet.

2 Click the Search down arrow, and, if necessary, click By Rows.

Excel will search across successive rows rather than down successive columns.

5 Click the Look In down arrow, and click Values.

Excel will search cells for values rather than formulas.

TROUBLESHOOTING

If you are searching for a value—either text or numeric—rather than a formula, make sure you click Values in the Look In box. If Formulas is currently selected in the Look In box and you want to find a value, the search will not locate any matches. You will learn about formulas in Lesson 7.

6 Click Find Next.

Excel selects the cell that contains the first occurrence of *Ski*.

ANOTHER METHOD

Press Enter.

If you can't see the search results in the worksheet, drag the title bar of the Find And Replace dialog box to move the dialog box out of the way.

7 **Click Find Next.**

Excel selects the cell that contains the next occurrence of *Ski.*

◆ **Leave the Find And Replace dialog box open for the next exercise.**

QUICK REFERENCE ▼

Find occurrences of a specific value in your worksheet

1 Click any cell.

2 On the Edit menu, click Find.

3 In the Find What box, type the value to find.

4 Click the Search down arrow, and choose to search by rows or columns.

5 Click the Look In down arrow, and click Values.

6 Click the Find Next button. You can click the Find Next button until there are no more matches.

Finding and Replacing Formats

You can use a distinctive text format to identify data that you may need to change later or that you want to highlight. For example, in the Rentals workbook, you could apply an italic format to all equipment items that were rented more than 20 times a month. If you wanted to find all of these items, you could use the Find Format dialog box, accessible through the Find And Replace dialog box, to seek out that specific format. In the Find And Replace dialog box, you'd click the Format button, click the Font tab, and select the Italic font

You can narrow the focus of a find operation by selecting the Match Case and Match Entire Cell Contents check boxes in the Find And Replace dialog box. The Match Case check box, when selected, requires that the text in cells match the uppercase and lowercase characters that you enter for the search string. Select the Match Entire Cell Contents check box when you want to specify that the search string be the *only* contents in a cell for it to be considered a match.

Replacing Data

When you edit worksheets, you might need to find a certain character string within the worksheet and replace it with a different character string. For example, the sales manager at Adventure Works wants to change the Rental workbook so that all prices that end with *.95* as the decimal amount are changed to *.99*. (For example, an item that currently rents for $4.95 per hour would now cost $4.99 per hour.) The change doesn't appreciably increase rental costs for visitors, but over time, it can significantly increase the total revenue from rentals.

You can quickly find and replace all or some occurrences of a character string in a worksheet using the Replace tab of the Find And Replace dialog box. Being able to replace data with the click of a button can save you the time of finding occurrences of the data and repeatedly typing replacement data.

Replace data in a worksheet

In this exercise, you find and replace the first occurrence of a search string and then replace every occurrence of a string in the worksheet with a different string.

1 **In the Find And Replace dialog box, click the Replace tab.**

FIGURE 2-15

Replace tab in the Find And Replace dialog box

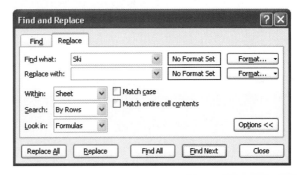

2 **In the Find What text box, replace Ski with .95, and press Tab.**

The search string that you want to locate is entered, and the insertion point is positioned in the Replace With text box.

3 **In the Replace With text box, type .99.**

The contents of the Replace With text box will be used to replace occurrences of the specified search string.

4 **Click the Search down arrow, and click By Columns.**

Excel will search down successive columns rather than across successive rows.

5 **Click Find Next.**

Excel locates the first occurrence of the search string .95.

ANOTHER METHOD

Press Enter.

6 **Click Replace.**

Excel replaces the first occurrence of .95 with .99 and locates the next occurrence of the search string.

7 **Click Replace All.**

Excel replaces all occurrences of *.95* with *.99*—the values in the Price per Rental column.

8 **Click OK to close the message box that tells you how many replacements were made.**

9 **Click Close.**

The Find And Replace dialog box is closed.

10 **On the File menu, click Save As, type** Rentals 2, **and click Save.**

The workbook is saved with the new name.

◆ **Keep this file open for the next exercise.**

TIP

You might wonder why you can't just enter *95* as the search string and *99* as the replacement string—without including the decimal point. If you were to do this, Excel would replace any value in the worksheet that contained *95*, rather than only those values that include the decimal point in front of *95*. For example, if the quantity *95* appeared in any of the Rentals per Month columns, Excel would replace it with *99*, which is not what you want. When you want to replace only the partial contents of a cell, as you do in this exercise, be as specific as possible in entering the search string; otherwise, Excel might make incorrect replacements.

QUICK REFERENCE ▼

Find and replace all occurrences of a specific value in your worksheet

1 Click any cell.

2 On the Edit menu, click Replace.

3 In the Find What box, type the value to find.

4 In the Replace With box, type the new value.

5 Click the Search down arrow, and choose to search by rows or columns.

6 Click Replace All.

7 Click Close.

Inserting and Deleting Cells, Rows, and Columns

THE BOTTOM LINE

You can insert rows or columns in which you want to enter new data, or you can insert rows and columns and leave them blank to enhance the appearance of the worksheet or to serve as dividers between sections of data. You can also easily delete cells and entire rows and columns.

After setting up a worksheet, you might find that you need to insert a blank cell, column, or row to create space for entering additional information. For instance, if the sales manager wants to add new rental items in the Rentals worksheet, he'll need to insert a new row for each new rental item. Alternatively, he might want to delete an existing cell, column, or row to eliminate unnecessary information. In the Rentals worksheet, column C is used to indicate the total number of rentals for each item in the year. The sales manager finds that this column is unnecessary and wants to delete it.

You can insert cells, columns, or rows using the Insert menu, and you can delete them using the Edit menu. When you insert a cell or a range of cells in a worksheet, you either shift the existing cells in that row to the right or shift the existing cells in the column down. To insert one or more rows, begin by selecting the number of rows that you want to insert. You do this by clicking and dragging across at least one cell for each row that you want to add. The number of rows that you select is then inserted *above* the first row that you selected, as shown in Figure 2-16.

FIGURE 2-16

Inserting rows

In this example, cells in rows 5, 6, and 7 were selected, as shown in the illustration on the left. When you click Rows on the Insert menu, three new rows are inserted above the first selected row, as shown in the illustration on the right.

Inserting columns is similar. When you want to insert one or more columns, you begin by selecting the number of columns that you want to insert. You do this by clicking and dragging at least one cell for each column that you want to add. In the following illustration on the left, cells in columns C and D are selected. When you click Columns on the Insert menu, Excel inserts two new columns—to the *left* of column C, as shown in the illustration on the right.

FIGURE 2-17

Columns are inserted to the left

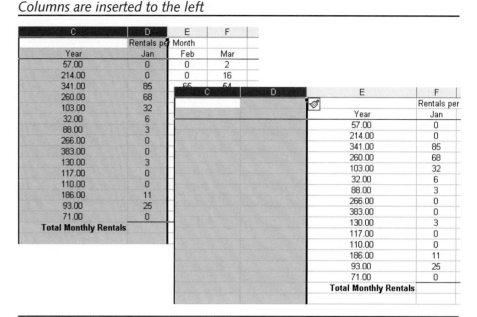

When you insert a row, column, or cell in a worksheet with existing formatting, such as the Currency format, the Insert Options button appears. Clicking the Insert Options button displays a list of choices about how the inserted row or column should be formatted. These options are summarized in the following table.

Option	Action
Format Same As Above	Apply the format of the row above the inserted row to the new row
Format Same As Below	Apply the format of the row below the inserted row to the new row
Format Same As Left	Apply the format of the column to the left of the inserted column to the new column
Format Same As Right	Apply the format of the column to the right of the inserted column to the new column
Clear Formatting	Apply the default format to the new row or column

Insert and delete rows, columns, and cells

In this exercise, you delete a column, insert cells (shifting the adjacent cells in the same row to the right), and insert rows.

1   Click cell C3.

C3 is now the active cell.

2   On the Edit menu, point to Clear, and click Contents.

The contents of the active cell are deleted, but the column is not removed.

ANOTHER METHOD

Right-click the selection, and click Clear Contents on the shortcut menu.

3 **On the Edit menu, click Delete.**

The Delete dialog box appears.

ANOTHER METHOD

Right-click the cell, and select Delete on the shortcut menu.

FIGURE 2-18

Delete dialog box

4 **Click the Entire Column option, and click OK.**

The Year column, along with all of its contents, is deleted.

5 **Select C1:F1.**

Four cells are selected.

6 **On the Insert menu, click Cells.**

The Insert dialog box appears.

ANOTHER METHOD

Right-click the selection, and select Insert on the shortcut menu.

FIGURE 2-19

Insert dialog box

7 **Click the Shift Cells Right option, and click OK.**

Excel inserts four new cells and shifts the contents of existing cells (in the same row) to the right.

8 **Select cells A10:A12.**

Three rows are selected.

> **TIP**
>
> It does not matter which column you use to select cells when you want to insert rows.

9 **On the Insert menu, click Rows.**

Excel inserts three rows above what was row 10 (now row 13). You now have room to add three new rental items.

FIGURE 2-20

Inserting three rows

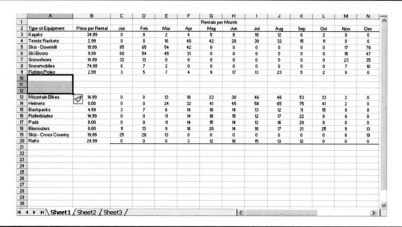

10 **Click the Undo button twice.**

Excel removes the inserted rows and cells.

11 **On the Standard toolbar, click the Save button.**

The workbook is saved with the current name.

◆ **Close Rentals 2. Keep Excel open for the next exercise.**

QUICK REFERENCE ▼

Insert a cell in a worksheet

1 Select the cell or cells above or to the left of where you want to insert the cell.

2 On the Insert menu, click Cells.

3 Choose whether to shift the cells down or to the right.

4 Click OK.

Or

1 Select the cell or cells above or to the left of where you want to insert the cell.

2 Right-click the selection.

3 Click Insert on the shortcut menu.

4 Make a selection, and click OK.

Insert a column or row

1 Select a cell to the left of the column or above the row where you
want to insert the column or row.

2 On the Insert menu, click Columns or Rows, as appropriate.

Or

3 Right-click the column or row heading.

4 Click Insert on the shortcut menu.

5 In the Insert dialog box, click Entire Row or Entire Column, and
click OK.

Cutting, Copying, Pasting, and Clearing Cells

THE BOTTOM LINE

Once you've entered raw data in a worksheet, you'll probably want
to rearrange or reorganize some of it to make the worksheet, as a
whole, easier to read and interpret. You might want to move sections
of data to another location in the worksheet or copy existing data to
another location so you don't need to retype it. You also might want
to "clear" cells of values, formats, or both.

When you're entering data in a worksheet, you might find yourself
changing your mind about where you've placed the contents of a cell,
row, or column. Or you might simply make a mistake by entering data
in a particular row or column when you meant to place it in a different
row or column.

When you want to change where you've placed data in your worksheet,
you do not need to delete the existing data and then retype the data at the
new locations. Excel lets you move the existing contents of one or more
cells to a different location. This approach is called **cut** and **paste** because
you cut (remove) data from its original location and then paste (insert) the
data at a different location. When you cut data, Excel stores it in the
Windows Clipboard, a temporary storage location in your computer's
memory. The data is removed from the worksheet but is still available for
you to paste at a different location. You can even paste data from the
Clipboard into a file created by a different application, such as Microsoft
Word or Microsoft PowerPoint.

At times, you'll want to reuse data that you've already entered. For instance, the sales manager at Adventure Works has created a worksheet containing sales amounts for the first quarter. He wants to **copy** many of the cells from one worksheet and paste them in another worksheet, which he'll use to create sales amounts for the second quarter. In Figure 2-21, the illustration on the left shows that the range A3:A7 on sheet Q1 has been selected and copied. The illustration on the right shows the same range pasted to sheet Q2.

FIGURE 2-21

Copying data from one location to another

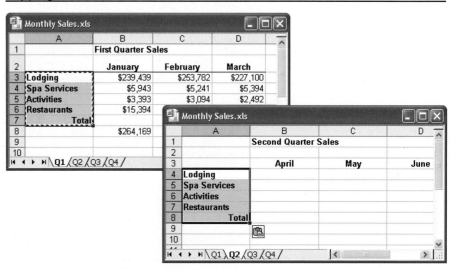

This approach is especially useful when you've applied number formatting to cells or text formatting to titles and labels. The sales manager can copy many of the labels and sales amounts (formatted as currency) to a different worksheet for the second quarter. He can then change the text labels without losing the current text formatting, and he can **clear** the sales amounts without losing the currency formatting stored in the cells. When you clear cells, you can specify whether you want to clear the values stored in the cells but keep the formatting, clear any formulas stored in the cells, clear the formatting in the cells but keep the values, or clear everything in the cells.

TIP

When you are pasting a range of cells—for example, a selection that contains three cells across in two adjacent rows—select an area with the same number of cells across and down as the data you cut or copied. You can also select a single cell to paste into; the pasted data will fill cells below and to the right of the selected cell.

◆ **Open Monthly Sales from the Excel Practice/Lesson02 folder.**

Copy, move, and clear data

In this exercise, you move and copy data to a new location, clear the formatting in a selected range, and clear the contents in a selected range.

1 **Click cell A7, and on the Standard toolbar, click the Cut button.**

The contents of cell A7 are copied to the Windows Clipboard, and a flashing marquee appears around cell A7, as shown in the following illustration. The marquee indicates the contents that will be cut.

ANOTHER METHOD

- Click Cut on the Edit menu.
- Right-click the selection, and click Cut on the shortcut menu.
- Press Ctrl+X.

FIGURE 2-22

Cutting data

	A	B	C	D
1		First Quarter Sales		
2		January	February	March
3	Lodging	$239,439	$253,782	$227,100
4	Spa Services	$5,943	$5,241	$5,394
5	Activities	$3,393	$3,094	$2,492
6	Restaurants	$15,394	$12,100	$12,812
7	Total			
8		$264,169	$274,217	$247,798
9				

2 **Click cell A8, and on the Standard toolbar, click the Paste button.**

The contents of the Windows Clipboard (from cell A7) are pasted in cell A8, and the marquee no longer appears around cell A7.

ANOTHER METHOD

- Click Paste on the Edit menu.
- Right-click the cell, and click Paste on the shortcut menu.
- Press Ctrl+V.

3 **Select B3:D6, and on the Standard toolbar, click the Copy button.**

The contents of the selected cells are copied to the Windows Clipboard, and a flashing marquee appears around the selected cells, indicating what has been copied to the Windows Clipboard.

ANOTHER METHOD

- Click Copy on the Edit menu.
- Right-click the selection, and click Copy on the shortcut menu.
- Press Ctrl+C.

TIP

If you decide you don't want to cut or copy data after you've already executed the Cut or Copy command, simply press the Esc key to abort the procedure.

4 **Click the Q2 sheet tab near the bottom of the Excel window.**

Excel displays the Q2 worksheet.

ANOTHER METHOD

Another way to cut and paste data is to select the cells and drag the selection by its border to the cells where you want to paste the data. To copy using the same method, hold down the Ctrl key while you drag.

5 **Click cell B4, and on the Standard toolbar, click the Paste button.**

The contents of the Windows Clipboard are copied to the Q2 worksheet, starting at the location of the active cell (B4).

6 **On the Edit menu, point to Clear, and click Formats.**

The currency formatting is removed from the selected cells.

7 **On the Standard toolbar, click the Undo button.**

The currency formatting is reapplied to the selected cells.

8 **On the Edit menu, point to Clear, and click Contents.**

The contents are removed from the selected cells, but the formats are still present and will be applied to any data entered in those cells.

9 **Type 3444, and press Enter.**

Excel converts your entry to currency format.

10 **On the File menu, click Save As, type Monthly Sales 2, and click Save.**

The workbook is saved with the new name.

◆ **Keep this file open for the next exercise.**

QUICK REFERENCE ▼

Cut or copy and then paste data in a worksheet

1 Select the desired cell or cells.

2 On the Standard toolbar, click the Cut button to remove the data or the Copy button to make a duplicate of the data.

3 Select the cell or cells into which you want to paste the data.

4 On the Standard toolbar, click the Paste button.

Or

1 Select the desired cell or cells.

2 On the Edit menu, click Cut or click Copy.

QUICK CHECK

Q: What is the difference between cutting and copying data?

A: When you cut data, you remove it from its original location. When you copy data, you make a duplicate of the data so that it can be pasted to a different location.

3 Select the cell or cells into which you want to paste the data.

4 On the Edit menu, click Paste.

Clear a cell or range of cells

1 Select the desired cell or range of cells.

2 On the Edit menu, point to Clear and click Formats to clear the formatting only, or click Contents to clear the contents only, or click All to clear both the contents and formatting.

Using Additional Paste Features

THE BOTTOM LINE

Excel provides a number of other features for organizing and customizing the data you paste to a new location. The Paste Special command lets you choose among values, formats, formulas, and other options to paste. The Paste Options button lets you specify how the data you paste is formatted. And the Office Clipboard allows you store up to 24 cut or copied items, any of which you can retrieve to paste in a new location. These features give you greater control over the appearance of data and help eliminate the need to repeatedly apply the same formatting to data that's copied.

As illustrated in the previous section, you can use the Standard toolbar buttons for cutting, copying, and pasting text. Excel provides other useful techniques that extend your editing capabilities. When you cut or copy text, you can use the **Paste Special** command (on the Edit menu) to display the Paste Special dialog box.

FIGURE 2-23

Paste Special dialog box

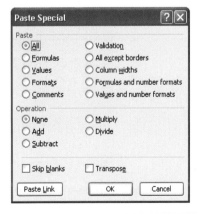

This dialog box gives you a number of options for specifying what you want to paste. For instance, if you copy a range of cells from one worksheet, you can use the Paste Special command to paste only the formatting from the copied cells to a different location. In the previous exercise, you pasted a range of cells to a different worksheet; then you used the Clear command to clear the contents from the pasted cells without losing the cell formatting. The Paste Special dialog box provides a more efficient way to achieve the same result.

An even more efficient and convenient way to perform some of these actions is through the Paste Options button. This button appears next to data you copy from a cell and paste in another cell.

FIGURE 2-24

Paste Options button

July	August	June
$239,439	$253,782	$227,100
$5,943	$5,241	$5,394
$3,393	$3,094	$2,492
$15,394	$12,100	$12,812

Clicking the Paste Options button displays a list of actions Excel can take regarding the pasted cells. The formatting options are valuable tools in helping to achieve a consistent look among the worksheets in a workbook.

FIGURE 2-25

Paste Options menu

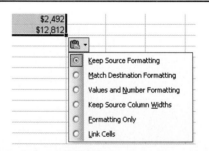

TIP

The options you see in your Paste Options list will vary depending on the content of the cell you are pasting.

These options are summarized in the following table.

Option	Action
Keep Source Formatting	Paste the contents of the Clipboard (which holds the last information selected via the Cut or Copy commands) in the target cells, and format the data as it was formatted in the original cells
Match Destination Formatting	Paste the contents of the Clipboard in the target cells, keeping any numeric formats
Values And Number Formatting	Paste the contents of the Clipboard in the target cells, and resize the columns of the target cells to match the widths of the columns of the source cells
Keep Source Column Widths	Paste the contents of the Clipboard in the target cells, and resize the columns of the target cells to match the widths of the columns of the source cells
Formatting Only	Apply the format of the source cells to the target cells, but do not copy the contents of the source cells
Link Cells	Display the contents of the source cells in the target cells, updating the target cells whenever the content of the source cells changes
Values Only	Paste the values from a column in the target column, and use the existing format to the target column
Values And Source Formatting	Paste a column of cells in the target column, and apply the format of the copied column to the new column

TROUBLESHOOTING

If the Paste Options button does not appear, you can turn the feature on by clicking Options on the Tools menu. In the dialog box that appears, click the Edit tab; then select the Show Paste Options buttons check box.

Use Paste Options

In this exercise, you use the Paste Options button to paste only the formatting of the data that's been copied.

1 **Click the Q1 sheet tab.**

Excel displays the Q1 worksheet. The range B3:D6 should still be selected. If this range is not selected, select it now.

2 **On the Standard toolbar, click the Copy button.**

The contents of the selected range are copied to the Windows Clipboard.

3 **Click the Q3 sheet tab, and click cell B4.**

Excel displays the Q3 worksheet, and B4 is the active cell.

4 **On the Standard toolbar, click the Paste button.**

The selected cells are pasted in the Q3 worksheet.

5 **Click the Paste Options button.**

6 **Click the Formatting Only option.**

Excel pastes the formatting from the copied cells, starting at the location of the active cell, but does not paste the contents.

7 **Type 3444, and press Enter.**

Excel converts your entry to currency format.

8 **Click the Q1 sheet tab.**

Excel displays the Q1 worksheet.

◆ **Keep this file open for the next exercise.**

QUICK REFERENCE ▼

Copy the formatting in a cell or range of cells

1 Select the cell or range of cells whose formatting you want to copy.

2 On the Standard toolbar, click the Copy button.

3 Select the cell or range of cells into which you want to paste the formatting.

4 On the Standard toolbar, click the Paste button.

5 Click the Paste Options button.

6 Click the Formatting Only option.

Working with the Office Clipboard

The **Office Clipboard** provides additional features for pasting data. Although the Office Clipboard has a name similar to the Windows Clipboard, it works in a different way. The Windows Clipboard stores the contents from only one copy or cut operation at a time. When you copy or cut another selection, the contents of the Windows Clipboard are replaced with the new contents. By contrast, the Office Clipboard can store the contents of up to 24 copy or cut operations at one time from any Office application.

Why is this valuable? Consider that the sales manager at Adventure Works wants to create a worksheet for third-quarter sales. However, he wants to see how the worksheet will look if each row label is separated by a blank row. He could copy the row labels from the Q1 worksheet, paste them in the Q3 worksheet, and insert a blank row between each row label. But the Office Clipboard, which has its own task pane, provides an easier way. The sales manager displays the Clipboard task pane and then quickly copies the row labels in Q1, one row at a time. The Office Clipboard stores each row as a separate entry. The sales manager then switches to the Q2 worksheet and uses the Office Clipboard to paste each entry, one at a time, where he wants the entry to appear. The ability to copy multiple selections, store them collectively in the Office Clipboard, and paste each selection separately is called **collect and paste**.

As shown in Figure 2-26, the Clipboard task pane includes two buttons—Paste All and Clear All. Each selection on the Clipboard appears as a page icon (with some portion of the copied information) on the task pane and indicates from which application the selection was cut or copied. When the task pane is open, any time you use the Copy button the selected cells are copied to the Office Clipboard. Use the Paste All button to paste all of the selections from the Office Clipboard at one time. Use the Clear All button to empty the contents of the Office Clipboard. Click one of the page icons to paste the selection in the current cell or range of cells. When you want to delete specific items from the Clipboard, point to the item and click on the arrow that appears next to it. From the menu that opens, you can select Delete to remove a specific item from the Clipboard.

FIGURE 2-26

Clipboard task pane

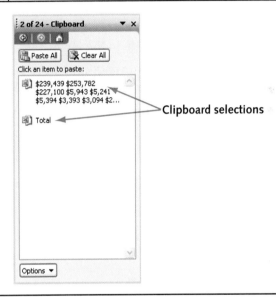

Paste selections to and from the Clipboard

In this exercise, you use the Office Clipboard to organize and manage items to paste.

1 To display the Office Clipboard task pane, on the Edit menu, click Office Clipboard.

The Clipboard task pane appears.

2 If you see any page icons on the Clipboard task pane, click the Clear All button.

3 In the worksheet, click cell A3, and on the Standard toolbar, click the Copy button.

The contents of the cell are copied as a selection to the Office Clipboard, and the Clipboard task pane shows a page icon for the copied selection.

4 **In the worksheet, click cell A4, and then click the Copy button.**

The contents of the cell are copied as a selection to the Office Clipboard, and the Clipboard task pane shows two page icons.

FIGURE 2-27

Pasting selections to the Clipboard

5 **In the worksheet, click cell A5, and then click the Copy button.**

The contents of the cell are copied as a selection to the Office Clipboard, and the Clipboard task pane shows three page icons.

6 **In the worksheet, click cell A6, and then click the Copy button.**

The contents of the cell are copied as a selection to the Office Clipboard, and the Clipboard task pane shows four page icons.

7 **Click the Q4 sheet tab, and click cell A5.**

Excel displays the Q4 worksheet, and A5 is the active cell.

8 **On the Clipboard task pane, click the Spa Services icon.**

The selection is pasted in cell A5.

9 **Click cell A7, and on the Clipboard task pane, click the Lodging icon. The selection is pasted in cell A7.**

10 **Repeat step 9 to paste Activities to cell A9 and Restaurants to cell A11.**

Your worksheet should look similar to the following illustration.

FIGURE 2-28

Selections pasted to the worksheet

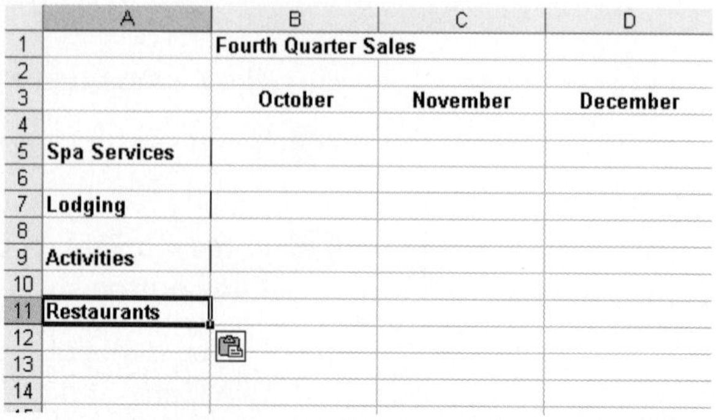

	A	B	C	D
1		Fourth Quarter Sales		
2				
3		October	November	December
4				
5	Spa Services			
6				
7	Lodging			
8				
9	Activities			
10				
11	Restaurants			
12				
13				
14				

11 On the Clipboard task pane, click the Clear All button.

The Office Clipboard is now empty.

12 Click the Save button to save your changes.

◆ Close Monthly Sales 2.

◆ If you are continuing to other lessons, leave Excel open.

◆ If you are not continuing to other lessons, close Excel.

QUICK REFERENCE ▼

Copy and paste multiple objects using the Office Clipboard

1 If necessary, click Office Clipboard on the Edit menu to display.

2 Select the cell or range of cells whose contents you want to copy.

3 On the Standard toolbar, click the Copy button.

4 Repeat steps 1 and 2 for up to 23 more cells (or ranges of cells) whose contents you want to copy.

5 Select the cells into which you want to paste the data.

6 On the Clipboard task pane, click the object you want to paste.

7 Repeat steps 4–5 for the remaining items on the Clipboard task pane.

Key Points

✔ *Applying accurate formatting to numeric data makes the data more useful and easier to interpret and analyze.*

✔ *Modifying column width and row height can make a worksheet's contents easier to read and work with.*

✔ *Proper alignment of data enhances readability and ensures that the data conforms to customary standards of displaying data (i.e., aligning decimal points in entries that are used for accounting purposes).*

✔ *The Find and Replace options let you locate specified data quickly and, if necessary, replace it with different data. These features are most effective in large worksheets where it can take a significant amount of time to scan numerous rows and/or columns to find the data you're looking for.*

✔ *You can insert rows or columns in which you want to enter new data, or you can insert rows and columns and leave them blank to enhance the appearance of the worksheet. You can also easily delete cells and entire rows and columns.*

✔ *Once you've entered raw data in a worksheet, you'll probably want to rearrange or reorganize some of it to make the worksheet, as a whole, easier to read and interpret. You might want to move sections of data to another location in the worksheet or copy existing data to another location so you don't need to retype it. You can copy and paste cell formats.*

> *These features give you greater control over the appearance of data and help eliminate the need to repeatedly apply the same formatting to data that's copied.*
>
> ✔ *The Office Clipboard allows you store up to 24 cut or copied items, any of which you can retrieve at any time to paste in a new location.*

Quick Quiz

True/False

T   F   **1.** The Number format displays data exactly as you enter it.

T   F   **2.** You can apply only those formats that are available in the Category list box of the Format Cells dialog box.

T   F   **3.** A series of pound signs (#####) in a cell indicates that the entry is too long for the current column width.

T   F   **4.** You can manually adjust the width of a column, but not the height of a row.

T   F   **5.** The Office Clipboard holds up to 24 items that you've cut or copied, whereas the Windows Clipboard holds only the most recent item.

Multiple Choice

1. Which number format would you apply to display values as currency?
   a. Number
   b. Currency
   c. Monetary
   d. Financial

2. Which of the following is *not* a method for opening the Format Cells dialog box?
   a. Select Cells on the Format menu.
   b. Press Ctrl+1.
   c. Click the Format Cells button on the Formatting toolbar.
   d. Right-click the selection, and select Cells on the shortcut menu.

3. To find data using the Find and Replace dialog box, you must enter a sequence of characters called a(an)
   a. string.
   b. range.
   c. address.
   d. condition.

4. When you insert a cell in a worksheet with existing formatting, which button appears, giving you options about how the inserted cell should be formatted?
   a. Paste Options
   b. Paste Special
   c. Insert Options
   d. Format Options

5. Which Clipboard can store up to 24 items?
   a. Windows
   b. Excel
   c. Collect and Paste
   d. Office

Short Answer

1. If you wanted to insert two rows above row 7 in your current worksheet, what steps would you use?

2. What is the difference between the Accounting and Currency number formats?

3. How can you drag to change the height of a row or the width of a column?

4. How do you display the Office Clipboard task pane?

5. How can you find the third occurrence of a value in your worksheet?

On Your Own

◆ **Open Five Year Sales02 from the Excel Practice/Lesson02 folder.**

Exercise 1

Insert a row between rows 1 and 2. Resize row 1 to a height of 25 pixels. Move the *Yearly Sales* title text to cell A1. Delete the row you added.

Exercise 2

Still using the Five Year Sales02 workbook, format cells B3:F6 as Accounting. Replace every occurrence of *12* in the worksheet with **13**. Find all entries that are bold, and change the formatting to bold italics.

Exercise 3

Still using the Five Year Sales02 workbook, in Sheet1, copy the range A3:F7 to the Office Clipboard. Switch to Sheet2, and paste the selected cells beginning at cell A3. In Sheet2, change the width of columns A through F to 15 characters. Then select the range B3:F6, delete its contents, but retain the formatting.

◆ **Save and close Five Years Sales02.**

One Step Further

Exercise 1

Create a worksheet to track your physical activity on a weekly basis. The rows should be the days of the week; the physical activities you do on a regular basis (walking, running, specific sports, aerobics, and so on) should go in the columns. Insert a row above row 1, and center the heading *Minutes per Day* above the days of the week. Improve the appearance of the worksheet by adjusting column widths, changing font colors, and so on. Change the name of the sheet to reflect the ending date for this week. Save the workbook as **My Physical Activity**. Use this worksheet to log how many minutes you spend on physical activity each day.

Exercise 2

Continuing with the workbook you created in Exercise 1, select all of the content from your first worksheet and copy it to Sheet 2. Clear any of the minute values that were entered. Rename this sheet with the date of the ending day for next week. Copy the contents of the second sheet to Sheet 3, and rename that sheet to reflect the ending date for two weeks from now. Save your worksheets. Use these sheets to log your physical activity for the next several weeks. If desired, add additional sheets to continue monitoring your activity level.

Formatting Cells

After completing this lesson, you will be able to:

- ✔ *Format text.*
- ✔ *Format numbers as currency.*
- ✔ *Use Format Painter.*
- ✔ *Add borders to cells.*
- ✔ *Add shading to cells.*
- ✔ *Use AutoFormat.*
- ✔ *Create and apply styles.*
- ✔ *Merge cells.*

KEY TERMS

- ▪ attribute
- ▪ AutoFormat
- ▪ font
- ▪ Format Painter
- ▪ merge cells
- ▪ style

Excel provides dozens of ways to format labels and values in a worksheet. If your worksheet or workbook will be printed or viewed by others, especially if it is part of a report or presentation, you'll want it to look as attractive and comprehensible as possible. For example, to improve the design, you can enlarge the text for headings and format the headings and labels in bold, italics, or both. You can also format text in different fonts (type styles) and in different colors.

In this lesson, you will learn how to format text and numbers, including headings, labels, and values. You will learn how to use Excel's Format Painter feature, which allows you to quickly pick up all of the formatting for selected text and then apply the same formats to different text. You will also learn how to add borders and shading around selected cells. Then you will learn how to apply one of Excel's built-in worksheet designs to add colors and design effects to a worksheet using only a few mouse clicks. Next you will learn how to create a style, which is a collection of formatting characteristics that can be applied at any time simply by clicking the name of the style in a list. Finally, you will learn how to combine multiple cells into a single cell.

IMPORTANT

Before you can use the practice files in this lesson, you must install them from the book's companion CD to their default location. For additional information on how to find and open files used in this book, see the "Using the CD-ROM" section at the beginning of this book.

Formatting Text

Making Data Easier to Read
Changing the Appearance of
Data

THE BOTTOM LINE

Excel's formatting tools enable you to give your worksheets a professional, customized look. You can use certain formats to call out important or unique data, such as the title of the worksheet. You can also use formatting that matches what's used in other documents, such as letterhead, to give all of your documents a consistent look.

In Lesson 2, you learned that applying certain formats to numeric data can make it more meaningful and easier to interpret. You also learned how alignment and spacing can improve the readability of data. Now you will see how applying different fonts in different sizes and styles can add a professional, polished look to your worksheets.

A **font** is the design of type, including letters, numbers, and other character symbols. The different characters of a particular font have a similar design to provide a consistent look. Excel's default font is 10-point Arial. In typography, one point is 1/72 inch. So characters in a 10-point font are about 1/6 inch high.

You can change to different fonts and different font sizes to add visual interest to a worksheet and to call attention to specific data. For example, in a budget worksheet, you might use a font in a large point size, in bold, and in a different color to make the title stand out. You might use a different font, such as the default 10-point Arial, for the budget data and the same font but in a different style, such as bold italics, for the column and row labels.

The Font tab of the Format Cells dialog box contains options to change the font, the font style (such as bold and italics), and the point size of a cell entry. You can apply some of these same formatting options by selecting buttons on the Formatting toolbar. You'll use this toolbar throughout this lesson.

FIGURE 3-1

Selected buttons on the Formatting toolbar

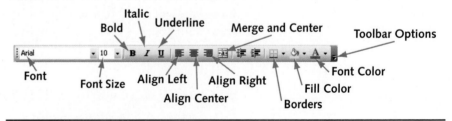

◆ To complete the procedures in this lesson, you must use the practice files Lodging Analysis03 and AW Guest Supplies in the Lesson03 folder in the Excel Practice folder that is located on your hard disk.

◆ Open Lodging Analysis03 from the Excel Practice/Lesson03 folder.

Format text

In this exercise, you format text in a worksheet.

1 **Click cell B1, and on the Formatting toolbar, click the Bold button.**

B

The title appears in bold, making it easier to determine the kind of data on the worksheet.

ANOTHER METHOD

Select Cells on the Format menu; or right-click the selection, and click Format Cells on the shortcut menu; or press Ctrl+1. In the Format Cells dialog box, click the Font tab, and click Bold in the Font Style list box.

Press Ctrl+B.

2 **Select the range B3:E3, and on the Formatting toolbar, click the Center button.**

The year labels are centered.

ANOTHER METHOD

Select Cells on the Format menu; or right-click the selection, and click Format Cells on the shortcut menu; or press Ctrl+1. In the Format Cells dialog box, click the Alignment tab, and click Center in the Horizontal list box.

TIP

You can customize the Formatting toolbar by placing buttons on it that you use frequently and removing those you don't. To customize your toolbar, click the Toolbar Options button, and then click Add or Remove Buttons. Click menu options to select or deselect the buttons on the list.

3 **Click the Bold button on the Formatting toolbar.**

B

The year labels appear in bold.

4 **Right-click the area you've selected, click Format Cells on the shortcut menu, and click the Font tab.**

The Font tab of the Format Cells dialog box appears.

FIGURE 3-2

Font tab in the Format Cells dialog box

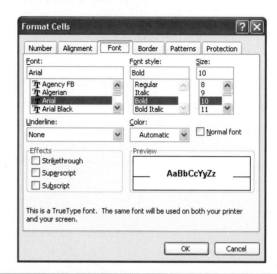

ANOTHER METHOD

- Select Cells on the Format menu.
- Press Ctrl+1.

5 On the Font list, scroll down and click Times New Roman.

ANOTHER METHOD

Click the Font button down arrow, and select Times New Roman.

6 On the Size list, scroll down and click 12.

ANOTHER METHOD

Click the Font Size down arrow, and select 12.

7 Click the Color down arrow, click the Red square (third row, first square), click OK, and click a blank area of the worksheet.

The range is deselected and appears in 12-point, red, Times New Roman text. The new formats applied to the year labels make them stand out.

ANOTHER METHOD

Click the Font Color button down arrow, and select Red.

8 Select the range A4:A8, and click the Bold button.

The row labels appear in bold.

B

9 On the Format menu, click Cells, and click the Alignment tab.

The Format Cells dialog box appears with the Alignment tab on top.

10 **Double-click in the Indent box, type 1, and click OK.**

The sales categories in the selected cells are indented one character to the right.

FIGURE 3-3

Indenting entries

	A	B	C	D	E
1		Yearly Income - Lodging			
2					
3		2002	2003	2004	2005
4	Teepees	23393	30094	32492	38262
5	Cabins	75943	79241	88394	89000
6	Condos	239439	653782	927100	954111
7					
8	Total	338775	763117	1047986	1081373
9					

ANOTHER METHOD

Click the Increase Indent button.

11 **On the File menu, click Save As, type Lodging Analysis, and click Save.**

The workbook is saved with the new name.

◆ **Keep this file open for the next exercise.**

ANOTHER METHOD

You can also change the file name by selecting only the numbers *03* at the end of the current file name, deleting them, and clicking the Save button.

QUICK REFERENCE ▼

Format text

1. Select the cell or cells to be formatted.
2. On the Format menu, click Cells.
3. Click the Font tab.
4. Select the desired font, style, and size options.
5. Click OK.

Or

Select the cell or cells to be formatted, and click the appropriate button on the Formatting toolbar.

QUICK CHECK

Q: What is a commonly used font style?

A: **Bold, italic, and underline are commonly used font styles.**

Formatting Numbers as Currency

THE BOTTOM LINE

You might use a worksheet to track your investments, to set your income and expenses, or to list the value of household items. Worksheets such as these contain monetary, or currency, values. Applying the appropriate currency format to these values makes them more meaningful and easier to interpret.

When you type numbers in worksheet cells, Excel formats the cells in the General format by default—which means that all text and numeric entries appear exactly as you've entered them. In the previous lesson, you learned about the various formats, such as Currency, Date, and Percentage, that you can apply to numbers using the Number tab in the Format Cells dialog box. For example, you can display large numbers with comma separators between thousands digit positions, you can display numbers as currency with dollar signs and decimal positions for fractions of a dollar, and you can display numbers as fractions or even percentages.

Some common number formats can be applied to selected cells more easily by using the Formatting toolbar. The following table shows some of the buttons on the Formatting toolbar that you can click to format numbers.

Button	Button Name	Description
$	Currency Style	Formats numbers with dollar signs, comma separators for thousands, and two decimal places
%	Percent Style	Multiplies numbers by 100 and displays them with percent signs
,	Comma Style	Inserts commas between groups of thousands
←.0 .00	Increase Decimal	Adds one decimal position each time you click the button
.00 →.0	Decrease Decimal	Removes one decimal position each time you click the button

Format numbers using the Formatting toolbar

In this exercise, you use the Formatting toolbar to format numbers as currency and to remove decimal positions.

1 Select the range B4:E8, and on the Formatting toolbar, click the Currency Style button.

The numbers in the selected cells appear with dollar signs, comma separators, and two decimal positions. Notice that none of the numbers includes fractions of a dollar, so the decimal positions are not necessary.

ANOTHER METHOD

Select Cells on the Format menu; or right-click the selection, and click Format Cells on the shortcut menu; or press Ctrl+1. In the Format Cells dialog box, click the Number tab, and click Currency in the Category list box.

2 Click the Decrease Decimal button twice, and click an empty cell in the worksheet.

The decimal positions are removed from the selected range of numbers, and the range is deselected. Your worksheet should look similar to the following illustration:

FIGURE 3-4

Numbers with decimals removed

	A	B	C	D	E
1		**Yearly Income - Lodging**			
2					
3		2002	2003	2004	2005
4	**Teepees**	$ 23,393	$ 30,094	$ 32,492	$ 38,262
5	**Cabins**	$ 75,943	$ 79,241	$ 88,394	$ 89,000
6	**Condos**	$ 239,439	$ 653,782	$ 927,100	$ 954,111
7					
8	**Total**	$ 338,775	$ 763,117	$ 1,047,986	$ 1,081,373

ANOTHER METHOD

Select Cells on the Format menu; or right-click the selection, and click Format Cells on the shortcut menu; or press Ctrl+1. In the Format Cells dialog box, click the Number tab, and change the value in the Decimal Places text box to the desired number.

QUICK CHECK

Q: By default, how many decimal places appear in a value when you format it using the Currency Style button on the Formatting toolbar?

A: The value has two decimal places by default.

◆ **Keep this file open for the next exercise.**

QUICK REFERENCE ▼

Use the Formatting toolbar to apply number formatting to a range of cells

1 Select the range of cells to which you want to apply number formatting.

2 On the Formatting toolbar, click the desired number format button (Currency Style, Percent Style, or Comma Style).

Using Format Painter

THE BOTTOM LINE

The Format Painter allows you to quickly copy the attributes, or characteristics, of data that you have already formatted and apply these attributes to other data, thus eliminating the need for you to apply the same formats repeatedly.

The **Format Painter** feature is available in most Microsoft Office programs. It allows you to copy formatting from a cell or range of cells and apply it to another cell or range of cells.

You can copy formats, including font, font size, font style, font color, alignment, indentation, number formats, and borders and shading, which you'll learn about in the next section. To apply all of these formats, you must make a number of selections, either from the Formatting toolbar or from the Format Cells dialog box. For example, in a sales worksheet, you record sales data at the end of each month in the next open column and label the column with the name of the month. You can use the Format Painter to copy the formatting on the previous month's column to the current month's column. This feature saves you time and helps ensure formatting consistency.

TROUBLESHOOTING

If the Format Painter button doesn't appear on the Standard toolbar, click the Toolbar Options button to display the rest of the buttons; then click the Format Painter button.

Use the Format Painter to apply formats

In this exercise, you use the Format Painter button to copy a format from one cell to a range of cells.

1 **Click cell B3.**

The first column label cell is selected.

 2 **Click the Format Painter button on the Standard toolbar.**

A flashing marquee appears around the selected cell, and the mouse icon changes to a plus sign with a paintbrush next to it.

FIGURE 3-5

Copying a format with the Format Painter

Flashing marquee

	A	B	C
1		Yearly Income - Lodging	
2			
3		2002	2003
4	Teepees	$ 23,393	$ 30,094
5	Cabins	$ 75,943	$ 79,241
6	Condos	$ 239,439	$ 653,782
7			
8	Total	$ 338,775	$ 763,117

Format Painter mouse icon

3 Select the range A4:A8 (the row labels).

Excel copies the formatting in cell B3 to the range you selected. The row labels now appear in red, bold, and 12-point Times New Roman font.

4 On the Standard toolbar, click the Save button.

The workbook is saved with the current name.

ANOTHER METHOD

- Select Save on the File menu.
- Press Ctrl+S.

◆ Keep this file open for the next exercise.

TIP

You can use the Format Painter to copy formatting to more than one nonadjacent cell or range of cells. Just *double-click* the Format Painter button, and then click the individual cells or ranges you want to format. When you are done, click the Format Painter button again to deactivate it.

QUICK REFERENCE ▼

Use Format Painter to copy formats from one cell to other cells

1 Select a cell that contains formatting that you want to copy.

2 On the Standard toolbar, click the Format Painter button.

3 Select the cell or range to which you want to apply the format.

Adding Borders to Cells

THE BOTTOM LINE

You can emphasize a cell or range of cells by adding borders. Borders are especially useful for demarcating sections in a worksheet, such as a row of labels or totals.

Adding borders to a cell or range of cells can enhance the visual appeal of your worksheet, make it easier to read, and highlight specific data. Borders can also clearly separate sections of a worksheet. For example, in a sales worksheet, you might add a border under the cells containing the names of each month in the year, you might add a border between each column of monthly sales data, and you might add a border around the row containing the sales totals for each month.

Excel provides more than a dozen border styles—including single lines of varying widths, dotted lines, and dashed lines. You can also change the color of a border. When you create a border for a cell or range of cells, you don't need to apply the border to all four sides. You can specify that the border be applied to any side or combination of sides. For instance, you can apply a double line border to only the bottom border of the first row of a worksheet to separate the title from the rest of the worksheet.

Excel provides three methods for applying borders:

- You can select the cell or cells to which you want to add the border and use the options available under the Formatting toolbar's Borders button.
- You can draw borders directly on the worksheet using the Borders toolbar, as shown in Figure 3-6. To draw a border around a group of cells, click the mouse pointer at one corner of the group and drag it to the diagonal corner. You will see your border expand as you move the mouse pointer. When you want to add a border in a vertical or horizontal line, drag the mouse pointer along the target grid line. You can also change the characteristics of the border you draw through the options on the Borders toolbar.

FIGURE 3-6

Borders toolbar

TIP

You display the Borders toolbar by opening the View menu, pointing to Toolbars, and clicking Borders.

- You can apply borders using the Borders tab in the Format Cells dialog box. With this method, you choose where you want the border, the line style, and the line color all from one tab.

Add borders

In this exercise, you use all three methods to add borders to your worksheet.

1 Select the range B8:E8.

 2 On the Formatting toolbar, click the down arrow to the right of the Borders button.

A menu of border line styles and locations appears.

FIGURE 3-7

Borders menu

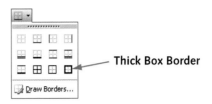

Thick Box Border

3 Click the Thick Box Border button (fourth button, third row, as identified in Figure 3-7).

A thick border is added around all sides of the selected cells.

4 Select the range A3:E3.

5 On the Format menu, click Cells, and click the Border tab.

The Format Cells dialog box appears with the Border tab on top.

FIGURE 3-8

Border tab in the Format Cells dialog box

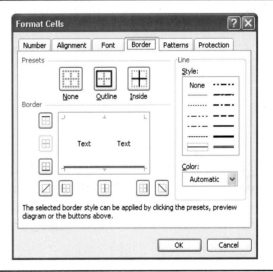

ANOTHER METHOD

Right-click the selection, and click Format Cells on the shortcut menu; or press Ctrl+1. In the Format Cells dialog box, click the Border tab.

6 In the Style list, click the second line style in the second column.

7 Click the Color down arrow, and click the Blue square (second row, sixth square).

8 In the Border section of the dialog box, click the bottom border.

In the dialog box, Excel shows a preview of what the chosen border will look like.

FIGURE 3-9

Preview of borders

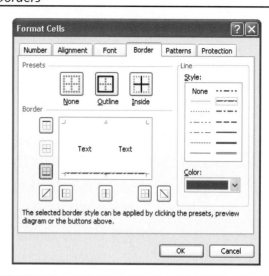

9 **Click OK, and click a blank cell in the worksheet.**

The Format Cells dialog box closes, and the blue border is added to your worksheet.

10 **Point to Toolbars on the View menu, and click Borders to open the Borders toolbar.**

ANOTHER METHOD

Click the Borders button down arrow, and select Draw Borders.

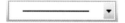

11 **Click the down arrow on the Line Style button, and select the double line.**

The mouse pointer changes to a pencil with a line next to it, and the Line Style button reflects the selection you have made.

12 **Click and drag under the text in cell B1. Then click the Draw Border button on the Borders toolbar to toggle the mouse icon back to the regular selection arrow.**

A double line is drawn under the text, and your worksheet should look similar to the following illustration.

QUICK CHECK

Q: What are two ways to display the Borders toolbar?

A: You can display the Borders toolbar by selecting Toolbars on the View menu and then clicking Borders or by clicking the Borders button down arrow and selecting Draw Borders.

FIGURE 3-10

Adding more borders

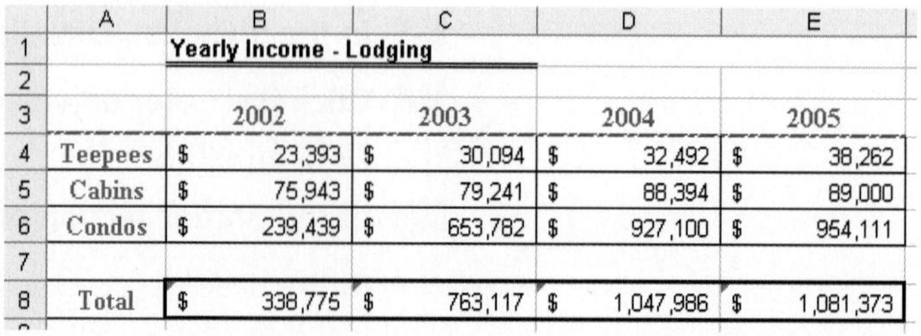

	A	B	C	D	E
1		Yearly Income - Lodging			
2					
3		2002	2003	2004	2005
4	Teepees	$ 23,393	$ 30,094	$ 32,492	$ 38,262
5	Cabins	$ 75,943	$ 79,241	$ 88,394	$ 89,000
6	Condos	$ 239,439	$ 653,782	$ 927,100	$ 954,111
7					
8	Total	$ 338,775	$ 763,117	$ 1,047,986	$ 1,081,373

◆ **Keep this file open for the next exercise.**

Adding Shading to Cells

THE BOTTOM LINE

Shading can draw attention to selected data as well as add color to your worksheet. Applying a light shade to every other column or row in a large worksheet is a good technique for improving the readability of data.

As with borders, you can add shading and patterns to one cell or a range of cells to set off the selection. For example, you might have a worksheet with numerous rows of data that span across 15 columns. You could apply a light shade of color to every other row so that it's easier to follow the data for a certain entry across the long series of columns, as shown in Figure 3-11.

FIGURE 3-11

Using shading to make data easier to read

	Type of Equipment	Price per Rental	Year	Jan	Feb	Mar	Apr	May	Jun	Jul	Aug	Sep
3	Kayaks	34.95	57.00	0	0	2	4	5	8	18	12	6
4	Tennis Rackets	2.95	214.00	0	0	16	40	42	28	30	32	15
5	Skis - Downhill	19.95	341.00	65	65	54	42	0	0	0	0	0
6	Ski Boots	9.95	260.00	68	54	45	31	0	0	0	0	0
7	Snowshoes	14.95	103.00	32	13	0	0	0	0	0	0	0
8	Snowmobiles	74.95	32.00	6	7	2	0	0	0	0	0	0
9	Fishing Poles	2.95	88.00	3	5	7	4	9	17	13	23	5
10	Mountain Bikes	14.95	266.00	0	0	13	18	23	30	46	48	53
11	Helmets	0.00	383.00	0	0	24	32	41	45	58	65	75
12	Backpacks	4.95	130.00	3	7	6	14	18	14	13	12	11
13	Rollerblades	14.95	117.00	0	0	11	14	18	15	12	17	22
14	Pads	0.00	110.00	0	0	11	14	15	14	12	16	20
15	Binoculars	0.00	186.00	11	13	9	16	20	14	18	17	21
16	Skis - Cross Country	19.95	93.00	25	28	13	0	0	0	0	0	0
17	Rafts	24.95	71.00	0	0	0	3	12	16	15	13	12

Shading can be a shade of gray or a color. Although colors can add significantly to the appearance of a worksheet, colors appear in a printed worksheet only when you are using a color printer. A pattern is a set of lines or dots that fill selected cells. Applying patterns is especially useful when you want to call attention to one or more cells in a printed worksheet but you do not have a color printer. If you have a color printer or plan to view your worksheet only on the screen, you can combine color shading with a pattern in selected cells. However, make sure the text in the cells is still easy to read.

Apply shading and patterns to cells

In this exercise, you add shading to cells in the worksheet and preview the patterns that you can apply to cells.

1 **Select the range B8:E8.**

You will add shading to the cells that show total projected income for each year.

2 **On the Format menu, click Cells, and click the Patterns tab.**

The Format Cells dialog box appears with the Patterns tab on top.

FIGURE 3-12

Patterns tab in the Format Cells dialog box

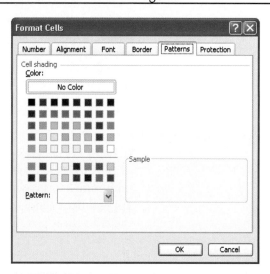

ANOTHER METHOD

Right-click the selection, and click Format Cells on the shortcut menu; or press Ctrl+1. In the Format Cells dialog box, click the Patterns tab.

3 In the Color area, click the Yellow square in the bottom row of colors.

ANOTHER METHOD

Click the Fill Color button's down arrow, and click Yellow.

4 Click the Pattern down arrow.

The fill patterns that you can add to cells appear.

FIGURE 3-13

Available fill patterns

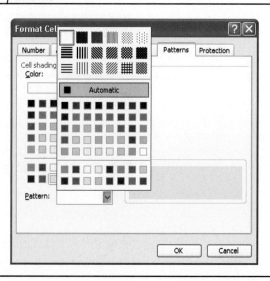

> **TIP**
>
> Patterns work best with row and column labels—especially for labels that are in a large font size or that are bold. When a pattern is applied to cells that contain numbers, the numbers can often be difficult to read.

5 **Click the Pattern down arrow again.**

The Pattern list closes without a pattern selected.

6 **Click OK, and click a blank area of the worksheet.**

The cells are deselected and appear with yellow shading.

7 **On the Standard toolbar, click the Save button.**

The workbook is saved with the current name.

◆ **Keep this file open for the next exercise.**

Using AutoFormat

Applying Styles and Formats to Data

THE BOTTOM LINE

The AutoFormat feature is another of Excel's handy time-saving devices. Simply select a range of cells and choose from among a number of predesigned formats to apply to it. This saves you the time of adding worksheet formats such as borders, shading, and font styles and sizes.

With the **AutoFormat** feature, you can format the data in your worksheets using a professionally designed template. The AutoFormat feature is ideal for a range of data that consists of these basic components:

- A top row with labels
- A first column with labels
- The raw data that's being stored
- A row or column (or both) with totals

When you apply an AutoFormat to a range with these components, they are automatically identified and formatted with the borders, shading, and font effects that are appropriate for that type of data. An AutoFormat is not permanent—you can modify it or change it completely using any formatting techniques you choose.

Apply an AutoFormat to a worksheet

In this exercise, you explore the AutoFormat dialog box and format a worksheet area with AutoFormat.

1 **Select the range A3:E8.**

All of the row labels, column labels, and data cells are selected.

2 **On the Format menu, click AutoFormat.**

The AutoFormat dialog box appears.

FIGURE 3-14

AutoFormat dialog box

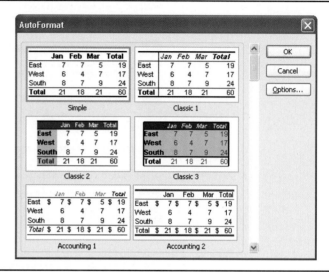

3 **Scroll down on the formats list to view all of the available formats.**

4 **Scroll back to the top of the formats list, click the Classic 2 format preview, click OK, and click a blank area of the worksheet.**

The range is deselected and appears in the Classic 2 format.

FIGURE 3-15

Applying the Classic 2 format

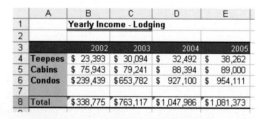

TIP

When an AutoFormat is applied, Excel removes any existing formatting in the selected cells so that the AutoFormat can be applied correctly.

---

5 **On the Standard toolbar, click the Save button.**

The file is saved with the current name.

◆ **Keep this file open for the next exercise.**

QUICK CHECK

Q: How do you open the AutoFormat dialog box?

A: **Open the AutoFormat dialog box by selecting AutoFormat on the Format menu.**

Apply a design with AutoFormat

1 Make sure your data is well organized.

2 Select the range to which you want to apply AutoFormat.

3 On the Format menu, click AutoFormat.

4 Select the desired AutoFormat style, and click OK.

Creating and Applying Styles

Applying Styles and Formats to Data

THE BOTTOM LINE

Styles, which are a defined set of formats, can save you time and provide consistency in the look of your worksheets.

A **style** is a set of formatting attributes that you can apply to a cell or range of cells more easily than setting each attribute individually.

Excel comes with several ready-made styles that you can use to format data quickly. You've already learned that the raw data you enter is formatted by default in the Arial 10- point font. This is Excel's "Normal" style. You can create a style that incorporates any of the following formatting attributes:

- Number
- Alignment
- Font
- Border
- Patterns
- Protection

An **attribute** is a formatting characteristic of a cell (such as a dotted line border) or the data in a cell (such as a font or font size). You can modify the attributes of the Normal style or Excel's other ready-made styles, or you can create your own styles. For example, the financial manager for a chain of fast-food restaurants records receipts by month on a separate worksheet for each location. The worksheet titles, subtitles, and row and column labels are basically the same in each worksheet. He creates a style for the title, a style for the subtitle, a style for the row labels, and a style for the column labels. All he does is select the data and apply the appropriate style. He doesn't need to spend time applying the individual formats that make up the style, and all the worksheets are consistent in their appearance.

When you create a new style, you must base it on an existing style; however, you don't need to keep any of the formatting that composes the original style.

Create and apply styles

In this exercise, you create a style that applies a font, a font size, alignment, and a font style to the contents of selected cells. You then apply the new style to other cells.

1 **Click cell B1, and on the Format menu, click Style.**

The Style dialog box appears, with Normal as the default style, as shown in Figure 3-16.

FIGURE 3-16

Style dialog box

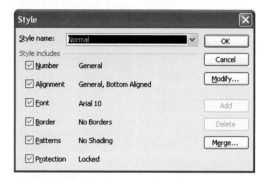

2 **Click in the Style Name box at the end of the word Normal, type 2, and click the Add button.**

A style named Normal2 is created.

3 **Click the Modify button.**

The Format Cells dialog box appears. In this dialog box, you define the attributes of the style.

4 **Click the Font tab, click Times New Roman on the Font list, click Bold on the Font Style list, and click 14 on the Size list.**

The contents of any cell to which you apply the Normal2 style will appear in 14-point, Times New Roman, bold text.

5 **Click OK.**

The Style dialog box reappears, showing the changes you made to the Normal2 style.

6 **Click OK again.**

The contents of cell B1 appear with the formatting you specified for the Normal2 style.

7 **Click cell A8, and on the Format menu, click Style.**

The Style dialog box appears.

TIP

You can apply styles more easily when you add the Style list to the Formatting toolbar. To do so, on the Tools menu, click Customize to display the Customize dialog box. Click the Commands tab, click Format on the Categories list, and drag the Style list box from the Commands list to the Formatting toolbar.

8 **Click the Style Name down arrow, click Normal2, and click OK.**

The contents of cell A8 appear with the formatting you specified for the Normal2 style.

FIGURE 3-17
_____
Applying a new style to a cell
_____

	A	B	C	D	E
1		**Yearly Income - Lodging**			
2					
3		2002	2003	2004	2005
4	**Teepees**	$ 23,393	$ 30,094	$ 32,492	$ 38,262
5	**Cabins**	$ 75,943	$ 79,241	$ 88,394	$ 89,000
6	**Condos**	$239,439	$653,782	$ 927,100	$ 954,111
7					
8	**Total**	$338,775	$763,117	$1,047,986	$1,081,373

9 **On the Edit menu, click Undo Style.**

The contents of cell A8 appear with the previous formatting.

ANOTHER METHOD

- Click the Undo button on the Standard toolbar.
- Press Ctrl+Z.

10 **On the Standard toolbar, click the Save button.**

The file is saved.

ANOTHER METHOD

- Select Save on the File menu.
- Press Ctrl+S.

◆ **Close Lodging Analysis.**

QUICK REFERENCE ▼

Create and apply a style

1 On the Format menu, click Style.

2 Click the Style Name down arrow, and click the style on which you want to base the new style.

3 Type a name for the new style on the Style Name list.

4 Click OK.

5 Select the cell or range of cells to which you want to apply the style.

6 On the Format menu, click Style.

7 Click the style you want to apply on the Style Name list.

8 Click OK.

QUICK **CHECK**

Q: What is an attribute?

A: **An attribute is a formatting characteristic of a cell or the data in a cell.**

Merging Cells

THE BOTTOM LINE

Merging multiple cells into a single cell gives you control over the alignment and spacing of a data entry that might be unusually long—such as a worksheet title—in comparison to other entries in the same row or column.

You already know that you can adjust the width of a column so that the longest number or text entry in the column fits within the column width. You can also **merge cells** to support additional formatting capabilities. Merging cells combines two or more cells into a single cell so that the text or value within the cell can be formatted more easily. For example, you might want to merge several cells in the title row of a worksheet so that the title is contained within a single cell. Then you could align the title so that it's centered within the cell and over the worksheet data.

You can also merge cells in adjoining rows so that you have more control over the alignment and placement of text in the cells. For example, suppose several of the column labels for your worksheet are lengthy. If you widen the columns to fit the lengthy column labels, the columns might be much longer than the longest value in the column. For example, suppose you have a column label called *Quantity Ordered*. This label occupies 16 character positions. Now consider that the largest order amount is 9,999—five character positions. If you widen the *Quantity Ordered* column to fit the column label, the column is wider than necessary. You'll see how this technique works in the following exercise.

A better approach is to merge the *Quantity Ordered* cell with the cell below it. After you've merged the cells, you can use the Format Cells dialog box to format *Quantity Ordered* so that the text wraps from the top line into the line below it and is centered horizontally and vertically in the merged cell. You can then narrow the column so that the values fit better within the column.

◆ **Open AW Guest Supplies from the Excel Practice/Lesson03 folder.**

Merge cells

In this exercise, you merge cells horizontally (multiple cells in the same row) and vertically (multiple cells in the same column) and reformat the merged cells.

1 **Click cell A1 to select it, if necessary.**

2 **Hold down the Shift key, and click cell F1.**

The range A1:F1 is selected.

ANOTHER METHOD

Although you can click and drag to select any range of cells, the technique used in steps 2 and 3 provides an easier way to select a lengthy range of cells.

3 Click the Merge And Center button.

The selected cells are merged into one cell, and the text is centered in the cell.

ANOTHER METHOD

To open the Format Cells dialog box, select Cells on the Format menu; right-click the selection, and select Format Cells on the shortcut menu; or press Ctrl+F1. Click the Alignment tab; click the Horizontal down arrow, and select Center Across Selection; and click Merge Cells in the Text Control section.

4 Click cell A3, hold down the Shift key, and click cell F3.

The range A3:F3 is selected.

5 Click the Merge And Center button.

The selected cells are merged into one cell, and the text is centered in the cell.

FIGURE 3-18

Merging cells and centering their content

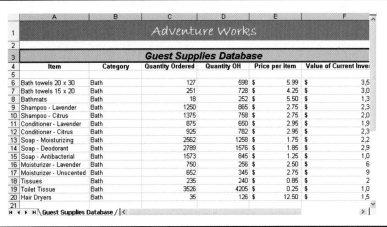

6 Select the range C4:C5; right-click the selected cells; and on the shortcut menu, click Format Cells.

The Format Cells dialog box appears.

7 Click the Alignment tab.

The Alignment tab of the Format Cells dialog box appears on top.

FIGURE 3-19

Alignment tab in the Format Cells dialog box

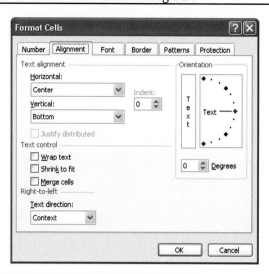

8 Click the Vertical down arrow, and click Center.

The selected cells will be centered vertically in the merged cell.

9 In the Text control section of the dialog box, select the Wrap text check box.

The text in the selected cells will wrap to two or more lines if the text does not fit on one line.

TIP

You can unmerge a merged cell at any time by selecting the cell, displaying the Alignment tab of the Format Cells dialog box, and clearing the Merge Cells check box.

10 In the Text control section of the dialog box, select the Merge Cells check box, and click OK.

The cells are now merged into a single cell, and the text is centered vertically and horizontally in the merged cell.

11 Click the right edge of the column selector for column C, and drag to the left until the column is about 9 characters in width.

The text in the merged cell wraps to a second line.

FIGURE 3-20

Wrapping text

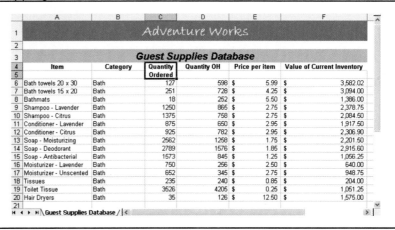

TIP

The column width, measured in the number of characters, appears and changes as you drag the column selector.

12 On the Standard toolbar, double-click the Format Painter button. Select the range D4:D5, then E4:E5, and finally F4:F5.

Excel copies the merge formatting to the selected cells.

13 Click the Format Painter button.

Excel copies the merge formatting to the selected cells, the Format Painter is no longer activated, and the cell selection marquee around cell C4 disappears.

14 On your own, use the column selectors to reduce the width of columns D, E, and F so that the text in the merged cells wraps to two lines for each column.

FIGURE 3-21

Decreasing column width to wrap column labels

	A	B	C	D	E	F
1			Adventure Works			
2						
3			Guest Supplies Database			
4	Item	Category	Quantity Ordered	Quantity OH	Price per item	Value of Current Inventory
5						
6	Bath towels 20 x 30	Bath	127	598	$ 5.99	$ 3,582.02
7	Bath towels 15 x 20	Bath	251	728	$ 4.25	$ 3,094.00
8	Bathmats	Bath	18	252	$ 5.50	$ 1,386.00
9	Shampoo - Lavender	Bath	1250	865	$ 2.75	$ 2,378.75
10	Shampoo - Citrus	Bath	1375	758	$ 2.75	$ 2,084.50
11	Conditioner - Lavender	Bath	875	650	$ 2.95	$ 1,917.50
12	Conditioner - Citrus	Bath	925	782	$ 2.95	$ 2,306.90
13	Soap - Moisturizing	Bath	2562	1258	$ 1.75	$ 2,201.50
14	Soap - Deodorant	Bath	2789	1576	$ 1.85	$ 2,915.60
15	Soap - Antibacterial	Bath	1573	845	$ 1.25	$ 1,056.25
16	Moisturizer - Lavender	Bath	750	256	$ 2.50	$ 640.00
17	Moisturizer - Unscented	Bath	652	345	$ 2.75	$ 948.75
18	Tissues	Bath	235	240	$ 0.85	$ 204.00
19	Toilet Tissue	Bath	3526	4205	$ 0.25	$ 1,051.25
20	Hair Dryers	Bath	35	126	$ 12.50	$ 1,575.00
21						

Guest Supplies Database

15 On the File menu, click Save As, type AW Guest Supplies 03, and click the Save button.

The file is saved with the new name.

◆ Close AW Guest Supplies 03.

◆ If you are continuing to other lessons, leave Excel open.

◆ If you are not continuing to other lessons, save and close all open workbooks, then close Excel.

QUICK REFERENCE ▼

Merge cells

1 Select the range of cells that you want to merge into a single cell.

2 On the Formatting toolbar, click the Merge and Center button.

Or

Display the Alignment tab of the Format Cells dialog box, and select the desired merge options.

Key Points

✔ *Excel's formatting tools enable you to give your worksheets a professional, customized look. You can format text and numbers using the Format Cells dialog box or buttons on the Formatting toolbar.*

✔ *The Format Painter allows you to quickly copy the attributes, or characteristics, of data that you have already formatted and apply these attributes to other data, thus eliminating the need for you to apply the same formats repeatedly.*

✔ *You can emphasize a cell or range of cells by adding borders or shading. Borders are especially useful for demarcating sections in a worksheet, such as a row of labels or totals. You can use shading to draw attention to selected data as well as add color to your worksheet.*

✔ *You can automatically apply professionally designed formats to a range by using the AutoFormat feature. This saves you the time of adding worksheet formats such as borders, shading, and font styles and sizes.*

✔ *Styles, which are a defined set of formatting options, can save you time and provide consistency in the look of your worksheets.*

✔ *Merging multiple cells into a single cell gives you control over the alignment and spacing of a data entry that might be unusually long in comparison to other entries in the same row or column.*

Quick Quiz

True/False

T F **1.** You cannot change the alignment of numeric values.

T F **2.** Bold and italics are examples of font styles.

T F **3.** By default, the General format is applied to numbers you enter in a cell.

T F **4.** The best way to add a line under a row of column labels is to apply the Underline font style.

T F **5.** To modify a style, open the AutoFormat dialog box and make your changes there.

T F **6.** You can merge cells horizontally, but not vertically.

Multiple Choice

1. Which of the following is *not* an alignment option?
   a. Underline
   b. Align Left
   c. Alight Right
   d. Center

2. Which of the following is the measurement unit for font sizes?
   a. leader
   b. tick
   c. millimeter
   d. point

3. If you wanted to change the entry *131.2543* to *131.25*, which button on the Formatting toolbar would you click?
   a. Increase Decimal
   b. Decrease Decimal
   c. Align Right
   d. Increase Indent

4. Which feature lets you apply a predesigned format to a range?
   a. AutoFormat
   b. Format Painter
   c. Format Wizard
   d. Style Painter

Short Answer

1. What is the easiest way to convert selected cells to currency format?

2. What are two ways to apply shading to selected cells?

3. How can you display a button that isn't showing on a toolbar?

4. What purpose do styles serve?

5. How can you apply a border to a cell or range of cells you've selected?

On Your Own

◆◆ **Open Lodging Analysis03 from the Excel Practice/Lesson03 folder.**

Exercise 1

Move the title text to cell A1, and then merge and center it over the worksheet data. Right-align the column headings. Change the column headings to a size, font, and style that you like. Then use the Format Painter to copy the format of the column labels to the row labels.

Exercise 2

Using the Lodging Analysis03 workbook, select the labels and data in the worksheet. Apply different AutoFormats to see how they look. Then create a style, and apply it to the Total row.

◆◆ **Save and close Lodging Analysis03.**

One Step Further

Exercise 1

Create a worksheet in which to log your daily physical activities. (If you created this worksheet in the previous lesson, you can continue to use that worksheet.) This worksheet should contain a list of your regular physical activities in column A and should include a column for each day of the week. In a row above the days of the week, insert a heading that reads **Minutes per Day**. Merge and center this heading. Change the heading format to 14-point, Arial, bold. Select the entire range that includes all of the days of the week and all of the activities (do not include the heading), and apply the Colorful 1 AutoFormat.

Exercise 2

In reviewing the worksheet that you created in Exercise 1, you decide that you like the basic Colorful 1 format; however, you're not fond of the colors and think you would like the borders to be somewhat different. What methods can you use to alter these features? Which method do you like the best? Write a brief answer to these questions.

Exercise 3

While learning to format cells in a worksheet, you have selected individual cells as well as ranges of cells. Use Excel's Help files to determine if there is a quick way to select an entire worksheet and apply formatting changes to all of the cells at once. Write a brief explanation of your findings.

LESSON

Changing Print Options

After completing this lesson, you will be able to:

✔ *Add a header and footer to a worksheet.*
✔ *Change margins and center a worksheet.*
✔ *Change the orientation and the scale of a worksheet.*
✔ *Add and delete page breaks.*
✔ *Set and clear a print area.*
✔ *Set other print options.*

KEY TERMS

- footer
- header
- orientation
- resolution
- scaling

One of the easiest ways to share information in a worksheet or workbook is to print copies for others to review. For instance, every year at the annual briefing for the Adventure Works resort, the activities coordinator passes out copies of an Excel worksheet that summarizes the yearly revenue for sports equipment rentals. She takes advantage of several Excel features that make worksheets more readable and more attractive.

By adding headers and footers, the activities coordinator can print information about the worksheet (such as the title, the date the worksheet was printed, and the author) on every page. She can adjust the size of the margins and change the orientation of the worksheet. She can even enlarge or reduce the size of the worksheet so all of the information fits on one page. She can center the content on a page for readability. To keep some worksheet information confidential, she can specify which parts of the worksheet to print and which parts not to print. Finally, she can insert page breaks to improve readability.

IMPORTANT

Before you can use the practice files in this lesson, you must install them from the book's companion CD to their default location. For additional information on how to find and open files used in this book, see the "Using the CD-ROM" section at the beginning of this book.

Adding a Header and Footer

THE BOTTOM LINE

Headers and footers are useful for documenting important information about a worksheet, such as the date it was created or last modified, who prepared it, the page number, and so on.

A **header** is a line of text that appears at the top of each page of a printed worksheet. A **footer** is a line of text that appears at the bottom. Headers and footers commonly contain information such as a page number, the title of a worksheet, and the date a worksheet was printed. This information provides another tool for helping users identify the contents, author, and status of a worksheet.

You can create headers and footers by picking from a list of header and footer options that Excel provides. These options include page numbers, workbook names, worksheet names, author names, company names, and combinations of these. The same options are available for both headers and footers.

You also can create headers and footers by typing the text that you want to appear or by clicking buttons to insert codes that form your own combinations of the options Excel provides. Then whenever you print the worksheet, Excel replaces the codes with the name of the workbook, the current page number, the current date, and so on. Doing this is an easy way to ensure that header and footer information is up to date.

The Header dialog box, where you create custom headers, looks similar to Figure 4-1

FIGURE 4-1

Header dialog box

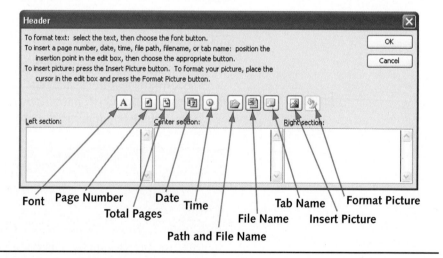

Information in the Left Section box is aligned with the left margin of the worksheet, information in the Center Section box is centered, and text in the Right Section box is aligned with the right margin. When you want to change the font, font size, or font style of a header or footer, click the Font button to open the Font dialog box.

◆ To complete the procedures in this lesson, you must use the practice file Sports Income in the Lesson04 folder in the Excel Practice folder that is located on your hard disk.

◆ Open Sports Income from the Excel Practice/Lesson04 folder.

Add a header and footer

In this exercise, you add a header and footer to a worksheet.

1 On the View menu, click Header And Footer.

The Page Setup dialog box appears with the Header/Footer tab displayed.

FIGURE 4-2

Page Setup dialog box

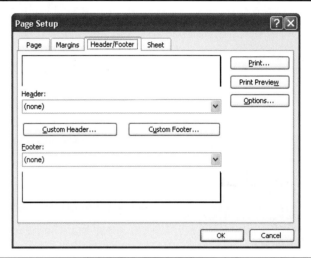

2 Click the Custom Header button.

The Header dialog box appears.

3 Click in the Right Section box, and click the Date button. Refer to Figure 4-1, where the buttons are identified.

A code for the date is inserted.

TIP

If you want to use an ampersand (&) within the text of a header or a footer, type two ampersands (&&). Otherwise, Excel interprets the single ampersand as part of the code.

4 In the Header dialog box, click OK.

The Header dialog box closes. The current date appears in the Header preview box in the Page Setup dialog box.

5 Click the Footer down arrow. On the list that appears, scroll down and click Sports Income.xls, Page 1.

The footer you chose appears in the Footer preview box.

6 **Click OK.**

The Page Setup dialog box closes. The header and footer would appear on a printed copy of the worksheet, although you can't see them on the screen.

7 **On the Standard toolbar, click the Print Preview button.**

The worksheet appears in the Preview window with the header and footer you specified, as shown in Figure 4-3.

FIGURE 4-3

Previewing a worksheet with the header and footer

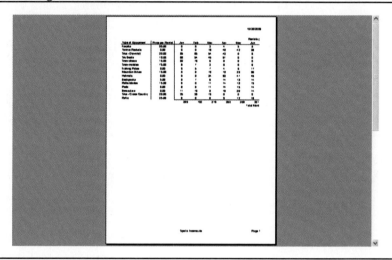

8 **On the Print Preview toolbar, click the Next button.**

Note that the header and footer also appear on the second page of the worksheet.

9 **On the Print Preview toolbar, click the Close button.**

The workbook window appears.

10 **Save the workbook with the current name.**

◆ **Keep this file open for the next exercise.**

QUICK CHECK

Q. How do you modify the format of text in a header?

A: In the Page Setup dialog box, click the Custom Header button. In the Header dialog box, select the text in the section box that you want to modify, and then click the Font button. The Font dialog box opens where you can change the font, font size, and font style.

QUICK REFERENCE ▼

Select a header or a footer

1 On the View menu, click Header And Footer.

2 Click the Header or Footer down arrow, and click the desired header or footer.

3 Click OK.

Customize a header or footer

1 On the View menu, click Header And Footer.

2 Click the Custom Header button or the Custom Footer button.

3 In the Header or Footer dialog box, type the desired text, and click buttons to enter codes in the Left, Center, or Right sections.

4 Format the text, if desired, and click OK twice.

Changing Margins

Making Printed Worksheets
Easier to Read

THE BOTTOM LINE

Margins are an effective way to control and optimize the white space on a printed worksheet. Achieving balance between data and white space adds considerably to the readability and appearance of a worksheet.

By default, worksheet margins are 1 inch on the top and the bottom and 0.75 inch on the left and right. When you add a header or footer to the worksheet, it is separated from the body of the worksheet by 0.5 inch.

You can change the margins to suit the needs of each workbook. For example, the activities coordinator at Adventure Works wants to print the Sports Income worksheet on company letterhead for the annual briefing, so she sets the top margin of the worksheet to 1.5 inches, leaving room for the company logo, address, and phone number.

Another technique for adding balance to a worksheet is centering its contents on the page. You can center the contents vertically between the top and bottom edges of the page or horizontally between the left and right edges of the page.

Change margins and alignment

In this exercise, you change the margins of a worksheet and center the worksheet on the page.

1 On the File menu, click Page Setup.

The Page Setup dialog box appears.

2 Click the Margins tab, if necessary.

The current margins are listed in the Top, Bottom, Right, Left, Header, and Footer boxes.

FIGURE 4-4

Margins tab in the Page Setup dialog box

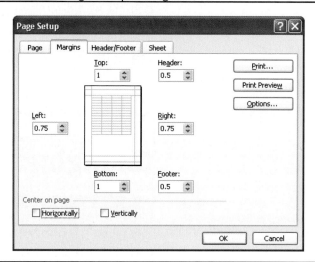

3 **Click the up arrow in the Top box twice.**

The top margin changes to 1.5 inches.

4 **Click the up arrow in the Bottom box twice.**

The bottom margin changes to 1.5 inches.

ANOTHER METHOD

You also can alter the margins in the Print Preview window by clicking the Margins button on the Print Preview toolbar and dragging the dotted margin indicators.

5 **In the Center On Page section at the bottom of the dialog box, select the Horizontally and Vertically check boxes.**

6 **Click the Print Preview button in the dialog box.**

The preview shows this change, as shown in Figure 4-5.

FIGURE 4-5

Previewing page setup

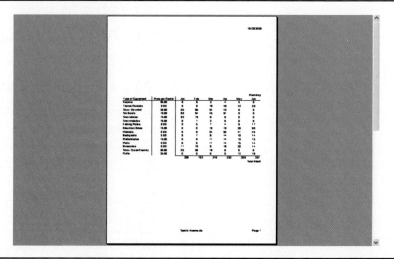

7 **On the Print Preview toolbar, click the Close button.**

The Print Preview window closes.

◆ **Keep this file open for the next exercise.**

QUICK REFERENCE ▼

Change margin settings, and center a worksheet on a page

1 On the File menu, click Page Setup, and click the Margins tab.

2 In the Top, Bottom, Left, Right, Header, or Footer boxes, click the arrow buttons, or type a new margin.

3 Select the Horizontally and Vertically check boxes, and click OK.

Changing the Orientation and Scale

THE BOTTOM LINE

Printed worksheets are easiest to read and analyze when all of the data appears on one piece of paper. Excel's orientation and scaling features give you more control over the number of pages that worksheet data prints on.

Positioning Data on a Printed Page

You can change the **orientation** of a worksheet so that it prints either vertically or horizontally on a page. A worksheet printed vertically uses the Portrait setting and looks like the document shown in Figure 4-5. Portrait orientation is the default setting. A worksheet printed horizontally uses the Landscape setting, shown in Figure 4-6.

FIGURE 4-6

Landscape orientation

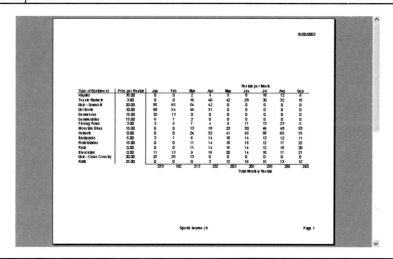

You may decide to use the Landscape setting if the width of the area you want to print is greater than the height. For example, the Sports Income workbook is currently set to print in Portrait orientation, and it needs two pages to accommodate all of the columns of data. The data would be much easier to read if it were all on one page. This can be accomplished by changing the orientation to landscape.

If you still can't fit all of the data on one printed page by changing the orientation, you can shrink or reduce it by using Excel's **scaling** options. The most common reason for scaling a worksheet is to shrink it so that you can print it on one page, but you also can enlarge the sheet so that data appears bigger and fills up more of the printed page. To scale a worksheet, you specify how much to enlarge or shrink it or you specify the number of pages on which you want it to fit.

Change the orientation and scaling of a worksheet

In this exercise, you change the orientation of a worksheet and set it up to print on one page.

1   On the File menu, click **Page Setup.**

The Page Setup dialog box appears.

2   Click the **Page tab.**

FIGURE 4-7

Page tab in the Page Setup dialog box

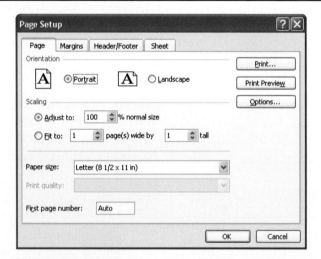

3   Click the **Landscape option.**

The orientation of the worksheet changes from portrait to landscape.

4   On the Page tab, click the **Print Preview button.**

The preview displays the first page of the worksheet.

5   On the Print Preview toolbar, click the **Close button.**

The Print Preview window closes.

6   On the File menu, click **Page Setup.**

The Page tab of the Page Setup dialog box appears.

7 In the Scaling section in the middle of the tab, click the Fit To option. Keep the default settings of 1 page wide by 1 page tall.

The worksheet is scaled to fit on one page.

8 On the Page tab, click the Print Preview button.

The scale of the worksheet decreases so that the worksheet fits on one page. It should look similar to the following illustration.

FIGURE 4-8

Setting up the data to fit on one page

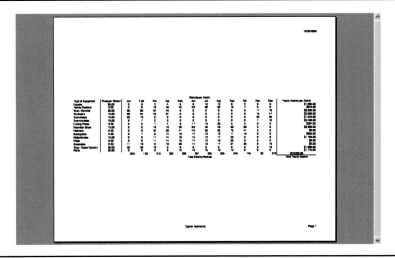

9 On the Print Preview toolbar, click the Close button.

The Print Preview window closes.

10 Save the workbook with the current name.

◆ Keep this file open for the next exercise.

TIP

You can limit a vertically oriented worksheet to one page wide but still allow it to extend several pages down. To do this, display the Page tab in the Page Setup dialog box, type 1 in the Page(s) Wide By box, and delete the number in the Tall box. Do the opposite to allow a worksheet to extend horizontally.

QUICK REFERENCE ▼

Change the page orientation of a worksheet

1 On the File menu, click Page Setup, and click the Page tab.

2 In the Orientation section, click the Portrait or Landscape option, and click OK.

QUICK CHECK

Q. What is the difference between orientation and scaling?

A: Orientation refers to the direction in which the worksheet prints—either portrait, in which the sheet is longer than it is wide, or landscape, in which the sheet is wider than it is long. Scaling refers to enlarging or reducing the data.

Scale a worksheet

1 On the File menu, click Page Setup, and click the Page tab.

2 Click the Adjust To option. In the Adjust To box, enter the percentage of the normal size at which you want the worksheet to appear.

Or

Click the Fit To option. In the two Fit To boxes, enter the number of pages wide by the number of pages tall that you want the worksheet to appear.

3 Click OK.

Adding and Deleting Page Breaks

THE BOTTOM LINE

When worksheet data prints on more than one page, you can control where the page breaks occur. This allows you to break data where it's most logical, resulting in a well-organized, easy-to-read document.

Excel determines the number of pages on which a worksheet will print based on the size of the worksheet, the margin settings, the orientation, and the scaling. The places where Excel breaks the content from one page to the next are called automatic page breaks, and Excel adjusts these automatically when you add and delete worksheet content.

You also can add and delete your own page breaks, but Excel won't adjust them as you change worksheet content. When you want to change your own page break positions, you must do it manually in the Page Break Preview window. Manual page breaks help you organize the content by letting you break pages based on content rather than dimensions. For instance, the activities coordinator at the Adventure Works wants to see how a worksheet would look if she added a page break between the rentals per month for each type of equipment and the total monthly rentals for all equipment.

Add and delete page breaks

In this exercise, you insert and delete page breaks.

1 the File menu, click Page Setup.

The Page Setup dialog box appears with the Page tab displayed.

2 In the Adjust To box, type 100, and then click OK.

The worksheet scale returns to 100%.

3 Click cell A18. On the Insert menu, click Page Break.

Excel inserts a page break in the worksheet below row 17. The page break appears as a dashed line on the worksheet, similar to that shown in Figure 4-9.

FIGURE 4-9

Inserting a page break

	A	B	C	D	E	F	G	H	I	J
1								Rentals per Month		
2	Type of Equipment	Price per Rental	Jan	Feb	Mar	Apr	May	Jun	Jul	Aug
3	Kayaks	35.00	0	0	2	4	5	8	18	12
4	Tennis Rackets	3.00	0	0	16	40	42	28	30	32
5	Skis - Downhill	20.00	85	65	54	42	0	0	0	0
6	Ski Boots	10.00	68	54	45	31	0	0	0	0
7	Snowshoes	15.00	32	13	0	0	0	0	0	0
8	Snowmobiles	75.00	6	7	2	0	0	0	0	0
9	Fishing Poles	3.00	3	5	7	4	9	17	13	23
10	Mountain Bikes	15.00	0	0	13	18	23	30	46	48
11	Helmets	0.00	0	0	24	32	41	45	58	65
12	Backpacks	5.00	3	7	6	14	18	14	13	12
13	Rollerblades	15.00	0	0	11	14	18	15	12	17
14	Pads	0.00	0	0	11	14	15	14	12	16
15	Binoculars	0.00	11	13	9	16	20	14	18	17
16	Skis - Cross Country	20.00	25	28	13	0	0	0	0	0
17	Rafts	25.00	0	0	0	3	12	16	15	13
18			233	192	213	232	203	201	235	255
19								Total Monthly Rentals		
20										

IMPORTANT

A manual page break occurs immediately above and to the left of the selected cell.

 4 **On the Standard toolbar, click the Print Preview button.**

A preview of the worksheet appears with the page break you just inserted.

5 **On the Print Preview toolbar, click the Close button.**

The Print Preview window closes.

TIP

You must select a cell directly below the manual page break in order for the Remove Page Break option to appear on the Insert menu.

6 **On the Insert menu, click Remove Page Break.**

The manual page break is removed, and the page breaks return to their default positions.

ANOTHER METHOD

You can move page breaks by dragging them in the Page Break Preview window. You display this window by clicking the Page Break Preview button on the Print Preview toolbar or by clicking Page Break Preview on the View menu.

7 **Save the workbook with the current name.**

◆ **Keep this file open for the next exercise.**

QUICK CHECK

Q. If you want to insert a page break between columns G and H and rows 20 and 21, which cell should you select before executing the Page Break command on the Insert menu?

A: **You should click cell H21.**

QUICK REFERENCE ▼

Add a page break

1 Select the cell directly below and to the right of where you want the page break.

2 On the Insert menu, click Page Break.

Delete a page break

1 Select the cell directly below and to the right of the page break you want to delete.

2 On the Insert menu, click Remove Page Break.

Setting and Clearing a Print Area

Printing Part of a Worksheet

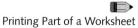

THE BOTTOM LINE

Defining an area or a section in a worksheet to print gives you more control over exactly what shows up on the printed page.

If you don't want to print an entire worksheet, you can print only an area you specify by setting a print area. For example, you might have a worksheet in which you're recording data for each month in the year. You want to print only data recorded for the first three months. You can set the print area to include this data only. Any other printing options you've set, such as margins or orientation, apply to the print area. The print area you set is the only part of the worksheet that prints until you clear it or change it.

TIP

Setting a print area works differently from choosing to print a selection using the Print dialog box. If you set a print area, only cells in that area will print, regardless of what cells are selected when you execute the Print command. Also, when you set a print area, you do not need to select a range before you print.

The activities coordinator at Adventure Works decides to scale the worksheet to fit on one page. She also sets a print area to print only the revenue generated by sports equipment rentals and not the maintenance cost of the equipment.

Set and clear a print area

In this exercise, you set and clear a print area in a worksheet.

1 **On the File menu, click Page Setup.**

The Page Setup dialog box appears with the Page tab displayed.

2 In the Scaling section in the middle of the tab, click the Fit To option. Keep the default settings of 1 page wide by 1 page tall.

The worksheet is scaled to fit on one page.

You also can specify a print area in the Page Setup dialog box. On the Sheet tab, enter the cell range in the Print Area box.

3 Click OK.

4 Select the range A2:E18.

5 On the File menu, point to Print Area, and click Set Print Area.

 6 Click in any cell, and on the Standard toolbar, click the Print Preview button.

The Print Preview window appears, showing what would print if you printed the worksheet with the current settings.

FIGURE 4-10

Previewing the sheet

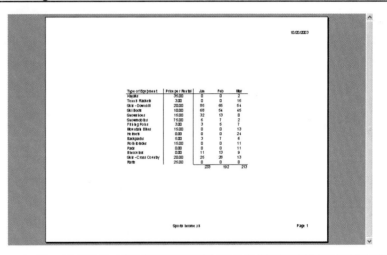

7 On the Print Preview toolbar, click the Print button. In the Print dialog box that appears, click OK.

The selection prints.

8 On the File menu, point to Print Area, and click Clear Print Area.

The print area is cleared.

9 Save the workbook with the current name.

◆ Keep this file open for the next exercise.

ANOTHER METHOD

To print an area of a worksheet without setting a print area, select the area. On the File menu, click Print. In the Print dialog box in the Print What section, click Selection, and click OK.

QUICK REFERENCE ▼

Set and clear a print area

1 Select the portion of the worksheet you want to print.

2 On the File menu, point to Print Area, and click Set Print Area.

3 Clear the print area by pointing to Print Area on the File menu and clicking Clear Print Area.

QUICK CHECK

Q. Which menu contains the commands to set and clear a print area?

A: The File menu contains the commands to set and clear a print area.

Setting Other Print Options

THE BOTTOM LINE

Worksheets that print on two or more pages may benefit from having certain row and column labels (and even row numbers and column letters) repeated on every page. These can be helpful in clearly identifying data and eliminating the need to flip through pages to determine what the data represents. You also can save on ink or toner by selecting options to control the quality of printouts.

To further customize your worksheet printout, you can print row and column labels, gridlines, row numbers, and column letters on each page. You also can choose whether to print in color or black and white, and you can select the quality of the printing. These options appear on the Sheet tab of the Page Setup dialog box, shown in Figure 4-11.

FIGURE 4-11

Sheet tab in the Page Setup dialog box

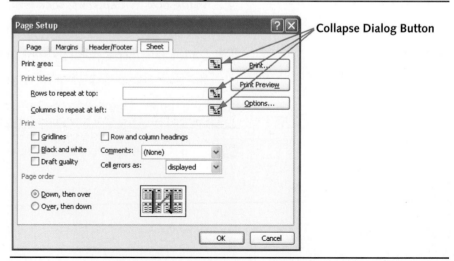

Options include:

- **Rows To Repeat At Top or Columns To Repeat At Left** Print row or column text labels on each page by specifying the row or rows to repeat at the top of each page and the column or columns to repeat at the left of each page. Printing titles on each page of a multiple-page worksheet makes it easy to identify the data on subsequent pages.
- **Gridlines** Print the gridlines that appear in the worksheet window.
- **Black And White** Print color worksheets more quickly and save ink or toner by printing them in black and white.
- **Draft Quality** Print the worksheet at a reduced **resolution** in order to print faster and to save ink or toner.
- **Row And Column Headings** Print the row numbers and column letters that appear in the worksheet window.

Apply additional print settings

In this exercise, you apply print settings from the Sheet tab in the Page Setup dialog box.

1 On the File menu, click **Page Setup.**

The Page Setup dialog box appears with the Page tab displayed.

2 In the Scaling section in the middle of the tab, click the **Adjust To** option, type **100** in the text box, and then click **OK.**

The worksheet scale returns to 100%.

3 On the View menu, click **Page Break Preview.** If the Welcome to Page Break Preview message box appears, click **OK.**

The worksheet appears in Page Break Preview.

4 Click and drag the dashed blue page break line to the left until it's between columns H and I.

The worksheet should have a vertical page break between the columns for June and July.

5 On the View menu, click **Normal.**

The worksheet is displayed in Normal view.

6 On the File menu, click **Page Setup,** and then click the **Sheet tab.**

The Page Setup dialog box appears with the Sheet tab displayed.

 7 Click the Collapse Dialog button on the Print Area box.

The Page Setup dialog box collapses, and you are returned to the worksheet.

 8 Select the range A2:N18, and then click the Expand Dialog button, as shown in Figure 4-12.

FIGURE 4-12

Selecting the print area

Expand Dialog button

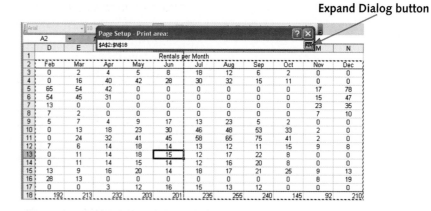

The Page Setup dialog box redisplays with the range you selected in the Print Area box.

9 **Click the Collapse Dialog button on the Columns To Repeat At Left box.**

The Page Setup dialog box collapses, and you are returned to the worksheet. The mouse pointer icon changes to a down arrow.

10 **Position the mouse pointer on the column A selector and click, and then click the Expand Dialog button.**

The Page Setup dialog box redisplays with column A displayed in the Columns To Repeat At Left box.

11 **Click the Row And Column Headings box, and then click the Print Preview button.**

The worksheet appears in the Preview window with page 1, which contains the data for the first six months and the row and column headings, as shown in Figure 4-13.

FIGURE 4-13

Previewing the sheet

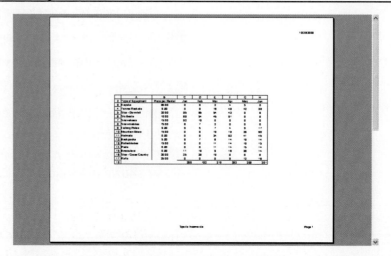

12 Click the Next button to preview page 2.

The column labels should be repeated on page 2, and the row and column headings should appear.

13 Click the Close button in the Print Preview window.

The worksheet appears in Normal view.

14 On the File menu, click Page Setup, and click the Sheet tab, if necessary.

15 Delete the selections in the Print Area box and the Columns To Repeat At Left box. Click the Row And Column Headings box to deselect it, and then click OK.

The additional print options are removed.

16 Save the workbook with the current name.

◆ Close Sports Income.

◆ If you are continuing to other lessons, leave Excel open.

◆ If you are not continuing to other lessons, save and close all open workbooks, then close Excel.

QUICK CHECK

Q. Which option on the Sheet tab in the Page Setup dialog box lets you print a worksheet at a reduced resolution?

A: The Draft Quality option lets you print at a reduced resolution.

Key Points

✔ *Headers and footers are useful for documenting important information about a worksheet, such as the date it was created or last modified, who prepared it, the page number, and so on.*

✔ *Margins are an effective way to control and optimize the white space on a printed worksheet.*

✔ *Centering the content in a worksheet can help you achieve balance between data and white space, which adds considerably to the readability and appearance of a worksheet.*

✔ *Printed worksheets are easiest to read and analyze when all of the data appears on one piece of paper. Excel's orientation and scaling features give you more control over the number of pages that worksheet data prints on.*

✔ *When worksheet data prints on more than one page, you can control where the page breaks occur. This allows you to break data where it's most logical, resulting in a well-organized, easy-to-read document.*

✔ *Defining an area or a section in a worksheet to print gives you more control over exactly what shows up on the printed page.*

✔ *Worksheets that print on two or more pages may benefit from having certain row and column labels (and even row numbers and column letters) repeated on every page. These can be helpful in clearly identifying data and eliminating the need to flip through pages to determine what the data represents.*

✔ *You can save on ink or toner by selecting options to control the quality of printouts.*

Quick Quiz

True/False

T F **1.** A header prints at the top of the first page only of a printed worksheet.

T F **2.** You can insert graphics in the header or footer of a worksheet.

T F **3.** In landscape orientation, the sheet appears longer than it is wide.

T F **4.** You can change margins by adjusting settings in the Page Setup dialog box or by dragging margin indicators in the Print Preview window.

T F **5.** Once you insert a manual page break, you cannot remove it.

Multiple Choice

1. If you wanted to change the point size of text in a custom header, which button in the Header dialog box would you click?
   a. Format
   b. Font
   c. Font Size
   d. Size

2. What are the default margin settings for a worksheet?
   a. top and bottom at .5 inch; left and right at 1 inch
   b. top and bottom at 1 inch; left and right at .5 inch
   c. top and bottom at .75 inch; left and right at 1 inch
   d. top and bottom at 1 inch; left and right at .75 inch

3. Which option lets you enlarge or reduce the size of a worksheet?
   a. orientation
   b. scaling
   c. resolution
   d. centering

4. In which view can you manually adjust page breaks?
   a. Print Preview
   b. Page Break Preview
   c. Zoom view
   d. Expand Dialog view

5. In which orientation does the page print longer than it is wide?
   a. Portrait
   b. Picture
   c. Landscape
   d. Horizontal

Short Answer

1. How can you automatically add the date to the bottom of every page when you print a worksheet?

2. How can you change a worksheet's page orientation?

3. What are two ways to print an area of a worksheet you've selected?

4. What are the default page margins of a worksheet?

5 Why would you want to repeat row or column labels on subsequent pages of a worksheet printout?

IMPORTANT

In the On Your Own section below, you must complete Exercise 1 before continuing to Exercise 2.

On Your Own

◆ Open Sports Income from the Excel Practice/Lesson04 folder.

Exercise 1

Delete the existing header and footer. Add the header Sports Income by Month, Year, and Activity in the top right corner of the worksheet. Add a footer that always prints the current date and time at the bottom center of the worksheet. Change the font of the header and footer to one of your choice.

◆ Save Sports Income and leave the file open for Exercise 2.

Exercise 2

Set the Sports Income workbook to print in Portrait orientation with grid-lines, and adjust the scaling to print at 100% of normal size. Preview the location of the page breaks, and scale the worksheet to print on a single page. Set the print area to A1:P20, and preview the worksheet.

◆ Close Sports Income.

One Step Further

Exercise 1

You want to create a footer that includes your name, the file name (including its location), and the current page number out of the total number of pages. You want this information to be left-aligned, centered, and right-aligned. Briefly describe how you would do this.

Exercise 2

You want to create a header for your worksheet that includes the current date and time in the left corner and your company logo in the right corner. Briefly describe how you would you do this.

Exercise 3

On the Sheet tab of the Page Setup dialog box are a few additional options that were not discussed in this lesson. Explore this tab of the dialog box, and use the Help system, if necessary, to determine how you can choose to print cell comments and where they can be placed. Additionally, determine the significance of the Page Order section of this sheet. When would one page order be preferred over the other?

LESSON

5

Organizing Worksheets and Window Display

After completing this lesson, you will be able to:

✔ *Magnify and shrink a worksheet on-screen.*
✔ *Hide and unhide rows and columns.*
✔ *Freeze and unfreeze rows and columns.*
✔ *Move between worksheets in a workbook.*
✔ *Add and delete worksheets in a workbook.*
✔ *Copy and move worksheets in a workbook.*
✔ *Sort data.*
✔ *Apply filters to data.*

KEY TERMS

- ascending order
- descending order
- filter
- freeze
- hide
- zoom

As you work with Excel, you will probably create worksheets that contain more data than can be viewed all at once on screen. You also might find that you need to distribute related data among several worksheets and workbooks. Fortunately, Excel provides several methods that allow you to work with the content in large worksheets or with the content spread across multiple worksheets and workbooks. These methods include assorted viewing options, the ability to add or delete worksheets in a workbook, and ways to sort and limit the data that's displayed.

The viewing options are particularly useful when you have a lot of data in your worksheet. You can magnify a worksheet to enlarge cells and see the content more easily, or you can shrink a worksheet so that you can see more of the content in the worksheet at once. Hiding worksheet rows and columns lets you focus on specific information in your worksheet by concealing data that is not relevant. When you want to see those rows and columns again, you unhide them. You can *freeze* one or more rows or columns so that they always remain in view, no matter how far you scroll down or across the worksheet. This is helpful when you want to keep data labels in sight. You can easily unfreeze the rows or columns to restore the look of your worksheet.

When you want to include related, but somewhat different, data in an existing workbook, you can add one or more worksheets. This allows you to keep the data in one workbook without creating overly large or complex worksheets. You can easily delete worksheets that are no longer necessary. You can also rearrange the order of worksheets and copy worksheets.

An important aspect of working with large amounts of data is the ability to organize it in a certain order and focus on the most important data in a worksheet, whether that data represents the best ten days of sales in a month or slow-selling product lines that you may need to reevaluate. Excel provides a number of powerful, flexible tools with which you can sort and limit the data displayed in your worksheet. In this lesson, you'll learn how to sort and *filter* the data that appears in your worksheets.

IMPORTANT

Before you can use the practice files in this lesson, you must install them from the book's companion CD to their default location. For additional information on how to find and open files used in this book, see the "Using the CD-ROM" section at the beginning of this book.

Magnifying and Shrinking a Worksheet On-Screen

THE BOTTOM LINE

Excel's Zoom feature lets you zoom in on a portion of a worksheet so that it appears larger and the data is easier to read. Or you can zoom out to get a better overall view of the worksheet, which makes it easy to identify formatting inconsistencies or awkward spacing or alignment.

If you've ever operated a video camcorder, you probably know how useful the zoom feature can be. You can zoom in to get a close-up view of your subject and zoom out to get a broader view of the subject and its surroundings. Excel's Zoom feature works in the same way.

When you create a worksheet, the cells and any data they contain appear at a standard size of 100%, which means basically that the size they appear on the screen is the size they appear on the printed page. You can magnify a worksheet to make each cell appear bigger. For example, in a large worksheet with cell after cell of numeric data, you might want to zoom in on a section so that the numbers are larger and, therefore, less stressful on your eyes to read. Or you can shrink the worksheet to see more rows and columns at a time. Again, in a large worksheet where all of the data does not fit on the screen, reducing the view of it lets you easily assess the overall appearance of the data.

To magnify or shrink a worksheet, you "**zoom**" it. To zoom in (magnify), you select a size greater than 100%; to zoom out (shrink), you select a size less than 100%.

◆ To complete the procedures in this lesson, you must use the files **Sports Income05**, **Food**, and **Filter** in the **Lesson05** folder in the Excel Practice folder located on your hard disk.

◆ Open **Sports Income05** from the Excel Practice/Lesson05 folder.

Zoom in and out

In this exercise, you zoom in and out on a worksheet.

1 Click cell C7. On the View menu, click Zoom.

The Zoom dialog box appears.

FIGURE 5-1

Zoom dialog box

2 Click the 200% option, and click OK.

Each cell of the worksheet appears twice its original size.

ANOTHER METHOD

On the Standard toolbar, click the down arrow on the Zoom button, and select 200%.

TROUBLESHOOTING

If the Zoom button doesn't appear on the Standard toolbar, click the Toolbar Options button, click Add Or Remove Buttons, click Standard, and then click Zoom on the list of buttons that appears.

3 On the Standard toolbar, click in the Zoom box.

4 In the Zoom box, type 60, and press Enter.

The worksheet shrinks to 60 percent of its original size and looks similar to the following illustration.

FIGURE 5-2

Zooming out

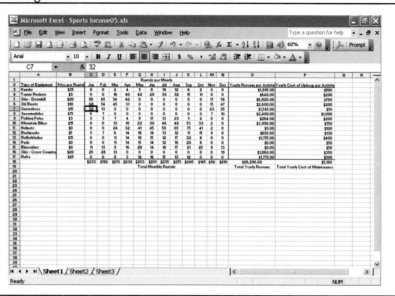

100% ▼

5 Click the down arrow on the Zoom box, and click 100%.

The worksheet returns to its original size.

◆ Keep this file open for the next exercise.

QUICK REFERENCE ▼

Zoom in and out on a worksheet

1 On the View menu, click Zoom.

2 In the Zoom dialog box, select the percentage by which you want to shrink or magnify the worksheet.

QUICK CHECK

Q. If you changed the zoom setting to 75%, would you be zooming in or zooming out?

A: You would be zooming out.

Hiding Rows and Columns

THE BOTTOM LINE

Not all of the data in a worksheet is relevant all of the time to all of the people who view it. You can hide specified rows and columns so that only the data you want to focus on is displayed.

Sometimes you have more rows or columns in a worksheet than you want to see at one time. In such situations, you can **hide** rows or columns so that they don't appear on your screen or in worksheet printouts. When you want to see them again, you unhide them.

For example, the activities coordinator at Adventure Works wants to focus on equipment rented during December, January, and February. On the worksheet, she hides the columns for the rest of the year. She already knows that no one rents kayaks during the winter, so she hides that row as well. When she's finished viewing the winter rentals, she reveals the hidden columns and the row so that she can view the rentals for the entire year.

Hide and unhide rows and columns

In this exercise, you hide and unhide worksheet rows and columns.

1 **Click the column selector for column D (Feb), hold the Shift key, and click the column selector for column L (Oct).**

Excel selects the columns.

ANOTHER METHOD

Click the column selector for column D, and drag the mouse pointer to the column selector for column L.

2 **On the Format menu, point to Column, and click Hide.**

The columns are hidden. Notice that the column labeling has not changed and that a dark line indicates where the hidden columns D through L are.

FIGURE 5-3

Hiding columns

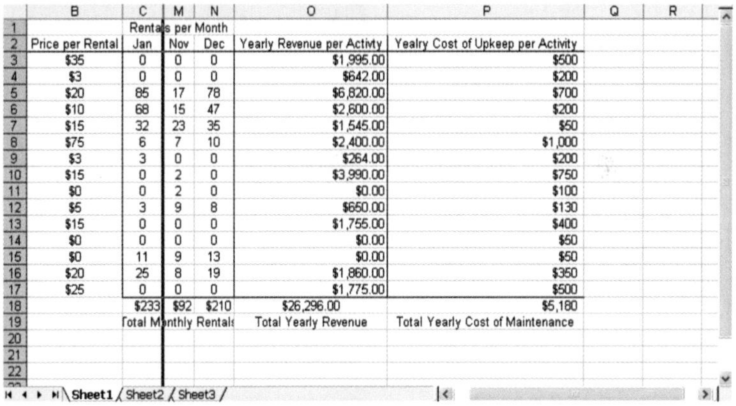

	B	C	M	N	O	P	Q	R
1		Rentals per Month						
2	Price per Rental	Jan	Nov	Dec	Yearly Revenue per Activity	Yealry Cost of Upkeep per Activity		
3	$35	0	0	0	$1,995.00	$500		
4	$3	0	0	0	$642.00	$200		
5	$20	85	17	78	$6,820.00	$700		
6	$10	68	15	47	$2,600.00	$200		
7	$15	32	23	35	$1,545.00	$50		
8	$75	6	7	10	$2,400.00	$1,000		
9	$3	3	0	0	$264.00	$200		
10	$15	0	2	0	$3,990.00	$750		
11	$0	0	2	0	$0.00	$100		
12	$5	3	9	8	$650.00	$130		
13	$15	0	0	0	$1,755.00	$400		
14	$0	0	0	0	$0.00	$50		
15	$0	11	9	13	$0.00	$50		
16	$20	25	8	19	$1,860.00	$350		
17	$25	0	0	0	$1,775.00	$500		
18		$233	$92	$210	$26,296.00	$5,180		
19		Total Monthly Rentals			Total Yearly Revenue	Total Yearly Cost of Maintenance		
20								
21								
22								

H ◀ ▶ H \Sheet1 ⟨ Sheet2 ⟨ Sheet3 /

3 **Click the row selector for row 3 (Kayaks).**

The row is selected.

4 **On the Format menu, point to Row, and then click Hide.**

The row is hidden. Notice that the row numbering has not changed and that a dark line indicates where the hidden row 3 is.

5 **Click the column selector for column C, and drag to the column selector for column M.**

Excel selects columns C and M.

ANOTHER METHOD

Click the column selector for column C, hold the Shift key, and click the column selector for column M.

6　**On the Format menu, point to Column, and click Unhide.**

Columns D through L are redisplayed.

7　**Click a blank area of the worksheet outside of the selected area.**

The columns are deselected.

8　**Click the row selector for row 2, and drag to the row selector for row 4.**

Rows 2 and 4 are selected.

ANOTHER METHOD

Click the row selector for row 2, hold the Shift key, and click the row selector for row 4.

9　**On the Format menu, point to Row, and then click Unhide.**

Row 3 is redisplayed.

◆　**Close the workbook without saving your changes.**

QUICK REFERENCE ▼

Hide a row or column

1　Click the row or column selector for the row or column you want to hide.

2　On the Format menu, point to Row or Column, and click Hide.

Unhide a row or column

1　Select the rows or columns on both sides of the hidden row or column.

2　On the Format menu, point to Row or Column, and click Unhide.

Freezing Rows and Columns

THE BOTTOM LINE

When you scroll in a large worksheet to bring rows and columns of data into view, you can implement the freezing feature to keep specified data, such as row or column labels, from moving off the screen. With the label always visible, you can easily identify what the data represents.

When your worksheet is larger than you can display on-screen at once, you need to scroll right and down to see all of your columns and rows. If your leftmost column and top row contain labels, scrolling can make the labels disappear off the edge of your screen—leaving you to wonder what exactly is in the cells you're seeing.

To remedy this problem, you can **freeze** rows and columns so that they remain on the screen even when you scroll down and across the worksheet. For example, the chef at Adventure Works uses a workbook to track the amount of food that is prepared by the popular restaurant at the resort. Doing this helps him determine what supplies to order from month to month. He freezes the rows and columns that have labels so that he can keep them in view as he scrolls down and across a worksheet.

◆ **Open Food from the Excel Practice/Lesson05 folder.**

Freeze and unfreeze rows and columns

In this exercise, you freeze and unfreeze rows and columns.

1 Scroll the worksheet to the right and then back to column A.

When you scroll the worksheet to the right, the leftmost columns disappear.

2 Click cell B3.

This cell is just below the row you want to freeze and just to the right of the column you want to freeze.

3 On the Window menu, click Freeze Panes.

The month row and Type of Food column are now frozen.

4 Scroll the worksheet to the right.

The leftmost column, with the category labels, remains visible on the screen.

5 Scroll down the worksheet.

The month row remains visible on the screen.

FIGURE 5-4

Freezing the month row and category labels column

	A	I	J	K	L	M	N	O	P	Q
1		Ordered per Month in Pounds								
2	Type of Food	Jul	Aug	Sep	Oct	Nov	Dec	Total Yearly Consumption	Total Yearly Cost	
21	Pork Chops	0	0	0	0	15	47	202	$252.50	
22	Pork Loin	40	40	40	25	25	25	370	$370.00	
23	Porterhouse Steak	35	30	25	20	15	15	250	$437.50	
24	Prime Rib	40	40	40	25	25	25	370	$740.00	
25	Ribeye Steak	40	40	30	25	25	20	330	$577.50	
26	Roast Beef	85	85	75	70	65	65	810	$688.50	
27	Salmon	30	30	20	15	10	10	210	$315.00	
28	Shrimp	70	70	55	40	30	20	500	$1,000.00	
29	Sirloin Steak	75	75	50	30	30	40	550	$825.00	
30	Sole	30	30	20	20	10	10	240	$300.00	
31	Swordfish	35	35	30	25	10	10	255	$459.00	
32	T-Bone Steak	75	75	50	30	30	40	550	$1,072.50	
33	Tuna	30	30	20	20	10	10	240	$360.00	
34	Turkey	0	0	0	0	200	150	350	$192.50	
35	Veal	35	30	25	20	10	10	235	$470.00	
36								13697	$18,879.25	
37										

H ◀ ▶ H \ Meats ⟋ Dry Goods ⟋ Produce ⟋

6 Press Ctrl+Home.

Excel scrolls to the top left unfrozen cell.

7 On the Window menu, click Unfreeze Panes.

The panes are unfrozen.

◆ **Keep this file open for the next exercise.**

QUICK REFERENCE ▼

Freeze rows and columns

1 Click a cell below the bottom row you want to freeze and to the right of the rightmost column you want to freeze.

2 On the Windows menu, click Freeze Panes.

Unfreeze rows and columns

On the Windows menu, click Unfreeze Panes.

QUICK CHECK

Q. If you click a cell in column D and then execute the Freeze Panes command, which columns will be frozen?

A: Columns A, B, and C will be frozen.

Managing Worksheets in a Workbook

Organizing Data

THE BOTTOM LINE

Each Excel workbook is made up of individual worksheets that you can add to, delete from, move, and copy as desired. This gives you the flexibility to group worksheets with similar subject matter together in one file and enables you to be more effective in organizing and managing data.

Storing related worksheet data in one workbook file has many organizational benefits. By using this method of organization, you can open all associated worksheets in a workbook at once, which saves time and ensures that all necessary data is available for a specific task. This also lets you quickly view related information and copy necessary data from one worksheet to the next without having to open and close various workbooks.

Moving between Worksheets

As you learned in Lesson 1, you can navigate from worksheet to worksheet by using the sheet tabs at the bottom of the worksheet window.

FIGURE 5-5

Using the sheet tabs to display different worksheets

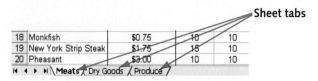

Sheet tabs

18	Monkfish	$0.75	10	10
19	New York Strip Steak	$1.75	15	10
20	Pheasant	$3.00	10	10

⊮ ◄ ► ⊯ \ Meats / Dry Goods / Produce /

The chef at Adventure Works uses several worksheets in one workbook. He orders different types of foods from different suppliers: one supplier provides meat, such as beef and poultry; another provides dry goods, such as flour and sugar; and a third provides produce. The chef tracks all of the food that he orders from each supplier on a separate worksheet in the same workbook. He can view each worksheet in the Food workbook by clicking the appropriate sheet tab.

Navigate among worksheets

You have learned how to customize the display of data in a single worksheet. In this exercise, you will display and view the various worksheets in a workbook.

1 **Click the Dry Goods tab.**

The Dry Goods worksheet is displayed.

2 **Click the Produce tab.**

The Produce worksheet is displayed.

3 **Click the Meats tab.**

The Meats worksheet is displayed.

◆ **Keep this file open for the next exercise.**

QUICK REFERENCE ▼

Navigate between worksheets in a workbook

Click the sheet tab of the worksheet you want to display.

Adding and Deleting Worksheets in a Workbook

By default, each new workbook contains three blank worksheets. If you don't need all three worksheets, you can easily delete the unnecessary ones. If you want more worksheets, you can insert as many new ones as you need. For example, the chef at Adventure Works decides to add a new worksheet to the Food workbook. Because he wants this new worksheet to contain summaries of figures from the other three worksheets, he names this worksheet *Summary*.

Add and delete a worksheet

In this exercise, you add and delete a worksheet.

1 **Click the Produce tab.**

The Produce worksheet is displayed.

2 **On the Insert menu, click Worksheet.**

A new worksheet named Sheet1 is inserted to the left of Produce.

ANOTHER METHOD

Right-click the sheet tab, select Insert, click Worksheet on the General tab of the Insert dialog box, and click OK.

3 Select any cell, type Test, and press Enter.

4 On the Edit menu, click Delete Sheet.

An alert message box opens.

FIGURE 5-6

Warning message

ANOTHER METHOD

Right-click the sheet tab, and select Delete on the shortcut menu.

5 Click Delete.

The new worksheet is deleted, and the Produce worksheet is redisplayed.

6 Click the Meats tab.

The Meats worksheet is displayed.

7 On the Insert menu, click Worksheet.

A new worksheet named Sheet2 is inserted to the left of Meats.

FIGURE 5-7

Inserting a new sheet

8 Double-click the Sheet2 tab.

9 Type Summary, and press Enter.

The name of the worksheet is changed.

◆ Keep this file open for the next exercise.

QUICK REFERENCE ▼

Add a worksheet to a workbook

On the Insert menu, click Worksheet.

Delete a worksheet in a workbook

1 In your workbook, click the sheet tab for the worksheet you want to delete.

2 On the Edit menu, click Delete Sheet.

Moving and Copying Worksheets

Just as you can move and copy data in a worksheet, you can move and copy the worksheets within a workbook. For example, you might want to move a worksheet in order to change the order of sheets in the workbook. You might want to copy a worksheet so that you can overwrite existing data with new data in the copy. When you copy the worksheet, you retain the structure and formatting of the original so that you don't need to "rebuild" it from scratch.

The chef at Adventure Works wants the Summary worksheet that was just added to appear as the last sheet in the workbook instead of the first. He also wants the workbook to include a worksheet for beverages. He decides to copy one of the existing sheets so that he can simply overwrite the data with the new beverage data.

Move and copy a worksheet

In this exercise, you move a worksheet to another location in the workbook and make a copy of a worksheet.

1 Click the Summary sheet tab, press and hold the mouse button, and drag until the small, black sheet insertion arrow is at the right corner of the Produce tab, as shown in Figure 5-8.

FIGURE 5-8

Moving a worksheet

The Summary sheet is moved from its position as the first sheet to follow the Produce sheet.

ANOTHER METHOD

Right-click the sheet tab, select Move Or Copy on the shortcut menu, click (Move To End) in the Before Sheet list box, and click OK.

2 Click the Produce sheet tab, hold the Ctrl key, and drag until the sheet insertion arrow is between the Produce and the Summary sheet tabs, as shown in Figure 5-9.

FIGURE 5-9

Copying a worksheet

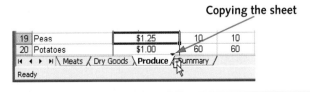

A copy of the Produce sheet, named *Produce (2)*, is inserted between the Produce and Summary worksheets.

ANOTHER METHOD

Right-click the sheet tab, select Move Or Copy on the shortcut menu, click Summary in the Before Sheet list box, click the Create A Copy box, and then click OK.

3 **Double-click the Produce (2) sheet tab, type** Beverages, **and press Enter.**

The copied sheet is renamed.

4 **Click the Save button on the Standard toolbar.**

ANOTHER METHOD

- Select Save on the File menu.
- Press Ctrl+S.

◆ **Close Food.**

QUICK REFERENCE ▼

Move a worksheet

1 Click the sheet tab.

2 Drag the sheet tab to the desired location.

Copy a worksheet

1 Click the sheet tab.

2 Hold the Ctrl key, and drag the copy to the desired location.

QUICK CHECK

Q. You have a worksheet that contains four sheets. You want to insert a sheet between sheets 2 and 3. How do you do it?

A: Click the Sheet3 tab, and select Worksheet on the Insert menu. Or right-click the Sheet3 tab, click Insert on the shortcut menu, click Worksheet on the General tab of the Insert dialog box, and click OK.

Sorting Data

THE BOTTOM LINE

The order in which you enter data is not necessarily the most logical order for interpreting or analyzing it. Sorting data (from highest to lowest or smallest to largest, for example) lets you quickly and easily identify trends and generate forecasts or predictions.

Sorting a Data List

The data you enter in a worksheet may be in an arbitrary order. For example, in a list of employees, an employee's name is added to the list as he or she joins the company. It might be more useful to the human resources manager, for example, to view the list of employees according to the department they're in or by their starting salary.

You can sort rows of data according to the contents of a particular column or columns. You can sort in **ascending order,** in which alphabetic data appears from A to Z, numeric data appears from lowest to highest or smallest to largest, and dates appear from the oldest to the most recent. If you sort in **descending order,** data appears just the opposite.

◆ **Open Sports Income05 from the Excel Practice/Lesson05 folder.**

Sort data

In this exercise, you sort equipment by the cost per rental and by the yearly revenue per type of equipment.

1 **Select the range A2:P17.**

This is the list you will sort.

2 **On the Data menu, click Sort to open the Sort dialog box.**

FIGURE 5-10

Sort dialog box

3 **Click the down arrow on the Sort By text box, and select Price per Rental.**

4 **Click OK.**

The data is sorted from lowest to highest price per rental.

FIGURE 5-11

Sorting by the Price per Rental column

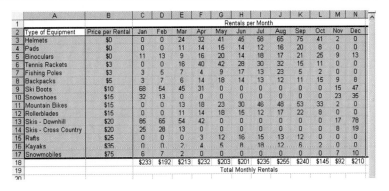

	A	B	C	D	E	F	G	H	I	J	K	L	M	N
1							Rentals per Month							
2	Type of Equipment	Price per Rental	Jan	Feb	Mar	Apr	May	Jun	Jul	Aug	Sep	Oct	Nov	Dec
3	Helmets	$0	0	0	24	32	41	45	58	65	75	41	2	0
4	Pads	$0	0	0	11	14	15	14	12	16	20	8	0	0
5	Binoculars	$0	11	13	9	16	20	14	18	17	21	25	9	13
6	Tennis Rackets	$3	0	0	16	40	42	28	30	32	15	11	0	0
7	Fishing Poles	$3	3	5	7	4	9	17	13	23	5	2	0	0
8	Backpacks	$5	3	7	6	14	18	14	13	12	11	15	9	8
9	Ski Boots	$10	68	54	45	31	0	0	0	0	0	0	15	47
10	Snowshoes	$15	32	13	0	0	0	0	0	0	0	0	23	35
11	Mountain Bikes	$15	0	0	13	18	23	30	46	48	53	33	2	0
12	Rollerblades	$15	0	0	11	14	18	15	12	17	22	8	0	0
13	Skis - Downhill	$20	65	65	54	42	0	0	0	0	0	0	17	78
14	Skis - Cross Country	$20	25	28	13	0	0	0	0	0	0	0	8	19
15	Rafts	$25	0	0	0	3	12	16	15	13	12	0	0	0
16	Kayaks	$35	0	0	2	4	5	8	18	12	6	2	0	0
17	Snowmobiles	$75	6	7	2	0	0	0	0	0	0	0	7	10
18			$233	$192	$213	$232	$203	$201	$235	$255	$240	$145	$92	$210
19							Total Monthly Rentals								
20														

5 **On the Standard toolbar, click the Undo button.**

The rows of data are returned to their original order.

6 **Select the range A2:P17.**

7 **On the Data menu, click Sort.**

The Sort dialog box opens.

8 **Click the down arrow on the Sort By text box, and select Yearly Revenue per Activity.**

9 **Click the Descending button, and then click OK.**

The data is sorted from the type of equipment with the highest yearly revenue to the lowest yearly revenue.

10 **Click cell B3, and on the Window menu, click Freeze Panes.**

You will freeze the column labels so that you can scroll to bring the Yearly Revenue per Activity column into view.

11 **Click the right scroll arrow so that column O is next to column A.**

You can now see which type of equipment rentals generated the most yearly revenue.

FIGURE 5-12

Sorting equipment by yearly revenues

	A	O	P	Q
1				
2	Type of Equipment	Yearly Revenue per Activity	Yearly Cost of Upkeep per Activity	
3	Skis - Downhill	$6,820.00	$700	
4	Mountain Bikes	$3,990.00	$750	
5	Ski Boots	$2,600.00	$200	
6	Snowmobiles	$2,400.00	$1,000	
7	Kayaks	$1,995.00	$500	
8	Skis - Cross Country	$1,860.00	$350	
9	Rafts	$1,775.00	$500	
10	Rollerblades	$1,755.00	$400	
11	Snowshoes	$1,545.00	$50	
12	Backpacks	$650.00	$130	
13	Tennis Rackets	$642.00	$200	
14	Fishing Poles	$264.00	$200	
15	Helmets	$0.00	$100	
16	Pads	$0.00	$50	
17	Binoculars	$0.00	$50	
18		$26,296.00	$5,180	
19		Total Yearly Revenue	Total Yearly Cost of Maintenance	
20				

12 **On the Window menu, click Unfreeze Panes.**

Columns B through N are redisplayed.

◆ **Close the workbook without saving your changes.**

QUICK REFERENCE ▼

Sort data

1 Select the range to be sorted.

2 Click Sort on the Data menu.

3 In the Sort dialog box, specify the column or columns by which the rows are to be sorted and the sort order.

4 Click OK.

Filtering Data

THE BOTTOM LINE

You can display a subset of rows that meet certain rules, or criteria, by applying a filter to data. The rest of the rows are temporarily "filtered out," enabling you to focus on the data that's pertinent to your review or analysis.

Excel spreadsheets can hold as much data as you need them to, but you may not want to work with all of the data in a worksheet at the same time. You can find data that meets certain rules by creating a filter. A **filter** is a rule or a set of criteria that when applied, temporarily filters out those entries that don't meet the criteria and displays only those that do. For example, you might want to see the entries for only those employees in the Marketing Department. You would set up a filter to temporarily hide the rows of those employees who are not in the Marketing Department.

To create a filter, you click the cell in the group you want to filter and use the Data menu to turn on AutoFilter. When you turn on AutoFilter, which is a built-in set of filtering capabilities, a down arrow button appears in the cell that Excel recognizes as the column's label, as shown in Figure 5-13.

FIGURE 5-13

Turning on AutoFilter

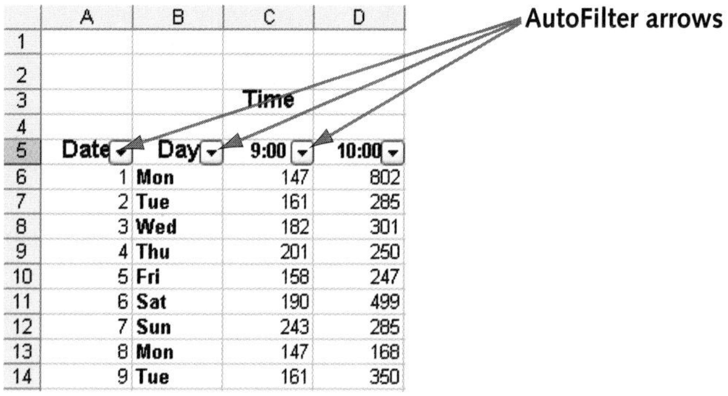

	A	B	C	D	
1					
2					
3			Time		
4					
5	Date	Day	9:00	10:00	
6	1	Mon	147	802	
7	2	Tue	161	285	
8	3	Wed	182	301	
9	4	Thu	201	250	
10	5	Fri	158	247	
11	6	Sat	190	499	
12	7	Sun	243	285	
13	8	Mon	147	168	
14	9	Tue	161	350	

AutoFilter arrows

TIP

When you turn on filtering, Excel treats the cells in the active cell's column as a range. To ensure that the filtering works properly, the column you want to filter should always have a label.

Clicking the down arrow displays a list of values and options, as shown in Figure 5-14. The Sort Ascending and Sort Descending options are new in Excel 2003. You can select them to sort the list according to the values in the selected column. The next few items on the menu are filtering options, such as whether you want to display the top ten values in the column, create a custom filter, or display all values in the column (that is, remove the filter). The rest of the items on the menu are the unique values in the column—clicking one of those values displays only the row or rows containing that value.

FIGURE 5-14

AutoFilter menu

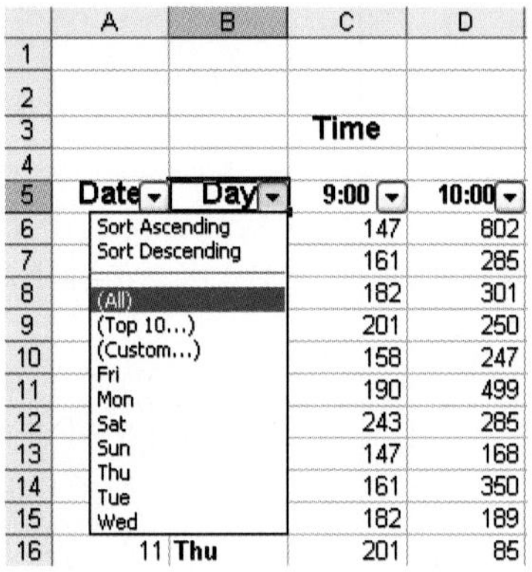

Choosing the Top 10 option from the list doesn't just limit the display to the top ten values. Instead, it opens the Top 10 AutoFilter dialog box. From within this dialog box, you can choose whether to show values from the top or bottom of the list, define the number of items you want to see, and choose whether the number in the middle box indicates the number of items or the percentage of items to be shown when the filter is applied. Using the Top 10 AutoFilter dialog box, you can find your top ten salespeople or identify the top 5 percent of your customers.

◆ **Open Filter from the Excel Practice/Lesson05 folder.**

Create a filter

In this exercise, you create a filter to show the top five sales days in January and show sales figures for Mondays during the same month.

1 If necessary, click the January sheet tab.

2 Click cell O5.

3 On the Data menu, point to Filter, and then click AutoFilter.

A down arrow appears in all the label cells.

4 In cell O5, click the AutoFilter arrow, and click (Top 10...) from the list that appears.

The Top 10 AutoFilter dialog box appears.

FIGURE 5-15

Top 10 AutoFilter dialog box

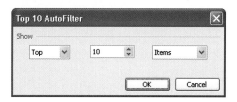

5 Click in the middle box, delete 10, type **5**, and click OK.

Only the rows containing the five largest values in column O are shown.

FIGURE 5-16

Displaying the five largest values

	F	G	H	I	J	K	L	M	N	O
1										
2	es Summary for January									
3										
4										
5	12:00 ▾	13:00 ▾	14:00 ▾	15:00 ▾	16:00 ▾	17:00 ▾	18:00 ▾	19:00 ▾	20:00 ▾	Total ▾
8	187	189	285	302	277	189	750	404	300	3766
11	150	206	189	602	401	206	601	388	135	3802
14	299	147	166	385	400	147	1028	385	243	4013
20	401	166	135	192	385	412	849	382	190	3794
21	187	187	206	166	277	602	1003	400	101	3710
37										
38	7276	8072	6948	8659	7553	7529	13930	8704	6111	97925
39										

Q. How do you apply a filter that displays the 15 highest-paid employees in a list?

A: Click a cell in the column that shows the pay or salary for employees. On the Data menu, click Filter and then AutoFilter. Click the AutoFilter arrow on the column label cell, and click (Top 10...) from the list that appears. In the Top 10 AutoFilter dialog box, click in the middle box, delete 10, type 15, and click OK.

6 In cell O5, click the AutoFilter arrow, and click Sort Descending.

The values are sorted from largest to smallest, with 4013 at the top.

7 On the Data menu, point to Filter, and then click AutoFilter.

The filtered rows reappear.

8 Click cell B5.

9 On the Data menu, point to Filter, and then click AutoFilter.

A down arrow appears in the label cells.

10 In cell B5, click the down arrow, and from the list of unique column values that appears, click Mon.

Only rows with *Mon* in column B are shown in the worksheet.

11 On the Data menu, point to Filter, and then click AutoFilter.

The filtered rows reappear.

◆ Close the workbook without saving your changes.

◆ If you are continuing to other lessons, leave Excel open.

◆ If you are not continuing to other lessons, save and close all open workbooks, then close Excel.

Key Points

✔ *Excel's Zoom feature works much like the zoom feature on a video camcorder. You can zoom in on a portion of a worksheet so that it appears larger and the data is easier to read. Or you can zoom out to get a better overall view of the worksheet.*

✔ *Not all of the data in a worksheet is relevant all of the time to all of the people who view it. You can hide specified rows and columns so that only the data you want to focus on is displayed.*

✔ *When you scroll in a large worksheet to bring rows and columns of data into view, you can implement the freezing feature to keep specified data, such as row or column labels, from moving off the screen. With the label always visible, you can easily identify what the data represents.*

✔ *Each Excel workbook is made up of individual worksheets that you can add to, delete from, move, and copy as desired. This gives you the flexibility to group worksheets with similar subject matter together in one file and enables you to be more effective in organizing and managing data.*

✔ *The order in which you enter data is not necessarily the most logical order for interpreting or analyzing it. Sorting data lets you quickly and easily identify trends and generate forecasts or predictions.*

✔ *You can display a subset of rows that meet certain rules, or criteria, by applying a filter to data. The rest of the rows are temporarily "filtered out," enabling you to focus on the data that's pertinent to your review or analysis.*

Quick Quiz

True/False

T   F   1. If you set your Zoom magnification at 50%, the cells in the worksheet would look about twice as large as normal.

T   F   2. The only way to reset the magnification of a worksheet to its default setting is to close the workbook and reopen it.

T   F   3. If you want to freeze columns A and B, you need to click a cell in column A before executing the Freeze Panes command.

T   F   4. In a descending sort, numbers appear from largest to smallest.

T   F   5. The AutoFilter menu contains options for sorting.

Multiple Choice

1. Which feature would you use if you wanted to enlarge the appearance of the worksheet?
   a. Zoom
   b. Freeze Panes
   c. AutoFilter
   d. Focus

2. Which feature would you use if you wanted to keep a column of row labels displayed as you scrolled other columns into view?
   a. Zoom
   b. Freeze Panes
   c. AutoFilter
   d. Hide

3. If you wanted to freeze the column headings in row 2 and the row headings in column A, which cell should you click on before executing the command to freeze?
   a. A1
   b. A2
   c. B2
   d. B3

4. How would you copy a worksheet using the keyboard and mouse?
   a. Click the sheet tab, hold the Ctrl key, and drag the sheet tab icon to the desired location.
   b. Click the sheet tab, hold the Shift key, and drag the sheet tab icon to the desired location.
   c. Click the sheet tab, hold the Alt key, and drag the sheet tab icon to the desired location.
   d. Click the sheet tab, and drag the sheet tab icon to the desired location.

5. Your workbook contains three sheets: Sheet1, Sheet2, and Sheet3. If you select the Sheet2 tab and insert a new worksheet, where would it be positioned?
   a. as the first sheet in the workbook
   b. as the last sheet in the workbook
   c. before Sheet2
   d. after Sheet2

Short Answer

1. How do you navigate between multiple worksheets in a workbook?

2. How can you display a worksheet on your screen at 60% of normal size?

3. Explain the difference between an ascending sort and a descending sort.

4. If your worksheet is so large that rows and columns with data labels disappear when you scroll down and to the right, what should you do?

5. If you want simultaneously to display certain columns or rows on your screen but columns or rows in the middle make it impossible, what should you do?

On Your Own

◆ **Open Sports Income05 from the Excel Practice/Lesson05 folder.**

Exercise 1

Zoom in on Sheet1 by 50%, and zoom out by 100%. Hide and then un-hide column B. Freeze column B and row 2, and then unfreeze them.

◆ **Close Sports Income05.**

◆ **Open Food from the Excel Practice/Lesson05 folder.**

Exercise 2 Open the Food workbook. On the Meats worksheet, sort the data in descending order by Total Yearly Consumption. Which type of meat generated the most orders? The fewest? Perform the same sort on the Dry Goods and Produce worksheets, and determine which items generated the most and the fewest orders.

Exercise 3

On the Meats worksheet in the Food workbook, apply an AutoFilter to the Total Yearly Consumption column that finds the top five items, and then sort them in ascending order. What are the top five meats? Apply the same AutoFilter on the Total Yearly Consumption columns in the Dry Goods and Produce worksheets. List the top five items on both of those sheets.

◆ **Close Food.**

One Step Further

Exercise 1

In this lesson, you learned how to insert and delete worksheets. You know that the default number of worksheets in a workbook is three, but is there a limit to the number of worksheets that can be added? If there is a limit, what determines this limit? Is there a limit to the number of rows or columns in a workbook? Use the Ask A Question box to determine the answer to these questions.

◆ **Open Filter from the Excel Practice/Lesson05 folder.**

Exercise 2

As you explored AutoFilter, you may have noticed the Custom option in the AutoFilter list. Use the Filter workbook to explore the Custom option. What can it be used for? If necessary, use Excel's Help files to determine the filtering possibilities made available through the Custom option. Briefly describe your findings.

◆ **Close Filter.**

Working with Charts

After completing this lesson, you will be able to:

✔ *Create charts using the Chart Wizard.*
✔ *Move, resize, and delete charts.*
✔ *Modify chart titles.*
✔ *Move and format chart elements.*
✔ *Change chart types and organize source data.*
✔ *Update data and format the axes.*
✔ *Add gridlines and arrows.*
✔ *Preview and print charts.*

KEY TERMS

- axis labels
- Category axis
- charts
- chart sheet
- embedded charts
- legend
- source data
- Value axis

Excel allows you to track and work with substantial amounts of data. At times, you may not be able to understand the larger picture from looking only at the details. With Excel **charts,** you can summarize, highlight, or reveal trends in your data that might not be obvious when looking at the raw numbers.

At the vacation resort Adventure Works, the sales manager records expense data and estimates future revenue in the Five Year Sales workbook. He intends to use charts to summarize the annual sales projections and quickly see which business area has the highest percentage of expenses. The activities coordinator tracks the pledges collected from members at resort events, and she uses charts to analyze the trend in pledge rates at various levels over the year.

In this lesson, you will learn what types of charts are available in Microsoft Excel and how to create them. Then you will learn how to modify, move, and format charts and chart elements. Finally, you will learn how to preview and print your charts.

IMPORTANT

Before you can use the practice files in this lesson, you must install them from the book's companion CD to their default location. For additional information on how to find and open files used in this book, see the "Using the CD-ROM" section at the beginning of this book.

Creating Charts Using the Chart Wizard

Creating a Chart

THE BOTTOM LINE

The Chart Wizard automates the tasks involved in creating a chart, saving you the time of manually adding elements such as titles, axis labels, and legends.

The Chart Wizard guides you through the process of creating a chart. As you complete each step, the wizard prompts you for your next selection. To start, you select the type of chart you want.

Excel offers 14 types of charts, with each type having two or more subtypes. Using the Chart Wizard, you can preview the chart types and choose the chart that best suits your data. For example, revenue and sales projections are easily summarized with a column, bar, or line chart, while expenses might be best represented as a pie chart.

The following table gives a brief description of each chart type.

Icon	Chart Name	Function
	Column	Compares individual values across time or other categories; represents values as vertical bars
	Bar	Compares individual values across time or other categories; represents values as horizontal bars
	Line	Shows the trend of values across time or other categories; represents values as points along a line
	Pie	Shows values as parts of a whole; represents values as sections of a circular pie
	XY (Scatter)	Compares the values of two sets of data across time or other categories; values are represented as data points, which might be connected by lines
	Area	Shows the trend of values across time or other categories; represents values as shaded areas
	Doughnut	Shows values as parts of a whole; represents values as sections of a circular band
	Radar	Shows the trend of values relative to a center point; represents values as points that radiate from the center; each category has its own axis; lines connect all of the values in the same series

	Surface	Shows the trend of values across two sets of data; values are represented as a 3-D surface that illustrates the relationship between the sets
	Bubble	Compares three sets of values
	Stock	Shows the trend of sets of values across time; often used to illustrate stock price changes with markers for High, Low, Close, and Open values; represents values as points, lines, or columns
	Cylinder	Compares individual values across time or other categories; represents values as vertical or horizontal cylinders
	Cone	Compares individual values across time or other categories; represents values as vertical or horizontal cones
	Pyramid	Compares individual values across time or other categories; represents values as pyramidal shapes

In preparation for a budget meeting, the sales manager for Adventure Works wants to create a chart to show the projected trend in each of four revenue categories over the next five years. A line chart clearly shows that the largest increase is expected in lodging sales.

TIP

In the Step 1 Of 4 – Chart Type dialog box, you can click the Press And Hold To View Sample button to see a preview of your chart.

◆ **To complete the procedures in this lesson, you must use the files Five Year Sales and Member Pledges in the Lesson06 folder in the Excel Practice folder located on your hard disk.**

◆ **Open Five Year Sales from the Excel Practice/Lesson06 folder.**

Create a chart using the Chart Wizard

In this exercise, you open a workbook and create a chart using the Chart Wizard.

1 Select cells A2:F6 in the Sales Projections worksheet.

2 On the Standard toolbar, click the Chart Wizard button.

The Step 1 Of 4 – Chart Type dialog box appears.

FIGURE 6-1

Step 1 of 4 Chart Wizard

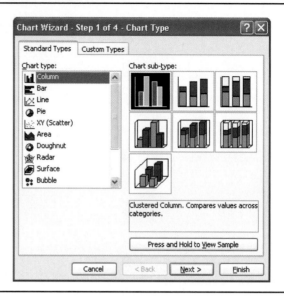

3 In the Chart Type list, click Column, if necessary.

4 In the Chart Sub-type box, click the Stacked Column sub-type in the center of the top row, and click Next.

The Step 2 Of 4 – Chart Source Data dialog box appears with a preview of your chart.

FIGURE 6-2

Step 2 of 4 Chart Wizard

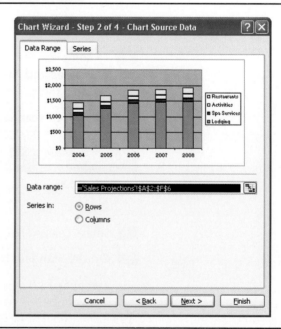

5 On the Data Range tab, verify that the Rows option is selected, and click Next.

The Step 3 Of 4 – Chart Options dialog box appears.

FIGURE 6-3

Step 3 of 4 Chart Wizard

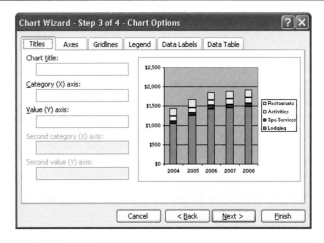

6 In the Chart Title box, type Yearly Sales, and click Next.

The Step 4 Of 4 – Chart Location dialog box appears.

FIGURE 6-4

Step 4 of 4 Chart Wizard

IMPORTANT

Charts are either embedded as objects in an existing worksheet or placed in a separate sheet. **Embedded charts** appear on a worksheet with other data. A **chart sheet** appears as a separate sheet in the workbook.

ANOTHER METHOD

To quickly create a chart with the default chart options, select a range of cells, and then press F11. The chart will be created in a new worksheet.

7 Click the As Object In option, if necessary, and click the Finish button.

The chart appears in the worksheet, and the Chart toolbar displays. The data that's charted is outlined in blue.

FIGURE 6-5

Creating a chart on the same sheet

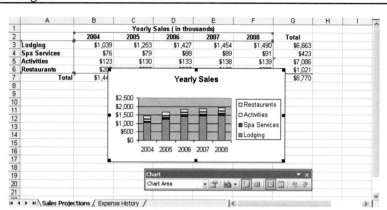

◆ **Keep this file open for the next exercise.**

QUICK REFERENCE ▼

Create a chart

1 Select the range of cells to be represented.

2 On the Standard toolbar, click the Chart Wizard button.

3 In the Step 1 Of 4 – Chart Type dialog box, click the chart type and chart subtype, and click Next.

4 In the Step 2 Of 4 – Chart Source Data dialog box, click the Rows or Columns option to specify whether the data is organized in rows or columns, and click Next.

5 In the Step 3 Of 4 – Chart Options dialog box, type titles for the chart and axes, and click Next.

6 In the Step 4 Of 4 – Chart Location dialog box, click As New Sheet to create a chart sheet or As Object In to create an embedded chart. Then click the Finish button.

Moving and Resizing Charts

THE BOTTOM LINE

You can reposition and change the size of a chart to present your data more effectively and to enhance the overall appearance of a worksheet.

Once a chart is created, you can position it in the worksheet, change its size, or delete it altogether. It is often useful to place the chart just before or immediately after the data it summarizes. For readability, detailed or complex charts may need to be larger, while simple charts can be smaller.

To move, resize, or delete a chart, you must select the chart. You select a chart by clicking in the Chart Area, which is the background or blank area of a chart. Clicking in other areas of the chart might select an element or elements of the chart. You will work with chart elements later in this lesson.

TIP

When selecting or dragging a chart, be sure to click the Chart Area and not the legend, labels, or Plot Area itself. To find the Chart Area, point to different parts of the chart to display the ScreenTips.

Modify a chart

In this exercise, you move, resize, delete, and restore a chart.

1 If necessary, click a blank area of the chart to select it.

2 Drag the chart to a position below the data and along the left edge of the worksheet.

FIGURE 6-6

Moving a chart

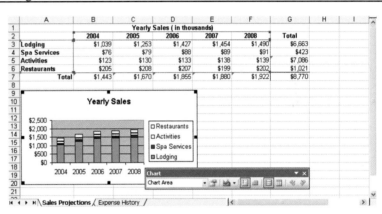

3 Drag the sizing handle on the right edge of the chart to the right side of column F to make the chart wider.

TIP

If the Chart toolbar is in the way, you can move it by dragging it by its title bar.

---

4 Drag the bottom sizing handle to the bottom of row 27 to make the chart longer.

FIGURE 6-7

Adjusting the size of the chart

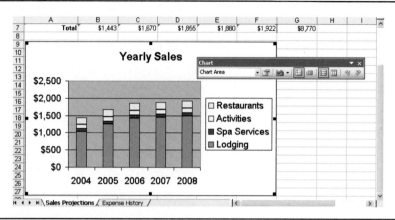

5 Click the Chart Area, and press the Delete key.

The chart disappears from the worksheet.

6 On the Standard toolbar, click the Undo button.

The chart reappears on the worksheet.

7 Save the workbook with the current name.

◆ Keep this file open for the next exercise.

QUICK REFERENCE ▼

Move a chart

1 Click the Chart Area to select the chart.

2 Drag the chart to the desired location.

Resize a chart

1 Click the Chart Area to select the chart.

2 Drag the appropriate sizing handle until the chart is the desired size.

Delete a chart

1 Click the Chart Area to select the chart.

2 Press the Delete key.

Modifying Chart Titles and Adding Axis Labels

Customizing Chart Labels and Numbers

THE BOTTOM LINE

A meaningful title and descriptive labels can clarify the meaning of a chart and enhance its impact.

Charts are useful for displaying statistical data in an eye-catching manner. When you create a chart using the ChartWizard, category labels and a **legend** are added to the chart if the selected range of cells includes the necessary information. You also can add a title and **axis labels** during the wizard operation, or you can add them later by changing the chart options.

For example, the sales manager at Adventure Works can add a label to the value axis to clearly show that revenue figures are reported in thousands of dollars. He also can rephrase the chart title so that it is more descriptive of the data that's being charted.

Change the title of a chart and insert axis labels

In this exercise, you change the title of the chart and add labels for the X and Y axes.

1 **Right-click a blank area of the chart, and click Chart Options.**

The Chart Options dialog box appears with the Titles tab displayed.

TIP

If the Titles tab is not displayed, click it.

ANOTHER METHOD

Select the chart and on the Chart menu, select Chart Options.

2 **In the Chart Title box, select "Yearly Sales," and type Five-Year Revenue Projection.**

The new title appears in the chart preview.

3 **In the Category (X) Axis box, type Fiscal Year.**

The axis title appears in the chart preview.

FIGURE 6-8

Previewing the chart

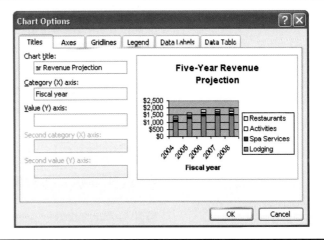

4 In the Value (Y) Axis box, type Revenue (in thousands), and click OK.

The chart appears with the new title and axis labels.

FIGURE 6-9

Changing the title and adding labels

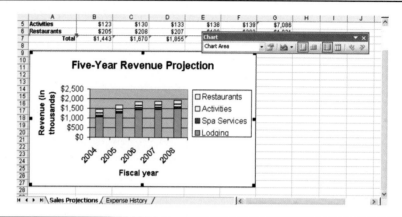

5 Right-click the chart title, and click Format Chart Title.

The Format Chart Title dialog box appears.

ANOTHER METHOD

- Click the chart title, and on the Chart toolbar, click the Format Chart Title button.
- On the Chart toolbar, click the Chart Objects down arrow, click Chart Title, and click the Format Chart Title button.

6 Click the Font tab, if necessary, and on the Size list, click 12. Click OK.

The chart title appears smaller.

ANOTHER METHOD

You can edit the chart title and axis labels like other text. Simply click the title or label to place your insertion point and begin typing. You also can format the chart title or axis labels by selecting the text and using the Formatting toolbar.

7 Save the workbook with the current name.

◆ Keep this file open for the next exercise.

QUICK REFERENCE ▼

Edit a chart title or an axis label

1 Right-click the Chart Area, and click Chart Options.

2 On the Titles tab, type the desired chart title or axis label, and click OK.

QUICK CHECK

Q. What are the two methods for editing the title of a chart?

A: You can edit a chart title by opening the Chart Options dialog box, selecting the Titles tab, and typing the new chart title in the Chart Title text box. Or you can click the chart title and click it again to place the insertion point within it and then start typing.

Moving and Formatting Chart Elements

THE BOTTOM LINE

Just as you format data to enhance the appearance of the worksheet and to highlight important entries, you can modify parts of a chart to make it easier to read and more effective in graphically depicting raw data and trends.

You can customize the appearance of your charts in many ways. To make the best use of the Chart Area, you can reposition the title or legend. To emphasize certain values, you can add labels to each data point on a line chart. To draw attention to a crucial piece of a pie chart, you can move that piece away from the rest of the chart. Other types of charts offer different formatting options.

The sales manager at Adventure Works has created a chart to represent data he needs for the budget meeting. Using a pie chart, he is able to show the percentage of costs spent in each business area for the past five years. To set the legend apart from the rest of the chart, he adds a border to it. He repositions other chart elements to highlight the least costly business area.

Format the legend and the pieces of a pie chart

In this exercise, you reposition and format the legend and draw out pieces of the pie chart.

1 Click the **Expense History** sheet tab.

The sheet contains a pie chart.

FIGURE 6-10

Sheet with a pie chart

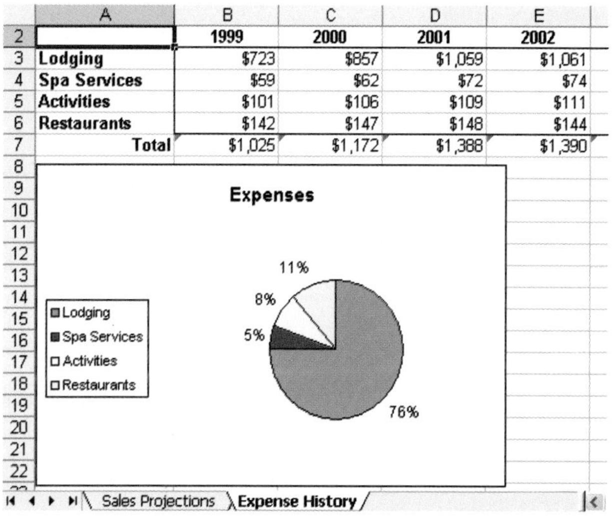

	A	B	C	D	E
2		1999	2000	2001	2002
3	Lodging	$723	$857	$1,059	$1,061
4	Spa Services	$59	$62	$72	$74
5	Activities	$101	$106	$109	$111
6	Restaurants	$142	$147	$148	$144
7	Total	$1,025	$1,172	$1,388	$1,390

Expenses

11%
8%
5%
76%

Lodging
Spa Services
Activities
Restaurants

Sales Projections \ Expense History

2 Drag the chart legend to the lower left corner of the Chart Area.

3 Right-click the chart legend, and click Format Legend.

The Format Legend dialog box appears.

ANOTHER METHOD

- Click the legend, and on the Chart toolbar, click the Format Legend button.
- On the Chart toolbar, click the Chart Objects down arrow, click Legend, and click the Format Legend button.

4 Click the Patterns tab, select the Shadow check box, and click OK.

The legend appears with a shadowed border.

FIGURE 6-11

Formatting the legend

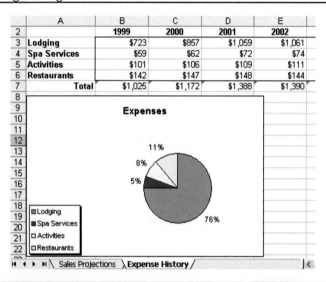

TIP

On the Placement tab of the Format Legends dialog box, you can choose from a list of predetermined locations for the legend. You can place the legend at the top, at the bottom, at the right, at the left, or in the corner of the chart.

5 Click the pie area, and click the smallest piece of the pie.

Sizing handles appear around the piece.

6 Drag the piece a short distance away from the pie.

The piece appears separated from the rest of the pie.

FIGURE 6-12

Manipulating a piece of the pie

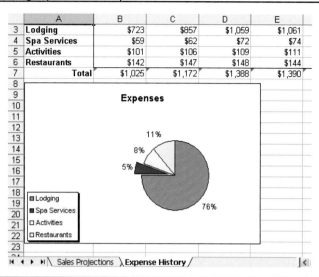

	A	B	C	D	E
3	**Lodging**	$723	$857	$1,059	$1,061
4	**Spa Services**	$59	$62	$72	$74
5	**Activities**	$101	$106	$109	$111
6	**Restaurants**	$142	$147	$148	$144
7	**Total**	$1,025	$1,172	$1,388	$1,390

◆ **Save and close the Five Year Sales workbook.**

Changing the Chart Type and Organizing the Source Data

THE BOTTOM LINE

You can manipulate data and chart it in different ways, which enables you to develop the most comprehensive assessment and analysis of it.

As you have learned, Excel offers a wide variety of chart types. Because each type emphasizes a particular aspect of the source data, several types might be useful for representing the same set of data. For budget discussions, a pie chart shows the proportion of expenses allocated to each category. For income projections, a column chart shows the trend of income over the past five years. You select a chart type when using the ChartWizard. After the chart is created, you can change it to a different chart type.

When you create a chart, the Chart Wizard interprets the **source data** as being organized in rows or columns. The organization of data in a chart depends on the range selected when creating the chart. When you select a range of cells with the same number of rows and columns, or more columns than rows, the data is plotted by rows. When you select a range that contains more rows than columns, the data is plotted by columns. For different chart types, it may be necessary to change the way the organization of the data is interpreted. In other words, you may need to indicate whether the data is organized in rows or columns. Also, when changing the chart type, you may want to exclude certain data (such as a column of totals) or include additional data.

By changing a column chart to a stacked area chart, the activities coordinator at Adventure Works can show the trend of member pledges collected at her events over the past year. Also, she has just recorded the final contributions for December, so she can include those figures in her chart.

◆ **Open Member Pledges from the Excel Practice/Lesson06 folder.**

Change the chart type, and organize the data

In this exercise, you change the chart type and organize the source data.

1 **Click the Chart sheet tab.**

The sheet contains a column chart showing pledges collected in each category.

FIGURE 6-13

Column chart showing pledges

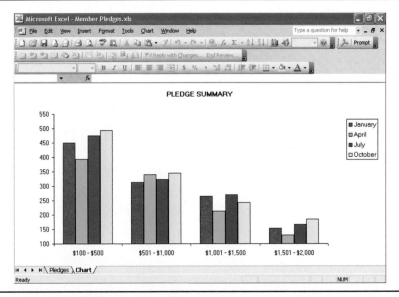

TIP

Close the Chart toolbar if it obscures your view of parts of the chart.

2 **Right-click the Chart Area, and click Chart Type.**

The Chart Type dialog box appears.

ANOTHER METHOD

Click the Chart Area, and on the Chart menu, click Chart Type.

3 **On the Chart Type list, click Area.**

4 **Click the Stacked Area chart sub-type in the center of the first row.**

FIGURE 6-14

Selecting the Stacked Area chart

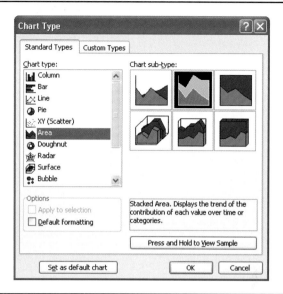

5 Click OK in the Chart Type dialog box.

A stacked area chart appears.

6 Right-click the Chart Area, and click Source Data.

The Source Data dialog box appears, and the worksheet from where the data was taken opens with a flashing marquee around the range of the source data.

FIGURE 6-15

Viewing the source data

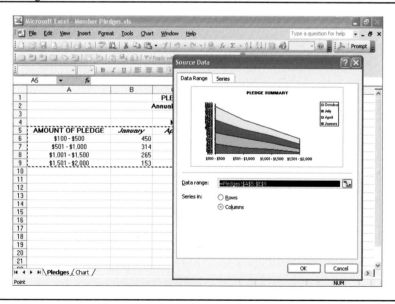

ANOTHER METHOD

Click the Chart Area, and on the Chart menu, click Source Data.

7 On the Data Range tab, click the Rows option, and click OK.

The updated chart appears.

FIGURE 6-16

Editing the source data

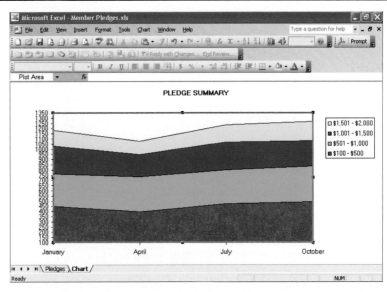

TIP

You might need to move the Source Data – Data Range dialog box in order to see the entire range of cells to be selected.

8 Right-click the Chart Area, and click Source Data.

The Source Data dialog box appears, and the source data worksheet opens.

 9 On the Data Range tab in the Data Range box, click the Collapse Dialog button.

10 Select A5:F9, and click the Expand Dialog button in the Source Data – Data Range dialog box.

 11 In the Source Data dialog box, click OK.

The chart appears with the data added for the month of December.

◆ Save and close the Member Pledges workbook.

QUICK REFERENCE ▼

Change a chart type

1 Right-click the Chart Area, and click Chart Type.

2 Select the chart type and chart sub-type, and click OK.

Reorganize the source data

1 Right-click the Chart Area, and click Source Data.

2 On the Data Range tab, click the Columns or Rows option, and click OK.

Updating Data and Formatting the Axes

THE BOTTOM LINE

The relationship between data and the chart that plots it is dynamic, so when you make changes to data entries, any charts that are based on that data are automatically updated. This saves you time and ensures that charts are accurate and up to date.

Typically, the data stored in Excel worksheets requires periodic updating. When you change any data that is source data, the corresponding chart updates automatically.

At Adventure Works, the sales manager learns that the new marketing campaigns are expected to increase restaurant revenues by 50 percent and spa revenues by 60 percent. When he enters the new figures on the Sales Projections sheet, the Five-Year Revenue Projection chart changes to reflect the new data.

As data values change, you may need to change various aspects of the axes in a chart. Using Scale options, you can format the **Value axis** (Y axis) to display a meaningful range of values for your data. Scale options for the **Category axis** allow you to control the display of category labels.

For example, the sales manager can set the minimum and maximum dollar values displayed on the Expected Annual Sales chart to be sure that the new values are properly represented.

Open Five Year Sales from the Excel Practice/Lesson06 folder.

Update source data, and format axes

In this exercise, you update the source data for a chart and format the axes.

1 Switch to the Sales Projections sheet, and type the following values.

Cell	B4	C4	D4	E4	F4
Value	122	126	141	142	146

Cell	B6	C6	D6	E6	F6
Value	308	312	311	299	303

The chart updates to reflect the new values.

FIGURE 6-17

Updating values in the chart

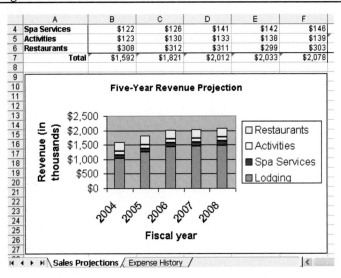

	A	B	C	D	E	F
4	Spa Services	$122	$126	$141	$142	$146
5	Activities	$123	$130	$133	$138	$139
6	Restaurants	$308	$312	$311	$299	$303
7	Total	$1,592	$1,821	$2,012	$2,033	$2,078

Five-Year Revenue Projection

TIP

The Y axis is the Value axis, and the X axis is the Category axis.

2 **Right-click the Value axis, click Format Axis, and click the Scale tab in the Format Axis dialog box.**

The Format Axis dialog box appears with the Scale tab displayed.

FIGURE 6-18

Format Axis dialog box

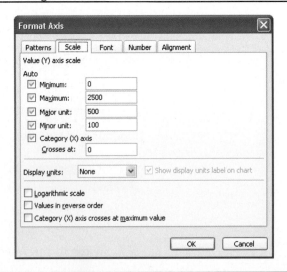

ANOTHER METHOD

- Click the Value axis, and on the Chart toolbar, click the Format Axis button.
- On the Chart toolbar, click the Chart Objects down arrow, click Value Axis, and click the Format Axis button.

The Auto check boxes clear when you change the various default values (Minimum, Maximum, Major Unit, and so on). To use the default value, simply select the Auto check box to restore that value.

3 In the Minimum box, type 500.

4 In the Maximum box, type 2100, and click OK.

The chart appears with the updated axis.

FIGURE 6-19

Updating the chart's axis information

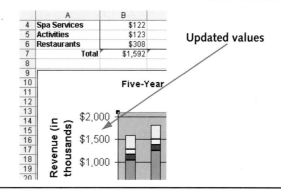

◆ Keep this file open for the next exercise.

Q. What does the Category axis typically display?

A: The Category axis typically displays labels that identify the categories of data you are plotting.

QUICK REFERENCE ▼

Change the scale of an axis

1 Right-click the axis, and click Format Axis.

2 On the Scale tab, type the desired values for minimum, maximum, major unit, and minor unit.

3 Click OK.

Adding Gridlines and Arrows

THE BOTTOM LINE

Horizontal and vertical gridlines help identify the value of each data marker in a chart. Arrows are useful for highlighting a particular data marker or for calling attention to certain information in a chart.

Adding a Graphic to a Worksheet

You can add gridlines to correspond with values on one or both axes in a chart. Gridlines are an effective tool for helping you identify more exact values for the categories of data being plotted on the chart. For example, you might have a line chart that plots income by week for the year. The Value axis is organized by units of $200, with $0 being the minimum and

$2000 being the maximum. Without the gridlines, you would more or less need to eyeball where the weekly values fall on the Value axis. You add major gridlines (appearing at bigger intervals) or minor gridlines (appearing at smaller intervals) using the Chart Options dialog box.

Using the Drawing toolbar, you can add picture objects, such as lines or arrows, to your chart. A well-placed arrow clearly indicates the most important piece of data in your chart.

You also can add a picture to the worksheet by clicking Picture on the Insert menu. Doing so displays a submenu that lists several sources from which you can choose to add a picture, including an existing file or clip art.

Once you've added a graphic element (picture, clip art, arrow, line, and so on) to your worksheet, you can change the graphic's location on the worksheet by dragging it to the desired location. You can change the graphic's size by right-clicking the picture and choosing Format Picture from the shortcut menu that appears. You also can resize a graphic by clicking the picture and then dragging one of the handles that appears on the graphic. However, using the Format Picture dialog box ensures that the aspect ratio (the relationship between the picture's height and width) doesn't change.

The sales manager would like to draw attention to the effects of the new marketing campaigns. Adding gridlines will more clearly define the impact of the new revenue levels. An arrow will emphasize the largest change in revenue.

Add gridlines and graphic objects to a chart

In this exercise, you add gridlines to the chart and add and move an arrow. You also add a text box to label the arrow.

1 **Right-click the Chart Area, and click Chart Options.**

The Chart Options dialog box appears.

2 **Click the Gridlines tab, select the Minor Gridlines check box in the Value (Y) Axis section, and click OK.**

The chart appears with major and minor horizontal gridlines.

FIGURE 6-20

Adding gridlines

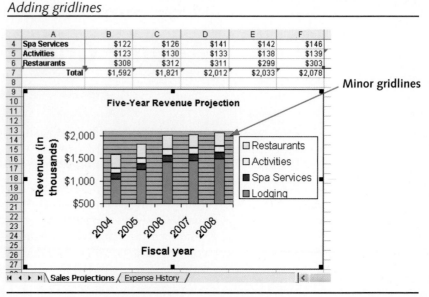

3 Click the Drawing button on the Standard toolbar.

The Drawing toolbar appears.

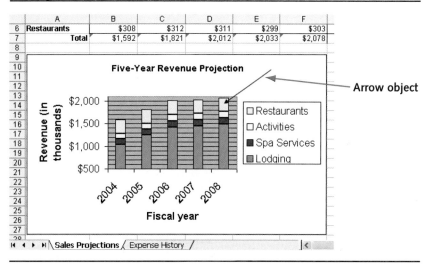

4 Click the Arrow button. Click a blank area in the upper right corner of the chart, drag the mouse pointer to the top of the tallest column on the chart, and click away from the chart.

An arrow appears on the chart.

FIGURE 6-21

Adding an arrow

	A	B	C	D	E	F
6	Restaurants	$308	$312	$311	$299	$303
7	Total	$1,592	$1,821	$2,012	$2,033	$2,078

Five-Year Revenue Projection — Arrow object

Sales Projections / Expense History /

IMPORTANT

When you select a chart or any element of a chart that contains picture objects, the chart moves to the front, causing the picture objects to seemingly disappear. To bring the picture objects back to the front, simply click outside of (deselect) the chart and any of its elements.

5 Click the arrow to select it, and drag the arrow so that it points to the top of the center column on the chart.

6 On the Drawing toolbar, click the Text Box button.

TIP

If the text box isn't big enough, you can drag the resize handles to increase its size.

7 Click a blank area of the chart at the tail of the arrow, and drag to draw a rectangular text box.

8 In the text box, type Largest Projected Increase!

The text appears in the text box.

FIGURE 6-22

Adding text

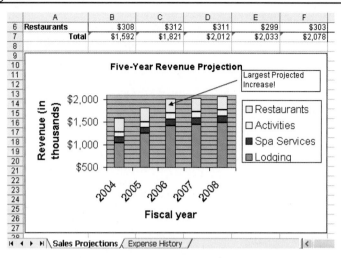

9 **If all of the text is not displayed in the text box, click the text box, and drag its handles until you can see all of the text.**

10 **On the Standard toolbar, click the Drawing button.**

The Drawing toolbar closes.

11 **Save the workbook.**

◆ **Keep this file open for the next exercise.**

QUICK REFERENCE ▼

Display gridlines

1 Right-click the Chart Area, and click Chart Options.

2 On the Gridlines tab, select the desired options, and click OK.

Add an object to a chart

1 On the Standard toolbar, click the Drawing button.

2 On the Drawing toolbar, click the desired object button.

3 Drag to create the object in the chart.

QUICK **CHECK**

Q. Which type of gridline appears at smaller intervals?

A: **Minor gridlines appear at smaller intervals.**

3 Click the Drawing button on the Standard toolbar.

The Drawing toolbar appears.

4 Click the Arrow button. Click a blank area in the upper right corner of the chart, drag the mouse pointer to the top of the tallest column on the chart, and click away from the chart.

An arrow appears on the chart.

FIGURE 6-21

Adding an arrow

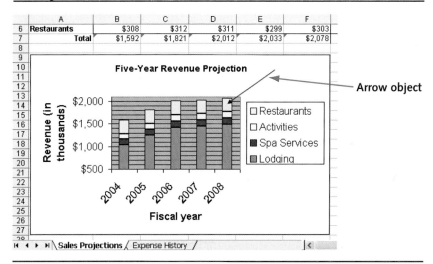

IMPORTANT

When you select a chart or any element of a chart that contains picture objects, the chart moves to the front, causing the picture objects to seemingly disappear. To bring the picture objects back to the front, simply click outside of (deselect) the chart and any of its elements.

---

5 Click the arrow to select it, and drag the arrow so that it points to the top of the center column on the chart.

6 On the Drawing toolbar, click the Text Box button.

TIP

If the text box isn't big enough, you can drag the resize handles to increase its size.

---

7 Click a blank area of the chart at the tail of the arrow, and drag to draw a rectangular text box.

8 In the text box, type Largest Projected Increase!

The text appears in the text box.

FIGURE 6-22

Adding text

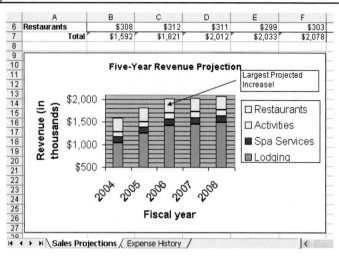

 9 If all of the text is not displayed in the text box, click the text box, and drag its handles until you can see all of the text.

10 On the Standard toolbar, click the Drawing button.

The Drawing toolbar closes.

11 Save the workbook.

◆ Keep this file open for the next exercise.

QUICK REFERENCE ▼

Display gridlines

 1 Right-click the Chart Area, and click Chart Options.

2 On the Gridlines tab, select the desired options, and click OK.

Add an object to a chart

1 On the Standard toolbar, click the Drawing button.

2 On the Drawing toolbar, click the desired object button.

3 Drag to create the object in the chart.

Previewing and Printing Charts

Printing a Chart

THE BOTTOM LINE

You should preview a chart before printing it, especially if the printout is part of a presentation to be reviewed by others. Previewing the chart, and any data that will print with it, helps you identify formatting problems and awkward page breaks.

You can preview and print Excel charts in the same way that you preview and print worksheets. Whether the chart is embedded or on a chart sheet, the Print Preview command displays the chart just as it will be printed, allowing you to verify the appearance and layout of your chart before printing.

As you have learned, you can choose to print the entire workbook, a single sheet in a workbook, a selected range of data, or a selected chart. If your chart appears as an object in a worksheet and you want to print a selected range of data, select the cells that include your chart. If your chart appears as an object in a worksheet and you want to print only the chart, select the chart before choosing the Print command. If your chart is on a chart sheet, simply go to the chart sheet and choose the Print command.

IMPORTANT

You must have a printer to complete the following exercise.

Preview and print a chart

In this exercise, you preview and print charts.

1 **Click a blank area of the Sales Projections worksheet, and click the Print Preview button on the Standard toolbar.**

The worksheet and embedded chart appear in the Preview window, as shown in Figure 6-23.

FIGURE 6-23

Previewing an embedded chart

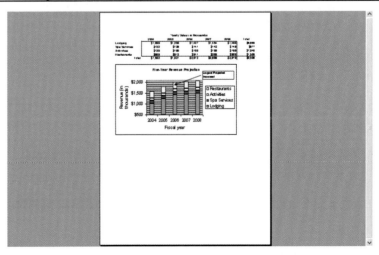

2 Click the Print button on the Preview toolbar.

The Print dialog box appears, and the Preview window closes.

3 Review your print settings, and click OK to print the chart.

4 Click a blank area of the chart, and then click the Print Preview button.

Only the chart appears in the Preview window, as shown in Figure 6-24.

FIGURE 6-24

Previewing a chart

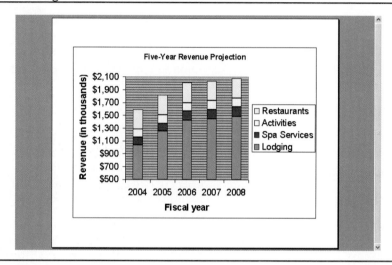

5 Click the Close button.

6 With the chart still selected, on the File menu, click Print.

ANOTHER METHOD

Press Ctrl+P.

7 Review your print settings, and click OK to print the chart.

◆ Save and close Five Year Sales.

◆ If you are continuing to other lessons, leave Excel open.

◆ If you are not continuing to other lessons, save and close all open workbooks, then close Excel.

QUICK REFERENCE ▼

Preview and print a chart

1 For an embedded chart, click the Chart Area to select the chart. For a chart on its own sheet, click the chart sheet tab.

2 On the Standard toolbar, click the Print Preview button.

3 On the Preview toolbar, click the Print button.

QUICK **CHECK**

Q. When you select a chart that's embedded on a worksheet, what do you see in the Print Preview window?

A: **You see only the selected chart.**

Key Points

✔ *The Chart Wizard automates the tasks involved in creating a chart, saving you the time of manually adding elements such as titles, axis labels, and legends.*

✔ *You can reposition and change the size of a chart so that it's easier to read and complements other data or elements on the sheet.*

✔ *You can apply formats to parts of a chart to highlight certain data and to enhance the overall appearance of the sheet.*

✔ *Excel has many different chart types. You can apply a different type of chart to your data and manipulate how the data is plotted. This enables you to interpret the data in different ways.*

✔ *When you make changes to data entries, any charts that are based on that data are automatically updated. This saves you time and ensures that charts are accurate and up to date.*

✔ *Horizontal and vertical gridlines help identify the value of each data marker in a chart.*

✔ *You can use graphics, such as lines, arrows, and text boxes, to highlight a particular data marker or to call attention to certain information in a chart.*

✔ *You should preview a chart before printing it. This helps you identify formatting problems and awkward page breaks.*

Quick Quiz

True/False

T F **1.** A column chart represents values as vertical bars.

T F **2.** A bar chart represents values as horizontal bars.

T F **3.** An embedded chart is one that appears on its own sheet in the workbook.

T F **4.** Every chart must have a legend.

T F **5.** The Y axis also is referred to as the Value axis because it typically displays a range of values for your data.

Multiple Choice

1. Which chart type shows values as parts of a whole?
   a. column
   b. bar
   c. area
   d. pie

2. A(an) _____ chart appears on a worksheet with other data.
   a. filtered
   b. embedded
   c. source
   d. destination

3. A chart's X axis also is referred to as what?
   a. Value axis
   b. Category axis
   c. Data axis
   d. Legend

4. Which toolbar contains buttons for graphic objects, such as arrows and lines, that you can add to a chart?
   a. Chart
   b. Formatting
   c. Drawing
   d. Picture

5. What part of a chart do you click when you want to select the entire chart?
   a. Chart Area
   b. Plot Area
   c. Chart Title
   d. Legend

Short Answer

1. What are five types of charts you can create with the Chart Wizard?

2. How do you move a chart in a worksheet?

3. How do you move individual elements within a chart?

4. How can you format an axis of a chart?

5. How can you change the title of a chart?

6. How can you change the type of a chart?

IMPORTANT

In the On Your Own exercises that follow, you must complete Exercise 1 before continuing to Exercise 2.

On Your Own

◆ **Open Five Year Sales from the Excel Practice/Lesson06 folder.**

Exercise 1

On the Expense History worksheet, change the pie chart to a doughnut chart comparing the percentage of expenses allocated to each category in 1999–2003. View the ScreenTips to see what year the outer ring represents.

Exercise 2

In the Five Years Sales workbook, move the legend to the left side of the chart. Change the chart title to read *Cost Allocation, 1999–2003*. Add a text box to the chart explaining which ring represents which year. Preview and print the chart.

◆ **Close Five Year Sales.**

One Step Further

Exercise 1

In this lesson, Value (Y) axis major and minor gridlines were included in a chart for the Five Year Sales worksheet. Would major or minor Category (X) axis gridlines have been useful in this chart? Why or why not? In what types of charts are X axis gridlines likely to be most useful?

Exercise 2

In the Five Year Sales workbook, a section of the Expenses History pie chart was pulled apart from the rest of the pie. This is often referred to as an "exploded view." Is there a way to "explode" the entire pie without having to click and drag each component after the pie chart is made? Explore Excel's chart types or use Excel's Help files to find the answer.

Exercise 3

Most companies have a company logo—something that identifies them to their customers. To be effective, these logos need to be visible in as many locations as possible. This includes any worksheets that the company provides to customers, shareholders, and business partners. How would you include an existing logo in a worksheet?

LESSON

Performing Basic Calculations

After completing this lesson, you will be able to:

✔ *Build formulas.*
✔ *Copy formulas.*
✔ *Use absolute and relative cell references.*
✔ *Edit formulas.*
✔ *Use the SUM function and AutoSum.*
✔ *Insert Date functions.*
✔ *Understand basic statistical functions.*
✔ *Work with three-dimensional formulas.*

KEY TERMS

- absolute reference
- AutoSum
- formula
- Formula bar
- function
- relative references
- three-dimensional formula

With Microsoft Excel, you can easily perform common and complex calculations. In addition to adding, subtracting, multiplying, and dividing, you can calculate the total and compute the average of a set of values. With basic calculations, you can figure profit values from revenue and expenses and you can compute an employee's wages from hours worked and pay rates. These are just a few examples of the calculations Excel can perform.

At the Adventure Works resort, the reservations manager is preparing a report on annual vacancy rates. To start, he finds the total number of nights that each type of room was occupied. Then he calculates the average number of rooms occupied per night. Finally, he figures the occupancy rate for each type of room. The results of these calculations help him plan the upcoming season and schedule cabin renovations for the time of year when demand is lowest.

Also at Adventure Works, the accountant is calculating income generated from equipment rentals for various activities. With those numbers, he can compute the average income earned from each activity each month. The activities coordinator uses these figures to plan her strategy for activities in the upcoming year.

In this lesson, you will learn how to perform basic Excel calculations with formulas and functions. You also will learn how to create and edit formulas, use mathematical operators, and use Excel's built-in functions.

> **IMPORTANT**
>
> Before you can use the practice files in this lesson, you must install them from the book's companion CD to their default location. For additional information on how to find and open files used in this book, see the "Using the CD-ROM" section at the beginning of this book.

Building Formulas

Creating Formulas to Calculate Values

> **THE BOTTOM LINE**
> -
> The real strength of a spreadsheet program like Excel is its feature for calculating and crunching numbers. Simple to complex formulas entered in a worksheet are calculated instantaneously, giving you results and solutions that help you assess and analyze your data.

A **formula** is the written expression of a calculation to be performed by Excel. When you enter a formula in a cell, the formula is stored internally while the calculated result is what you see in the cell.

A formula consists of two elements: operands and mathematical operators. The operands identify the values to be used in the calculation. An operand can be a constant value, another formula, or a reference to a cell or range of cells. Mathematical operators specify what calculations are to be performed with the values.

You can use any of the following mathematical operators in a formula:

Operator	Meaning
^	Exponentiation
*	Multiplication
/	Division
+	Addition
-	Subtraction

When a formula contains two or more operators, operations are not necessarily performed in the order in which you read the formula—that is, left to right. The order in which operations are performed is determined by operator priority, as defined by the rules of mathematics. For example, exponentiation is performed before any other operation. Multiplication and division are next on the priority list, performed sequentially from left to right. Finally, addition and subtraction are performed, again from left to right. Consider the following equation:

$$2 + 4 * 6 / 3 - 1 = 9$$

First, four is multiplied by six, and the result is divided by three. Two is then added to the result, and one is subtracted. See Figure 7-1.

FIGURE 7-1

Structure of a formula

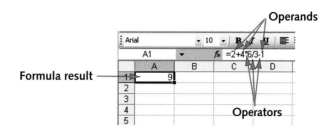

You can override the standard operator priorities by using parentheses. Operations contained within parentheses are completed before those outside parentheses. Thus, the following equation is calculated differently than the previous one.

$$(2 + 4) * 6 / (3 - 1) = 18$$

In this formula, two and four are added first, and the result is multiplied by six. Finally, that result is divided by the result of three minus one. See Figure 7-2.

FIGURE 7-2

Using parentheses to control the order of operations

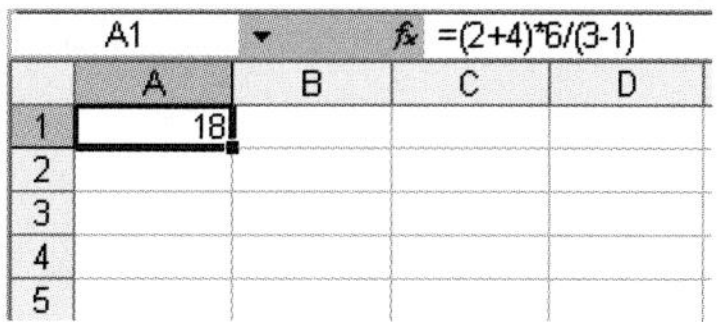

Creating a formula is similar to entering text and numbers in cells. To begin, you select the cell in which you want the formula to appear. To allow Excel to distinguish formulas from data, all formulas begin with an equal sign (=) or a plus sign (+).

Then you use one of two methods to create the formula:

- Type an equal sign to mark the entry as a formula. Then type the formula, including cell addresses, constant values, and mathematical operators, directly into the cell.
- Type an equal sign. When entering the formula, type any operators, constant values, or parentheses directly in the cell, but you can click a cell or range of cells included in the formula instead of typing the cell or range address. This method is typically quicker and eliminates the possibility of typing an incorrect cell or range address.

As you build a formula, it appears in the **Formula bar** and the cell itself. When you have completed the formula, the cell displays the result of the formula and the Formula bar displays the formula itself, as you saw in Figures 7-1 and 7-2.

The reservations manager at Adventure Works has tracked the number of nights each type of room was occupied each month for the last year. To calculate occupancy rates, he must find the total number of nights occupied for each month, divide that total by the number of rooms, and divide that result by the number of nights in the month.

◆ **To complete the procedures in this lesson, you must use the files Lodging Usage, Activity Rentals, and Food07 in the Lesson07 folder in the Excel Practice folder located on your hard disk.**

◆ **Open Lodging Usage from the Excel Practice/Lesson07 folder.**

Enter formulas in a worksheet

In this exercise, you open a worksheet and create basic formulas using different methods to enter the formulas.

1 **Click cell C9, and type** =C5+C6+C7.

As you type each cell address (or reference), the cell being referred to is selected and the selection border appears in a specific color. This color matches the color of the text used for the cell reference, as shown in Figure 7-3.

FIGURE 7-3

Color-coordinating cell references

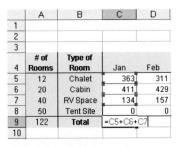

TIP

When you type a cell address in a formula, you can use uppercase or lowercase letters. For example, references *B8* and *b8* refer to the same cell.

2 **Press Enter.**

The total of the cells (908) appears in cell C9.

3 **Click cell C13, type =, and click cell C5.**

C5 is added to the formula. The cell you click is color-coded and shows a flashing marquee border, as shown in Figure 7-4.

FIGURE 7-4

Referencing a cell in a formula

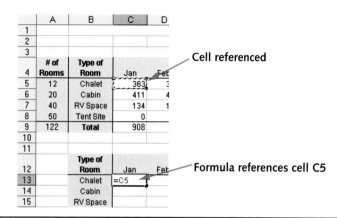

✓ **4** Type **/**, click cell **A5**, and click the Enter button on the Formula bar.

Excel completes the formula and displays the ratio of cells C5 and A5 (30.25).

5 Scroll down, if necessary, and click cell **C21**. Click in the Formula bar, type **=C13/31**, and click the Enter button on the Formula bar.

Excel calculates the occupancy rate of chalet rooms for the month of January (0.97581), and the results appear in cell C21.

6 On the Format menu, click **Cells**.

ANOTHER METHOD

- Right-click the selected cell, and select Format Cells on the shortcut menu.
- Press Ctrl+1.

7 Switch to the Number tab, if necessary, and click **Percentage** in the Category list.

8 Click **OK** to accept the default number of decimal places (2).

The value in C21 appears as a percentage.

FIGURE 7-5

Formatting formula results

	A	B	C	D	E	F	G	H	I	J	K	L	M	N	
1					Lodging Usage and Vacancy, Fiscal Year 2004										
2															
3					Number of Nights Occupied										
4	# of Rooms	Type of Room	Jan	Feb	Mar	Apr	May	Jun	Jul	Aug	Sep	Oct	Nov	Dec	
5	12	Chalet	363	311	247	176	143	121	154	218	239	275	303	358	
6	20	Cabin	411	429	396	292	254	484	501	555	493	366	245	371	
7	40	RV Space	134	157	323	467	792	1028	1143	1096	888	637	244	141	
8	50	Tent Site	0	0	11	47	431	962	1381	1426	1011	68	6	0	
9	122	Total	908												
10															
11					Average Number of Nights Occupied per Room										
12		Type of Room	Jan	Feb	Mar	Apr	May	Jun	Jul	Aug	Sep	Oct	Nov	Dec	Av
13		Chalet	30.25												
14		Cabin													
15		RV Space													
16		Tent Site													
17		Total													
18															
19					Occupancy Rate										
20		Type of Room	Jan	Feb	Mar	Apr	May	Jun	Jul	Aug	Sep	Oct	Nov	Dec	Av
21		Chalet	97.58%												
22		Cabin													

H ◀ ▶ H \ Usage /

◆ **Keep this file open for the next exercise.**

> **TIP**
>
> By default, Excel calculates formulas automatically. To change when a formula is calculated, open the Tools menu and click Options; on the Calculation tab, select the desired option.

QUICK REFERENCE ▼

Enter a formula in a cell

1 Click the cell and type =.

2 Type the formula, including cell references, constant values, mathematical operators, functions, and parentheses.

3 Press Enter.

QUICK CHECK

Q. In a formula, what is a cell reference?

A: A cell reference is the cell's address.

Copying Formulas

THE BOTTOM LINE

You can avoid entering formulas repeatedly and save a considerable amount of time by copying a cell with a completed formula and pasting it in the destination cells.

You may find that a similar formula is needed in several adjacent cells. For example, if you have a list of items and each item contributes to the total income for one year, you might want to add the items to total the income for that year. To total the income for consecutive years, you can create formulas to sum the income for each year.

Instead of entering the formula repeatedly for each year, you can simply copy it and paste it in the destination cells. You also can use the Fill feature to copy formulas to adjacent cells.

When selecting a cell, you may have noticed the small black square in the bottom right corner, as shown in Figure 7-6. This is the Fill handle. When you click a cell containing a formula and drag the Fill handle, the formula is copied to the cells. When the formula contains cell references, Excel changes them to match those of the column or row to which the formula has been copied.

FIGURE 7-6

Fill handle on a selected cell

Fill handle

The reservations manager does not want to type the same formula over and over to calculate the occupancy rate for each type of room for each month. Instead, he copies his formulas to several locations.

Copy formulas

In this exercise, you copy formulas in your worksheet.

1 **Click cell C13, and on the Edit menu, click Copy.**

A flashing marquee border appears around the cell.

ANOTHER METHOD

- Select the cell you want to copy, and then click the Copy button.
- Select the cell you want to copy, and press Ctrl+C.

2 **Click cell C14, and on the Edit menu, click Paste.**

The formula is pasted in cell C14, and the Paste Options button appears next to the cell.

ANOTHER METHOD

- Select the cell to which you want to paste, and then click the Paste button.
- Select the cell to which you want to paste, and press Ctrl+V.

TIP

For more information on the Paste Options button, see Lesson 2, "Editing and Formatting Worksheets."

3 **Repeat step 2 for cells C15 and C16.**

ANOTHER METHOD

To copy data, including a formula, that is in the cell directly above the selected cell, press Ctrl+D. To copy data that is in the cell to the immediate left of the selected cell, press Ctrl+R.

4 **Click cell C9, and point to the Fill handle.**

The mouse pointer turns into a crosshair pointer when properly positioned.

TIP

When you copy a formula to a different cell, Excel also copies the formatting.

5 **Drag the Fill handle to cell D9.**

The formula in cell C9 is copied to cell D9, and the Auto Fill Options button appears next to the cell.

FIGURE 7-7

Copying a formula using the Fill handle

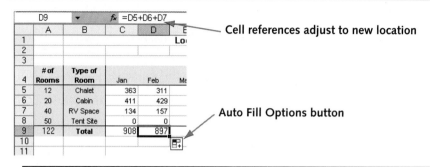

Cell references adjust to new location

Auto Fill Options button

6 **Click cell D9, and observe its formula in the Formula bar.**

The formula is copied from C9, and the column letter is adjusted to match the column of the new cell.

7 **Point to the Fill handle in cell D9, and drag the handle to cell N9.**

The formula is copied to cells E9:N9. The total number of nights occupied for each month is displayed in cells E9:N9.

FIGURE 7-8

Formula copied to a range of cells

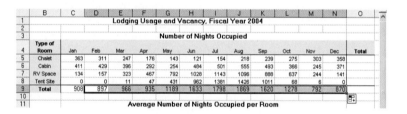

◆ **Save the file, and leave it open for the next exercise.**

Q. If you wanted to copy a formula from cell A5 to cell C5, would you use the Fill handle method or would you use the Copy and Paste commands?

A: **You would use the Copy and Paste commands because you can use the Fill handle only to copy to adjacent cells.**

TROUBLESHOOTING

If you inadvertently delete or change a formula, press Ctrl+Z or click the Undo button on the Standard toolbar to reverse the action.

QUICK REFERENCE ▼

Copy a formula using the Fill handle

1 Select the cell that contains the formula you want to copy.

2 Drag the Fill handle to the last cell in the desired range.

Working with Cell References

THE BOTTOM LINE

Cell references are frequently used in formulas. Being able to copy formulas without having to manually change cell references is a time-saver as well as an effective way to ensure accuracy in your calculations.

As you have learned, you can copy (and move) cells that contain formulas with cell references, and the references automatically adjust to reflect their new location. These are referred to as **relative references.** For example, if you enter =(C4+C5) in cell C6, the resulting value in C6 will be the sum of the values in C4 and C5. If you copy this formula to cell D6, the formula in D6 will appear as =(D4+D5) and the resulting value in cell D6 will be the sum of the values in D4 and D5. Excel automatically adjusts the cell references relative to their new location, which is why they are called "relative" cell references.

In some cases, however, you need cell references that don't change when you copy them from one location to another. For example, a formula might refer to a rate of interest that is always stored in a particular cell. This is referred to as an **absolute reference.** A cell reference also may have an absolute reference to a row but not to a column, and vice versa. To make a cell reference absolute, type a dollar sign ($) before either or both of the column or row references.

For example, C1 is an absolute reference to cell C1. $C1 is an absolute reference to column C, but the reference to row 1 is relative. C$1 is a relative reference to column C, but the reference to row 1 is absolute.

At Adventure Works, the reservations manager is having trouble copying the formulas in his worksheet that calculate simple averages. Using a combination of absolute and relative references, however, he is able to replicate easily the formulas to compute the necessary averages.

Use cell references in formulas

In this exercise, you use absolute references and relative references to build and copy a formula.

1 **Double-click cell C13.**

2 **Type a dollar sign ($) before the A in the reference to cell A5, and press Enter.**

The formula reads =C5/$A5.

3 **Copy the formula in cell C13 to cell D13, and click cell D13, if necessary, to select it.**

The formula in cell D13 reads =D5/$A5. Because the column reference to cell A5 is absolute, that reference does not change when the formula is copied. The reference to the first cell in the formula is entirely relative.

4 **Copy the formula in cell C13 to cell C14, and click cell C14.**

The formula in cell C14 reads =C6/$A6. Because the reference to column A is absolute, that reference does not change when the formula is copied. However, the row reference is still relative, so that value is updated when the formula is copied. The reference to the first cell is entirely relative.

5 **Using the Fill handle, copy the formula in cell C14 to cells C15 and C16. Click cell D13 and use its Fill handle to copy the formula to E13:N13. Use the Fill handles on C14, C15, and C16 to copy their formulas to D14:N14, D15:N15, and D16:N16, respectively.**

That section of the worksheet should look like the worksheet shown in Figure 7-9.

FIGURE 7-9

Copying formulas with cell references

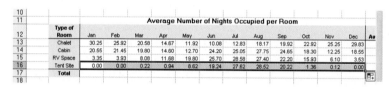

	Type of Room	Jan	Feb	Mar	Apr	May	Jun	Jul	Aug	Sep	Oct	Nov	Dec	Av
	Average Number of Nights Occupied per Room													
13	Chalet	30.25	25.92	20.58	14.67	11.92	10.08	12.83	18.17	19.92	22.92	25.25	29.83	
14	Cabin	20.55	21.45	19.80	14.60	12.70	24.20	25.05	27.75	24.65	18.30	12.25	18.55	
15	RV Space	3.35	3.93	8.08	11.68	19.80	25.70	28.58	27.40	22.20	15.93	6.10	3.53	
16	Tent Site	0.00	0.00	0.22	0.94	8.62	19.24	27.62	28.52	20.22	1.36	0.12	0.00	
17	Total													

◆ **Save and close Lodging Usage.**

Q. Which type of cell reference changes to reflect a location to which it is copied or moved?

A: A relative cell reference changes "relative" to its new location.

QUICK REFERENCE ▼

Create an absolute reference

- Type a dollar sign ($) before the column reference to make the column reference absolute.
- Type a dollar sign ($) before the row reference to make the row reference absolute.
- Type a dollar sign ($) before the column and row references to make the entire cell reference absolute.

Editing Formulas

THE BOTTOM LINE

You may want to change a formula to produce a different result on specified data or because an error was made in entering a formula.

You can edit a formula just like you edit any data you've already entered in a cell. For example, instead of summing the values in a range of cells, you may want to find the average for the range. You can edit a formula using one of the following methods:

- Double-click the cell, type your changes directly in the cell, and press Enter.

  Or

- Click the cell, click in the Formula bar, type your changes, and click the Enter button on the Formula bar or press Enter.

To delete a formula, click the cell and press the Delete key or the Backspace key.

◆ **Open Food07 from the Excel Practice/Lesson07 folder.**

Edit formulas

In this exercise, you revise formulas.

1 **Click cell P3, and click to the right of the formula in the Formula bar.**

The insertion point flashes at the end of the formula.

2 **Press the Backspace key three times, click cell O3, and then press Enter.**

The Total Yearly Consumption figure, which also is shown in cell O3, is deleted from the formula, and the cell reference for that data replaces it. Using a cell reference in the formula instead of a constant allows you to copy the formula.

ANOTHER METHOD

Double-click the cell, edit the formula by typing the new values or by referencing other cells, and press Enter.

3 **Copy the formula to cells P4:P35 by using the Fill handle in cell P3.**

Excel calculates and displays the yearly costs per item.

TROUBLESHOOTING

Before you drag the Fill handle, make sure the mouse pointer icon is the shape of a crosshair. If it's the shape of a four-headed arrow, you will move the cell when you drag.

FIGURE 7-10

Edited worksheet

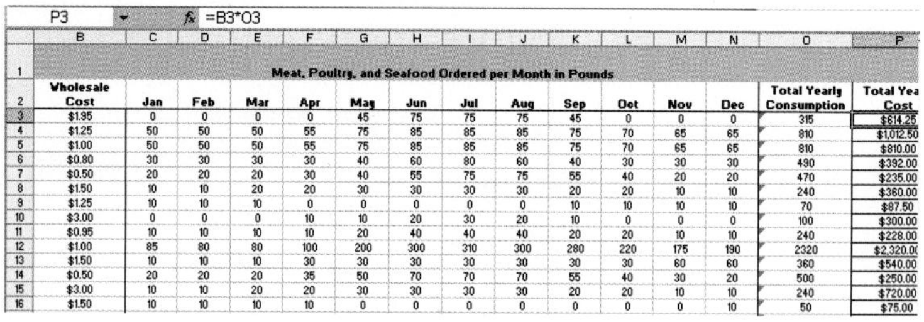

P3 | fx =B3*O3

	B	C	D	E	F	G	H	I	J	K	L	M	N	O	P
1	Meat, Poultry, and Seafood Ordered per Month in Pounds														
2	Wholesale Cost	Jan	Feb	Mar	Apr	May	Jun	Jul	Aug	Sep	Oct	Nov	Dec	Total Yearly Consumption	Total Yea Cost
3	$1.95	0	0	0	0	45	75	75	75	45	0	0	0	315	$614.25
4	$1.25	50	50	50	55	75	85	85	85	75	70	65	65	810	$1,012.50
5	$1.00	50	50	50	55	75	85	85	85	75	70	65	65	810	$810.00
6	$0.80	30	30	30	30	40	60	80	60	40	30	30	30	490	$392.00
7	$0.50	20	20	20	30	40	55	75	75	55	40	20	20	470	$235.00
8	$1.50	10	10	20	20	30	30	30	30	20	20	10	10	240	$360.00
9	$1.25	10	10	10	0	0	0	0	0	10	10	10	10	70	$87.50
10	$3.00	0	0	0	10	10	20	30	20	10	0	0	0	100	$300.00
11	$0.95	10	10	10	10	20	40	40	40	20	20	10	10	240	$228.00
12	$1.00	85	80	80	100	200	300	310	300	280	220	175	190	2320	$2,320.0(
13	$1.50	10	10	10	30	30	30	30	30	30	30	60	60	360	$540.00
14	$0.50	20	20	20	35	50	70	70	70	55	40	30	20	500	$250.00
15	$3.00	10	10	20	20	30	30	30	30	20	20	10	10	240	$720.00
16	$1.50	10	10	10	10	0	0	0	0	0	0	0	10	50	$75.00

◆ **Save and close Food07.**

QUICK CHECK

Q. What are the two methods for editing a formula?

A: Double-click the cell, type your changes directly in the cell, and press Enter. Or click the cell, click in the Formula bar, type your changes, and click the Enter button on the Formula bar or press Enter.

QUICK REFERENCE ▼

Revise a formula

1. Click the cell that contains the formula.
2. Click in the Formula bar.
3. Edit the necessary formula, functions, or arguments, and click the Enter button on the Formula bar or press Enter.

Exploring Functions

THE BOTTOM LINE

Functions are designed to perform all sorts of calculations—from simple to complex. When you apply one of Excel's built-in functions to specified data, you eliminate the time involved in manually constructing a formula and ensure the accuracy of the formula's result.

One of the most common calculations performed in a worksheet is adding a range of cells. You can add a range of cells by creating a formula that includes each cell label separated by the addition (+) operator. An easier way to achieve the same result is to use the SUM function.

A **function** is a predefined formula that performs a calculation. For example, the SUM function adds values or a range of cells. A typical SUM function totaling cells C13 through C16 looks like this: *=SUM(C13:C16)*.

A function consists of two components: the *function name* and, in most cases, an *argument list*. See Figure 7-11. The argument list, which is enclosed in parentheses, contains the data (or operands) that the function requires to produce the result. Depending on the function, an argument can be a constant value, a single-cell reference, a range of cells, a range name, or even another function. When a function contains multiple arguments, the arguments are separated by commas. In this lesson, you explore some of the more commonly used functions, including the SUM, AVERAGE, and various date functions.

FIGURE 7-11

Structure of a function

	B	C	D	E	F	
	C17		▼	f_x	=SUM(C13:C16)	
1					Lodging Usage	← Argument
2						
3						N ← Function name
4	Type of Room	Jan	Feb	Mar	Apr	
5	Chalet	363	311	247	176	
6	Cabin	411	429	396	292	
7	RV Space	134	157	323	467	
8	Tent Site	0	0	11	47	
9	Total	908	897	966	935	
10						
11					Average Nu	
12	Type of Room	Jan	Feb	Mar	Apr	
13	Chalet	30.25	25.92	20.58	14.67	
14	Cabin	20.55	21.45	19.80	14.60	
15	RV Space	3.35	3.93	8.08	11.68	
16	Tent Site	0.00	0.00	0.22	0.94	
17	Total	54.15				

Inserting a Function

You can enter a function in a cell just as you enter any formula: by typing it directly in the cell or in the Formula bar. With this method, you must know the exact name and syntax (or structure) of the function. You might find that an easier way to enter a function is to use the Insert Function feature, which guides you through the process of "building" the formula that the specified function will execute.

Once you've selected a function in the Insert Function dialog box, the Function Arguments dialog box opens. This is where you build your function. The Function Arguments dialog box lists the selected function's arguments, provides a description of each argument, and shows the calculated result of the function.

At Adventure Works, the accountant uses the Insert Function feature to calculate the annual income generated through the rental of various types of sporting equipment.

◆ **Open Activity Rentals from the Excel Practice/Lesson07 folder.**

Insert functions

In this exercise, you use the Insert Function feature to enter functions in a worksheet.

1 **Click cell O3, and click the Insert Function button on the Standard toolbar.**

The Insert Function dialog box opens.

FIGURE 7-12

Insert Function dialog box

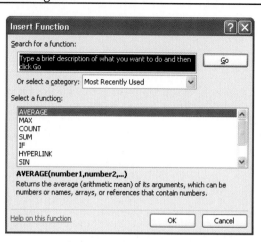

ANOTHER METHOD

- On the Insert menu, click Function.
- Click the cell, and click the Insert Function button on the Formula bar.

TROUBLESHOOTING

If the Office Assistant appears asking if you want help with this feature, click No, Don't Provide Help Now.

2 In the Or Select A Category box, click the down arrow, and select Most Recently Used, if necessary.

3 In the Select A Function list, click SUM, and then click OK.

The Function Arguments dialog box appears, showing the SUM function totaling cells C3:N3.

FIGURE 7-13

Function Arguments dialog box

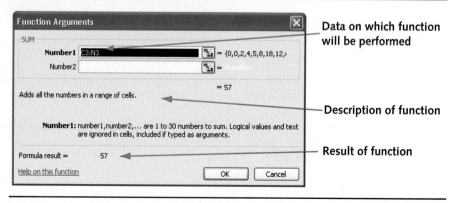

If you do not see the SUM function in the Select A Function list, click the arrow on the *Or Select A Category* box, and click All. All of Excel's functions are listed alphabetically in the Select A Function list.

4 **Click OK in the Function Arguments dialog box.**

The Function Arguments dialog box closes, and the result of the calculation (57) appears in cell O3.

5 **Click cell A20, and then click the Insert Function button on the Standard toolbar.**

The Insert Function dialog box appears.

6 **In the Or Select A Category box, click the down arrow, and select Statistical.**

7 **In the Select A Function list, click COUNT, and then click OK.**

The Function Arguments dialog box appears.

8 **In the Value1 text box, type A3:A17, and click OK.**

Excel counts 15 numeric entries in cells 3 through 17 of column A.

◆ **Save Activity Rentals, and then close the workbook.**

QUICK REFERENCE ▼

Enter a function using the Function Arguments dialog box

1 Click the cell that will contain the function.
2 On the Standard toolbar, click the Insert Function button.
3 Select the function, and enter arguments into the Function Arguments dialog box.
4 Click OK.

Q. What is the argument in the function formula *=AVERAGE(A4:A9)*?

A: The argument is the portion in parentheses (A4:A9).

Using AutoSum

Excel's **AutoSum** feature offers a shortcut for entering SUM functions to total ranges of cells. When you click the AutoSum button on the Standard toolbar, Excel totals cells directly above or to the left of the cell containing the function.

If there are any nonnumeric cells within the range of cells you want to total, AutoSum will, by default, calculate the total only from the active cell to the first nonnumeric cell. To get around this problem, either alter the arguments to include the full range of cells or select only the range of cells you want to total.

The reservations manager learns that AutoSum makes it even easier for him to complete his occupancy calculations. He can use AutoSum to calculate the many totals he needs.

◆ **Open Lodging Usage from the Excel Practice/Lesson07 folder.**

Use AutoSum

In this exercise, you use AutoSum to total a range of cells.

Σ ▾

1 **Click cell C17, and click the AutoSum button on the Standard toolbar.**

A SUM formula appears in cell C17 and the Formula bar, and the range C13:C16 is surrounded by a flashing marquee border.

2 **Press Enter.**

The formula is entered in cell C17, and the result (54.15) is displayed.

3 **Click cell O5, and then click the AutoSum button.**

A SUM formula is displayed in cell O5 and in the Formula bar, and the range C5:N5 is surrounded by a flashing marquee border.

4 **Press Enter.**

The formula is entered in cell O5, and the result (2908) is displayed.

FIGURE 7-14

Applying the AutoSum feature

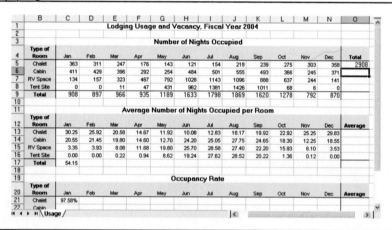

◆ **Leave the file open for the next exercise.**

QUICK REFERENCE ▼

Automatically total a row or column of cells

1 Select the cell that will contain the total.

2 On the Standard toolbar, click the AutoSum button.

3 Modify the arguments, if desired, and press Enter.

QUICK CHECK

Q. Which Excel function does AutoSum use?

A: AutoSum incorporates the SUM function.

Using Date Functions

Excel's Date and Time functions allow you to use dates and times in formulas. To perform calculations on these values, Excel converts each date and time to a serial number. The Date function performs that conversion for any year, month, and day combination you enter. The Time function converts any hour, minute, and second combination you enter.

NOW and TODAY are two of the most frequently used date functions. NOW returns the date and time that the function was entered in a worksheet. TODAY returns only the date. Each time you open a workbook that uses one of these functions, the date or time is updated automatically.

In March, the reservations manager needs to figure the occupancy rate for the winter season, which runs from November 1 through the end of February. He wants to confirm the number of days in that season.

Enter Date functions

In this exercise, you use Date functions to calculate the amount of time between two dates.

1 Click cell A20, and click the Insert Function button.

2 Select Date & Time from the Or Select A Category list.

3 Select DATE from the Select A Function list, and click OK.

The Function Arguments dialog box opens.

4 In the Year box, type 2004.

5 In the Month box, type 2.

6 In the Day box, type 29.

The serial number for the date 02/29/2004 appears as the formula result at the bottom of the Function Arguments dialog box.

7 With the Function Arguments dialog box still open, click to the right of the function in the Formula bar, press the spacebar, and type a minus sign (-).

TROUBLESHOOTING

Be sure you include a space between the closing parenthesis of the DATE argument and the minus sign.

8 On the Functions list to the left of the Formula bar, click Date, as shown in Figure 7-15.

The Function Arguments dialog box opens.

FIGURE 7-15

Entering a second DATE function

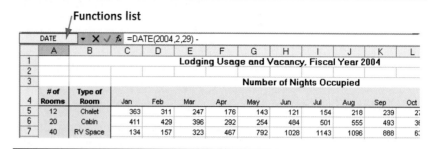

Functions list

TIP

Date functions are most useful when the date arguments are formulas rather than constants.

9 In the Year, Month, and Day boxes, type 2003, 11, and 1, respectively, and click OK.

The total number of days (120) between 11/1/2003 and 2/29/2004 appears in the cell. The formula reads =DATE(2004,2,29) - DATE(2003,11,1).

10 In the Formula bar, click the first Date function.

A ScreenTip appears with a description of each item in that portion of the formula.

11 Click the word year in the ScreenTip to select 2004, and type 2005.

12 In the Formula bar, click to the right of the formula.

13 Press the Backspace key to remove the second date function of DATE(2003,11,1).

14 Type TODAY(), and press Enter.

The total number of days between 2/29/2005 and the current date appears in the cell.

◆ Close the workbook without saving your changes.

TIP

To calculate quickly the number of days between two dates that already appear in cells in your worksheet, simply subtract one cell from the other. For example, if cell A1 contains the date 11/1/2004 and cell A2 contains the date 2/29/2005, the number of days between them will be calculated with the following formula: =A2-A1.

Make sure you choose the number format for the cell containing this formula. Otherwise, Excel displays the result in the same format as the cells used in the calculation (in this case, as a date).

QUICK REFERENCE ▼

Use the NOW or TODAY function

1 Click the cell in which you want the date or date and time to appear.

2 Type **=NOW()** or **=TODAY()** in the cell, and press the Enter key.

Using Basic Statistical Functions

Statistical functions are typically used to compile and classify data so as to present significant information. For example, a teacher wants to determine the highest score (MAX) and the lowest score (MIN) on an exam, a sales manager wants to set pay increases based on sales reps' average sales over a 12-month period (AVERAGE), and a market researcher wants to figure out the middle income for a group of survey participants (MEDIAN). Some of the more commonly used statistical functions are shown in the following table.

QUICK CHECK

Q. What is the difference between the NOW and the TODAY functions?

A: The NOW function displays the current date and time; the TODAY function displays the current date.

Function	Meaning	Example
SUM	Totals the numeric arguments	=SUM(B5:B10)
AVERAGE	Computes the average (arithmetic mean) of the numeric arguments	=AVERAGE(B5:B10)
COUNT	Within the argument list, counts only the cells that contain numbers	=COUNT(B5:B10)
MIN	Returns the smallest number within the arguments	=MIN(B5:B10)
MAX	Returns the largest number within the arguments	=MAX(B5:B10)

The activities manager at Adventure Works is learning which Excel functions can help her devise a strategy for activities in the upcoming year.

◆ **Open Activity Rentals from the Excel Practice/Lesson07 folder.**

Insert statistical functions

In this exercise, you create formulas using the AVERAGE, MIN, and MAX functions.

fx

1 **Click cell A21, and click the Insert Function button.**

The Insert Function dialog box appears.

2 **Select Statistical in the Or Select A Category list, click AVERAGE in the Select A Function list, and click OK.**

The Function Arguments dialog box appears.

3 **In the Number 1 box, click the Collapse Dialog button.**

The Function Arguments dialog box collapses, allowing you to select the range of cells to be averaged.

4 **Select cells C15:N15, and click the Expand Dialog button in the Function Arguments dialog box.**

The Function Arguments dialog box appears with the completed AVERAGE function.

FIGURE 7-16

Entering the AVERAGE function

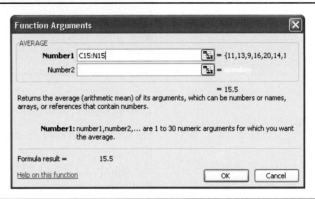

5 **In the Function Arguments dialog box, click OK.**

The average number of pairs of binoculars rented per month (15.5) appears in cell A21.

6 **Click in the Formula bar, and select the word AVERAGE.**

7 **Click the Functions down arrow to the left of the Formula bar (currently displaying the text AVERAGE), and click MAX.**

The Function Arguments dialog box opens with the range previously used already entered.

TROUBLESHOOTING

If MAX does not appear in your list of functions, click More Functions. This opens the Insert Functions dialog box, from which you can select MAX in the Statistical category.

FIGURE 7-17

Entering the MAX function

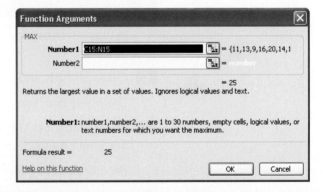

TIP

If you forget the syntax for a function you want to use, type = and the name of the function in a cell and press Ctrl+A. The Function Arguments dialog box appears so you can enter the arguments for your function.

8 **In the Function Arguments dialog box, click OK.**

The highest number of pairs of binoculars rented in a month (25) appears in cell A21.

9 **Click cell A22, type =MIN(C15:N15), and press Enter.**

The lowest number of pairs of binoculars rented in a month (9) appears in cell A22.

10 **Delete the entries in cells A20:A22.**

◆ **Save and close Activity Rentals.**

Creating a Three-Dimensional Formula

THE BOTTOM LINE

Formulas can reference cells in any worksheet within a workbook as well as in other workbooks. Using three-dimensional formulas, you can compile data and prepare summaries that are vital to forecasts and analyses.

So far you've learned how to enter formulas and functions that calculate data on a single worksheet. You also can enter formulas to calculate data from multiple worksheets within a workbook. A formula that contains a reference (referred to as a 3-D reference) to data or cells on one or more other worksheets is called a **three-dimensional formula.** When data is adjusted on a worksheet, any formula that references that data also is adjusted.

Three-dimensional formulas are widely used to create a summary sheet that totals figures from different sheets in a workbook file. For example, the chef at Adventure Works wants to see how much the restaurant has paid for food in a year. To calculate the total amount spent, he uses a three-dimensional formula on the Summary worksheet. The formula refers to the cells in each worksheet that contain the amount spent in a particular food category and adds these amounts together.

As with any formula, you can specify a reference by typing the cell coordinates. The references in the formula, however, must begin with the name of the worksheet to which the formula is linking, followed by an exclamation point and then the cell coordinates. Commas separate the references.

IMPORTANT

When a worksheet has a name consisting of two or more words, the name must be put in single quotation marks in the formula.

◆ **Open Food07 from the Excel Practice/Lesson07 folder.**

Create a three-dimensional formula

In this exercise, you create a formula in one worksheet that adds together data in other worksheets.

1 Click the **Summary sheet tab**, click cell **A3**, type **Total Cost of Food,** and **press Enter.**

Excel adds the text to cell A3 and moves the insertion point to cell A4.

2 In cell **A4,** type **=SUM(.**

3 Click the **Meats sheet tab, click cell P36, and type a plus sign (+).**

In the Formula bar on the Meats worksheet, the first argument and addition operator are added to the formula, as shown in Figure 7-18.

FIGURE 7-18

Building a three-dimensional formula

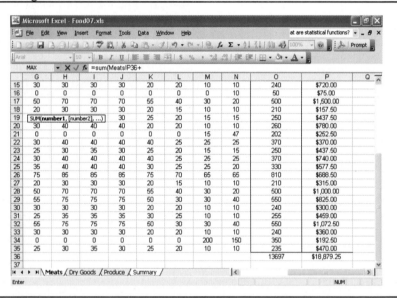

4 Click the **Dry Goods sheet tab, click cell P26, and type a plus sign (+).**

The second argument is added to the formula.

5 Click the **Produce sheet tab, click cell P28, and press Enter.**

The last argument is added to the formula, and the result of the formula appears in cell A4 on the Summary worksheet.

FIGURE 7-19

Result of a three-dimensional formula

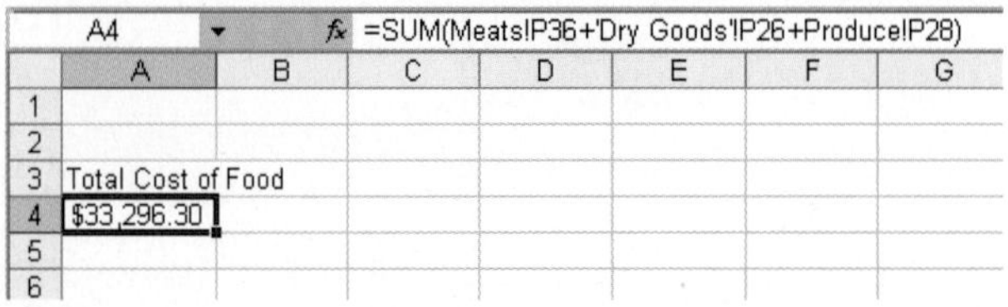

◆ Save and close Food07.

◆ If you are continuing to other lessons, leave Excel open.

◆ If you are not continuing to other lessons, save and close all open workbooks, then close Excel.

QUICK CHECK

Q. How would you type a three-dimensional formula that totals the values in cell A10 on worksheets named *January*, *February*, and *March*?

A: You type =SUM(January!A10+February!A10+March!A10).

CHECK THIS OUT ▼

Using AutoComplete
Excel has another timesaving feature called AutoComplete. AutoComplete automatically finishes text entries for you. When the first few letters that you type match an existing entry in the same column, Excel assumes you are typing the same entry again and completes it for you. You can disable AutoComplete by clicking Options on the Tools menu, clicking the Edit tab, and clearing the Enable AutoComplete For Cell Values check box.

QUICK REFERENCE ▼

Create a three-dimensional formula

1 Click the cell where you want to insert the formula.

2 Enter the formula using the appropriate worksheet and cell references.

3 Press Enter.

Key Points

✔ *In a spreadsheet program like Excel, formulas that range from simple to complex are calculated instantaneously, giving you results and solutions that are timely and accurate. You can enter and edit formulas just as you enter and edit other data.*

✔ *You can avoid entering formulas repeatedly and save a considerable amount of time by copying a cell with a completed formula and pasting it in the destination cells. You also can copy a cell's contents by using the Fill feature.*

✔ *Cell references are frequently used in formulas. Being able to copy formulas without having to manually change cell references is a time-saver as well as an effective way to ensure accuracy in calculations.*

✔ *Excel comes with hundreds of functions that are designed to perform all sorts of calculations. When you apply one of Excel's built-in functions, you eliminate the time involved in manually constructing a formula and ensure the accuracy of the formula's result.*

✔ *You can use three-dimensional formulas to compile data from multiple worksheets and to prepare summaries.*

Quick Quiz

True/False

T F **1.** A lowercase *x* is the multiplication operator.

T F **2.** In a formula with addition and multiplication operators, the multiplication operation is performed first.

T F **3.** You can use the Fill handle to copy a cell's contents only to adjacent cells.

T F **4.** In a function, the argument includes the name of the function.

T F **5.** You would use the DATE function if you wanted to display the current date in a worksheet.

T F **6.** The COUNT function is an example of a statistical function.

Multiple Choice

1. Which of the following is *not* a mathematical operator?
   a. ^
   b. @
   c. +
   d. *

2. If you entered the formula, =(2 + 4) * 6 / (3 − 1) in a cell, what would the result be?
   a. 7.6
   b. 9
   c. 11
   d. 18

3. Which function automatically totals cells directly above or to the left of the cell containing it?
   a. AutoSum
   b. Auto Fill
   c. AutoComplete
   d. COUNT

4. Which character designates a cell reference as absolute?
   a. ^
   b. @
   c. #
   d. $

Short Answer

1. How can you enter a formula in a cell?

2. What is the quickest way to total a column of values?

3. How can you copy a formula to a range of adjacent cells?

4. What are two ways to edit a formula in a cell?

5. List and identify the five mathematical operators discussed in this lesson.

On Your Own

◆ Open Lodging Usage from the Excel Practice/Lesson07 folder.

Exercise 1

In cell O5, use AutoSum to total the data in C5:N5. Do the same for the data in C6:N9. Complete the row of totals in the next table, and then create a formula to compute the average number of nights occupied in each room type for the year. In the third table, compute the occupancy rates. To do this, divide the average number of nights occupied per room by the number of days in the month (use 29 days for February). Then figure the average occupancy rate of each room type for the year.

◆ Close Lodging Usage.

◆ Open Activity Rentals from the Excel Practice/Lesson07 folder.

Exercise 2

Calculate the total number of rentals each month, the total yearly rentals, the yearly income for each type of activity/equipment, and the total annual income. Use the NOW function to display the current date and time in cell A1. Insert a column to the right of Yearly Rentals, label it **Average Monthly Rentals**, and use the AVERAGE function to find the average monthly rentals for each type of equipment.

◆ **Close Activity Rentals.**

One Step Further

Exercise 1

In this lesson, you used the COUNT function, which is a statistical function. Review the other categories of functions available from the Insert Function dialog box. What category would you likely use the most?

Exercise 2

This lesson illustrated how to find the number of days between two days by entering the dates in a formula that subtracted one date from the other. Is there a function that can do this automatically? Is there a way to calculate just the number of workdays between two dates (not counting weekends)? Explore the Date & Time category of the Insert Function dialog box or use Excel's Help files to find the answers to these questions. Write a brief summary of your findings.

Exercise 3

This lesson briefly touched on the Auto Fill feature and the Auto Fill Options button that appears whenever you fill cells. Return to the Activity Rentals workbook, and explore the filling and copying options available through the Auto Fill Options button. Briefly describe how these options can be useful.

Part

3

Microsoft Outlook

LESSON

Introduction to Outlook

After completing this lesson, you will be able to:

✔ *Start Outlook.*
✔ *Navigate within Outlook.*
✔ *Use the Office Assistant.*

KEY TERMS

- Folder List
- folder
- item
- Office Assistant

- Navigation pane
- profile
- Reading pane
- shortcut

Managing work-related data often means recording and tracking information on paper stored in several different places. For example, a businessperson might record appointments and meetings in a day planner, while keeping phone numbers and addresses in a card file. Brief reminders were jotted down on small sticky notes. Other important business information was stored in files and folders in a desk drawer or filing cabinet.

Although many people have grown accustomed to these organizational approaches, Microsoft Office Outlook 2003 provides a better way to store, track, and integrate business and personal information. With Outlook, you can store and access important information in a single location on a personal computer. For example, you can use Outlook's electronic calendar to record meetings and appointment dates and times. Outlook can even sound an alarm or display a reminder on your computer screen when you have an appointment. You can record brief reminders to yourself on Outlook notes, which resemble sticky notes, and these notes can be displayed on your screen at any time for easy reference. You can use Outlook to record your daily or weekly tasks and check them off as you complete them. Outlook has an address book in which you can record phone numbers, addresses, e-mail addresses, and other information about your business and personal contacts. You can even view Web sites directly from Outlook, as well as open other Microsoft Office System documents. The power of Outlook lies in knowing how to use all of its capabilities to organize information efficiently.

Outlook 2003 has several improvements since the previous version. The most obvious change is the interface. The new interface simplifies navigation and dramatically improves the ease of reading messages.

In this lesson, you will tour many of the elements of Outlook to become familiar with it. You will start Outlook and view different folders, which are containers for programs and files. You will also use the new Navigation pane to display the contents of the selected folder or file. The new Reading pane provides a larger vertical area for displaying and reading messages. Finally, you will learn how to use the Help system in Outlook to find answers to your questions about using Outlook as a powerful tool to organize your data.

FIGURE 1-1

Outlook icon

Microsoft Office
Outlook 2003

Starting Outlook

THE BOTTOM LINE

Microsoft Office Outlook 2003 requires a profile that includes all the information required to access your e-mail accounts and send messages. You establish this profile when you first sart Outlook.

As with all Microsoft Office System programs, there are several different ways to open Outlook. One method is to click the Start button on the Windows taskbar, point to All Programs, point to Microsoft Office, and click Microsoft Office Outlook 2003. This option is always available, even if you are using another Microsoft Office System program.

TROUBLESHOOTING

Be sure that you can see the Start menu and a clear area on your desktop before you start the process of adding the Outlook icon to your desktop.

You can also add the Outlook icon to your desktop, and then simply double-click the icon to start Outlook. Using the icon is faster and easier than using the Start button on the Windows taskbar. To add an Outlook icon to your desktop, click the Start button on the Windows taskbar, point to All Programs, point to Microsoft Office, hold down the Ctrl key, and drag the Microsoft Office Outlook 2003 icon onto your desktop. This process adds the icon to your desktop without removing it from the Start menu.

When you start Outlook, you are asked to select a profile. The Outlook **profile** is a set of data required to enable Outlook to access your e-mail accounts and address book. It includes the name of your e-mail account, the servers used to send and receive e-mail, and your passwords.

TROUBLESHOOTING

See the Appendix for more information about setting up a profile.

Start Microsoft Outlook:

In this exercise, you start Microsoft Office Outlook 2003.

1 **On the Windows taskbar, click the Start button, point to All Programs, point to Microsoft Office, and click Microsoft Office Outlook 2003.**

Outlook starts. The available Outlook profiles are listed.

ANOTHER METHOD

Double-click the Outlook icon on your desktop.

FIGURE 1-2

Outlook profiles

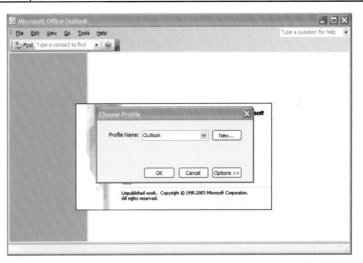

2 **If necessary, select your Outlook profile. Click the OK button.**

The main Outlook window is displayed, placing all of Outlook's functionality at your fingertips.

TROUBLESHOOTING

If you are opening Outlook for the first time, the Office Assistant (the animated paper clip character) might be displayed. To close the Office Assistant, right-click the paper clip, and click Close on the shortcut menu that appears. You will learn more about the Office Assistant later in this lesson.

3 **If necessary, click the Maximize button in the upper-right corner of the Outlook window.**

The Outlook window expands to fill the entire screen. This enables you to view the Outlook application at its best, providing a clear view of the information available in Outlook.

◆ **Keep Outlook open for the next exercise.**

QUICK CHECK

Q: What is the purpose of the Maximize button?

A: **The Maximize button expands the window to fill the entire screen.**

QUICK REFERENCE ▼

Start Outlook

1 On the Windows taskbar, click the Start button.

2 Point to All Programs.

3 Point to Microsoft Office.

4 Click Microsoft Office Outlook 2003.

5 Select your profile and click OK.

6 If necessary, click the Maximize button.

Navigating Within Outlook

THE BOTTOM LINE

Microsoft Office Outlook 2003 has a new interface that enables you to save and access information quickly.

Now that you have opened the Outlook application, you can examine each element in the Outlook window. The Outlook window contains buttons, icons, menu commands, and other elements that enable you to navigate within Outlook and use Outlook effectively. The contents of this window change as you click buttons and icons and choose options. The table on the following page describes the basic functions of the elements displayed in the Outlook window.

TROUBLESHOOTING

If you used a previous version of Outlook, you will notice significant differences in the appearance of the Outlook window.

FIGURE 1-3

Outlook window

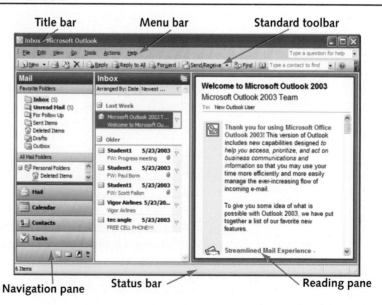

Title bar   Menu bar   Standard toolbar

Navigation pane   Status bar   Reading pane

Element	Description
Title bar	Identifies the application currently running (in this case, Outlook) and the active Outlook folder.
Menu bar	Lists the names of the menus available in the current Outlook window. A menu displays a list of commands the application can perform.
Standard toolbar	Displays buttons that enable you to quickly access commonly used commands for the application.
Navigation pane	Provides access to the contents of folders that are available in Outlook, such as the Inbox and Calendar. The **Navigation pane** replaces the Outlook bar used in previous versions. To hide or display the Navigation pane, open the View menu and click Navigation pane. You will learn how to use the Navigation pane later in this lesson.
Item	Information displayed in Outlook. For example, in the Inbox, each message is an **item**; in Contacts, the contact record (phone and address information about an individual) is an item.
Status Bar	As you switch to different Outlook folders, the Status bar displays the number of items that are in a specific folder. For example, when you open Contacts, the Status bar displays the number of contacts in the folder.
Reading pane	A section of the Inbox window that displays the text of the selected message. The **Reading pane** can be moved, but the default location is the right side of the window. This provides the most vertical space to read longer messages without needing to scroll the text.

Using Personalized Menus

THE BOTTOM LINE

Personalized menus provide fast access to the commands you use frequently.

Like other Microsoft Office System applications, Outlook has a default feature that enables you to personalize your menus. The first time you open a menu in Outlook, you see a short menu that displays the commands that are most frequently used by Outlook users. You also see two small arrows at the bottom of the menu. These arrows are used to expand the menu to display more options. You can expand the menu in two ways: click the arrows at the bottom of the menu or wait a few seconds for the menu to expand on its own. When you click a command on the expanded menu, Outlook immediately displays this command on the short menu. Outlook continues to adapt. Over time, if you stop using this command, it is removed from the short menu. The command will be displayed on the expanded menu.

TIP

If you prefer to see the expanded menus instead of the short menus, open the Tools menu, click Customize, click the Options tab, select the Always Show Full Menus check box, and click Close.

Outlook 2003 includes a new menu. The Go menu contains a link to each of the main Outlook folders. This simply provides another way to move around in the Outlook application. Like the other menus, the short menu contains your most selections.

Use Outlook menus:

With Outlook open, you will now learn to use the Outlook menus.

TROUBLESHOOTING

Your short menu may display more commands than the samples in this exercise.

FIGURE 1-4

Short Tools menu

1. **On the menu bar, click Tools.**

   The short Tools menu is displayed. The short Tools menu contains the options used most frequently by the majority of Outlook users. All of the menu options are not displayed.

2. **Click anywhere outside the menu.**

   The menu closes. The focus shifts to the location you clicked.

3. **On the menu bar, click Tools.**

   The short Tools menu is displayed. Again, only the most frequently used commands are displayed.

4. **Click the double arrows at the bottom of the short Tools menu.**

   The expanded Tools menu is displayed. All commands available on the Tools menu are available for your use.

ANOTHER METHOD

To display the expanded menu, open the short menu and wait several seconds.

◆ **Keep Outlook open for the next exercise.**

QUICK CHECK

Q: What is the meaning of the double arrows at the bottom of an open menu?

A: **The double arrows indicate that additional options are available.**

QUICK REFERENCE ▼

To expand a short menu

1. Click the desired menu.
2. Click the double arrows at the bottom of the menu.

Using the Navigation Pane

THE BOTTOM LINE

The new Navigation pane contains buttons that provide one-click access to the standard Outlook folders.

You have used menus in the Outlook window to access commands and information. However, the Navigation pane provides faster access to most Outlook folders and items. It contains buttons that represent the components available in Outlook, such as the Mail, Calendar, and Contacts folders. When you click one of the buttons, the contents of the folder are displayed. For example, if you click the Calendar button, the content of the Calendar folder—a calendar containing your appointments—is displayed.

FIGURE 1-5

Navigation pane

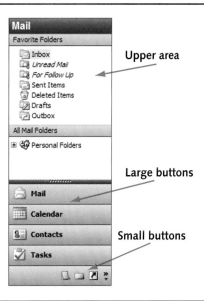

Buttons are displayed in the lower area of the Navigation pane. The buttons used frequently are large. Additional buttons are smaller. The content of the upper area of the Navigation pane depends on the button you select.

Outlook uses the term **folder** to describe how Outlook's functions and common items are divided within Outlook. For example, the Inbox folder contains e-mail messages that you have received and enables you to create messages within the Inbox folder. The Tasks folder contains a list of activities that you need to perform and enables you to create tasks. You cannot create a task in the Inbox folder or create a message in the Tasks folder. When you view the folders in Outlook, you'll notice that the appearance and options differ in each folder. For that reason, you can think of each folder as a separate program within Outlook, even though the functions work together without a seam.

TIP

Even though the Inbox, Contacts, Tasks, and other Outlook features are called "folders" in this book, you will sometimes see them referred to by name alone (for example, "the Inbox") rather than by name and identifier (for example, "the Inbox folder").

The Outlook folders directly accessed by the buttons are described in the following table.

Folder	Description
Mail	Displays the folders used to send and receive e-mail messages
Calendar	Displays a calendar and appointment book to track your schedule
Contacts	Stores the names, phone numbers, addresses, and other information about the people with whom you communicate
Tasks	Displays a to-do list of your personal and business tasks
Notes	Stores information on electronic sticky notes, such as ideas, grocery lists, or directions
Folder List	Displays a list of available folders; can be used to move items from one folder to another folder, create folders within folders, and much more (If your organization uses Microsoft Exchange Server, you might also see public folders that can be accessed by other network users.)
Shortcuts	Enables you to add links to additional files and folders that can be accessed by your computer
Journal	Displays a history of your Microsoft Office activities in a timeline format

Use the Navigation pane

You will now use the Navigation pane to view different Outlook folders.

1 **If necessary, on the Navigation pane, click the Mail button.**

The contents of the Mail folder are displayed. You will learn how to use the Inbox to send and receive e-mail messages in the next lesson.

FIGURE 1-6

Mail folder

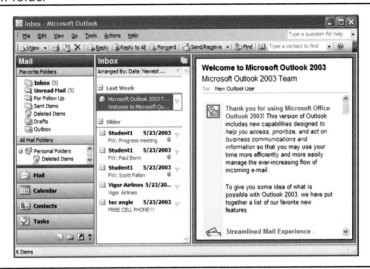

2 **On the Navigation pane, click the Calendar shortcut.**

The contents of the Calendar folder are displayed. You will learn how to use the Calendar in Lesson 5, "Using the Calendar."

FIGURE 1-7

Calendar folder

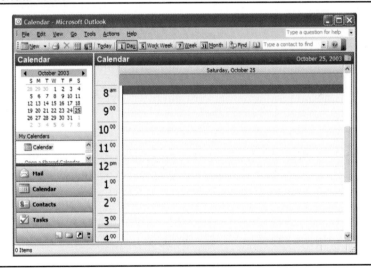

3 **On the Navigation pane, click the Contacts shortcut.**

The contents of the Contacts folder are displayed. You will learn how to create and edit contacts in Lesson 3, "Using Contacts."

FIGURE 1-8

Contacts folder

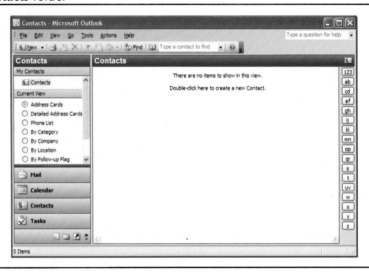

4 **On the Navigation pane, click the Tasks shortcut.**

The contents of the Tasks folder are displayed. You will learn how to create and edit tasks in Lesson 5, "Using Tasks."

FIGURE 1-9

Tasks folder

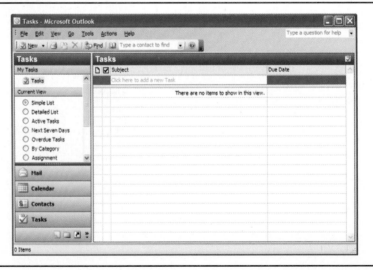

TROUBLESHOOTING

The remaining shortcuts in the Navigation pane are small buttons.

5 **On the Navigation pane, click the Notes shortcut.**

The contents of the Notes folder are displayed. We will not be studying notes in this text, but you can learn a great deal from the Help system and by experimentation.

FIGURE 1-10

Notes folder

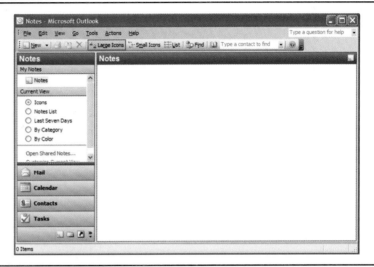

TROUBLESHOOTING

The information displayed on the right side of the window may not change when you select a different button. For example, the right side of the window doesn't change when you click the Folder List button.

6 **On the Navigation pane, click the Folder List button.**

The folders you can access are listed in the upper area of the Navigation pane.

FIGURE 1-11

Folder list

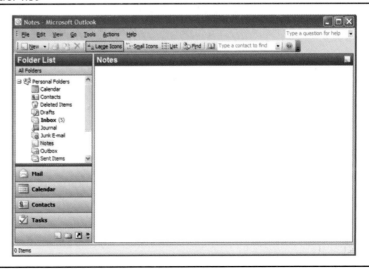

7 **On the Navigation pane, click the Shortcuts button.**

This area enables you to add new groups and **shortcuts**, creating links to additional folders and documents.

ANOTHER METHOD

Use the Folder List to access each folder.

FIGURE 1-12

Shortcuts

◆ **Keep Outlook open for the next exercise.**

QUICK REFERENCE ▼

Use the Navigation pane

Click a button to access a specific folder.

Using the Folder List

THE BOTTOM LINE

Improvements in the Folder List have increased its usefulness and provided fast access to Outlook folders.

You can also view Outlook folders and their contents by using the **Folder List**. The Navigation pane displays buttons that provide access to frequently used folders. The Folder List displays additional folders available in Outlook, including folders such as Drafts and Sent Items used to store draft copies of e-mail messages you compose and copies of e-mail messages you send to other recipients.

The Folder List displays each folder as a small icon followed by the name of the folder. When you click a folder's icon, the contents of the folder are displayed. For example, if you click the Contacts shortcut in the Folder

List, Outlook displays the contents of the Contacts folder, enabling you to view contact records.

Use the Folder List to display folders:

Now that you know how to use the Navigation pane, you will learn to use the Folder List to display Outlook folders.

1 **Click the Folder List button on the Navigation pane.**

The Folder List is displayed.

2 **In the Folder List, click Inbox.**

The contents of the Inbox folder are displayed on the right side of the window. The Folder List is still displayed.

FIGURE 1-13

Folder List and Inbox

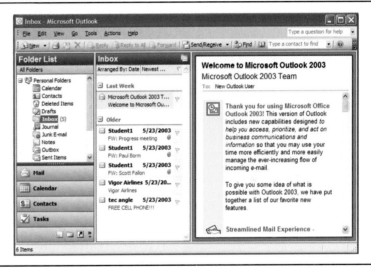

3 **In the Folder List, click Tasks.**

Outlook displays the contents of the Tasks folder. The Folder List is still displayed.

◆ **Keep Outlook open for the next exercise.**

QUICK CHECK

Q: How do you display the Folder List?

A: **Click the Folder List button on the Navigation pane.**

ANOTHER METHOD

Use the buttons in the Navigation pane to access each folder.

QUICK REFERENCE ▼

Display a folder using the Folder List

1 Click the Folder List button on the Navigation pane.

2 Click the name of the Outlook folder that you want to display.

Using the Office Assistant

THE BOTTOM LINE

The Office Assistant lets you use normal phrasing and key words to search for information in Outlook Help.

Outlook, like all Microsoft Office System applications, includes an extensive Help system that you can use to learn more about features and options available in Outlook. The **Office Assistant** is an animated character that provides helpful information about Outlook topics. By default, the Office Assistant appears as an animated paper clip named Clippit. However, you can choose to display the Office Assistant as an animated dog, cat, or any one of several other characters.

Help is readily available in Outlook. To view help when the Office Assistant is displayed, click the Office Assistant and type your question in the displayed box. Use your language of choice to phrase your request— for example, in Standard English, you might write, "How do you send a message?" or "What is in the Journal?" You can simply type a few words, such as "send message" or "Journal," to view information related to those topics. The Office Assistant interprets your request and displays topics that match one or more words in your request. Click the topic that most closely matches your request.

CHECK THIS OUT ▼

Office Assistant
To change the Office Assistant, right-click the Office Assistant and click Choose Assistant. Click Next to view the various animations available and click OK when you find one that you like. All available animations may not be saved onto your hard drive during installation, so you may need to insert the Microsoft Office (or Microsoft Outlook) CD-ROM to install a new animation.

Use the Office Assistant:

In this exercise, you display the Office Assistant and use it to view help on an Outlook topic. You will then hide the Office Assistant to complete the exercise.

1 **On the menu bar, click Help and click Show the Office Assistant.**

The Office Assistant is displayed.

ANOTHER METHOD

Click the Microsoft Outlook Help button on the Standard Toolbar to access Outlook Help.

FIGURE 1-14

Office Assistant

2 **Click the Assistant.**

A box that asks you to type a question and click the Search button is displayed.

3 **Type** How do I send a message? **and click the Search button.**

The Office Assistant displays Help topics that are relevant to the question you asked.

FIGURE 1-15

Help topics

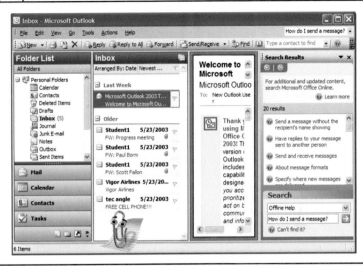

TROUBLESHOOTING

Additional search results are available if Outlook is online when the search is performed.

4 **Click the Send and Receive Messages option.**

An Outlook Help window is displayed that explains how to send messages.

5 **In the upper-right corner of the Help window, click the Close button.**

The Outlook Help window closes.

6 **In the upper-right corner of the task pane, click the Close button.**

The task pane containing the search results is closed.

7 **Right-click the Office Assistant and click Hide.**

The Office Assistant disappears.

TIP

Keep the Office Assistant hidden unless you are using Microsoft Outlook Help.

◆ **On the Navigation Bar, click the Mail button.**

◆ **If you are continuing to other lessons, keep Outlook open.**

◆ **If you are not continuing to the next lesson, close Outlook.**

QUICK REFERENCE ▼

Use the Office Assistant

1 Open the Help menu and select the option Show the Office Assistant.

2 Click the Assistant, type a question, and click the Search button.

3 In the list of displayed topics, click the topic that most closely matches your help request.

Hide the Office Assistant

1 Right-click the Office Assistant.

2 Click Hide.

Key Points

✔ *The Outlook 2003 window provides a number of ways to navigate through the main Outlook components.*

✔ *You can use the Navigation pane and the Folder List to display different Outlook folders.*

✔ *The Office Assistant can be used to view more information about Outlook.*

Quick Quiz

True/False

T F   1. You can enter additional commands to personalize Outlook menus.

T F   2. Microsoft Outlook Help is the last option on every expanded Outlook menu.

T F   3. You can start Outlook from an icon on your desktop.

T F   4. Deleted Items is a small button on the Navigation pane.

T F   5. The Reading pane enables you to read information from Outlook Help.

Multiple Choice

1. To place a command on a short menu, _____.
   a. use the command once.
   b. don't use the command at all.
   c. use the command frequently.
   d. click the double-arrows at the bottom of the short menu.

2. To view your schedule, click the button labeled _____.
   a. Contacts.
   b. Schedule.
   c. Tasks.
   d. Calendar.

3. To access any Outlook folder, use the _____.
   a. Folder List.
   b. short menus.
   c. expanded menus.
   d. Outlook Help.

4. Each individual e-mail message you receive is a(n) _____.
   a. folder.
   b. item.
   c. attachment.
   d. shortcut.

5. Outlook Help will provide answers if you use the search field to _____.
   a. enter complete sentences that identify the information you need.
   b. enter key words.
   c. ask a question.
   d. all of the above.

Short Answer

1. What are the main functions in Outlook?
2. How do you use the Office Assistant to view help topics in Outlook?
3. How is the appearance of a command on a short menu determined?
4. Identify two ways to display an expanded menu.
5. List two ways to display an Outlook folder such as the Inbox.

On Your Own

Exercise 1

Display the View menu and display the expanded View menu. When you open the expanded View menu, move your mouse pointer across different menus on the Menu bar to view the results.

Exercise 2

Use the Folder List to display the contents of the Contacts folder and the Tasks folder. Use the Office Assistant to find out how to hide the Navigation pane. Hide the Navigation pane and redisplay it.

One Step Further

Exercise 1

Use the Navigation pane to display the Inbox, Calendar, Contacts, Tasks, and Notes. Observe the differences in the Standard toolbar as you select each shortcut in the Outlook Shortcuts group.

Exercise 2

Make a list of folders on your hard drive or network that you would like to access through Outlook to work more efficiently.

Exercise 3

Display the Office Assistant. Type **new message** in the box and view the available help topics.

LESSON 2

Using E-Mail in Outlook

After completing this lesson, you will be able to:

✔ *Compose, address, and send messages.*
✔ *Format the body of a message.*
✔ *Attach a file to a message.*
✔ *Check for e-mail messages.*
✔ *View messages.*
✔ *Read messages.*
✔ *Reply to and forward messages.*
✔ *Print messages.*
✔ *Find messages.*
✔ *Recall messages.*
✔ *Delete messages.*

KEY TERMS

- arrangement
- attachment
- AutoPreview
- Deleted Items folder
- Drafts
- e-mail
- file
- flag
- forward
- icon
- Inbox
- interoffice mail
- mail queue
- message header
- Microsoft Exchange Server
- Outbox
- recall
- reply
- Sent Items folder

Gone are the days when the telephone was the main way to communicate with other people immediately and postal mail was the chief way to send letters and documents to others. Today, e-mail enables you to communicate and share information with others in a way that is faster and more versatile than methods that were available in the past. **E-mail** refers to any communication that is sent or received via computers, either over the Internet or through a messaging program used with an organization's internal network, or intranet.

Creating, sending, receiving, and reading e-mail messages are the activities that you will probably perform most frequently with Microsoft Outlook. E-mail provides a fast way to send and receive messages, files, and documents such as reports, worksheets, and pictures.

In this lesson, you will learn how to create, address, format, and send an e-mail message. You will learn how to attach a file; check for and read messages; and reply to and forward messages you receive. You will learn how to flag messages with a reminder to yourself or to the recipient to follow up on the message. You will also learn how to print, find, and recall messages that you've sent. You will learn how to save e-mail messages that you aren't ready to send in Drafts, a folder that stores incomplete messages. Finally, you will learn how to delete messages.

IMPORTANT

Before you can use the practice files in this lesson, you need to install them from the companion CD for this book to their default location. For additional information on how to find and open files used in this book, see the "Using the CD-ROM" section at the beginning of this book.

To complete the exercises in this lesson, you will need to use the files named Map and Syllabus in the Outlook Practice folder that is located on your hard disk.

IMPORTANT

To complete some of the exercises in this lesson, you will need to exchange e-mail messages with a class partner. If you don't have a class partner or you are performing the exercises alone, you can send the message to yourself. Simply enter your own e-mail address instead of a class partner's address.

Composing, Addressing, and Sending Messages

THE BOTTOM LINE

Creating New Messages

Sending an e-mail message is similar to sending any type of correspondence. Outlook provides the tools for you to accomplish exactly what you need with your message.

If you've used other e-mail programs, you'll probably find that creating and sending messages is similar in Outlook. To create a new mail message, click the New button when you are in the **Inbox** folder. The message you create can be any length and contain any information. The following illustration displays the window used to create an e-mail message.

TROUBLESHOOTING

Your toolbars may be placed in different positions than the toolbars in these images.

Figure 2-1

Message window

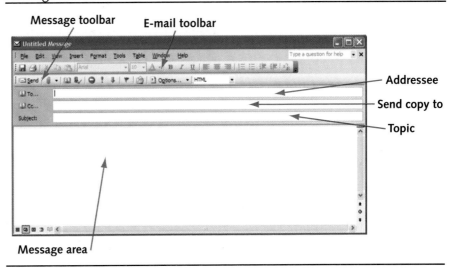

Just as you must address an envelope before mailing it, you must also pro-vide at least one e-mail address in the To box of your message. E-mail can be addressed to any number of recipients and the message is sent to all recipi-ents simultaneously. To send a message to multiple recipients, type a semi-colon after each recipient's e-mail address in the To box. After you type one or more e-mail addresses, enter the subject of your message, type the mes-sage, and click the Send button to send the message. Typically, your e-mail message arrives in the recipient's Inbox within seconds after you send it.

It is easy to address an e-mail message if you have sent a message to the same recipient before or the recipient's e-mail address is stored in Outlook's address book. The AutoComplete addressing function automati-cally completes the address as you start to type it. If the address Outlook suggests is correct, press the Tab key to enter the complete address. If Outlook finds several matches, it presents a list of possible matches. Use the arrow keys to select the correct entry and press the Enter key.

Below the To button is the Cc button. Cc is an acronym for carbon copy, re-ferring to the days of printed letters when copies were made by using carbon paper. The copy contains the same content sent to the recipient identified in the To box. However, a copy of a message is sent to others for information purposes only; the Cc recipients are not required to take any action.

The Cc function is optional: You can send a message without sending any copies. However, there are times when it is valuable to be able to copy a message to others. To send a copy, simply enter the individual's e-mail ad-dress in the Cc box. To send a copy to multiple recipients, type a semicolon after each recipient's e-mail address. When the Cc recipient receives the message, his or her address appears in the message header as a Cc.

The subject of the message is usually a brief description of the information in the message. All of the message recipients will see the message header when the message arrives in their Inboxes. A **message header** includes the name of the sender, the subject of the message, and the date and time when the message was sent. This information enables recipients to quickly iden-tify the purpose of the e-mail message without opening the message.

IMPORTANT

- Microsoft Office Outlook 2003 supports several types of Internet e-mail accounts. Account types include POP3, IMAP, and HTTP.
- Post Office Protocol 3 (POP3)—Common type of e-mail account provided by an ISP (Internet Service Provider). To receive messages, you connect to an e-mail server and download messages to your local computer.
- Internet Message Access Protocol (IMAP)—Messages are stored on the e-mail server. When you connect to an e-mail server, you read the headers and select the messages to download to your local computer.
- Hypertext Transfer Protocol (HTTP)—Messages are stored, retrieved, and displayed as Web pages. MSN Hotmail, a free, Web-based e-mail service offered by Microsoft, provides HTTP accounts.

◆ **Be sure to start Outlook before beginning this exercise.**

Compose and send a message

Now that you have learned the basics of working within Outlook, you will compose a message and send it to your class partner.

 1 **If necessary, click the Mail button and click the Inbox folder. Click the New Mail Message button on the Standard toolbar.**

A message window is displayed. The message and all the information necessary to deliver the message are entered in this window.

ANOTHER METHOD

You can create a new e-mail message from any folder. Open the File menu, point to New, and click Mail Message to display a new message window.

2 **In the To box, type the e-mail address of your class partner or type your e-mail address if you are working alone.**

This identifies the recipient who will receive the message.

TROUBLESHOOTING

Your To box will contain your class partner's e-mail address.

3 **Press Tab twice.**

The insertion point skips through the Cc box and moves to the Subject box.

4 **Type Picnic Reminder and press Enter.**

The subject is entered and the insertion point moves to the message area.

5 **Type** Just a reminder... Our 5th annual Fun in the Sun picnic is on Saturday, June 6th.

Your message window contains all the necessary information.

Figure 2-2

Message ready to be sent

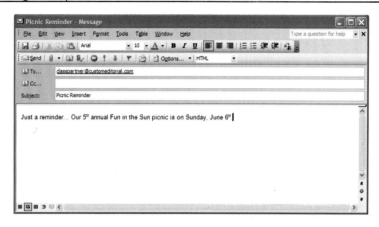

TROUBLESHOOTING

If the server is down or if there is a problem with the connection to the Internet, messages are placed in the **Outbox** until a connection is established.

6 **On the Message toolbar in the message window, click the Send button.**

The message is sent to the recipient.

IMPORTANT

Although you clicked the Send button, the message has not necessarily been sent over the Internet (or over the intranet) yet. By default, Outlook connects to your server (Workgroup, Corporate, or Internet service provider) to send and receive e-mail every 10 minutes. Messages that have been sent but have not yet made it to the server are stored in your Outbox. To send and receive e-mail immediately, click the Send/Receive button on the standard toolbar in the Mail folder. This action connects your computer to your server, sends all e-mail messages in the Outbox, and retrieves any messages that the server has for you. To avoid delays while performing the exercises in this book, click the Send/Receive button immediately after you click the Send button.

◆ **Keep Outlook open for the next exercise.**

QUICK REFERENCE ▼

Compose and send a message

1 In the Inbox, click the New Mail Message button on the Standard toolbar.

2 In the To text box, type an e-mail address.

3 Press Tab and type another e-mail address in the Cc box, if necessary.

4 Press Tab, type the message description in the Subject text box, and press Enter.

5 Type your message and click the Send button.

Formatting a Message

THE BOTTOM LINE

Microsoft Word is the default e-mail editor. Its formatting power can be used to enhance a message sent in Outlook.

Formatting Messages

Looks aren't everything, but a message that looks good makes a positive impact on the recipient. Microsoft Outlook uses Microsoft Word as the default e-mail editor, placing the power of Word's formatting options at your fingertips. The toolbar has been redesigned to group the Word functions that apply to e-mail. A few clicks of the mouse can apply formatting that highlights important information or gives your message a bit of flash to make it stand out in the crowd of messages that fill many Inboxes.

The Formatting buttons on the toolbar are familiar if you use Microsoft Word. They enable you to apply formats that create the image you want to present. Color the name of your product. Make the dates of a conference bold so recipients can see them at a glance. Highlight the important numbers in a sales report. Make your point with a bulleted list. Your options are endless.

Figure 2-3

E-mail toolbar

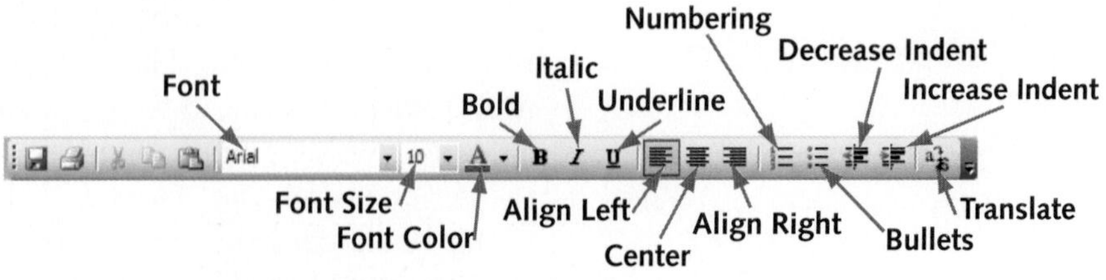

QUICK CHECK

Q: What application is used to format e-mail messages?

A: Microsoft Word is the default editor.

Applying formats is easy. Type the body of the e-mail message in the message area. Select the text you want to format. Click the appropriate button on the toolbar. The selected text immediately takes the new format.

You can include a Web site address in an e-mail message. When a recipient clicks the Web address, it automatically starts the default Web browser and displays the Web site. Including a Web site address in the message is helpful because the recipient does not need to leave the message to open a Web browser and type the Web site address to access the site. To include a Web site address in a message, just type it in the message. Outlook automatically formats the address (or URL, an acronym for Uniform Resource Locator) as a link to a Web page—for example, www.microsoft.com.

Flagging Messages

Flagging Messages for Follow-Up

> **THE BOTTOM LINE**
>
> You can use flags to alert a recipient to important messages or remind yourself to perform some action.

Sometimes it's necessary to remind yourself or notify recipients of the importance of a message that you are sending. Perhaps you sent a message about an event with a specific deadline or asked for input on a particular topic. You can **flag** the message to remind yourself to follow up on an issue or you can flag an outgoing message with a request for someone else to follow up with a reply.

When you create a new message, click the Message Flag button on the New Message toolbar in the message window. A dialog box is displayed that enables you to identify the reason you flagged the message, such as requesting a reply, requesting follow-up action, and stating that no response is necessary. You also can set the due date for the follow-up action. When a recipient receives a message with a flag, the purpose of the flag is displayed at the top of the message. If a date was set, that date appears as well. The message appears in the recipient's Inbox with either a red flag, indicating that action still needs to be taken, or a gray flag, indicating that the request is complete.

Figure 2-4

Flag for Follow Up dialog box

You can also flag messages you receive in your Inbox. Quick Flags is a new feature in Outlook 2003. Click the shaded flag **icon** to the right of the messages in your Inbox to flag the message. Click the flag icon a second time to mark the item as completed. Right-click the icon to clear the flag or change the color of the flag.

QUICK REFERENCE ▼

Flag a message to be sent

1 Create an e-mail message.

2 On the Standard toolbar in the message window, click the Message Flag button.

3 Select your options and click OK.

QUICK CHECK

Q: Can you flag messages after you receive them?

A: **Quick Flags is a new feature that enables you to flag messages you receive.**

Flag a message you received

1 Click on an e-mail message in your Inbox.

2 Click the flag icon next to the message.

Setting Message Priority

Changing Message Settings and Delivery Options

THE BOTTOM LINE

Outlook enables you to identify high-priority messages for the recipients.

You can also specify the priority for a message. When you mark a message as High priority, the message header appears in the recipient's Inbox with a red exclamation point, indicating that the message is important. You want the recipient to reply to or read the message as soon as possible. When you mark a message as Low priority, a blue, downward-pointing arrow appears in the message header, indicating that the message is not important. The recipient can reply to or read the message when it is convenient.

QUICK CHECK

Q: How can you identify a high-priority message?

A: **Mark the message with the Importance: High flag.**

QUICK REFERENCE ▼

Set message priority

◆ On the Standard toolbar in the message window, click the Importance: High button.

◆ On the Standard toolbar in the message window, click the Importance: Low button.

Saving Drafts

THE BOTTOM LINE

If you are interrupted before you can send a message, Outlook automatically saves your working draft.

If you are interrupted while composing a message, you can save it in your **Drafts** folder. You can complete and send the message later. You can create a draft of a message in two ways:

✖

- In the top-right corner of the message window, click the Close button. Outlook will ask if you want to save the message. Click Yes to save the message without sending it.

💾

- On the E-mail toolbar in the message window, click the Save button and click the Close button in the top-right corner of the message window.

QUICK REFERENCE ▼

Retrieve a draft:

1 Display the Folder List and click the Drafts folder.

2 Double-click the message to open it.

3 Complete or edit the message and send it just as you normally would.

Attaching a File to a Message

THE BOTTOM LINE

Outlook items and other files can be attached to a message and sent to a recipient.

Attaching Files to Messages

In today's fast-paced workplaces, you need to be able to get information to several people in a short amount of time. As an example, the sales manager at Adventure Works, an outdoor vacation resort, likes to distribute Microsoft Excel sales forecast workbooks to other managers at the resort. Rather than distributing printed copies or retyping the contents of these documents into an e-mail message, the sales manager can make the workbook file an **attachment**—an external document included as part of a message— and send the message and the attachment to all recipients at one time.

An attachment can be a file, a document stored on a disk, or another Outlook item. A **file** can be any type of document, such as a Microsoft Word document, an Excel spreadsheet, or a picture. An item is an Outlook object, such as a contact, task, or note. You will learn how to create and use these and other Outlook items later in this course.

The selected attachment appears in a new field, the Attach box, located below the Subject box. The attachment is displayed as an icon, or graphic representation of the attached file. The name and size of the file are also displayed. When you send the message, the message recipient can double-click the icon to open and view the file or item.

To attach a file to a message, compose the message just as you normally would and click the Insert File button on the New Message toolbar in the message window. Navigate to the folder that contains the file, click the file name, and click the Insert File button. Repeat this procedure to attach multiple files to a message.

To attach an Outlook item to a message, click the down arrow next to the Insert File button on the New Message toolbar. Select Insert Item to display the Insert Item dialog box. In the Look In list, click the folder name for the type of Outlook item, such as a contact, that you want to attach. In the Items list in the bottom pane, click the item that you want to attach and click OK. The icon representing the attached Outlook item is displayed in the Attach box.

Figure 2-5

Insert Item dialog box

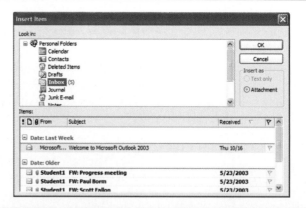

Send a message with an attachment

You will now practice many of the concepts you have learned. You will compose a message, attach a picture to the message, and send the message and file attachment to the recipient.

1 **On the Mail toolbar, click the New Mail Message button.**

A message window is displayed.

2 **In the To box, type the e-mail address of the recipient.**

3 **Press Tab twice and type** Fun in the Sun Picnic Invitation **in the Subject box.**

4 **Press Enter. In the message area, type** Hope to see you at the picnic on June 6th at 1:00 P.M. For directions to Cherry Creek Park, please see the attached map. See you there!

5 **On the New Message toolbar in the message window, click the Insert File button.**

The Insert Item dialog box is displayed.

6 **Click the Look In down arrow and navigate to the Outlook Practice folder on your hard disk.**

The items in the Outlook Practice folder are displayed.

Figure 2-6

Insert File dialog box

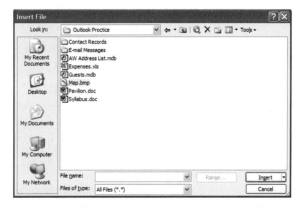

TROUBLESHOOTING

If you send an e-mail attachment to someone who connects to the Internet using a slow modem (33.6 Kbps or slower), you should limit the attachment size to 300 KB or less. Messages with large attachments can take a long time for the recipient's e-mail program to receive. A small pane may be displayed, asking if you want to resize the attachment (decrease its size) to send it faster. If the pane is not displayed, click the Attachment Options button.

7 **Double-click the Map file to attach it to your e-mail message.**

Outlook attaches the Map file to the e-mail message and the Insert File dialog box closes. Your screen should look similar to the following.

Figure 2-7

New message with attachment

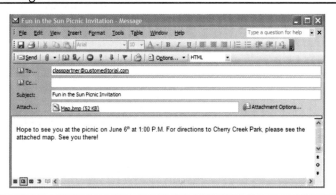

8 On the New Message toolbar in the message window, click the Send button.

The message is sent to the recipient.

◆ Keep Outlook open for the next exercise.

QUICK REFERENCE ▼

Attach a file to a message

1 Compose and address a message.

2 On the New Message toolbar in the message window, click the Insert File button.

3 Click the Look In down arrow and navigate to your file.

4 Double-click the file to attach it to the e-mail message.

5 On the New Message toolbar in the message window, click the Send button.

QUICK **CHECK**

Q: Can an Outlook item be sent as an attachment?

A: An Outlook item can be attached to an e-mail message.

Checking for E-Mail Messages

THE BOTTOM LINE

Messages are sent and received at regular intervals (intervals that you can adjust) and when you click the Send/Receive button.

Just as Outlook sends e-mail every 10 minutes, Outlook automatically checks for new mail every 10 minutes. Later in this course, you will learn how to change this setting to a longer or shorter interval. You can manually check for messages at any time. Simply click the Send/Receive button on the toolbar in the Mail folder. Any messages that are on the mail server are sent to your Inbox.

IMPORTANT

Interoffice mail—e-mail sent over a local area network (LAN) or to a **Microsoft Exchange Server** post office—is usually sent almost instantaneously. However, when you send e-mail to someone outside of your LAN or Exchange Server, you send the message over the Internet. Your Internet service provider's mail server places incoming messages in a mail queue. The **mail queue** is a list of messages received by a mail server organized in the order in which the messages are received. In turn, messages are sent to recipients in the order in which the server received them. Sometimes, this means you have to wait a few minutes to receive an Internet mail message that was sent to you.

Check for e-mail messages

Now that you have sent messages, it's time to check for incoming e-mail messages.

1 **If necessary, click the Mail button in the Navigation pane and select the Inbox folder.**

The contents of the Inbox folder are displayed. It contains the message headers for messages that you've already received.

ANOTHER METHOD

If you are using Exchange Server to send and receive e-mail messages, or if you have multiple e-mail accounts, point to Send/Receive on the Tools menu and click the account that you want to send to and receive from.

Figure 2-8

Message headers in the Inbox

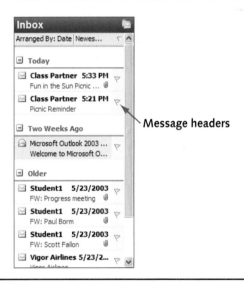

Message headers

2 **On the Standard mail toolbar, click the Send/Receive button.**

A progress bar indicating that Outlook is sending and receiving messages is displayed briefly before new message headers appear in the middle pane. The messages were created and sent in previous exercises by you or your class partner.

◆ **Keep Outlook open for the next exercise.**

QUICK REFERENCE ▼

Check for e-mail messages

1 If necessary, on the Navigation pane, click the Mail button and the Inbox folder.

2 On the Standard mail toolbar, click the Send/Receive button.

QUICK CHECK

Q: When does Outlook check for new messages?

A: **Outlook checks for messages every 10 minutes and when you click the Send/Receive button.**

View Messages

Viewing and Printing Messages

THE BOTTOM LINE

Outlook lets you arrange messages in a variety of predefined views which make it easier to find specific items you are looking for or to sort your messages.

You can gather some important information about the messages that arrive in your Inbox without actually reading the messages. The message header tells you who sent the message, the time the message arrived, and the subject of the message.

AutoPreview provides additional information. The message header for each message is displayed above a sample of the message's content. Up to three lines of each message is displayed. This enables you to scan for important messages and read a message without opening it in a separate window. AutoPreview is useful if you receive dozens of e-mail messages each day and want to scan through them quickly to determine which messages to read first. You can quickly spot junk e-mail messages that have deceptive headers.

A new feature in Outlook 2003, known as **arrangements**, enables you to view messages in 13 different ways. Each arrangement focuses on a different characteristic of the messages in your Inbox. For example, you can base your arrangement on the date the message was received or the individual who sent the message. By default, messages are arranged by the date they were received. The most recent message is displayed at the top of the list. However, one or more of the standard views may help you find information received in a specific message or group of messages. The following table describes the standard views.

Arrangement	Result
Date	Messages are grouped by the date they are received. This is the default arrangement.
Conversation	Messages are grouped by the subject of the message. By default, only flagged messages and messages you haven't read are displayed in the group.
From	Messages are grouped by the name in the From line of each message.
To	Messages are grouped by the name in the To line of each message.
Folder	Messages are grouped by the folder where they are stored. This arrangement is only available when you are viewing search results.
Size	Messages are grouped by the size of each message.
Subject	Messages are grouped alphabetically by the text in the Subject line of each message.
Type	Messages are grouped by the type of message. Types include meeting requests, task requests, and so on.
Flag	Messages are grouped by the color of the flag you assigned to the message. Messages flagged by the sender are not included in the groups of flagged messages.

Arrangement	Result
Attachments	Messages with attachments are placed in one group. Messages without attachments are placed in a second group.
E-mail account	If you have more than one e-mail account, messages are grouped by the e-mail account that received the message.
Importance	Messages are grouped by the importance assigned to each message. Groups are high, normal, and low importance.
Categories	Messages assigned to a specific category are placed with messages in the same category. You can add categories to the Master Category List or modify existing categories.

Besides using arrangements, you can also sort messages by any column. Simply click the column heading above the list of messages.

TROUBLESHOOTING

The Reading pane was turned off in this figure to display the column headings available in the Inbox.

Figure 2-9

Messages grouped by the From column

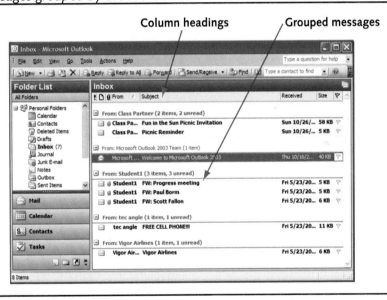

Messages that you have read are shown with an open envelope icon to the left of the message header; unread messages appear with a closed envelope icon. To read the body of a message in the Reading pane, click the message header in the Inbox. Double-click a message header to open the message in a separate window.

Select an arrangement

Since you have sent and received messages, you now select an arrangement to group mail messages.

1 **If necessary, click the Mail button in the Navigation pane and select the Inbox folder.**

The contents of the Inbox folder are displayed. It contains the message headers for messages that you've already received.

2 Open the View menu. Point at the Arrange By option. Click on Attachments.

ANOTHER METHOD

Click the Sort by: Attachments column heading.

Messages with attachments are grouped in the upper area. Messages without attachments are grouped in the lower area.

TROUBLESHOOTING

The Reading pane was turned off in this figure to display the arrangement and message headers.

Figure 2-10

Messages arranged by attachments

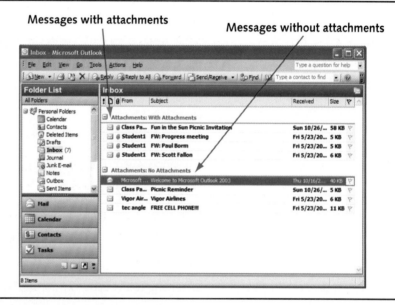

Messages with attachments   Messages without attachments

◆ Keep Outlook open for the next exercise.

QUICK REFERENCE ▼

Select an arrangement for e-mail messages

1 If necessary, on the Navigation pane, click the Mail button and the Inbox folder.

2 Open the View menu, point at the Arrange By option, and click on an arrangement.

Sort e-mail messages by column heading

1 If necessary, navigate to a mail folder.

2 Click on one of the column headings.

QUICK CHECK

Q: What is an arrangement?

A: **An arrangement is a method of viewing messages.**

Reading Messages

Viewing and Printing Messages

THE BOTTOM LINE

The Reading pane displays the content of an e-mail message. This allows you to get a quick glance at a message witout opening it.

Outlook 2003 incorporates several improvements that make it easier to read your e-mail messages. Many of the changes are visible the first time you open your Inbox. The new Reading pane is one of the obvious improvements. The Reading pane is designed for the way you read. By default, it is placed on the right side of the Outlook window. Like a sheet of paper, it is taller rather than wider. This enables you to read long messages without using the scroll bars or opening a separate window. Open attachments directly from the Reading pane, rather than opening them from a separate viewing window.

Read e-mail messages

Now you will read the e-mail messages that your class partner sent to you.

1 **Click the Fun in the Sun message header.**

The message is displayed in the Reading pane. The message header is displayed above the message. The name and size of the attachment are clearly identified. The icon representing the attachment tells you which application can be used to view the attachment. Images can usually be viewed by the Windows Picture and Fax Viewer. This eliminates your need for the application used to create the image.

Figure 2-11

Message displayed in the Reading pane

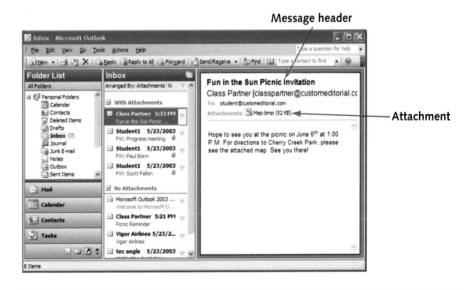

TROUBLESHOOTING

Be sure to single-click the Picnic Reminder message in Step 1. Double-clicking the message has a different result.

2 Double-click the Fun in the Sun Picnic Invitation message header.

The message is displayed in a separate window. Notice the attachment icon in the message.

Figure 2-12

Message displayed in a separate window

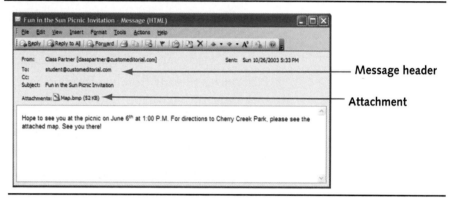

3 Double-click the Map attachment icon in the message window.

ANOTHER METHOD

You can also open the attachment from the Reading pane. In the message header, double-click the icon that represents the attachment.

The map is displayed in a separate window by the application your computer uses to view graphics.

Figure 2-13

Attachment displayed in a separate window

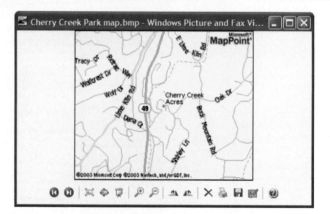

4 In the top-right corner of the window that contains the map, click the Close button.

The application closes.

5 In the top-right corner of the message window, click the Close button.

The message closes.

◆ Arrange the content of the Inbox by date.

◆ Keep Outlook open for the next exercise.

QUICK REFERENCE ▼

Read e-mail messages and messages with attachments

1 In the Inbox, click the message header of the message to display it in the Reading pane.

2 Double-click the attachment icon in the message (if one is included) to read the attachment.

Replying to and Forwarding Messages

Responding to Messages

THE BOTTOM LINE

Outlook enables you to respond to messages you receive and share the information in a message with additional recipients.

If you receive an advertisement via postal mail, you might read it or discard it. If you receive a letter from a friend sent via postal mail, you might respond by writing and sending a reply to your friend.

E-mail is similar. Sometimes, you'll read an e-mail message without replying to the message. At other times, you'll reply to e-mail messages sent by friends or co-workers. A **reply** sends a copy of the original message and additional text that you type, if any. The recipient sees the text RE: and the original subject in the message header. When you reply to a message, your response is automatically addressed to the sender. If the original message was sent to you and several other recipients, you can choose to reply to the sender or the sender and all the other recipients.

After you receive an e-mail message, you might decide that the information contained in the message will be useful to others. If so, you can **forward** the message to other recipients. Forwarding a message lets you send a message to individuals who were not originally on the recipient list. Select the message and click the Forward button on the Standard toolbar in the Inbox folder, type the e-mail addresses of the additional recipients in the To box, and click the Send button. You can also type additional information at the beginning of the forwarded message before you send it.

Respond to a message

As are typical actions, you will now reply to the message that you receive and forward the message to another individual.

1 In the Inbox, verify that the Fun in the Sun Picnic Invitation message header is selected.

The message content is displayed in the Reading pane.

2 On the standard mail toolbar, click the Reply button.

A reply window containing the original message is displayed. The insertion point is already in the message area.

3 In the message area, type Yes, I will attend the picnic.

The text you add is included in the reply.

4 On the New Message toolbar in the message window, click the Send button.

The reply is sent to your class partner.

5 On the standard mail toolbar, click the Send/Receive button.

A reply from your class partner arrives in the Inbox.

Figure 2-14

Reply from your Class Partner

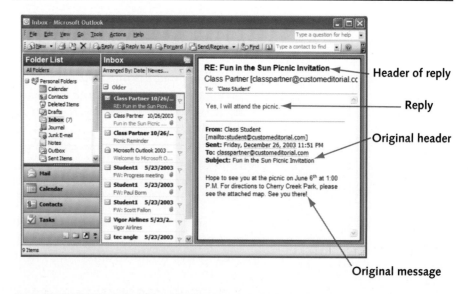

6 In the Inbox, click the original Fun in the Sun Picnic Invitation message header again.

The message is displayed in the Reading pane.

7 Click the Forward button on the toolbar.

A forward window opens with the original message displayed.

8 In the To box, type an e-mail address for a class member other than your class partner.

The message will be forwarded to this recipient.

> **TIP**
>
> When you forward a message you can add new text in the message area before you send it.

9 On the New Message toolbar in the message window, click the Send button.

The message is forwarded to a class member.

10 On the standard mail toolbar, click the Send/Receive button.

A forwarded message from a class member arrives in the Inbox.

Figure 2-15

Forwarded message

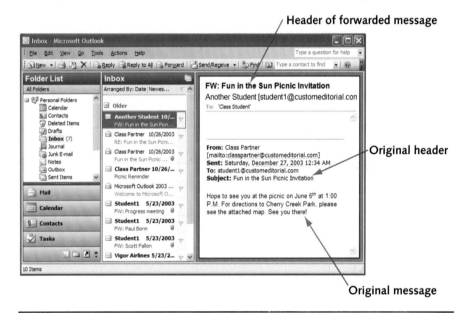

> **ANOTHER METHOD**
>
> You can also reply to or forward a message by clicking Reply or Forward on the Actions menu.

◆ Keep Outlook open for the next exercise.

QUICK REFERENCE ▼

Reply to a message

1 Click the message header for the message to which you want to reply.

2 On the standard mail toolbar, click the Reply button.

3 Type your message.

4 On the New Message toolbar in the message window, click the Send button.

Forward a message

1 In the Inbox, click the message header for the message that you want to forward.

2 On the standard mail toolbar, click the Forward button.

3 In the To box, type an e-mail address.

4 On the New Message toolbar in the message window, click the Send button.

Printing Messages

THE BOTTOM LINE

Though much work can be done electronically, there are times when you need printed documnets. With Outlook, you can print messages and attachments.

Viewing and Printing Messages

It's often convenient to print a copy of a message so you can read the message when you are not at your computer or so you can give the printed message to somebody who does not have access to e-mail. For example, Adventure Works employees found it useful to print a copy of a message that provided directions to the company picnic so they could follow the directions to get to the park.

TROUBLESHOOTING

When printing an attachment, Outlook might display an alert box warning you of the possible danger of viruses hidden within attached messages. Click the Print button in the message box to continue the printing process.

You can also print message attachments if the application used to create the attachment is installed on your computer. You can print an attachment by opening the attachment and using the Print command of the program that opens the attachment. You can also right-click the attachment icon in the message window and click Print on the shortcut menu. The attachment is printed by the default printer for your computer.

Outlook includes several options for printing e-mail messages when you are in the Inbox folder. Messages can be printed in Table style or Memo style. If you print using the Table style, the document contains a list of messages in a table format that resembles the Inbox; the message headers that are currently in your Inbox are listed under column headings, such as From, Subject, and Received. If you print using the Memo style, the document contains your name at the top of the page, information about the selected message (who the message was from, when the message was sent, who the message was sent to, and the subject of the message); the actual message is printed last.

TROUBLESHOOTING

Print Preview isn't available for HTML formatted items.

Select Page Setup on the File menu to open the Page Setup dialog box. This enables you to preview the page style, the size of the columns and rows (if you selected the Table style), and the fonts in which the message will be printed. Click the Paper tab in the Print Setup dialog box to change the paper type and select a page style. Paper options include letter, legal, and A4. Page styles include the Day-Timer and Franklin Day Planner styles.

Print an e-mail message and attachment

In this exercise, you print an e-mail message in the Memo style and set up Outlook to print an e-mail message and its attachment.

1 **In the Inbox, click the Picnic Reminder message header.**

The Picnic Reminder message header is selected.

2 **On the standard mail toolbar, click the Print button.**

One copy of the e-mail message is printed.

3 **Click the original Fun in the Sun Picnic Invitation message header.**

The Picnic Reminder message header is selected again.

4 **On the File menu, click Print.**

The Print dialog box is displayed. The options in the dialog box will be different if you choose Table Style.

TROUBLESHOOTING

The appearance of the Print dialog box and the printing process are based on your printer. Your options may differ from those illustrated.

Figure 2-16

Print dialog box

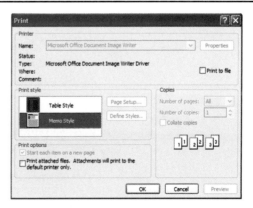

5 In the Print Options section of the dialog box, select the Print Attached Files check box, and click OK.

Outlook prints the e-mail message in the Memo style and prints the attachment.

◆ Keep Outlook open for the next exercise.

QUICK REFERENCE ▼

Print a message

1 In the Inbox, click the message header for the message that you want to print.

2 On the standard mail toolbar, click the Print button.

Print a message with an attachment

1 In the Inbox, click the message header for the message that you want to print.

2 On the File menu, click Print.

3 In the Print Options section in the Print dialog box, select the Print Attached Files check box and click OK.

Finding Messages

Finding and Categorizing Messages

THE BOTTOM LINE

One of Outlook's many features lets you search messages for a specific word or phrase.

If you send and receive a lot of messages on a regular basis, your Inbox and **Sent Items folder** might contain dozens or even hundreds of messages. At some point, you might need to track down a specific message sent to a recipient or a message received from a particular e-mail address. For example, one of the new employees at Adventure Works said he didn't receive directions to the picnic. The sender opened the Sent Items folder and searched for a key word or phrase (such as picnic directions) that she knew was contained in the message. She forwarded the message to the employee who had not received the directions.

Find message

In this exercise, you find the messages that contain the word *directions*.

Find

1 On the standard mail toolbar, click the Find button.

A small pane is displayed that enables you to enter search criteria.

2 In the Look For box, type directions.

This defines the text to be found in the messages.

Find Now

3 **Select the location or mail folders to be searched.**

This defines the folder to be searched.

4 **Click the Find Now button.**

The results are displayed. The messages containing *directions* should be the only messages listed.

Figure 2-17

Search for text

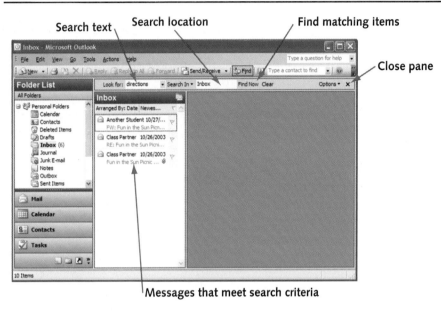

Messages that meet search criteria

5 **Click the Close button in the small search pane.**

The pane closes.

◆ **Keep Outlook open for the next exercise.**

QUICK REFERENCE ▼

Find a message

1 On the standard mail toolbar, click the Find button.

2 In the Look For and Search In boxes, type the search criteria.

3 Click the Find Now button.

Recalling Messages

THE BOTTOM LINE

There may be occasions when, after you have sent a message, you realize that you need to make a correction to that message. With Outlook, you can retrieve messages before they are read and substitute a different message to issue a correction.

If you are connected to a network that uses Microsoft Exchange Server, you can **recall** a message and send an updated message. Use this feature to reissue information that might have been sent incorrectly the first time or to retrieve messages sent to the wrong recipient. For example, the recreation director at Adventure Works sent a message to the planning team announcing an upcoming event and accidentally typed the wrong price for attending the event. He recalled the message, made the correction to the date, and sent the corrected message.

To be recalled, a message must meet four criteria. The recipient must be logged on to the network. The recipient must use Microsoft Outlook. The message must be in the recipient's Inbox. The message must be unread.

Recall a message

To recall a message, take these steps:

1 **Open the Sent Items folder.**

Messages you sent are listed.

2 **Double-click the message to be recalled.**

The message opens in a separate window.

3 **Click Recall This Message on the Actions menu.**

The Recall This Message dialog box is displayed.

Figure 2-18

Recall This Message dialog box

4 **Choose to delete the unread messages or delete the unread messages and send a replacement message.**

Select one of the options to deal with the message.

5 Click OK to recall the message.

All copies of the sent message that meet the recall criteria are recalled. If the option is selected, a replacement message is sent.

◆ **Keep Outlook open for the next exercise.**

QUICK REFERENCE ▼

Recall a message

1 Open the Sent Items folder.

2 Double-click the message header for the message that you want to recall.

3 On the Actions menu, click Recall This Message.

4 Click OK.

Deleting Messages

THE BOTTOM LINE

When a message is no longer needed, it can be deleted. The two-step process used to delete messages prevents you from accidentally deleting critical information.

After reading new messages, you can leave them in the Inbox. However, you will find that over time your Inbox can become cluttered if you don't organize or remove messages regularly. You can choose to delete any outdated e-mail messages by clicking the message header and then clicking the Delete button on the standard mail toolbar or pressing the Delete key.

TIP

To select multiple message headers that are displayed together, click the first message header, hold down the Shift key, and click the last message header. To select multiple message headers that are not displayed together, click the first message header, hold down the Ctrl key, and click each additional message header.

When you delete messages, they are not permanently removed from Outlook. Instead, they are placed in the **Deleted Items folder** until you decide to empty it. This safeguard makes it possible to restore your messages if you accidentally delete them or realize that you still need certain deleted messages.

Delete messages

Since you are done with the Picnic Reminder message, you will delete this message from the Inbox and then empty the Deleted Items folder.

1 In the Inbox, click the Picnic Reminder message header.

The message is selected. The content is displayed in the Reading pane.

2 On the standard mail toolbar, click the Delete button.

The message moves to the Deleted Items folder.

TIP

To restore a deleted message, drag the message from the Deleted Items folder to the Inbox shortcut on the Outlook bar.

3 **In the Folder List, click Deleted Items.**

The Deleted Items folder opens, displaying the message that you deleted.

4 **Click the message.**

The message is selected.

5 **Press Delete.**

An alert box asks you to confirm the deletion.

ANOTHER METHOD

You can also delete all messages in the Deleted Items folder by clicking Empty "Deleted Items" Folder on the Tools menu.

6 **Click Yes.**

The items are removed from the Deleted Items folder and permanently deleted.

◆ **If you are continuing to the next lesson, keep Outlook open.**

◆ **If you are not continuing to the next lesson, close Outlook.**

QUICK CHECK

Q: Where is a message placed after it is deleted from the Inbox?

A: **It is placed in the Deleted Items folder.**

QUICK REFERENCE ▼

Delete a message

1 In the Inbox, click the message header for the message that you want to delete.

2 On the standard mail toolbar, click the Delete button.

Empty the Deleted Items folder

1 In the Folder List, click Deleted Items.

2 Select the message or messages that you want to delete.

3 Press Delete and click Yes.

Key Points

✔ *You can use Outlook to read an electronic message.*
✔ *Outlook provides the tools to reply to and forward messages.*
✔ *You can include an attachment in an e-mail message.*
✔ *Messages received and sent can be sorted and searched.*
✔ *Messages which are no longer needed can be deleted.*
✔ *Outlook items can be moved between folders.*

Quick Quiz

True/False

T   F   **1.** Messages can be recovered from the Deleted Items folder.

T   F   **2.** Message headers are not displayed in the Reading pane.

T   F   **3.** Double-click a message header to display the message in the Reading pane.

T   F   **4.** Only graphics can be sent as attachments.

T   F   **5.** A message cannot be longer than 1,500 characters.

Multiple Choice

1. To permanently delete a message, _____.
   a. press the Delete key
   b. empty the Deleted Items folder
   c. click the Delete button
   d. select the Delete command from the Edit menu

2. Attachments can include _____.
   a. graphics
   b. Excel files
   c. Outlook items
   d. all of the above

3. Messages in the Sent Items directory have been _____.
   a. sent to other recipients
   b. received from other users
   c. stored because they are incomplete
   d. forwarded to you by other users

4. To be recalled, a message must be _____.
   a. incomplete
   b. deleted
   c. unread
   d. all of the above

5. A(n) _____ is sent to the person who sent the original message.
   a. forwarded message
   b. attachment
   c. reply
   d. draft

Short Answer

1. How do you manually check for messages in Outlook without waiting for messages to be sent or received at the preset interval?

2. What are the steps you take to create an e-mail message?

3. What happens to a message when you delete it from your Inbox?

4. What information is contained in the header of a message?

5. How do you read an e-mail message?

6. How do you save a message without sending it so that you can complete or edit the message later?

7. What is the Inbox?

8. What can you insert into an Outlook e-mail message?

9. What is the value of AutoPreview?

On Your Own

Exercise 1

The training director at Adventure Works must send an Outlook 2003 class announcement to those who signed up for the class. The date, time, and location of the class should be included in the message. Use the date, time, and location for your Outlook class to provide this information. A syllabus for the class must be sent as an attachment. You can find the syllabus in the Outlook Practice folder on your hard disk.

Send the class announcement with the syllabus—and include a flag—to your partner, to another member of your class, and to yourself. When you receive the message, print the syllabus.

Exercise 2

After you sent the class announcement, you discovered that the location of the class has changed. Notify the recipients that the location of the class has changed. After you've completed this task, delete the message.

One Step Further

Exercise 1

Create a message describing the benefits of using Outlook 2003. Use the Formatting toolbar to create visual interest. Set a flag to request a reply in 10 days. Send the message.

Exercise 2

Move the messages you sent about the picnic from the Sent Items folder to the Deleted Items folder. Delete the messages.

Exercise 3

A co-worker complains that it takes several minutes for his mail messages to be sent and he frequently experiences a delay in receiving messages. Use Microsoft Outlook Help to explain the delay in sending and receiving mail. Describe how he can fix the problem.

Using Contacts

After completing this lesson, you will be able to:

✔ *Open the Contacts folder.*
✔ *Create and edit contacts.*
✔ *Create multiple contact records for people at the same company.*
✔ *Delete and restore contacts.*
✔ *Use folders, views, and categories.*
✔ *Assign items to a category.*
✔ *Modify the Outlook Master Category List.*
✔ *Sort contacts.*
✔ *Send e-mail from the Address Book and the Contacts folder.*
✔ *Send and receive contact information by e-mail.*
✔ *Create a letter for a contact by using the Letter Wizard.*

KEY TERMS

- Address Book
- Address Cards
- category
- contact

- contact record
- Contacts folder
- Master Category List
- vCard

To communicate efficiently with personal and business associates, many people keep important phone and fax numbers, addresses, and other relevant information in an address book or a business card holder. The tools in Microsoft Outlook help you create and organize contact information on your computer. In Outlook, a **contact** is a collection of information about a person or a company. Contact information is stored in the **Contacts folder**, which is essentially an electronic organizer that you can use to create, view, sort, and edit contact information. Contacts are integrated with other components of Outlook and other Microsoft Office System programs so that name, address, and phone information is available for use with other Outlook folders and Office programs.

Efficiency is one of the chief values of the Contacts folder. Each time you create a new contact, the name, e-mail address, and phone numbers are added to your Address Book. When you compose an e-mail message, use the Address Book to insert the appropriate e-mail address in the To or Cc box—you don't have to manually type the addresses.

In this lesson, you learn how to create, edit, and delete contacts. You also learn how to sort contacts and organize them by using folders and views. In addition, you learn how to use the Address Book and Contacts to send e-mail messages as well as how to send contact information as a vCard, or a virtual business card. At the end of this lesson, you learn how to compose and send letters in Microsoft Word by using contact information from Outlook.

The practice file Eric_Lang is required to complete the exercises in this lesson.

Viewing Contacts

Creating and Updating
Contact Information

THE BOTTOM LINE

Contact records can contain a variety of useful information about the people you know.

Click the Contacts button in the Navigation pane or open the Go menu and click the Contacts option to view the contents of the Contacts folder. Outlook provides several formats for viewing contact information. Contacts are displayed in the Address Cards view by default. From the **Address Cards** view, you can see a contact's title bar, a follow-up flag (if one is present), a mailing address, and the associated company. You can also see four fields that hold telephone and fax information, and up to three of the contact's e-mail addresses.

Figure 3-1

Outlook contacts

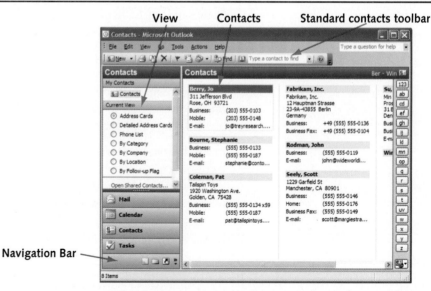

The Financial Information tab is not present for every contact.

Double-click the contact to view more detailed information in the contact window. It contains a menu bar, a Standard toolbar, and six tabs—General, Financial Information, Details, Activities, Certificates, and All Fields. The General tab contains the most frequently used information. Use the Details tab to add more information about contacts.

Figure 3-2

General information about the contact

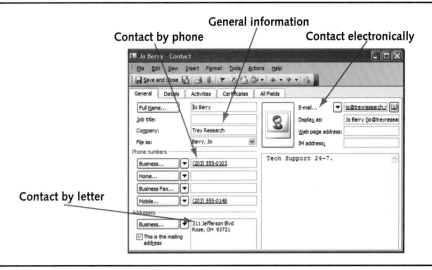

View contact information from any Outlook folder. On the Tools menu, point at Find, and click Advanced Find. Select Contacts in the Look For box. In the Search For The Words box, type the first few letters of the contact's name and click the Find Now button. The contact will be displayed in the bottom pane of the Advanced Find window. Double-click the contact to view information in the contact window.

Figure 3-3

Find a contact

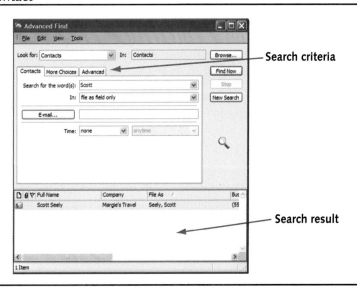

The General tab is displayed when you open a contact window. The General tab contains all the information that appears about the contact in the Address Cards view, as well as a box for a Web page address, an area for notes, links to other contacts, and assigned Outlook categories. When you create a new contact, you must enter at least a full name, a company name, or an e-mail address. (Only one of these is required so that the contact can be sorted properly.) All other entries are optional. If you enter an e-mail address but don't include a full name or company name, Outlook suggests that you provide one of these names before you save the contact.

The Details tab contains more specific information about the contact—the contact's office, department, profession, manager's name, assistant's name, the contact's nickname, spouse's name, and the contact's birthday and anniversary. All entries on the Details tab are optional.

Figure 3-4

Contact Details

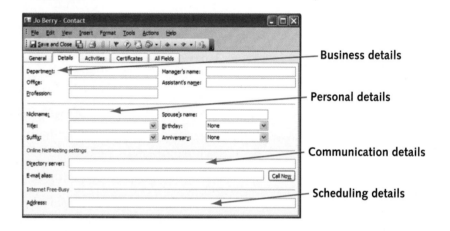

To close a contact window, click the Save And Close button or click the Close button in the top-right corner of the contact window.

◆ **Be sure to start Outlook before beginning this exercise.**

View contact information

You begin this lesson by viewing contact information.

1 **On the Navigation pane, click the Contacts button.**

ANOTHER METHOD

Open the Go menu and select Contacts.

The contents of the Contacts folder are displayed.

2 **Double-click the title bar of the Fabrikam, Inc. contact.**

The Fabrikam, Inc. contact window opens. Information on the General tab is displayed.

Figure 3-5

General information about Fabrikam

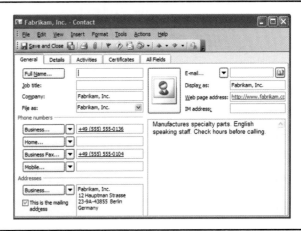

3 Click the Details tab.

The Details tab is displayed. Entering detailed information for any contact is optional. There is no information in the Details section for this contact.

Figure 3-6

Details have not been entered about Fabrikam

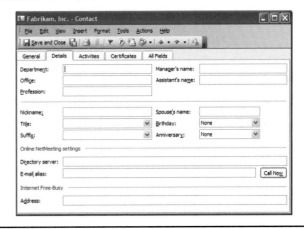

4 Click the General tab.

The General tab is displayed.

5 In the top-right corner of the contact window, click the Close button.

The contact window closes.

◆ Keep Outlook open for the next exercise.

QUICK REFERENCE ▼

View a contact

1 On the Navigation pane, click the Contacts button.

2 Double-click the contact record.

Creating and Editing a New Contact

Creating and Updating
Contact Information

THE BOTTOM LINE

You should keep your contact records up to date by creating new records and editing existing contact records.

Creating a contact is simply a matter of typing information in boxes in the contact window. Each box represents a field, or a single item of contact information, such as an individual's name, a company's name, or a phone number. All the used fields form a **contact record**. On the standard contacts toolbar, click the New Contact button to display a blank contact window. To enter information in a box (field), click the box and type the information. To move to the next box, press Tab or click in the next box.

When you create a contact for a company rather than a specific person at the company, enter the company name in the Company box and leave the Full Name box blank. Outlook interprets any information in the Full Name box as an individual's name. It attempts to store the contact by name, placing the last name first. For example, if you create a contact for Adventure Works, enter Adventure Works in the Company box. If you type Adventure Works in the Full Name box, the contact is stored as Works, Adventure.

Figure 3-7

Enter the name of a company

Full <u>N</u>ame...	
<u>J</u>ob title:	
Co<u>m</u>pany:	Adventure Works
Fil<u>e</u> as:	Adventure Works ⌄
Phone numbers	
Business... ▼	
Home... ▼	
Business Fax... ▼	
Mobile... ▼	

Because some people have multiple phone numbers, addresses, and e-mail addresses, the Address, Phone, and E-Mail boxes can have multiple entries. To enter more than one number, address, or e-mail address, click the arrow next to the box to display a list of entry descriptions. Select the mix of fields that works for your contact.

Figure 3-8

Select the type of information you store

As you enter contact information, click the most appropriate entry description and enter the information in the box. For example, a customer service representative at Adventure Works is entering information for a contact who has both a pager and a mobile phone. In the first box, the representative selects Pager and types the pager number. In the next box, the representative selects Mobile and types the mobile phone number.

You can also store a contact's Web page address in the contact window. Unlike e-mail addresses, you can store only one Web page address at a time.

If you open a contact window for an existing contact and close Outlook, the contact window remains open so you can continue to view or modify the contact information.

To help you remember which contacts are related to certain activities, link the contact record to activities—such as tasks or e-mail messages. To link an activity, display the contact window, open the Actions menu, point to Link, and click Items. In the Look In list on the dialog box, click a folder that contains the activity that you want to link to the contact. In the Items list, click an item, such as an appointment, and click OK. You can see the linked activities on the contact's Activities tab.

Contact records in Microsoft Office Outlook 2003 can contain more than text. Include a photograph or other image in the contact record. On the General tab, click the large box next to the e-mail and Web page address. Browse to locate and select a graphic for the contact record. The image is automatically resized to fit into the box.

When you finish entering or modifying information for a contact, click the Save And Close button on the Standard toolbar in the contact window to save the information as a contact record and close the contact window.

Create Contact Records

Now that you have explored the Contact options, you will create three contact records.

1 **On the standard contacts toolbar, click the New Contact button.**

ANOTHER METHOD

Open the File menu, point at New, and click Contact.

A contact window is displayed. The insertion point is positioned in the Full Name box.

TROUBLESHOOTING

When you type a name in the Full Name box and move to a different box, the window's title bar replaces Untitled with the contact's name.

2 **In the Full Name box, type Eric Lang and press Tab.**

The insertion point moves to the Job Title box. Outlook automatically inserts Lang, Eric in the File As box.

3 Type Director **and press Tab.**

The insertion point moves to the Company box.

4 Type Coho Vineyard.

5 **Click in the Business box and type** 5555550142.

6 **Click the Mobile down arrow.**

A list of fields is displayed. Notice that Business has a check mark next to it because you already entered a phone number in the Business field.

7 **Click Pager.**

The label for the field changes to Pager.

8 **In the Pager box, type** 5555550143. **Click in the Address box, type** 4567 Coolidge St. **and press Enter. Type** Cherry Hills, NY 09472.

The address is entered into the record.

9 **Click the Add Contact Picture box. Navigate to the Outlook Practice folder and select the Eric_Lang file. Click the OK button.**

The picture of Eric Lang is placed in the contact record.

10 **Click in the E-Mail box. Type** eric@cohovineyard.com **and press Tab.**

A line is displayed under the e-mail address and the Display as box is filled with the contact's name and e-mail address. This identifies how the contact's name is displayed in the To box when you send the contact an e-mail message.

11 **Click in the Display As box if necessary. Delete the e-mail address, leaving Eric's first and last name.**

When you use Outlook's e-mail function to send a message, Eric's first and last name are displayed in the To field. The e-mail address is not displayed. This feature makes your e-mail messages look more "friendly" and less "technical."

12 **Click in the Web Page Address box. Type** www.cohovineyard.com **and click in the Notes box.**

A Web page link is created and the insertion point is placed in the Notes box.

13 **Type** Eric is a mountain bike enthusiast.

Figure 3-9

General information about Eric Lang

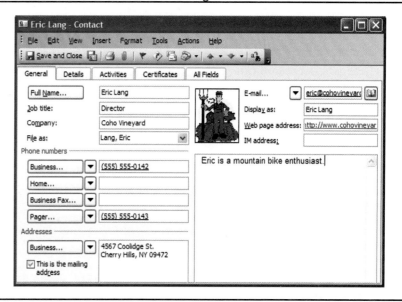

14 **On the Standard toolbar in the contact window, click the Save And New button.**

The contact record is saved and a blank contact window is displayed. This saves a step when you are entering several new contacts at the same time.

TROUBLESHOOTING

The exercises in this lesson use the contact information entered for you and your class partner. To perform these exercises alone, create contact records for you and a fictional class partner. Enter your e-mail address for both contact records. This enables you to complete the exercises by using only your e-mail address. However, your Inbox will not look the same as the samples in this lesson because messages for your class partner will also be in your Inbox.

15 **Add a new record using your contact information. Type your name in the Full Name box and the e-mail address used for this class in the E-mail box. Press the Tab key.**

Do not include personal information such as home phone or address. You will add this information later.

16 **On the Standard toolbar in the contact window, click the Save And New button.**

A contact record containing your information is saved.

17 **Add a new record using your class partner's contact information. Type your class partner's name in the Full Name box and your class partner's e-mail address in the E-mail box.**

Do not include personal information such as home phone or address. You will add this information later.

18 On the Standard toolbar in the contact window, click the Save And Close button.

The contact is saved. The three contacts that you've added are displayed in the Contacts folder.

◆ Keep Outlook open for the next exercise.

QUICK REFERENCE ▼

Create a contact

1 On the standard contacts toolbar, click the New Contact button.

2 Enter contact information.

3 Click the Save And Close button.

Creating Multiple Contacts for the Same Company

Creating and Updating Contact Information

THE BOTTOM LINE

You can simplify the process of entering a second contact at the same company by creating a record that inherits information from the original record.

When entering multiple contacts for different people at the same company, you don't have to type company information for each new contact. Click an existing contact for the company, open the Actions menu, and click New Contact From Same Company. A new contact window is displayed. The company name, address, business phone, and business fax number are automatically inserted. Simply enter new information about the individual, such as the person's name and home phone number.

TIP

To store a copy of several selections at the same time and paste the items in different locations in a contact record or in different folders, use the Office Clipboard. The difference between the Office Clipboard and the general Windows Clipboard is the ability to collect and paste several items at the same time. The Windows clipboard stores only one item. If you copy or cut an item, it replaces the existing content of the Windows Clipboard. With the Office Clipboard, however, you can copy and store up to 24 items at the same time and select which stored item you want to paste. To use the Office Clipboard, open the Edit menu and select the Office Clipboard option.

Create another record for contact with the same company

Now you will create a new record for a contact who works at the same company as an existing contact.

TIP

You can change any information inherited from the original record.

1 In the Contacts folder, click the contact record for Eric Lang that you created in the previous exercise.

The contact is selected.

TROUBLESHOOTING

Outlook does not automatically add the same e-mail address for employees at the same company because most employees have different e-mail addresses. Simply type an e-mail address in the appropriate box.

2 Open the Actions menu and select the option New Contact From Same Company.

A new contact window is displayed. It contains the same company name, address, business phone number, and Web page address as the contact record for Eric Lang.

Figure 3-10

Inherited data for a new contact from a company in an existing record

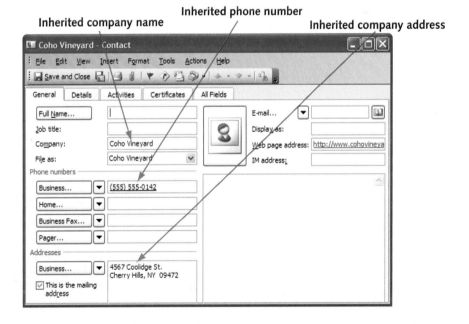

TROUBLESHOOTING

Change the Pager field to a Mobile field to enter a mobile phone number.

3 Type the following contact information in the appropriate boxes:
Full Name Wendy Wheeler
Job Title Sales Representative
Mobile 5555550110
E-Mail wendy@cohovineyard.com

4 **Remove the e-mail address from the Display As field.**

This makes the address on any e-mails appear friendlier and less technical.

Figure 3-11

General data entered for a new contact from a company in an existing record

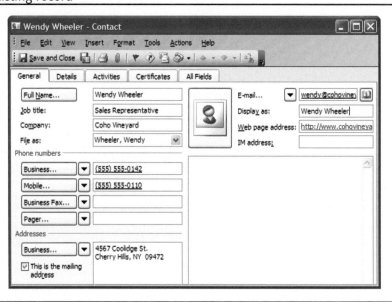

Save and Close

5 **Click the Details tab.**

The Details tab is displayed.

6 **If necessary, click in the Department box and type Sales.**

This entry specifies a different department for Wendy.

7 **On the standard contacts toolbar in the contact window, click the Save And Close button.**

The information about Wendy Wheeler is saved as a new contact and the record is displayed in the Contacts folder.

◆ **Keep Outlook open for the next exercise.**

QUICK REFERENCE ▼

Create multiple contacts for the same company

1 Select a record.

2 Open the Actions menu and select the option New Contact From Same Company.

3 Enter or modify any contact information.

4 Click the Save And Close button.

Deleting and Restoring Contacts

Organizing Contact Information

THE BOTTOM LINE

In Outlook, contacts are not really deleted until the Deleted Items folder is emptied. This provides a safety net in case you accidentally delete a contact.

Just as it is important to clean up your e-mail folders by deleting old messages occasionally, it's important to remove outdated contacts. If you no longer do business with a particular company or an employee leaves your company, delete the corresponding contact records in Outlook. Deleting old or unwanted contact records helps you find and organize the contacts you use regularly.

The Deleted Items folder can be set to empty—permanently delete—all items in the folder when you exit Outlook. To set the Deleted Items folder to be emptied when you exit Outlook, open the Tools menu, click Options, and click the Other tab. Select the Empty The Deleted Items Folder Upon Exiting check box, click Apply, and click OK.

Figure 3-12

Options dialog box

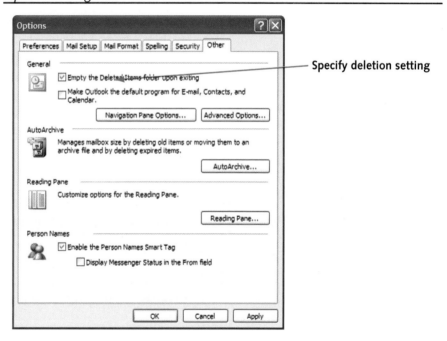

When you delete a contact, Outlook doesn't ask for confirmation. Outlook simply moves the contact to the Deleted Items folder. The contact is not permanently deleted when you do this; you can open the Deleted Items folder and double-click the contact. However, if you delete a contact from the Deleted Items folder or you empty the contents of the Deleted Items folder, the contact is permanently deleted.

If the last step you performed was to delete a contact record, you can quickly restore the record. Open the Edit menu and select the Undo option.

You can restore a deleted contact if you haven't emptied the Deleted Items folder since the item was deleted. To return a deleted contact to the Contacts folder, drag the contact from the Deleted Items folder onto the Contacts button on the Navigation pane.

Delete and restore a contact

As practice, in this exercise, you delete and restore a contact.

1 **Click the Min Su contact record.**

The contact record is selected.

2 **On the standard contacts toolbar, click the Delete button.**

The record is moved to the Deleted Items folder.

3 **On the Navigation pane, click the Folder List button.**

The folders are displayed.

4 **Click the Deleted Items folder.**

The contact record is in the Deleted Items folder.

Figure 3-13

Deleted contact record

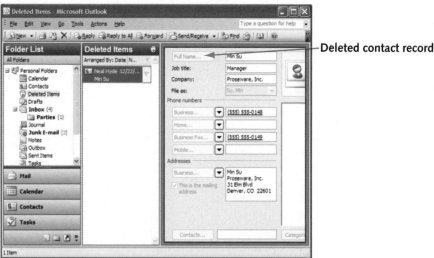

5 **Drag the Min Su contact to the Contacts button on the Navigation pane.**

The Min Su contact moves to the Contacts folder.

ANOTHER METHOD

Open the Edit menu and select the Undo option.

6 **On the Navigation pane, click the Contacts button.**

The contents of the Contacts folder are displayed. The Min Su contact record has been restored to the Contacts folder.

◆ **Keep Outlook open for the next exercise.**

QUICK CHECK

Q: How do you restore a contact?

A: Drag it to the Contacts folder.

QUICK REFERENCE ▼

Delete a contact

1 Select a record.

2 Click the Delete button.

Restore a deleted contact

1 Select a record in the Deleted Items folder.

2 Drag the record to the Contacts folder.

Using Folders to Organize Contacts

THE BOTTOM LINE

Create folders to hold contact records that are related by a common characteristic.

You can use folders to organize your contacts just as you used folders to organize your e-mail messages. Create new folders to meet your needs and organize your contacts more efficiently. For example, Adventure Works uses many different contractors to perform maintenance at the resort. The office manager decided to move all the contact information for these contractors into a folder named Maintenance so she can easily locate a particular contractor without looking through her long list of contacts.

Create a folder and move a contact

So far we have worked within the folders that are available within Outlook. Now you will create a folder and move a contact into it.

1 **Open the Tools menu and click the Organize command.**

The Organize pane is displayed.

2 **In the Organize pane, click the Using Folders link.**

The Using Folders section of the Organize pane is displayed.

3 **In the top-right corner of the Organize pane, click the New Folder button.**

The Create New Folder dialog box is displayed.

ANOTHER METHOD

Create a new folder in the Folder List.

4 **In the Name box, type** Personal**.**

This identifies the content of the folder.

Figure 3-14

Create a new contact folder

5 **In the Folder Contains box, verify that Contact Items is displayed and click OK.**

The Personal folder is added to the Contacts folders listed on the left.

6 **Click the Wingtip Toys contact record in the Contacts pane.**

The contact record is selected.

7 **In the Organize pane, click the Move button.**

The Wingtip Toys contact moves to the Personal folder.

8 **Click the Personal folder listed on the left.**

The contact Wingtip Toys is displayed in the Personal folder.

Figure 3-15

Move a contact into the new folder

9 Click the Contacts folder.

The contents of the Contacts folder are displayed.

TROUBLESHOOTING

Occasionally, a file may not be displayed in the expected location. A filter may be applied to the folder. To clear the filter, open the View menu, point at the Arrange option, point at the Current View option, and select the Customize Current View option to display the dialog box. Click the Filter button to display the Filter dialog box. Click the Clear All button to remove all filters for the selected folder and click the OK button in each dialog box to return to the main window.

◆ Keep Outlook open for the next exercise.

QUICK REFERENCE ▼

Create a folder

1 Open the Tools menu and click the Organize command.

2 In the Organize pane, click the Using Folders link.

3 In the top-right corner of the Organize pane, click the New Folder button.

4 Name the folder and click the OK button.

Move a contact record to a folder

1 Select the record.

2 Select the folder in the Organize pane.

3 Click the Move button.

Using Views to Organize Contacts

THE BOTTOM LINE

Displaying contact records in a selected Outlook view makes it simple to find a specific contact record.

Organizing Contact Information

Like e-mail messages, contact records can appear in several different views, or groups, which can help you find contacts faster and easier. For example, if you are looking for a particular contact and you know the contact's company, you could group your contact records by Company to search more effectively.

ANOTHER METHOD

To use views to organize contacts, open the Tools menu and click the Organize option. In the Organize pane, click the Using Views option, and select a view in the Change Your View box.

In the Address Cards (the default view) and Detailed Address Cards views, contacts are displayed as cards, similar to business cards in a card file. In all other views, contacts are displayed in a table format with columns and rows. Each contact is displayed in a row, separated by columns that correspond to fields in the contact, such as Company and Business Phone. The contents of the columns change to reflect the contents of the selected view. When contacts are displayed in tables, the contacts are divided into groups with expandable gray bars that summarize the contents of each group. For example, when you display your contacts in the By Location view, you see several gray bars that display the text Country/Region: (location) ([number] items). If you had four contacts located in the United States and two in the United Kingdom, you see two gray bars that display the text Country/Region: United States of America (4 items) and Country/Region: United Kingdom (2 items). To see the contacts, click the plus sign (+) located at the left end of the bar. To hide the contacts, click the minus sign (–) located at the left end of the bar. The following table details each view.

View	Description
Address Cards	Contacts appear similar to business cards. They are arranged in alphabetical order.
Detailed Address Cards	The view resembles the Address Cards view, but it displays more information.
Phone List	Contacts are arranged in rows and columns; most telephone fields are displayed. As the name suggests, this view makes it easy to find a contact's telephone number.
By Category	Contacts are grouped by categories. Categorizing contacts emphasizes the characteristics the contacts have in common. (Learn about categories in the next section of this lesson.)
By Company	Contacts appear grouped by company. This view is useful for finding contacts based on the contents of the Company box. If you have several contacts employed by the same company, use this view to identify the job title and the department for each contact.
By Location	Contacts are grouped by Country/Region based on the content in the Address box. This view is useful when you have international contacts.
By Follow-Up Flag	Contacts are grouped by Follow-Up Flag. This view is useful when you have marked contacts for follow-up. For example, add a follow-up flag for a contact who requested additional information or registered for a conference.

Display contact records

Next you will experiment with displaying contact records in different views.

1 **In the Current View area of the Navigation pane, select Detailed Address Cards.**

ANOTHER METHOD

You can also change views through the menu. Open the View menu, point at Arrange By, point at Current View, and click an available view.

The Contacts view changes to display your contacts in Detailed Address Cards view.

Figure 3-16

Detailed address cards

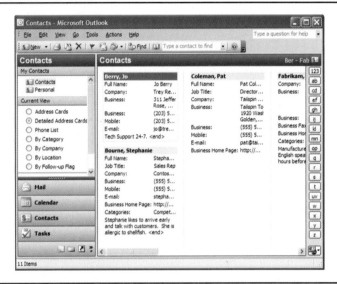

2 **In the Current View area of the Navigation pane, select Phone List.**

The Contacts view changes to list your contacts by name, company, and phone numbers.

Figure 3-17

View contacts by phone list

3 In the Current View area of the Navigation pane, select By Category.

The Contacts view changes to list your contacts by category. Each category is represented by a gray bar. Expand a bar to view the contact records it contains.

Figure 3-18

View contacts by category

Click to expand or contract each category

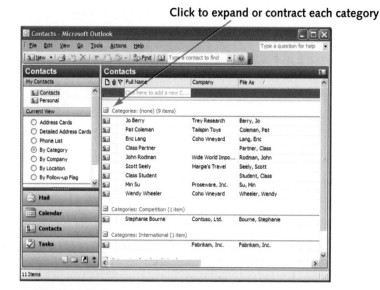

4 In the Current View area of the Navigation pane, select By Company.

The Contacts view changes to list your contacts in alphabetic sequence based on the name of the company. Contacts without a company are listed first.

Figure 3-19

View contacts by company

5 In the Current View area of the Navigation pane, select By Location.

The Contacts view changes to list your contacts by geographic location. Contacts that don't provide information for this category are listed first.

Figure 3-20

View contacts by location

6 In the Current View area of the Navigation pane, select By Follow-up Flag.

The Contacts view changes to list your contacts based on the follow-up flag currently assigned to the contact. All contacts don't have follow-up flags.

Figure 3-21

View contacts by follow-up flag

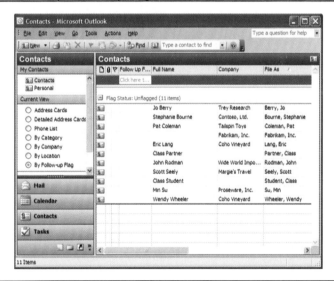

QUICK CHECK

Q: Can you change the method of viewing your contact records?

A: Yes, you can view contact records in several different arrangements.

7 In the Current View area of the Navigation pane, select Address Cards.

The Contacts view changes to display the default view of contacts as address cards.

◆ Keep Outlook open for the next exercise.

QUICK REFERENCE ▼

Display contact records

In the Current View of the Navigation pane, select a view.

Using Categories to Organize Contacts

Organizing Contact Information

> **THE BOTTOM LINE**
>
> You can organize contacts when you assign contact records to categories that describe an important characteristic of each record.

Outlook provides other approaches that you can use to organize and group contacts, including the use of categories. A **category** is a keyword or phrase associated with an Outlook item, such as a contact. A category is typically a brief description of the method used to group contacts. Categories are based on common characteristics, such as *business, personal,* and *customers.*

To assign a contact to a category, select the contact, and click the Using Categories link in the Organize pane. In the first line, select an existing category such as Holiday, Business, or International, and click the Add button. The contact is added to the selected category.

Assigning Items to a New Category

Finding and Categorizing Messages

> **THE BOTTOM LINE**
>
> If Outlook's existing categories don't meet your needs, you can create new categories.

Outlook provides dozens of ready-made category descriptions, but you can create more categories to meet your specific needs. For example, the operations manager at Adventure Works assigned the ready-made Outlook category Suppliers to all companies that sell products and services to the resort. When she needs a list of the resort's suppliers, she can view her Contacts folder by category. All contacts that have been assigned to the Suppliers category are displayed in a group. She could narrow the categorization further by creating custom categories for each department, such as Restaurant Suppliers, Business Office Suppliers, and Housekeeping Suppliers.

Figure 3-22

Organize contacts by categories

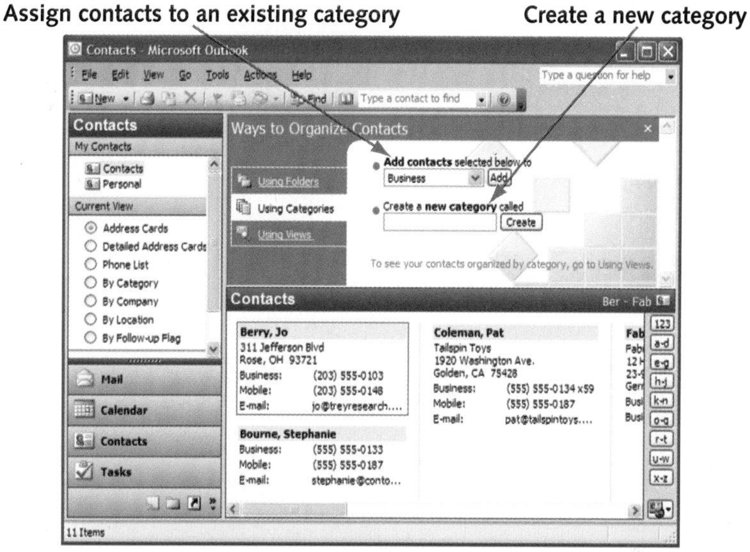

Assign contacts to an existing category   Create a new category

To create a new category, open the Organize pane and click the Using Categories link. In the second box, enter the name of the new category. Click the Create button to create the category. Assign any appropriate existing contacts to the new category.

Assign contacts to a new category

Since you have created contacts, you will create a new category, assign two contacts to the category, and then view your contacts by category.

1 **Open the Tools menu and click the Organize command.**

The Organize pane is displayed.

2 **In the Organize pane, click the Using Categories link.**

The Using Categories section of the Organize pane is displayed.

3 **Click in the Create A New Category Called box, type Finance, and click the Create button.**

The Finance category is created and Finance becomes the selected category in the upper box. This makes it easy to assign contacts to the category immediately.

Figure 3-23

New category

4 **In the Contacts folder, click the John Rodman contact record.**

The contact record is selected.

5 **In the Organize pane, click the Add button.**

The contact record is assigned to the new Finance category.

Figure 3-24

Record assigned to a new category

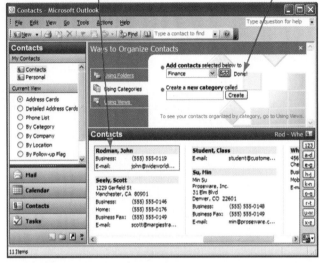

Selected record   Record successfully added to a category

6 **In the Contacts folder, click the Scott Seely contact record.**

The contact record is selected.

7 **In the Organize pane, click the Add button.**

The contact record is assigned to the Finance category.

8 **In the Current View area of the Navigation pane, select By Category.**

Scott Seely and John Rodman are displayed as the contacts in the Finance category.

Figure 3-25

Records displayed by category

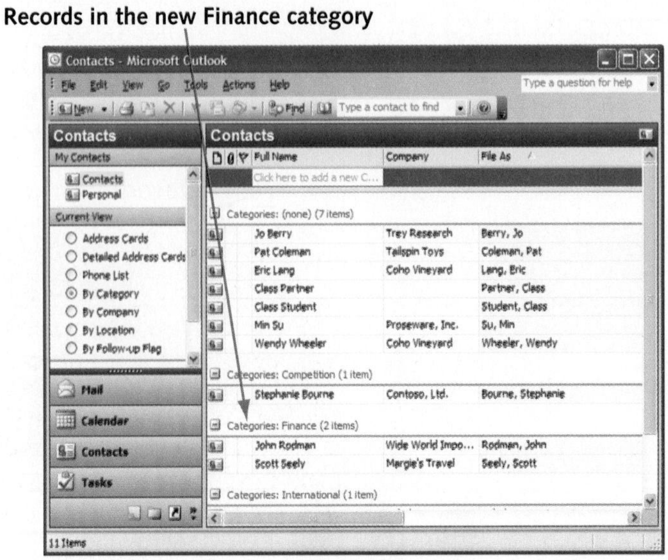

Records in the new Finance category

ANOTHER METHOD

In the Navigation pane, click the Address Cards option.

QUICK CHECK

Q: What is the basis for creating or using categories?

A: **Categories are based on common characteristics.**

9 If necessary, reopen the Organize pane. Select the Address Cards view.

The Contacts folder returns to the Address Cards view.

◆ Keep Outlook open for the next exercise.

QUICK REFERENCE ▼

Assign contacts to a new category

1 Open the Tools menu and click the Organize command.

2 In the Organize pane, click the Using Categories link.

3 Enter the category in the Create A New Category Called box and click the Create button.

4 Select a contact record and click the Add button in the Organize pane.

Assigning Items to Multiple Categories

THE BOTTOM LINE

If you want to view a record for different reasons, you can assign a contact record to more than one category.

Finding and Categorizing Messages

Relationships with contacts can be complex, so it's not unusual when a contact doesn't fit neatly into a single category. For example, Adventure Works hosts an international convention organized by a company in Mexico. The contact record for the convention organizer can be assigned to the International, Key Customer, or Business category—or to all three categories.

Over time, your relationship with each contact changes. Update category assignments as necessary to reflect a contact's current status.

Fortunately, you can assign contacts to more than one category. By assigning multiple categories to a contact, you make the contact record more accurately reflect your relationship to the contact and you enhance your ability to sort that contact by a particular category. However, don't assign a contact to more categories than necessary. The benefit of sorting contacts by category is undermined if a contact appears in almost every category.

To assign a contact to an additional category or change an existing category, select the contact, open the Edit menu, and select the Categories option. Select the appropriate check box to assign a category. Select a check box that already has a check mark in it to remove the contact from that category.

Assign a contact to multiple categories

Now you will assign the contact Scott Seely to two additional categories—Business and Supplier.

TIP

You can open a contact record from any view in the Contacts folder.

1 In the Contacts folder, click the contact record for Scott Seely.

The contact is selected.

ANOTHER METHOD

Double-click a contact to open it in a new window.

2 Open the Edit menu and select the Categories option.

The Categories dialog box is displayed. Scott Seely is already assigned to the Finance category.

Figure 3-26

Categories dialog box

3 In the Categories dialog box, select the Business check box and the Suppliers check box. Click OK.

The categories are added to the contact record.

4 In the Current View area of the Navigation pane, select By Category.

Scott Seely is listed in three categories. Notice that Fabrikam, Inc., is also listed in the Suppliers category.

Figure 3-27

Scott Seely assigned to multiple categories

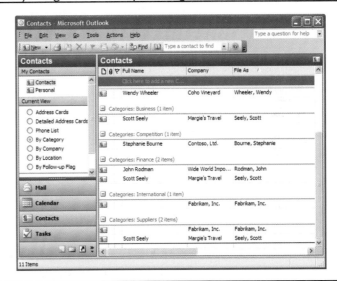

QUICK CHECK

Q: Why would you assign a contact to more than one category?

A: **This makes it easier to find a contact.**

5 **If necessary, reopen the Organize pane. Select the Address Cards view.**

The Contacts folder returns to the Address Cards view.

◆ **Keep Outlook open for the next exercise.**

QUICK REFERENCE ▼

Assign contacts to multiple categories

1 Select the record.

2 Open the Edit menu and select the Categories option.

3 Select the additional categories and click OK.

Modifying the Outlook Master Category List

THE BOTTOM LINE

You can modify the Master Category List as needed or reset the list to Outlook's original categories.

Outlook's ready-made list of categories is the **Master Category List.** It contains many useful categories, such as Hot Contacts, Holiday, and VIP, but you can add your own categories. In a previous exercise, you used the Organize pane to create a new category named Finance. Outlook automatically added that category to the Master Category List. You can open the Master Category List directly and add more custom categories to the list. In fact, you can customize the Master Category List in many ways, even deleting categories that you don't use. You can also reset the Master Category List to restore the default categories if you decide you want a fresh start.

Figure 3-28

Master Category List

Notice that the Finance category that you created in the previous exercise appears in the Master Category List.

Modify and reset the Master Category List

You will now work with the Master Category List. First you add a category to the Master Category List. Then you delete a category from the Master Category List. And, last, you reset the Master Category List to its original content.

1 **Open the Edit menu in the main Outlook window. Click Categories.**

ANOTHER METHOD

Right-click any contact record and click the Categories option.

The Categories dialog box is displayed.

2 **Click the Master Category List button.**

The Master Category List dialog box is displayed.

3 **In the New Category box, type Charities and click the Add button.**

Charities is added to the Master Category List.

4 **In the Master Category List, click Ideas and click the Delete button.**

Ideas is deleted from the Master Category List.

5 **Click the Reset button.**

An alert box states that the Master Category List will be reset to contain only the categories that were installed with Outlook and items assigned to deleted categories keep their assignments. In this case, the Finance and Charities categories will be deleted because neither category is part of the original Master Category List. However, the two contacts that have been assigned to the Finance category will retain their category assignments.

6 Click OK.

The Master Category List is reset. The custom Finance and Charities categories are deleted and the Ideas category is restored.

Figure 3-29

Reset Master Category List

7 Click OK twice.

The Master Category List dialog box closes and the Categories dialog box closes.

◆ **Keep Outlook open for the next exercise.**

QUICK REFERENCE ▼

Modify the Master Category List

1 Open the Edit menu in the main Outlook window. Click Categories.

2 Click the Master Category List button.

3 Make any needed changes and click OK twice.

Sorting Contacts

THE BOTTOM LINE

Contact records can be sorted to find a specific record.

Organizing Contact Information

Sorting contacts can help you find a contact faster and easier. You can sort contacts in any view, in either ascending order (A to Z) or descending order (Z to A) by a specific field, or by a particular column header that appears at the top of the view's table, such as Company, Job Title, or Personal Home Page. When you sort in a view, the contacts remain in the same view; however, they are displayed in a different sequence.

TIP

Remember, a filter hides contacts that don't meet a set of criteria. When you use the Sort command, all contacts are displayed.

For example, the human resources manager at Adventure Works needed to find a contact but could only remember that the contact's first name was Kim. After she sorted her Contacts folder by First Name, the contacts were displayed in alphabetical order based on each contact's first name. She could have also used the Find button on the standard toolbar to search for Kim. However, because the Find feature looks for a match in the name, company, address, and categories fields, it might find matches that she definitely did not want. For example, Kimborough Museum of Science matched because Kim is part of the museum's name. Sorting by a particular column heading is often faster than the Find feature.

Add a second field to perform a sort within a sort. When you include a second field, the second sort narrows the first sort criterion even further. For example, you can sort contacts by Country/Region in ascending order and then sort by Business Address in ascending order. The contacts are sorted by Country/Region. Within the Country/Region groups, contacts are sorted by Business Address.

Sort contacts

To practice sorting you will sort the list of contacts in Phone List view by Business Phone number.

1 **In the Current View area of the Navigation pane, select Phone List.**

The Contacts view changes to list your contacts by name, company, and phone numbers.

2 **Open the Tools menu and select the Organize option.**

The Organize pane is displayed.

3 **In the Organize pane, click the Using Views link. Click the Customize Current View button.**

The Customize View dialog box is displayed.

Figure 3-30

Customize View dialog box

4 **Click the Sort button.**

The Sort dialog box is displayed.

ANOTHER METHOD

Many times, you can sort contacts for your needs by clicking a column heading.

5 **In the Sort Items By section, click Business Phone. Verify that the Ascending option is selected.**

Figure 3-31

Sort dialog box

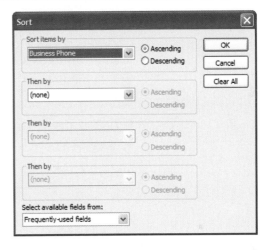

6 **Click OK twice.**

The contents of the selected Contacts folder are sorted by Business Phone.

Figure 3-32

Sorted records

Records sorted by business phone number

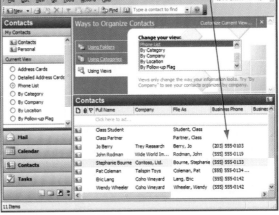

7 **In the Organize pane, click the Customize Current View button.**

The Customize View dialog box is displayed.

8 Click the Sort button.

The Sort dialog box is displayed.

9 Click the Clear All button and click OK twice to close the dialog boxes.

The contents of the Contacts folder are no longer sorted by Business Phone.

10 In the Organize pane, select the Address Cards view.

The Contacts view is changed to Address Cards.

◆ Keep Outlook open for the next exercise.

QUICK REFERENCE ▼

Sort contact records

1 Select a view in the Navigation pane.

2 Open the Tools menu and select the Organize option.

3 In the Organize pane, click the Using Views link.

4 Click the Customize Current View button.

5 Click the Sort button.

6 Select the Sort criteria.

7 Click OK twice to return to the main Contacts folder.

Using the Address Book to Send E-Mail

Using Address Books

THE BOTTOM LINE

Outlook lets you use the Address Book in any Outlook folder to send an e-mail message.

When you create a new contact record, some of the information is copied to the **Address Book**, which stores names, e-mail addresses, and phone numbers. To open the Address Book from any folder in Outlook, click the Address Book button on the Standard toolbar.

Figure 3-33

Address Book

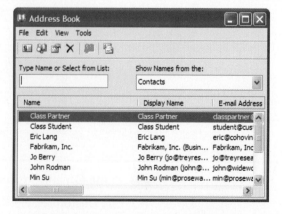

If your computer is set up for the Corporate or Workgroup e-mail service, your Address Book will look slightly different (and have different options) than the one discussed in this lesson.

Within the Address Book window is a toolbar and a list of contact information for each record in the Contacts folder. The toolbar contains six buttons—New Entry, Find Items, Properties, Delete, Add to Contacts, and New Message. The buttons are described in the following table.

Button	Description
New Entry	Add a new contact or a distribution list to the Address Book.
Find Items	Open the Find dialog box that enables you to search for names containing a specific sequence of letters.
Properties	Display the General tab of a contact record. You can add or edit contact information.
Delete	Permanently delete an entry from the address book.
Add to Contacts	The Address Book and Contacts list interact.
New Message	Open a blank e-mail message addressed to the selected contact.

If a contact has an e-mail address, you can send messages to the contact directly from the Address Book. You don't need to copy or manually type the e-mail address into the To box of a new message window.

Send mail from the Address Book

Now you will open the Address Book, select an e-mail address, and send an e-mail message through the Address Book.

TIP

The Address Book button is on the standard toolbar for each Outlook folder.

 1 On the standard contacts toolbar, click the Address Book button.

The Address Book is displayed.

Figure 3-34

Address Book

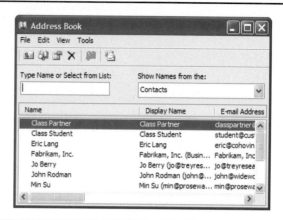

 2 Click your class partner's name and click the New Message button.

A new message window is displayed. Your class partner's address is in the To box.

Figure 3-35

Message sent from Address Book

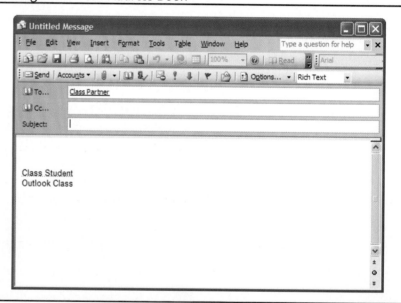

3 In the Subject box, type Address Book.

 4 Click in the message area and type You are in my address book. On the toolbar in the message window, click the Send button.

The message is sent to your class partner.

 5 In the top-right corner of the Address Book, click the Close button.

QUICK CHECK

Q: Where can you open the Address Book?

A: **The Address Book can be opened from the standard toolbar in each Outlook folder.**

◆ **Keep Outlook open for the next exercise.**

QUICK REFERENCE ▼

Send e-mail using the Address Book

1 On the standard contacts toolbar, click the Address Book button.

2 Select a contact and click the New Message button.

3 Write the message and click the Send button.

Using Contacts to Send E-Mail

THE BOTTOM LINE

Just as you were able to send a message from the Address Book, you can also send a message to one of your contacts without moving to the Mail folder.

You can send e-mail directly from the Contacts folder without opening the Inbox folder first. To send an e-mail message to a contact from the Contacts folder, select the contact record in the Contacts folder. On the standard contacts toolbar, click the New Message To Contact button. A message window is displayed. The e-mail address of the selected contact is in the To box. You can type additional information in the e-mail message and click the Send button.

You can send e-mail messages from Contacts even when the recipient is not a contact. On the Standard toolbar, click the down arrow to the right of the New Contact button, and click Mail Message. A blank message window is displayed, enabling you to create and send a message to someone who isn't in your Contacts.

TIP

In a message window, click the Address Book button in the To field. This displays the Address Book and enables you to insert or add addressees to the message.

Send a message from a Contact folder

You will now send a message to your class partner directly from a contact window.

1 **In the Contacts folder, double-click your class partner's contact record.**

Your class partner's contact record is displayed in a new window.

TIP

You can send a new message from the standard toolbar in any of the Outlook folders.

2 **On the Standard toolbar in the contact window, click the New Message To Contact button.**

A message window is displayed. Your class partner's e-mail address is located in the To box. The insertion point is in the Subject box.

3 **Type Outlook Class and press Enter.**

The insertion point moves to the message area.

TIP

These messages are not used in another part of the lesson. It is not necessary to send or receive the messages.

4 **Type How is the Outlook class going? Click the Send button.**

The message is sent.

5 **In the top-right corner of the contact window, click the Close button.**

The contact window closes. Your class partner's contact record is still selected.

6 **On the Navigation pane, click the Mail button. If necessary, go to the Inbox.**

Messages you have received are displayed.

7 **Click the Send/Receive button.**

The message sent by your class partner is received.

Figure 3-36

Message sent from Contacts folder

◆ **Keep Outlook open for the next exercise.**

QUICK CHECK

Q: Can you send a message to someone who isn't one of your contact records?

A: **You can send a message to someone who isn't one of your contact records.**

QUICK REFERENCE ▼

Send a message from a Contact folder

1 Double-click a contact record.

2 On the standard toolbar in the contact window, click the New Message To Contact button.

3 Type your message and click the Send button.

Sending and Receiving Contact Information via E-Mail

Sending and Receiving
Contact Information

THE BOTTOM LINE

A vCard creates or updates a contact record without the recipient typing in the new information.

IMPORTANT

To use vCards in Outlook, you must have the VcViewer program installed and Outlook must be set up using the Internet Only configuration. If an alert box states that you do not have the VcViewer program installed, you can install it from the Outlook or Microsoft Office 2003 CD-ROM.

A **vCard** is a virtual business card. It enables you to send information about yourself, your contacts, and others who send you information. Send and receive contact information as an e-mail attachment so it can be added easily to a recipient's Contacts folder. You can create a vCard for yourself, forward a vCard sent to you from another person, send a contact as a vCard to other recipients so they can add it to their Contacts folder or Address Book, and include a vCard as part of a signature.

Sending a vCard

THE BOTTOM LINE

Sending a vCard ensures that others have current contact information for you.

Exchanging contact information using vCards is fast and convenient. If you send a text message containing contact information, the recipient must type it into Outlook as a new contact. It is much easier for the sender and the receiver to use vCards. You can send a vCard and the recipient can add it directly to his or her Contacts folder. For example, the head chef of Adventure Works attaches a vCard with his address and phone information to his signature. When he sends e-mail to other people, they receive the vCard and can easily add it to their Contacts folder. To send a vCard from Contacts, click the contact record you want to send, open the Actions menu, and select the Forward as vCard option. A new message window opens. The contact information is a vCard attached to the message. In the To box, type the recipient's e-mail address and click the Send button.

Use vCards

In this exercise, you forward your contact information as a vCard to a member of your class, make the vCard part of your signature, and send a message to a class member with a vCard as part of your signature.

TIP

A vCard can be sent as an attachment in a specific message or included in a signature that is automatically added to each message you compose.

1 In the Contacts folder, double-click your contact record.

Your contact window is displayed.

2 In the Address box, type the address for your company, your home address, or a fictitious address.

This provides additional contact information.

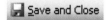

3 On the standard contacts toolbar, click the Save And Close button.

The contact window closes. Your contact record is still selected in the Contacts folder.

4 Right-click your contact record and click Forward.

A new message window is displayed with FW: [Your Name] in the Subject box. The vCard is located in the bottom of the message window as an attachment.

5 Click the To button.

The Select Names dialog box is displayed.

6 In the Select Names dialog box, click your class partner's name, click the To button, and click OK.

The Select Names dialog box closes and your class partner's name is displayed in the To box.

7 On the toolbar in the message window, click the Send button.

Your contact information is sent as a vCard.

8 Open the Tools menu and click Options.

The Options dialog box is displayed.

9 Click the Mail Format tab, and click the Signatures button.

The Create Signature dialog box is displayed.

10 Verify that the signature you created in a previous lesson is selected and click the Edit button.

The Edit Signature dialog box is displayed.

Figure 3-37

Edit Signature dialog box

11 At the bottom of the dialog box, click the New vCard From Contact button.

The Select Contacts To Export As vCards dialog box is displayed.

Figure 3-38

Select Contacts To Export As vCards

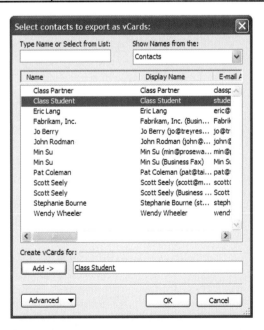

12 Click your name, click the Add button, and click OK.

In the Edit Signature dialog box, notice that your name is displayed in the Attach This Business Card (vCard) To This Signature box.

13 Click OK three times to return to the Contacts folder.

Your contacts are displayed.

14 Click your class partner's contact record. On the standard toolbar, click the New Message To Contact button.

A new message window is displayed. Your class partner's e-mail address is located in the To box, your signature is displayed in the message area, and a vCard is attached to the message.

15 In the Subject box, type My new signature. In the message area, type Look at my new signature. and click the Send button on the Message toolbar.

The message is sent to your class partner.

TIP

You will view the message sent by your class partner in the next exercise.

◆ Keep Outlook open for the next exercise.

QUICK REFERENCE ▼

Send a vCard

1 Right-click a contact record and click Forward.

2 Address the message and click the Send button.

Receiving a vCard

THE BOTTOM LINE

You can keep your contact records current by saving the vCards you

When you receive a vCard, it is displayed as an attachment to an e-mail message. Open it by double-clicking the vCard icon just like any other attachment. The vCard opens as a contact window. You can insert additional information, such as who sent you the card, or edit existing information. Click the Save And Close button to add the vCard to your Contacts folder.

If the vCard is a duplicate of an existing contact, an alert box is displayed. You can choose to add the contact as a second record or add updated information from the new contact to the existing contact.

Receive a vCard

In this exercise, you receive and save the vCard sent by your class partner.

TIP

A vCard can be received as an attachment or part of the sender's signature.

1 **Double-click the My New Signature message you received from your class partner in the previous exercise.**

A message window is displayed. The vCard is an attachment to the message.

Figure 3-39

Received vCard in signature of message sent by your class partner

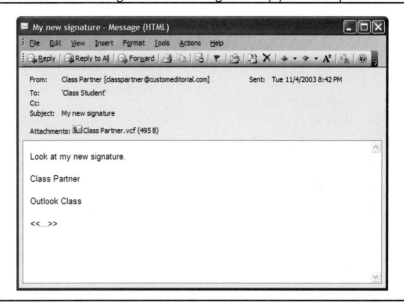

An alert box might be displayed. Continue to open the vCard.

2 **Double-click the vCard.**

The vCard is displayed as a contact record.

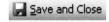 **3** **Click the Save And Close button.**

An alert box indicates that this is a duplicate record.

Figure 3-40

Alert box for duplicate record

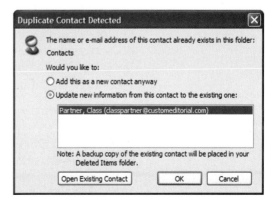

4 **Choose to update the existing record and click OK.**

Outlook saves the vCard as a contact record in the Contacts folder.

5 Close the message window. On the Navigation pane, click the Contacts button.

The Contacts folder is displayed.

6 In the Contacts folder, find your class partner's contact record and verify that the information in the vCard has been added to the contact record.

The contact record has been modified.

Figure 3-41

Updated contact information from vCard

Partner, Class
Suite 5
1104 Main Street
Smallville, MO 80909
E-mail: classpartner@cus...

◆ Keep Outlook open for the next exercise.

QUICK REFERENCE ▼

Receive a vCard

1 Double-click a message containing a vCard attachment.

2 Double-click the vCard.

3 Click the Save And Close button.

Creating a Letter for a Contact

THE BOTTOM LINE

With Microsoft Word's Letter Wizard you can create letters addressed to your contacts.

Outlook e-mail capabilities are integrated with all other Microsoft Office applications. This means you can initiate some activities directly in an Office application that you would otherwise have to do from within Outlook. For example, you can use your Address Book to create and send documents in Microsoft Word. After you create a document in Word, click the E-Mail button on Word's Standard toolbar to quickly send the document as an e-mail message.

Conversely, you can also initiate an e-mail message in letter format from within Outlook, which can launch Word so you can compose the body of the letter. You don't need to type the recipient's address in the letter if it already exists in a contact record.

For example, an administrative assistant at Adventure Works needs to write a letter to a client regarding his account. Instead of opening Word and typing the client's information in the upper-left corner of the letter, the assistant creates the letter from the contact record in Outlook, and the contact information is automatically added to the letter.

QUICK CHECK

Q: What happens if you receive the same vCard twice?

A: **You can update the contact record.**

Although Outlook starts the letter-creation process, you actually create and compose the letter in Microsoft Word. The Letter Wizard dialog box is displayed in Word to walk you through the steps in the letter-creation process. In the first step, on the Letter Format tab, choose a letter format, including letterhead, page design, and letter style. In the second step, on the Recipient Info tab, select the recipient's name, mailing address, and a salutation. In the third step, on the Other Elements tab, select options concerning reference lines, mailing instructions, attentions, subjects, and courtesy copies. In the fourth and final step, on the Sender Info tab, select information about the person sending the letter (either yourself or someone else), and letter closing options. After the fourth step is finished, the Letter Wizard closes and you can type the body of the letter.

IMPORTANT

To complete the next exercise, you must have Microsoft Word installed on your computer.

Use the Letter Wizard

Now you will use the Letter Wizard to format and compose a letter to contact Scott Seely.

TROUBLESHOOTING

If the Office Assistant is displayed, right-click the Assistant and click Hide on the shortcut menu that is displayed.

1 **In the Contacts folder, click the Scott Seely contact record. Open the Actions menu and select the New Letter To Contact option.**

Word opens and the first dialog box of the Letter Wizard is displayed.

2 **Complete the Letter Wizard and click the Finish button.**

The Letter Wizard closes and the letter is displayed in Word. You can now add the body text to the letter.

TIP

Although you made many formatting decisions in the Letter Wizard, you can change the format after the letter is created.

3 **Complete the letter by typing the following body text.** Adventure Works is now taking bids for new signs. If you would like to obtain more information and place a bid, contact us at 555-555-0129.

4 **Save the letter in the Outlook Practice folder on your hard disk as Letter to Scott Seely.**

The letter is saved in the Outlook Practice folder.

◆ **Close Microsoft Word.**

◆ **If you are continuing to the next lesson, keep Outlook open.**

◆ **If you are not continuing to the next lesson, close Outlook.**

QUICK REFERENCE ▼

Use the Letter Wizard

1 Select a contact record.

2 Open the Actions menu and select the New Letter To Contact option.

3 Complete the Letter Wizard and click the Finish button.

4 Complete and save the letter.

Key Points

✔ *Contacts can be viewed, edited, deleted, and restored.*
✔ *You can create multiple contact records for people at the same company.*
✔ *In Outlook, you can sort and organize contacts using folders, views, and categories.*
✔ *The Outlook Master Category List can be modified.*
✔ *The Address Book as well as the contacts can be used to send e-mail messages directly. You do not need to be in the Mail folder.*
✔ *You can send and receive contact information as a vCard.*
✔ *Using Microsoft Word, you can create a letter to a contact.*

True/False

T F 1. Contact records are deleted immediately when you click the Delete button.

T F 2. Every contact record should be assigned to every category.

T F 3. Sort contact records in some views by clicking a column heading.

T F 4. The Address Book contains only contact records for individuals who have received a letter from you.

T F 5. You can send a message to a contact from any Outlook folder.

Multiple Choice

1. Contacts can be assigned to _____ category(categories).
  a. one
  b. three
  c. every
  d. All of the above

2. When a vCard is received, it is a(n) _____.
  a. attachment
  b. part of the message body
  c. chore to type the new information
  d. All of the above

3. The _____ enables you to add an address to an e-mail message without typing it.
   a. Master Category List
   b. Address Book
   c. Letter Wizard
   d. All of the above

4. A deleted contact is _____.
   a. removed immediately
   b. stored until you enter a new contact record
   c. stored in the Deleted Items folder
   d. assigned to the Deleted category

5. Organize contacts by _____.
   a. assigning them to categories
   b. moving them to folders
   c. sorting them
   d. All of the above

Short Answer

1. How can the Address Book save you time in addressing a new message?

2. Can you add categories to the Master Category List? If so, how do you make the changes?

3. What is a category?

4. How do you enter multiple contacts for the same company?

5. What is a vCard?

6. What happens when you click the Save And New button after entering contact data?

7. For a contact record to be complete, which fields in the contact window are required?

8. In general, what is the purpose of the Contacts folder?

9. Where does a contact go when you delete it, and how do you permanently delete a contact?

On Your Own

Exercise 1

The new marketing director at Adventure Works needs to add two new contacts for the advertising agency of Contoso, Ltd. The members of the agency are Susan W. Eaton, President, and Eva Corets, Ad Consultant. The address for the company is 55 Pine Terrace, Suite 400, San Jose, CA 11111. Each contact is to be assigned to the Business and Strategies categories. The additional information the marketing director has for each person is the business phone, mobile phone, pager, and e-mail address.

Enter the following contact information for Susan W. Eaton:

Name	Susan W. Eaton
Job Title	President
Business Phone	555-555-0177
Pager	555-555-0132
Mobile Phone	555-555-0151
E-Mail Address	susan@contoso.com

Enter the following contact information for Eva Corets:

Name	Eva Corets
Job Title	Ad Consultant
Pager	555-555-0163
Mobile Phone	555-555-0184
E-Mail Address	eva@contoso.com

TROUBLESHOOTING

You must complete Exercise 1 before you can continue to Exercise 2.

Exercise 2

Compose a formal letter to the president of Contoso, Ltd. indicating what a pleasure it was to meet with her team and expressing confidence that the advertising campaign for Adventure Works is in good hands. Save or print the letter.

One Step Further

Exercise 1

Send two vCards to your class partner using the information you entered in the first exercise.

Exercise 2

Add the vCards you receive from your class partner to your Contacts folder.

Exercise 3

Assign the vCards you receive from your class partner to a category for suppliers. If necessary, create the category. Delete the vCards from your Contacts folder.

Using the Calendar

After completing this lesson, you will be able to:

- ✔ *Navigate within the Calendar.*
- ✔ *Change Calendar views.*
- ✔ *Schedule appointments and events.*
- ✔ *Create recurring appointments.*
- ✔ *Set reminders.*
- ✔ *Edit appointments.*
- ✔ *Delete appointments.*
- ✔ *Organize appointments using categories and views.*
- ✔ *Plan meetings with others.*
- ✔ *Print a calendar.*
- ✔ *Save a calendar as a Web page.*
- ✔ *Integrate the Calendar with other Outlook components.*

KEY TERMS

- Appointment Area
- appointment
- Calendar
- Date Navigator
- event

- meeting
- recurring appointment
- TaskPad
- Work Week

For many busy businesspcople, there never seems to be enough time in the day to finish all their tasks. To keep track of all your day-to-day duties, meetings, and appointments, it is important to stay organized. To do this, you can jot down your appointments and other scheduling information in a day planner or enter the information into a palm-size computer. You can also use Microsoft Office Outlook 2003 to plan your day and your week. Because Outlook uses the full power of your computer, you can often take advantage of features not available with a day planner or a palm-size computer. For example, in Outlook, you can set an alarm to notify you of an upcoming appointment. You certainly can't expect your day planner to sound an alarm.

The Outlook Calendar is just as easy to use as the calendar hanging on your wall or buried on your desk. Use the Calendar, to set reminders, create a list of daily tasks to perform, change appointment times, and automatically mark meetings that occur on a regular basis (such as a weekly department meeting). You can print your daily, weekly, or monthly calendar and take it with you when you are away from your desk or your office, and you can make your schedule available to others over a network (via Microsoft Exchange Server) or over the Internet so co-workers can see when you are available for meetings.

In this lesson, you will learn how to navigate within the Calendar. You will use the Calendar to schedule and edit appointments and events. You will set reminders and plan meetings with others. Finally, you will print a copy of your calendar to take with you or distribute and you will see how the Calendar is integrated with other Outlook components.

Using the Outlook Calendar

THE BOTTOM LINE

The Outlook Calendar can help you organize a busy schedule by tracking your appointments, meetings, and events.

Looking at Calendars in Different Ways

Outlook places many features at your fingertips. The **Calendar** is a component of Outlook that can be used like a desk calendar or a day planner. In the Calendar, you can create information about activities that take place at scheduled times, called **appointments**. You can track and plan events, which are activities that occupy long periods of time, such as vacations or conventions. You can also schedule **meetings**, which are appointments that you invite or request others to attend.

Understanding Appointments and Meetings

Many people use the terms *appointment* and *meeting* interchangeably. In the Outlook Calendar, however, there is a clear distinction between an appointment and a meeting.

In the Outlook Calendar, an *appointment* is anything that is scheduled—a doctor's appointment, a business trip, a management meeting, a luncheon engagement, a racquetball game, and so on. A *meeting*, though, is a kind of appointment. Specifically, a meeting is an appointment in which you use the Outlook Calendar to request the attendance of other people. For example, if you plan a management meeting for two hours on Tuesday and use the Calendar to e-mail invitations to the other managers, Outlook considers this to be a meeting. If you plan the management meeting, use the telephone to call each manager to request his or her attendance, and then schedule the meeting time in the Outlook Calendar, Outlook does not consider this to be a meeting, just an appointment.

Therefore, if you schedule an activity, but don't use the Outlook Calendar to request the attendance of others, you are scheduling an appointment. If you use the Outlook Calendar to request the attendance of others at a scheduled activity, you are creating a type of appointment called a meeting. Even if you call something a meeting, Outlook might not.

Navigating Within the Calendar

When you click the Calendar shortcut on the Outlook Bar, the Calendar opens and the Day view of your schedule appears by default. This view shows the Calendar divided into four sections—the **Appointment Area**, the **Date Navigator**, the Navigation pane, and the **TaskPad**.

Figure 4-1

Outlook Calendar window

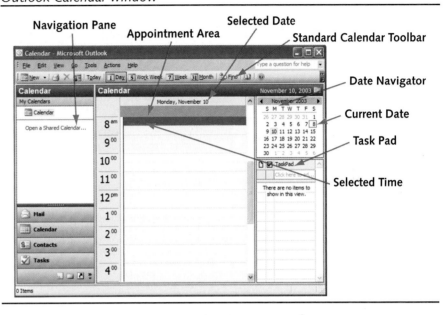

TIP

The selected date is displayed above the Appointment Area and shaded on the Date Navigator. The current date is outlined in the Date Navigator.

Section	Description
Appointment Area	The Appointment Area resembles a daily planner. Use the area to schedule activities, which can be displayed by day, work week, week, or month. By default, the workday starts at 8:00 A.M. and ends at 5:00 P.M. The time slots outside this workday period are shaded. Use the scroll bars to display entry lines for any time of the day or night.
Date Navigator	The Date Navigator displays a full-month calendar, regardless of the number of days displayed in the Appointment Area. It may be displayed on the Navigation pane on the left side of the Appointment Area or on the right side of the Appointment Area. Its location is determined by the presence or absence of the TaskPad. Scroll backward and forward through different months and years to find dates by using two different options. First, use the left or right arrows at the top of the Date Navigator to scroll backward and

(Continued)

(continued)

	forward through the months. Second, click and hold the name of the month to display a list of months and click a month in the list to display it in the Calendar. You can also click a different date in the Date Navigator to display the day in the Appointment Area.
Navigation pane	The Navigation pane enables you to move from one Outlook folder to another. It also may contain the Date Navigator, which enables you to move back and forth in time.
Task Pad	Use the TaskPad to record tasks that you want to accomplish. This function works directly with Outlook's Tasks folder.

◆ **Be sure to start Outlook before beginning this exercise.**

Navigate the Calendar

We begin this lesson by learning to navigate through the Calendar's Appointment Area and Date Navigator.

TROUBLESHOOTING

The first view displayed in this exercise may be different on your computer. Click the Day button and select TaskPad on the View menu to see the correct view.

1 **On the Navigation pane, click the Calendar button.**

The contents of the Calendar folder are displayed.

Figure 4-2

Outlook Calendar day view

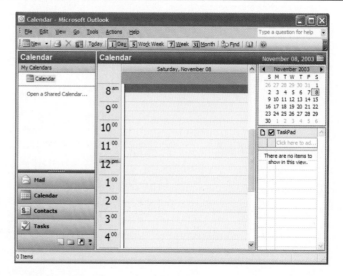

2 **In the Appointment Area, drag the scroll bar to the top.**

The Appointment Area is divided into 30-minute increments. Dark lines separate each hour. Light lines separate each half-hour. Only the start of each hour is labeled. The time slot between the hours (12:30, 1:30, etc.) isn't labeled. The day starts at 12:00 A.M.

3 **Scroll to the bottom of the Appointment Area.**

The day ends at 11:30 P.M.

4 **In the Date Navigator, click tomorrow's date.**

The Appointment Area displays tomorrow's date.

5 **At the top of the Date Navigator, click the left arrow.**

The previous month is displayed, but the date in the Appointment Area remains the same.

6 **At the top of the Date Navigator, click and hold the right arrow on the month bar for a few seconds.**

Time moves forward rapidly in the Date Navigator.

7 **In the Date Navigator, click and hold the name of one of the currently displayed months.**

A menu of months is displayed.

8 **Move the pointer to the month at the top of the list and release the mouse button.**

The Date Navigator displays the selected month.

9 **On the Standard Calendar toolbar, click the Go To Today button.**

The current day is displayed in the Appointment Area and the Date Navigator.

ANOTHER METHOD

You can quickly display a different date. Right-click in the Appointment Area, select the Go To Date option, click the Date down arrow, select a date, and click OK.

◆ **Keep Outlook open for the next exercise.**

QUICK REFERENCE ▼

Navigate through the Calendar

Use the Date Navigator to view different dates.

Changing the Calendar View

Looking at Calendars in Different Ways

THE BOTTOM LINE

Using standard views and arrangements helps you stay on top of your schedule.

Many personal planners show appointment and task information in a variety of ways. The Outlook Calendar also provides a variety of views. Although the default display in the Calendar is the Day view, you can change the view to display a **Work Week** (five business days), Week (seven days), or a Month.

Several standard arrangements are also available. Arrange your calendar by day/week/month, active appointments, events, annual events, recurring appointments, and category. To select an arrangement, open the View menu, point at Arrange By, point at Current View, and select a view.

The days of the work week are normally Monday through Friday, but you can change them to fit a different work schedule. Open the Tools menu and select Options. On the Preferences tab, click the Calendar Options button. In the Calendar Work Week section, select the check boxes of the days of the week that you want to display and click OK twice.

Change the Calendar view

Now that you are familiar with the default Calendar view you will now learn how to change the view of the Calendar.

1 On the Standard Calendar toolbar, click the Work Week button.

The five days of a standard work week are displayed in five columns.

Figure 4-3

Work week view

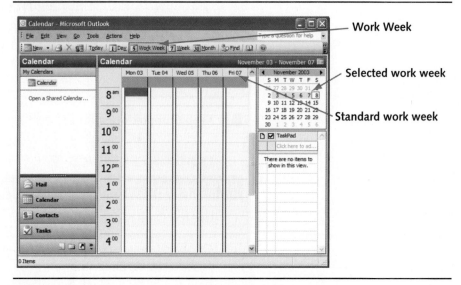

2 On the Standard Calendar toolbar, click the Week button.

The view changes to seven days.

Figure 4-4

Week view

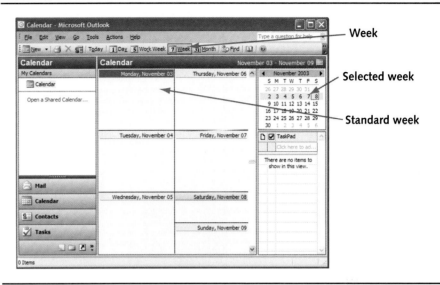

Days that are not part of the current month are shaded. You can still view activities entered for these days.

3 **On the Standard Calendar toolbar, click the Month button.**

The view changes to display a month.

Figure 4-5

Month view

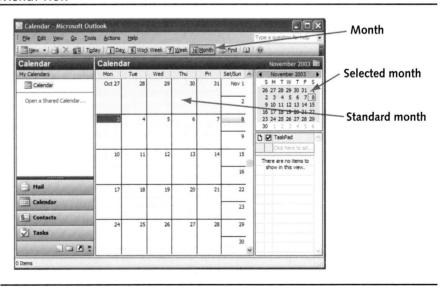

4 **On the View menu, point at Arrange By, point at Current View, and click Active Appointments.**

A list of active appointments is displayed. The list is empty if you haven't created appointments yet. Notice that the toolbar changes and a label appears above the list that tells you a filter has been applied.

Figure 4-6

Active appointments arrangement

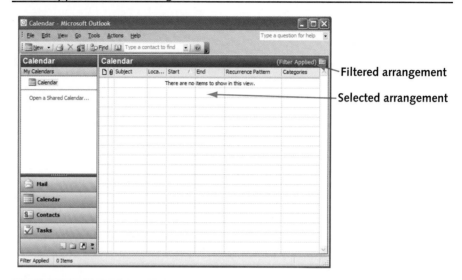

Filtered arrangement

Selected arrangement

5 **On the View menu, point to Arrange By, point to Current View, and click Day/Week/Month.**

The filter is removed. The standard calendar toolbar and the month view are displayed.

6 **On the Standard Calendar toolbar, click the Day button.**

The view returns to the day view.

◆ **Keep Outlook open for the next exercise.**

QUICK CHECK

Q: What is the difference between an appointment and a meeting?

A: **You must use Outlook to invite others to a meeting.**

QUICK REFERENCE ▼

View the Calendar

On the Navigation pane, click the Day, Week, or Month button.

Scheduling Appointments and Events

THE BOTTOM LINE

Scheduling appointments and events in Outlook helps you manage your time efficiently.

Scheduling Appointments and Events

An appointment is an activity that takes place at a scheduled time that does not require you to request the attendance of other people. Examples of appointments include meeting with a sales representative, visiting a doctor, picking up your dry cleaning, or any other activity that can be scheduled. When you enter an appointment into the Calendar, the appointment is displayed in one slot. Because the slots are measured in increments of 30 minutes, by default, an appointment takes 30 minutes to perform.

However, you can increase the duration of an appointment by dragging the top or bottom border of the blue box that surrounds the appointment entry. For example, the marketing director at Adventure Works has a doctor's appointment Monday morning at 9:00 A.M. Her doctor always seems to run at least an hour behind schedule, so the marketing director wants to specify that the appointment end at 11:00 A.M. She scheduled the appointment time by clicking the bottom border of the 9:00 A.M. time slot in the Appointment Area and dragging the border down to the top of the 11:00 A.M. time slot.

Figure 4-7

Appointment scheduled in the Appointment Area

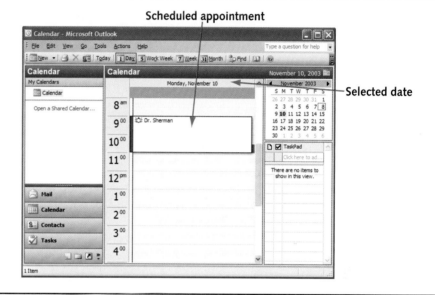

To add details to an appointment, double-click the scheduled time slot. The detailed appointment window is displayed. Enter the details that are necessary and use the Memo Area to enter notes about the appointment.

Figure 4-8

Appointment detail window

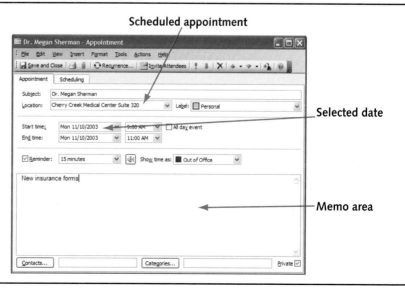

The following basic components are displayed in the window:

Component	Description
Subject	Change the topic or purpose of the appointment directly within the Appointment Area or change it in the Subject box.
Location	Use this box to identify where the appointment occurs. Outlook maintains a list of previously entered locations. Scroll through the Location box to select a previous appointment location.
Label	Assign a color to color-code appointments. This enables you to identify the type of appointment at a glance.
Start Time	Outlook uses the starting time in the Appointment Area by default. You can change the starting time in the appointment window.
End Time	Outlook automatically inserts the ending time in the Appointment Area. You can change the ending time in the appointment window.
Reminder	Use this field to specify when Outlook informs you about the meeting. The entry is based on the amount of time before the meeting. If you do not want a reminder, clear the Reminder check box.
Show Time As	Use this option to let others know that you are busy, free, or out of the office, or that the appointment is tentative.
Memo Area	Use the text area at the bottom of the dialog box to type any notes or additional reminders. If you add text to the memo area, you can see the text in the Calendar by opening the Preview pane.

You can also schedule a lengthy event in the Calendar. An **event** is a function that usually makes you unavailable for the entire day or for multiple days—such as a vacation, business trip, or an off-site seminar. Events are displayed in the Calendar as a banner at the top of the Appointment Area. You can schedule appointments and meetings during an event. For example, you could mark the next two days as an event because you will be attending a convention. You can still make appointment entries for different lectures and presentations that you will be attending during the convention. Double-click an event to open an event window, which is very similar to the appointment window.

Schedule an appointment

You will now create two appointments and one multiday event.

1 **In the Date Navigator, click the next workday.**

The Appointment Area displays the date.

TROUBLESHOOTING

A bell icon to the left of the appointment indicates that Outlook will remind you to attend the appointment. Setting reminders is discussed later in this lesson.

2 **In the Appointment Area, click the 12:00 P.M. time slot.**

The 12:00 P.M. time slot is selected.

3 **Type** Lunch with caterer **and press Enter.**

The half-hour appointment is entered.

4 **Click in the 2:00 P.M. and type** Meeting with Picnic Planning Committee. **Press Enter.**

Two appointments for tomorrow are created.

5 **Select the bottom border of the 2:00 P.M. time slot and drag the mouse pointer down to the top of the 3:30 P.M. time slot.**

Three slots are selected, indicating an hour-and-a-half appointment.

Figure 4-9

Scheduled appointments

Scheduled appointments

Selected date

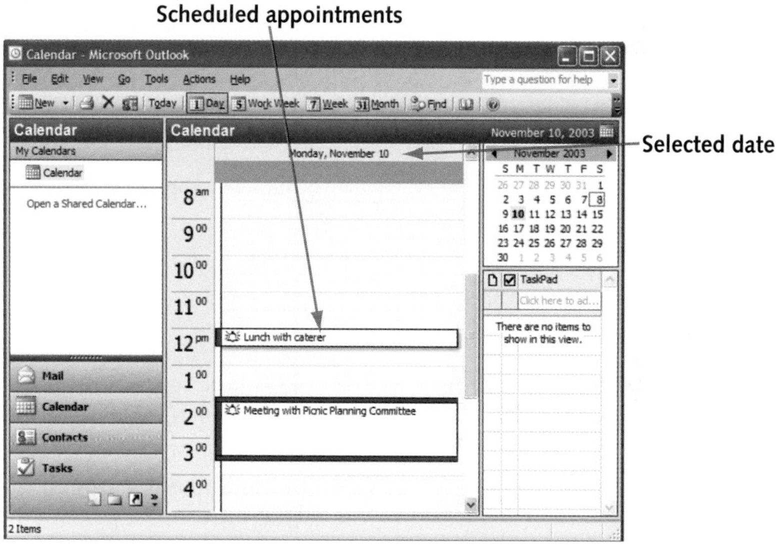

6 **In the Date Navigator, click Monday of the following week.**

The Appointment Area displays the Monday of the following week.

7 **On the Standard Calendar toolbar, click the New Appointment button.**

Open the File menu, point at New, and click Appointment.

An appointment window is displayed. The insertion point is already in the Subject box.

8 **In the Subject box, type** Vacation **and press the Tab key.**

The insertion point moves to the Location box.

9 **In the Location box, type** Hawaii **and select the All Day Event check box.**

Notice that the window is now called Vacation - Event.

10 **Click the End Time down arrow.**

A mini-calendar is displayed.

11 **In the mini-calendar, click a date two weeks from the shaded date.**

When you close the appointment window and return to the Calendar, it will display a two-week vacation.

12 **Click the Show Time As down arrow and select Out Of Office.**

Your Calendar indicates to others that you are out of the office for this two-week period.

13 **Select Personal in the Label box.**

The color you assign to an appointment indicates the type of appointment.

Figure 4-10

Vacation-Event window

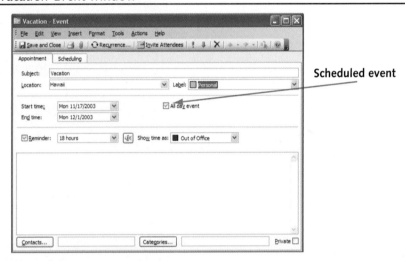

Scheduled event

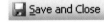

14 **On the Standard toolbar in the event window, click the Save And Close button.**

The window closes. The event, Vacation (Hawaii), is displayed at the top of the Appointment Area. In the Date Navigator, the vacation days are displayed in bold type.

Figure 4-11

Scheduled event

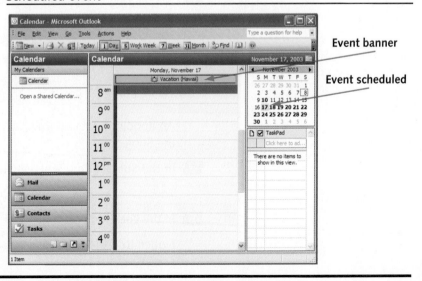

Event banner

Event scheduled

◆ **Keep Outlook open for the next exercise.**

QUICK REFERENCE ▼

Schedule an appointment

1 Enter the appointment in the Appointment Area.

2 Drag the borders to set the appointment time.

QUICK CHECK

Q: What is the difference between an appointment and an event?

A: An event lasts a day or more.

Creating Recurring Appointments

Scheduling Appointments and Events

THE BOTTOM LINE

You can create a recurring appointment to save time. Outlook enables you to schedule a regular appointment once rather than entering it every time it occurs.

Some meetings and appointments are held on a regular basis at the same time and on the same day each week. These appointments are referred to as **recurring appointments**. For example, the office manager at Adventure Works calls a supplier to place an order every Friday morning at 10:00 A.M. To remind herself of this task, she creates a recurring appointment in her calendar.

For daily appointments, you can specify whether they occur every day (Monday, Tuesday, Wednesday, Thursday, Friday, Saturday, and Sunday) or every weekday (Monday, Tuesday, Wednesday, Thursday, and Friday). For weekly appointments, you can specify the number of weeks that pass before repeating the appointment (every two weeks, for example), and the day of the week (such as every other Monday). For monthly appointments, you can specify the day of the month, and for yearly appointments, you can specify the day of the year.

Create a recurring appointment

Now you will create a recurring appointment.

1 **In the Date Navigator, select the date that is four Tuesdays into the future.**

The fourth Tuesday into the future is displayed in the Appointment Area.

TIP

When creating a recurring appointment in the Appointment Area, the date does not have to be on the same day of the week as the appointment. You can change the day of the week in the Appointment Recurrence dialog box.

2 **In the Appointment Area, click the 8:00 A.M. time slot, type** Weekly sales meeting, **and press Enter.**

The weekly sales meeting is entered as an appointment.

3 Drag the bottom border to the top of the 10:00 A.M. time slot.

Four slots are selected, indicating a two hour appointment.

4 Double-click the appointment.

The appointment window is displayed. The subject of the appointment is the same name that you just typed in the Appointment Area.

TIP

Recurring meetings, appointments, and events can be scheduled on multiple days in one week.

5 On the toolbar in the appointment window, click the Recurrence button.

The Appointment Recurrence dialog box is displayed. Notice that the appointment time is the same time you specified in the Appointment Area.

Figure 4-12

Appointment Recurrence dialog box

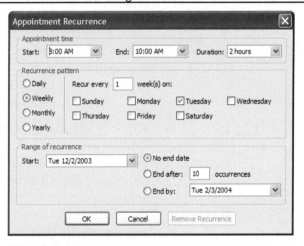

6 In the Recurrence Pattern section, click the Weekly option if necessary.

7 If necessary, select the Tuesday check box and clear the check boxes for all other days.

8 In the Range Of Recurrence section, click the End After option. In the End After box, double-click 10, and type 8.

The appointment recurs on Tuesdays for eight weeks.

TROUBLESHOOTING

If the recurring appointment conflicts with another appointment in the future, Outlook displays a warning. You can reschedule or cancel the appointment.

---

9 Click OK.

The dialog box closes and you can access the appointment window.

10 Click in the Location box and type Adventure Works Pavilion.

The information for this appointment is complete.

Figure 4-13

Recurring appointment

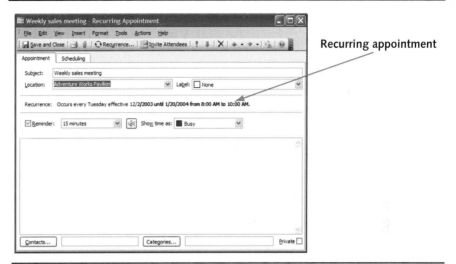

Recurring appointment

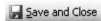

11 On the Standard toolbar in the appointment window, click the Save And Close button.

The recurring appointment is saved.

12 In the Date Navigator, click several Tuesdays into the future.

The recurring meeting message continues to appear in the Appointment Area.

13 On the Standard Calendar toolbar, click the Go To Today button.

Today's date is displayed in the Calendar.

ANOTHER METHOD

You can change an existing appointment into a recurring appointment. Double-click the existing appointment and click the Recurrence button on the Standard toolbar in the appointment window. Enter the recurrence information, click OK, and click the Save And Close button.

◆ Keep Outlook open for the next exercise.

QUICK REFERENCE ▼

Create a recurring appointment

1 Enter the appointment in the Appointment Area.

2 Double-click the appointment.

3 Click the Recurrence button.

4 Select the recurrence pattern.

5 Save the appointment.

QUICK **CHECK**

Q: Why would you schedule a recurring appointment?

A: **The appointment happens at a regular interval**

Setting Reminders

Scheduling Appointments and Events

THE BOTTOM LINE

A visual reminder and a sound can ensure that you make it to meetings on time. Give yourself time to prepare by setting the reminder to announce the appointment 10 minutes or more before the scheduled time.

When you are extremely busy or preoccupied with a particular task, you can easily forget about an upcoming appointment. With Outlook, you can let the Calendar remind you. When you set up an appointment, you can choose to be reminded before the appointment occurs. If you choose this option, you can also select when the reminder is displayed before the appointment. The appointment is displayed with a bell next to its description, indicating that you will be reminded of the appointment. You can also choose a sound that will play (if any) when the reminder is displayed on the screen. The following reminder dialog box is displayed before the appointment begins.

Figure 4-14

Reminder

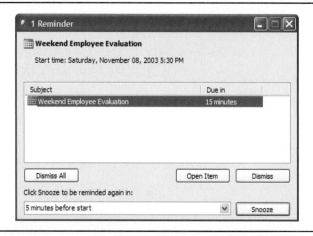

IMPORTANT

Outlook must be running to display the Reminder dialog box. If you are using a different program and Outlook is running, the Reminder dialog box is displayed on top of any open windows and documents.

Set a reminder

In this exercise, you set a reminder for the appointment *Meeting with Picnic Planning Committee* that you entered in a previous exercise.

1 **In the Date Navigator, click the next workday.**

The appointments for tomorrow are displayed.

2 Double-click the appointment Meeting with Picnic Planning Committee.

The appointment window is displayed.

3 If necessary, select the Reminder check box. In the Reminder field, select 10 minutes.

Outlook will remind you that you have an appointment 10 minutes before the scheduled appointment.

Figure 4-15

Reminder dialog box

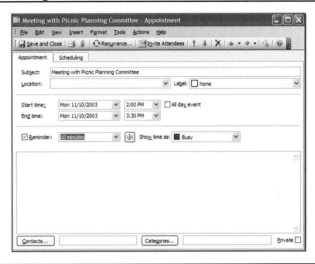

TROUBLESHOOTING

To hear the reminder sound, your computer must have a sound card and speakers that are turned on. Whether or not you have sound capabilities, Outlook still displays the Reminder dialog box.

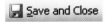

4 On the Standard toolbar in the appointment window, click the Save And Close button.

The reminder is set.

◆ Keep Outlook open for the next exercise.

QUICK REFERENCE ▼

Set a reminder

1 Double-click the appointment.

2 Select the Reminder check box.

3 Select the time period in the Reminder field.

4 Save the appointment.

Editing Appointments

Updating and Organizing
Appointments

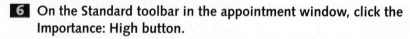

THE BOTTOM LINE

You change details about an appointment so your information is up
to date.

In addition to setting reminders for appointments, you can add information about the appointment—such as who is involved or additional topics discussed—and you can attach files for reference or mark the appointment as private. You can also set the level of importance for an appointment. By default, the level of an appointment is Medium, but you can change this to High or Low. Use the appointment window or the Appointment Area to change appointment information—such as the start and end times or the location—at any time.

For example, when the marketing director at Adventure Works meets with clients, she jots down the attendees' names and the topics she wants to discuss in the memo area of her appointment window. If her appointment has to be rescheduled for later in the day, she changes the start and end times and sets a reminder.

Edit an appointment

You will edit the appointment *Lunch with caterer* created earlier in the lesson and change the date of the appointment.

1 **Double-click the appointment "Lunch with caterer."**

The appointment window is displayed.

2 **Click in the Location box and type** Mom's Kitchen Cafe.

The location will be added to the appointment information.

3 **Click the first Start Time down arrow.**

A mini-calendar is displayed.

4 **In the mini-calendar, click the day after the currently scheduled date.**

The date of the appointment will be changed.

5 **Click the Show Time as down arrow and click Out Of Office.**

Others who view your schedule will see that you are out of the office for the appointment.

6 **On the Standard toolbar in the appointment window, click the Importance: High button.**

The importance of the appointment is elevated.

7 **In the bottom-right corner of the window, select the Private check box.**

The appointment will be considered private. Others with access to this schedule can see that there is an appointment and that you will be out of the office, but they can't see any details.

Figure 4-16

Edited appointment

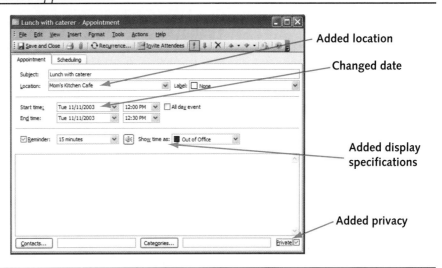

Added location

Changed date

Added display specifications

Added privacy

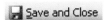

8 On the Standard toolbar in the appointment window, click the Save And Close button.

The modifications are saved.

9 On the Navigation Bar, click the day of the appointment.

The appointment is displayed on the schedule. The location of the appointment is displayed next to the subject. A key icon is displayed to the left of the subject, indicating that the appointment is private.

Figure 4-17

Additional information displayed in Appointment Area

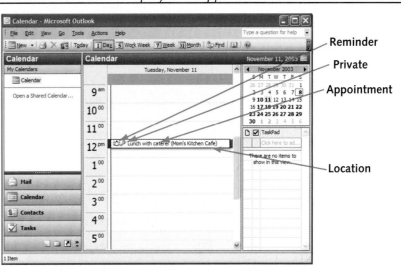

Reminder

Private

Appointment

Location

ANOTHER METHOD

Change the time or duration of an appointment in the Appointment Area by dragging an appointment from one time entry to another. In Month view, which displays multiple days, you can drag an appointment to a different day.

QUICK CHECK

Q: How do you edit an appointment?

A: Double-click the appointment, make the changes, and save the appointment again.

◆ **Keep Outlook open for the next exercise.**

QUICK REFERENCE ▼

Edit an appointment

1 Double-click the appointment.

2 Make any necessary changes.

3 Save the appointment.

Deleting Appointments

Updating and Organizing
Appointments

THE BOTTOM LINE

Keep your schedule clean and uncluttered by removing unnecessary appointments.

If an appointment is cancelled or its occurrence has already passed, you can remove the appointment from the Calendar. When you delete an appointment, it is moved to the Deleted Items folder, like e-mail messages and contacts. The deleted appointments remain there until you empty the Deleted Items folder. You can restore an appointment from the Deleted Items folder by dragging it back into the Calendar folder.

IMPORTANT

When you try to delete a recurring appointment, Outlook will ask if you want to delete the current selected appointment or all occurrences of the appointment.

Delete and restore an appointment

Working with existing appointments, you delete a normal appointment and a recurring appointment, and restore an appointment.

1 Click the appointment "Lunch with caterer."

The appointment is selected.

2 On the Standard Calendar toolbar, click the Delete button.

The appointment moves to the Deleted Items folder.

3 In the Date Navigator, click one of the Tuesdays that are displayed in bold (after the vacation days).

The recurring appointment for the selected date is displayed in the Appointment Area.

4 Click anywhere on the appointment Weekly Sales Meeting. Click the Delete button.

An alert box is displayed, as shown in Figure 4-18. It asks if you want to delete the currently selected appointment or all occurrences. If you

Figure 4-18

Confirm Delete dialog box

select the Delete All Occurrences option, Outlook deletes every occurrence of the appointment Weekly sales meeting. The option to delete this one is already selected.

5 **Click OK.**

The selected appointment is deleted, but all other occurrences remain.

6 **In the Navigation pane, click the Folder List button. When the folders are displayed, click the Deleted Items folder.**

The contents of the Deleted Items folder are displayed.

7 **Drag the appointment "Lunch with caterer" onto the Calendar button on the Navigation pane. Click the Calendar button.**

The Calendar is displayed.

8 **On the Date Navigator, click the original date for the lunch meeting with the caterer.**

Notice that the appointment *Lunch with caterer* has returned to its original date and time.

ANOTHER METHOD

You can also right-click an appointment that is not currently selected and click Delete on the shortcut menu.

◆ **Return to today's date.**

◆ **Keep Outlook open for the next exercise.**

QUICK REFERENCE ▼

Delete an appointment

1 Click the appointment.

2 On the Standard Calendar toolbar, click the Delete button.

Organizing Appointments by Using Categories

THE BOTTOM LINE

In Outlook, you can assign appointments to categories to track appointments by purpose, associated events, or other meaningful groups.

Looking at Calendars in Different Ways

Like contacts, appointments can be organized by categories to view just the appointments you need to see. In the Using Categories section of the Organize pane, you can select one of the existing categories, such as Holiday, Business, or Gifts. You can also create your own categories and assign appointments or events to the new categories.

Create and assign a category

Now will you create a category and assign a category to the appointment *Meeting with Picnic Planning Committee* that you entered in a previous exercise.

1 Open the Tools menu and click the Organize option.

The Organize pane is displayed.

Figure 4-19

Organize pane in the Calendar folder

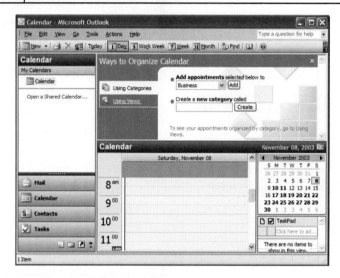

2 In the Organize pane, click in the Create A New Category Called box, type Planning and click the Create button.

The category, Planning, is created. It is displayed in the Add Appointments Selected Below To box in the Organize pane. This enables you to quickly add appointments to the new category. Later, you can use the category to locate an appointment.

3 In the Date Navigator, locate and click the appointment "Meeting with Picnic Planning Committee."

The appointment is selected.

4 In the Organize pane, click the Add button.

The appointment is assigned to the Planning category.

Figure 4-20

Appointment assigned to a category

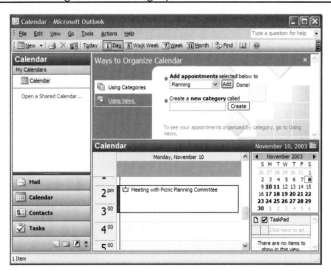

ANOTHER METHOD

Double-click any appointment. Enter the category in the Categories field and save the appointment.

◆ **Keep Outlook and the Organize pane open for the next exercise.**

QUICK REFERENCE ▼

Assign an appointment to a category

1 Open the Tools menu and click the Organize option.

2 In the Organize pane, elect an existing category or create a new category.

3 In the calendar, select the appointment.

4 In the Organize pane, click the Add button.

Organizing Appointments by Using Arrangements

THE BOTTOM LINE

Outlook's Arrangements feature helps you keep track of appointments by displaying those that meet specific requirements.

Looking at Calendars
in Different Ways

You've already used the basic arrangements to view Calendar items. With Outlook, you can also determine which appointments are displayed in the Calendar so that you see only a specific type of appointment or only appointments for a particular period. Arrangements include Active Appointments, Events, Annual Events, Recurring Appointments, and By Category. Changing the view in this manner enables you to quickly identify a particular type of appointment. For example, if you want to see only appointments that require a full day or multiple days, display the Calendar Events arrangement. If you've assigned appointments to different categories, view appointments by category so you can identify related appointments. To view a different arrangement, use the Organize pane or on the View menu, point at Arrange By, point at the Current View option and select the desired arrangement.

Display different Calendar views

Next you will use the Organize pane to display appointments in different arrangements.

1 In the Organize pane, click the Using Views link.

The Using Views section of the Organize pane is displayed.

Figure 4-21

Using Views option in the Organize pane

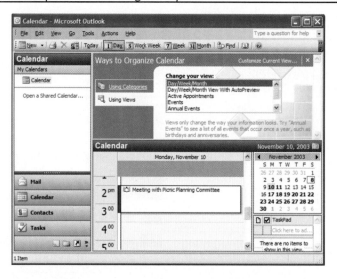

2 In the Change Your View list, select By Category.

The appointments are divided into categories displayed below the Organize pane. Each bar identifies the number of items in the category. The Planning category contains one item.

Figure 4-22

View appointments by category

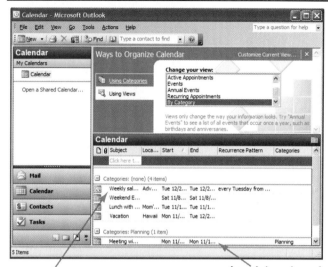

Appointments not assigned to a category

Appointments assigned to a category

TIP

If necessary, scroll to view the entire list of appointments.

---

3 If necessary, click the plus sign (+) on the left side of the Planning gray bar.

The appointment you added to the Planning category in the previous exercise is displayed.

4 In the Organize pane, click Recurring Appointments in the Change Your View list.

Only recurring appointments are displayed.

Figure 4-23

View recurring appointments

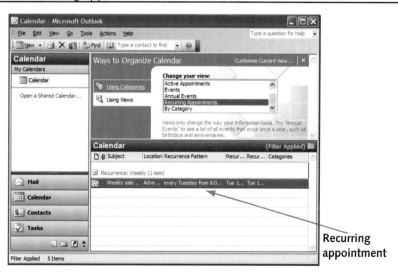

Recurring appointment

5 In the Change Your View list, click Active Appointments.

All upcoming appointments are displayed in table format.

Figure 4-24

View active appointments

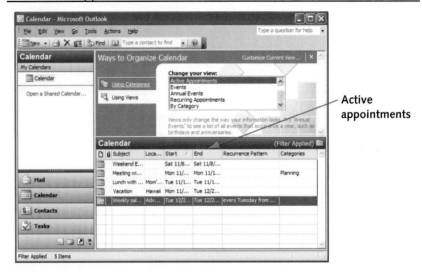

Active appointments

6 In the Change Your View list, click Day/Week/Month.

The view returns to the default Calendar view.

7 In the Tools menu, click the Organize option.

The Organize pane closes.

◆ Keep Outlook open for the next exercise.

QUICK REFERENCE ▼

Display an arrangement

1 Open the Tools menu and click the Organize option.

2 Click Using Views in the Organize pane.

3 Select a view in the Change Your View list.

Planning Meetings

THE BOTTOM LINE

Planning meetings and gathering the participants into a single time and location can be difficult. Outlook's scheduling functions can help you match up available times, locations, and resources.

Scheduling Meetings

Arranging a time for a meeting can be difficult because you have to coordinate multiple schedules. You can play phone tag all day with your prospective meeting attendees, attempting to schedule them for a commonly available meeting time, or you can use the Outlook Calendar.

Sending a Meeting Request

Scheduling Meetings

When you set up a meeting in Outlook, you send each prospective attendee a meeting request. For each prospective attendee, you can specify that his or her attendance is required or optional. (If you specified that a particular attendee's attendance is required and he or she declines the invitation to attend the meeting, you need to reschedule it.) The meeting request is an e-mail message that tells people what the meeting is about, where it will be held, and when the meeting will take place.

IMPORTANT

In an Exchange Server environment, Outlook makes it easy to view co-workers' busy schedules and enable them to view your schedule. You can't see the actual appointments for other people on your network, but you can see the time periods that have been blocked off as busy for a particular employee. This approach helps to ensure that you have scheduled a meeting for a time that is available to all your prospective attendees. When you send your meeting requests via e-mail in this environment, you are more likely to receive acceptances from most or all of the prospective attendees.

Send a meeting request

To practice scheduling a meeting, you will create a meeting and invite your class partner to the meeting. In the next exercise you will respond to your partner's meeting request.

1 On the Date Navigator, click the last Monday of next month and click the 9:00 A.M. time slot.

The last Monday of next month is displayed in the Appointment Area.

2 On the Standard Calendar toolbar, click the down arrow to the right of the New Appointment button, and select the Meeting Request option.

The meeting window is displayed.

Figure 4-25

Meeting Request window

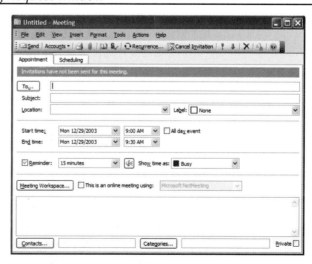

3 **Click the To button.**

The Select Attendees And Resources dialog box is displayed.

Figure 4-26

Select Attendees And Resources dialog box

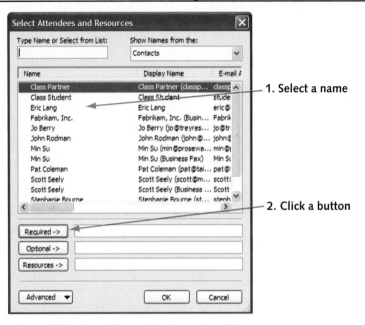

4 **Select your class partner's name, click the Required button, and click OK.**

The meeting window becomes active. Your class partner's name is now in the To box.

5 **Click in the Subject box, type Client Review meeting, and press Tab.**

The insertion point moves to the Location box.

6 **In the Location box, type Conference Room 3.**

The date, start time, and end time are already specified.

7 **Click in the memo box and type I'm looking forward to discussing the project's requirements.**

TIP

To invite attendees who are not required to attend a meeting, click the attendee and click the Optional button.

Figure 4-27

Meeting request

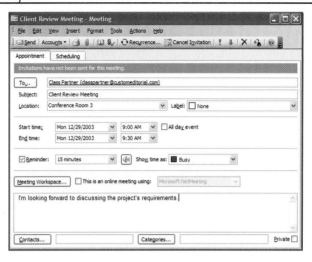

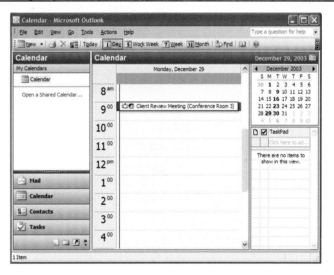

8 On the Standard toolbar in the meeting window, click the Send button.

The meeting request is sent to your class partner. The meeting is displayed in the Calendar with a bell icon (indicating that a reminder has been set) and an icon that resembles two heads (indicating that other people are invited to the meeting).

Figure 4-28

The meeting request has been sent

ANOTHER METHOD

If necessary, after a meeting has been set up in the Calendar, you can add and remove attendees. Double-click the meeting, open the Actions menu, and click Add Or Remove Attendees to display the Select Attendees And Resources dialog box. To delete an attendee, click the attendee in the Message Recipients list and press the Delete key. To add

ANOTHER METHOD (continued)

an attendee, click the attendee's name in the Name list and click the Required or Optional button. When you are finished, click OK and click the Save And Close button on the Standard toolbar. In the alert box, you can choose to send updates to attendees.

9 **In the Appointment Area, click the meeting. On the Standard toolbar, click the Delete button.**

An alert box is displayed, stating that attendees have not been notified that the meeting has been cancelled. You can either send a cancellation and delete the message or delete the meeting in your calendar without sending a cancellation.

10 **Click the Delete without sending a cancellation option and click OK.**

The meeting is deleted.

IMPORTANT

You deleted this message for training purposes. Normally, you would not delete a meeting you just organized (unless you made a mistake). You need to delete the meeting because you will receive a meeting request to attend this same meeting from your class partner. You need to have this time open so that Outlook will not find a scheduling conflict.

◆ **Keep Outlook open for the next exercise.**

QUICK REFERENCE ▼

Send a meeting request

1 On the Standard Calendar toolbar, click the down arrow to the right of the New Appointment button, and select the Meeting Request option.

2 Select the attendees and resources.

3 Identify the subject, location, and time of the meeting.

4 Click the Send button.

Responding to a Meeting Request

Responding to Meeting Requests

When somebody sends you a meeting request via e-mail, a message is displayed that includes buttons that you can use to accept, decline, tentatively accept the invitation, or propose a new time for the meeting. If you accept, the meeting is added to your calendar and an e-mail response accepting the invitation is sent to the meeting organizer. If you decline, you can choose to decline with or without a response. For example, you might want to decline, but let the person who sent the meeting request know when you are available. If you select the Tentative option, the meeting is added to your calendar, but your time for the meeting is classified as tentatively scheduled. Select the Tentative response if you think you can attend the meeting, but something more important may require your attention at that time.

The last option for responding to a meeting request is Propose New Time. Select this option if you can't meet at the time selected by the sender requesting the meeting, but you can attend at a different time or date. For example, a co-worker requests a meeting for 1:00 PM tomorrow. However, you have a lunch meeting scheduled that you think could run a little long. Send a response to the meeting request that proposes the new meeting time of 2:00 PM.

Respond to a meeting request

In this exercise, you receive a meeting request from your class partner and propose a new time for the meeting.

1 **Open the Go menu and click Mail. If necessary, click the Inbox in the Navigation pane.**

The contents of the Inbox are displayed.

2 **On the Standard Mail toolbar, click the Send/Receive button.**

A meeting request from your class partner arrives in the Inbox.

3 **Click the meeting request.**

The meeting request opens in the Reading pane.

Figure 4-29

The meeting request has been received

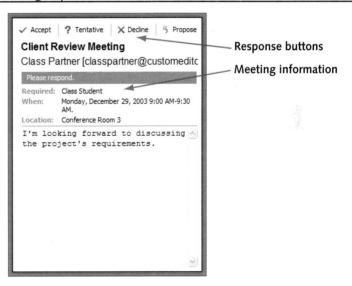

4 **On the message, click the Propose button.**

The Propose New Time dialog box is displayed.

TROUBLESHOOTING

A dialog box inviting you to join a Microsoft service that enables you to view calendars for other members may be displayed. Click Cancel in the dialog box to continue.

Figure 4-30

Propose New Time dialog box

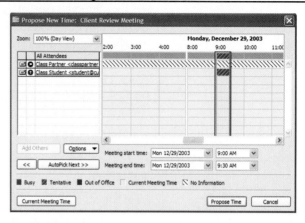

5 **Drag the borders of the current meeting time to the right to propose the new time of 10:00 A.M. to 10:30 A.M. Click the Propose Time button.**

An e-mail response is created. It contains the current time and the proposed time. You can add text to the body of the e-mail.

Figure 4-31

New time proposed for meeting

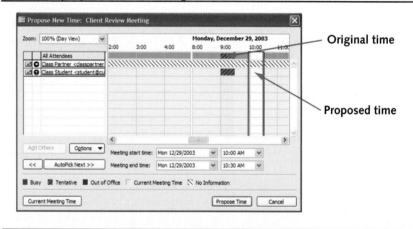

TROUBLESHOOTING

If you had accepted the meeting, your class partner would have received an e-mail with the subject Accepted: Client Review meeting. The meeting would be scheduled in your calendar.

6 **On the Message toolbar, click the Send button.**

The e-mail containing the proposed time is sent to your class partner. Your response is considered to be a "tentative acceptance." Your class partner is responsible for rescheduling the meeting and sending a new meeting request.

Figure 4-32

Message proposing a new time for meeting

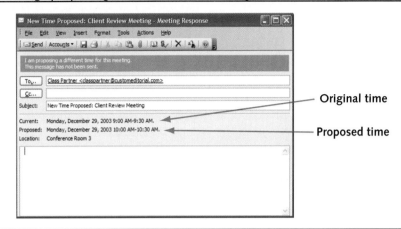

Original time

Proposed time

◆ **Keep Outlook open for the next exercise.**

QUICK REFERENCE ▼

Respond to a meeting request

1 In the Inbox, click the meeting request.

2 On the meeting request, click a button to accept, decline, or propose a new time.

3 If you propose a new time, drag the borders to the new time and click Propose Time. If you accept or decline the meeting, indicate in the alert box if you wish to include comments with your response.

4 Click the Send button.

Reserving Meeting Resources

Scheduling Meetings

In addition to inviting people to meetings, you can schedule resources, such as conference rooms, flip charts, or computers. For example, when the office manager at Adventure Works scheduled the budget review meeting for the president, she booked a large conference room and an overhead projector through Outlook.

To schedule a resource, the resource must have its own mailbox on your server. One person, usually the office manager, sets up and administers the mailbox for the resource. The resource is self-sufficient because it automatically accepts and rejects invitations. For example, if you attempt to reserve a conference room for a particular time period but somebody has already reserved the conference room, your meeting request will be rejected for the conference room resource.

To reserve a resource, invite it to the meeting, just as you would invite a person. In the Select Attendees And Resources dialog box, click the resource, and click the Resources button. The resource is added to your message list. If the resource you scheduled is free, the meeting is automatically entered in the resource's calendar so that no one else can reserve the same resource at the same time.

QUICK CHECK

Q: Why would you invite a conference room to a meeting?

A: It reserves the resource for the meeting.

QUICK REFERENCE ▼

Reserve meeting resources

1 On the Standard Calendar toolbar, click the down arrow to the right of the New Appointment button, and select the Meeting Request option.

2 Select the resources.

3 Identify the subject, location, and time of the meeting.

4 Click the Send button.

Printing Calendars

Printing Calendars

THE BOTTOM LINE

Print a calendar to take with you or distribute to others who can't access your schedule electronically.

Many people who use Outlook as their scheduling tool like to take a printed copy of their schedule with them when they leave their desk or their office. As you might expect, Outlook provides several printing options for your Calendar. Specifically, you can print different views of the Calendar, such as a daily, weekly, or monthly view. Use the Print dialog box to specify the range of days and style that you want to print. The Print dialog box includes five styles:

- Daily—The days that you specify will be printed. The printout contains one day per page.
- Weekly—The weeks that you specify will be printed. The printout contains one week per page.
- Monthly—The months that you specify will be printed. The printout contains one month per page.
- Tri-fold—The printout is divided into three columns. The first column contains a day view. The second column is the TaskPad. The third column is a week view.
- Calendar Details—Appointments, meetings, and events scheduled in the Calendar are described and listed under the day they occur.

The events coordinator at Adventure Works likes to attach a printout of a calendar in the Monthly Style to her newsletter. The calendar notifies readers of upcoming events at the resort.

Print a calendar

Sometimes, after you create appointments in your calendar, you need a printed copy of your schedule. In this exercise, you specify print options and print a two-month calendar in the Monthly Style.

1 **On the Standard Calendar toolbar, click the Print button.**

The Print dialog box is displayed.

Figure 4-33

Print dialog box

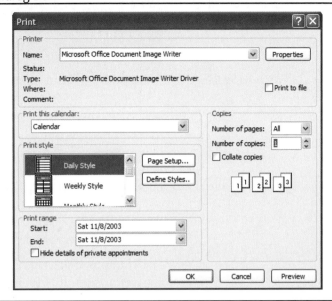

Q: Can you print a calendar for a specific day?

A: **You can specify the time period before you print a calendar.**

2 **In the Print Style section, click Monthly Style. In the Print Range section, click the Start down arrow.**

A mini-calendar is displayed.

3 **Click the first day of this month. Also in the Print Range section, click the End down arrow.**

A mini-calendar is displayed.

4 **Click the last day of next month and click OK.**

The Print dialog box closes and a two-month calendar prints in the Monthly Style.

ANOTHER METHOD

You can also print the Calendar in a Day-Timer or a Franklin Day Planner format. In the Print dialog box, click the Page Setup button, click the Paper tab, and select the desired page size in the Size list.

◆ **Keep Outlook open for the next exercise.**

QUICK REFERENCE ▼

Print a calendar

1 On the Standard Calendar toolbar, click the Print button.

2 Select the printing options.

3 Click OK.

Saving a Calendar as a Web Page

Saving a Calendar as a Web Page

THE BOTTOM LINE

With Outlook you can create a calendar that can be viewed by others on the Internet or your intranet.

Save your calendar as a Web page so people can access your calendar via the Internet or a company intranet. When you save a calendar as a Web page, Outlook converts the calendar to HTML (Hypertext Markup Language) format. HTML is the formatting language that all Web browsers (such as Microsoft Internet Explorer) use to display text and graphics. A calendar can be placed on a Web site or it can remain in a file that others can download for later access. When you save a calendar as a Web page, you can specify the calendar time frame that you want to share, include appointment details, or add a background.

For example, the events coordinator at Adventure Works used to attach a copy of the monthly events calendar to the employee newsletter. However, after the company's intranet was established, she began to post the calendar to the company's Web site.

Save your Calendar

With a calendar created, you will now save your Calendar as a Web page.

1 On the File menu, click Save As Web Page.

The Save As Web Page dialog box is displayed.

2 In the Duration section, click the Start Date down arrow and click the first day of the current month. Click the End Date down arrow and click the last day of the current month.

This selects the time period for the calendar. Only the current month will be saved.

3 In the Calendar Title box, type your name (if necessary), press the spacebar, and type Class Calendar.

4 Click the Browse button.

The Calendar File Name dialog box is displayed.

5 Click the Save In down arrow, and navigate to the Outlook Practice folder.

You will store the calendar in this directory.

6 In the File Name box, type MyClassCalendar.

The HTML file will be named MyClassCalendar. Commonly, the name of the file may include your name and the time period covered by the calendar.

CHECK THIS OUT ▼

Sending Schedules
You can save a schedule as a Web page so you can send it as an attachment to a message.

IMPORTANT

Do not include any spaces when you name a Web page file. If the name of the file is part of a Web address (such as www.calendars.microsoft.com/MyClassCalendar.htm), the space will not be recognized and the file can't be viewed on the Web.

7 Click the Select button.

The Save As Web Page dialog box becomes active.

Figure 4-34

Save As Web Page dialog box

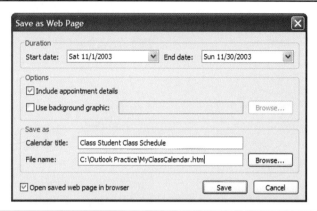

> **IMPORTANT**
>
> If Internet Explorer does not automatically display the Web calendar, you can manually open the calendar through Windows Explorer. Display Windows Explorer. Navigate to the location you selected to store the files. Many files were created as a result of saving the Web calendar. Double-click the main HTML file. Internet Explorer opens and displays the Web calendar.

8 Click the Save button.

The calendar is saved as a Web page that can be displayed in Internet Explorer. By default, the Web page is displayed immediately.

Figure 4-35

Calendar displayed as a Web page

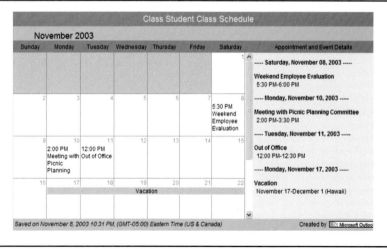

 9 In the top-right corner of the Internet Explorer window, click the Close button.

QUICK CHECK

Q: In what format is a
calendar saved to
become a Web page?

A: **The calendar is saved in
HTML format.**

QUICK REFERENCE ▼

Save a calendar as a Web page

1 On the File menu, click Save As Web Page.

2 Select the time period and enter a name for the Web page.

3 Select the file destination.

4 Save the file.

Integrating the Calendar with Other Outlook Components

THE BOTTOM LINE

Outlook's TaskPad lets you create tasks, keep track of their progress, and mark when they are complete.

Creating and Updating Tasks

The Calendar includes the Appointment Area, Date Navigator, and TaskPad. Use the Appointment Area and the Date Navigator to schedule appointments and meetings. Use the TaskPad to enter task descriptions, such as creating a weekly status report or listing phone calls that you need to make. Each row on the TaskPad indicates a separate task. The tasks in Calendar are also displayed in the Outlook Tasks folder, which you can access by clicking the Tasks button on the Navigation pane.

Create and complete a task

In this exercise, you create a task and mark it as completed.

1 **In the TaskPad, click in the box that contains the text Click Here To Add A New Task.**

The text is replaced with a blank line and an insertion point.

2 **Type Call park about picnic and press Enter.**

The task *Call park about picnic* is displayed in the task list.

Figure 4-36

Task list

Tasks

3 **On the Navigation pane, click the Tasks button.**

The contents of the Tasks folder are displayed. The task *Call park about picnic* is displayed in the task list.

Figure 4-37

Tasks folder

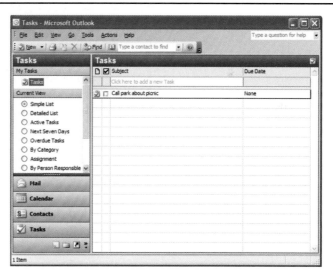

Figure 4-38

Task completed in the Calendar folder

4 **On the Navigation pane, click the Calendar button.**

The contents of the Calendar folder are displayed.

5 **In the TaskPad, select the check box to the left of the task.**

A check is displayed in the check box and the task has a strikeout line through it, as shown in Figure 4-38.

6 On the Navigation pane, click the Tasks button.

The contents of the Tasks folder are displayed. The task *Call park about picnic* also has a line through it.

ANOTHER METHOD

Create a task in the Tasks folder and view it in the Calendar's TaskPad.

◆ On the Navigation pane, click the Calendar button.

◆ If you are continuing to the next lesson, keep Outlook open.

◆ If you are not continuing to the next lesson, close Outlook.

QUICK REFERENCE ▼

Create and complete a task

1 In the TaskPad, click in the box that contains the text Click Here To Add A New Task.

2 Type the task and press Enter.

3 In the TaskPad, select the check box to the left of the task.

4 Save the file.

Key Points

✔ *In Outlook, you can navigate through the Calendar, change views, and create and edit appointments and events.*

✔ *You can create recurring appointments and meetings as well as set reminders to yourself.*

✔ *Appointments and meetings can be organized by category and views.*

✔ *Through Outlook you can plan meetings with others and send meeting invitations by e-mail.*

✔ *Outlook lets you print a calendar and save the calendar as a Web page.*

✔ *The task list lets you keep track of items which you need to complete. As you accomplish the tasks you can mark them as complete.*

Quick Quiz

True/False

T   F   1. All tasks must be created in the Tasks folder.

T   F   2. Appointments cannot be assigned to a category.

T   F   3. Calendars can only be distributed to others by printing.

T   F   4. The Date Navigator enables you to view a date six months in the future.

T   F   5. Recurring appoints must be scheduled for the same day every week.

Multiple Choice

1. To view a different date, use the _____.
   a. Navigation pane
   b. Date Navigator
   c. TaskPad
   d. All of the above

2. Propose a new meeting time _____.
   a. every time you receive a meeting request
   b. by clicking the Accept button
   c. by clicking the Propose button in a meeting request
   d. All of the above

3. The Calendar enables you to _____.
   a. plan meetings
   b. set recurring appointments
   c. schedule appointments
   d. All of the above

4. A(n) _____ is a function that usually makes you unavailable for the entire day or for multiple days.
   a. recurring appointment
   b. meeting
   c. event
   d. appointment

5. Organize your calendar by _____.
   a. assigning appointments to categories
   b. saving it as a Web page
   c. printing it
   d. All of the above

Short Answer

1. How do you invite others to a meeting?
2. What is the Appointment Area?
3. Time slots in the Calendar are divided into what increment of time?
4. Can you change the Work Week view to include days other than Monday through Friday?
5. What is the Date Navigator?
6. In what styles can you print a calendar?
7. What are two ways you can view a calendar?
8. What is a recurring appointment?
9. How can you tell that you will be reminded of a meeting?
10. In addition to printing your calendar, how can you make it accessible to others?

On Your Own

Exercise 1

The marketing director at Adventure Works wants to get her team on board for the new ad campaign. She wants to schedule a weekly team meeting on Fridays from 10:00 A.M. until noon in Conference Room 2 for the next four months. At the meeting, they will discuss the progress and status of the ad campaign project. Schedule this as a meeting, invite any member of your class to attend, and indicate that this class member's attendance is required.

Exercise 2

The marketing director will be taking a vacation to Tahiti after the ad campaign project is underway—five months from now. She wants anyone who looks at her schedule to know that she is out of the office for the two weeks she is in Tahiti. Schedule this event for a two-week period five months from now.

One Step Further

Exercise 1

You have been placed in charge of the company picnic. Make a list of tasks you must perform before the picnic. Mark three of the tasks as completed.

Exercise 2

Your company recently announced a new intranet. Your supervisor requests that everyone in her department place their calendars on the intranet. Prepare your calendar and save it as a Web page.

Exercise 3

You will be conducting interviews for a new receptionist. Schedule the following appointments.

Monday	8:30 A.M.	Aaron Con
Monday	10:00 A.M.	Jim Hance
Tuesday	1:00 P.M.	Britta Simon
Tuesday	2:30 P.M.	Debra E. Keiser
Wednesday	9:00 A.M.	Bradley Beck

Using Tasks

After completing this lesson, you will be able to:

✔ *Create tasks in Outlook.*
✔ *Change the task view.*
✔ *Add task details.*
✔ *Sort tasks.*
✔ *Print a task list*
✔ *Organize tasks by using folders.*
✔ *Organize tasks by using categories.*
✔ *Assign tasks to others.*
✔ *Accept or decline tasks.*
✔ *Mark tasks as complete.*
✔ *Manually record a task in the Journal.*
✔ *Delete tasks.*

KEY TERMS

- Journal
- owner
- ownership
- task
- task list
- Tasks folder

Sometimes, a project can be so big that it seems overwhelming. It can become difficult to keep track of everything you have to do each day. A to-do list is a great way to manage big projects and your daily activities. Seeing a list of the things you have to do helps you organize and prioritize more efficiently. Breaking a large project into smaller tasks makes it seem more manageable and ensures that you won't forget a critical step. Also, checking off the items creates a sense of accomplishment. For example, the marketing director at Adventure Works creates a daily list of things to do based on her current activities, special projects, and obligations to friends, family, and business associates.

The Microsoft Office Outlook 2003 task list provides a place for you to record a to-do list or track tasks required to complete a project. In Lesson 4, you saw the TaskPad that appears in the Calendar. When you make entries in the Calendar TaskPad, the entries are also recorded in the task list, which provides several options for organizing and viewing tasks that are not available in the Calendar TaskPad.

In this lesson, you will learn how to enter a **task**—a personal or work item to be completed. You will add details to a task, mark tasks as complete, and delete a task in the **Tasks folder**. You will sort and organize tasks by using folders and categories. Finally, you will learn how to assign tasks to others, accept or decline tasks assigned to you, mark tasks as complete, and manually record a task in the Journal.

Creating Tasks

THE BOTTOM LINE

With Outlook you can create a task list that can keep you on-track in completing any project.

Creating and Updating Tasks

Tasks can be as basic as a to-do list of personal errands, such as grocery shopping, picking the kids up at baseball practice, and going to doctor appointments. They can also be as elaborate as a list of milestones that need to be completed during a lengthy or complex work project. Breaking down a project into tasks helps you keep track of items that are accomplished and items that still need attention.

To create a **task list**, identify your priorities. Decide exactly what needs to be done and know the dates the task items are due. Some tasks are more important than others. If possible, the most important tasks should be completed first. Sometimes, the most difficult part of a task is deciding how to break it into smaller, more manageable steps or additional and more specific tasks. Finally, you can assign a due date. Although you do not need to give a task a due date, a due date keeps tasks in order and keeps you aware of deadlines.

Click the Tasks button on the Navigation pane to display the task list in the default view, called Simple List. The task list is divided into Subject and Due Date columns. Tasks that are overdue are displayed in red; tasks that you have completed appear with a strikeout line through them.

Figure 5-1

Outlook Tasks window

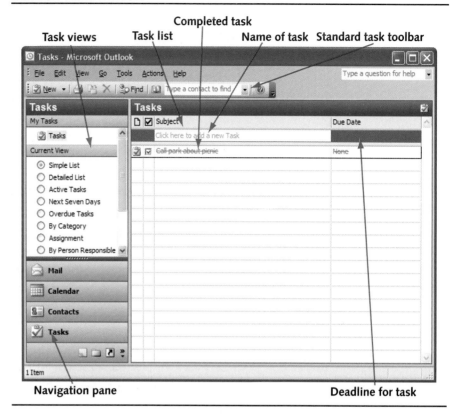

You can create a task in one of four ways—click the New Task button on the standard toolbar, type in the TaskPad window in the Calendar, type a task in the task list, or drag an item to the Tasks button on the Navigation pane.

◆ **Be sure to start Outlook before you begin exercise.**

Create tasks

We will begin the exercises in this lesson by creating four tasks using the task list.

1 **On the Navigation pane, click the Tasks button.**

The contents of the task folder are displayed.

2 **Click in the box that contains the text "Click here to add a new Task." Type** Call band to check availability for the picnic.

This will become the name of the task.

3 **To the right of the task that you just created, click in the Due Date column.**

The insertion point and a down arrow are displayed in the Due Date column.

TIP

To access other months, click the arrows to the right and left of the month.

4 Click the down arrow to display the mini-calendar.

The current month and year are displayed and today's date is shaded.

5 Click the Today button.

Today's date is entered in the Due Date column.

6 Press Enter.

The new task is placed in the task list. The insertion point remains in the first row of the Subject column to add more tasks.

7 Type Make a dentist appointment for Emily. **Press Enter.**

The new task is placed in the task list and the insertion point remains in the first row of the Subject column. A due date is not assigned.

8 Type Call Cherry Creek Park to reserve sheltered picnic area. **To the right of the task, click in the Due Date column.**

The insertion point and a down arrow are displayed in the Due Date column.

9 Click the down arrow to display the mini-calendar. Click the date four days from today. Press Enter.

The date four days from today is placed in the Due Date column. The new task is placed in the task list and the insertion point remains in the first row of the Subject column.

10 Type Complete the Outlook class. **Press Enter.**

The new task is placed in the task list.

Figure 5-2

Tasks added to the task list

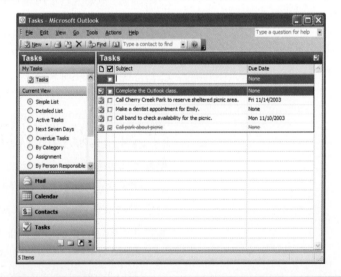

ANOTHER METHOD

Drag an item to the Tasks button on the Navigation pane.

◆ **Keep Outlook open for the next exercise.**

QUICK REFERENCE ▼

Create a task

1 On the Navigation pane, click the Tasks button.

2 Click in the box that contains the text "Click here to add a new Task."

3 Enter the name of the task.

4 Optionally, enter additional details.

5 Press Enter.

Changing Task Views

Organizing Tasks

THE BOTTOM LINE

When you use different views of your tasks it can help you focus your priorities.

As you learned in previous lessons, when you change the view of a folder, new criteria determine how items are displayed. The same is true for the task list. Different views can present your tasks in greater or more meaningful detail. For example, you might want to display only tasks that are due on a specific day. In the past, you had to use the View menu to change the view of the task list. The Navigation pane has streamlined this into a single click.

When you change the task list view, different columns are displayed. This makes it an excellent organization tool. Focus on tasks due today or this week. Improve your long-term planning by increasing your awareness of upcoming due dates.

You can change details about a task by clicking the appropriate column. If you click in the Importance, Due Date, Date Complete, or Status column, a down arrow is displayed. Click the down arrow to display a list of available options.

Change the task view

Continuing to work with the tasks we entered in the previous exercise, you will change the view of the task list several times.

1 **Click the Detailed List option in the Current View area of the Navigation pane.**

This view contains information about the status, percent complete, and categories for each task.

Figure 5-3

Detailed task list contains additional information

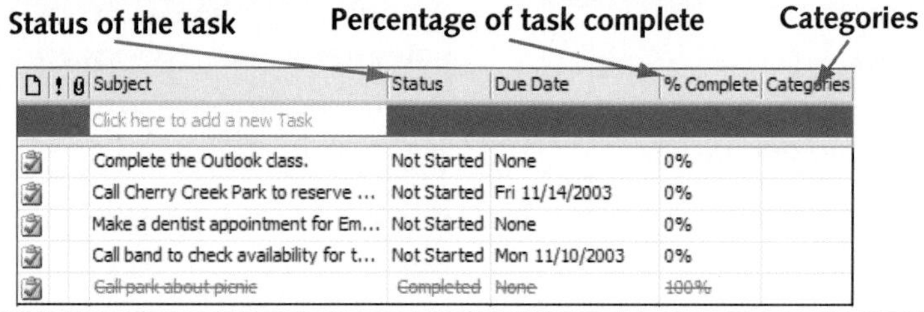

Status of the task
Percentage of task complete
Categories
Subject
Status
Due Date
% Complete
Categories
Click here to add a new Task
Complete the Outlook class.
Not Started
None
0%
Call Cherry Creek Park to reserve ...
Not Started
Fri 11/14/2003
0%
Make a dentist appointment for Em...
Not Started
None
0%
Call band to check availability for t...
Not Started
Mon 11/10/2003
0%
Call park about picnic
Completed
None
100%

2 **Click the Next Seven Days option in the Current View area of the Navigation pane.**

This view contains information about tasks that are due in the next seven days. Because this view applies a filter, tasks without a due date are not displayed.

Figure 5-4

Tasks due in the next seven days

Subject
Status
Due Date
% Complete
Categories
Call band to check availability for t...
Not St...
Mon 11/10/2003
0%
Call Cherry Creek Park to reserve s...
Not St...
Fri 11/14/2003
0%

3 **Click the Task Timeline option in the Current View area of the Navigation pane.**

This view contains a unique look at the task list. Again, tasks without a due date are not displayed.

TROUBLESHOOTING

You might need to scroll to view both items.

Figure 5-5

Task timeline view

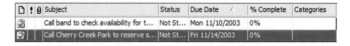

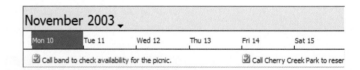

November 2003
Mon 10
Tue 11
Wed 12
Thu 13
Fri 14
Sat 15
Call band to check availability for the picnic.
Call Cherry Creek Park to reser

◆ **Return to the Detailed List view for the next exercise.**

QUICK CHECK

Q: Why is selecting a different view a good organization tool?

A: **It enables you to focus on different columns of information.**

ANOTHER METHOD

Open the View menu, point at Arrange By, point at Current View, and click one of the available views.

QUICK REFERENCE ▼

Change the task view

Click one of the view options in the Navigation pane.

Adding Task Details

Creating and Updating Tasks

THE BOTTOM LINE

When you include details such as due dates, status, and percent complete it can help you view and organize your task list in ways that will help you achieve your goals.

Often the Simple List view for the task list does not show all the columns you need for adding information about a more complicated task. For example, the marketing director at Adventure Works set up a task to create a project plan for the upcoming advertising campaign. Because this task is crucial to the project, it has a high priority and a definite due date. The marketing director created the task, assigned the task a high priority flag, assigned a due date, and assigned the task to a category.

When you want to add several details to a task, it's often easiest to use the task window or switch to the Detailed List view. The task window has two tabs—Task and Details. Most of the information that is displayed in the task list is on the Task tab. The Details tab contains boxes to add information regarding the actual hours of work needed to complete a task, data about mileage and billing, and information regarding any companies involved with the task.

Figure 5-6

Task window

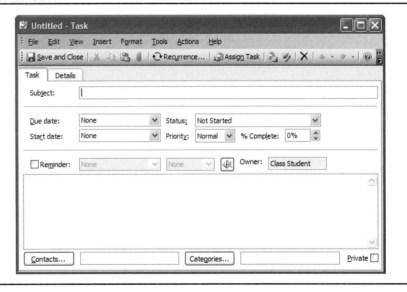

The task window is displayed when you double-click a task or click the New Task button. In the task window, the boxes on the Task tab correspond to the column headings displayed in the different task list views. The options you select in these boxes or the information you enter can be used as criteria for organizing your tasks. Some of the options on the Task tab are described in the following table.

Box/Button	Description
Subject	The text of the task is the Subject. You can change the task by editing it here.
Due date	Specify a deadline for completing the task.
Start date	Set a date for beginning the task.
Status	Mark a task's progress as Not Started, In Progress, Completed, Waiting On Someone Else, or Deferred.
Priority	Set the importance of the task to Low, Normal, or High.
% Complete	Indicate the amount of work done on a task. Enter any percentage from 0% to 100%. The task status changes to reflect the percentage.
Reminder	Identify the length of time between the reminder and the due date. If you don't want to be reminded, clear the Reminder check box. Click the appropriate down arrows to display a list of dates or times.
Owner	Identify the person responsible for the task. By default, the task creator is the task owner.
memo area	Use the text area at the bottom of the window to record notes or additional reminders.
Contacts	Click this button to display the Select Names dialog box and select contacts that you can link to this task.
Categories	Click this button to display the Categories dialog box and assign the task to a category.
Private	By selecting this check box, you can hide this task so others who have access to your schedule cannot see it.

TIP

Outlook understands natural language in most date boxes. For instance, in the Due Date or Start Date box, you can type *yesterday* to display yesterday's date, type *next Monday* to display next Monday's date, or type *one week from today* to display the date seven days from the current date. Be specific. If you type a vague expression like *soon* or *ASAP*, Outlook displays an error message. You can also enter a natural-language date in the Due Date column of the task list.

Add details to a task

Continuing to work with tasks, you now change the task view, create a new task with details, and add information to an existing task.

1 **Click the New Task button.**

The task window is displayed. The insertion point is already placed in the Subject box.

ANOTHER METHOD

You can also press Ctrl+N to display a new task window.

2 **In the Subject box, type** Call Jen to arrange a birthday dinner for Dad.

This becomes the name of the task.

3 **Click the Due Date down arrow.**

A mini-calendar is displayed.

4 **Click the date two days from today.**

The selected date is displayed in the Due Date box.

5 **Click the Status down arrow and click In Progress.**

In Progress is displayed in the Status box.

6 **Click the Priority down arrow and click High.**

High is displayed in the Priority box.

Figure 5-7

Task window with information

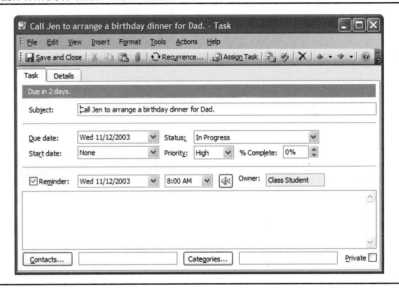

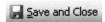

7 **On the Standard toolbar in the task window, click the Save And Close button.**

The task window closes, and the task is placed in the task list. Notice that an exclamation point appears in the Priority column, indicating that the task is high priority.

8 **Double-click the task "Call Cherry Creek Park to reserve sheltered picnic area."**

A task window is displayed. A note at the top of the task window indicates that the task is due in four days. The Subject box already contains the text you entered in the previous exercise.

9 **Click the Start Date down arrow and click tomorrow's date.**

Tomorrow's date is displayed in the Start Date box.

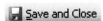

10 **On the Standard toolbar in the task window, click the Save And Close button.**

The task is updated.

11 **Click the Active Tasks view on the Navigation pane.**

The updated information is displayed.

Figure 5-8

Active Tasks view with updated information

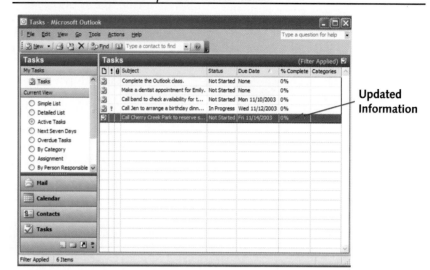

Updated Information

◆ **Keep Outlook open for the next exercise.**

QUICK REFERENCE ▼

Add details to a task

1 Create a task or double-click an existing task.

2 Add new details to the task information.

3 Click the Save And Close button.

Sorting Tasks

Organizing Tasks

THE BOTTOM LINE

In Outlook you can sort tasks when you focus on one or two characteristics of your tasks to select a sort sequence.

You can sort tasks by a field in the task list, such as Status, Priority, or Due Date. For example, the marketing director at Adventure Works sorted her task list for the ad campaign by Due Date so she could plan her upcoming deadlines.

To sort the task list, click a column heading. The task list is sorted according to the contents of that column. Click the same column heading a second time to reverse the sort order. For example, if you click the Subject column heading, Outlook sorts tasks alphabetically from Z to A. If you click the Subject column heading again, Outlook sorts tasks alphabetically from A to Z.

Figure 5-9

Tasks sorted in alphabetic order

	!	0	Subject	Status	Due Date	% Complete	C...
			Call band to check availability for the pi...	Not Started	Mon 11/10/2003	0%	
			Call Cherry Creek Park to reserve shelt...	Not Started	Fri 11/14/2003	0%	
			Call Jen to arrange a birthday dinner fo...	In Progress	Wed 11/12/2003	0%	
			Complete the Outlook class.	Not Started	None	0%	
			Make a dentist appointment for Emily.	Not Started	None	0%	

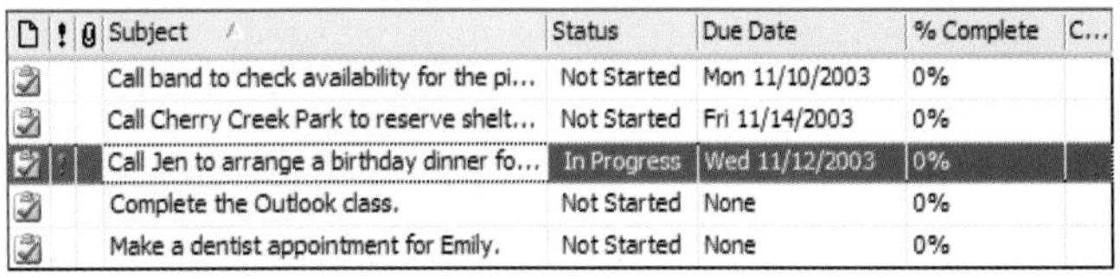

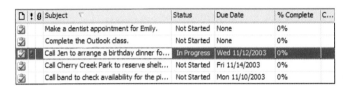

Figure 5-10

Tasks sorted in reverse alphabetic order

	!	0	Subject	Status	Due Date	% Complete	C...
			Make a dentist appointment for Emily.	Not Started	None	0%	
			Complete the Outlook class.	Not Started	None	0%	
			Call Jen to arrange a birthday dinner fo...	In Progress	Wed 11/12/2003	0%	
			Call Cherry Creek Park to reserve shelt...	Not Started	Fri 11/14/2003	0%	
			Call band to check availability for the pi...	Not Started	Mon 11/10/2003	0%	

To quickly add or change a due date in the task list, click the task's Due Date box and click the down arrow that appears to the right of the column. Click a date or click the Today button to choose the current date.

Sort tasks

To practice sorting, in this exercise, you sort tasks by Due Date and by Status.

1 Click the Detailed List option on the Navigation pane.

The Detailed List view is displayed.

2 Click the Due Date column heading.

The tasks are sorted by due date. The due date the farthest in the future is displayed first. Tasks without a due date appear last.

3 Click the Due Date column heading again.

The tasks are sorted again by due date. The tasks without a due date appear first, and the due date the farthest in the future appears last.

4 Click the Status column heading.

The tasks are sorted by status. The tasks that have the Not Started status appear first, the In Progress tasks are displayed next, and the Completed tasks are listed last.

5 Click the Status column heading again.

The tasks are sorted by status again. The Completed tasks appear first, the In Progress tasks are displayed next, and the Not Started tasks are listed last.

6 Click the Subject column heading.

The tasks are sorted alphabetically.

ANOTHER METHOD

To sort tasks, you can also right-click an empty area of the tasks list and select the Sort option from the displayed menu. Select the desired sort criteria in the Sort dialog box and click OK. This enables you to sort by more than a single criterion.

◆ **Keep Outlook open for the next exercise.**

QUICK REFERENCE ▼

Sort tasks

Click a column heading.

Printing a Task List

Organizing Tasks

THE BOTTOM LINE

You can print your task list to make it portable, separating it from your computer.

You can print a task list to carry with you, distribute to co-workers, or hang on the refrigerator. For example, if you create a task list to identify the milestones of a project, you probably want to print a copy of the task list and bring it with you to the next project status meeting. To print a task list, click the Print button on the Standard toolbar to display the Print dialog box. Select the print style. You can click the Page Setup button to choose options, such as text formatting, different paper sizes, and types of paper. When you are finished selecting options, click OK.

Two print styles are available—Table Style and Memo Style. The Table Style option prints the task list in columns, similar to the way it appears in Outlook. The Memo Style option prints selected tasks in a two-column list. The name of the task is displayed in the left column and the due date is displayed in the right column. Additional information about the tasks, such as the subject, status, and percent complete, appears in paragraph form below the columns. If you've created several columns for a task list and they won't fit within the page margins, Memo Style might be a better printing option. When you select Memo Style, you can print tasks one after another or print each task on a separate page.

Organizing Tasks by Using Folders

Organizing Tasks

THE BOTTOM LINE

As you can do with other features in Outlook, you can use folders to store related Outlook tasks.

If you work on several projects at the same time, it can be helpful to place the tasks for each project in a different folder. For example, the events coordinator at Adventure Works is planning a banquet. She created a folder called Banquet so she could have a centralized location for all the planning tasks related to the banquet.

Organize tasks by folders

Since you have a number of tasks related to the picnic, you create a folder and move the picnic tasks into it.

1 **Open the Tools menu and click the Organize option.**

The Organize pane is displayed.

2 **Click the Using Folders link.**

The Using Folders section of the Organize pane is displayed.

3 **In the top-right corner of the Organize pane, click the New Folder button.**

The Create New Folder dialog box is displayed. The insertion point is already located in the Name box.

4 **Type Picnic Tasks. In the Select Where To Place The Folder box, verify that the Tasks folder is selected, and click OK.**

The new folder is created.

Figure 5-11

Create New Folder dialog box

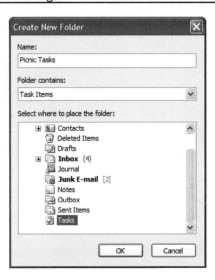

5 Click the task "Call Cherry Creek Park to reserve sheltered picnic area." Press and hold the Ctrl key and click the task "Call band to check availability for the picnic."

Both tasks are selected.

6 In the Organize pane, click the Move button.

ANOTHER METHOD

Drag the task to a different folder.

The tasks are moved to the Picnic Tasks folder.

Figure 5-12

Tasks have been moved to the Picnic Tasks folder

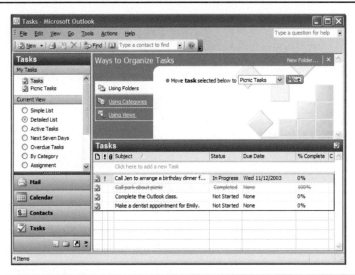

7 On the Navigation pane, click the Folder List button.

Folders are listed.

8 Click on the plus sign next to the Tasks folder in the folder list. Click the name of the folder you just created.

The tasks moved to the Picnic Tasks folder are displayed.

Figure 5-13

Contents of the Picnic Tasks

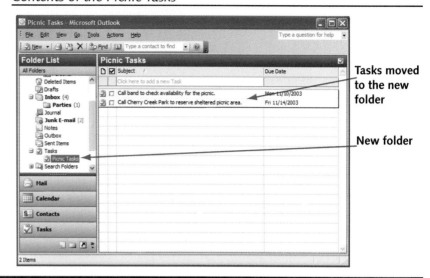

Tasks moved to the new folder

New folder

◆ **Keep Outlook open for the next exercise.**

QUICK REFERENCE ▼

Organize tasks by folder

1 Open the Organize pane.

2 Click the Using Folders link.

3 Create a new folder or select an existing folder.

4 In the task list, select a task.

5 In the Organize pane, click the Move button.

Organizing Tasks by Using Categories

THE BOTTOM LINE

Organizing Tasks

Categories provide another means to sort tasks into related groups.

Categories have helped you organize many Outlook items. Categories can also be used to organize tasks. Categorizing tasks makes it easier to access specific related tasks. In the Using Categories section of the Organize pane, select one of the existing categories, such as Holiday, Business, or Gifts. You can also create your own category.

Assign a task to a category

You will now assign a task to a category and apply the By Category view to your task list.

1 **Click the Tasks button on the Navigation pane and click the Tasks folder in the list of available folders.**

The tasks in the Tasks folder are displayed.

Figure 5-14

Contents of the Tasks folder

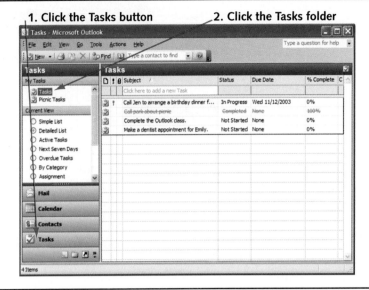

1. Click the Tasks button   2. Click the Tasks folder

2 **Open the Tools menu and click the Organize option.**

The Organize pane is displayed.

3 **If necessary, click the Using Categories link.**

The Using Categories section of the Organize pane is displayed.

4 **Select the existing "Personal" category in the Add Tasks Selected Below To box.**

The category is selected.

5 **In the task list, click the task "Call Jen to arrange a birthday dinner for Dad" and click the Add button in the Organize pane.**

The task is added to the Personal category. The text Personal is displayed in the Categories column of the task.

Figure 5-15

Task assigned to a category

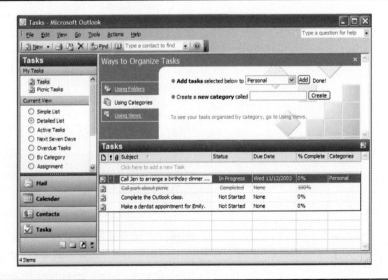

TIP

If necessary scroll the list of tasks to the right or drag the borders of the columns to resize the columns to display the categories.

6 **In the Organize pane, click the Using Views link.**

The Using Views section of the Organize pane is displayed.

7 **In the Change Your View list, select By Category. If necessary, click the plus sign (+) to expand the categories.**

The By Category view is displayed. Notice that there are two gray bars. One category is none. The other category is Personal. The Personal category contains the single task *Call Jen to arrange a birthday dinner for Dad.*

Figure 5-16

Task assigned to the Personal category

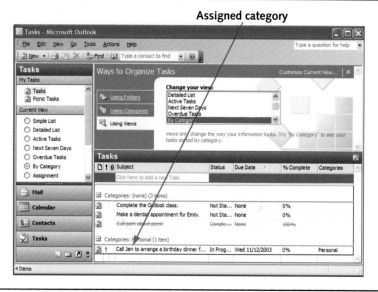

8 **In the Organize pane, select Detailed List in the Change Your View box and click the Close button in the Organize pane.**

The tasks are displayed in Detailed List view and the Organize pane is closed.

◆ **Keep Outlook open for the next exercise.**

Organize tasks by category

1 Open the Organize pane.
2 Click the Using Categories link.
3 Create a new category or select an existing category.
4 In the task list, select a task.
5 In the Organize pane, click the Move button.

QUICK CHECK

Q: Why would you assign tasks to categories?

A: **This makes it easier to access specific related tasks.**

Assigning Tasks to Others

Accepting, Declining, and
Delegating Tasks

THE BOTTOM LINE

Often, particularly on large projects, it is necessary to divide tasks. With Outlook you can assign tasks to others. This allows you to manage each aspect of a project.

Many projects involve more than one person. In addition to setting up tasks for a project, you might also need to assign different tasks to various members of a team. In Outlook, you can easily assign a task to someone else. When you assign a task, you send that person a task request as an e-mail message generated by Outlook. The recipient can accept or decline the task.

When you create a task in your task list, you are the **owner** of the task. As the owner, you are the only person who can edit the task. If you assign the task to someone else and the recipient accepts the task, the **ownership** (the ability to make changes to the task) passes to the recipient. If you assign a task to someone and he or she accepts it, you can choose to keep an updated copy in your task list and receive status reports when the task is edited or completed.

Assign tasks

You will now create two tasks and assign them to your class partner.

1 **On the standard tasks toolbar, click the New Task button.**

ANOTHER METHOD

You can also open the Actions menu and click New Task Request to display a task request.

The task window is displayed. The insertion point is already in the Subject box.

TROUBLESHOOTING

The name of the brochure should not be the same as the brochure name used by your class partner. When you receive the task assignment in the next exercise, using the same brochure name would cause conflict.

2 **Type** Edit the [insert name here] brochure. **Click the Priority down arrow and select High.**

Notice that you are currently the owner of the task.

Figure 5-17

The creator of a task owns the task

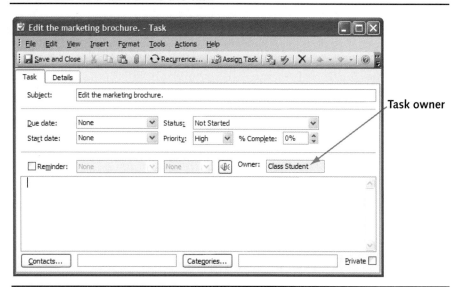

Task owner

Assign Task

3 **On the toolbar in the task window, click the Assign Task button.**

A task request window, which is similar to the task window, appears. A note at the top of the window indicates that the task request has not been sent yet.

4 **Click the To button.**

The Select Task Recipient dialog box is displayed.

5 **In the Select Task Recipient dialog box, click your class partner's name, and click OK.**

Your class partner's name is displayed in the Message Recipients box. The Select Task Recipient dialog box closes.

TROUBLESHOOTING

The addressee cannot be the same as the sender. If you don't have a class partner, use a second address entry for yourself that has a different e-mail address.

Figure 5-18

Task request to be sent

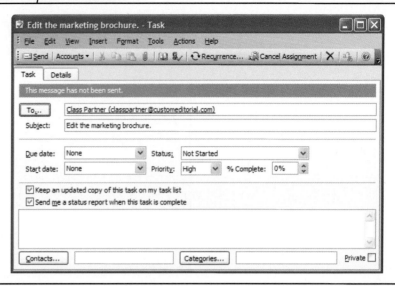

TROUBLESHOOTING

An alert box may be displayed when you assign a task. It states that the task reminder has been shut off because you are no longer the owner of the task. Click OK.

6 **On the Standard toolbar in the task window, click the Send button.**

The task is sent to your class partner.

7 **On the Standard Tasks toolbar, click the New Task button.**

The task window is displayed.

8 **In the Subject box, type Arrange printing for [insert name here] brochure. Click the Due Date down arrow and click "Tuesday of next week."**

This provides basic task information.

9 **On the Standard toolbar in the task window, click the Assign Task button.**

A task request window is displayed. A note at the top of the window indicates that the task request has not been sent yet and gives the number of days until the task is due.

10 **Click the To button.**

The Select Task Recipient dialog box is displayed.

11 **In the Select Task Recipient dialog box, click your class partner's name and click the To button.**

Your class partner's name is placed in the Message Recipients box.

12 **Click OK.**

The Select Task Recipient dialog box closes.

13 **On the Standard toolbar in the task window, click the Send button.**

The task is sent to your class partner.

◆ **Keep Outlook open for the next exercise.**

Assign a task

1 Create or select a task.

2 In the task request window, click the Assign Task button.

3 Click the To button, select the assignee, and click OK.

4 Click the Send button.

Accepting or Declining Tasks

Accepting, Declining, and Delegating Tasks

THE BOTTOM LINE

To keep a project moving, accept or decline task requests when you receive them. Accepting a task request adds it to your task list. Declining a task returns it to the previous task owner.

Sending a task request does not mean that the recipient automatically agrees to perform the task. The recipient must respond to the message, either by accepting or declining it. If the recipient declines a task request, the sender can reassign the task to someone else. If the recipient accepts a task request, the recipient receives ownership of the task and the sender receives a message of acceptance. This process prevents tasks from falling between the cracks in large projects. For example, the marketing director at Adventure Works assigned a task related to the picnic to the head chef. Because the chef had prior obligations, he declined the task. After receiving the chef's reply, the marketing director assigned the task to the head chef's assistant, who accepted the task.

If you receive a task request, you become the temporary owner of the task until you decide what to do with it—to accept or decline the task. If you accept a task, you become the permanent owner of the task. If you decline a task, you return ownership of the task to the person who sent the task request.

A task request arrives in your Inbox as an e-mail message. Double-click the message to open the task request. To accept a task request, click the Accept button. To decline a task request, click the Decline button. Although it is not necessary, you can include a comment with your reply, such as providing a start time, asking questions, or stating a reason for declining the task. To reply without a comment, click the Send The Response Now option. To enter a comment before sending the reply, click the Edit The Response Before Sending button. Type your comment and click the Send button to send the response.

Respond to a task request

In the last exercise, your class partner sent you task requests. In this exercise, you accept a task request and send a response without comment to the original sender. You also decline a task request and send a response with a comment to the original sender.

1 On the Navigation pane, click the Mail button. If necessary click the Inbox folder.

The contents of the Inbox are displayed.

2 On the Standard toolbar, click the Send/Receive button.

Two task requests from your class partner arrive in the Inbox.

TROUBLESHOOTING

Depending on when your class partner sends task requests, you might need to click the Send/Receive button (in the Inbox) again to receive these task request messages.

3 In the Inbox, click the task request "Edit the [insert name here] brochure."

The task request is displayed in the Reading pane.

Figure 5-19

Task request received in the Inbox

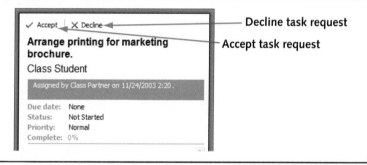

ANOTHER METHOD

You can also right-click the message header of a task request in the Inbox and click Accept to accept a task request or Decline to refuse the assignment.

Figure 5-20

Accepting a task request

4 On the message in the Reading pane, click the Accept button.

An alert box is displayed. The Send The Response Now option is already selected.

5 Click OK.

The response is sent as an e-mail message. Notice that the task request, Edit [insert name here] brochure is no longer in the Inbox.

6 In your Inbox, click the task request "Arrange printing for [insert name here] brochure."

The task request is displayed in the Reading pane.

7 On the Standard toolbar in the task request window, click the Decline button.

An alert box is displayed. The Send The Response Now option is already selected.

8 **Click the Edit The Response Before Sending option and click OK.**

A task window is displayed. The insertion point is already in the memo area.

9 **In the memo area, type I'm sorry, but my schedule doesn't allow me to accept this task.**

You have provided a reason for declining the task.

Figure 5-21

Declining a task request

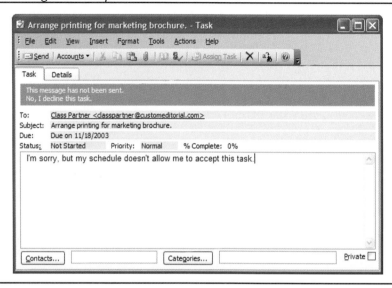

10 **On the Standard toolbar in the task window, click the Send button.**

The response to the task request is sent as an e-mail message.

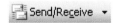

11 **On the Standard toolbar in the Mail folder, click the Send/Receive button.**

Two responses from your class partner about the task requests you sent arrive in your Inbox. One message accepts a task and one message declines a task.

12 **On the Navigation pane, click the Tasks button.**

The contents of the Tasks folder are displayed. The task you accepted is displayed in the task list. The task you declined is not in your task list.

◆ **Keep Outlook open for the next exercise.**

QUICK CHECK

Q: Can a task be assigned automatically?

A: **No, the task must be accepted by the new owner.**

QUICK REFERENCE ▼

Accept or decline a task

1 Receive the task request.

2 View the task request in the Reading pane.

3 Click the Accept or Decline button.

4 If necessary, add a comment to the message and send the message.

Marking Tasks as Complete

Managing Tasks Assigned to You

THE BOTTOM LINE

Completed tasks remain in the task list to show progress, but they are marked so that you can tell which are completed and which remain to be done.

When you mark a task as complete, the task is listed with a strikeout line through it and the task no longer appears in the Active Tasks view. New tasks marked as complete remain in the task list. You can make a task that has been completed active again by changing its status. To mark a task as complete, double-click the task to display the task window, click the Status down arrow, and click Completed. If you click the Details tab, you can also enter a different completion date (other than the current date) and additional completion information (such as total number of hours worked).

Mark a task as complete

Now you mark a task as complete using the Details tab of the task window, mark a task as complete using the Status box of the task window, and mark a task as complete in the task list.

1 Double-click the task "Make a dentist appointment for Emily."

The task window is displayed.

2 Click the Details tab and click the Date Completed down arrow.

A mini-calendar is displayed.

TROUBLESHOOTING

Select today's date or any previous date to complete the task. You cannot use a date in the future.

3 Click the date for yesterday.

Yesterday's date is displayed in the Date Completed column.

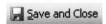

4 On the toolbar in the task window, click the Save And Close button.

A line is placed through the task Make a dentist appointment for Emily.

5 In the Navigation pane, click the Picnic Tasks folder.

The contents of the Picnic Tasks folder are displayed.

6 Double-click the task "Call band to check availability for the picnic."

The task window opens.

7 Click the Status down arrow.

The Status list is displayed.

8 Click Completed.

The task is marked as complete.

9 On the Standard toolbar in the task window, click the Save And Close button.

[Save and Close button icon]

The task is displayed with a line through it.

10 Right-click the task "Call Cherry Creek Park to reserve sheltered picnic area." Click the Mark Complete option.

ANOTHER METHOD

To mark a task as complete in the task list, right-click the task and click Mark Complete on the shortcut menu that appears. If the task list is displayed in Detailed List view, you can type 100 in the % Complete column for the task. In most views, you can simply click the checkbox in front of a task.

The task is displayed with a line through it.

Figure 5-22

Completed tasks

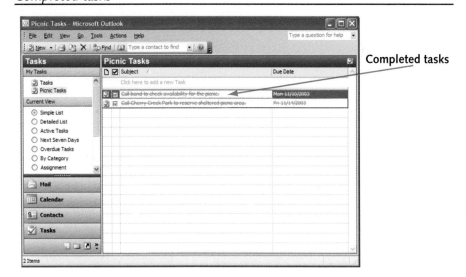

Completed tasks

Keep Outlook open for the next exercise.

QUICK REFERENCE ▼

Mark a task as complete

1 Double-click a task.

2 Click the Details tab.

3 Enter today's date or a previous date.

4 Click the Save And Close button.

QUICK CHECK

Q: How can you tell that a task has been completed?

A: A completed task has a strikeout line through it.

Manually Recording a Task in the Journal

Tracking Dealings with Contracts

THE BOTTOM LINE

Outlook's Journal helps you track the amount of time spent on each task.

The **Journal** is a folder in Outlook that displays information in a timeline format. The Journal can record when you create, use, and modify Microsoft Office System documents (such as Microsoft Excel, Access, Word, and PowerPoint). When the Journal tracks an Office document, it displays each document's type, name, date, the amount of time the document was open, and the path in which the document is stored on your computer. The document path is useful if you can't remember where you stored a document. Double-click any Office document or Outlook item recorded in the Journal to open the item.

To set the Journal to automatically track Office documents, open the Tools menu, click Options, and click the Journal Options button in the Options dialog box. In the Journal Options dialog box, select the check boxes next to the Office applications you want to track, and click OK twice.

Figure 5-23

Journal Options dialog box

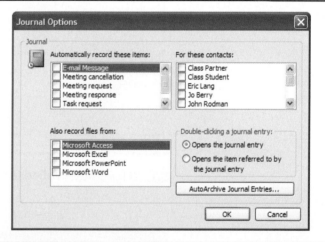

You can also use the Journal to track various Outlook activities, such as e-mails and tasks. To track an Outlook item, such as a task, you need to manually record it in the Journal.

For example, the marketing director at Adventure Works likes to record tasks in the Journal so she can have a record of the time she spends on a task. This information helps her schedule future projects and gives her a clear picture of where her time goes each week.

Use the Journal

You will now work with the Journal. First you create a task and record it in the Journal. Then you access the task from within the Journal and update it.

1 **In the Navigation pane, click the folder Picnic Tasks.**

The tasks in the Picnic Tasks folder are displayed.

2 **In the task list, click in the box that contains the text "Click here to add a new Task." Type Create brochures. Press Enter.**

The new task is created.

3 **Drag the new task to the Journal button on the Navigation pane.**

A Journal entry window is displayed.

Figure 5-24

Journal entry for a task

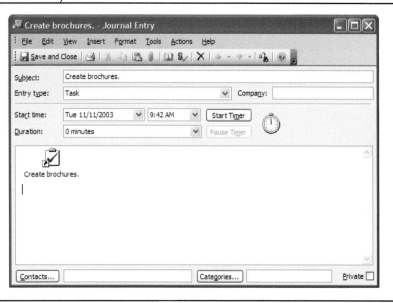

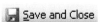

4 **On the toolbar in the Journal entry window, click the Save And Close button.**

The task will be tracked in the Journal.

5 **In the Navigation pane, click the Journal button.**

The contents of the Journal are displayed.

6 If necessary, on the Standard toolbar, click the Day button and the By Type view.

The current day appears in the Journal. The task is displayed in the Journal under the time at which you created the task.

Figure 5-25

Journal view of the day

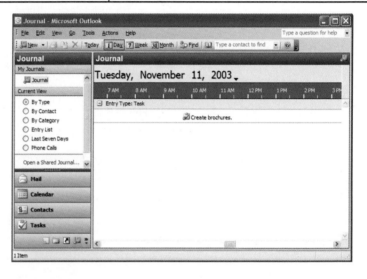

7 Right-click the task and click Open Item Referred To.

The task is displayed in a task window.

8 In the % Complete box, select the 0% and type 100. On the toolbar in the task window, click the Save And Close button.

The task is updated.

9 Click the Tasks button on the Navigation pane. If necessary, click the Picnic Tasks folder.

Notice that the task has been updated in the task list. It is marked as completed. A line has been placed through it.

QUICK CHECK

Q: What is the purpose of the Journal?

A: It can record when you create, use, and modify Microsoft Office System documents and various Outlook items.

Figure 5-26

The task is completed

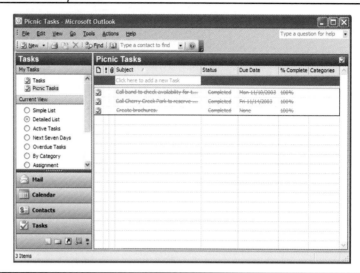

◆ Keep Outlook open for the next exercise.

QUICK REFERENCE ▼

Manually record a task in the Journal

1 Drag a task to the Journal button on the Navigation pane.

2 Click the Save And Close button.

Deleting Tasks

THE BOTTOM LINE

When a project is over, you need to delete the associated tasks to reduce clutter.

Managing Tasks Assigned to You

If you complete a task and mark it as complete, the task still remains as an entry in your task list. Because completed tasks appear with a strikeout line, you can easily identify which tasks have been completed and which tasks are still in progress or have not yet begun. When you know a task has been completed and you don't want the task to clutter your task list, you can delete it. If you delete a task, it is moved to the Deleted Items folder, like other Outlook items. The deleted tasks remain in the Deleted Items folder until you empty the Deleted Items folder or restore the task.

Delete a task

Since you have completed your task, you delete the completed task.

1 If necessary, click the Picnic Tasks folder on the Navigation pane.

The contents of the Picnic Tasks folder are displayed.

2 Click the completed task "Call band to check availability for the picnic" and click the Delete button.

The appointment moves to the Deleted Items folder.

ANOTHER METHOD

Right-click on a task and click Delete.

◆ If you are continuing to the next lesson, keep Outlook open.

◆ If you are Not continuing to the next lesson, close Outlook .

QUICK REFERENCE ▼

Delete a task

1 Click the task.

2 Click the Delete button.

QUICK CHECK

Q: How do you permanently delete a task?

A: Delete the task and empty the Deleted Items folder.

Key Points

✔ *Outlook lets you create and add details to a task.*

✔ *You can sort and organize tasks by using folders and categories.*

✔ *When you assign tasks to others they can accept or decline the tasks. Likewise, you can accept or decline tasks sent to you.*

✔ *Outlook allows you to mark tasks as complete.*

✔ *You can manually record a task in the Journal.*

✔ *When a task is completed and a record of the task is no longer needed, the task can be deleted from the task list.*

Quick Quiz

True/False

T   F   **1.** All tasks must be assigned to a category.

T   F   **2.** Tasks can be stored only with other task items.

T   F   **3.** Overdue tasks are automatically deleted.

T   F   **4.** You must be the owner of a task to assign it to someone else.

T   F   **5.** The Journal automatically tracks all tasks.

Multiple Choice

1. When you receive a task request, you _____.
   a. must accept the task
   b. become the temporary task owner
   c. become the permanent task owner
   d. All of the above

2. When you decline a task, _____.
   a. it is added to your task list
   b. it can be claimed by any Outlook user in your group
   c. it reverts to the previous owner who sent the task request
   d. All of the above

3. The Tasks folder enables you to _____.
   a. track your tasks
   b. receive e-mail
   c. schedule appointments
   d. All of the above

4. A(n) _____ task is red.
   a. in-progress
   b. deleted
   c. completed
   d. overdue

5. A folder containing tasks _____.
   a. must be named Tasks folder
   b. can contain any Outlook item
   c. can hold only task items
   d. can be assigned to another user

Short Answer

1. Identify the columns that appear in the Detailed List view of the task list but do not appear in the Simple List view.
2. How does a completed task appear in a task list?
3. Describe one way to enter a task.
4. If you receive a task request, how do you respond to the request?
5. How can you organize tasks?
6. What happens to deleted tasks?
7. Can you assign a task to someone else? Explain your answer.
8. What is a task?
9. What is the Journal?
10. If you send a task request to someone, how and where does it show up?

On Your Own

Exercise 1

The events coordinator at Adventure Works must begin to plan the company's holiday party. She wants to put all the tasks into Outlook and store them in a folder called Holiday Party. The tasks include the following: find a location, plan the food, buy gifts, book a band or DJ, create invitations, send invitations, and buy decorations. Group all the tasks under the Holiday category. The events coordinator will handle most of the tasks. However, she wants to assign the task of creating invitations to the graphic designer and the task of buying decorations to her assistant (your class partner). Create the tasks and organize them as specified. Use a different name and e-mail address for the graphic designer.

Exercise 2

The following week, the events coordinator needs to update the task list for the holiday party. So far, she has found a location and booked a band. She is halfway through planning the food. She realizes that she needs to buy the gifts quickly. Update the task list.

One Step Further

Exercise 1

The events coordinator wants to track the amount of time she is spending on the holiday party. Record the tasks created for the holiday party in the Journal.

Exercise 2

Use the Journal to access each task. Mark the tasks *Buy decorations* and *Create invitations* as complete.

Exercise 3

The director of marketing asked the events coordinator for a status report. Create a status report for all the tasks related to the holiday party.

Microsoft PowerPoint

Creating a Presentation

After completing this lesson, you will be able to:

✔ *Start Microsoft PowerPoint.*
✔ *Explore the PowerPoint window.*
✔ *Choose a method to start a presentation.*
✔ *Create a presentation using a wizard.*
✔ *Move around in a presentation.*
✔ *Change text in the Outline/Slides pane.*
✔ *Reverse one or more actions.*
✔ *Change and add text in the Slide pane.*
✔ *Change presentation views.*
✔ *Save a presentation.*

KEY TERMS

- bullet text
- menus
- Normal view
- Notes Page view
- Notes pane
- Outline/Slides pane
- paragraph
- presentation window
- ScreenTip
- selection box
- Slide pane
- Slide Show view
- Slide Sorter view
- status bar
- task pane
- text object
- title slide
- title text
- toolbars
- window

With Microsoft PowerPoint, you can create overhead slides, speaker notes, audience handouts, and outlines—all in a single presentation file. PowerPoint offers powerful tools to help you create and organize a presentation step by step.

As an example, suppose that you are the vice president of sales for the public relations firm Contoso, Ltd, and are responsible for developing a new employee training program. The president of Contoso has asked you to create a brief presentation to describe the project at the annual stockholders' meeting.

In this lesson, you will learn how to start PowerPoint, explore the PowerPoint window, create a presentation using the AutoContent Wizard, move around in a presentation, change and insert text, reverse changes that you make, look at content in different views, and save your work.

◆ Before you can use the practice files for this course, you must install them from the book's companion CD to their default location. See "Using the CD-ROM" at the beginning of this book for more information. You will not need any practice files for this lesson. Instead, you will create all of the files and folders that you need during the course of the lesson.

Starting Microsoft PowerPoint

THE BOTTOM LINE

Before you can create a new presentation or work on an existing one, you need to start PowerPoint on your computer. Starting PowerPoint opens the PowerPoint window, giving you access to PowerPoint's tools and features.

After you install PowerPoint, you are ready to start PowerPoint. As with other programs, there are several ways to start PowerPoint. One way is to use the Start button on the taskbar. Clicking the Start button displays the Start menu, where you can click All Programs to see a list of the programs available on your computer.

Depending how you installed PowerPoint, you may find an icon for it directly on the All Programs menu. If you installed PowerPoint as a part of the Microsoft Office system, you may find a Microsoft Office folder on the All Programs menu. Click the Microsoft Office folder to see a submenu of Office applications, including PowerPoint.

ANOTHER METHOD

You can also start PowerPoint by creating a shortcut icon on the Windows desktop. Shortcut icons allow you to launch the associated program by simply double-clicking. To create a shortcut, click the Start button, point to All Programs, right-click Microsoft Office PowerPoint 2003, point to Send To, and then click Desktop (create shortcut). A desktop shortcut is represented by an icon with a curved arrow in the left corner.

Use Start to open PowerPoint

1 **On the taskbar, click Start.**

The Start menu appears.

2 **On the Start menu, point to All Programs or Programs.**

The Programs menu appears, displaying all the programs on your hard disk drive, including Microsoft PowerPoint. A portion of the All Programs menu should look like the following illustration.

FIGURE 1-1

Portion of the All Programs menu

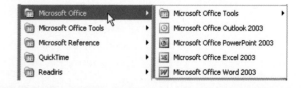

3 **Click Microsoft Office PowerPoint 2003 on the All Programs menu, or point to Microsoft Office and then click the Microsoft Office PowerPoint 2003 icon to start PowerPoint.**

◆ **Keep PowerPoint open for the next exercise.**

QUICK CHECK

Q: What do you call the Windows submenu that shows you all the applications available on your computer?

A: This menu is called All Programs.

Opening, Saving, and Closing a Presentation

QUICK REFERENCE ▼

Use Start to open PowerPoint

1 On the taskbar, click Start, and then point to All Programs.

2 Click Microsoft Office, if necessary, and then click Microsoft Office PowerPoint 2003.

Exploring the PowerPoint Window

THE BOTTOM LINE

The PowerPoint Window gives you access to important tasks and features you use to create and work with presentations. Becoming familiar with the presentation window elements allows you to work more quickly and efficiently with PowerPoint.

When Microsoft PowerPoint opens, it displays the program window. A **window** is an area of the screen that is used to display a PowerPoint program or presentation window. The **presentation window** is the electronic canvas on which you type text, draw shapes, create graphs, add color, and insert objects. As with any Microsoft Windows XP program, you can adjust the size of the PowerPoint and presentation windows with the Minimize and Restore Down/Maximize buttons, and you can close PowerPoint or the presentation window with the Close button.

FIGURE 1-2

Elements of the PowerPoint window

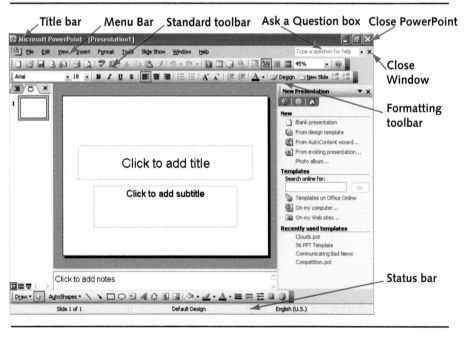

Along the top of the PowerPoint window are the menus and buttons you use to perform the most common presentation tasks. Another row of buttons appears along the bottom of the screen. The **menus** are lists of commands or options available in PowerPoint. The buttons you see are organized on **toolbars**. Toolbar buttons are shortcuts to commonly used menu commands and formatting tools. You simply click a button on the appropriate toolbar for one-step access to tasks such as formatting text and saving a presentation. At the top of the program window, you will also find the Ask a Question box, which you can use to type questions that the PowerPoint help system will answer for you.

TROUBLESHOOTING

What you see on your screen might not match the graphics in this book exactly. When you first open PowerPoint after installation, the Standard and Formatting toolbars share one row and show only the most frequently used buttons. The graphics in this book show the Standard and Formatting toolbars on two rows to make it easier for you to see the buttons you will be using. You can change your setup to match the graphics by clicking Customize on the Tools menu. On the Options tab, select the Show Standard And Formatting Toolbars On Two Rows check box, and then click Close.

The Standard and Formatting toolbars are located directly below the menu bar. Only the most commonly used commands appear on the toolbars by default. The toolbars on your computer might display buttons different from the ones shown in the figures in this lesson. To see the rest of the commands on either toolbar, click the Toolbar Options down arrow, shown in the margin. Once you use a button on the Toolbar Options list, it replaces a less frequently used button on the visible part of the toolbar. In this book, if you are instructed to click a button and you don't see it, click the Toolbar Options down arrow to display all of the buttons on a toolbar.

PowerPoint uses personalized menus and toolbars. When you click a menu name, a short menu appears, containing the most frequently used commands. These short menus save you time by displaying only the commands you use regularly. To make the complete long menu appear, you can leave the pointer over the menu name for several seconds, you can double-click the menu name, or you can click the menu name and then click the small double arrow at the bottom of the short menu.

IMPORTANT

You can turn off the personalized menus feature so that all commands appear all the time on the menus. On the Tools menu, click Customize, click the Options tab, click the Always Show Full Menus check box, and then click Close.

Messages appear at the bottom of the window in an area called the **status bar**. These messages describe what you are seeing and doing in the PowerPoint window as you work.

To find out about different items on the screen, you can display a **ScreenTip**. To display a ScreenTip for a toolbar button, you simply place the pointer over the button without clicking it, and a ScreenTip appears, telling you the name of the button, as shown in the margin.

TIP

You can turn toolbar ScreenTips on and off. On the Tools menu, click Customize, click the Options tab, clear the Show ScreenTips On Toolbars check box, and then click Close.

The default view, Normal, is made up of three panes: Outline/Slides, Slide, and Notes. The **Outline/Slides pane** has tabs that allow you to alternate between an outline of the slide text (the Outline tab) and a list of the presentation's slides displayed as thumbnails (Slides tab). The **Slide pane** shows the currently selected slide as it will appear in the presentation. The **Notes pane** is where you enter speaker notes. You can resize any of the panes by dragging the light-colored bar that separates them.

At the right side of the PowerPoint window is the **task pane**. The task pane displays commands and features you use often in working with presentations. Task panes let you work with commands without having to display menus or use toolbar buttons. Some task panes display automatically. For example, the Getting Started task pane opens along with PowerPoint each time the program starts. Other task panes display in response to a specific request. For instance, when you tell PowerPoint you want to insert a clip art picture, the Clip Art task pane opens to help you find a picture.

ANOTHER METHOD

To open the task pane manually, click Task Pane on the View menu. This command opens the task pane if it is hidden or closes it if it is open.

You can quickly switch from one task pane to another by clicking the Other Task Panes down arrow on any task pane to display the other task panes. When you're finished with a task pane, click its Close button to hide it.

FIGURE 1-3

Task pane in the PowerPoint window

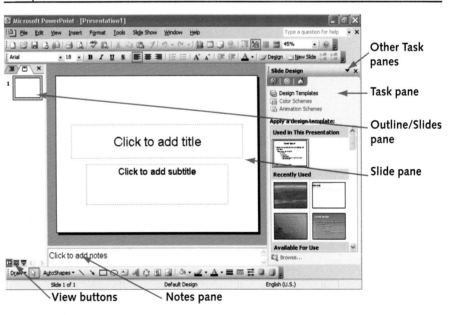

At the bottom of the Outline/Slides pane are view buttons that allow you to display the presentation's slides in different ways. When you open PowerPoint, the presentation is displayed in Normal view.

Work with PowerPoint window elements

In this exercise, you work with a PowerPoint menu, ScreenTips, and the task pane to become familiar with the PowerPoint window.

1 **On the menu bar, click Window.**

The Window menu appears.

2 **Click the arrows at the bottom of the Window menu to view the expanded menu.**

The expanded menu appears.

ANOTHER METHOD

You can also view the expanded menu by clicking the menu and waiting a few seconds for the expanded menu to appear or by double-clicking the menu name.

3 **Click Next Pane.**

4 **On the menu bar, click Window again.**

Notice that the Next Pane command is now displayed on the Window menu. PowerPoint has personalized the Window menu for you.

5 **Position the pointer on the slide icon in the Slides tab of the Outline/Slides pane.**

A ScreenTip appears when you position the pointer over the icon to identify the Slides tab.

6 **Click the Other Task Panes down arrow.**

The Other Task Panes menu opens, showing a list of all available task panes.

7 **Click New Presentation on the Other Task Panes menu.**

The Other Task Panes menu closes, leaving the New Presentation task pane open.

◆ Keep PowerPoint open for the next exercise.

Choosing a Method to Start a Presentation

THE BOTTOM LINE

Use the New Presentation task pane to start a new presentation when you open PowerPoint or at any time while you're working with another presentation. Choose the New Presentation task pane option that best fits the new presentation you want to create.

QUICK CHECK

Q: What are the three panes displayed in PowerPoint's Normal view?

A: The three panes are the Outline/Slides pane, the Slide pane, and the Notes pane.

When you start PowerPoint, the Getting Started task pane displays along with a blank presentation. If you have created presentations recently, their names appear in the Open section of the Getting Started task pane. In this case, you can simply click the presentation name to open it and continue working with it.

If you want to create a new presentation, you can simply start adding text to the blank presentation in the Slide pane or display the New Presentation task pane to select from several options in the New section for creating a new presentation. Below are the default options available in the New Presentations task pane.

- Click Blank Presentation to start a new presentation from scratch.
- Click From Design Template to apply one of PowerPoint's design templates to a new, blank presentation.
- Click From AutoContent Wizard to let a wizard help you with both presentation content and a design.
- Click From Existing Presentation to base a new presentation on the content of a presentation you have already created.
- Click Photo Album to create an album of pictures or other images.

CHECK THIS OUT ▼

Create a Photo Album
The Photo Album feature allows you to create a presentation that contains nothing but photos or other images. This is a great way to display pictures from a trip to show your friends or organize images you intend to use in other projects.

Creating a Presentation Using a Wizard

Using a Wizard to Start a New Presentation

THE BOTTOM LINE

Use the AutoContent Wizard to help you create a sophisticated presentation with a design and suggested content. After you have answered the wizard's questions and the wizard has completed the presentation, you can replace the suggested content with your own text.

Creating a presentation with the AutoContent Wizard can save you time by helping you organize and write the presentation. The wizard takes you through a step-by-step process, prompting you for presentation information, beginning with the **title slide**, which is the first slide in the presentation. Although the AutoContent Wizard creates business-related presentations, you can adapt them to a wide variety of uses and save yourself a lot of planning and formatting time.

Create a presentation with the AutoContent Wizard

Now that you're more familiar with the PowerPoint window, you're ready to create your first presentation. You'll use the AutoContent Wizard for the new presentation.

1 **In the New Presentation task pane, click From AutoContent Wizard under New.**

The AutoContent Wizard dialog box opens, displaying the Start screen. On the left side of the dialog box is a list of the screens in the wizard.

2 **Read the introduction, and then click Next.**

The second screen in the AutoContent Wizard appears, and the square next to Presentation Type on the left of the dialog box turns green to indicate that this is the current screen. The AutoContent Wizard prompts you to select a presentation type. To help you identify presentation types quickly, the wizard organizes presentations by category.

3 **Click Projects.**

A list of project-related presentations displays.

4 **In the list on the right, click Project Overview if necessary.**

Your AutoContent Wizard dialog box should look like the following illustration.

FIGURE 1-4

Step 2 of the Wizard

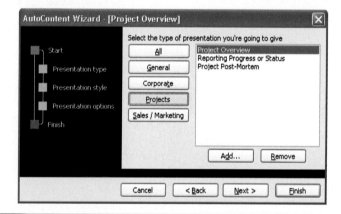

5 **Click Next.**

The AutoContent Wizard now prompts you to select a type of output, based on the media type you will be using for the presentation.

6 **Click the On-Screen Presentation option, if necessary, to select that presentation type.**

7 **Click Next.**

The AutoContent Wizard now prompts you to enter information for the title slide and for footer information to be included on each slide.

IMPORTANT

In the steps throughout this book, bold red type indicates text that you should type exactly as it appears. If you make a mistake as you type the information, press Backspace to delete the error, and then type the correct text.

8 **Click in the Presentation Title box, type New Employee Training Program and then press Tab.**

Pressing Tab takes you automatically to the next text box in the dialog box. You can also click inside the text box in which you would like to enter information.

9 **In the Footer box, type** Contoso, Ltd.

10 **Verify that the Date Last Updated and the Slide Number check boxes are selected.**

The Date Last Updated setting inserts the current date on each slide, and the Slide Number setting applies consecutive numbers to the slides.

FIGURE 1-5

Title and footer information for the new presentation

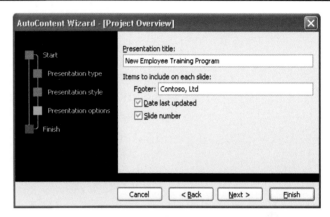

TROUBLESHOOTING

If you want to change any of the information you previously entered, click the Back button.

11 **Click Next, and then click Finish.**

The PowerPoint presentation window appears with content provided by the AutoContent Wizard in outline form in the Outline tab of the Outline/Slides pane and the title slide in the Slide pane. The name on the title slide is the name of the registered user. The task pane closes automatically.

◆ **Keep this file open for the next exercise.**

QUICK REFERENCE ▼

Use a wizard to create a new presentation

1 In the New Presentation task pane, click From AutoContent Wizard.

2 Read the introduction, click Next, and then click All.

3 In the list box on the right, click a presentation, and then click Next.

4 Click a presentation style, and then click Next.

5 Click the Presentation Title box, type a presentation title, and then press Tab.

6 In the Footer box, type footer text.

7 Select the Date Last Updated and the Slide Number check boxes.

8 Click Next, and then click Finish.

Moving Around in a Presentation

Viewing a Presentation

THE BOTTOM LINE

Because most presentations contain a number of slides, you need to master methods of moving from one slide to another so you can work efficiently with the slides. PowerPoint allows you to use both keys and mouse operations to move from slide to slide.

As you work with a presentation, you will find that you are constantly jumping from one slide to another to finalize content, add graphics, modify formats, and so on. Learning how to navigate a presentation quickly is an important skill.

You can move around in a presentation in several ways in PowerPoint. You can click the scroll arrows in the Slide pane to scroll slide by slide, click either side of the scroll box to scroll window by window, or drag the scroll box to move immediately to a specific slide. In the Slide pane, you can click the Next Slide and Previous Slide buttons, which are located at the bottom of the vertical scroll bar. You can also press the Page Up or Page Down key to scroll slide by slide.

FIGURE 1-6

Scroll bars and boxes in the PowerPoint window

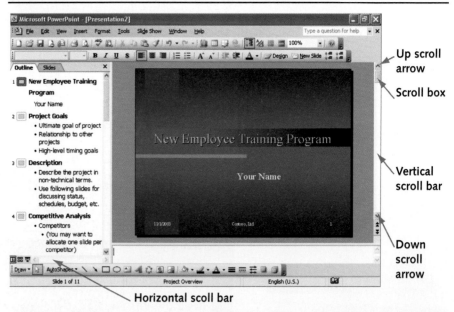

Move around in a PowerPoint presentation

In this exercise, you move around in the Outline tab and from slide to slide in the Slide pane.

1 **Click the down scroll arrow in the Outline tab a few times to see the text below the current pane.**

Each time you click a scroll arrow, PowerPoint changes the screen to show you one more line.

When you click below or above the scroll box, PowerPoint scrolls slide by slide.

2 **Click below the scroll box in the scroll bar in the Outline tab.**

The next window of information in the outline appears.

3 **Drag the scroll box to the bottom of the scroll bar—you cannot drag it off the scroll bar.**

The end of the outline appears. With this method, you can quickly jump to anywhere in the outline.

4 **Click below the scroll box in the vertical scroll bar in the Slide pane.**

Slide 2 appears in the Slide pane. Notice that the Outline tab jumps to slide 2 as well, and the slide icon next to slide 2 in the Outline tab is gray to indicate that this is the current slide.

5 **Click the Previous Slide button.**

Slide 1 appears in the Slide pane and is highlighted in the Outline tab

6 **Click the Next Slide button until you reach the end of the presentation.**

Each slide contains suggestions for developing and organizing the presentation.

7 **Drag the scroll box up the vertical scroll bar to view the slide 3 slide indicator box, but don't release the mouse button.**

Your presentation window should look like the following illustration.

FIGURE 1-7

Drag the scroll box to display the slide 3 indicator box

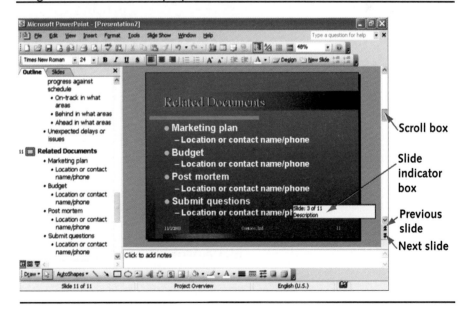

As you drag the scroll box, a slide indicator box appears, telling you the slide number and title of the slide to which the scroll box is pointing. The scroll box indicates the relative position of the slide in

the presentation on the scroll bar. To display the slide named in the indicator box, simply release the mouse button.

8 **Release the mouse button.**

The status bar changes from Slide 11 of 11 to Slide 3 of 11.

◆ **Keep this file open for the next exercise.**

ANOTHER METHOD

You can click the slide icon next to a slide in the Outline tab. The Slide pane jumps to the slide you clicked. Or, on the Slides tab, click on the thumbnail of the slide you want to display.

QUICK REFERENCE ▼

Move from slide to slide in the Slide pane

1 Click the Previous Slide button or the Next Slide button.

2 Click above or below the scroll box in the vertical scroll bar in the Slide pane.

3 Drag the scroll box up or down the vertical scroll bar.

Changing Text in the Outline/Slides Pane

Editing Text

THE BOTTOM LINE

Use the Outline tab when you want to concentrate on the text of a presentation rather than its design. You can see the text of a number of slides at a time in the Outline tab, making it easy for you to ensure consistency from slide to slide and to get information you might need from other slides.

You can edit presentation text in either the Outline tab of the Outline/Slides pane or in the Slide pane. When you are concentrating on the text of a presentation, the Outline tab is the most useful pane in which to work because you can easily see the text of the entire presentation.

Change text in the Outline tab

The AutoContent Wizard helps you get started with a suggested presentation outline. Now your job is to modify the suggested outline text to meet your specific needs.

1 **In the Outline tab, scroll up to slide 2, position the pointer (which changes to the I-beam) to the right of the text "Project Goals" in slide 2, and then double-click to select the title text.**

PowerPoint highlights the selected text so that once you select it, the subsequent text you type—regardless of its length—replaces the selection.

2 Type Program Overview.

If you make a typing mistake, press Backspace to erase it. Note that the text changes in the Slide pane also.

3 Position the I-beam pointer (which changes to the four-headed arrow) over the bullet in the Outline tab next to the text "Ultimate goal of project" in slide 2, and then click to select the bullet text.

4 Type Contoso's Goals.

5 In slide 2, click the bullet next to the text "Relationship to other projects," and then type Training Sessions.

6 In slide 2, click the bullet next to the text "High-level timing goals," and then press Delete or Backspace.

The text is deleted but the grayed-out bullet remains in view.

7 Press Backspace twice.

The first time you press Backspace, you remove the grayed-out bullet. The second Backspace removes the blank line and moves the insertion point back to the end of the second bullet item. Your presentation window should look like the following illustration.

FIGURE 1-8

New text added to slide

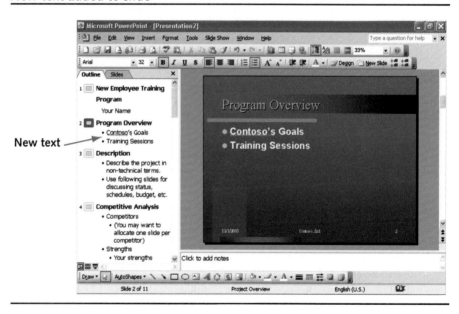

◆ Leave this file open for the next exercise.

QUICK REFERENCE ▼

Change text in the Outline/Slides pane

1 In the Outline/Slides pane, click the Outline tab.

2 Position the pointer (which changes to the I-beam) to the right of the text, and then select the text.

3 Type the replacement text.

Reversing One or More Actions

Editing Text

THE BOTTOM LINE

As you work on a presentation, you may want to "take back" changes you have made to text, formatting, or other parts of the presentation. The Undo and Redo commands give you a very helpful "safety net" that allows you to feel comfortable making changes.

Whenever you perform an action that is not what you intended, you can reverse the action with a handy PowerPoint feature called the Undo command. Located on the Standard toolbar or the Edit menu, the Undo command can reverse up to the last 20 actions by default, one at a time. For example, choosing the Undo command now will restore the text you just deleted. If you decide that the undo action is not what you wanted, you can restore the undone action by clicking the Redo button or by clicking Redo on the Edit menu.

You must undo or redo actions in the order in which you performed them. That is, you cannot undo your fourth previous action without first reversing the three actions that followed it. To undo a number of actions at the same time, you can use the Undo button down arrow.

Use Undo and Redo

In the last exercise, you made some changes to the text on slide 2. In this exercise, you undo and redo these changes.

1 **On the Standard toolbar, click the Undo button to reverse your last action.**

The blank line reappears below the two bullet items on the slide.

ANOTHER METHOD

- Press Ctrl + Z.
- On the Edit menu, click Undo Typing. (The command name will change depending on what action has just been taken.)

2 **On the Standard toolbar, click the down arrow next to the Undo button.**

The Undo button menu appears.

3 **Click the third item in the list, Typing.**

The second bullet in slide 2 reverts to the AutoContent Wizard's text. Notice that the third bullet, which you deleted after changing the second bullet's text, also reappears.

4 **On the Standard toolbar, click the Redo button.**

The text you typed for the second bullet item reappears.

ANOTHER METHOD

- Press Ctrl + Y.
- On the Edit menu, click Redo.

5 On the Standard toolbar, click the Redo button down arrow, and then click the item in the list, Typing, to restore the changes you just undid.

You should now see only the two bullet items you typed.

◆ Leave this file open for the next exercise.

TIP

You can change the number of actions the Undo command will undo by adjusting the number of Undo actions that appear on the Undo list. To do this, click Options on the Tools menu, click the Edit tab, change the maximum number of undos near the bottom of the dialog box, and then click OK.

QUICK REFERENCE ▼

Use Undo and Redo

- On the Standard toolbar, click the Undo or Redo button.
- On the Standard toolbar, click the down arrow next to the Undo or Redo button, and then click an item in the list.

Changing and Adding Text in the Slide Pane

Editing Text

THE BOTTOM LINE

Besides editing text in the Outline pane, you can add and change text in the Slide pane, right on the slide. Working in the Slide pane lets you see your text at a larger size with the presentation's formatting applied, so you have a better idea how the slide will look when displayed during the presentation.

You can also work with presentation text in the Slide pane. In the Slide pane, you work with one slide at a time. An object containing slide text is called a **text object**. A typical slide contains a title, called **title text**, and the major points beneath the title, called a **paragraph** or **bullet text**. To add more bulleted text to the text object, you place the insertion point at the end of a line of text, press Enter, and then add another line of text.

Change and add text in the Slide pane

In this exercise, you work in the Slide pane to change and enter text.

1 Click the Next Slide button in the Slide pane to display slide 3.

2 Position the pointer (which changes to the I-beam) over the title text in slide 3, and then click the title text.

The text is surrounded by a rectangle of gray slanted lines called a **selection box**, with the blinking insertion point placed in the high-lighted text. The selection box lets PowerPoint know what object you want to change on the slide.

FIGURE 1-9

Click in the title text to display the selection box

3 Double-click the title text "Description" to select it.

The text background becomes white to let you know the word is selected.

4 Type Training Session Development.

The new text replaces the selected text.

5 Position the pointer (which changes to the I-beam) over any of the bulleted text in slide 3, and then click the bulleted text.

6 Select all the text in the first bullet "Describe the project ...".

You can drag over the text to select it.

7 Type Content development stage.

8 Position the pointer (which changes to the four-headed arrow) over the bullet next to the text "Use following slides ..." in slide 3, and then click the bullet.

9 Type Lining up speakers for video and then press Enter.

A new bullet appears in the slide. The new bullet appears black until you add text.

10 Type Program will be ready in two weeks.

11 **Click outside of the selection box to deselect the text object.**

Your slide should look like the following illustration.

FIGURE 1-10

Text changed in Slide pane

◆ **Keep this file open for the next exercise.**

QUICK REFERENCE ▼

Change or add text in the Slide pane

1 Position the pointer (which changes to the I-beam) over the text, and then select the text to change or click the text to which you want to add.

2 Type text.

Changing Presentation Views

THE BOTTOM LINE

PowerPoint's views let you perform different tasks to prepare a presentation for viewing. Switching frequently among these views helps you to identify problems and fine-tune the organization and content of a presentation.

Viewing a Presentation

PowerPoint has four views to help you create, organize, and display presentations: Normal, Slide Sorter, Notes Page, and Slide Show. You can click the view buttons at the bottom of the presentation window to switch among the different views. You can also access all of these view commands on the View menu. There is no view button for Notes Page view. Instead, to display this view you click Notes Page on the View menu.

You have been working in Normal view. In **Normal view,** you can work with your presentation in four different ways: Modify text in the Outline tab of the Outline/Slides pane; select slide miniatures in the Slides tab of the Outline/Slides pane; work with the slide and its design in the Slide pane; or add speaker notes to slides in the Notes pane.

In **Slide Sorter view,** you can preview an entire presentation as slide miniatures—as if you were looking at photographic slides on a light board—and easily reorganize the slides in a presentation.

Notes Page view differs slightly from the Notes pane. You can add speaker notes in the Notes pane, but if you want to add graphics as notes, you must be in Notes Page view.

Slide Show view allows you to preview slides as an electronic presentation. Slide Show view displays slides as you would see them in Normal view, but the slides fill the entire screen. Use this view at any time during the development of the presentation to check slides for accuracy and appearance.

Illustrations of Normal, Slide Sorter, Notes Page, and Slide Show view are shown below.

FIGURE 1-11

Four PowerPoint views

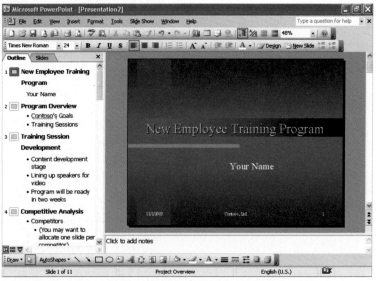

Normal view

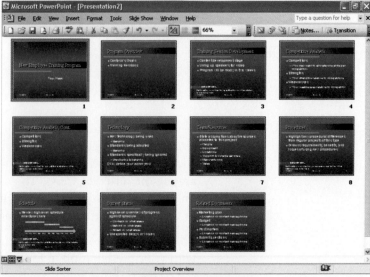

Slide Sorter view

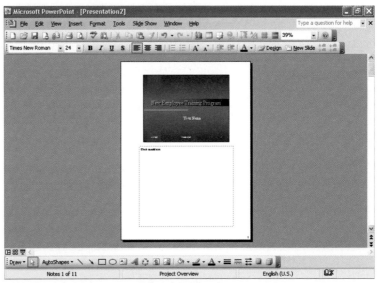

Notes Page view

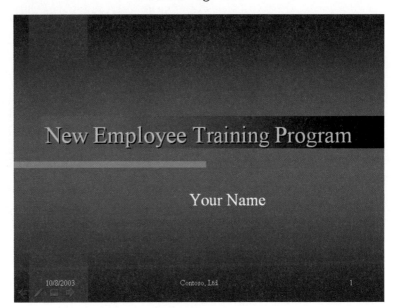

Slide Show view

Switch to different PowerPoint views

1 **In Normal view, click the Slides tab in the Outline/Slides pane.**

The Slides tab displays all slides in the presentation as slide miniatures. Click a slide in the Slides tab to display that slide in the Slide pane.

2 **Click slide 4 in the Slides tab.**

Your presentation should look like the following illustration:

FIGURE 1-12

Display slide 4

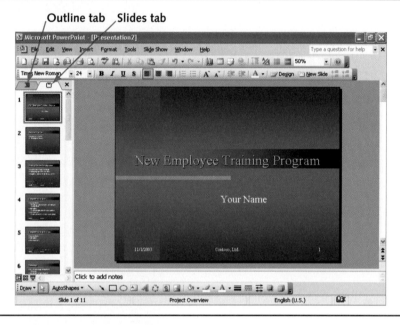

3 **Click the Slide Sorter View button.**

All the slides now appear in miniature on the screen, and the slide that you were viewing in Normal view is surrounded by a dark box, indicating that the slide is selected. You can scroll through the slides in Slide Sorter view to view all of the slides in a presentation.

ANOTHER METHOD

On the View menu, click Slide Sorter.

4 **Drag the scroll box on the vertical scroll bar to see the slides at the end of the presentation.**

TIP

If your screen is large enough to display all the slides in Slide Sorter view, you may not need to scroll.

5 **Drag the scroll box to the top of the scroll bar.**

The beginning slides of the presentation appear. Your presentation window should look like the following illustration.

FIGURE 1-13

Presentation in Slide Sorter view

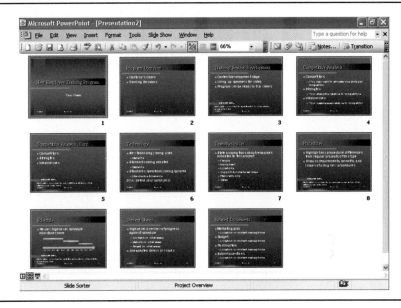

Note that your screen might display a different number of slides than shown in the illustration.

When PowerPoint displays slides that are formatted in Slide Sorter view, titles might be hard to read. You can suppress the slide formatting to read the slide titles.

6 **Hold down Alt, and then click an individual slide.**

The formatting for the slide disappears, and the title appears clearly. When you release the mouse button, the display format reappears.

7 **Double-click slide 1 to switch to Normal view.**

The presentation view changes back to Normal view, showing slide 1.

ANOTHER METHOD

- On the View menu, click Normal.
- Click the Normal View button.

◆ **Keep this file open for the next exercise.**

QUICK REFERENCE ▼

Switch to different PowerPoint views

- Click the Normal View button.
- Click the Slide Sorter View button.
- Click the Slide Show button.
- On the View menu, click Notes Page.

Saving a Presentation

Opening, Saving, and
Closing a Presentation

THE BOTTOM LINE

Saving a presentation is an important skill to learn because saving stores the information on your system. Though you can recover presentations if the computer shuts down accidentally, it is better to save a presentation as soon as possible and to save changes frequently while you work.

The work you have completed so far is stored only in your computer's temporary memory. To save your work for further use, you must give the presentation a name and store it on your computer's hard disk drive.

The first time you save a new presentation, the Save As dialog box opens when you choose the Save command. In the Save As dialog box, you can name the presentation and choose where to save it. Once you name a presentation, you can save the changes you just made by clicking the Save button on the Standard toolbar or by selecting Save on the File menu. In other words, the newer version overwrites the original version. If you want to keep both the original file and the new version, you can choose the Save As command on the File menu to save the new version with a new name.

TIP

PowerPoint saves presentations for recovery in case the program stops responding or you lose power. Changes are saved in a recovery file based on the settings in the AutoRecover save features. On the Tools menu, click Options, click the Save tab, select the Save AutoRecover Info check box, specify the period of time in which to save, and then click OK.

Save a new presentation

You're finished working on this presentation, so you can save the presentation and close it.

1 **On the Standard toolbar, click the Save button.**

PowerPoint displays the Save As dialog box. The text in the box next to the label File Name shows the title of the presentation by default. This default name is selected so that you can type a different file name if you want.

FIGURE 1-14

Save As dialog box

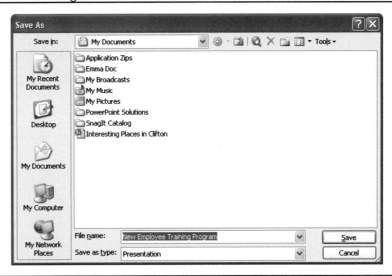

- Press Ctrl + S.
- On the File menu, click Save As.

2 **In the File Name box, type** Contoso Employee Training Report Pres 01.

The word *Pres* in the file name is an abbreviation for Presentation.

3 **Click the Save In down arrow, and then click the letter of your hard drive, which is usually C.**

If your hard disk uses a letter other than C, substitute the appropriate drive letter in place of C.

4 **In the list of file and folder names, double-click the PowerPoint Practice folder, and then double-click the Lesson01 folder.**

5 **Click Save or press Enter to save the presentation.**

The title bar name changes to Contoso Employee Training Report Pres 01.

◆ **If you are continuing to other lessons, close the Contoso Employee Training Report Pres 01 presentation and leave PowerPoint open. If you are not continuing to other lessons, click the Close button in the title bar of the PowerPoint window.**

To create a new presentation from existing slides, click File on the menu bar, click Save As, type a new name in the File Name box, and then click Save.

QUICK CHECK

Q: What command do you use to give a new name to an existing presentation?

A: Use the Save As command to give a new name to a presentation.

QUICK REFERENCE ▼

Save a new presentation

1 On the Standard toolbar, click the Save button.

2 In the File Name text box, type a file name.

3 In the Save In box, navigate to the location where you want to save the presentation.

4 Click Save or press Enter to save the presentation.

Key Points

✔ *Starting PowerPoint opens the PowerPoint window, giving you access to the features and tools you can use to create and work with presentations.*

✔ *The PowerPoint window contains typical features such as a menu bar, toolbars, and sizing and closing buttons. The default window displays Normal view, which consists of the Outline/Slides pane, the Slide pane, and the Notes pane.*

✔ *Choose one of four options in the New Presentation task pane to create a presentation: Blank Presentation, From Design Template, From AutoContent Wizard, or From Existing Presentation. You can also quickly create a Photo Album by clicking this link in the task pane.*

✔ *The AutoContent Wizard provides a slide design and suggested content on a number of business-related presentation topics. Use this option to quickly generate content you can change to suit your purpose.*

✔ *Text can be entered and modified in either the Outline tab or the Slide pane. Use the Outline tab when you want to concentrate on the text and the Slide pane when you want to concentrate on the presentation's appearance.*

✔ *To move from slide to slide in a presentation, use keys such as Page Up or use the mouse and the scroll bars.*

✔ *The Undo and Redo commands allow you to reverse or repeat actions. You can undo or redo one action at a time or a whole series of actions.*

✔ *PowerPoint's four views let you work with a presentation in specific ways. To switch from one view to another, use the view buttons or menu commands.*

✔ *It is important to save a presentation soon after you create it and at frequent intervals while working on it. Saving a presentation guards against loss from unexpected computer failure.*

Quick Quiz

True/False

T   F   **1.** There is only one way to start PowerPoint.

T   F   **2.** When you first open PowerPoint after installing the program, the Standard and Formatting toolbars appear on one row.

T   F   **3.** You can find the names of previously created presentations in the New Presentation task pane.

T   F   **4.** Using Redo is like undoing an Undo action.

T   F   **5.** After you have saved a presentation once, you can simply click the Save button to store your most recent changes.

Multiple Choice

1. To add toolbar buttons not on the Standard toolbar, click the _____.
  a. More Buttons arrow
  b. Toolbar Buttons arrow
  c. Toolbar Options arrow
  d. More Options button

2. The small message that tells you the name of a toolbar button is called a _____.
  a. What's This?
  b. ScreenTip
  c. ScreenName
  d. ToolHint

3. To create a presentation that suggests slide content as well as supplies a design, click _____.
  a. From Another Presentation
  b. From Design Template
  c. From Slide Wizard
  d. From AutoContent Wizard

4. To add more bulleted text to a slide in the Slide pane, place the insertion point at the end of a line of text and press _____.
  a. Enter
  b. Tab
  c. Down arrow
  d. Insert

5. The view that doesn't have a button at the bottom left of the screen is _____.
  a. Normal view
  b. Slide Sorter view
  c. Notes Page view
  d. Slide Show view

Short Answer

1. What are the options for starting a new presentation?
2. How do you create a presentation using a wizard?
3. How do you display a presentation as an outline?
4. What are the four PowerPoint views?
5. How do you clearly display a slide title in Slide Sorter view?
6. How do you save two versions of the same file?

On Your Own

Exercise 1

Your manager asks you to create a business plan. To help you get started, use the AutoContent Wizard to create the new presentation. Create an on-screen business plan presentation with the title **Business Plan** and the footer **Contoso, Ltd.** Save the presentation as **Business Plan** in the Lesson01 folder that is located in the PowerPoint Practice folder.

Exercise 2

A colleague needs a presentation slide on your current project for a larger presentation that he is working on for an upcoming business strategy meeting. Create a blank presentation. Change the new title slide to a Title and Text slide as follows: Display the Slide Layout task pane and select the second layout from the top at the left side of the task pane (use the ScreenTips to help you select the correct layout). Add the following title and bulleted list to the slide:

Brandson Ad Campaign
- Print media
- Commercial coverage
- Completion in Q4

Save the presentation as **Brandson** in the Lesson01 folder that is located in the PowerPoint Practice folder.

One Step Further

Exercise 1

You work for a computer services company named A. Datum Corporation that customizes systems for small businesses. Your company was counting on winning a contract to supply 25 new computers to a local school but was underbid by a new firm in your area. Use the AutoContent Wizard's Communicating Bad News template to break the news to your other employees. Modify the suggested content of the slides to fit your situation. Save the presentation as **Badnews** in the Lesson01 folder that is located in the PowerPoint Practice folder.

Exercise 2

A. Datum Corporation, your company, wants to avoid losing more contracts. Your boss has scheduled a sales meeting and wants you to put together a presentation that will help the sales force focus on A. Datum Corporation's services and strengths. Use the AutoContent Wizard's Selling a Product or Service template and then customize the slides to explain the needs of A. Datum Corporation's clients and how A. Datum Corporation can meet them with customer service and price strategies. Save the presentation as Selling in the Lesson01 folder that is located in the PowerPoint Practice folder and leave it open for the next exercise.

Exercise 3

View the Selling presentation in Slide Sorter view. Then change back to Normal view and display the Slides tab. Click the last slide in the tab to display the last slide in the Slide pane. Change the name on the first slide to that of your supervisor. Save and close the presentation.

LESSON

2

Working with a Presentation

After completing this lesson, you will be able to:

✔ *Create a new presentation using a design template.*
✔ *Enter text in the Slide pane.*
✔ *Create a new slide.*
✔ *Enter text in the Outline tab.*
✔ *Edit text in Normal view.*
✔ *Enter speaker notes in the Notes pane and Notes Page view.*
✔ *Insert slides from other presentations.*
✔ *Rearrange slides in Slide Sorter view.*
✔ *Show slides in Slide Show view.*

KEY TERMS

▪ design template
▪ text object
▪ text placeholder

To work efficiently with Microsoft PowerPoint, you need to become familiar with the important features of the product. In the previous lesson, you learned how to create a presentation using the AutoContent Wizard, change title and paragraph text, change views, move from slide to slide, and save a presentation.

After creating a progress report presentation for the employee training program at Contoso, Ltd, you decide to use PowerPoint to develop the program content. The next step is to start a new presentation and develop the content for the first training session, "Recruiting New Clients." Your sales manager has given you several slides to include in the presentation.

In this lesson, you will learn how to start a new presentation using a design template, enter and edit slide text, create new slides, enter speaker notes, insert slides from other presentations, rearrange slides, and show slides using the entire screen on your computer.

◆ Before you can use the practice files in this lesson, you must install them from the book's companion CD to their default location. See "Using the CD-ROM" at the beginning of this book for more information. To complete the procedures in this lesson, you will need to use a file named 02 PPT Lesson in the Lesson02 folder in the PowerPoint Practice folder located on your hard disk.

Creating a New Presentation Using a Design Template

Using a Template to Design a Presentation

THE BOTTOM LINE

Starting a new presentation with a design template displays a blank presentation with design formatting already applied. Design templates give you professional-looking formats and designs at the click of a button and save you considerable time in creating a good-looking presentation.

In addition to starting a presentation with sample text from the AutoContent Wizard as you did in Lesson 1, you can also start a new presentation without having PowerPoint insert any sample text. You can choose a design template or a blank presentation.

A **design template** is a presentation with a professionally designed format and color scheme to which you need only add text. Typically, design templates include background graphics that range from formal to playful. Each design template specifies where text placeholders appear on the slide and how the text in the placeholder is formatted. For example, some design templates specify round bullets for bullet text, whereas others use graphic pictures for bullets.

You can use one of the design templates that come with PowerPoint, or you can create your own. Design templates are displayed in the Slide Design task pane and can be applied to a presentation with a single click of the mouse. After you apply a design template, all slides you add to a presentation use the same template automatically.

◆ **If you quit PowerPoint at the end of the last lesson, restart PowerPoint now.**

Create a new presentation with a design template

In this exercise, you explore another option for creating a new presentation. You choose a design template and then save the presentation.

1 **On the View menu, click Task Pane, if necessary, to display the task pane.**

ANOTHER METHOD

Press Ctrl + F1.

2 **If necessary, click the Other Task Panes arrow, and then click New Presentation.**

3 **In the New Presentation task pane, click From Design Template.**

The Slide Design task pane appears with a variety of design templates shown as thumbnails.

4 In the Slide Design task pane, point to any design template.

The name of the design template appears as a ScreenTip, and a down arrow appears on the right side of the design.

5 In the Slide Design task pane, click the down arrow on the right side of any design template.

A menu appears with commands that let you apply the design template to the entire presentation or to selected slides, use the template as the default for all new presentations, or change the size of the preview design templates in the Slide Design task pane.

6 In the Slide Design task pane, drag the scroll box down until the Maple slide design appears in the task pane, and then click the Maple slide design.

The Maple slide design is applied to the blank slide in the Slide pane.

FIGURE 2-1

New slide design in place

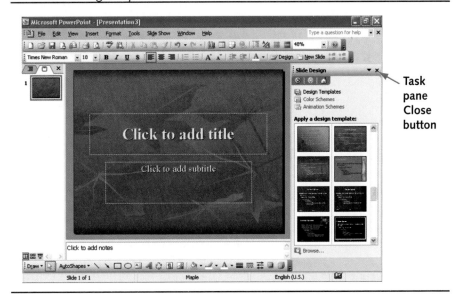

7 In the Slide Design task pane, click the Close button to close the task pane.

Closing the task pane gives you more room for the slide in the Slide pane.

ANOTHER METHOD

- Click Ctrl + F1.
- On the View menu, click Task Pane.

8 On the File menu, click Save As.

The Save As dialog box opens. Verify that the PowerPoint Practice folder appears in the Save In box.

9 In the File Name box, type Contoso Recruiting Pres 02, and then click Save.

PowerPoint saves the presentation, and the title bar changes to the new name.

◆ Keep this file open for the next exercise.

You can create a folder in which to store presentations that relate to a particular topic. This is a good way to keep your presentations organized by subject. When you save a presentation for the first time, click the Create New Folder button in the Save As dialog box. Give the folder a name that relates to the subject. When you click OK, PowerPoint automatically opens the new folder so you can save your presentation in it.

QUICK CHECK

Q: Why would you want to apply a design template to one or more selected slides?

A: Applying a design template to selected slides emphasizes the slides in the presentation.

QUICK REFERENCE ▼

Create a new presentation with a design template

1 In the New Presentation task pane, click From Design Template.

2 Click a design template in the Slide Design task pane.

Entering Text in the Slide Pane

THE BOTTOM LINE

Adding text in the Slide pane lets you see the text in its formatted form, so you know how it will look in the final presentation.

Creating Slides and
Revising Their Layouts

To add text to a presentation, including titles and subtitles, you can enter text into either the Slide pane or the Outline tab in Normal view. The Slide pane allows you to enter text on a slide using a visual method, whereas the Outline tab allows you to enter text using a content method.

The Slide pane displaying the Title Slide layout includes two text boxes called **text placeholders**. The upper box is a placeholder for the slide's title text. The lower box is a placeholder for the slide's subtitle text. Each placeholder on a PowerPoint slide includes text that tells you how to use it. For example, the title placeholder contains the text *Click To Add Title*. When you click this text, it disappears and an insertion point appears, ready for you to type your own title text. After you enter text into a placeholder, the placeholder becomes a **text object**, a box that contains text in a slide.

Most presentations begin with a title slide, which contains two placeholders: one for a title and one for a subtitle. You do not have to use all placeholders on a slide. If you choose not to use a placeholder, it won't display when you run the presentation.

Title a slide and add a subtitle

Now that you have applied a design template and saved the presentation, you're ready to begin entering text into the presentation.

1 **Click the Outline tab, if necessary, in the Outline/Slides pane.**

Though you will work in the Slide pane in this exercise, displaying the Outline tab lets you view the text not only on the slide but also as an outline.

TIP

You can resize the Outline tab by dragging its border to allow more room for the slide in the Slide pane.

2 **In the Slide pane, click the text placeholder Click To Add Title.**

A selection box surrounds the placeholder, indicating that the placeholder is ready for you to enter or edit text. The placeholder text disappears, and a blinking insertion point appears.

3 **Type Recruiting New Clients.**

Notice that the text appears in the Outline tab at the same time.

TIP

If you make a typing error, press Backspace to delete the mistake, and then type the correct text.

4 **Click the text placeholder Click To Add Subtitle.**

The title object is deselected, and the subtitle object is selected.

5 **Type Your Name, and then press Enter.**

Insert your own name in the placeholder rather than the words *Your Name* to customize the presentation.

6 **Type Contoso, Ltd.**

Your presentation window should look like the following illustration.

FIGURE 2-2

Completed title slide

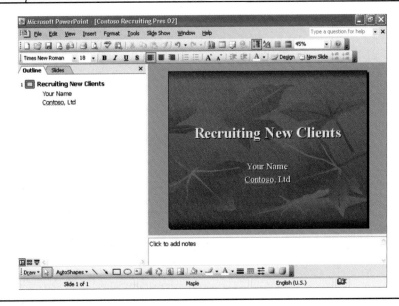

◆ **Keep this file open for the next exercise.**

QUICK **CHECK**

Q: What do you call a placeholder after text has been entered into it?

A: A placeholder that contains text is called a text object.

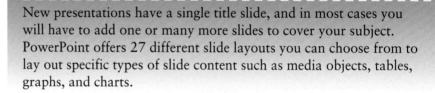

QUICK REFERENCE ▼

Enter text in the Slide pane

1 In the Slide pane, click the text placeholder Click To Add Title or click the text placeholder Click To Add Subtitle.

2 Type your text.

Creating Slides and
Revising Their Layouts

Creating a New Slide

THE BOTTOM LINE

New presentations have a single title slide, and in most cases you will have to add one or many more slides to cover your subject. PowerPoint offers 27 different slide layouts you can choose from to lay out specific types of slide content such as media objects, tables, graphs, and charts.

You can quickly and easily add more slides to a presentation in two ways: by clicking the New Slide button on the Formatting toolbar directly above the task pane or by clicking the New Slide command on the Insert menu. When you use either of these methods, PowerPoint inserts the new slide into the presentation immediately following the current slide, and the Slide Layout task pane appears with 27 predesigned slide layouts, any of which you can apply to your new slide. You select a layout by clicking it in the Slide Layout task pane. The layout title for the selected slide layout appears as you roll the mouse over each choice.

Slide layouts allow you to create slides with specific looks and functions. For example, you can choose a layout that displays only a title on a slide or a layout that provides placeholders for a title and a graph. The wide variety of different slide layouts means that you will most likely find one with exactly the layout you need, so you won't have to take the time to create it from scratch yourself.

Create a new slide

In this exercise, you add a slide to your presentation and then enter text on the new slide.

1 **On the Formatting toolbar, click the New Slide button.**

The Slide Layout task pane appears. A new, empty slide is added after the current slide in the Slide pane and is created a new slide icon in the Outline tab. The default Title and Text slide layout (a title and bulleted list) is applied to the new slide. The status bar displays Slide 2 of 2.

- Press Ctrl + M.
- On the Insert menu, click New Slide.

2 **Type** Develop a Plan.

TIP

If you start typing on an empty slide without first having selected a placeholder, PowerPoint enters the text into the title object.

3 **In the Slide Layout task pane, click the Close button to close the task pane.**

◆ **Keep this file open for the next exercise.**

Q: Where does a new slide appear in relation to the current slide?

A: **A new slide appears after the current slide.**

QUICK REFERENCE ▼

Create a new slide

1 On the Formatting toolbar, click the New Slide button.

2 In the Slide Layout task pane, select a slide layout.

Entering Text in the Outline Tab

THE BOTTOM LINE

Working in the Outline tab lets you concentrate on the text of a presentation. The Outlining toolbar can help you work efficiently with an outline.

Creating Slides and Revising Their Layouts

The Outline tab shows the presentation text in outline form just as if you had typed the text using Outline view in Microsoft Word. The Outline tab allows you to enter and organize slide title and paragraph text for each slide in a presentation. In the Outline tab, the slide title text appears to the right of each slide icon, and the paragraph text appears underneath each title, indented one level.

To enter text in the Outline tab, you click where you want the text to start, and then you begin typing. While working in the Outline tab, you can also create a new slide and add title and paragraph text by using the New Slide command or the Enter key.

PowerPoint offers an Outlining toolbar that supplies a number of tools useful for working efficiently with outlines. For example, the Promote and Demote buttons let you change the outline level of paragraph text. You can display the Outlining toolbar (or any toolbar) by clicking the View menu, clicking Toolbars, and selecting the toolbar name.

Enter text and create a new slide in the Outline tab

In this exercise, you enter text and create a new slide in the Outline tab.

1 **Position the pointer—which changes to the I-beam pointer—to the right of the title in slide 2 in the Outline tab, and then click the blank area.**

A blinking insertion point appears to the right of the slide title.

2 **Press Enter.**

PowerPoint adds a new slide in the Slide pane and a new slide icon in the Outline tab, with the blinking insertion point next to it. To add paragraph text to slide 2 instead of starting a new slide, you need to change the outline level from slide title to a bullet.

3 **Press Tab.**

Pressing Tab indents the text to the right one level and moves the text from slide 3 back to slide 2. The slide icon changes to a small gray bullet on slide 2 in the Outline tab.

4 **Type Develop a list of contacts, and then press Enter.**

PowerPoint adds a new bullet at the same indent level. Notice that once you press Enter after typing bulleted text, the preceding bullet becomes black. Also note that the text wraps to the next line in the Outline tab without your having to press Enter.

5 **Type Schedule periodic phone calls to prospective clients, and then press Enter.**

6 **Type Re-evaluate your strategy regularly, and then press Enter.**

Now you will display the Outlining toolbar and use one of its tools to work with the current outline.

7 **On the View menu, click Toolbars, and then click Outlining.**

The Outlining toolbar appears vertically to the left of the outline in the Outline tab.

ANOTHER METHOD

Right-click any displayed toolbar, and then click Outlining.

8 **On the Outlining toolbar, click the Promote button.**

PowerPoint creates a new slide with the insertion point to the right of the slide icon.

9 **Type Make the Client Number One, press Enter, and then press Tab.**

PowerPoint creates a new indent level for slide 3.

10 **Type Be creative, and then press Enter.**

A new bullet appears.

11 **Type Stay positive, press Enter, and then type Be tenacious.**

12 **Hold down Ctrl, and then press Enter.**

A new slide appears.

13 Type Summary, **press Enter, and then press Tab.**

PowerPoint creates a new indent level for slide 4.

14 Type Create a plan suitable to your temperament, **and then press Enter.**

15 Type Try to avoid cold calls, **and then press Enter.**

16 Type Keep current with the client's industry trends.

Your presentation window should look like the following illustration.

FIGURE 2-3

Summary slide with new text

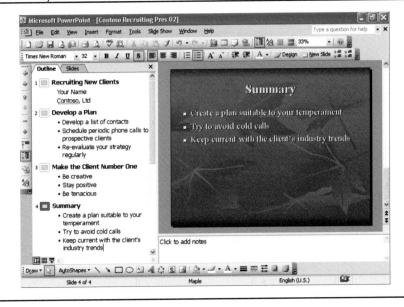

◆ **Keep this file open for the next exercise.**

QUICK REFERENCE ▼

Enter paragraph text in the Outline pane

1 Click in the blank area to the right of the slide title in the Outline tab.

2 Press Enter, and then press Tab.

3 Type your text.

Editing Text in Normal View

THE BOTTOM LINE

Editing Text

Most presentations require a certain amount of editing before they are finished. You can edit text in Normal view in either the Outline tab or the Slide pane. Editing can mean inserting text, changing text, or rearranging text on a slide.

After you have created a presentation, you frequently need to revise it. You may need to insert more text, for example, to "beef up" the content of a slide. Or, you may need to change existing content as you receive more recent information on the presentation's subject.

You can easily modify the text in a presentation using either the Outline tab or the Slide pane. Editing text in either location requires some basic skills that you should already be familiar with if you have worked with programs such as Microsoft Word. To insert text, for instance, you must click in the proper location to position the insertion point. To change text, you must first select it. You can select text by dragging the I-beam pointer over it or by double-clicking a word. In either the Outline tab or the Slide pane, you can select an entire bulleted item by simply clicking the bullet.

Besides modifying the text, you may want to rearrange it. For example, you may want to move the second bullet of paragraph text to be the first item, or even move one bullet item to another slide. You can easily re-arrange text in this fashion by dragging it in the Outline tab.

Edit text in Normal view

In this exercise, you insert new text, select and replace text, and then select and rearrange text in the Outline tab.

1 **In the Outline tab, click the blank area to the right of the word "regularly" in slide 2.**

The blinking insertion point appears where you want to begin typing.

FIGURE 2-4

Place the insertion point

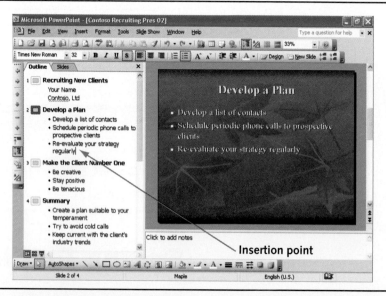

IMPORTANT

If you want to move the insertion point, reposition the I-beam pointer to the desired location, and then click the desired location.

2 **Press the Spacebar, and then type** and make adjustments as needed.

PowerPoint makes room in the outline for the new text.

3 **In the Outline tab, double-click the word "tenacious" in the third bullet point of slide 3.**

The text is now highlighted, indicating that it is selected.

ANOTHER METHOD

To select paragraph text or an individual slide in the Outline tab, click the associated bullet or slide icon to its left.

4 **Type** persistent.

The new word replaces the text in both the Outline tab and Slide pane.

5 **Move the pointer over the bullet next to "Be persistent" in slide 3.**

The pointer changes to the four-headed arrow.

6 **Click the bullet to select the entire line.**

7 **Drag the selected item up until a horizontal line appears above the bullet entitled "Stay positive," but do not release the mouse button yet.**

The horizontal line indicates where the selected text will go. The pointer changes to the two-headed arrow.

FIGURE 2-5

Moving selected text

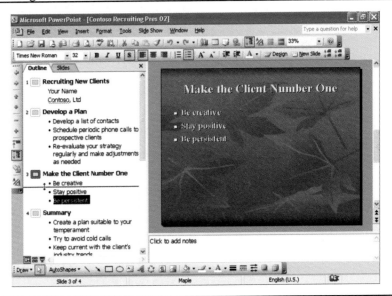

8 **Release the mouse button.**

The entire line moves up one line. You have now repositioned the text on this slide.

◆ **Keep this file open for the next exercise.**

QUICK CHECK

Q: What shape does the pointer take when you're dragging an entire bullet item in the Outline tab?

A: **The pointer takes the shape of a two-headed arrow.**

QUICK REFERENCE ▼

Select and replace text

1 Position the I-beam pointer over any part of the text that you want to replace.

2 Double-click or drag the text to select it.

3 Type the replacement text.

Select and rearrange bulleted text

1 Click the bullet to the left of the text.

2 Drag the selected item with the two-headed arrow until a horizontal line appears above the area where you want to place it.

3 Release the mouse button.

Entering Speaker Notes

THE BOTTOM LINE

Speaker notes supply additional information about a slide that a speaker can use when delivering the presentation. Using speaker notes helps you keep slide content relatively simple and uncluttered while also reminding you of important points to cover.

If you are going to deliver a presentation to a live audience, you may want to enter speaker notes on some or all of the slides in the presentation. Speaker notes relate to the content of the slide. For example, you may want to have available statistics associated with bullet items on a slide, or you may want to be able to give your audience more information about a person or place mentioned on a slide. Using speaker notes for this supplementary information can help you keep slide content simple for easy comprehension by your audience.

Speaker notes don't display along with the slides when you deliver the presentation. To have access to your speaker notes, you can print them, as you learn in the next lesson, or you can view them on one screen while you show the presentation on another, as you learn in Lesson 7.

You have two options for entering speaker notes: You can use the Notes pane or you can use Notes Page view. Which option you choose depends to some degree on how extensive the notes are as well as on your own working style.

Entering Notes in the Notes Pane

The Notes pane appears below the Slide pane in Normal view. If you have one or two sentences of notes to add, this is an appropriate place to insert the notes, because you don't have to change views.

To enter speaker notes in the Notes pane, click the Notes pane placeholder text, and then begin typing to insert text. You can modify the notes text the same way you would on a slide or in the Outline tab. If your notes run to more lines than the pane can display at one time, you can use the Notes pane's scroll bar to see them. You may also want to drag the top border of the Notes pane upward to increase the size of the pane.

Enter text in the Notes pane

You add a speaker note in the Notes pane in this exercise.

1 **Click the Notes pane in slide 3.**

The notes placeholder text disappears, and a blinking insertion point appears, as shown in the following illustration.

FIGURE 2-6

Insertion point in Notes pane

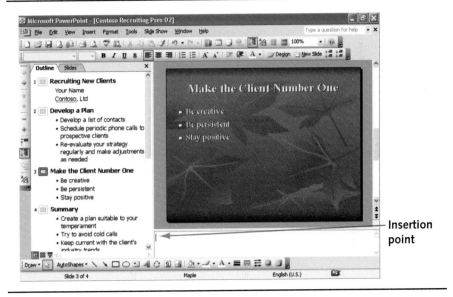

2 **Type the sentence below, but do not press Enter.**

Being persistent without being annoying is a skill you will need to perfect.

The Notes pane shows your new entry.

TIP

If you make a mistake, press Backspace to delete the mistake, and then type the correct text.

◆ **Keep this file open for the next exercise.**

QUICK CHECK

Q: What is the purpose of speaker notes?

A: These are notes on additional information relating to the slide's content that a speaker may want to share with an audience.

QUICK REFERENCE ▼

Enter text in the Notes pane

1 In Normal view, click the Notes pane.

2 Type your text.

Entering Notes in Notes Page View

PowerPoint's Notes Page view displays each slide in a presentation along with the notes that have been inserted for that slide. After you have inserted notes in the Normal view Notes pane, for example, you can see those notes under the slides in Notes Page view. To check all the speaker notes in a presentation, you can move from slide to slide using the Next Slide and Previous Slide buttons just as in Normal view.

Notes Page view is not just for displaying slides and their associated notes. You can also enter notes directly in Notes Page view. Because this view provides a much larger area for inserting notes, this is the option to choose if you want to enter a number of notes or a long note. You can also insert graphics such as a chart or picture into the notes area in this view.

By default, Notes Page view displays at a size that will fit the entire page in the window, such as 33% or 39%. At this size, you will have trouble inserting and reading speaker notes. You can use the Zoom box on the Standard toolbar to change the zoom percentage so you can read text more easily.

Enter notes in Notes Page view

In this exercise, you change the zoom percentage and add a note in Notes Page view to see how this compares to using the Notes pane.

1 **On the View menu, click Notes Page.**

Notes Page view appears at approximately 33% view on most screens to display the entire page. Your presentation window should look like the following illustration.

FIGURE 2-7

Notes Page view displays entire page

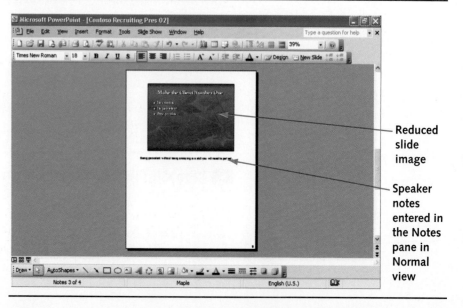

Reduced slide image

Speaker notes entered in the Notes pane in Normal view

Your view scale might be different, depending on the size of your monitor.

`42%` ▾

2 **On the Standard toolbar, click the Zoom button down arrow, and then click 75%.**

The view scale increases to 75%.

⯯ **3** **Click the Next Slide button.**

The status bar displays *Notes 4 of 4*.

4 **Select the Notes placeholder.**

The selection box surrounds the area that contains the notes text and the placeholder text disappears.

5 **Type** Experienced sales reps will lead a question-and-answer session immediately following this presentation.

6 **On the Standard toolbar, click the Zoom down arrow, and then click Fit.**

Choosing this option displays the page at the largest size that will fit in the window.

▦ **7** **Click the Normal View button.**

ANOTHER METHOD

- Double-click the reduced slide image in Notes Page view.
- On the View menu, click Normal.

◆ **Keep this file open for the next exercise.**

Q: How would you change the display size of a notes page to the actual page size?

A: Click the Zoom button down arrow, and then click 100%.

QUICK REFERENCE ▼

Enter speaker notes in Notes Page view

1 On the View menu, click Notes Page.

2 Select the Notes placeholder.

3 Type your text.

Inserting Slides from Other Presentations

THE BOTTOM LINE

To save time when creating a presentation, you can insert slides that have already been created in other presentations. This is also a good way to maintain consistency when creating a number of presentations on one subject or for one client.

Creating presentations can be a time-consuming process. You can save time while creating a presentation by using slides that you or someone else has already made. For example, you can pick up your company's title slide or a slide that contains contact information to avoid having to recreate these slides every time you do a company presentation.

PowerPoint's Slides From Files command allows you to pick up one or more—or all—slides from another presentation to insert into the current presentation. You don't have to worry if the other presentation has the same design template as your current presentation. When you insert slides from one presentation into another, the slides conform to the color and design of the current presentation, so you don't have to make many changes.

TIP

If you want to keep the original formatting for inserted slides, click the Keep Source Formatting check box in the Slide Finder dialog box.

Insert slides from one presentation into another

You're now ready to add slides from another presentation your sales manager has given you to beef up your presentation.

1 On the Insert menu, click Slides From Files.

The Slide Finder dialog box appears.

2 Click the Find Presentation tab if necessary, and then click Browse.

The Browse dialog box appears.

3 In the Look In box, verify that your hard disk is selected.

4 In the list of file and folder names, double-click the PowerPoint Practice folder, and then double-click the Lesson02 folder.

5 Click the file titled 02 PPT Lesson, and then click Open.

The Slide Finder dialog box reappears.

6 Click Display, if necessary.

All of the slides in the selected presentation are displayed as thumbnails.

TIP

If you use one or more slides in several presentations, you can click Add To Favorites to save the selected slides in the List Of Favorites tab in the Slide Finder dialog box.

7 Click slide 2, click slide 3, click the right scroll arrow, and then click slide 4 to select the slides you want to insert.

The Slide Finder dialog box should look like the following illustration.

FIGURE 2-8

Slide Finder dialog box

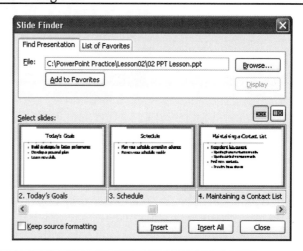

8 **Click Insert.**

PowerPoint inserts the slides into the new presentation after the current slide. The Slide Finder dialog box remains open so you can insert other slides from the same or a different presentation if desired.

9 **Click Close.**

The Slide Finder dialog box closes, and the last inserted slide appears in the Slide pane. The inserted slides adopt the design template of the current presentation.

◆ **Keep this file open for the next exercise.**

QUICK REFERENCE ▼

Insert slides from other presentations

Q: How do you tell PowerPoint to keep the original formatting for slides you insert from another presentation?

A: **Click the Keep Source Formatting check box in the Slide Finder dialog box.**

1 On the Insert menu, click Slides From Files.

2 Click the Find Presentation tab, and then click Browse.

3 In the Look In box, navigate to the location of the presentation that you want to insert.

4 In the list of file names, click the presentation you want to open, and then click Open.

5 Click Display, if necessary.

6 Click the slides that you want to insert.

7 Click Insert.

8 Click Close.

Rearranging Slides in Slide Sorter View

THE BOTTOM LINE

Use Slide Sorter view to quickly reorganize a presentation so you can make sure the slides are arranged in the best order. The advantage of using this view is that you can usually see all slides of a presentation at one time, making it easy to move them around.

Creating a presentation often requires reorganizing slides. You want to make sure they appear in the best order to communicate your message effectively. For example, you may want to move a slide that reviews the presentation content from the end of the presentation to the beginning, to give the audience a preview of the presentation's topics.

Although you can rearrange slides in both the Outline and Slides tabs, you will find reorganizing slides to be easiest in Slide Sorter view. This view shows you all slides as thumbnails. To rearrange slides, you simply click a slide and drag it to its new position. As you drag, a vertical gray line appears to show where you can "drop" the slide. You can move a slide to the end or the beginning of the presentation or between existing slides. After you drop the slide, PowerPoint renumbers the slides to reflect their new order.

Rearrange slides in Slide Sorter view

After you added slides from the other presentation in the last exercise, your Summary slide is no longer the last slide in the presentation. You reorganize the presentation in this exercise.

1 Click the Slide Sorter View button.

Notice that the Slide Sorter toolbar appears above the presentation window.

ANOTHER METHOD

On the View menu, click Slide Sorter.

2 Click slide 4 ("Summary"), and then drag it to the empty space after slide 7 ("Maintaining a Contact List").

Slide 4 displays a heavy blue border to indicate it is selected. Notice that the pointer changes to the drag pointer when you begin to drag (see illustration below). When you release the mouse button, slide 4 moves to its new position, and the other slides in the presentation are repositioned and renumbered.

FIGURE 2-9

Repositioning a slide

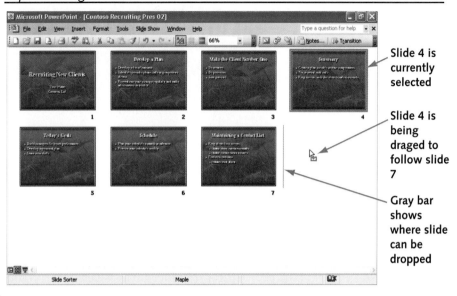

Slide 4 is currently selected

Slide 4 is being draged to follow slide 7

Gray bar shows where slide can be dropped

3 Click the current slide 4 ("Today's Goals").

4 Drag slide 4 between slides 1 and 2.

Drop the slide when you see the vertical gray bar appear between slides 1 and 2.

ANOTHER METHOD

In Slide Sorter view, you can also move slides between two or more open presentations. Open each presentation, switch to Slide Sorter view, and then click Arrange All on the Window menu. Drag the slides from one presentation window to another.

5 Double-click slide 1 to return to the previous view, Normal view.

ANOTHER METHOD

- Click the Normal View button.
- On the View menu, click Normal.

◆ Keep this file open for the next exercise.

QUICK CHECK

Q: What visual aid helps you to choose a place to drag a slide?

A: A vertical gray bar shows you where a slide will display when moved.

QUICK REFERENCE ▼

Rearrange slides in Slide Sorter view

1 Click the Slide Sorter View button.

2 Click a slide to select it.

3 Drag the slide to a new position.

4 Release the mouse button to "drop" the slide in its new position.

Showing Slides in Slide Show View

Viewing a Presentation

THE BOTTOM LINE

Slide Show view lets you see the slides in a presentation in order from first to last at full-screen size. Previewing a presentation in this view lets you review content and flow and identify errors or problems on the slides.

PowerPoint's Slide Show view gives you a full-screen view of the slides in a presentation. This allows you to see the presentation more nearly as it will appear when presented to an audience (or on-screen, if you are presenting the slides over the Internet or on an intranet). Slide Show view displays the slides in order by slide number.

It is a good idea to preview a presentation often as you create it. You can quickly and easily review the slides for accuracy and flow in Slide Show view. When you see slides at full-screen size, you can often catch errors that you missed in Normal view. You can also determine if slides are too crowded or need additional content, if the design template isn't exactly what you want, if you can easily read text, and so on.

To move from slide to slide in Slide Show view, click on the screen with the mouse button or use the Page Down or Enter key. If you want to end a slide show before you reach the last slide, click the Esc button.

Display slides in Slide Show view

1 **In the Outline tab, click the slide 1 icon, if necessary.**

The slide show begins with the currently selected slide, so displaying slide 1 ensures that you see the presentation from the beginning.

2 **Click the Slide Show button.**

PowerPoint displays the first slide in the presentation.

ANOTHER METHOD

- Press F5.
- On the View menu, click Slide Show.

3 **Click the screen to advance to the next slide.**

You can also press the Page Down or the Enter key to move to the next slide.

4 **Click one slide at a time to advance through the presentation. After the last slide, click to exit Slide Show view.**

PowerPoint returns to the current view.

◆ If you are continuing to other lessons, save the Contoso Recruiting Pres 02 presentation with the current name and then close it. If you are not continuing to other lessons, save and close the Contoso Recruiting Pres 02 presentation, and then click the Close button in the title bar of the PowerPoint window.

QUICK REFERENCE ▼

Show slides in Slide Show view

1 Verify that slide 1 appears in the Slide pane.

2 Click the Slide Show button.

3 Click the screen (or press Page Down or Enter) to advance to the next slide.

4 Click one slide at a time to advance through the presentation.

Key Points

✓ *You can create a new presentation using a design template that supplies professionally designed background color and graphics, text formatting, and layout.*

✓ *Use either the Outline tab or the Slide pane to enter and edit slide text. Working in the Outline tab allows you to concentrate on the presentation's text, whereas working in the Slide pane lets you see how text will look when presented.*

✓ *Most presentations need more than the single slide of a blank or design template presentation. You can select the layout of a new slide from the Slide Layout task pane.*

✓ *Speaker notes allow you to keep track of additional information you might want to share with your audience. Enter speaker notes in the Notes pane in Normal view or in Notes Page view.*

✓ *If another presentation contains slides you can use in your current presentation, you can use the Slides From Files command on the Insert menu to locate that presentation and select slides from it to insert. Inserted slides take on the design template of the current presentation by default.*

✓ *Use Slide Sorter view to rearrange slides so they appear in the best order to communicate your message. Because you can usually see all slides in the presentation at once, you can easily drag slides to new positions to reorganize them.*

✓ *To see how a presentation will look when delivered onscreen, use Slide Show view. Slide Show view displays slides using the entire screen on your computer, allowing you to easily check the presentation's flow and accuracy.*

Quick Quiz

True/False

T F **1.** You can create your own design template if you want.

T F **2.** One way to insert a new slide is to click New Slide on the Edit menu.

T F **3.** If you need to enter only a sentence or two of notes, the Notes pane in Normal view is your best bet.

T F **4.** To rearrange slides in Slide Sorter view, you can simply drag them from one location to another.

T F **5.** If a slide has speaker notes, they display at the bottom of a slide in Slide Show view.

Multiple Choice

1. If you are most concerned about how text is going to look on a slide, you should enter text in the _____.
   a. Outline tab
   b. Slides tab
   c. Slide pane
   d. Notes pane

2. If you want to select an entire bullet item at once, click _____.
   a. the bullet symbol
   b. the first word of the bullet item
   c. the last word of the bullet item
   d. anywhere in the bullet item

3. To insert a graphic speaker note, you should use _____.
   a. Normal view's Notes pane
   b. the Outline tab
   c. the Slide pane
   d. Notes Page view

4. If you don't see slides in the Slide Finder dialog box, click the _____.
   a. Show Slides button
   b. Display button
   c. Insert button
   d. Browse button

5. The easiest way to move from slide to slide in Slide Show view is to _____.
   a. use the Advance command on a shortcut menu
   b. press Esc
   c. click the screen
   d. press Ctrl + Enter

Short Answer

1. How do you start a new presentation using a design template with PowerPoint already running?

2. How do you add title text to a slide?

3. What are the ways you can create a new slide?

4. How do you change a paragraph text indent level in the Outline tab?

5. How do you move an entire line of text?

6. How do you enter text in the Notes pane?

7. How do you view the slides you want to insert from another presentation?

8. How do you move a slide in Slide Sorter view?

9. How do you advance to the next slide in Slide Show view?

On Your Own

Exercise 1

Your sales team has nominated you to choose the new design template for the monthly sales reports. You decide to use the following text to create a new presentation using a design template with a title slide, a new slide with a title and bullets, and speaker notes.

Southwest Sales Review Agenda	{title}
Today's Date	{subtitle}
Agenda	{title}
Introduction	{bullet}
Discussion	{bullet}
Summary	{bullet}
Elaborate only where projections significantly varied from actuals	{notes}

Save the presentation as **SW Sales** in the Lesson02 folder in the PowerPoint Practice folder.

Exercise 2

Your supervisor has asked you to help with a motivational presentation. You begin by creating a new presentation using a design template with the following slides:

Personal Strategic Planning	{title}
Sales Force	{subtitle}
Topics	{title}
Planning for Change	{bullet}
Identifying Barriers to Success	{bullet}
Getting the Right Skills and Knowledge	{bullet}

Switch the order of the second and third bullets on the slide. Insert slide 2 ("Today's Goals") at the end of the presentation from the file 02 PPT Lesson in the Lesson02 folder in the PowerPoint Practice folder. Move the slide so that it becomes the second slide.

Save the presentation as **Motivate** in the Lesson02 folder in the PowerPoint Practice folder.

One Step Further

Exercise 1

The personnel department at A. Datum Corporation wants to create several presentations to remind employees of company policies. Begin by creating a new presentation using a design template with the following slides:

A. Datum Corporation	{title}
Holidays and Personal Time	{subtitle}
Holidays	{title of Title Only slide}
Standard Holidays	{title of Title and Text slide}
New Year's Day	{bullet}
Memorial Day	{bullet}
Independence Day	{bullet}
Labor Day	{bullet}
Thanksgiving Day	{bullet}
Christmas Day	{bullet}

In the Outline tab, create a new slide with the title **Expanded Holidays**. Then type the following bullet items in the Outline tab:

Available to senior staff only
Six standard holidays
Day after Thanksgiving
Christmas Eve
New Year's Eve

Move the first bullet so that it becomes the last bullet on the slide. Save the presentation as **Holidays 02** in the Lesson02 folder in the PowerPoint Practice folder.

Exercise 2

Create another new presentation for A. Datum Corporation's personnel department. Use the same design template as for the previous exercise and save the presentation as **Vacation 02** in the Personnel folder. Create slide content as follows:

A. Datum Corporation	{title}
Vacation Policies	{subtitle}
Administration Staff	{title}
Less than 1 year, 0 days	{bullet}
From 1 to 5 years, 7 days	{bullet}
From 6 to 10 years, 14 days	{bullet}

Add the following note to the slide: **Special arrangements may be made for employees with less than a full year's employment.** Save and close the presentation.

Exercise 3

Create a new presentation using a design template for your company's cafeteria. The cafeteria staff want to inform the company's employees about new "lite" entrees and a coffee bar that offers coffee drinks such as those sold at chain coffee establishments. Develop the slide content and modify slide order as desired. Then view the slides in Slide Show view.

Printing a Presentation

After completing this lesson, you will be able to:

✔ *Open an existing presentation.*
✔ *Add a header and a footer.*
✔ *Preview a presentation.*
✔ *Change the page setup.*
✔ *Choose a printer.*
✔ *Print slides, audience handouts, and speaker notes.*

KEY TERMS

- Grayscale
- Landscape
- Portrait
- Print Preview
- Pure Black and White

Microsoft PowerPoint gives you flexibility in printing the slides of a presentation and any supplements. For example, you can add headers and footers, preview your presentation in grayscale or black and white to see how color slides will look after printing, and print presentation slides, speaker notes, audience handouts, and outlines. You can easily customize the printing process by selecting the paper size, page orientation, print range, and printer type to meet your needs. When you are ready to print, you can preview your presentation on the screen to make sure it appears the way you want.

There are a number of reasons why you might want to print your presentation materials. Preparing a printed copy of the slides lets you review them easily or file the presentation hard copy for future reference. Printing the speaker notes gives you a hard copy of the notes to refer to during your presentation. You may also want to distribute printed handouts or the outline of the slides to your audience so they can refer to the material later or take notes during the presentation.

As the vice president of sales for Contoso, Ltd, you need to develop presentations for a new employee training program. In the previous lesson, you created a presentation for the first training session, "Recruiting New Clients," and now you want to open and print the presentation and accompanying speaker notes pages.

In this lesson, you will learn how to open an existing presentation; add a header and a footer; preview slides; change the page setup; choose a printer; and print slides, audience handouts, and speaker notes.

◆ Before you can use the practice files in this lesson, you must install them from the book's companion CD to their default location. See "Using the CD-ROM" at the beginning of this book for more information. To complete the procedures in this lesson, you will need to use a file named 03 PPT Lesson in the Lesson03 folder in the PowerPoint Practice folder located on your hard disk.

Opening an Existing Presentation

Opening, Saving, and Closing
a Presentation

THE BOTTOM LINE

Before you can open an existing presentation, you have to find it. Use the Getting Started task pane or the Open dialog box to help you locate and open an existing presentation.

You can open an existing presentation—for example, one that you or a coworker has already created—and work on it in the same way that you would a new presentation. To open an existing presentation, you must first identify the presentation and its location.

One of the easiest ways to open an existing presentation that you have worked on recently is to look at the list of files in the Open section of the Getting Started task pane. This task pane displays automatically each time you start PowerPoint. To open one of the presentations listed near the bottom of this pane, simply click it. The task pane closes as the presentation opens.

If the presentation you want to work with doesn't appear in the Getting Started task pane, you can use the Open dialog box to locate the presentation. To display the Open dialog box, click the More link in the Open section of the Getting Started task pane or click the Open button on the Standard toolbar.

ANOTHER METHOD

If you can't remember the name of a presentation but you know part of the name or some of its contents, you can search for the presentation using the Basic or Advanced File Search task pane. Click File Search on the File menu or click the Search button on the Standard toolbar to open the Basic File Search task pane. You can specify a partial name and locations to search in the task pane. Use the Advanced File Search task pane if you want to be able to specify properties and conditions for the search.

◆ **If you quit PowerPoint at the end of the last lesson, restart PowerPoint now.**

Open an existing presentation

In this exercise, you open an existing presentation and then save the presentation with a new name.

1 **On the Standard toolbar, click the Open button.**

PowerPoint displays the Open dialog box, which is where you specify the name and location of the presentation you want to open.

FIGURE 3-1

Open dialog box

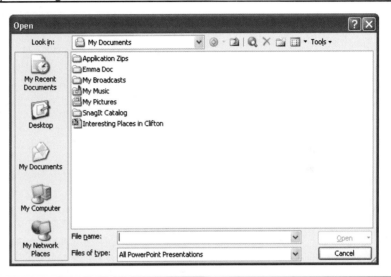

ANOTHER METHOD

- Press Ctrl + O.
- On the File menu, click Open
- On the Getting Started task pane, click More in the Open section of the task pane.

2 **In the Look In box, verify that your hard disk is selected.**

3 **In the list of file and folder names, double-click the PowerPoint Practice folder to open it.**

You can also click My Recent Documents in the Places bar in the dialog box to see a list of documents that you have worked on recently.

4 **In the list of file and folder names, double-click the Lesson03 folder, and then click 03 PPT Lesson, if it is not already selected.**

TIP

The Open button down arrow in the Open dialog box provides additional ways to open a file.

5 **Click Open.**

PowerPoint displays the presentation 03 PPT Lesson in Normal view. Your presentation window should look like the following illustration.

FIGURE 3-2

Presentation opens in Normal view

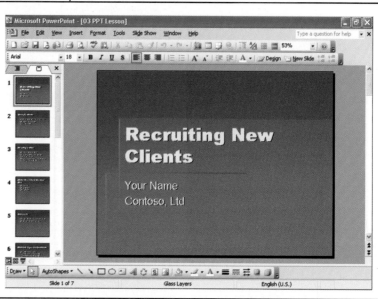

TROUBLESHOOTING

If the Outlining toolbar is open in Normal view, right-click the toolbar and select Outlining to close the toolbar.

6 **On the File menu, click Save As.**

The Save As dialog box opens. Verify that the PowerPoint Practice folder appears in the Save In box.

7 **In the File Name box, type** Contoso Recruiting Pres 03**, and then click Save.**

PowerPoint saves the presentation, and the title bar changes to the new name.

◆ **Keep this file open for the next exercise.**

QUICK REFERENCE ▼

Open an existing presentation

1 On the Standard toolbar, click the Open button.

2 In the Look In box, navigate to the location of the presentation that you want to open.

3 In the list of file names, click the presentation that you want to open.

4 Click Open.

Adding a Header and a Footer

Adjusting Headers and Footers

THE BOTTOM LINE

Headers and footers give additional information on a slide or page such as the date, the slide or page number, company name, author, and so on. This information helps you identify the slides and keep them organized.

Before you print your work, you can add a header or a footer, which will appear on every slide, handout, or notes page. Headers and footers contain useful information about the presentation, such as the author or company name, the date and time, and the page or slide number. This information helps you keep slides organized and can give a customized look to a presentation.

You can quickly and easily add a header and a footer to your slides, audience handouts, outlines, and speaker notes with the Header And Footer command on the View menu. This command opens the Header And Footer dialog box, which contains one tab for slides and one tab for notes and handouts. You can enter footers on each tab, so you can specify a footer on a notes page that differs from the footer on the presentation's slides. You can apply your header and/or footer information on the current slide or on all slides in the presentation. You can also choose to apply the slide footer information to all slides *except* the title slide, so the title slide has a clean look.

TROUBLESHOOTING

You can enter headers on notes pages and handouts only. Slides do not offer a placeholder for header information.

Header and footer information appears on the *slide master*, a slide that controls the display of items such as placeholders, background graphics, and text formatting. As you select items such as the date or slide numbers for a header or footer, these items appear in a specific location on the slide controlled by the slide master.

Add a header and a footer to a presentation

In this exercise, you apply footer information to the presentation's slides, and you also apply both header and footer information to the notes and handouts pages.

1 On the View menu, click Header And Footer.

The Header And Footer dialog box appears with the Slide tab on top.

2 **Select the Footer check box, and then type** Employee Training **to the right of the phrase Contoso, Ltd.**

In the Preview box, a black rectangle highlights the placement of the footer on the slides. Your dialog box should look like the following illustration.

FIGURE 3-3

Header And Footer dialog box

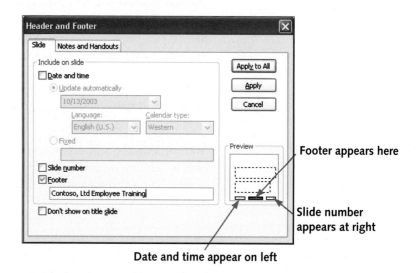

3 **Click the Notes And Handouts tab.**

The header and footer settings for the notes and handout pages appear. All four check boxes are selected.

4 **Click the Header box, and then type** Recruiting New Clients.

5 **Click the Footer box, and then type** Contoso, Ltd.

6 **Clear the Date And Time check box.**

PowerPoint includes the header, footer, and page number on each note or handout page you print.

7 **Click Apply To All.**

The header and footer information is applied to the slides, notes pages, and handouts pages. Notice that the current slide appears with the slide footer in place.

◆ **Keep this file open for the next exercise.**

QUICK CHECK

Q: Where does a footer appear on a slide by default?

A: A footer appears at the bottom center of the slide by default.

QUICK REFERENCE ▼

Add a header and footer to slides

1 On the View menu, click Header And Footer.

2 Click the Slide or Notes And Handouts tab.

3 Select date and time, slide or page number, or header or footer options.

4 Click Apply To All.

Previewing a Presentation

Previewing and Printing a Presentation

THE BOTTOM LINE

Print Preview allows you to check slides, handouts, notes pages, or an outline page before printing, which is a good way to identify errors or problems. You can change the color mode to pure black and white or grayscale in either Print Preview or Normal view to see how slides will look when printed to a black and white printer.

Print preview allows you to see how your presentation will look before you print it. While in print preview, you have the option of switching between various views, such as notes, slides, outlines, and handouts, and changing the print orientation. You can also view the current object close up by clicking the pointer on the slide or page. The pointer takes the shape of a magnifying glass in Print Preview. Click once to enlarge the view, and then click again to restore the previous size. Using the Print Preview tools can help you identify problems on slides or handouts before you commit them to paper or another medium.

If you are using a black and white printer to print a color presentation, you need to verify that the printed presentation will be legible. For example, dark red text against a shaded background shows up well in color, but when seen in black and white or shades of gray, the text tends to be indistinguishable from the background. To prevent this problem, you can preview your color slides in pure black and white or grayscale in Print Preview to see how they will look when you print them. **Pure Black and White** displays colors in black and white, whereas **Grayscale** displays colors in shades of gray.

You can also display your slides in black and white or grayscale in Normal view. Click the Color/Grayscale button on the Standard toolbar and select the desired option. Using this view allows you not only to see how your slides look in different color modes but also allows you to work with the text. When you change to black and white or grayscale in Normal view, the slide miniatures in the Slides tab retain the original design template colors.

Preview a presentation

You're ready to check your presentation before printing it. In this exercise, you preview your presentation, view your slides in Grayscale and Pure Black and White, and then change black and white settings.

 1 **On the Standard toolbar, click the Print Preview button.**

The screen switches to Print Preview and shows your presentation in the currently selected settings.

FIGURE 3-4

Print Preview window

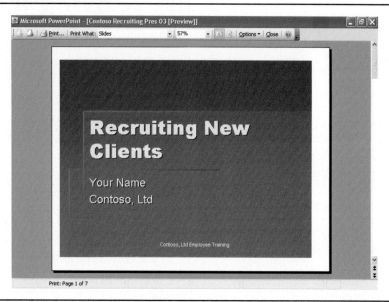

ANOTHER METHOD

On the File menu, click Print Preview.

IMPORTANT

If you are printing to a grayscale printer, your slides are shown in grayscale in Print Preview.

2 **On the Print Preview toolbar, click the Print What down arrow, and then click Handouts (2 Slides Per Page).**

The preview screen displays your presentation in handout format with two slides per page.

3 **On the Print Preview toolbar, click the Options down arrow, point to Color/Grayscale, and then click Grayscale.**

The preview screen displays your presentation in a shaded grayscale.

 4 **On the Print Preview toolbar, click the Next Page button.**

The preview screen displays the next handout page.

5 Position the pointer (which changes to a magnifying glass with a plus sign) in the preview area, and then click anywhere in the top slide.

The preview screen magnifies to display a close-up view of the slide.

6 Position the pointer (which changes to a magnifying glass with a minus sign) in the preview area, and then click anywhere in the slide.

The preview screen zooms out to display the original preview of the two handout slides.

7 On the Print Preview toolbar, click the Previous Page button.

The preview screen displays the previous handout page.

8 On the Print Preview toolbar, click the Close Preview button.

The preview screen closes, and your slide appears in the previous view.

9 Click the Normal View button, if necessary, and then click the Slides tab if necessary to display slide miniatures in the Outline/Slides pane.

ANOTHER METHOD

On the View menu, click Normal.

10 On the Standard toolbar, click the Color/Grayscale button, and then click Grayscale.

The slide switches from color to grayscale and the Grayscale View toolbar opens. You can still view the slide miniatures in color on the Slides tab, making it easier to compare the color slides with the grayscale slides.

ANOTHER METHOD

On the View menu, point to Color/Grayscale, and then click Grayscale.

FIGURE 3-5

Slide in grayscale

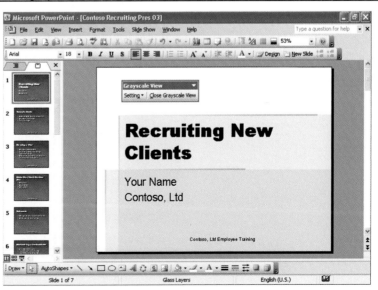

11 **On the Standard toolbar, click the Color/Grayscale button and then click Pure Black And White.**

The slide displays in pure black and white.

ANOTHER METHOD

On the View menu, point to Color/Grayscale, and then click Pure Black And White.

12 **On the Grayscale View toolbar, click the Setting button, and then click Black With Grayscale Fill.**

The slide background changes from white to gray.

13 **On the Grayscale View toolbar, click the Setting button, and then click White.**

The slide background is white again.

14 **On the Grayscale View toolbar, click the Close Black And White View button.**

The slide switches back to color.

◆ **Keep this file open for the next exercise.**

QUICK REFERENCE ▼

Preview a presentation

1 On the Standard toolbar, click the Print Preview button.

2 On the Print Preview toolbar, click the Print What down arrow, and then click an option on the list.

Preview slides in pure black and white or grayscale

1 On the Standard toolbar, click the Color/Grayscale button or if in Print Preview, click the Options down arrow, and point to Color/Grayscale.

2 On the menu, click Pure Black And White or Grayscale.

Changing the Page Setup

THE BOTTOM LINE

Besides the default page size, you can specify 10 other page size options to allow you to print to various paper sizes, set up 35mm slides, or create a Web page banner. Use the Page Setup dialog box to make a page size selection.

Choosing the Correct Print Settings

Before you print a presentation, you can use the Page Setup dialog box to set the proportions and orientation of your slides, notes pages, handouts, and outlines on the printed page. For a new presentation, PowerPoint opens with default slide page setup: on-screen slide show, **Landscape** orientation (10 x 7.5 inches), and slide numbers starting at 1. Notes, handouts, and outlines are printed in **Portrait** orientation (7.5 x 10 inches). You can change these options at any time to customize your presentation for a particular type of output.

PowerPoint has 11 slide sizes from which to choose:

- **On-Screen Show** Use this setting when you are designing an on-screen slide show. The slide size for the screen is smaller than the Letter Paper size.
- **Letter Paper (8.5x11 in)** Use this setting when you are printing a presentation on U.S. letter paper.
- **Ledger Paper (11x17 in)** Use this setting when you are printing a presentation on legal-size paper.
- **A3 Paper (297x420 mm), A4 Paper (210x297 mm), B4 (ISO) Paper (250x353 mm), B5 (ISO) Paper (176x250 mm)** Use one of these settings when you are printing on international paper.
- **35mm Slides** Use this setting when you are designing a presentation for 35mm slides. The slide size is slightly reduced to produce the slides.
- **Overhead** Use this setting when you are printing overhead transparencies for an overhead projector (8.5 x 11 inch).
- **Banner** Use this setting when you are designing a banner (8 x 1 inch) for a Web page.
- **Custom** Use this setting to design slides with a special size.

TIP

You can print with the slides sized for any of the formats, but if you first choose the correct slide format, PowerPoint properly scales the slide for that medium.

Change the page setup

In this exercise, you change the slide size setting from On-Screen Show to Letter Paper.

1 On the File menu, click Page Setup.

The Page Setup dialog box appears.

2 Click the Slides Sized For down arrow, and then click Letter Paper (8.5x11 in).

3 Click OK.

The slide size changes to Letter Paper. You will not see a change in the slide size in Normal view.

◆ Keep this file open for the next exercise.

Choosing the Correct Print Settings

QUICK REFERENCE ▼

Change the slide size

1 On the File menu, click Page Setup.
2 Click the Slides Sized For down arrow.
3 Click a format in the list.
4 Click OK.

Choosing a Printer

THE BOTTOM LINE

PowerPoint uses the Windows default printer unless you choose another printer to print a presentation. You may want to select a printer other than the default to print in color or if your default printer is busy.

PowerPoint prints presentations on your default Microsoft Windows printer unless you select a different printer. Your default printer is set up in the Windows print settings in the Control Panel.

TIP

To change the default printer in Windows XP, click Start on the taskbar, point to Control Panel, double-click Printers and Faxes in the Control Panel, right-click the printer you want to set as the default, and then click Set As Default Printer. For Windows 2000 users, point to Settings, click Control Panel, and then double-click Printers.

You can select another printer in PowerPoint's Print dialog box. After you have added a new printer to your system, it will appear on the list of available printers when you click the Name down arrow. Just click the printer to select it as the presentation's printer. You might select a different printer if it will do a better job of printing your presentation materials (for example, if it is a color printer and your default printer is black and white), if there is a problem with your default printer, or if your default printer is currently busy.

ANOTHER METHOD

If you are using Microsoft Windows 2000 or Windows XP and the Active Directory service, you can search for and use printers across your network, intranet, or the Web. Click the Find Printer button in the Print dialog box, and then click Find Now to locate all printers on the network, intranet, or Web site. You can then select the desired printer and it appears in the Name box in PowerPoint's Print dialog box.

Select a printer for a presentation

You've previewed the presentation and adjusted its page size. You're now ready to choose a printer to print the presentation materials.

1 **Verify that your printer is turned on, connected to your computer, and loaded with paper.**

Verifying these points can eliminate some common reasons why your presentation doesn't print when you tell it to.

2 **On the File menu, click Print.**

The Print dialog box appears.

FIGURE 3-6

Print dialog box

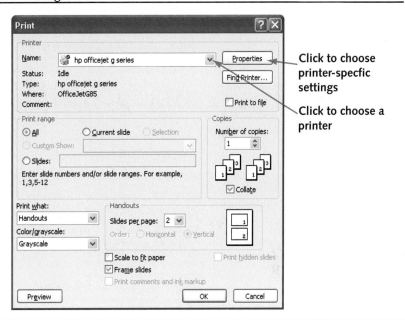

Click to choose printer-specfic settings

Click to choose a printer

3 **In the Printer area, click the Name down arrow.**

A drop-down list appears with the printers installed on your computer.

4 **Click one of the printers in the list.**

After choosing a printer, you can customize your printer settings.

5 **Click Properties.**

The Properties dialog box appears, showing the current printer settings. The Properties dialog settings differ depending on the specific printer you selected.

6 **Click OK in the Properties dialog box.**

The Properties dialog box closes to display the Print dialog box.

◆ **Keep this dialog box open for the next exercise.**

QUICK REFERENCE ▼

Choose a printer

1 On the File menu, click Print.

2 In the Printer area, click the Name down arrow.

3 Click a printer in the list.

4 Click Properties and make any necessary setting adjustments for the selected printer.

5 Click OK in the Properties dialog box.

Printing a Presentation

Previewing and Printing a Presentation

THE BOTTOM LINE

To make a hard copy of presentation materials, print them. You can print slides, notes pages, handouts, or the presentation outline. Choose other options in the Print dialog box to change output color, select slides or number of handouts to print, frame slides, and so on.

You can print your PowerPoint presentation in several ways: as slides, speaker notes, audience handouts, or an outline. PowerPoint makes it easy to print your presentation. It detects the type of printer that you chose—either color or black and white—and prints the appropriate version of the presentation. For example, if you select a black and white printer, your presentation will be set to print in shades of gray (grayscale).

TIP

If you are working with a professional printer to print your slides, you will need to print your slides to a file instead of a printer. To print your slides to a file, select the Print To File check box in the Printer section of the Print dialog box.

Slides and supplements are printed based on the settings in the Print dialog box. In the Print dialog box, you can select a printer or the option to print to a file. You set the print range, which defines which slides to print. You can choose to print multiple copies of a presentation, and if you do print more than one copy of each slide, you can choose to collate the presentation as you print. When you collate the presentation, a complete set of pages is printed before the next set starts printing. The Print dialog box also contains a Preview button that takes you to the Print Preview window, allowing you to preview any changes you might have made.

By clicking the Print What down arrow in the Print dialog box, you can choose to print a presentation as one of four output types:

- **Slides** Prints slides as they appear on the screen, one per page. You can print a slide as an overhead transparency in the same way that you print any other slide, except you put transparency film in the printer instead of paper.
- **Handouts** Prints one, two, three, four, six, or nine slides per page, with the option of ordering them horizontally or vertically.
- **Notes Pages** Prints each slide with the speaker notes under it.
- **Outline View** Prints an outline with formatting according to the current view setting. What you see in the Outline tab is what you get on the printout.

An example of each printing type is shown below.

FIGURE 3-7

PowerPoint printouts

Slide (landscape)

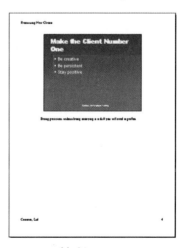

Notes page

Handout page

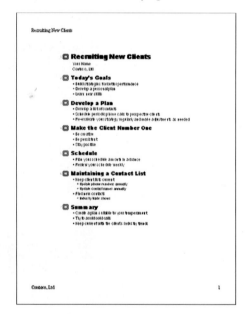

Outline page

By using the Color/Grayscale down arrow in the Print dialog box, you can choose to print a presentation as one of three color options:

- **Color** Use this option to print a presentation in color on a color printer. If you select a black and white printer with this option, the presentation prints in grayscale.
- **Grayscale** Use this option to print a presentation in grayscale on a color or black and white printer.
- **Pure Black And White** Use this option to print a presentation in black and white only with no gray on a color or black and white printer.

Finally, at the bottom of the Print dialog box, you can select from the following print options to enhance a printout:

- **Scale To Fit Paper** Use this option to scale slides to fit the paper size in the printer if the paper in the printer does not correspond to the slide size and orientation settings.
- **Frame Slides** Use this option to add a frame (a border) around the presentation slides when you print. This option is not available for the Outline print type.
- **Include Comments And Ink Markup** Use this option to print any comments and handwritten notes that you have inserted throughout the presentation. This option will be grayed out (unavailable) unless the presentation contains comments.
- **Print Hidden Slides** Use this option to print all hidden slides. This option will be grayed out (unavailable) unless the presentation contains hidden slides.

If you are satisfied with the current Print dialog box settings, you can click the Print button on the Standard toolbar to print directly without first viewing the settings. Otherwise, click the Print command on the File menu to adjust printer settings before printing.

Print presentation materials

Now that you have reviewed print output types and options, you're ready to print presentation slides, audience handouts, and speaker notes.

1 On the File menu, click Print (if the Print dialog is not already displayed).

The Print dialog box appears.

FIGURE 3-8

Options in the Print dialog box

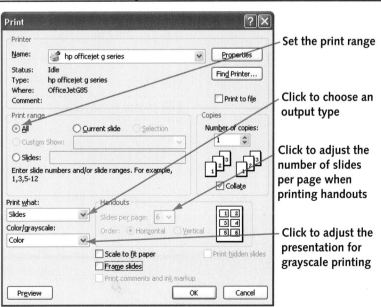

- Set the print range
- Click to choose an output type
- Click to adjust the number of slides per page when printing handouts
- Click to adjust the presentation for grayscale printing

2 In the Print Range area, click the Current Slide option.

3 Click the Print What down arrow, and then click Slides.

4 Click the Color/Grayscale down arrow, click Grayscale, and then click OK.

PowerPoint prints the current slide in the presentation. A small print icon appears on the status bar, showing the printing status.

> **TIP**
>
> Every printer prints text and graphics slightly differently. PowerPoint presentation slides are sized to the printer you choose. Using scalable fonts, such as TrueType fonts, you can print a presentation on different printers with the same great results. When you print a presentation with scalable fonts, the size of the text is reduced or enlarged in the presentation for each printer to get consistent results.

5 On the File menu, click Print.

The Print dialog box appears.

6 Click the Print What down arrow, and then click Handouts.

> **TIP**
>
> You can print audience handouts in six formats: one, two, three, four, six, or nine slides per page.

7 Click the Slides Per Page down arrow, and then click 2.

Notice that PowerPoint selects the Frame Slides check box when you select handouts.

8 Click OK.

PowerPoint prints the presentation slides as handout pages.

9 On the File menu, click Print.

The Print dialog box appears.

10 Click the Print What down arrow, and then click Notes Pages.

11 In the Print Range area, click the Slides option.

The insertion point appears in the range box next to the Slides option.

> **TIP**
>
> You can print notes pages or slides in any order by entering slide numbers and ranges separated by commas.

12 Type 1-4,7.

You are telling PowerPoint you want to print pages 1 through 4 and 7.

13 Click OK.

PowerPoint prints notes pages 1, 2, 3, 4, and 7.

◆ If you are continuing to other lessons, save the Contoso Recruiting Pres 03 presentation with the current name and then close it. If you are not continuing to other lessons, save and close the Contoso Recruiting Pres 03 presentation, and then click the Close button in the title bar of the PowerPoint window.

QUICK CHECK

Q: If you want a border to appear around each printed slide or page, what option do you choose in the Print dialog box?

A: **Select the Frame Slides check box in the Print dialog box.**

QUICK REFERENCE ▼

Print a presentation

1 On the File menu, click Print.

2 Click the down arrow to the right of the Print What box, and then click the part of the presentation you want to print.

3 Select any other print options you want to apply.

4 Click OK.

Key Points

✓ *If you need to continue working on a presentation, you can open it from the Getting Started task pane or using the Open dialog box.*

✓ *Headers and footers provide additional information about notes pages, handouts, and slides. Use the Header And Footer dialog box to insert the date and time, a header, slide number, or a footer on slides, notes pages, outlines, and handouts.*

✓ *Preview slides to check their accuracy and impact. In the Print Preview window, you can move from slide to slide, change the view to see notes pages, handouts with various numbers of thumbnails, and the outline.*

✓ *You can change to a grayscale or black and white view in either Print Preview or Normal view to see how slides will look if printed with a black and white printer.*

✓ *Change the page setup if you need to print to a specific paper size or to a medium such as overhead transparency film or 35mm slides.*

✓ *You can choose the printer that will print a presentation in the Print dialog box. This dialog box also allows you to modify the printer's properties, choose what to print, specify what slides or pages to print, and select other options such as a frame for slides.*

Quick Quiz

True/False

T F **1.** The New Presentation task pane has a section that allows you to open existing presentations.

T F **2.** By default, the slide number appears at the bottom right side of all slides.

T F **3.** If you want to see an outline in Print Preview at a larger size, simply click the pointer on the outline.

T F **4.** You can create a custom page size for slides if desired.

T F **5.** When you collate a presentation as you print several copies, PowerPoint prints all page 1s, then all page 2s, and so on.

Multiple Choice

1. You can add a footer to one or more slides that includes _____.
   a. date
   b. slide number
   c. footer text
   d. all of the above

2. If you have a black and white printer, you may want to display slides in _____ to see how colors will look when printed.
   a. Grayscale
   b. Pure Color
   c. Pure Black And White
   d. either a or c

3. The default orientation for slides is _____.
   a. Portrait
   b. Landscape
   c. On-Screen
   d. Banner

4. To change the default printer in Windows XP, open the Control Panel and double-click _____.
   a. Network Printers
   b. All Printers
   c. Printers and Faxes
   d. Default Printers

5. If the paper in the printer doesn't correspond to the slide size and orientation, you can make slides fit the paper size by selecting _____ in the Print dialog box.
   a. Page Setup
   b. Scale To Fit Paper
   c. Print Comments
   d. Print Slides At Current Paper Size

Short Answer

1. Describe two methods for opening an existing presentation.
2. How do you change to Pure Black and White view?
3. What are four options you can specify in a header or a footer?
4. How do you select On-Screen Show as your slide size?
5. What are the print types from which you can print a presentation?
6. How do you print audience handouts with four slides per page?
7. How can you preview a presentation outline before printing?

On Your Own

Exercise 1

Open the presentation Contoso Recruiting Pres 03 in the Lesson03 folder that is located in the PowerPoint Practice folder, and then print two slides per page without a frame.

Exercise 2

Open the presentation Contoso Recruiting Pres 03 in the Lesson03 folder that is located in the PowerPoint Practice folder, and then print audience handouts with six grayscale slides per page in vertical order.

One Step Further

Exercise 1

Open the Holidays 02 presentation you created in Lesson 2. Add a footer to all slides that displays the date (choose the date option that updates automatically), the slide number, and the footer text **A. Datum Corporation**. For notes and handouts pages, add a header that includes the date (update automatically) and the text **Holidays and Personal Time**. Add a footer with the text **A. Datum Corporation**. Save the file as **Holidays 03** in the Lesson03 folder and close the presentation.

Exercise 2

Open the Holidays 03 presentation and display the presentation in Print Preview. Change to Outline view. Magnify the view to see the header and footer text on the page. Print the presentation as an outline. Save and close the presentation.

Exercise 3

Open the Vacation 02 presentation you created in Lesson 2. Display the slides in Normal view in Pure Black and White. Change the view to Grayscale. Print Notes Pages in grayscale, with a frame around the pages. Save the file as **Vacation 03** in the Lesson03 folder and close the presentation.

Outlining Your Ideas

After completing this lesson, you will be able to:

✔ *Create a blank presentation.*
✔ *View and enter text in an outline.*
✔ *Insert an outline from Microsoft Word.*
✔ *Change the view of an outline.*
✔ *Select text and delete slides in the outline.*
✔ *Rearrange slides, paragraphs, and text.*
✔ *Format text in an outline.*
✔ *Send an outline or slides to Word.*
✔ *Save a presentation as an outline.*

KEY TERMS

- export
- import
- Rich Text Format (RTF)

Outlining your thoughts and ideas makes it easier to organize a presentation. In Microsoft PowerPoint, you can enter and organize your thoughts and ideas in the Outline tab on the Outline/Slides pane to see the slide title text and paragraph text for each slide in the presentation. You can also edit and rearrange both title and paragraph text in the Outline tab, **import** outlines created in other programs into a PowerPoint outline, and **export** the results when you are done.

In previous lessons, you created a presentation for Contoso, Ltd's new employee training program. Now you need to develop a presentation that can be customized for prospective clients. You will present the slide show to the other department heads and to the CEO of Contoso at the next monthly meeting.

In this lesson, you will create a blank presentation, enter text into a PowerPoint outline, insert a Microsoft Word outline into a presentation, change the way you view an outline, select text, delete slides, rearrange and format text, export the outline into Word for later use, and then save a presentation as an outline.

◆ Before you can use the practice files in this lesson, you must install them from the book's companion CD to their default location. See "Using the CD-ROM" at the beginning of this book for more information. To complete the procedures in this lesson, you will need to create a new blank presentation and use a file named 04 Marketing Outline in the Lesson04 folder in the PowerPoint Practice folder located on your hard disk.

Creating a Blank Presentation

THE BOTTOM LINE

Start a new blank presentation when you want to concentrate on slide content. You can apply a design template at any time after you have begun entering slide text.

If you are not sure how you want your presentation to look, you can start a new presentation from scratch. You can create a blank presentation when you first start PowerPoint or after you have already started PowerPoint. Either way, a blank presentation appears, ready for you to use.

Working in a blank presentation allows you to concentrate on getting content on the slides, rather than spending time selecting just the right design. You can always apply and tweak a design at any time after you have begun to insert slide content. Keep in mind, however, that even the blank presentation has a template that controls the placeholder positions and text formatting.

◆ If you quit PowerPoint at the end of the last lesson, restart PowerPoint now.

Create a blank presentation

To start your task of creating a customizable presentation, you create a blank presentation and then save the presentation.

1 Click the New button on the Standard toolbar.

PowerPoint displays a blank presentation with the default Title Slide layout, and the Slide Layout task pane appears, displaying various slide layouts.

ANOTHER METHOD

- Press Ctrl + N.
- On the File menu, click New.
- On the New Presentation task pane, click Blank Presentation.

FIGURE 4-1

PowerPoint displays a blank presentation with a title slide

2 On the title bar of the Slide Layout task pane, click the Close button to close the task pane.

Because you want to start with the default title slide already displayed, you don't need to specify another layout. Closing the task pane gives you more room to work.

3 On the File menu, click Save As, and then type Contoso Company Pres 04 in the File Name box.

4 Navigate to the Lesson04 folder in the PowerPoint Practice folder, and then click Save.

◆ Keep this file open for the next exercise.

QUICK REFERENCE ▼

Create a blank presentation

On the Standard toolbar, click the New button or in the New Presentation task pane, click Blank Presentation under New.

QUICK CHECK

Q: What is one way you can start a new presentation while working on another presentation?

A: Click the New button on the Standard toolbar, click New on the File menu, press Ctrl + N, or if the task pane is open, select New Presentation from Other Task Panes.

Entering Text in an Outline

Creating Slides and Revising
Their Layouts

THE BOTTOM LINE

Enter slide text in the Outline tab when you want to be able to see the content of a number of slides at one time. Working in the Outline tab makes it easy to create a proper outline structure for your slides.

As you have already learned in Lesson 2, working in the Outline tab allows you to concentrate on the text of your presentation. The Outline tab displays the title and bullet points for each slide at a reduced size, making it possible for you to see most or all of the text in your presentation in one pane. This makes it simple for you to avoid repetition and stay on track with your main points. For example, after you create a slide that summarizes the topics that will be covered in the presentation, you can refer easily to that slide as you enlarge on each topic in subsequent slides.

If you are a skillful typist, working in the Outline tab has an additional benefit. You can do quite a lot of the labor of creating a presentation using keyboard keys. For example, you can insert a slide using keys so you don't have to take your hand away from the keyboard to use the mouse to click a command or button.

You need to know a few basic skills to work with an outline in the Outline tab. When you press Enter after inserting a title or paragraph, you automatically create another line at the same outline level. For instance, if you press Enter after typing a slide title, PowerPoint creates a new slide so you can enter the next title. Likewise, if you press Enter after typing a first-level bullet item, a new first-level bullet item is created.

To make sure your slide content is properly structured, you may need to *promote* or *demote* paragraphs. When you promote an item, you move it up to a higher level. For example, promoting a first-level bullet item turns it into a slide title. When you demote an item, you move it down to a lower level. Demoting a first-level bullet item turns it into a second-level bullet item. You can promote and demote using keyboard keys or buttons on the Outlining toolbar.

Enter text in the Outline tab

In this exercise, you use the Outline tab to complete the title slide.

1 **In the Outline/Slides pane, click the Outline tab, if necessary, and then click to the right side of slide 1 to place the insertion point.**

The slide icon for slide 1 is selected in the outline.

2 **On the View menu, point to Toolbars, and then click Outlining, if necessary, to display the Outlining toolbar.**

ANOTHER METHOD

Right-click any displayed toolbar, and then click Outlining.

FIGURE 4-2

Display the Outlining toolbar

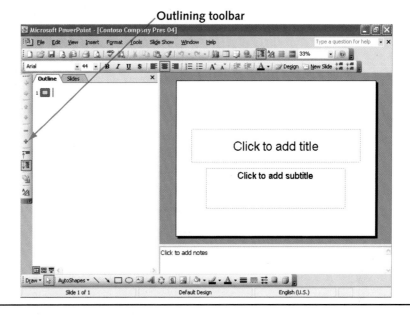

3 Type Give Your Image Impact, and then press Enter.

A new slide appears in the Outline tab.

4 On the Outlining toolbar, click the Demote button, or press Tab.

The insertion point shifts to the right to start a new paragraph for the title text above it. Because this is a title slide, the new paragraph will be the subtitle.

TIP

Notice that there is no bullet next to the subtitle text on the title slide.

5 Type Contoso, Ltd at the insertion point.

Your screen should look similar to the following illustration.

FIGURE 4-3

New text displays in Outline tab

Don't worry if a wavy red underline appears below the word *Contoso*. It means this word isn't in PowerPoint's spelling dictionary. You'll learn more about spelling in the next lesson.

6 **On the Outlining toolbar, click the Promote button.**

The paragraph text shifts to the left to create title text for a new slide. A slide icon appears next to the text.

7 **On the Outlining toolbar, click the Demote button.**

The title text shifts to the right to again create paragraph text for the title text above it.

◆ **Keep this file open for the next exercise.**

QUICK REFERENCE ▼

View and enter text in an outline

1 In the Outline/Slides pane, click the Outline tab.
2 Click to place the insertion point, type your text, and then press Enter.

Inserting an Outline from Microsoft Word

To save time, create slides using an outline typed in another program. You can insert text in Word (.doc) format, Rich Text Format (.rtf), or plain text format (.txt).

Importing an Outline from Word

If you already have text in other programs, such as Microsoft Word, you can insert the text into the Outline tab as titles and body text. Inserting an outline in this way can save considerable time because you don't have to retype the outline text in PowerPoint.

You can insert text in several formats, including Microsoft Word (.doc) format, Rich Text Format (.rtf), or plain text format (.txt). When you insert a Word or Rich Text Format document, PowerPoint creates an outline of slide titles and paragraphs based on the heading styles in the document. When you insert text from a plain text document, paragraphs without tabs at the beginning become slide titles, and paragraphs with tabs at the beginning become paragraph text. You can of course adjust the title and text levels after you have imported the outline into PowerPoint.

Imported slides are inserted into the presentation following the currently selected slide.

Insert an outline developed in another program into a presentation

You have created the title slide for your new presentation, and you're now ready to add content. You will use an existing Word outline to create new slides.

1 **On the Insert menu, click Slides From Outline.**

The Insert Outline dialog box appears.

2 **In the Look In box, verify that the Lesson04 folder in the PowerPoint Practice folder is listed and that All Outlines appears in the Files Of Type box.**

3 **In the list of file and folder names, click 04 Marketing Outline.**

4 **Click Insert.**

PowerPoint inserts the Word outline into the PowerPoint outline following the current slide.

If you receive a message telling you that PowerPoint needs a converter, install the converter as directed.

5 **Click a blank area of the Outline tab to deselect the text.**

Your screen should look similar to the following illustration.

FIGURE 4-4

New text displays in Outline tab

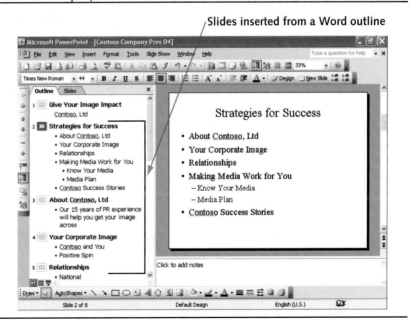

Slides inserted from a Word outline

◆ **Leave this file open for the next exercise.**

QUICK REFERENCE ▼

Insert an outline from Microsoft Word

1 In the Outline tab, click a blank area to place the insertion point where you want to insert the outline.

2 On the Insert menu, click Slides From Outline.

3 In the Look In box, navigate to the location of the outline that you want to insert.

4 In the list of file and folder names, click an outline.

5 Click Insert.

Changing the View of an Outline

Importing an Outline from Word

THE BOTTOM LINE

You can change the view of the outline in the Outline tab in a number of ways to make it easier to work with the outline. Zooming in or out lets you see more detail or more slides. Collapsing the outline lets you reorganize slides using only their titles. Showing formatting lets you see in the outline the same fonts and styles used on the slide.

The outline you are working on might contain more text than you can see on the screen at one time. To make it easier to view an outline, you can reduce the view scale of the presentation window. You can change the scale of your view by using the Zoom button on the Standard toolbar or the Zoom command on the View menu. When you change the view scale, the view of the presentation is increased or decreased in size, but the presentation itself does not change size.

The standard view scales available in the Outline tab are 25%, 33%, 50%, 66%, 75%, and 100%. Other panes use additional view scales: Fit, which means the view of the presentation is sized to fit your monitor; or 150%, 200%, 300%, and 400%, which are helpful for working on detailed items, such as graphics or objects. The Zoom command allows you to decrease the view size to see more of the presentation outline or increase the view size to see small text that is hard to read. You can also enter any view scale in the Zoom box on the Standard toolbar. The Zoom setting affects whatever pane is currently active.

To make it easier to work with the main points of an outline, PowerPoint lets you collapse and expand slide content to view entire slides or only slide titles. When you format text in the Outline tab, sometimes the text can be hard to read, so PowerPoint allows you to show or hide text formatting in the outline. The formatting information is not deleted or cleared. It is just turned off so that you can see the content more easily. When you print an outline, the outline will always appear with formatting on.

Change the view of the outline

Now that you have more content in the outline, you can become more familiar with some of the Outline tab's features. In this exercise, you change the view scale, and then you collapse and expand the outline.

42% ▼

1 Click in the Outline tab, if necessary. On the Standard toolbar, click the Zoom button down arrow, and then click 25%.

The view scale decreases from 33% to 25%. Your presentation window should look similar to the following illustration.

ANOTHER METHOD

On the View menu, click Zoom to open the Zoom dialog box.

TROUBLESHOOTING TIP

Your view scale might be different, depending on the size of your monitor.

FIGURE 4-5

Outline view scale decreased

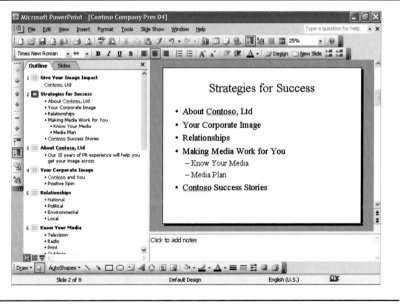

You can also enter a specific zoom percentage in the Zoom box.

2   **On the Standard toolbar, click in the Zoom box to type a percentage.**

3   **Type 38, and then press Enter.**

The view scale changes to 38%.

4   **Click the blank area to the right of the slide 2 title to place the insertion point in the line.**

5   **On the Outlining toolbar, click the Collapse button.**

Slide 2 collapses to show only the title. The rest of the outline remains fully expanded. Your presentation window should look like the following illustration.

FIGURE 4-6

Slide 2 is collapsed

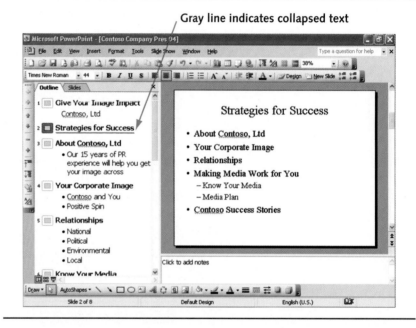

To make it easier to work on the main points of the outline, you can view slide titles only for the presentation.

6   **On the Outlining toolbar, click the Collapse All button.**

The view switches from titles and paragraphs to titles only.

7   **Click the blank area to the right of the slide 6 title to place the insertion point in the line.**

8   **On the Outlining toolbar, click the Expand button.**

Slide 6 expands to include the paragraph text again.

9   **On the Outlining toolbar, click the Expand All button.**

The view switches to show all of the text in the outline. Now you will change the view to show in the outline the same text formatting applied in the Slide pane.

10 **On the Outlining toolbar, click the Show Formatting button.**

The text in the Outline tab changes from plain to formatted text, as shown in the following illustration. The formatting reflects the styles that were applied in the Word source file.

FIGURE 4-7

Outline text shows formatting

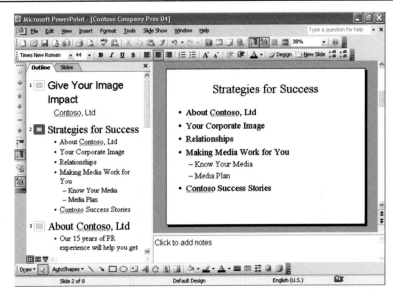

◆ **Keep this file open for the next exercise.**

QUICK REFERENCE ▼

Change the view of an outline

On the Standard toolbar, click the Zoom button down arrow, and then click a percentage.

Or

1 On the Standard toolbar, click in the Zoom box to select the current percentage size.

2 Type the percentage size, and then press Enter.

Collapse the outline

1 Click to the right of the slide title in the Outline tab to place the insertion point in the line.

2 On the Outlining toolbar, click the Collapse button or the Collapse All button.

Expand the outline

1 Click to place the insertion point in the line.

2 On the Outlining toolbar, click the Expand button or the Expand All button.

Show outline formatting

On the Outlining toolbar, click the Show Formatting button.

Selecting Text and Deleting Slides in an Outline

THE BOTTOM LINE

The Outline tab is the best location for making extensive text changes to a presentation because you can work in this tab just as in a word processing program to select, edit, and rearrange text.

The compact nature of the Outline tab makes it the best place to edit text because you can see a good part of the presentation's text in one place. Additionally, working in the Outline tab is similar to working in a word processor. In the Outline tab, you can select, edit, and rearrange slides, paragraphs, and text by using the Outlining toolbar buttons or by dragging the slides, paragraphs, or text.

As you will recall from Lesson 2, to edit or rearrange slides and paragraphs, you must first select the material you want to work with. To select a slide or paragraph, click the corresponding slide icon or paragraph bullet. To select a word, double-click the word. To select any portion of a title or paragraph, drag the I-beam pointer to highlight the text. In the Outline tab, you can also click the blank area at the end of a title or paragraph to select the entire line of text. This technique works especially well when selecting slide titles.

Select and delete slides and text in an outline

In this exercise, you select and delete a slide and a paragraph, and then you select text using different methods.

 1 **Position the I-beam pointer (which changes to the four-headed arrow) over the icon for slide 3, and then click the icon to select the slide.**

The entire slide, including all text, is selected. Your presentation window should look like the following illustration.

ANOTHER METHOD

You can also select a slide by clicking its slide number.

FIGURE 4-8

All text on the slide is selected

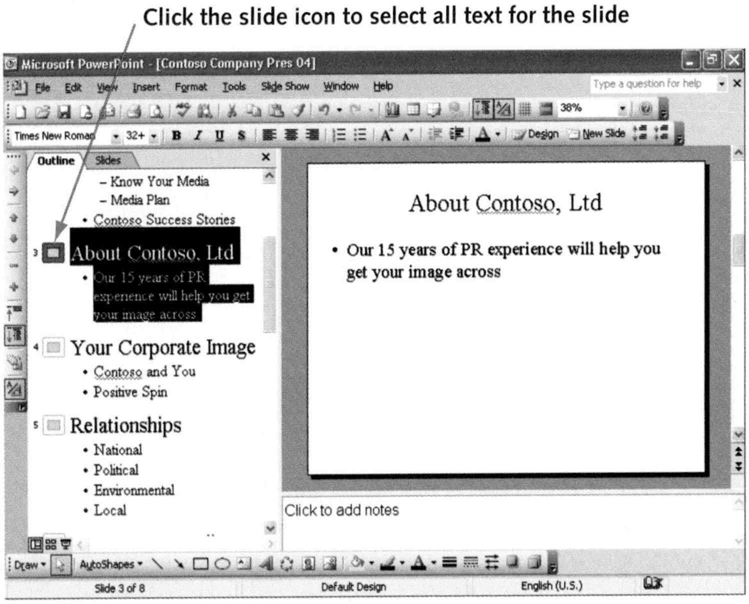

Click the slide icon to select all text for the slide

2 **Press Delete.**

PowerPoint deletes slide 3 and renumbers the other slides.

ANOTHER METHOD

On the Edit menu in any view, click Delete Slide.

3 **Scroll to the top of the outline and display slide 2.**

This slide's first paragraph refers to the slide you just deleted, so you will need to delete this paragraph. Selecting and deleting paragraphs works the same way as selecting and deleting slides.

4 **Position the I-beam pointer (which changes to the four-headed arrow) over the bullet next to the paragraph titled "About Contoso, Ltd" in slide 2, and then click the bullet.**

PowerPoint selects the paragraph.

5 **Press Delete.**

PowerPoint deletes the paragraph.

6 **Click the bullet next to the paragraph titled "Your Corporate Image" in slide 2.**

TIP

You can also select multiple paragraphs.

7 Hold down Shift, and then click the bullet for the paragraph titled "Media Plan." Notice that the bulleted text in between is also selected.

Your presentation window should look like the following illustration.

FIGURE 4-9

Multiple paragraphs are selected

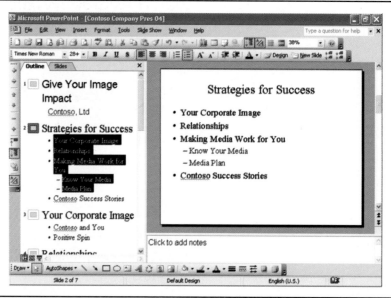

ANOTHER METHOD

You can also select multiple paragraphs by dragging the mouse. Click the I-beam pointer where you want the selection to begin, and then drag the I-beam pointer down to where you want the selection to end. PowerPoint selects everything between the first click and the ending point of the drag action.

8 Position the I-beam pointer in the middle of the word "Contoso" in the last paragraph in slide 2.

9 Drag the I-beam pointer to the right, through the text "Contoso Success Stories," to select all the text that follows in the line.

Although you started the selection in the middle of the word *Contoso*, because the Automatic Word Selection feature is turned on, PowerPoint selects the entire word.

◆ Keep this file open for the next exercise.

TIP

You can turn off the Automatic Word Selection command by clicking Options on the Tools menu, clicking the Edit tab, and then clearing the When Selecting, Automatically Select Entire Word check box.

QUICK REFERENCE ▼

Select text

1 Position the I-beam pointer.

2 Drag the I-beam pointer to select the desired text.

Select multiple paragraphs

1 Click the bullet next to a paragraph.

2 Hold down Shift, and the click the bullet next to another paragraph.

Select and delete a paragraph or slide

1 Position the I-beam pointer over a bullet or slide icon, and then click to select the bullet text or slide.

2 Press Delete.

Rearranging Slides, Paragraphs, and Text

Rearranging a Presentation

THE BOTTOM LINE

Take advantage of the Outline tab's Outlining toolbar to rearrange slides and slide text to improve your presentation's flow.

One of the most important tasks you can perform in the Outline tab is rearranging slide content. As you work with a presentation, you will often realize that a slide would fit better at some other location in the presentation, or that the paragraphs on a slide aren't in quite the right order. You may also feel that the phrasing of a particular paragraph could be improved by rearranging words.

You can rearrange slides and paragraphs in the Outline tab by using the Move Up button and the Move Down button on the Outlining toolbar or by dragging selected slides and paragraphs to the desired location. You can also drag a paragraph so that it becomes a part of another paragraph. To move selected words, you simply drag the selection to the new position.

Rearrange a slide, paragraphs, and words

You're ready to begin the process of fine-tuning the presentation outline. In this paragraph, you rearrange slides, paragraphs, and words.

1 Scroll down so that slide 4 is the top slide in the window.

2 Position the four-headed arrow over the slide icon for slide 4, Relationships, and click to select it.

3 Drag the slide icon down between slides 6 and 7.

As you drag, the pointer changes to the vertical two-headed arrow, and a horizontal line appears, showing you where you can place the slide. Your screen should look similar to the following illustration.

FIGURE 4-10

Moving a slide to a new location

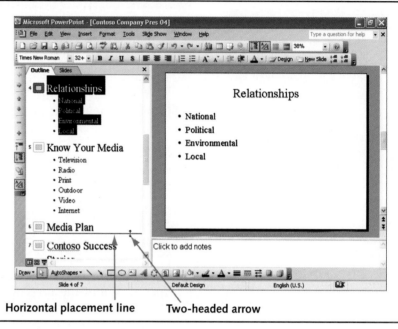

Horizontal placement line   Two-headed arrow

After you release the mouse button, the selected slide content is dropped into its new location, and PowerPoint reorders and renumbers the slides.

4 Click the bullet to the left of the word "Local" in slide 6.

The paragraph is selected.

5 On the Outlining toolbar, click the Move Up button three times.

Local becomes the first bulleted item.

6 Scroll to the top of the outline, and then in slide 2, position the four-headed arrow over the bullet of the text line titled "Know Your Media."

7 Drag the text line horizontally to the left one level, as shown in the following illustration.

FIGURE 4-11

Move a bullet item up one level by dragging

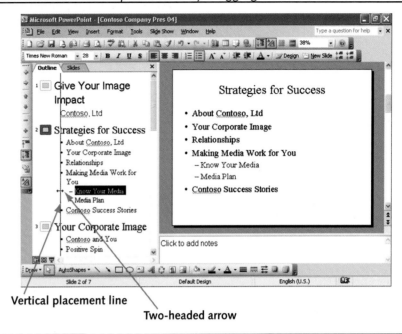

Vertical placement line

Two-headed arrow

As you drag, the pointer changes to the horizontal two-headed arrow, and a vertical line indicates at what level the text will be placed. The text line moves one indent level to the left. This is the same action as promoting the paragraph.

8 **Drag the text line titled Media Plan horizontally to the left one level.**

You have promoted this bullet item to the first level.

TIP

You can also drag a paragraph horizontally to the right to demote it.

---

9 **Click the bullet next to the text "Making Media Work for You," and then press Delete.**

10 **Scroll down so that you can see all of slide 7 at the bottom of the outline, and then position the I-beam pointer over the word "Bits" in slide 7.**

11 **Select the entire word, the comma, and the space that follows it, and then drag the selection to the left of the word "Bytes" on the same line.**

As you drag, a gray indicator line shows where the text will be placed. When you release the mouse button, the word *Bits* moves to its new position.

FIGURE 4-12

Indicator line shows where text will move

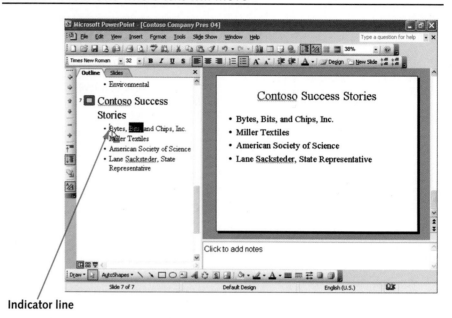

Indicator line

◆ **Keep this file open for the next exercise.**

QUICK REFERENCE ▼

Rearrange a slide

1 Position the four-headed arrow over the icon of the slide to rearrange.

2 Drag the slide icon between the slides where you want the selected slide to appear.

Rearrange paragraphs

1 Position the four-headed arrow over the bullet of your text line.

2 Drag the text line horizontally to the left or to the right to promote or demote one level.

Rearrange words

1 Position the I-beam pointer over a word in the slide, and then drag the I-beam pointer to select the words that you want to rearrange.

2 Drag the selection to a new position.

QUICK CHECK

Q: What happens when you select a bullet item and drag it to the left?

A: **The item is promoted one level.**

Formatting Text in an Outline

Formatting Text and Text Objects

THE BOTTOM LINE

Apply formatting right in the Outline tab to save time while you're working with outline text. You can change fonts, font sizes, and styles using Formatting toolbar buttons.

You can apply formatting in the Outline tab just as you would in the Slide pane. (You will learn more about formatting text in the Slide pane in the next lesson.) If you are working extensively in the Outline tab, it makes good sense to apply formatting to the outline text rather than switch to the Slide pane to do so.

TIP

If you prefer creating and formatting slide text as an outline, you can drag the Outline/Slides pane border to the right to provide plenty of room to work on the outline. This is especially useful if you're showing formatting in the Outline tab because you have room for the formatted text to display at a larger scale.

You can change fonts, sizes, and styles in the Outline tab. To format text, you first select it and then apply the specific formatting you want, using the commands on the Formatting toolbar. The Formatting toolbar includes commands to change the font type and size and to apply the bold, italic, and underline styles.

Format text in an outline

Now that you're satisfied with the reorganization of the presentation, you can turn your attention to formatting text. In this exercise, you change the style, font, and size of the text.

1 Scroll to the top of the outline.

2 Double-click the blank area to the right of the word "Impact" in the title of slide 1.

The title text is selected.

 3 On the Formatting toolbar, click the Bold button.

ANOTHER METHOD

Press Ctrl + B.

 4 Position the four-headed arrow pointer to the left of the word "Contoso" in the paragraph text of slide 1.

5 Click the blank area to select the entire line.

I **6** On the Formatting toolbar, click the Italic button.

The selected text is formatted. Your screen should look similar to the following illustration.

ANOTHER METHOD

Press Ctrl + I.

FIGURE 4-13

Text formatted with bold and italic styles

7 With the subtitle text still selected, on the Formatting toolbar, click the Font Size button down arrow, and then click 28.

The subtitle text is reduced in size.

8 Double-click the blank area to the right of the slide title "Give Your Image Impact."

The entire line is selected.

9 On the Formatting toolbar, click the Increase Font Size button.

The slide title font changes from 44 to 48 points. The Increase Font Size button increases the font size by a set increment and thus can be used when you just want to increase the size without worrying about a specific font size.

10 On the Formatting toolbar, click the Font down arrow, and then scroll down and click Times New Roman.

The selected text changes from Arial to Times New Roman.

11 On the Formatting toolbar, click the Font down arrow again.

Notice that the Times New Roman font is at the top of the list. PowerPoint places the fonts you recently used at the top of the list, separated by a double line, so you don't have to scroll down the list of fonts if you want to use the font again.

12 Click a blank space in the Outline tab.

The font list closes, and PowerPoint deselects the slide 1 title text, as shown in the following illustration.

FIGURE 4-14

Slide formatted with new styles

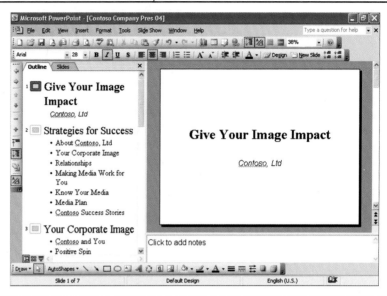

◆ Keep this file open for the next exercise.

QUICK REFERENCE ▼

Change text style

1 Select the text in which you want to change text style.

2 On the Formatting toolbar, click a formatting button such as Bold or Italic.

Change the font

1 Select the text in which you want to change the font.

2 On the Formatting toolbar, click the Font down arrow, and then click a font.

Change the font size

1 Select the text in which you want to change the font size.

2 On the Formatting toolbar, click the Font Size down arrow, and then click a size, or on the Formatting toolbar, click the Increase Font Size button or the Decrease Font Size button.

QUICK CHECK

Q: What is a quick way to make text larger without specifying an exact font size?

A: **Use the Increase Font Size button to increase font size by a set amount at each click.**

Sending an Outline or Slides to Word

Sending an Outline or Notes to Word

THE BOTTOM LINE

Send an outline or slides to Word when you want to take advantage of Word's formatting and text-handling features. Exported outlines and slides are editable documents that can provide good alternatives to printing presentation materials from PowerPoint.

You may find that you need output options other than simply printing a presentation's slides, pages, or outline. Suppose, for example, you want to study further and perhaps edit the outline you have created for Contoso in this lesson. You can use PowerPoint's Send To command to send the outline to Microsoft Word, where you can edit it just like any other Word document. (And you can then, if desired, insert the edited outline back into a PowerPoint presentation to eliminate the need for correcting each slide with your edits.)

As long as Word is installed on your computer, you can export a presentation outline or slides and their associated speaker notes directly from PowerPoint into a Word document. You can choose to arrange the presentation's slides in two different ways as well as choose whether to include the notes or instead create blank lines beside or beneath each slide. Because the slides and notes display in a Word table, you can use table-editing tools to adjust layout and format notes text. This is an excellent alternative to printing handouts or notes pages.

CHECK THIS OUT ▼

Link Presentation to Word Document

The Send To Microsoft Office dialog box, where you choose settings for exporting presentation materials to Word, allows you either to paste the presentation content or Paste Link it. When you use Paste Link, changes you make to the presentation will automatically be made to the Word document the next time you open it. Use this feature when you want to keep an archive copy of a presentation and don't want to have to keep exporting as the presentation is modified.

Send an outline to Word

You have finished tweaking the presentation outline. You're now ready to export the outline to Word, where you'll be able to edit it if you need to.

1 **On the File menu, point to Send To, and then click Microsoft Office Word.**

The Send To Microsoft Office Word dialog box appears with five page layout options and two pasting options. The page layout options determine the type of information you want to send to Word. The pasting options determine how you want to send the information.

2 **Click the Outline Only option, and then click OK.**

The pasting options gray out, indicating that you don't have the option to link the outline. PowerPoint launches Word and inserts the presentation slides with the title text and main text format into a blank Word document. Your Word document should look similar to the following illustration.

FIGURE 4-15

Exported outline in Word

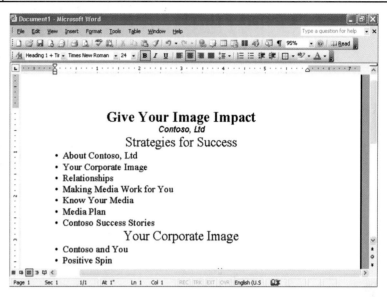

3 On the Word File menu, click Save As.

The Save As dialog box opens.

4 In the Save In box, verify that the Lesson04 folder in the PowerPoint Practice folder is open.

5 In the File Name box, type Contoso Company Doc 04 and click Save.

Word saves the presentation slide text in a document called Contoso Company Doc 04 in the Lesson04 folder.

6 On the Word File menu, click Exit.

Word closes, and PowerPoint is redisplayed.

TIP

If you don't have Word installed, you can save a presentation in a common file format called Rich Text Format (RTF). For more information on RTF, see "Saving a Presentation as an Outline" in the next section.

QUICK CHECK

Q: What is one reason why you might export a presentation to Word?

A: Exporting allows you to keep an archive copy, create an editable version of an outline, or prepare handouts that can be formatted.

◆ Keep this file open for the next exercise.

QUICK REFERENCE ▼

Send an outline or notes to Word

1 On the File menu, point to Send To, and then click Microsoft Office Word.

2 Click a layout option and pasting option.

3 Click OK.

Saving a Presentation as an Outline

Sending an Outline or Notes to Word

When you need the text portion of a presentation for use in another program, you can save the presentation text in a format called **Rich Text Format (RTF)**. Saving an outline in RTF allows you to save any formatting you made to the presentation text in a common file format that you can open in other programs. There are many programs, such as Word for Macintosh or older versions of PowerPoint, that can import outlines saved in RTF.

TIP

As with an outline created in Word, you can use the Slides From Outline command to create slides from an outline you have saved in RTF.

Save a presentation as an outline

For your last task, you'll save the current presentation, then save it as an outline in RTF format.

1 On the Standard toolbar, click the Save button.

The next time you open this presentation, PowerPoint opens it with the Outline displayed in the same view scale in which you last saved it. Now that you have saved the changes to a presentation in Normal view, you can save it as an RTF file.

ANOTHER METHOD

- Press Ctrl + S.
- On the File menu, click Save.

2 On the File menu, click Save As.

3 In the Save In box, verify that the Lesson04 folder in the PowerPoint Practice folder is open.

4 Type Contoso Outline RTF in the File Name box.

5 Click the Save As Type down arrow, and then click Outline/RTF.

6 Click Save.

PowerPoint saves the presentation slide text in RTF format in a document called Contoso Outline RTF in the Lesson04 folder.

◆ If you are continuing to other lessons, save the Contoso Company Pres 04 presentation with the current name, and then close it. If you are not continuing to other lessons, save and close the Contoso Company Pres 04 presentation, and then click the Close button in the title bar of the PowerPoint window.

QUICK REFERENCE ▼

Save a presentation as an outline

1 On the File menu, click Save As.

2 In the Save In box, navigate to the location in which you want to save the outline file.

3 In the File Name box, type the file name.

4 Click the Save As Type down arrow, and then click Outline/RTF.

5 Click Save.

QUICK CHECK

Q: What does RTF stand for?

A: RTF stands for Rich Text Format.

Key Points

✔ *Create a blank presentation when you want to concentrate more on content, rather than slide design.*

✔ *The Outline tab lets you see much of your presentation at one time, making it easy to avoid repetition and emphasize your main points.*

✔ *If text useful for slides has already been typed in a word processing outline, use the Slides From Outline command to import the text into a PowerPoint presentation. The text is designated as titles or bullet items according to the outline formatting in the word processing document.*

✔ *Change an outline's zoom setting to see the text at a larger or smaller size. Collapsing and expanding slide content makes it easier to reorganize slides. You can display the same text formatting in the outline as is shown in the Slide pane.*

✔ *Use the Outline tab to easily select and delete slides, paragraphs, or words.*

✔ *The Outline tab can be used to reorganize slides, paragraph text, and words just by dragging.*

✔ *Apply formats such as fonts, sizes, and styles right in the Outline tab to save time.*

✔ *Send an outline or slides to Word to create an editable document that can be used for archive purposes or as an alternative to PowerPoint's printed materials.*

✔ *Save a presentation as an RTF outline when you want to make it available to other programs.*

Quick Quiz

True/False

T   F   **1.** You can create a new blank presentation by starting to enter text in the first window that opens when you start PowerPoint.

T   F   **2.** When the Outline tab is active, changing the zoom setting scales text in the outline.

T   F   **3.** You can delete a slide in any view by clicking Delete Slide on the Format menu.

T   F   **4.** If you drag a first-level bullet to the left in the Outline tab, you turn it into a slide title.

T   F   **5.** You can easily send presentation handouts to Word for further editing.

Multiple Choice

1. If you drag a bullet item to the right, you have _____ the item.
   a. promoted
   b. demoted
   c. deleted
   d. formatted

2. You can import an outline in which of these formats?
   a. .doc
   b. .rtf
   c. .txt
   d. all of the above

3. To select all of the content for a slide in the Outline tab, click the _____.
   a. paragraph bullet
   b. slide icon
   c. slide number
   d. either b or c

4. To apply underline formatting to text, you would click a button on the _____ toolbar.
   a. Formatting
   b. Outlining
   c. Standard
   d. Drawing

5. In the Send To Microsoft Office Word dialog box, you select a layout option and a _____ option.
   a. formatting
   b. saving
   c. pasting
   d. color/grayscale

Short Answer

1. What are the two ways you can change the view scale?

2. How do you insert an outline from another file?

3. How do you delete multiple paragraphs?

4. How do you display the same text fonts and styles in the Outline tab that are displayed in the Slide pane?

5. How do you send an outline to Word?

6. How do you save a presentation in RTF?

On Your Own

Exercise 1

Open the Contoso Company Pres 04 in the Lesson04 folder that is located in the PowerPoint Practice folder. Move slide 6 after slide 3, and then add the following bulleted list to the Media Plan slide:

Target audience
Budget
Time frame

Save and close the presentation.

Exercise 2

Create a blank presentation, display the Outline tab, and then insert the Contoso Outline RTF from the Lesson04 folder that is located in the PowerPoint Practice folder. In the Outline tab, change the view scale to 100%, and then save the presentation as **Contoso Company Pres Outline** in the Lesson04 folder that is located in the PowerPoint Practice folder. Close the presentation.

One Step Further

Exercise 1

Open Holidays 03 from the Lesson03 folder that is located in the PowerPoint Practice folder and position the insertion point at the end of the last slide in the Outline tab. Insert the **04 Holiday Outline** from the Lesson04 folder that is located in the PowerPoint Practice folder so that its slides follow the original four slides. Delete the last slide in the outline. Move the *Vacation* slide to become slide 6. Change the view scale to 25% to see all the new slides at once. Save the presentation as **Holidays 04** in the Lesson04 folder that is located in the PowerPoint Practice folder and leave the presentation open for the next exercise.

Exercise 2

Demote the *Maternity leave* slide title so it becomes paragraph text on slide 9. Demote the next two slide titles to become second-level bullets below *Maternity leave*. Demote the *Disability* slide one level. On slide 8, demote *Immediate family only* one level. Collapse all text to see only the headings. Select all slides and change the font to another appropriate font. Expand all text again. Apply bold formatting to all slide titles, if they aren't already bold. Change paragraph formatting on the inserted slides to match that on the original slides (remove italic formatting as necessary). Increase the font size of the title text on the first slide. Save and close the presentation.

Exercise 3

You have been asked to lead a discussion on your company's wellness and enrichment programs, which include a new exercise room, classes in yoga and Pilates, smoking and diet counseling, company-supported teams for local running and cycle races, and so on. Create a new, blank presentation. Working in the Outline tab of the Outline/Slides pane, create several slides that list the company's programs and reasons for investing in the health and well-being of their workers. Use tools on the Outlining toolbar to re-organize slides and slide text. Format slide text as desired. Save the presentation as **Wellness 04** in the Lesson04 folder that is located in the PowerPoint Practice folder and close the presentation.

LESSON

Adding and Modifying Text

KEY TERMS

- dotted selection box
- object
- resize handles
- slanted-line selection box
- text label
- word processing box
- word wrap

In Microsoft PowerPoint, you can add to and modify your presentation text to fine-tune your message. PowerPoint offers several alternatives for placing text on your slides: text placeholders for entering slide titles and subtitles, text labels for short notes and phrases, and word processing boxes for longer text. You can also place text inside objects, such as circles, rectangles, or stars.

As the vice president of sales at the public relations firm Contoso, Ltd, you have been working on a presentation that you want to customize for new clients. After working with your presentation outline in the previous lesson, you are ready to fine-tune your message.

In this lesson, you will learn how to create several kinds of text objects, edit text, change the appearance of text, find and replace text, replace fonts, let PowerPoint correct text while you type, check spelling and presentation styles, and use PowerPoint's new Research task pane.

◆ Before you can use the practice files in this lesson, you must install them from the book's companion CD to their default location. See "Using the CD-ROM" at the beginning of this book for more information. To complete the procedures in this lesson, you will need to use a file named 05 PPT Lesson in the Lesson05 folder in the PowerPoint Practice folder located on your hard disk.

Selecting and Deselecting Objects

Editing Text

THE BOTTOM LINE

Knowing the ways you can select objects can speed editing. Click in an object to work with its content individually. Click on an object to work with the object as a single unit.

An **object** is anything that you can manipulate. For example, the title object on a slide is all the text in the title, which is treated as a unit. To make formatting changes to all of the text in a text object, you need to first select the object. To select an object, you click a part of the object by using the pointer. To deselect an object, you move the pointer off the object into a blank area of the slide and then click the blank area.

In PowerPoint, you can select a text object in two ways. First, you can click inside a text object. This places the insertion point in the object and surrounds the text object with a **slanted-line selection box**, consisting of gray slanted lines. When the slanted-line selection box is displayed, you can edit any content within the box. For example, you can insert or delete a word. Second, you can click on the outside edge of a text object. This surrounds the object with a fuzzy outline, called a **dotted selection box**. When the dotted selection box is displayed, the entire object is selected and ready for you to edit as an object. That is, you can manipulate it as a whole. The white circles at each corner of either type of selection box are **resize handles**, which you use to adjust and resize the object. A sample of each selection box is shown in the following illustrations.

FIGURE 5-1

Slanted-line and dotted selection boxes

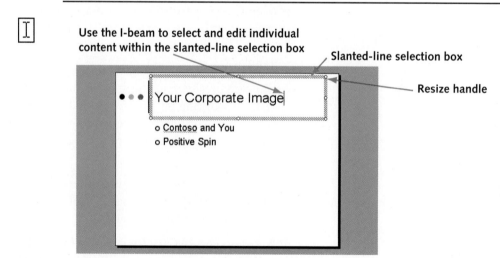

Use the selection pointer to select and edit
all of the content in the dotted selection box

Dotted selection box

Resize handle

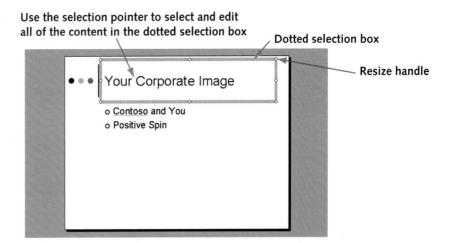

Select and deselect objects

In this exercise, you review selection boxes and then select and dese-lect a text object.

◆ **Start PowerPoint, if necessary, click the Open button on the Standard toolbar, navigate to the Lesson05 folder in the PowerPoint Practice folder, and then open the 05 PPT Lesson file. Save the file as Contoso Company Pres 05 in the same folder.**

1 Display slide 3 and click directly on top of the title object.

The text box is selected with the slanted-line selection box and an insertion point displays where you clicked.

2 Position the pointer directly on top of an edge of the slanted-line selection box.

The pointer changes to the selection pointer, shown in the margin.

3 Click the edge of the slanted-line selection box.

The selection box changes to a dotted selection box.

FIGURE 5-2

Placeholder shows dotted selection box

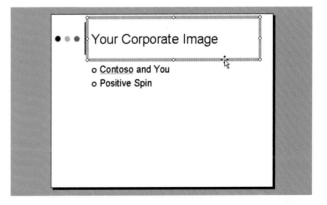

4 **Click outside the selection box in a blank area of the slide.**

The text box is deselected.

QUICK REFERENCE ▼

Select and deselect objects

- Click directly on top of the title object.
- Click directly on top of an edge of the slanted-line selection box.
- Click outside the selection box in a blank area of the slide to deselect it.

Adding Text to Slides

THE BOTTOM LINE

When you want to add text in a location that doesn't have a place-holder, add a text box. Use a text label for a single line of text and a word processing box for text that wraps.

Editing Text

Usually, slides contain text boxes for title and bulleted text into which you enter your main ideas. You can also place other text objects on a slide by using the Text Box button on the Drawing toolbar. You use text boxes when you need to include annotations or minor points that do not belong in a list.

You can create two types of text objects: a **text label,** which is text that does not **word wrap** within a defined box, and a **word processing box,** which is text that wraps inside the boundaries of an object. Use a text label to enter short notes or phrases and a word processing box for longer text or sentences.

You can create a text label on a slide by using the Text Box tool to select a place on the slide where you will begin typing your text. You can create a word processing box by using the Text Box tool to drag the pointer to create a text box of the appropriate width.

Once you have created a word processing box or a text label, you can change one object into the other by changing the word-wrap option and the fit text option in the Format Text Box dialog box. You can also change a text label to a word processing box by dragging one of the corner resize handles. The text rewraps to adjust to the new size.

Add text to slides

Your presentation would benefit from some additional information on several slides. In this exercise, you add text in an existing text object and then create a text label and a word processing box.

1 **Drag the scroll box in the Slide pane to slide 5.**

2 **Click immediately before the word "homework" in the first bulleted item.**

You will add a word in this text box to see how text wraps automatically in a placeholder.

3 **Type your, and then press the Spacebar.**

The paragraph wraps in the text object. Your slide should look like the following illustration.

FIGURE 5-3

Wrapping text in the text object

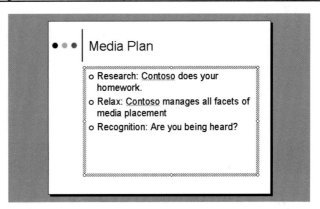

4 **Click anywhere outside the slanted-line selection box to deselect the text object.**

5 **On the Drawing toolbar, click the Text Box button.**

The pointer changes to the upside-down T-pointer.

ANOTHER METHOD

On the Insert menu, click Text Box.

6 **Position the pointer at the bottom center of the slide.**

7 **Click to create a text label.**

A small, empty selection box composed of gray slanted lines appears with the blinking insertion point in it.

8 **Type Media types are listed on slide 4.**

Text in a new text box uses the current default font and font size, such as 18 point Arial. Your slide should look like the following illustration.

FIGURE 5-4

Text box added to slide

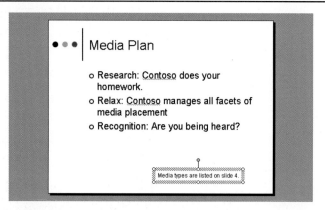

The text you create on a slide using the Text Box tool does not appear in the Outline tab. Only text entered in a title placeholder or a main text placeholder appears in the Outline tab.

9   Click a blank area of the slide to deselect the label.

10   Click the Next Slide button to advance to slide 6.

11   On the Drawing toolbar, click the Text Box button.

12   Position the pointer below the last bullet, about halfway between the bulleted item and the bottom of the slide, and then drag the pointer to create a box that extends a bit farther than the last bullet entry.

When you release the mouse button, a slanted-line selection box appears with the blinking insertion point in it. You can now enter your text.

13   Type **It is worth it to create community relationships on several levels.**

The width of the box does not change, but the words wrap, and the box height increases to accommodate the complete entry. Your slide should look like the following illustration.

FIGURE 5-5

Text box adjusts text automatically

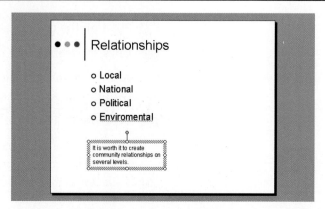

14 Click a blank area of the slide to deselect the text object.

◆ Keep this file open for the next exercise.

QUICK REFERENCE ▼

Create a text label

1 On the Drawing toolbar, click the Text Box button.

2 Click where you want the text label to appear.

3 Type the text.

Create a word processing box

1 On the Drawing toolbar, click the Text Box button.

2 Position the pointer on the slide, and then drag the pointer to create a box of the length you want.

3 Type the text.

QUICK CHECK

Q: What do you call a text box that allows text to wrap?

A: This type of text box is called a word processing box.

Adjusting Text Objects

Formatting Text and Text Objects

THE BOTTOM LINE

To ensure that text objects appear neatly on a slide, you can control word wrap and object size for both placeholders and text boxes you have added.

On occasion, you may need to adjust text objects to change object size or wrap options. For example, default bullet text placeholders usually take up a good portion of the slide, and if you want to insert a graphic or another text object near the bottom of the slide, you may want the unused portion of the placeholder out of the way. You may also want to change the wrap option for a text object to control the size of the object on the slide.

You can adjust text object settings for any text object on a slide—not only for text objects you have added, but also for the default text placeholders. Settings are adjusted in the Format Text Box or Format Placeholder dialog box. The Text Box tab in either of these dialog boxes offers check boxes that let you turn word wrap on or off and resize a placeholder to fit its text.

Adjust text objects

In this exercise, you experiment with changing word wrap options and adjust the size of a text placeholder.

1 Click the bottom text box on slide 6, and then click the edge of the text box to select it with the dotted selection box.

Remember that the dotted selection box means you can modify the object as a whole.

2 **On the Format menu, click Text Box.**

The Format Text Box dialog box opens. Note that the command on the menu is *Text Box* because this is a text box you added yourself.

ANOTHER METHOD

Right-click a text box, and click Format Text Box on the shortcut menu.

3 **Click the Text Box tab.**

FIGURE 5-6

Format Text Box dialog box

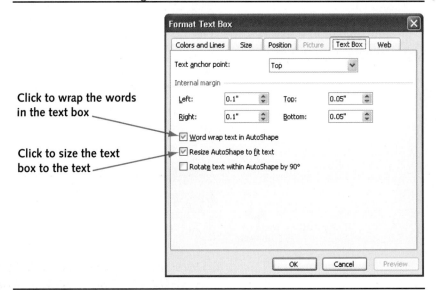

Click to wrap the words in the text box

Click to size the text box to the text

4 **Clear the Word Wrap Text In AutoShape check box.**

5 **Click OK.**

The word processing box changes to a text label and stretches across the slide.

TIP

You can also convert a text label to a word processing box by dragging a resize handle to reduce the width of the text box. The text inside wraps to adjust to the new dimensions of the text box.

6 **On the Standard toolbar, click the Undo button.**

ANOTHER METHOD

- Press Ctrl + Z.
- On the Edit menu, click Undo.

7 Position the pointer near the bulleted text on slide 6 until it changes to the selection pointer, and then click to select the paragraph text object.

Notice that the dotted selection box is larger than it needs to be. (There is additional white space at the bottom that overlaps the word processing box you added.)

8 On the Format menu, click Placeholder.

The Format AutoShape dialog box appears. The menu command is *Placeholder* in this case because you have selected a default text placeholder.

ANOTHER METHOD

Right-click a placeholder, and click Format Placeholder on the shortcut menu.

9 Click the Text Box tab.

10 Select the Resize AutoShape To Fit Text check box, and then click OK.

The object adjusts to fit the depth of the text. You now have clear space at the bottom of this slide if you want to add another text box or a graphic.

11 Click a blank area of the slide to deselect the text box.

◆ Keep this file open for the next exercise.

QUICK REFERENCE ▼

To adjust word wrap in a text object

1 Select the text object.
2 On the Format menu, click Text Box.
3 Click the Text Box tab.
4 Clear or select the Word Wrap Text In AutoShape check box.
5 Click OK.

To adjust a text placeholder to fit text

1 Select the text object.
2 On the Format menu, click Placeholder.
3 Click the Text Box tab.
4 Select the Resize AutoShape To Fit Text check box.
5 Click OK.

QUICK CHECK

Q: Which menu option should you select to format the text of a placeholder object?

A: **You use the Format Placeholder option on the Format menu.**

Formatting Text

Formatting Text and
Text Objects

THE BOTTOM LINE

Though a design template specifies text formatting, you can adjust
formats to suit your content or improve slide appearance. You can
turn bullets or numbering on and off and change font styles, color,
and size to add emphasis.

At any time while you work on a presentation, you can change text formatting. Although design templates specify fonts, font sizes, styles, colors,
and bullets, you can modify these settings to add special emphasis to text
or just to adjust the design's formats. With all text formatting changes, you
need to select the text object before you can apply new changes.

Apply or Remove Bullets and Numbers

By default, paragraphs on text slides use bullets to indicate each item. You
may sometimes want to remove bullets from paragraphs to achieve a different look on a slide or when you have only one paragraph on the slide.
To remove bullets, select the placeholder and click the Bullets button on
the Formatting toolbar. To reapply bullets, simply click the button again.

PowerPoint also has a Numbering button on the Formatting toolbar. You
can number paragraphs rather than use bullets if you want to show order
in the paragraphs. For example, you would use numbers rather than bullets when your paragraphs describe the process of applying for a credit
card or the steps necessary to prepare a floor for tile installation.

TIP

You can use AutoNumbering to start a numbered list by typing.
Remove any bullets at the beginning of the line, type a number 1,
letter A or a, or Roman numeral I or i followed by a period or
closing parenthesis, type text, and then press Enter. The numbering
continues automatically.

Work with bullets and numbers

In this exercise, you work with bullets and numbers to decide which
approach works best for the material on a slide.

1 Click the edge of the bulleted text box on slide 6 to select it with the
dotted selection box.

 2 On the Formatting toolbar, click the Bullets button.

You have turned off bullets, so the bullets for the four lines of text
disappear.

 3 On the Formatting toolbar, click the Numbering button to apply
numbers to the paragraphs.

The text changes to a numbered list. This list doesn't need to be in a particular order, however, so it will be best to return it to a bulleted list.

 4 **On the Formatting toolbar, click the Bullets button again.**

The text changes back to a bulleted list.

◆ **Keep this file open for the next exercise.**

QUICK REFERENCE ▼

Add bullets or numbering to a text object

1 Click the edge of a text box on a slide to select it with the dotted selection box.

2 On the Formatting toolbar, click the Bullets button or click the Numbering button.

Remove bullets or numbering from a text object

1 Select the text object.

2 On the Formatting toolbar, click the Bullets button or click the Numbering button to deselect the button.

Change Font Styles, Size, and Color

In all PowerPoint presentations, you can choose among three styles to emphasize text: **bold**, *italic*, and underline. Some design templates also make the shadow style available for use. Changing font style is as easy as clicking a button on the Formatting toolbar.

> **TIP**
>
> Additional font styles, bold italic and emboss, are available in the Font dialog box. This dialog box lets you make a number of font, size, and style selections at one time. To open this dialog box, click Font on the Format menu.

You already know that design templates provide the colors for text and background in a presentation. You can change text color at any time, however, to make text stand out by clicking the Font Color button, either on the Formatting toolbar or the Drawing toolbar. You can select another of the design template's colors, or you can choose a different color from PowerPoint's color palette.

Font size is also controlled by the design template, but you may want to adjust size to fill a placeholder better or to fit more text in placeholder. You can change the font size either by specifying an exact size in the Font Size box or by using the Increase Font Size or Decrease Font Size button, which increases or reduces font size by set intervals.

Change font styles

You will change text formatting in several ways in this exercise to emphasize portions of the presentation.

1 **Click the Next Slide button to go to slide 7.**

2 **Position the pointer near the edge of the quote in the text box until the pointer changes to the selection pointer, and then click to select it.**

A dotted selection box appears around the text object, indicating that it is selected.

3 **On the Formatting toolbar, click the Italic button.**

The text in the object changes to italics.

ANOTHER METHOD

Press Ctrl + I.

4 **On the Formatting toolbar, click the Decrease Font Size button to reduce the font size to 20 points.**

5 **On the Drawing toolbar, click the Font Color button down arrow.**

A text color palette of the current color scheme appears.

6 **Click the blue color as indicated in the following illustration.**

FIGURE 5-7

Use the blue color on the color palette

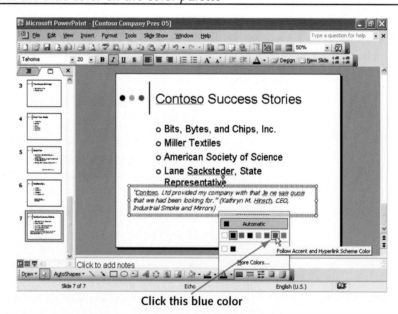

Click this blue color

The font color in the word processing box changes to blue.

TIP

The line on the Font Color button also changes, indicating the currently selected font color.

7 Select the words "Je ne sais quois."

The slanted-line selection box appears, and you can format individual text.

8 On the Formatting toolbar, click the Italic button.

You have turned off italic formatting. This is the usual way to emphasize text that is already italicized.

9 Click a blank area of the slide to deselect the text object.

◆ Keep this file open for the next exercise.

QUICK REFERENCE ▼

Format text in a text object

1 Select the text object.

2 On the Formatting toolbar, click a formatting button (such as Bold, Italic, Underline, Shadow, or Font Color).

3 Click a blank area of the slide to deselect the text object.

Changing Text Alignment and Spacing

THE BOTTOM LINE

To add emphasis to text, you can change how it lines up in a placeholder. Adjust the line spacing to fit more text in a placeholder or to fill space in a placeholder.

Formatting Text and
Text Objects

PowerPoint enables you to control the way text lines up on the slide. You can align text to the left or to the right or to the center in a text object. You can adjust the alignment of text in an object by selecting the object and clicking an alignment button on the Formatting toolbar. The Align Left button aligns text evenly along the left edge of the text box and is useful for paragraph text. The Align Right button aligns text evenly along the right edge of the text box and is useful for text labels. The Center button aligns text in the middle of the text box and is useful for titles and headings. You can also justify text in a paragraph so it lines up evenly along both edges of the text box.

You can adjust the vertical space between selected lines and the space before and after paragraphs by selecting the object and clicking a line spacing button (Increase Paragraph Spacing or Decrease Paragraph Spacing) on the Formatting toolbar or by using the Line Spacing command on the Format menu.

Change text alignment and spacing

In this exercise, you change the alignment of text in a text object, decrease paragraph spacing, and adjust line spacing.

1 Select the text box at the bottom of slide 7.

2 On the Formatting toolbar, click the Center button.

The text in the text object aligns to the center.

ANOTHER METHOD

- Press Ctrl + E.
- On the Format menu, click Alignment, and then click Center.

3 Click a blank area of the slide to deselect the text box.

4 Click the edge of the bulleted paragraph text box on slide 7 with the selection pointer.

The dotted selection box appears. You are now ready to change the paragraph spacing, but to do so, you may need to add a button to your Formatting toolbar.

5 On the Formatting toolbar, click the Toolbar Options down arrow, point to Add or Remove Buttons, and then point to Formatting.

A list of all the buttons currently available for the Formatting toolbar appears.

6 In the list of additional buttons, click the Decrease Paragraph Spacing button to place it on the toolbar.

A check mark appears next to the entry.

TROUBLESHOOTING

If a check mark appears by the button when you open the list of additional buttons, the button is already active. Don't click the button or you will deactivate it.

7 Click the Toolbar Options down arrow to close the list.

8 On the Formatting toolbar, click the Decrease Paragraph Spacing button.

The paragraph spacing in the text box decreases by 0.1 lines, from 1.0 to 0.9.

9 Click a blank area of the slide to deselect the text box.

10 Click the edge of the bulleted paragraph text object on slide 7 to select it.

11 On the Format menu, click Line Spacing.

The Line Spacing dialog box appears.

12 Click the Before Paragraph down arrow until 0.1 appears, and then click OK.

FIGURE 5-8

Line Spacing dialog box

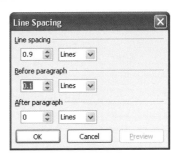

The paragraph spacing before each paragraph decreases by 0.1 lines.

13 **Click a blank area of the slide to deselect the text box.**

> **TIP**
>
> Everything you can do to manipulate a text label or word processing box you can also do to any text object, including title and paragraph text objects, and vice versa.

◆ **Keep this file open for the next exercise.**

QUICK REFERENCE ▼

Change text alignment

1 Select the text box.

2 On the Formatting toolbar, click an alignment button (such as Align Left, Center, or Align Right).

3 Click a blank area of the slide to deselect the text box.

Decrease or increase paragraph spacing

1 Select the text object.

2 On the Formatting toolbar, click the Decrease Paragraph Spacing button or the Increase Paragraph Spacing button.

Adjust line spacing

1 Select the text object.

2 On the Format menu, click Line Spacing.

3 Adjust the Line Spacing measurement to increase or decrease space between lines, or click the Before Paragraph or After Paragraph arrow to increase or decrease space above or below a paragraph.

4 Click OK.

Moving a Text Object

Editing Text

Move a text object to place it more attractively or usefully on a slide.

You can move a text object to any place on a slide to improve the appearance of a presentation. You can use the mouse to drag a text object from one location to another on a slide. Any text object on a slide can be moved, including both the default placeholders and text labels and word processing boxes you add yourself. The most efficient way to move a text object is to drag it from one location to another.

Move a text object

In this exercise, you move a text object by dragging the edge of the text object's selection box.

1 **Click the edge of the text box at the bottom of slide 7 with the selection pointer.**

The dotted selection box appears.

2 **Drag the edge of the selection box to center the text object between the bottom of the slide and the bulleted text box.**

ANOTHER METHOD

You can use the arrow keys on the keyboard to "nudge" an object by small increments in any direction.

TIP

To copy a text object, hold down Ctrl, and then drag the selection box of a text object to a new location on the slide.

3 **Click a blank area of the slide to deselect the text box.**

Your slide should look like the following illustration.

FIGURE 5-9

Text box has been repositioned

◆ Keep this file open for the next exercise.

QUICK REFERENCE ▼

To move a text object

1 Select the text object.

2 Drag the edge of the selection box to place the text object where you want it.

QUICK CHECK

Q: What key should you use if you want to copy a text box to another location?

A: **Use the Ctrl key to copy a text box.**

Finding and Replacing Text and Fonts

The Find and Replace commands on the Edit menu allow you to locate and change specific text in a presentation. Find helps you locate each occurrence of a specific word or set of characters, whereas Replace locates every occurrence of a specific word or set of characters and replaces it with a different one. You can change every occurrence of specific text all at once, or you can accept or reject each change individually.

The Find and Replace commands also give you options for more detailed searches. If you want to search for whole words so the search doesn't stop on a word that might contain only part of your search word, you select the check box for Find Whole Words Only. If you want to find a word or phrase that matches a certain capitalization exactly, you select the Match Case check box.

In addition to finding text, you can also find and replace a specific font in a presentation. The Replace Fonts command allows you to replace every instance of a font style you have been using with another. You cannot choose to replace a font only in certain locations.

Find and replace text and fonts

In this exercise, you use the Replace command to find and replace a word and then use Replace Fonts to replace a font.

1 On the Edit menu, click Replace.

The Replace dialog box appears.

ANOTHER METHOD

Press Ctrl + H.

2 Click in the Find What box, and then type facets.

3 Press Tab or click in the Replace With box.

4 Type aspects.

FIGURE 5-10

Replace dialog box

5 **Click Find Next.**

PowerPoint finds and selects the word facets on slide 5.

TROUBLESHOOTING

If the dialog box covers up the selected text, drag the Replace dialog box title bar out of the way so that you can see the text.

6 **Click Replace.**

An alert box appears, telling you that PowerPoint has finished searching the presentation. If you do not want to replace an instance, you could click Ignore, and if you want to replace all instances, you could click Replace All.

7 **Click OK, and then click Close in the Replace dialog box.**

The Replace dialog box closes.

8 **Click a blank area of the slide to deselect any text boxes.**

9 **On the Format menu, click Replace Fonts.**

The Replace Font dialog box appears.

10 **Click the Replace down arrow, and then click Tahoma.**

11 **Click the With down arrow, scroll down, and then click Arial.**

12 **Click Replace.**

Throughout the presentation, the text formatted with the Tahoma font changes to the Arial font.

13 **Click Close in the Replace Font dialog box.**

◆ **Keep this file open for the next exercise.**

QUICK REFERENCE ▼

Replace text

1 On the Edit menu, click Replace.

2 Click the Find What box, and then type the text you want to replace.

3 Press Tab or click in the Replace With box.

4 Type the replacement text.

5 Click Find Next, and then click Replace, Replace All, or Ignore.

6 Click OK, and then click Close in the Replace dialog box.

Replace fonts

1 On the Format menu, click Replace Fonts.

2 Click the Replace down arrow.

3 Click a font.

4 Click the With down arrow, and then click a font.

5 Click Replace.

6 Click Close in the Replace Font dialog box.

QUICK CHECK

Q: What is a drawback to using Replace Fonts?

A: You cannot choose where to replace the font; all instances are replaced at once.

Correcting Text While Typing

Checking Spelling and Word Choice

THE BOTTOM LINE

Automatic correction and text-fitting features can save time by fixing errors and adjusting layouts for you. AutoCorrect replaces common typing errors with correct words, and AutoFit reduces text size as necessary to fit in a placeholder.

As you type text in a presentation, you might be aware of making typographical errors, but when you look at the text, the mistakes have been corrected. PowerPoint's AutoCorrect feature corrects common capitalization and spelling errors as you type. For example, if you frequently type *tehm* instead of *them*, you can create an AutoCorrect entry named *tehm*. Then, whenever you type *tehm* followed by a space or a punctuation mark, PowerPoint replaces the misspelling with *them*. You can customize AutoCorrect to recognize or ignore misspellings that you routinely make or ignore specific text that you do not want AutoCorrect to change. You can also use AutoCorrect to recognize abbreviations or codes that you create to automate typing certain text. For example, you could customize AutoCorrect to type your full name when you type in only your initials.

When you point to a word that AutoCorrect has changed, a small blue box appears under the first letter. When you point to the small blue box, the AutoCorrect Options button appears. The AutoCorrect Options button gives you control over whether you want the text to be corrected. You can change text back to its original spelling, or you can stop AutoCorrect from automatically correcting text. You can also display the AutoCorrect dialog box and change AutoCorrect settings.

As you type text in a placeholder, PowerPoint's AutoFit feature resizes the text, if necessary, to fit into the placeholder. The AutoFit Options button, which appears near your text the first time that it is resized, gives you control over whether you want the text to be resized. The AutoFit Options button displays a menu with options for controlling how the option works. For example, you can stop resizing text for the current placeholder while still maintaining your global AutoFit settings. You can also display the AutoCorrect dialog box and change the AutoFit settings so that text doesn't resize automatically.

Correct text while typing

In this exercise, you add an AutoCorrect entry, use AutoCorrect to fix a misspelled word, and then use AutoFit to resize text in a placeholder.

1 **On the Tools menu, click AutoCorrect Options, and then click the AutoCorrect tab, if necessary.**

The AutoCorrect dialog box appears. Note that PowerPoint has already added a number of commonly mistyped words and their correct equivalents.

2 **Click in the Replace box, and then type** vidoe.

Video is commonly mistyped as *vidoe*.

3 **Press Tab, type** video, **and then click Add.**

FIGURE 5-11

AutoCorrect dialog box

Enter the misspelled word here —

Enter the correct word here —

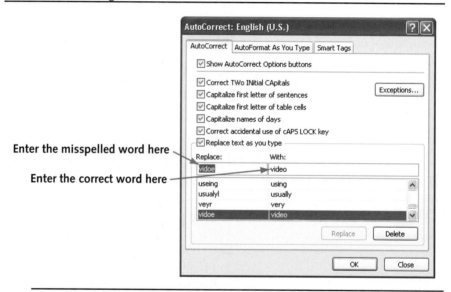

Now, whenever you type *vidoe* in any presentation, PowerPoint replaces it with *video*.

4 **Click OK.**

5 **Drag the scroll box to slide 4.**

6 **Click the blank space immediately after the word Outdoor.**

7 **Press Enter, and then type** Vidoe.

Press the Spacebar. The word corrects to *Video*.

8 **Point to the small blue box under the "V" of "Video" to display the AutoCorrect Options button, and then click the AutoCorrect Options down arrow.**

A short menu displays, as shown below, giving AutoCorrect options for the corrected word.

FIGURE 5-12

AutoCorrect options display

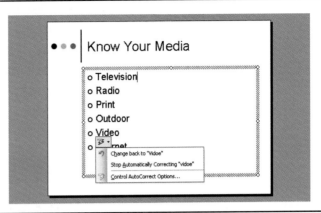

9 Click a blank area of the slide to deselect the AutoCorrect Options menu.

10 Click just to the right of the word "Television" at the top of the bulleted list.

11 Press Enter, and then press Tab.

12 Type Local.

13 Press Enter and then type National.

The text box automatically resizes to fit in the box. The AutoFit Options button appears at the bottom left of the text box.

14 Point to the AutoFit Options button, and then click the AutoFit Options down arrow.

The AutoFit Options menu gives you a number of options for fitting the text into the placeholder or creating a new slide to hold the runover content, as shown in the following illustration.

FIGURE 5-13

AutoFit options display

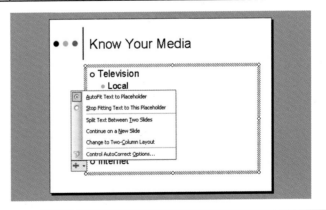

15 Click AutoFit Text To Placeholder if necessary and then click a blank area of the slide to deselect the text box.

PowerPoint reduces the font size to fit the text in the placeholder.

◆ Keep this file open for the next exercise.

Add an AutoCorrect entry

1 On the Tools menu, click AutoCorrect Options, and then click the AutoCorrect tab, if necessary.

2 Click the Replace box, and then type a misspelled word.

3 Press Tab, and then type the correctly spelled word.

4 Click Add.

5 Click OK.

Use AutoCorrect to fix a misspelled word

1 Click to position the insertion point where you want to type text.

2 Type the misspelled word.

3 Press the Spacebar or Enter.

Use AutoFit to fit text in a placeholder

1 Click the AutoFit button down arrow when the AutoFit button displays next to a text placeholder.

2 Select an option for fitting text in the current placeholder, changing slide layout, or creating a new slide to hold runover text.

Checking Spelling

Checking Spelling and Word Choice

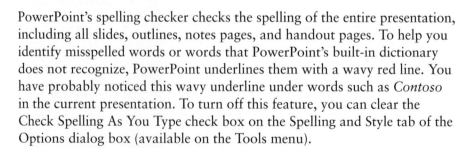

THE BOTTOM LINE

Even if you're a good typist, you should always check spelling in a presentation to identify possible errors. Nothing is more amateurish than a presentation with glaring spelling mistakes for all to see.

PowerPoint's spelling checker checks the spelling of the entire presentation, including all slides, outlines, notes pages, and handout pages. To help you identify misspelled words or words that PowerPoint's built-in dictionary does not recognize, PowerPoint underlines them with a wavy red line. You have probably noticed this wavy underline under words such as *Contoso* in the current presentation. To turn off this feature, you can clear the Check Spelling As You Type check box on the Spelling and Style tab of the Options dialog box (available on the Tools menu).

PowerPoint includes several built-in dictionaries so you can check presentations that use languages other than English. You can also create custom dictionaries in PowerPoint to check the spelling of unique words, or you can use custom dictionaries from other Microsoft programs. If a word is a foreign language word, you can mark it as such, and PowerPoint won't flag it as a misspelling anymore.

You can correct misspelled words in documents in two ways. You can use the Spelling button on the Standard toolbar (or select Spelling from the Tools menu) to check the entire presentation, or, when you encounter a wavy red line under a word, you can right-click the word and choose the correct spelling from the list on the shortcut menu.

Correct spelling

You have finished entering and formatting text in the presentation. Now you need to check if the text is accurately spelled.

1 Drag the scroll box to slide 7.

The words *Je ne sais quois* appear with a wavy red underline, indicating that they are misspelled or not recognized by the dictionary. They aren't recognized because this is a common French phrase.

2 Select the French phrase "Je ne sais quois" in the word processing box.

3 On the Tools menu, click Language.

The Language dialog box appears.

4 Scroll down, and then click French (France).

You are telling PowerPoint that this is a French phrase (French as it is spoken in France, to be precise) that is correct as it stands.

FIGURE 5-14

Language dialog box

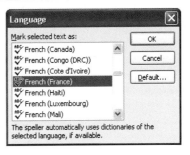

5 Click OK, and then click to deselect the selected text.

The dictionary now recognizes the words, though a wavy red line may still appear below *quois*.

6 Drag the scroll bar to slide 6.

7 Right-click the word "Enviromental," and then click Environmental on the shortcut menu.

PowerPoint corrects the misspelled word.

TIP

The custom dictionary allows you to add words that your dictionary doesn't recognize. Contoso is a proper name that you can add to your custom dictionary.

8 **On the Standard toolbar, click the Spelling button.**

PowerPoint begins checking the spelling in the presentation. The spelling checker stops and selects the proper name *Contoso*.

TROUBLESHOOTING

If you have just installed PowerPoint, the spelling feature may not be installed. PowerPoint may prompt you to install this feature before you can continue.

FIGURE 5-15

Spelling dialog box

Contoso does not appear in your dictionary, but you know it is a proper name that is spelled correctly.

9 **Click Add.**

The custom dictionary adds the word *Contoso* and continues to check the presentation. This word will no longer appear as an error in any presentation, because it has been added to the dictionary. The spelling checker stops on and selects the proper name *Sacksteder*.

TROUBLESHOOTING

Your spelling checker may not stop on the name *Sacksteder* if it has already been added to the custom dictionary.

10 **Click Ignore All if the spelling checker highlights "Sacksteder."**

The spelling checker may stop on *quois*, the French word that is part of the quote in the word processing box.

11 **Click Ignore if the spelling checker highlights "quois."**

The spelling checker ignores the proper name. The spelling checker stops when it fails to recognize the name *Hinsch*.

12 **Click Ignore All.**

The spelling checker now ignores all appearances of the word *Hinsch*. The spelling checker stops and selects the misspelled word *Realtionships*. The correct word spelling, *Relationships*, appears in the Suggestions list.

TIP

Click AutoCorrect in the Spelling dialog box to add the misspelling and the correct spelling of a word to the AutoCorrect table of entries.

13 Click Change to correct the spelling.

The spelling checker continues to check the presentation for misspelled words or words not found in the dictionary. A dialog box appears when PowerPoint completes checking the entire presentation.

14 Click OK, and then drag the scroll box up to slide 1.

◆ Keep this file open for the next exercise.

Using Smart Tags

You have just seen that you can add frequently used proper names to a spelling dictionary to make future presentations easier to check. PowerPoint 2003 offers another feature called *smart tags* that can help you keep track of information such as names, dates and times, addresses, and telephone numbers.

You control smart tags from the AutoCorrect dialog box's Smart Tags tab. Select the Label Text With Smart Tags check box, and then select the kinds of information you want to tag. Click Check Presentation to search for information that can be tagged. Applicable items are underlined on the slides with a purple dotted line. If you point to the smart tag, the Smart Tag Actions button displays, as shown in the illustration below.

FIGURE 5-16

Smart Tag Actions menu

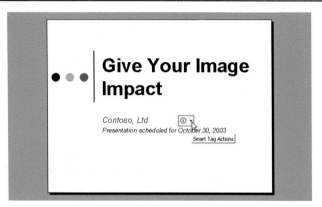

Click the Smart Tag Actions down arrow to display a menu of actions you can perform with the tagged information. For the date smart tag shown in the illustration above, for example, you can select Schedule A Meeting or Show My Calendar to schedule the presentation date in Microsoft Outlook.

Checking Presentation Styles

THE BOTTOM LINE

The presentation style checker helps you identify style and consistency errors in your presentation. This can save you a lot of time in the editing process.

PowerPoint's style checker works with the Office Assistant to help you correct common presentation style design mistakes so that your audience focuses on content and not on visual mistakes. When the Office Assistant is visible, the style checker reviews the presentation for typical mistakes, such as incorrect font size, too many fonts, too many words, inconsistent punctuation, and other readability problems. The style checker then suggests ways to improve the presentation. You can specify the style errors, such as text case or punctuation, that the style checker looks for.

TIP

As part of the style checking process, PowerPoint checks the text case, such as capitalization, of sentences and titles in the presentation, but you can independently change text case for selected text with a command on the Format menu. The Change Case command allows you to change text to sentence case, title case, uppercase, lowercase, or toggle case, which is a mixture of cases.

Check presentation styles

You have completed the spelling check. Now you need to check presentation styles to ensure that your slides are consistent.

1 On the Tools menu, click Options.

2 Click the Spelling And Style tab.

3 Select the Check Style check box.

If PowerPoint prompts you to enable the Office Assistant, click Enable Assistant.

4 Click Style Options.

The Style Options dialog box appears.

5 Select the Body Punctuation check box if necessary to check for consistent body punctuation in the presentation.

6 Click the down arrow in the box next to Body Punctuation, and then click Paragraphs Have Consistent Punctuation in the list, if necessary.

This style option will prompt the Office Assistant to point out paragraphs whose end punctuation differs from that of other paragraphs.

FIGURE 5-17

Style Options dialog box

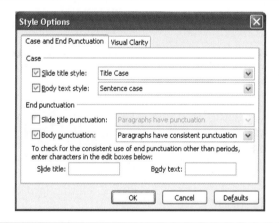

7 Click OK, and then click OK again.

The Options dialog box closes.

8 Drag the scroll box to slide 5.

A light bulb appears on slide 5.

TROUBLESHOOTING

If you don't see a light bulb, click Show the Office Assistant on the Help menu.

9 **Click the light bulb.**

A dialog balloon appears over the Office Assistant, as shown below. The Office Assistant noticed that the second bulleted item does not have a period at the end of the sentence. The default style for main text is to have a period at the end of each bulleted item.

FIGURE 5-18

Office Assistant suggests changes

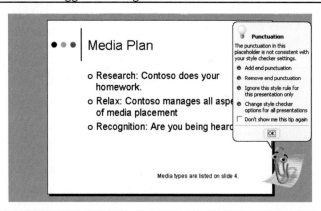

TIP

If you make a decision on a tip and then change your mind, you may need to display the tip again. To do this, you need to reset your tips so that the Office Assistant will display all of them again. To reset your tips, right-click the Office Assistant, click Options, click Reset My Tips, and then click OK.

10 **Click the Add End Punctuation option.**

PowerPoint adds a period at the end of the second bullet. The dialog balloon disappears.

11 **Click the Next Slide button twice to scroll to slide 7.**

12 **Click the light bulb on slide 7.**

The Office Assistant displays the same dialog balloon as before. The bulleted text items in this slide are not sentences, so they do not need end punctuation.

13 **Click OK in the Office Assistant dialog balloon.**

The Office Assistant closes.

14 **To hide the Office Assistant, if necessary, right-click the Office Assistant, and then click Hide on the shortcut menu.**

◆ **Keep this file open for the next exercise.**

QUICK REFERENCE ▼

Set style options

1 On the Tools menu, click Options.

2 Click the Spelling And Style tab.

3 Select the Check Style check box.

4 Click Style Options.

5 Select the style options that you want to set.

6 Click OK, and then click OK again.

Check the style of a presentation

1 On the Help menu, click Show The Office Assistant if necessary.

2 Click the light bulb.

3 Click the option that you want from the list.

4 Click OK in the Office Assistant's dialog balloon.

5 On the Help menu, click Hide The Office Assistant.

QUICK **CHECK**

Q: What does a light bulb signify on a slide?

A: **The light bulb signifies that the Office Assistant has identified a style error.**

Using the Research Task Pane

Checking Spelling and Word Choice

THE BOTTOM LINE

The Research task pane gives you access to a number of reference tools that you would otherwise have to have on hand to check facts, spelling, and word choice as you work.

As part of the process of entering and working with text, you need to make sure you're using correct information and words that exactly convey the meaning you intend. In the past, you might have turned to reference books on your bookshelf to locate the information you need. In PowerPoint 2003, you can use the Research task pane to open a reference and find information without leaving the program.

The Research task pane gives you access to a number of research sites such as encyclopedias, a thesaurus, a translation feature, and specialized search sites. Enter a word or phrase you want to research and choose the desired reference tool from the drop-down list. After the search is complete, information displays in the task pane.

PowerPoint's online Thesaurus works much the same way as a hard-bound thesaurus. It displays a list of synonyms for your selected word. If you don't find exactly the word you want, you can click one of the synonyms to display synonyms for that word.

CHECK THIS OUT ▼

Translate a Word
You can use the Research task pane's translation feature to translate a word from one language to another. This is a good way to check foreign language words or phrases you want to add to your presentation or add "local color" to a presentation. You need to have the desired languages installed before the translation feature will work.

Use the Thesaurus to replace a word

For your final action in fine-tuning the presentation, you will find a better word for one currently in the presentation.

1 Go to slide 5 and select the word "homework" in the first bullet item.

2 On the Standard toolbar, click the Research button.

The Research task pane opens and displays the word *homework* in the Search For box.

ANOTHER METHOD

On the Tools menu, click Research.

3 Click the All Reference Books down arrow, and then click Thesaurus: English (U.S.).

The task pane displays a list of synonyms for *homework*, as shown in the illustration below.

FIGURE 5-19

Synonyms display in the Research task pane

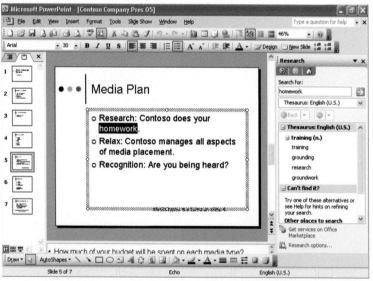

4 Point to the last synonym in the upper part of the task pane, groundwork.

A down arrow appears at the right of the word.

5 Click the down arrow and click Insert.

The word *homework* is replaced by the word *groundwork*.

6 Click the Close button to close the Research task pane.

QUICK REFERENCE ▼

Use the Thesaurus

1 Select the word you want to find a replacement for.

Q: Which research option should you select from the drop-down menu if you need to change a word to another language?

A: **Select the Translation option to change a word to another language.**

2 On the Standard toolbar, click the Research button.

3 Click the All Reference Books down arrow and select Thesaurus: English (U.S.).

4 Point to a word you want to use as a replacement to display the down arrow.

5 Click the down arrow and click Insert.

◆ If you are continuing to other lessons, save the Contoso Company Pres 05 presentation with the current name and then close it. If you are not continuing to other lessons, save and close the Contoso Company Pres 05 presentation, and then click the Close button in the title bar of the PowerPoint window.

Key Points

- ✔ *Click in an object to display the slanted-line selection box that allows you to edit content within the box. Click the outside border to display the dotted selection box that allows you to manipulate the object as a whole.*
- ✔ *You can add text objects to slides either as text labels (a single line of text) or as word processing boxes (word-wrapped text).*
- ✔ *Any text object can be modified to change word wrap options or adjust the size of the placeholder to fit the text.*
- ✔ *Change text formatting by removing bullets, applying numbers, using text styles such as bold and italic, and changing text color, font style, or font size.*
- ✔ *Modify the position of text in a placeholder by changing alignment or adjusting paragraph spacing and spacing before and after lines.*
- ✔ *You can move a text object anywhere on a slide by simply dragging and dropping it at its new location to improve the slide appearance or usefulness.*
- ✔ *Use the Find and Replace commands to locate and change text quickly throughout a presentation. The Replace Fonts command lets you replace one font with another on all slides.*
- ✔ *AutoCorrect makes many corrections as you type. You can add words to the AutoCorrect list that you commonly mistype. AutoFit helps you adjust text in placeholders when you have too many lines to fit on the slide.*
- ✔ *You can correct the spelling of any word underlined with a wavy red underline by right-clicking and choosing the correct word. Use the spelling checker to move from slide to slide to identify and correct errors.*
- ✔ *The style checker lets you specify a number of style options to check for throughout the presentation. The Office Assistant appears to suggest style changes.*
- ✔ *Use the Research task pane to look up words or find information without having to leave the PowerPoint window.*

Quick Quiz

True/False

T   F   **1.** To deselect an object, click in the middle of the object.

T   F   **2.** You should format a series of paragraphs explaining how to get from point A to point B with numbers rather than bullets.

T   F   **3.** If you used the Find Whole Words Only option in the Replace dialog box when searching for the word *cat*, PowerPoint would find both *cat* and *catastrophe*.

T   F   **4.** You could use AutoCorrect to insert your company name when you type its initials.

T   F   **5.** A wavy red line doesn't necessarily mean a word is misspelled.

Multiple Choice

1. To adjust the size of the default title text object, you would click _____ on the Format menu.
   - **a.** Text Box
   - **b.** Placeholder
   - **c.** AutoShape
   - **d.** Title

2. What is one text alignment option that you would probably not use for a slide title?
   - **a.** Align Left
   - **b.** Center
   - **c.** Align Right
   - **d.** Justify

3. To copy a text object, drag the object while holding down _____.
   - **a.** Ctrl
   - **b.** Alt
   - **c.** Shift
   - **d.** Ctrl + Alt

4. The style checker uses the _____ to offer suggested changes.
   - **a..** Presentation Assistant
   - **b.** Office Checker
   - **c.** Style Editor
   - **d.** Office Assistant

5. The Research task pane gives you access to _____.
   - **a.** an encyclopedia
   - **b.** a thesaurus
   - **c.** specialized search sites
   - **d.** all of the above

Short Answer

1. How do you create a 2-inch word processing box that will word wrap?
2. How do you remove numbering from a list and insert bullets instead?
3. How do you change font color?
4. How do you adjust the line spacing of several paragraphs to 1.3 lines?
5. How do you find and replace a particular word?
6. How do you specify another language for a word or phrase to prevent the spelling checker from showing it as an error?

On Your Own

Exercise 1

Open the Contoso Company Pres 05 in the Lesson05 folder that is located in the PowerPoint Practice folder. Display slide 3 in Normal view, and then make the following changes:

- Add a text box with the text **Create an image with impact!**
- Change the formatting of the text to Impact font, 36-point size, italic style, and red color.
- Move the text box to the bottom center of the slide.

Save and close the presentation.

Exercise 2

Open the Contoso Company Pres 05 in the Lesson05 folder that is located in the PowerPoint Practice folder. Display slide 4, and then make the following changes:

- Add a text box with the text **Create impact with the rigth media.**
- Correct the spelling of the word *right* by using the wavy red underline.
- Add a trademark symbol to the end of the text *Create impact with the right media* using the AutoCorrect replacement (tm).

Save and close the presentation.

One Step Further

Exercise 1

Open the Holidays 04 presentation from the Lesson04 folder that is located in the PowerPoint Practice folder. Save it as **Holidays 05** in the Lesson05 folder. Check the spelling of the entire presentation. On slide 3, add two new holidays after New Year's Day: Martin Luther King Day and Presidents Day. Solve the AutoFit problem by changing to a two-column format. Move half the holidays into the second text placeholder. Increase paragraph spacing to 1.2 lines for both placeholders. Save and close the presentation.

Exercise 2

Open the Holidays 05 presentation. Change the alignment of the subtitle on slide 1. (If the alignment is currently centered, right-align the subtitle, for example.) Replace one of the fonts in the presentation with another you like better. Change the color of the slide titles (except on slide 1) to another in the same group of colors offered by the design template. Save and close the presentation.

Exercise 3

Open Holidays 05. Add a new slide following slide 1 with the title **Contents**. (Format the title to match the other titles in the presentation.) Type the following paragraph text:

Holidays
Personal Time

Change the bulleted list to a numbered list. Replace the word *salary* with the word *wages* in all instances except the reference to *jury salary*. Use PowerPoint's thesaurus to find another word or phrase to use in place of *negotiable* on slide 10. Check presentation styles on each slide of the presentation and use your own judgment on how to solve any style problems. Save and close the presentation.

LESSON

6

Adding Graphics to PowerPoint

After completing this lesson, you will be able to:

✔ *Change the layout of a slide.*
✔ *Insert a clip art image.*
✔ *Scale an image.*
✔ *Recolor a clip art image.*
✔ *Insert and modify a picture.*
✔ *Insert and modify WordArt.*

KEY TERMS

■ clip art
■ scaling

Adding graphics to a Microsoft PowerPoint presentation can help you communicate your message as well as enhance the appearance of slides. Clip art pictures and photographs can act as illustrations for the slide content or impart the tone you wish to set for the presentation. For a light-hearted presentation topic, for example, humorous clip art pictures can amuse your audience. A travel presentation can be greatly improved with photographs illustrating the destination under discussion.

You use commands on the Insert menu and the Drawing toolbar to insert graphic objects such as clip art pictures, photographs, and stylized text. Once you have a graphic object on the slide, tools from the Picture toolbar and other specialized toolbars help you modify and customize your graphics.

As vice president of sales at Contoso, Ltd, you have been working on a company presentation. Now you are ready to add clip art, pictures, and stylized text to enhance your message.

In this lesson, you will learn how to change a slide layout; insert, modify, and resize clip art images; scale an image; recolor a clip art image; insert and modify a picture; and insert and modify WordArt.

◆ Before you can use the practice files in this lesson, you must install them from the book's companion CD to their default location. See "Using the CD-ROM" at the beginning of this book for more information. To complete the procedures in this lesson, you will need to use files named 06 PPT Lesson and 06 Future Picture in the Lesson06 folder in the PowerPoint Practice folder located on your hard disk.

Changing the Layout of a Slide

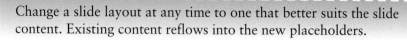

Creating Slides and
Revising Their Layouts

THE BOTTOM LINE

Change a slide layout at any time to one that better suits the slide content. Existing content reflows into the new placeholders.

As you work with the content of a slide, you may realize that you need a different slide layout. Suppose you have decided to add a clip art picture to a Title and Text slide, for example. Although you can insert a clip art picture anywhere on any slide layout, using a Title, Text, and Content or Title, Text and Clip Art layout can make it easier to size and position the clip art.

When you change a slide layout after you have already added content, you don't lose the existing content. Instead, it is repositioned in the placeholders of the new layout. You have considerable flexibility in adjusting layouts at any time during the creation of a presentation.

Change the layout of a slide

You begin this lesson by changing the layout of a slide to which you want to add a graphic image. The new layout will make it easy to position the image.

◆ Start PowerPoint, if necessary, click the Open button on the Standard toolbar, navigate to the Lesson06 folder in the PowerPoint Practice folder, and then open the 06 PPT Lesson file. Save the file as Contoso Company Pres 06 in the same folder.

1 In the Slides tab, click slide 4.

2 On the Format menu, click Slide Layout.

The Slide Layout task pane opens with the current slide layout style selected.

ANOTHER METHOD

Right-click a blank area of the slide, and then click Slide Layout on the shortcut menu.

3 In the Slide Layout task pane, scroll down until you reach the Text and Content Layouts heading.

The layouts in this section make it easy for you to add both text and graphic content to a slide.

4 Under the Text and Content Layouts heading, click the Title, Text, and Content slide layout.

The layout of slide 4 changes. The bulleted list now occupies only the left half of the screen. A content placeholder occupies the right half. The slide is now ready for you to insert content such as a table, a chart, a piece of clip art, a picture, a diagram or organization chart, or a media clip. Your presentation window should look like the following illustration.

Figure 6-1

Text fits to the new placeholder

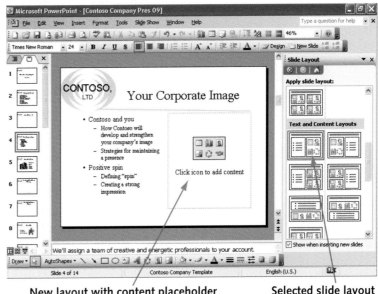

New layout with content placeholder   Selected slide layout

TROUBLESHOOTING

If the bulleted text doesn't automatically fit to the text placeholder, click the AutoFit button at the lower left corner of the text placeholder and choose to fit the text to the placeholder.

5 In the Slide Layout task pane, click the Close button to close the task pane.

◆ Keep this file open for the next exercise.

QUICK REFERENCE ▼

Change the layout of a slide

1 Display the slide to which you want to apply a different slide layout.

2 On the Format menu, click Slide Layout to display the Slide Layout task pane.

3 Click a new slide layout.

Inserting a Clip Art Image

THE BOTTOM LINE

Inserting Clip Art and Pictures

Use clip art to add graphic interest to a slide or to help illustrate the slide content. Use the Clip Art task pane to specify what kind of graphic content to insert and to search for images by keyword.

PowerPoint provides access to hundreds of professionally designed pieces of **clip art**. Clip art images include illustrations, symbols, borders, and other graphic images that can add impact to your slides. While it isn't necessary to illustrate every slide in a presentation, inserting clip art judiciously can provide "eye relief" for your audience.

In PowerPoint, as in all Microsoft Office applications, clip art is stored in the Microsoft Clip Organizer. The Clip Organizer organizes clips by category, and each clip is identified by several keywords. A picture of an eagle, for example, might be identified by the keywords *animals, bald eagles, birds.* Keywords that apply to multiple categories make it easy for you to search for an image.

You have several options for adding a clip art image to a slide. In a slide with a content placeholder, click the Insert Clip Art icon to open the Select Picture dialog box. This dialog box shows you all clip art on your system, as well as any other graphic images that the Clip Organizer has organized for you. You can search in the Select Picture dialog box to find images.

To have more control over the process of searching, you can display the Clip Art task pane. To do so, click the Insert Clip Art button on the Drawing toolbar or point to Picture on the Insert menu and then click Clip Art. The Clip Art task pane has a Search For box where you type a keyword to identify the type of clip you want to find, such as clips that show *clients* or *doctors.* The Search In box lets you select which collections to search in: your personal collections, the standard Office collections, collections on the Web, or all collections. The Results Should Be box lets you choose what type of media to search: clip art images, photographs, movies, or sounds. You can select any one of these, or select multiple options. After you have typed a keyword and selected options for the search, click Go to complete the search and display images that match your search criteria in the pane. You can then simply click the image to insert it on the slide.

If you don't find an image you like when you search in the Clip Art task pane, you can click Clip Art On Office Online at the bottom of the Clip Art task pane to connect to Microsoft's Clip Art And Media Web page. This Web page gives you access to many more clip art images.

You can also work directly in the Clip Organizer to locate images. Click Organize Clips to open the Clip Organizer. You can then browse through the categories for each collection. If you find a clip you want to use, you can copy it and paste it onto the slide.

Insert a clip art image

Now that you have changed the slide layout, you are ready to insert a clip art image in the content placeholder. You will use the Clip Art task pane to locate and insert the clip.

1 **With slide 4 displayed, click in a blank area inside the content placeholder to select the placeholder.**

Selecting the placeholder before you insert the clip art will ensure that the clip art uses the placeholder size and position.

2 On the Insert menu, point to Picture, and then click Clip Art.

The Clip Art task pane appears with search options.

ANOTHER METHOD

On the Drawing toolbar, click the Insert Clip Art button.

3 Click the Results Should Be down arrow and make sure only the Clip Art check box is selected.

The search will be restricted to clip art images, which will save time in searching and in evaluating the results of the search.

4 In the Search For text box, type peak, and then click Go.

All clip art pertaining to *peak* appears.

TIP

Clip art from the Clip Organizer appears with a small globe icon in the lower-left corner of the image.

5 Scroll down, if necessary, and then click a clip art picture similar to the one shown in the following illustration. (You may find it faster to scroll up from the bottom of the pane to locate this illustration.)

PowerPoint inserts the clip art in the placeholder. The picture is selected on the slide, and the Picture toolbar opens. When a picture is selected, PowerPoint automatically opens the Picture toolbar.

Figure 6-2

Select picture similar to this one

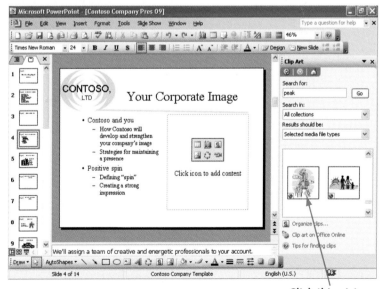

Click this picture

6 Click outside the image to deselect it.

The Picture toolbar is hidden.

✕

7 In the Clip Art task pane, click the Close button to close the task pane.

◆ Keep this file open for the next exercise.

QUICK REFERENCE ▼

Insert a clip art image using the Clip Art task pane

1 On the Insert menu, point to Picture, and then click Clip Art.

2 In the Clip Art task pane, in the Search For text box, type what you want to search for.

3 Make any necessary adjustments in Search In and Results Should Be boxes.

4 Click Go.

5 Click a clip art image to insert it into the placeholder or on the slide.

Scaling an Image

THE BOTTOM LINE

Modifying Clip Art and Pictures

If a graphic isn't exactly the right size on the slide, you can scale it to resize it precisely by percentage or by measurement.

Graphics that you insert on slides may not be the right size for the area where you want to place them. You can adjust image size by scaling. **Scaling** changes the size of an entire object by a set percentage. Scaling differs from simply dragging a resize handle in that you can specify an exact measurement for width or height or type a percentage to enlarge or reduce the image.

Use the Picture command on the Format menu to open the Format Picture dialog box, or right-click the picture and select Format Picture from the shortcut menu. The Size tab in this dialog box gives you access to several measurement boxes for scaling. By default, a change to one dimension of the picture will automatically change the other dimension so that the current ratio of width to height is maintained. The Size tab also displays the original dimensions of the image so you can reset the original size if you don't like the result of your scaling.

If you create a presentation specifically for giving a slide show, you can also optimize the size of an image for the size of the slide show screen by selecting the Best Scale For Slide Show check box on the Size tab.

Scale an object

An image you have already inserted in the presentation could be scaled for greater impact on the slide.

1 Scroll down to slide 8.

2 Select the clip art image.

The Picture toolbar appears.

TROUBLESHOOTING

If the Picture toolbar doesn't appear, click the View menu, point to Toolbars, and then click Picture.

 3 On the Picture toolbar, click the Format Picture button, or click Picture on the Format menu.

The Format Picture dialog box appears.

ANOTHER METHOD

Right-click the picture, and then click Format Picture on the shortcut menu.

4 Click the Size tab.

The Size tab displays a number of options for changing the scale of the image.

5 In the Scale area, select the number in the Height box.

6 Type 120.

Because the Lock Aspect Ratio check box is selected, the Width option setting will also automatically change to 120% when you click OK. If you are not sure about the new scale size, you can click Preview (next to Cancel) to view the object before you close the dialog box.

7 Click OK, and then deselect the object.

The dialog box closes, and you should see that the picture is larger. Your slide should look like the following illustration.

ANOTHER METHOD

You can also press Esc to deselect an object.

Figure 6-3

Image has been scaled

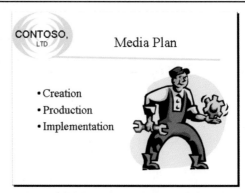

◆ Keep this file open for the next exercise.

QUICK REFERENCE ▼

Scale an object

1 Select the clip art image.

2 On the Picture toolbar, click the Format Picture button, or click Picture on the Format menu.

3 Click the Size tab.

4 In the Scale area, select the number in the Height box.

5 Type a number.

6 Click OK.

Recoloring a Clip Art Image

THE BOTTOM LINE

Recolor clip art images to make them coordinate with the color scheme of your current design template. This gives a custom look to the image.

Modifying Clip Art and Pictures

You can change the color of clip art images to create a different look or to match the current color scheme. Recoloring customizes the image so it looks as if it were created specifically for the current presentation.

The Recolor Picture command displays a dialog box with a preview of the picture and a list of all the colors in the picture. You can change any color in the list. By default, when you select a color to change, the color menu displays the current color scheme colors. Choose one of these colors to have the image blend in with slide colors already in use. You can also click More Colors to select any other color from the PowerPoint color palette.

Recolor an image

You have already inserted a clip art image on slide 5, but it would be improved by recoloring. You will change both image colors to colors that coordinate with the color scheme.

1 Scroll up to slide 5.

2 Select the clip art object.

 3 On the Picture toolbar, click the Recolor Picture button.

The Recolor Picture dialog box appears with the Colors option selected in the Change section. This image has only two colors, black and white.

4 Under New, click the down arrow next to the black color.

A color menu appears, showing the current color scheme colors.

5 Click in the dark blue color box.

The color swatch changes to dark blue, and the preview box on the right shows that all the parts of the image that were black—the lines—are now blue. Now you will choose a new color from the PowerPoint color palette to replace the white color.

6 Under New, click the down arrow next to the white color, click More Colors, and then click the first gray cell in the bottom row, as shown in the following illustration.

Figure 6-4

Select the light gray shown here

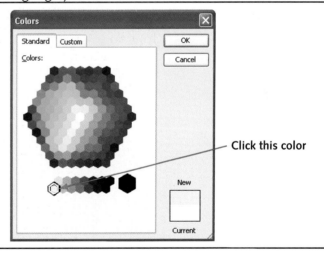

7 Click OK, and then click OK in the Recolor Picture dialog box.

PowerPoint recolors the clip art image so all white areas are light gray.

8 Deselect the object.

The Picture toolbar closes.

◆ Keep this file open for the next exercise.

QUICK CHECK

Q: How does PowerPoint determine which colors are shown in the drop-down menu of the New box?

A: **The colors shown are the current color scheme colors.**

QUICK REFERENCE ▼

Recolor a clip art image

1 Select a clip art object.

2 On the Picture toolbar, click the Recolor Picture button.

3 Under New, click the down arrow next to a color.

4 Click a color box or click More Colors, click a color, and then click OK.

5 Click OK.

Inserting a Picture

THE BOTTOM LINE

Pictures stored on your system, network, or removable media give you a great deal of flexibility for locating and inserting pictures to illustrate your slides. You can also save time by inserting pictures directly from your scanner or camera.

Inserting Clip Art and Pictures

Besides using PowerPoint's broad collection of clip art and photographs, you can insert pictures that are stored anywhere on your system, on a network, or on removable media such as disk or CD-ROM. You can also insert a picture directly from a scanner or digital camera to a slide, without having to first save it to a location on your system. Using the Picture submenu on the Insert menu gives you access to an almost limitless number of pictures that can add visual impact to your slides.

You already know that the Picture submenu gives you access to the Clip Art command that opens the Clip Art task pane. This submenu also offers the From File command, which you can use to locate a picture stored on any local or network drive, and From Scanner or Camera, which you can use to download a picture directly from either of these devices.

You do not have to use a placeholder to contain a picture. You can insert a picture on any slide and then adjust its size as desired.

TIP

You can also find the New Photo Album command on the Picture submenu. Use a photo album to display a collection of photos in a presentation using special layout options such as oval frames and captions under the pictures.

When you insert pictures from files on your hard disk drive, scanner, digital camera, or Web camera, PowerPoint allows you to select multiple pictures, view thumbnails of them, and insert them all at once.

Insert a picture

You have available a photograph that you think will illustrate the excitement of working with Contoso. In this exercise, you will insert the picture on a slide.

1 **In the Slides tab, click slide 10.**

2 **On the Insert menu, point to Picture, and then click From File.**

The Insert Picture dialog box appears.

ANOTHER METHOD

- Click the Insert Picture button on the Drawing toolbar.
- Click the Insert Picture button in any content placeholder.

3 **Navigate to the Lesson06 folder in the PowerPoint Practice folder.**

A thumbnail of the picture stored in the folder displays. (You may need to change the View option to see the thumbnail view.)

4 **Click 06 Future Picture, and then click Insert.**

The picture and the Picture toolbar appear. The picture is inserted at a very small size, as shown in the following illustration. You will adjust the size in the next exercise.

Figure 6-5

Picture inserted on slide

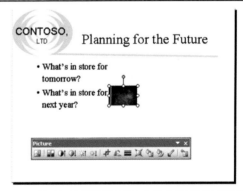

◆ **Keep this file open for the next exercise.**

QUICK REFERENCE ▼

Insert a picture

1 On the Insert menu, point to Picture, and then click From File.

2 In the Look In box, navigate to the location from which you want to insert a picture.

3 In the list of file names, click the picture you want to insert.

4 Click Insert.

QUICK CHECK

Q: Besides inserting clip art from the Picture submenu, what other options do you have for inserting graphics?

A: **You can insert a picture from a file, insert a picture from a scanner or digital camera, or create a new photo album.**

Modifying a Picture

Modifying Clip Art and Pictures

THE BOTTOM LINE

Change attributes such as size, brightness, and contrast to improve the look of a picture. Cropping can eliminate unnecessary parts of the picture, and compressing can help to keep file size reasonable.

You can enhance a photograph or scanned image by using tools on the Picture toolbar to control brightness, contrast, and color. Modifying a picture using these controls ensures that it will look its best on the slide. If you find that your changes don't improve the picture as you wanted, you can click the Reset Picture button on the Picture toolbar to reverse all changes.

Sometimes you need only a portion of a picture in the presentation. With the Crop command, you can mask portions of a picture so you do not see all of it on the screen. The picture is not altered, just covered up.

You can also compress pictures with PowerPoint to minimize the file size of the image. In doing so, however, you may lose some visual quality, depending on the compression setting. You can pick the resolution that you want for the pictures in a presentation based on where or how they'll be viewed (for example, on the Web or printed), and you can set other options, such as deleting cropped areas of a picture, to get the best balance between picture quality and file size.

Modify a picture

As you have already seen, the picture you inserted is too small. In this exercise, you will resize it as well as make other modifications to improve its appearance on the slide.

1 Click the picture on slide 10 to select it if necessary and display the Picture toolbar.

2 Hold down Shift, and then drag the corner resize handles on the picture to enlarge the picture on the slide.

Holding Shift as you drag maintains the current ratio of width to height so the picture doesn't become distorted.

IMPORTANT

If you are having trouble resizing the picture, you can press the Alt key while dragging the resize handles to turn off the Snap Objects To Grid feature.

3 On the Picture toolbar, click the Color button, and then click Washout.

The picture is converted to a watermark, which is a grayed version of the image.

4 On the Picture toolbar, click the Less Brightness button twice.

The picture brightness decreases to enhance the look of the picture.

5 On the Picture toolbar, click the More Contrast button twice.

The picture contrast increases to enhance the look of the picture.

6 Drag the picture up until it is aligned to the top of the text box on the slide.

For fine positioning of the picture, nudge it using the keyboard arrow keys.

7 On the Picture toolbar, click the Crop button.

The pointer changes to the cropping tool.

8 Position the center of the cropping tool over the left-middle resize handle, and then drag right to crop the left side of the picture to cover the pole.

While you are dragging, a dotted outline appears to show you the area that remains after cropping. The cropping tool also changes to a constrain pointer, indicating the direction in which you are cropping.

9 Position the center of the cropping tool over the right-middle resize handle, and then drag left to crop the right side of the picture to cover the pole.

10 On the Picture toolbar, click the Crop button, or click a blank portion of the slide.

The cropping tool changes back to the pointer.

11 Drag the corner and side resize handles to resize the picture so that it covers the right side of the slide.

12 On the Picture toolbar, click the Compress Pictures button.

The Compress Pictures dialog box appears. The current settings, shown in the illustration below, fit your needs.

Figure 6-6

Compress Pictures dialog box

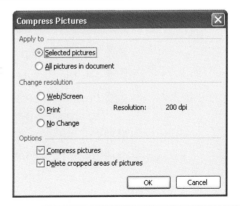

13 Click OK.

A warning box appears, letting you know that compressing pictures may reduce the quality of your images.

14 Click Apply to compress the image.

15 Deselect the picture.

Your presentation window should look like the following illustration.

Figure 6-7

Modified picture

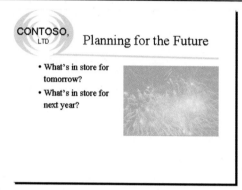

◆ **Keep this file open for the next exercise.**

QUICK REFERENCE ▼

Resize a picture

Select the picture, hold down Shift, and then drag the corner resize handles on the picture to enlarge the picture on the slide.

Move a picture

Drag the picture until it is properly aligned.

Enhance a picture

1 Select the picture.

2 On the Picture toolbar, click formatting buttons such as Color, Less Brightness, or More Contrast until you reach the effect you want.

Crop a picture

1 Select the clip art image.

2 On the Picture toolbar, click the Crop button.

3 Position the center of the cropping tool over a resize handle and drag to crop the picture.

4 On the Picture toolbar, click the Crop button or click a blank portion of the slide to deselect the Crop button.

Compress a picture

1 Select the picture.

2 On the Picture toolbar, click the Compress Pictures button.

3 Click the compression options that you want.

4 Click OK, and then click Apply.

Inserting and Modifying WordArt

Inserting and Modifying Stylized Text

THE BOTTOM LINE

WordArt creates a graphic from text and thus can add both information and visual appeal to a slide. Use the WordArt toolbar options to further customize a WordArt graphic for the presentation.

You can insert fancy or stylized text into a presentation with Microsoft's WordArt feature. WordArt allows you to add visual enhancements to your text that go beyond changing a font or font size. Most users apply WordArt to emphasize short phrases, such as *Our Customers Come First*, or to a single word, such as *Welcome*. You do not have to be an artist to create stylized text—WordArt provides you with a gallery of choices. You can insert stylized text by clicking the Insert WordArt button on the Drawing toolbar (or by clicking Picture on the Insert menu and then clicking WordArt) and then selecting a style.

Insert and modify WordArt

Your final enhancement to the presentation will be adding a WordArt graphic to the last slide.

1 Scroll down to slide 14.

2 On the Drawing toolbar, click the Insert WordArt button.

The WordArt Gallery dialog box appears, displaying a list of styles.

ANOTHER METHOD

On the Insert menu, point to Picture and then click WordArt.

3 Click the style in the third column, third row, as shown in the following illustration.

Figure 6-8

WordArt Gallery dialog box

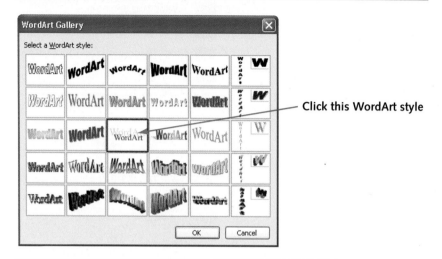

Click this WordArt style

4 **Click OK.**

The Edit WordArt Text dialog box appears.

5 **In the Text box, type** We bask in the glow of your image!

The WordArt text defaults to the Times New Roman font at 36 points. You can change this text at any time using the Edit Text button on the WordArt toolbar.

6 **Click OK.**

The text you typed and the WordArt toolbar appear. Notice that the shadow extends almost off the slide at the right.

7 **Drag the lower-right resize handle to the left to decrease the size of the WordArt object so it fits on the slide.**

8 **On the WordArt toolbar, click the WordArt Shape button, and then click the Double Wave 2 symbol, as shown in the following illustration.**

The new shape is applied to the WordArt, adding even more visual interest.

Figure 6-9

WordArt Shape menu

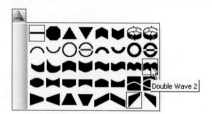

Double Wave 2

9 **On the WordArt toolbar, click the WordArt Character Spacing button.**

A submenu appears with character spacing types. Character spacing options increase or decrease the space between the letters in the words.

10 On the Character Spacing submenu, click Loose.

Space between letters increases slightly.

11 On the WordArt toolbar, click the Format WordArt button.

The Format WordArt dialog box opens.

12 Click the Colors and Lines tab, click the Color down arrow in the Fill section at the top of the dialog box, and then click in the dark blue box in the top row of color boxes (Follow Accent Scheme Color box).

The fill color changes from a green marble texture to the color scheme dark blue.

13 Click the Color down arrow in the Line section, and then click in the dark blue box in the top row of color boxes (Follow Accent Scheme Color box).

The line color now matches the fill color.

14 Click OK.

The text now coordinates better with the color scheme, but the shadow behind the text still has a greenish tint that can be modified to improve the graphic.

15 On the Drawing toolbar, click the Shadow Style button, and then click Shadow Settings.

The Shadow Settings toolbar appears.

16 On the Shadow Settings toolbar, click the Shadow Color button down arrow, and then click in the light blue box (Follow Accent And Hyperlink Scheme Color box).

17 Click the Close button on the Shadow Settings toolbar.

The shadow now coordinates with the text.

18 Drag the WordArt text object to the center of the slide, and then click a blank area of the presentation window to quit WordArt.

The WordArt toolbar closes.

◆ If you are continuing to other lessons, save the Contoso Company Pres 06 presentation with the current name and then close it. If you are not continuing to other lessons, save and close the Contoso Company Pres 06 presentation, and then click the Close button in the title bar of the PowerPoint window.

QUICK REFERENCE ▼

Insert WordArt in a slide

1 On the Drawing toolbar, click the Insert WordArt button.

2 Click a style, and then click OK.

3 In the Text box, type text.

4 Click OK.

QUICK CHECK

Q: What WordArt toolbar button can help you tighten up the space between letters?

A: **The WordArt Character Spacing button adjusts space between letters.**

Format the WordArt text

1 Click the WordArt text.

2 On the WordArt toolbar, click formatting buttons to adjust the graphic as desired.

3 To adjust a WordArt shadow, on the Drawing toolbar, click the Shadow Style button, and then click Shadow Settings.

4 On the Shadow Settings toolbar, click the Shadow Color button down arrow, and then click a color box.

5 Click the Close button on the Shadow Settings toolbar.

Key Points

✔ *Change the layout of a slide at any time to adjust the way content appears on the slide. Existing content reformats into the new placeholders.*

✔ *Use the Select Picture dialog box or Clip Art task pane to search for and insert clip art stored on your system. The Clip Art task pane gives you greater flexibility in searching for particular types of clip art.*

✔ *When you want to adjust an image's size precisely, use the scaling options in the Format Picture dialog box.*

✔ *Make a clip art image match your color scheme more closely by recoloring portions of it.*

✔ *You can insert a picture such as a photograph or illustration from any drive on your system, from a scanner, or from a digital camera. You can then modify the picture using the tools on PowerPoint's Picture toolbar.*

✔ *WordArt creates stylized text that can add visual impact as well as information to your slides. Format a WordArt graphic using the tools on the WordArt toolbar.*

Quick Quiz

True/False

T F   1. After you change a slide layout, you have to manually move information into the new placeholders.

T F   2. To search for clip art on a particular subject, you type a keyword in the Search For box in the Clip Art task pane.

T F   3. Most clip art images are created using only one or two colors.

T F   4. A picture must be inserted into a placeholder.

T F   5. It is probably best to limit WordArt graphics to short phrases or single words.

Multiple Choice

1. Clip art images can include _____.
   a. illustrations
   b. symbols
   c. borders
   d. all of the above

2. To scale an image, you use the _____ tab in the Format Picture dialog box.
   a. Scale
   b. Size
   c. Format
   d. Layout

3. To insert a picture from your digital camera, click Insert, _____.
   a. point to Import, and then click From Scanner or Camera
   b. point to Camera, and then click Insert Picture
   c. point to Picture, and then click From Scanner or Camera
   d. point to New, and then click Digital Image

4. To remove a portion of a picture you don't need, you use the _____ tool.
   a. Trim
   b. Reset
   c. Compress
   d. Crop

5. To change the color of a WordArt graphic, click the _____ button on the WordArt toolbar.
   a. Format WordArt
   b. Recolor
   c. WordArt Color
   d. Shadow Color

Short Answer

1. How do you scale an object disproportionately?
2. How do you recolor an image?
3. How do you search for a photograph using the Clip Art task pane?
4. How do you insert a picture stored on a CD-ROM?
5. How do you make an image into a watermark?
6. How do you crop a picture?
7. How do you insert WordArt?

On Your Own

Exercise 1

Open Contoso Company Pres 06 in the Lesson06 folder that is located in the PowerPoint Practice folder. Insert a new slide at the end of the presentation with the Title, Text, and Content layout, search for clip art with the keyword *communication*, and insert a clip art image into the content placeholder. Scale the image by 50 percent, recolor the image, and then save and close the presentation.

Exercise 2

Open Contoso Company Pres 06 in the Lesson06 folder that is located in the PowerPoint Practice folder. Insert a new slide at the end of the presentation with the Blank layout, insert WordArt in the slide with any style and the text Any Questions? with the Inflate shape, and then save and close the presentation.

One Step Further

Exercise 1

Start a new presentation for A. Datum Corporation, using any design template or the one you have been using in other lessons. Save the presentation as AD Sales 06 in the Lesson06 folder that is located in the PowerPoint Practice folder. In the title area of the title slide, insert a WordArt object using the text A. Datum Corporation, and modify styles and formats as desired. Add the subtitle **Annual Sales Conference**. Save and close the presentation.

Exercise 2

Open the AD Sales 06 presentation in the Lesson06 folder. In the Clip Art task pane, search for photographs only using the keyword *presentation*. Insert an appropriate picture on the slide. Scale the image as necessary to fit on the slide (you may want to move the title and subtitle to make room for the picture). Modify the picture properties and crop as necessary. Compress the picture. Save and close the presentation.

Exercise 3

Open the AD Sales 06 presentation in the Lesson06 folder. Add a new slide using the Title and Text layout. Type the title **Focus on Clients** and then insert in the text area the names of five clients (you can make up these names). Insert an appropriate clip art graphic (use the keyword *client*, for example) on this slide to the right of the bulleted list. Scale the clip art appropriately. Recolor the clip art to match the current design template colors. Save and close the presentation.

LESSON

Producing a Slide Show

After completing this lesson, you will be able to:

✔ *Navigate in Slide Show view.*
✔ *Annotate slides during a slide show.*
✔ *Set slide transitions.*
✔ *Animate slides.*
✔ *Hide a slide.*
✔ *Create and edit a custom show.*

KEY TERMS

■ Animation Schemes   ■ Custom shows

In Microsoft PowerPoint, you can display presentations on your computer monitor using Slide Show view. Slide Show uses your computer like a projector to display a presentation on one or two monitors using the full screen or, using special hardware, on an overhead screen. To make your slide shows more exciting and engaging, you can add animation to text and graphics on the slide to display during a slide show. As you present a slide show, you can also take notes to document discussion points that members of your audience express during the presentation.

As vice president of sales at Contoso, Ltd, you have been working on a company presentation. You are ready to rehearse the slide show for Wendy Beth Kahn, the CEO, who wants to see it before you give the presentation at next month's meeting of department heads.

In this lesson, you will learn how to navigate through a slide show, draw on a slide during a slide show, add slide transitions, animate text and objects, hide a slide, and create and edit a custom slide show.

◆ Before you can use the practice files in this lesson, you must install them from the book's companion CD to their default location. See "Using the CD-ROM" on at the beginning of this book for more information. To complete the procedures in this lesson, you will need to use a file named 07 PPT Lesson in the Lesson07 folder in the PowerPoint Practice folder located on your hard disk.

Navigating in Slide Show View

Delivering a Slide Show

THE BOTTOM LINE

Knowing how to get around in Slide Show view will make you a more comfortable and professional presenter. Use PowerPoint's keyboard and popup menu options to move from slide to slide.

In earlier lessons, you learned to click the mouse to advance to the next slide in a slide show. PowerPoint has several additional options for navigating through a slide show presentation, as shown in the table below. Mastering these options will help you navigate with ease and confidence during a presentation.

Table 7-1

Presentation navigation methods

Action	Mouse Options	Keyboard Options
Go to next slide	Click the slide	Press Spacebar
	Click Next button on popup toolbar	Press →
	Right-click and click Next	Press Enter
		Press Page Down
		Press N
Go to previous slide	Click Previous button on popup toolbar	Press ←
	Right-click and click Previous	Press Page Up
	Right-click and click Last Viewed	Press P
End show	Right-click and click End Show	Press Esc

You may have noticed a small toolbar in the bottom-left corner of slides when you used Slide Show view in previous lessons. This is the popup toolbar, which displays when you move the mouse pointer on the screen in Slide Show view. The popup toolbar is new in PowerPoint 2003. Its options streamline the process of navigating a presentation in Slide Show view. The popup toolbar has four buttons, as shown in the illustration at left.

Figure 7-1

Popup toolbar

As mentioned in Table 7-1, you can use the Previous and Next buttons on this toolbar to move forward and backward among the slides. Click the Pointer button to display a menu of pointer and annotation options. (You learn more about annotating in the "Annotating Slides During a Slide Show" section of this lesson.) Click the Navigation button to display a menu of additional options for moving to the next or previous slide, to the slide last viewed, or to a specific slide or custom show. You'll also find options on this menu for changing the screen color and ending the show.

As you fine-tune your presentation, you will often want to check a slide in Slide Show view. You don't have to start with slide 1 each time you check slides in Slide Show view. You can start a slide show with any slide by selecting the slide in the current view and then clicking the Slide Show button.

Navigate in Slide Show view

In this exercise, you use various keyboard and mouse techniques to navigate your slide show.

◆ **Start PowerPoint, if necessary, click the Open button on the Standard toolbar, navigate to the Lesson07 folder in the PowerPoint Practice folder, and then open the 07 PPT Lesson file. Save the file as Contoso Company Pres 07 in the same folder.**

1 Click the Slide Show button.

PowerPoint displays the first slide in the presentation.

2 Click anywhere on the screen, or press the Spacebar.

The slide show advances to the next slide.

3 Move the mouse to display the pointer.

The popup toolbar displays in the bottom-left corner of the slide.

4 Click the Next button on the popup toolbar.

The slide show advances to slide 3.

5 On the popup toolbar, click the Navigation button.

A shortcut menu displays, as shown in the following illustration, giving you multiple options for navigating in the presentation.

Figure 7-2

Navigation shortcut menu

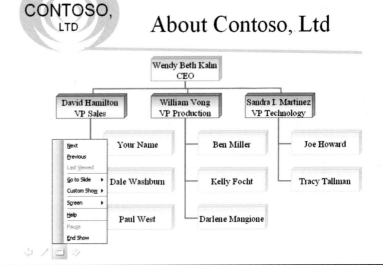

6 On the shortcut menu, point to Go To Slide, and then click 9 Relationships.

Slide 9 appears in Slide Show view.

7 Right-click anywhere on the screen, point to Go To Slide, and then click 14 Contoso, Ltd.

Right-clicking displays the same navigation shortcut menu that you open when you click the Navigation button on the popup toolbar. You have now displayed the last slide in the presentation.

8 Click the screen.

Slide 1 appears in Normal view. Now you will start the slide show from a slide other than slide 1.

If you see a black screen after the last slide, click to exit this screen and return to Normal view.

9 Click slide 3 in the Slides tab of the Outline/Slides pane.

10 Click the Slide Show button.

The slide show starts by displaying slide 3.

IMPORTANT

Pressing the F5 Shortcut key or clicking Slide Show on the View menu always displays the first slide in the presentation. To start a slide show with another slide in the presentation, use the Slide Show button.

11 On the popup toolbar, click the Previous button.

Slide 2 displays.

12 Right-click anywhere on the screen, and then click End Show or press Esc.

Slide 2, the current slide in the slide show, appears in Normal view.

◆ Keep this file open for the next exercise.

QUICK REFERENCE ▼

Navigate through a slide show

1 Click the Slide Show button.

2 Use keyboard or mouse options to move forward or back through the slides.

3 To go to a specific slide, click the Navigation button on the popup toolbar, point to Go To Slide, and click a slide title.

Start a show on a specific slide

1 Select a slide in the Slide pane, Slides tab, or Slide Sorter view.

2 Click the Slide Show button.

Using Presenter View with Multiple Monitors

If your computer is connected to two monitors, you can view a slide show on one monitor while you control it from another. This is useful when you want to control a slide show and run other programs that you don't want the audience to see. You can set up your presentation to use multiple monitors by choosing options in the Multiple Monitors area in the Set Up Show dialog box. When you display your slide show on multiple monitors, you can present it using PowerPoint's presenter tools in the Presenter view, which allows presenters to have their own view not visible to the audience. In addition to including details about what bullet or slide is coming next, this view enables you to see your speaker notes and lets you jump directly to any slide.

In order to use multiple monitors, you must first install the proper hardware and software.

To use presenter tools in Presenter view, select the Show Presenter View check box in the Set Up Show dialog box. If you clear the Show Presenter View check box, the slide show runs as it would on a single monitor.

To present a slide show on two monitors:

1. Connect the two computers as instructed by the manufacturer.

2. On the Slide Show menu, click Set Up Show.

3. In the Multiple Monitors area, click the Display Slide Show On down arrow.

4. Click the name of the monitor on which you want to project the slide show.

5. Select the Show Presenter View check box under the Multiple Monitors options.

6. Click OK.

7. Click the Slide Show button to start the slide show.

8. In Presenter view, use the navigation tools to deliver the presentation on multiple monitors.

Annotating Slides During a Slide Show

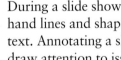
Delivering a Slide Show

THE BOTTOM LINE

To help your audience grasp a point, you can highlight text or write or draw on a slide during a presentation.

During a slide show presentation, you can annotate slides by drawing freehand lines and shapes to emphasize a point or by highlighting portions of the text. Annotating a slide can help you make your points more forcefully or draw attention to issues you want your audience to consider more closely.

PowerPoint 2003 has improved annotation features that give you more options for marking on a slide. Clicking the Pointer button on the popup toolbar displays the shortcut menu shown in Figure 7-3. You can choose from the Ballpoint Pen, the Felt Tip Pen, or the Highlighter to mark on the text, with the Ballpoint Pen giving the finest line and the Highlighter the thickest. Change the ink color by clicking Ink Color and selecting a new color from the color palette.

Figure 7-3

Pointer shortcut menu

In PowerPoint 2003, annotations remain on slides even after you move to another slide. To erase annotations, you can click Eraser on the Pointer shortcut menu to change the pointer to an eraser you can use to delete selected annotations. Or, click Erase All Ink On Slide (or press E) to remove all annotations. If you don't erase annotations, you will be asked when you end the slide show if you want to keep or discard the annotations.

IMPORTANT

When a marking tool is active in Slide Show view, clicking the mouse does not advance the slide show to the next slide. Click Arrow on the Pointer shortcut menu to reactivate the pointer, or press Esc.

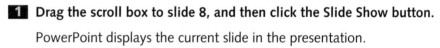

Annotate slides during a slide show

Now that you are more comfortable working in Slide Show view, you will practice marking on a slide to test the annotation tools.

1 Drag the scroll box to slide 8, and then click the Slide Show button.

PowerPoint displays the current slide in the presentation.

2 Move the mouse pointer to display the popup toolbar, and then click the Pointer button.

The Pointer shortcut menu displays PowerPoint's annotation options.

3 Click Highlighter.

The pointer changes to a thick vertical bar in the current ink color.

4 Drag the highlighter pointer over the word "Creation" in the first bullet.

The text is highlighted, just as if you were using an ink highlighter on a printed page.

5 Right-click anywhere on the slide, point to Pointer Options, point to Ink Color, and click the red color on the palette.

You have changed the ink color to red.

6 Click the Pointer button on the popup toolbar, click Felt Tip Pen, and then draw a line under the word "Implementation."

Your Slide Show window should look like the following illustration.

Figure 7-4

Annotations added to slide 8

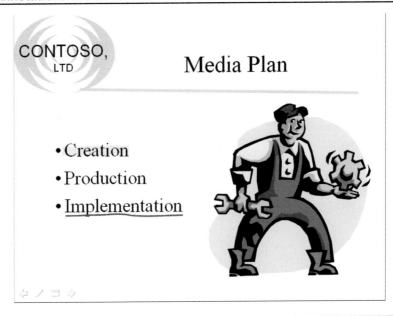

7 Click the Pointer button on the popup toolbar, and then click Erase All Ink On Slide.

All annotations are erased.

ANOTHER METHOD

Press E to erase all ink on the slide.

8 Press Esc twice.

The slide show ends, and PowerPoint displays slide 8 in Normal view.

◆ Keep this file open for the next exercise.

QUICK REFERENCE ▼

Draw an annotation in slide show

1 Click the Slide Show button.

2 Click the Pointer button on the popup toolbar, or right-click anywhere on the slide and point to Pointer Options.

3 Select a marking option and, if desired, an ink color, and drag to annotate the slide.

4 To erase annotations, click the Pointer button on the popup toolbar and click Eraser to erase individual annotations or Erase All Ink On Slide to remove all annotations.

Setting Slide Transitions

Adding Transition Effects

THE BOTTOM LINE

Transitions can help to hold audience interest while one slide is replaced by another. You can apply transitions to individual slides or to all slides in the presentation and change the speed to control the transition effect.

Transition effects help your presentation make more of an impact by varying the way one slide replaces another. A slide transition is the visual effect of a slide as it moves on and off the screen during a slide show. Slide transitions include such effects as Checkerboard Across, Cover Down, Cut, and Split Vertical Out.

Use the Slide Transition task pane to apply a slide transition effect, set the transition speed and transition sound, and determine settings for advancing a slide. You can set a transition for one slide or a group of slides by first selecting the slides in Slide Sorter view or in the Slides tab in Normal view and then applying the transition. Use Apply To All Slides to apply the settings to all slides in the presentation.

Set slide transitions

In this exercise, you apply a slide transition effect to a single slide, apply a transition to multiple slides, change the transition speed, and then remove all transitions.

1 **Click the Slide Sorter View button, and then select slide 1.**

ANOTHER METHOD

On the View menu, click Slide Sorter View.

2 **On the Slide Sorter toolbar, click the Slide Transition button.**

The Slide Transition task pane appears with current slide transition options.

ANOTHER METHOD

- On the Slide Show menu, click Slide Transition.
- Right-click a blank area of a slide in Normal view, and then click Slide Transition on the shortcut menu.

3 **Under Apply To Selected Slides, scroll down, and then click Dissolve.**

PowerPoint previews the transition effect on the slide miniature for slide 1 in Slide Sorter view and places a transition symbol below the lower-left corner of the slide, as shown in the illustration below. The symbol indicates that PowerPoint has applied a slide transition effect to this slide.

Figure 7-5

Slide Transition task pane

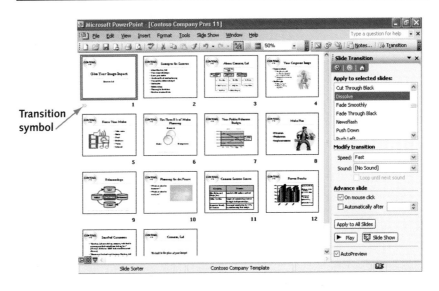

Transition symbol

4 Click the transition symbol below slide 1.

PowerPoint demonstrates the Dissolve transition effect on slide 1. Now you will apply another transition effect to the other slides in the presentation.

5 On the Edit menu, click Select All.

All of the slides in the presentation are selected. You need to deselect slide 1 because a transition has already been applied to it.

ANOTHER METHOD

Press Ctrl + A.

6 Hold down Ctrl, and then click slide 1 to deselect it.

Slide 1 is deselected, but all other slides remain selected.

7 In the Slide Transition task pane, under Apply To Selected Slides, scroll down and then click Random Bars Horizontal.

The slide miniatures demonstrate the transition effect.

8 Under Modify Transition, click the Speed down arrow, and then click Medium.

PowerPoint applies the transition effect to the selected slides. Notice that all of the slides have a transition symbol below their left corners.

9 Click the Slide Show button.

Slide Show view displays slide 2 with the Random Bars Horizontal effect.

10 Click the mouse several times to advance through the slides and watch the transition effect, and then press Esc to end the slide show.

PowerPoint returns you to Slide Sorter view.

11 Press Ctrl+A to select all the slides.

12 In the Slide Transition task pane, under Apply To Selected Slides, scroll up and click No Transition, and then click a blank area of the presentation window.

PowerPoint removes the transition effect from all of the slides.

13 In the Slide Transition task pane, click the Close button to close the task pane.

◆ Keep this file open for the next exercise.

QUICK REFERENCE ▼

Apply a slide transition effect

1 Click the Slide Sorter View button or select the Slides tab in Normal view, and then select one, several, or all slides.

2 On the Slide Show menu, click Slide Transition to open the Slide Transition task pane.

3 Under Apply To Selected Slides, click a transition effect.

4 Under Modify Transition, click the Speed down arrow, and then click the desired speed.

5 Click the transition symbol below the slide to preview the effect.

Animating Slides

Animating Slides

THE BOTTOM LINE

Add animation effects to text and slide objects such as shapes and charts to create greater visual interest on a slide. Animation also allows you to control how objects come into view on the slides during the presentation.

You can make a slide show more exciting and engaging by adding animation to the text and objects on your slides. You can apply a wide variety of animation effects to almost every object on a slide, including text placeholders, pictures, tables, charts and their individual series, and shapes you have drawn on the slide. Not only are the animation effects visually interesting, they allow you to control how you want to display the objects during the presentation. For example, you can apply an effect to a title that causes it to spin around when you click the mouse button during the show, or you can control a chart's elements so that you can display the data one column at a time.

You have two options for applying animation to slide objects. You can use an Animation Scheme, or you can create custom animations for various objects on slides. Your choice depends on how much time you want to spend animating your slides.

Applying an Animation Scheme

The easiest way to apply animation effects to a slide show is to use Animation Schemes in the Slide Design task pane. The **Animation Schemes** feature gives you one-click access to professionally designed animations divided into three categories: Subtle, Moderate, and Exciting. Some of these have sound connected to them, and they are designed to animate both the title and text on a slide. You can preview each animation scheme to find the animation you want. You can apply an Animation Scheme in either Normal View or Slide Sorter view.

TIP

If you apply both a transition effect and an animation effect to a slide, the transition effect will occur first, followed by the animation effect.

Apply an Animation Scheme

You will start the process of animating slides by applying Animation Schemes to several slides in the presentation.

1 In Slide Sorter view, select slide 8.

2 On the Slide Show menu, click Animation Schemes.

The Slide Design task pane opens with a selection of Animation Schemes.

ANOTHER METHOD

Click the Slide Design button, and then click the Animation Schemes link.

3 In the Slide Design task pane, under Apply To Selected Slides, click Fade In All.

PowerPoint applies the animation effect to the slide. An animation symbol appears below the left corner of slide 8, as shown in the following illustration.

Figure 7-6

Animation symbol displays below slide

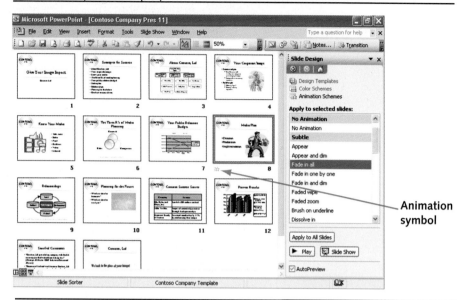

Animation symbol

4 Click slide 2, hold down Shift, and then click slides 3 and 4.

Slides 2, 3, and 4 are selected.

5 In the Slide Design task pane, under Apply To Selected Slides, click Faded Wipe.

PowerPoint applies the animation effect to all three slides. An animation symbol appears below the left corner of each slide.

6 With slide 2 selected, click the Slide Show button.

As the slide show starts, the slide 2 title fades into view. On a slide that has an Animation Scheme applied, the title displays automatically, but you have to click to display the other items.

ANOTHER METHOD

Click the Slide Show button at the bottom of the Slide Design task pane.

7 Click the mouse button to display each bullet item.

As you click, each bullet item fades into view.

8 Press Esc to stop the slide show.

You return to Slide Sorter view.

◆ Keep this file open for the next exercise.

QUICK REFERENCE ▼

Apply an animation scheme

1 Click a slide in Slide Sorter or Normal view.

2 On the Slide Show menu, click Animation Schemes.

3 In the Slide Design task pane, under Apply To Selected Slides, click an animation scheme.

Applying Custom Text Animation Effects

Although Animation Schemes offer a quick and easy way to animate text on a slide, you may want to customize text animation. To apply custom animation effects to text (as well as objects), you use the Custom Animation task pane in Normal view. You must work in Normal view because you need to choose the objects on the slide that you want to animate. You can create animation effects from scratch, or you can customize effects applied by an Animation Scheme.

After you have selected the object to which you want to add an effect, click the Add Effect button in the Custom Animation task pane and choose from Entrance, Emphasis, Exit, or Motion Paths. These options describe when or how the effect will take place. Each of these categories offers a number of effects to choose among. You can then choose how to start the effect, select a direction for the effect, and adjust its speed.

After you apply an effect, you can fine-tune it by opening the effect's dialog box to choose further options. For example, you can have a title display one word or one letter at a time. You can also determine which text indent levels to animate. If a slide has multiple paragraphs and more than one level of bulleted text, for example, you can customize the animation so that the levels of text in each bulleted item animate separately.

Apply custom text animation effects

You have applied an Animation Scheme to a few slides in the presentation. In this exercise, you use the Custom Animation options to animate text on several other slides.

1 In Slide Sorter view, double-click slide 1 to switch to Normal view.

2 On the Slide Show menu, click Custom Animation.

The Custom Animation task pane opens with the text prompt *Select An Element Of The Slide, Then Click "Add Effect" To Add Animation.*

3 Click the title text "Give Your Image Impact," and then click Add Effect in the Custom Animation task pane.

The Add Effect submenu appears with four effect categories: Entrance, Emphasis, Exit, and Motion Paths.

4 Point to Entrance, and then click Fly In.

The animation effect is demonstrated on slide 1. In the Custom Animation task pane, the title text (item 1) and a description of the effect appear in the Animation Order list. A small number 1 displays to the left of the title placeholder to indicate an effect has been applied to the title.

Figure 7-7

Animating the title

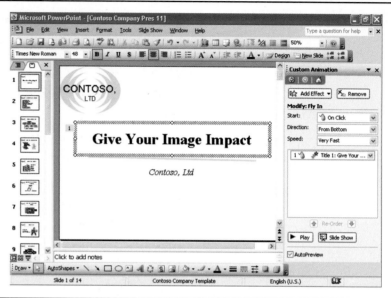

5 **Click the subtitle text "Contoso, Ltd."**

6 **In the Custom Animation task pane, click Add Effect, point to Emphasis, and then click Spin.**

The animation effect is demonstrated. In the Custom Animation task pane, the subtitle text (item 2) and a description of the effect appear in the Animation Order list. This list shows effects for the current slide only.

7 **In the Custom Animation task pane, click the first animated item in the Animation Order list to select it.**

A down arrow appears when the item is selected.

8 **Click the down arrow, and then click Effect Options to display the Fly In dialog box.**

The Fly In (the current effect) dialog box appears, showing the Effect tab.

Figure 7-8

Fly In dialog box

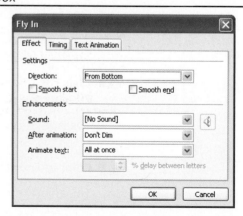

ANOTHER METHOD

Double-click an animation effect in the Animation Order list to open the effect's dialog box.

9 Click the Animate Text down arrow, and then click By Word.

This option animates the selected text one word at a time.

10 Click OK.

The dialog box closes and the revised effect previews on the slide.

11 In the Custom Animation task pane under Modify: Fly In, click the Start down arrow, and then click With Previous.

The animation effect is now set to play without having to click the screen during the slide show.

12 Click the Slide Show button to start the slide show and view the new animation effects.

The title appears one word at a time.

13 Click the screen to spin the subtitle, and then press Esc to end the Slide Show.

14 Click the Next Slide button three times to advance to slide 4.

The animation effects in the Animation Order list were supplied by the Animation Scheme you applied in the last exercise.

15 In the Custom Animation task pane, click the second animated item in the Animation Order list, click the down arrow, and then click Effect Options.

The Fade dialog box appears.

16 Click the Text Animation tab, click the Group Text down arrow, and then click By 2nd Level Paragraphs.

This option sets the text to animate the first- and second-level paragraph lines separately.

17 Click OK.

The Fade dialog box closes, and the effect is demonstrated. Each bullet item and subitem appears separately.

18 At the bottom of the Custom Animation task pane, click Slide Show.

The title fades in.

19 Click the screen to display each bullet item, and then press Esc to end the slide show.

◆ **Keep this file open for the next exercise.**

QUICK REFERENCE ▼

Apply custom text animation effects

1 In Normal view, select a slide and select an object on the slide.

2 On the Slide Show menu, click Custom Animation.

3 Click Add Effect in the Custom Animation task pane.

4 Point to an effect category, and then click an effect.

5 Adjust settings for start, direction, and speed if desired.

6 In the Animation Order list, click the down arrow for an effect.

7 Click Effect Options and modify settings on the dialog box tabs as required.

8 Click OK.

Animating Slide Objects

In addition to animating text in a slide show, you can customize the animation of slide objects, such as pictures or drawn objects. As with text, to set custom animation effects, you must be in Normal view.

If an object includes text, you have an additional choice. The default is for the object and its text to be animated at the same time. If you want, however, you can animate only the text so that it flies into the stationary shape, for example.

As you add effects to a slide, you may need to adjust the order in which the effects take place. By reordering the effects in the Animation Order list, you can control when each object appears on the slide.

As you customize the animation order, you should also pay attention to the Start settings for each object. The default setting is On Click, which requires you to click the mouse to start the animation effect. Use the With Previous setting to start an animation at the same time as the object above it on the list (or when the slide displays for the first effect on the list). Use After Previous to start an effect after the previous effect has finished.

Animate slide objects

In this exercise, you animate slide objects and change the order in which objects animate.

1 In Normal view, drag the scroll box to slide 6.

2 Drag the mouse to draw a selection marquee around the three shapes and the connectors.

All five objects are selected.

QUICK CHECK

Q: What are the four categories of effects you can add to a slide object?

A: **You can choose among Entrance, Emphasis, Exit, and Motion Paths.**

3 In the Custom Animation task pane, click **Add Effect**, point to **Entrance**, click **More Effects**, click **Peek In**, and then click **OK**.

The three objects and two connector lines are animated with the same effect. The number 1 appears next to each of the five parts to show that they will all take place at the same time.

Slide Show

4 At the bottom of the Custom Animation task pane, click the **Slide Show** button, and then click the screen.

The three objects and connector lines appear all at once.

5 Press **Esc** to end the slide show.

Because the current animation effect isn't as exciting as it could be, you will now adjust the animation order and start settings to improve the effect.

6 In the Animation Order list, click **Elbow Connector 6**, click the **Re-Order** up arrow at the bottom of the task pane two times, click the **Start** down arrow, and then click **After Previous**.

The Elbow Connector 6 animation order changes from fourth to second, and it will now start its animation after the Research shape has finished its animation.

7 In the Animation Order list, click **Elbow Connector 7**, click the **Re-Order** up arrow once, click the **Start** down arrow, and then click **After Previous**.

The Elbow Connector 7 animation order changes from fifth to fourth. Your Animation Order list should look like the one shown in the following illustration.

Figure 7-9

Object animation order has been adjusted

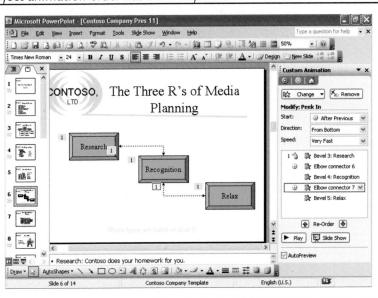

8 In the Animation Order list, click **Bevel 4: Recognition**, click the **Start** down arrow, and then click **After Previous**.

The Recognition shape will not animate until after the first connector has finished.

9 In the Animation Order list, click Bevel 5: Relax, click the Start down arrow, and then click After Previous.

This object will animate after the previous object has finished.

Slide Show

10 At the bottom of the Custom Animation task pane, click the Slide Show button, and then click the screen to view the revised animation.

The objects and connector lines appear one after another from top to bottom.

11 Press Esc to end the slide show.

◆ Keep this file open for the next exercise.

QUICK REFERENCE ▼

Animate slide objects

1 Select the object that you want to animate.

2 On the Slide Show menu, click Custom Animation to open the Custom Animation task pane.

3 In the Custom Animation task pane, click Add Effect, point to an effect category, and then click an effect.

Change animation order

1 In the Custom Animation task pane, click the item in the Animation Order list.

2 Click the Re-Order up or down arrow.

Change start option

1 In the Custom Animation task pane, click the item in the Animation Order list.

2 Click the Start down arrow, and then click On Click, With Previous, or After Previous.

Animating Chart Objects

You can also enhance a presentation by animating charts that are created with Microsoft Graph or imported from Microsoft Excel. For example, you can animate each data series in a chart to appear at a different time. This allows you to control the flow of information to the audience to add dramatic effect.

Animate chart objects

To complete your animation task, you will animate the chart to make its appearance more dramatic.

QUICK CHECK

Q: What Start option animates an object at the same time as the object above it on the Animation Order list?

A: The With Previous setting animates an object at the same time as the previous object.

CHECK THIS OUT ▼

Create a Motion Path Animation
The Motion Paths category in the Add Effects list lets you create a path for an object to follow on the slide. You can choose from a number of preset paths for the motion, from simple diagonals and straight lines to complex shapes such as parallelograms or arcs, or you can create your own path by drawing it. Adding motion in this way is similar to the kind of animation you can create in a program such as Macromedia Flash.

1 Scroll down to slide 12.

2 Click the chart object to select it.

3 In the Custom Animation task pane, click Add Effect, point to Entrance, and then click Blinds.

The Blinds effect is applied to the entire chart. Now you will modify settings to control the display of each data series column.

4 In the Animation Order list, select the chart effect, click the down arrow, and click Effect Options.

The Blinds dialog box opens.

5 Click the Chart Animation tab, click the Group Chart down arrow, and click By Series.

This setting displays the columns of the chart one by one as you click the mouse button.

6 Click OK.

The Custom Animation task pane looks like the following illustration. You could click the double arrow in the shaded bar below the animation effect to see the animation effect for each part of the chart.

Figure 7-10

Custom Animation task pane shows chart animation

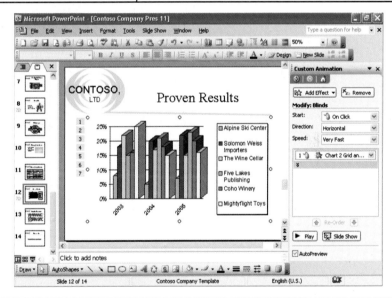

7 At the bottom of the Custom Animation task pane, click the Slide Show button, and then click the screen seven times to view the animation.

As you click, the chart framework and then each data series appears on the screen.

8 Press Esc to end the slide show.

9 In the Custom Animation task pane, click the Close button to close the task pane.

◆ Keep this file open for the next exercise.

QUICK CHECK

Q: What option do you choose in a chart effect's dialog box to have each column appear by itself?

A: **Choose By Series to animate each series separately.**

QUICK REFERENCE ▼

Animate a chart

1 Select the chart object that you want to animate.

2 On the Slide Show menu, click Custom Animation to open the Custom Animation task pane.

3 In the Custom Animation task pane, click Add Effect, point to an effect category, and click an effect.

4 In the Animation Order list, select the chart object's down arrow and click Effect Options.

5 Click the Chart Animation tab, click the Group Chart down arrow, and select an option.

6 Click OK.

Hiding a Slide

Customizing a Slide Show

THE BOTTOM LINE

Hide slides in a presentation when you don't want to display them during a slide show. This is a good way to safeguard some information or customize a show for a particular audience.

When you have a number of slides on a particular subject, you may find that you don't need to show all of them to a particular audience. If you have a presentation on the progress of putting in a new community pool, for example, you can leave out slides relating to costs when you deliver the presentation to the neighborhood children.

Rather than copy all the slides you want to use to a new presentation, you can simply hide the slides you don't want to show during a particular presentation but still want to keep in the presentation. To hide a slide, you select it in the Slides tab or in Slide Sorter view and click Hide Slide on the Slide Show menu (or click the Hide Slide button in Slide Sorter view, or right-click the slide and select Hide Slide from the shortcut menu). A hidden slide displays a special symbol below it in Slide Sorter view or the Slides tab so you know it is hidden. When you deliver the presentation, hidden slides are skipped automatically.

Even if you have hidden a slide, however, you can still display it during the slide show. Use the Navigation shortcut menu to display slide titles and then click the title of the hidden slide. Unhide a slide by using the same command or button you used to hide it.

Hide a slide

In this exercise, you hide a slide in the current slide show.

1 Click the **Slide Sorter View** button.

On the View menu, click Slide Sorter.

2 Select slide 10.

3 On the Slide Sorter toolbar, click the Hide Slide button.

A hide symbol appears over the slide number to indicate that the slide will be hidden in a slide show, as shown in the following illustration.

Figure 7-11

Slide shows hide symbol

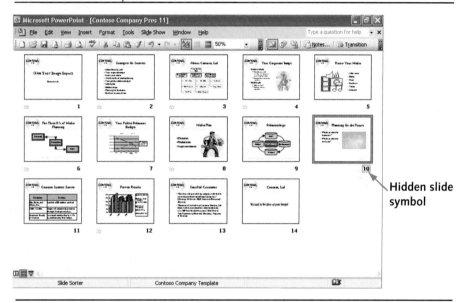

Hidden slide symbol

- With the slide selected in Slides tab or Slide Sorter view, click Hide Slide on the Slide Show menu.
- Right-click the selected slide, and then click Hide Slide on the shortcut menu.

4 Select slide 9.

5 Click the Slide Show button, and then click anywhere on the screen.

The slide show hides slide 10 and displays slide 11.

6 Press P to go back to slide 9.

7 Right-click anywhere on the screen, point to Go To Slide, and then click (10) Planning for the Future, or press the H key to show the hidden slide.

Slides are designated as hidden with parentheses around their slide numbers. The hidden slide appears in Slide Show view.

8 Press Esc to end the slide show.

◆ Keep this file open for the next exercise.

QUICK REFERENCE ▼

Hide a slide

1 Select the slide that you want to hide in Slides tab or Slide Sorter view.

2 On the Slide Sorter toolbar, click the Hide Slide button, or on the Slide Show menu, click Hide Slide.

Show a hidden slide during a presentation

1 Click the Slide Show button, and then click the screen.

2 Right-click anywhere on the screen, point to Go To Slide, and then click the hidden slide in parentheses, or press H on the previous slide to show the hidden slide.

Creating and Editing a Custom Show

Customizing a Slide Show

THE BOTTOM LINE

You can use the slides in a presentation to set up custom shows of specific slides for specific audiences. This is a more efficient way to customize a presentation than hiding slides.

If you plan to present slides on a topic to more than one audience, you don't have to create separate presentations for each audience. Instead of creating multiple, nearly identical presentations for different audiences, you can create one comprehensive presentation that includes all the slides you will need and then create **custom shows** that contain selected slides for each audience. This is a much more efficient way to customize a presentation than hiding slides for each audience.

When you create a custom show, you supply a name for the show and then select slides from the presentation to add to the show. You can create as many custom shows as you need, and each show can use any of the presentation's slides. After you have created the show, you can edit it to change the order of slides or remove slides. When you deliver the presentation, you can select the custom show to present, and only the slides in the custom show appear.

Create a custom show

For your last task in preparing your presentation, you create and edit a custom show.

1 **In Slide Sorter view, on the Slide Show menu, click Custom Shows.**

The Custom Shows dialog box appears.

2 **Click New.**

The Define Custom Show dialog box appears. The default custom show name is selected in the Slide Show Name box.

3 **In the Slide Show Name box, type** Contoso Custom Show 07.

4 **In the Slides In Presentation box, click slide 1, and then click Add.**

Slide 1 appears in the Slides In Custom Show box on the right.

5 **Select and add slides 3, 4, 6, 8, 13, and 14 to the custom slide show to match the following illustration.**

You can hold down the Ctrl key to select multiple slides.

Figure 7-12

Define Custom Show dialog box

6 **Click OK.**

The Custom Shows dialog box appears, with the newly created custom show selected in the Custom Shows list.

7 **Click Show.**

Slide 1 of the custom show displays.

8 **Click through all of the slides until Slide Sorter view appears, indicating the slide show is complete.**

Slide Sorter view appears. Now you will edit the custom show to r emove a slide.

9 **On the Slide Show menu, click Custom Shows.**

The Custom Shows dialog box appears.

10 **Verify that Contoso Custom Show 07 is selected, and then click Edit.**

The Define Custom Show dialog box appears.

11 In the Slides In Custom Show box, click slide 2, and then click Remove.

Slide 2 is removed from the show.

12 Click OK, and then click Close to close the Custom Shows dialog box.

◆ If you are continuing to other lessons, save the Contoso Company Pres 07 presentation with the current name and then close it. If you are not continuing to other lessons, save and close the Contoso Company Pres 07 presentation, and then click the Close button in the title bar of the PowerPoint window.

QUICK REFERENCE ▼

Create a custom show

1 On the Slide Show menu, click Custom Shows.

2 Click New.

3 In the Slide Show Name box, type the slide show name.

4 In the Slides In Presentation box, click a slide, and then click Add.

5 Select and add more slides to the custom slide show.

6 Click OK, and then click Close or Show.

Key Points

✔ *You can use a variety of keystrokes or mouse actions to navigate from slide to slide in Slide Show view. Use the new popup toolbar to display a shortcut menu that gives additional options for going to the last slide viewed and specific slides.*

✔ *Use several new pointer tools to mark on slides during a presentation. You can use the Ballpoint Pen, the Felt Tip Pen, or the Highlighter to emphasize slide content for the audience.*

✔ *Apply slide transitions to slides to hold audience attention between slides with graphical effects. You can apply a transition to one, several, or all slides and modify the speed as desired.*

✔ *For additional visual interest in a presentation, animate text and objects on slides. Use Animation Schemes to apply pre-designed effects to one or all slides, or create custom animations to control the effect's start options, direction and speed.*

✔ *Hide one or more slides in a presentation when you want to skip them automatically during the slide show. You can show hidden slides during the slide show using the Navigation shortcut menu.*

✔ *Create custom shows to organize slides in a presentation for different audiences. Name the show and then select the slides to include in it.*

Quick Quiz

True/False

T **F** 1. To go to a specific slide during a slide show, you can use the Go To Slide command on the Navigation shortcut menu.

T **F** 2. Once you have added a transition to a slide, you cannot remove it.

T **F** 3. You can apply an Animation Scheme in either Normal view or Slide Sorter view.

T **F** 4. You can start a slide show right from the Custom Animation task pane.

T **F** 5. Hidden slides cannot be seen in any PowerPoint view.

Multiple Choice

1. If you need to remove only one annotation on the slide, select _____ on the Pointer shortcut menu.
   a. Erase All Ink On Slide
   b. Remove Annotation
   c. Remove Ink
   d. Eraser

2. The default start option for new custom animation effects is _____.
   a. On Click
   b. With Previous
   c. After Previous
   d. On Hover

3. When you animate a shape that has text in it, you can choose to _____.
   a. animate the text only
   b. animate the text and the shape at the same time
   c. animate either the text or the shape.
   d. either A or B

4. A keyboard shortcut you can use to display a hidden slide during a slide show is _____.
   a. E
   b. S
   c. H
   d. P

5. If you need to give similar presentations to different audiences, the most efficient method to customize a presentation is to _____.
   a. hide slides as necessary
   b. create custom shows
   c. create separate presentations for each audience
   d. skip slides as you present them

Short Answer

1. How do you view the Custom Animation settings?
2. How do you eliminate a transition effect from all of the slides in a presentation?
3. How do you move forward in Slide Show view?
4. How do you animate a slide object?
5. How do you immediately end a presentation in Slide Show view?
6. How do you animate a chart?
7. How do you edit a custom show?
8. How do you change the color of the annotation marker tool?
9. How do you hide a slide during a slide show?
10. How do you create a new custom show?

On Your Own

Exercise 1

Open Contoso Company Pres 07 in the Lesson07 folder that is located in the PowerPoint Practice folder. Change the slide 1 transition to Box with a slow speed, hide slide 13, start a slide show, change the ink color to blue and select a pen tool, draw a line under the text *Contoso, Ltd* on slide 1, display each slide in the slide show, and then save and close the presentation.

Exercise 2

Open Contoso Company Pres 07 in the Lesson07 folder that is located in the PowerPoint Practice folder. Animate the clip art on slide 4 with the Fly In effect from the bottom, create and show a custom slide show named *Contoso Client* with the slides 1, 4, 6, 7, 8, 9, and 14, and then save and close the presentation.

One Step Further

Exercise 1

Open Holidays 07 from the Lesson07 folder that is located in the PowerPoint Practice folder. Save the presentation as Holidays 07 Revised in the Lesson07 folder. Apply an animation scheme to all slides. On slide 3, animate the fireworks objects and their dotted-line paths to appear one at a time on the slide. Use the After Previous Start option for the fireworks objects so you don't have to click to display them. On slides 9 and 10, remove the animation scheme and supply custom animations for the titles and animate bulleted lists by second-level paragraphs. Save and close the presentation.

Exercise 2

Open the Holidays 07 Revised presentation from the Lesson07 folder. Create two custom shows. In the first custom show, include all the slides relating to holidays. In the second custom show, include all the slides that relate to personal time. Supply appropriate names for the custom shows. Save and close the presentation.

Exercise 3

Open AD Sales 07 from the Lesson07 folder that is located in the PowerPoint Practice folder. Save the presentation as AD Sales 07 Revised in the Lesson07 folder. Animate the picture on slide 1 to fly in from the bottom at medium speed. Animate all slide titles with an appropriate custom animation effect and specify the With Previous start for all titles. Animate the table, chart, and diagram as desired. Select a slide transition and apply it to all slides. Hide slide 3. Start the slide show with slide 1. On slide 2, use the Felt Tip Pen to circle the April 29 agenda topic. Use the Navigation shortcut menu to display the hidden slide. Save and close the presentation.

Microsoft Access

Understanding Databases

After completing this lesson, you will be able to:

✔ *Start Access and open an existing database.*
✔ *Move around in Access.*
✔ *Open and close a table.*
✔ *View a table in Datasheet view and Design view.*
✔ *Navigate within a table using the mouse pointer.*
✔ *Navigate within a table using the keyboard.*

KEY TERMS

- cell
- data access page
- database
- database management system (DBMS)
- Database window
- Datasheet view
- Design view
- Edit mode
- fields
- field name
- forms
- group
- Groups bar
- HTML (Hypertext Markup Language)
- Leszynski naming convention
- macros
- modules
- navigation buttons
- Navigation mode
- object
- Objects bar
- pages
- queries
- records
- relational database
- reports
- shortcut
- shortcut keys
- tables
- task pane

A **database** is a collection of data, or information that is organized so that specific information can be easily located and retrieved. The phone book is an example of a noncomputerized database. The phone book contains names, addresses, and telephone numbers arranged alphabetically by last name so that it is easy to locate information for a particular person.

Microsoft Access is a **database management system (DBMS)** for creating and using computerized databases. A database management system is an integrated collection of programs that are used to create and manage information in a database. Computerized databases are much more powerful than noncomputerized databases (like the phone book) because users can reorganize data and search for information in hundreds of ways. For example, if a phone book were stored as an Access database, you could search by address, first name, or phone number, instead of just by last name.

As another example of the advantages of computerized databases, consider Adventure Works, a fictitious outdoor vacation resort outside Santa Barbara, California. The marketing manager for the resort wants to send a summer events newsletter to everybody who has visited the resort during the summer months within the past five years. If the records for guest visits were kept in ledger books, you would need to flip through the books page by page to create a list of past summer visitors. With a computerized database, however, you could create a list of previous summer visitors in seconds. If the marketing manager later decides to send a newsletter to winter visitors instead, a computerized database could create this new list almost instantly.

To complete the procedures in this lesson, you will need to use a file named Adventure Works 01 in the Access Practice folder that is located on your hard disk. This database tracks employees, human resources information, guests, reservations, and suite information for the fictional Adventure Works.

IMPORTANT

For maximum compatibility with existing databases, the default file format for new databases created with Access 2003 is Access 2000.

IMPORTANT

Before you can use the practice files in this lesson, be sure you install them from the book's companion CD to their default location. For additional information on how to find and open files used in this book, see the "Using the CD-ROM" section at the beginning of this book. To complete the procedures in this lesson, you will need to use the Adventure Works 01 database file.

Starting Access and Opening an Existing Database

THE BOTTOM LINE

Using a database is an efficient way of organizing, viewing, and retrieving your data. To access the data in the database, you must first open the database. There are several ways to open a database, including a task pane in the Access window, by using the Open dialog box, or by double-clicking a database file through My Computer or Windows Explorer.

You start Access by clicking the Start button on the Windows taskbar, pointing to All Programs, and clicking Microsoft Access. If the full Microsoft Office package was installed, you may need to point to the Microsoft Office folder on the programs menu, and then click Microsoft Access. As with other Microsoft Office applications, Access displays a menu bar and one or more toolbars across the top of the window, as shown in Figure 1-1. All Microsoft Office XP and 2003 applications also contain a **task pane,** which is shown at the right side of the figure.

In Access, a different version of the task pane appears when you click either New or File Search on the File menu, or click Office Clipboard on the Edit menu. Figure 1-1 shows the Getting Started task pane that appears by default. From the task pane, the toolbar, or the File menu, you can choose whether to create a new database or open an existing database.

FIGURE 1-1

Access user interface

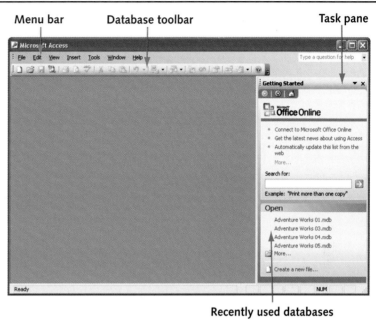

If you have recently worked with the database to be opened, it may be listed in the lower section of the task pane in the Open section. If so, click on the file name to open the database. If your database is not listed among the most recently opened files, click the More link at the bottom of the list. This will open a dialog box from which you can navigate your disk drives to find the file and open it.

ANOTHER METHOD

You can also open an existing database by finding the file on your hard disk and double-clicking the file name. Access and the database will open at the same time.

After you've opened the database, a separate window, called the **Database window**, appears below the menu bar and toolbar. The Database window is used to navigate in Access.

TROUBLESHOOTING

When you open an Access 2003 database, an introductory screen called a *splash screen* may appear. If the splash screen appears, close it by clicking the Close button in the top right corner of the screen. A second screen, called a switchboard screen, may then appear, and if you close that screen, the Database window will appear.

◆ The Adventure Works 01 database must be installed in the Access Practice folder before beginning this exercise.

Start Microsoft Access and Open a Database

Access is installed on your computer and the Access Practice folder should contain the database to be used in this lesson. The first step in working with a database is to open the database, as you will do now.

1 On the Windows taskbar, click the Start button.

The Windows XP Start menu will appear.

ANOTHER METHOD

You can also open Access by double-clicking the Access icon that is often created on your desktop when Access is installed, or you can create a desktop shortcut manually from the Start menu.

2 On the Start menu, point to All Programs, and click Microsoft Access.

Access starts, and the Getting Started task pane appears on the right side of the screen. The lower portion of the task pane displays the most recently opened database files.

TROUBLESHOOTING

If the Getting Started task pane does not appear, click the View menu, point to Toolbars, and then click the Task Pane option.

3 Click the More link near the bottom of the task pane.

The Open dialog box appears. You use this dialog box to locate the database file to be opened.

TROUBLESHOOTING

If you are using a newly installed version of Access, the More link may not be present in the Getting Started task pane. If you do not see that option, click the File menu and then click Open.

ANOTHER METHOD

If Access is already open, you can open an existing database by clicking the Open button on the Database toolbar and navigating to and selecting the desired file in the Open dialog box.

4 Click the Look In down arrow, click the icon for your hard disk, and then double-click the Access Practice folder.

The Open dialog box displays a list of files stored in the Access Practice folder, with Adventure Works 01 already selected.

FIGURE 1-2

The Open dialog box

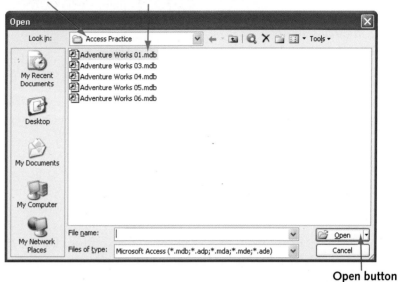

Look In box   Database files in the selected folder

Open button

5 **Click the Open button in the lower-right corner of the dialog box.**

The Database window for Adventure Works 01 appears within the main Access window.

◆ **Keep the database open for the next exercise.**

QUICK REFERENCE ▼

To start Access

1 On the Windows taskbar, click the Start button.

2 On the Start menu, point to All Programs, and click Microsoft Access.

To open an existing database

1 If Access is not already open, start Access, and in the Getting Started task pane that appears, click the More option near the bottom of the pane to cause the Open dialog box to appear.

Or

If Access is already open, click the Open button on the Database toolbar.

2 Click the Look In down arrow, and navigate to the location of the database that you want to open.

3 Click the database that you want to open, and click Open.

Moving Around in Access

The Office Assistant

All Office applications, including Access, have a Help feature called the Office Assistant. The Office Assistant is an animated character that helps you find answers to questions that you might have about Access. The first time that you start Access, the Office Assistant will appear. You can also display the Office Assistant at any time by clicking Show the Office Assistant on the Help menu. When you need help with a particular feature, type a specific question into the Office Assistant text box, and a list of possible answers will appear.

The Office Assistant displays help information at your request, but it tries to stay out of your way the rest of the time by moving to another part of the screen whenever it is in the way of the insertion point or of your typing. You can close the Office Assistant at any time by clicking Hide the Office Assistant on the Help menu.

THE BOTTOM LINE

The Objects bar and the Groups bar are the area of the Database window that allow you to select the types of Access objects you want to work with, such as tables, forms, queries, and so forth. Each object type is grouped within its own category on the Objects bar. You can create customized "groups" of different yet related objects in the Groups bar area. You could create a group to contain all tables, forms, and queries related to all personnel employed by a company to provide quick access to those objects.

When you opened the Adventure Works 01 database in the previous exercise, the Database window appeared on your screen. The Database window toolbar appears along the top of the Database window and contains the Open button, Design button, New button, Delete button, and options for displaying the items listed in the Database window.

The **Objects bar** and **Groups bar** appear along the left side of the Database window. The Objects bar includes the part of the Database window under the word *Objects*. **Object** is a generic term that refers to any component of an Access database. The Objects bar lists the major types of objects in an Access database: **tables, queries, forms, reports, pages, macros,** and **modules.**

FIGURE 1-3

The Database Window and the Objects bar

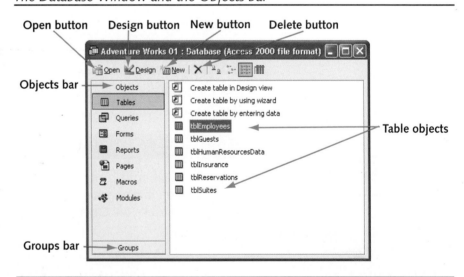

TIP

If you are working in a table datasheet or in Design view and need to access the Database window, you can switch to the Database window from any other window in Access by pressing F11. The Database window will immediately appear in front of your current window and will be the active window.

You can also display the Database Window at any time by clicking the Database Window button that appears on several of the Access toolbars, such as the Table Design and the Table Datasheet toolbars.

The foundation for all other types of objects in Access is the table, because tables store the data that the other objects use to perform procedures and activities in Access. A table is made up of **fields** and **records** that are displayed in a row-and-column format with fields as the columns and records as the rows. A field can contain data about a person, place, product or service, event, or other entity. For example, a field would contain all the last names or phone numbers in a table. Each field in a table has a **field name**, also called a label, which appears at the top of the column. For example, a field that holds all the last names for the guests at Adventure Works could be called LastName.

A collection of related fields forms a record. For example, a resort guest's FirstName, LastName, Address, City, State, and PostalCode fields might make up a single guest record, as shown in Figure 1-4. In this book, the intersection of a record (row) and a field (column) is called a **cell**.

TIP

When referring to the individual fields in a record, the words cell and field can be used interchangeably.

FIGURE 1-4

Some commonly used Access terminology

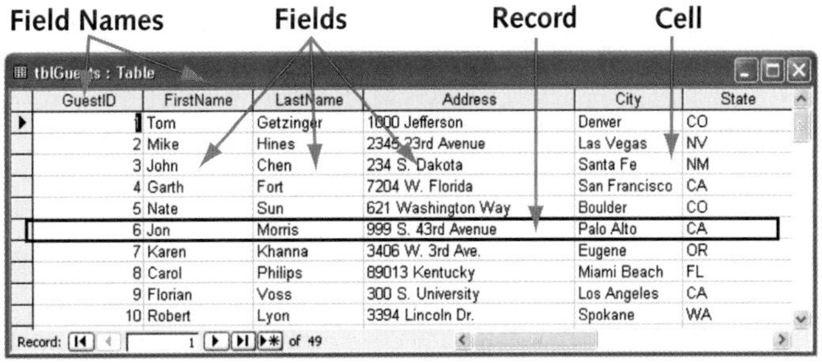

Tables store all the information in a database, but if you want to view only selected fields and records in the database, you use a query. A query extracts specific data from one or more tables based on search criteria. For example, you could create a query for the reservations table for Adventure Works to only list records for guests who have made reservations after June 2004. The query might list each guest's identification number (or guest ID), reservation dates, number of occupants, and reserved room number.

TIP

Queries are explained in more depth in Lesson 4, "Creating and Using Queries."

Another way to view information in a database is to use a form, as shown in the following figure. A form displays a single record at a time in a specified format. Forms can also be used to add new information to a database.

FIGURE 1-5

An Access form

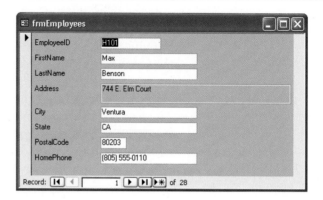

Forms are explained in more depth in Lesson 5, "Designing a Form."

If you want to display or print the data from a table or query, you can also create a report. Unlike a form, a report can be used to display multiple records. Although this sounds similar to a table, a report can be formatted in different ways to make the information easier to use and more attractive than a table. For example, you could create a report that contains a formatted title, a header or footer, and an attractive background. Reports, like queries, can also be customized to show data from only specific fields in a table instead of from all fields.

FIGURE 1-6

An Access report

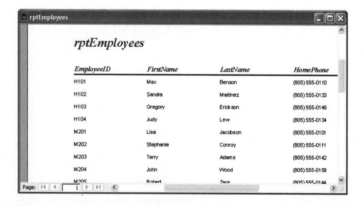

Reports are explained in more depth in Lesson 6, "Designing a Report."

Besides tables, queries, reports, and forms, the Objects bar also includes these three types of objects:

- Pages. A page object is a shortcut to a **data access page** in a database. A data access page displays selected data from a database, but it is an **HTML (Hypertext Markup Language)** file that can be displayed as a Web page.
- Macros. A macro is a sequence of actions that are performed automatically.
- Modules. A module is a program written in Microsoft Visual Basic or another programming language.

When you click the icon for a particular type of object on the Objects bar, Access displays a list of the names of all objects of that type in the database. (Fields and records don't have their own icons because they are not objects; fields and records are stored within tables, which are objects.)

TIP

The Groups bar contains groups of shortcuts to objects of different types.

The Groups bar is located under the word *Groups* in the Database window and contains one or more groups. A **group** holds a list of shortcuts to different types of objects in the database. A **shortcut** is a quick way to get to an object stored somewhere else in the database. The object shortcut is stored in the group, while the object itself is stored in the appropriate list on the Objects bar. Groups allow you to keep related objects of different types together. For example, you could create a group that holds shortcuts to all the objects in the database that relate to the guests at Adventure Works, such as the table that lists reservation information, the query that extracts reservations for the coming week, and the form that allows you to enter new guest information. On the Groups bar, the Favorites group is created by default and contains the names of the most frequently used objects in a database.

Use the Access Objects bar

You have just learned how to open a database, and the database should still be open. You will now use the Objects bar of the Database window to determine what types of objects exist in this database.

1 **On the Objects bar, click Tables, if necessary.**

The names of the tables in Adventure Works 01 appear, along with options to Create Table In Design View, Create Table By Using Wizard, and Create Table By Entering Data.

2 **On the Objects bar, click Queries.**

The options to Create Query In Design View and Create Query By Using Wizard appear. There are currently no queries in the Adventure Works 01 database.

3 **On the Objects bar, click Forms.**

One form name, frmEmployees, appears, along with the options to Create Form In Design View and Create Form By Using Wizard.

4 **On the Objects bar, click Reports.**

The options to Create Report In Design View and Create Report By Using Wizard appear. Currently the Adventure Works 01 database contains no reports.

5 **On the Objects bar, click Pages.**

The options to Create Data Access Page In Design View, Create Data Access Page By Using Wizard, and Edit Web Page That Already Exists appear. There are no data access pages in the Adventure Works 01 database.

> **IMPORTANT**
>
> There are no shortcut options to create macros or modules as there were for the previous objects.

6 **On the Objects bar, click Macros.**

There are no macros in the Adventure Works 01 database.

7 **On the Objects bar, click Modules.**

There are no modules in the Adventure Works 01 database.

◆ **Keep the database open for the next exercise.**

About Object Naming Conventions

As you navigated through the database in the previous exercise, you probably noticed that the names of the objects followed a standard convention. The file names used in this course follow the **Leszynski naming convention**, which was developed by Access expert and author Stan Leszynski to encourage a standard for naming database objects. The Leszynski naming convention also makes it easier to convert objects to formats used by other database management systems without a loss of data or data organization.

This convention requires each object to be identified by including the object type in the object name. This way, you can tell at a glance whether an object is a table, query, form, or other type of object. The following table identifies the naming prefixes that are used for each type of object.

Access Object	Object Prefix
table	tbl
form	frm
query	qry
report	rpt

The Leszynski naming convention extends to field names, pictures, and all objects used in Access, but only the prefixes listed above are used in this book. Following the Leszynski naming convention:

- The first three letters of an object name are lowercase and identify the object type.
- The name that follows the object prefix begins with a capital letter.
- Spaces are never used in object names.
- Object names contain only letters and numbers.

The following table shows some examples of Access objects that might be within a database, and the table shows a valid name for the object using the Leszynski naming convention. The table also shows an invalid name for each of the objects.

Object Type	Object Name	Valid Name	Invalid Name
table	Customer Order	tblCustomerOrder	Customer order
form	New Employee	frmNewEmployee	New_Employee
query	Orders By Cust	qryOrderByCust	orders by cust

QUICK REFERENCE ▼

Move around the Database window

◆ On the Objects bar, click the icon or button for the type of object for which you want to view a list of the currently defined objects.

QUICK CHECK

Q. What is the generic term that refers to any component of an Access database, such as a table or a form?

A. Access database components are called Objects.

Understanding Datasheet View and Design View

THE BOTTOM LINE

Access allows you to create and modify database tables in table Design view. Design view allows you to enter or view the field definitions for the table, and the properties associated with each field. You view the data contained within a table in Datasheet view. Table Datasheet view shows you the data contained in each field that is defined for the table.

Every Access object has two or more views. Tables are most commonly viewed in one of two formats, or views: **Datasheet view** and **Design view.** You switch between the two views by clicking the View button on the Table Design and Table Datasheet toolbars. You can choose other views by clicking the down arrow to the right of the View button and selecting a view from the drop-down list.

TIP

All Access objects (such as tables, queries, forms, and reports) can be opened in Design view and are generally created in this view.

Design view allows you to design the structure of a table by deciding what fields will appear in the table, customizing the process of entering data into the fields, and determining how the data will appear to users. The Adventure Works database includes tblEmployees, a table that contains basic information, such as addresses and phone numbers, about the resort's employees. Figure 1-7 shows the tblEmployees table opened in Design view:

FIGURE 1-7

tblEmployees in Design view

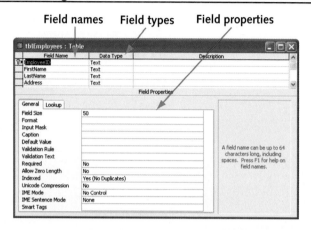

TIP

Using Design view to create and modify tables is explained further in Lesson 2, "Creating Tables."

The Field Name column contains the names of the fields in the table. The Data Type column allows you to decide what kind of data (for example, alphabetical or numerical) can be entered into a field. The lower part of the Table Design view window allows you to set specific properties for each field.

When you display the table in Datasheet view, the actual data in the table appears. For example, in tblEmployees, the field names, displayed in the Field Name column in Design view, appear from left to right across the top of the table.

FIGURE 1-8

tblEmployees in Datasheet view

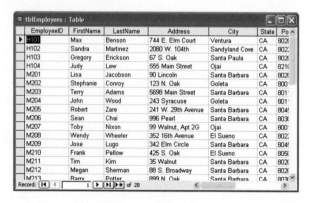

TROUBLESHOOTING

The data displayed in some of the fields may be partially cut off. This is because Access does not automatically adjust column widths. Changing column widths is discussed in Lesson 3, "Working with Tables," and also in Lesson 4, "Creating and Using Queries."

Switch Access views

You have now opened Access, and explored the Objects bar in the Database window. You will now open the table tblGuests in Datasheet view, switch to Design view, and then switch back to Datasheet view.

1 **On the Objects bar, click Tables.**

The list of tables presently in this database appears.

2 **Click the tblGuests table name.**

Access selects the table, as indicated by the blue rectangle around the table name.

3 **On the Database window toolbar, click Open.**

The table appears in Datasheet view. When you switch between Datasheet view and Design view, the picture on the View button changes to show which view the object will appear in *after* the button is clicked. The View button currently shows the Design view icon, indicating that is the view you will go to if you click the button.

ALTERNATE METHOD

You can also double-click a table name in the Database window to open it in Datasheet view.

FIGURE 1-9

tblGuests in Datasheet view

View button shows Design view icon   tblGuests datasheet

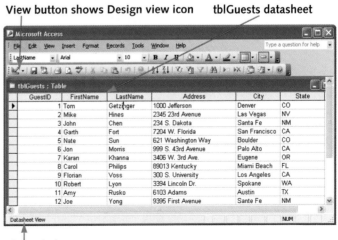

Current view

To open a table in Design view, click the table name, and click the Design button on the Database window toolbar.

4 **On the Table Datasheet toolbar, click the View button.**

The table appears in Design view. Note that the View button now shows the Datasheet icon. That is the view you will switch to the next time you click the button.

FIGURE 1-10

tblGuests in Design view

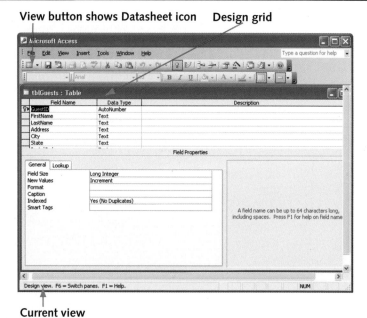

5 **On the Table Design toolbar, click the View button.**

The table appears in Datasheet view.

TROUBLESHOOTING

To open or close a toolbar, you can right-click on any blank area of the toolbar and then click the name of the toolbar that you want to open or close on the menu that appears.

◆ Keep the database open for the next exercise.

QUICK REFERENCE ▼

Switch between Datasheet and Design views

◆ Click the View button to switch from one view to the other.

Using the Mouse Pointer to Navigate in Datasheet View

THE BOTTOM LINE

In any database, you can use the mouse and/or the navigation buttons to move from the current record or field to a new record or field. In large databases where not all records fit on one screen, you can use the mouse, navigation buttons, and scroll bars to move among the records and fields.

Many databases contain large tables that, when opened, do not fit on your screen. For example, when you opened tblGuests in the last exercise, only the information for about the first 25 guest records appeared on your screen, depending on the size of your monitor and view window. To view the last record, which is number 49, you might have to navigate down through the table to show the record on your screen. To edit and view all the data in a database, you need to know how to move around within a table.

TROUBLESHOOTING

The number of records that you can view at a time depends on your monitor size, screen resolution, and the size of the table window. A 15-inch monitor set to 800 x 600 resolution can display about 25 records.

In Datasheet view, you can use the mouse pointer to select a cell for editing simply by clicking the cell that you want to select. Using the mouse pointer is often the fastest way to navigate if the cell that you want to edit is visible on the screen, and if it is not close to the currently selected cell. You can also use the mouse pointer in conjunction with the scroll bars to move to parts of the table not visible on the screen. You can drag the scroll boxes within the scroll bars, click in the empty area above or below the scroll box to advance or go back one page at a time (on the vertical scroll bar), click to the left or right of the scroll box to move left or right one screen at a time (on the horizontal scroll bar), or click the scroll arrows to scroll one record or field at a time.

Vertical and horizontal scroll bars

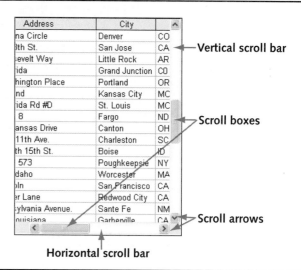

When a table is open in Datasheet view, Access supports two general viewing and updating modes: **Edit mode** and **Navigation mode**. When you open a table, it is in Navigation mode. In Navigation mode, you can navigate within the table, allowing you to view data easily. When the data in an entire cell is selected (highlighted), Access is in Navigation mode. In Edit mode, as the name suggests, you can navigate within a cell in the table and edit individual characters in the cell. When a blinking insertion point appears in the cell, Access is in Edit mode. To switch between Navigation mode and Edit mode, press the F2 key.

Another way to navigate within a table is to use the **navigation buttons** in the bottom-left corner of a table. The navigation buttons are shown in Figure 1-12.

FIGURE 1-12

The navigation buttons

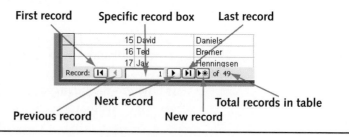

The navigation buttons are described in the following table.

Button Name	Button Result
First Record button	First record in the table.
Previous Record button	Previous record (for example, to go from the tenth to the ninth record).
Next Record button	Next record (for example, to go from the tenth record to the eleventh record).
Last Record button	Final record in the table.

Button Name	Button Result
New Record button	First blank record after the final record in the table so that you can enter a new record.

Additionally, typing a number in the Specific Record box moves the insertion point to that record. For example, if you type 5, the insertion point will move to the fifth record. This is useful in very large tables when you don't want to spend a lot of time clicking buttons to get to the record that you want.

TIP

You can move the insertion point to the Specific Record box by pressing F5.

Use Access Navigation buttons

You previously opened the tblGuests table and switched between Design and Datasheet view. It should still be open in Datasheet view. In this exercise, you will use the mouse pointer to select a cell in tblGuests, and then you will use the navigation buttons and scroll bars to navigate to different locations within the table.

1 **In the Address field of the first record, click between 1000 and Jefferson.**

A blinking insertion point appears in the field.

2 **On the scroll bar on the right side of the table, drag the scroll box down until the record for guest ID 49, Kim Ralls, is visible.**

The insertion point has not moved, and is currently invisible. It is still in the first record in the database. Moving the scroll bar displayed different data, but did not affect the location of the insertion point.

TIP

The total number of records in the table appears to the right of the navigation buttons. The table used in this exercise contains 49 records.

---

3 **In the FirstName field, click after the word Kim.**

The insertion point now appears in this record after the word *Kim*.

4 **On the scroll bar at the bottom of the table, click the right scroll arrow button until the MailingList field is visible, if necessary.**

The table scrolls to the right one field each time you click the scroll arrow.

5 **On the scroll bar at the bottom of the table, click the left scroll arrow button until the GuestID field appears.**

The table scrolls to the left, again one field at a time each time you click the arrow.

6 **In the GuestID field, click in the record for Kim Ralls.**

The insertion point appears in the GuestID field. The location of the insertion point depends on where in the field you clicked.

IMPORTANT

In tblGuests, the records are sorted in sequential order based on the GuestID field. Consequently, when you type **35** in the record number box, the selected record is for guest ID 35. But if the table were sorted in a different way, record number 35 would probably not contain guest ID 35. For example, record number 35 might contain guest ID B206.

---

7 **Click in the Specific Record box, delete the existing number, type 35, and then press Enter.**

Access selects the GuestID field in record number 35.

FIGURE 1-13

GuestID field selected in record 35

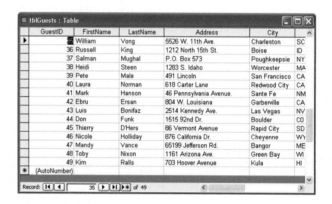

8 **Click the Previous Record button.**

Access selects the GuestID field in record number 34.

9 **Click the Next Record button.**

Access selects the GuestID field in record number 35.

10 **Click the Last Record button.**

Access selects the GuestID field in record number 49.

FIGURE 1-14

GuestID field selected in record 49

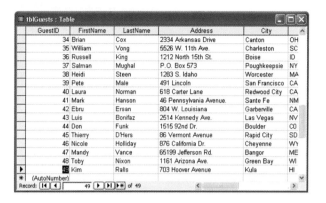

TIP

Notice that the GuestID field remains the selected field as you change from record to record using the navigation buttons.

[◄] **11** **Click the First Record button.**

Access selects the GuestID field in record number 1.

◆ Keep the database open for the next exercise.

QUICK REFERENCE ▼

Move around in a database table

- To move from field to field or record to record using the mouse, click in the new field or record.
- To move from record to record using the navigation buttons, click the button for the action you want, such as next record, previous record, first or last record, or new record.
- To go to a specific record, enter the record number in the Specific Record box.
- To move up or down, or left to right using the scroll bars, click the scroll bar arrows, or drag the scroll bar slider (scroll box), or click in the empty area of the scroll bar.

QUICK CHECK

Q. Where do you find the navigation buttons when a table is open in Datasheet view?

A. They are found in the lower-left corner of the Datasheet window.

Using the Keyboard to Navigate in Datasheet View

THE BOTTOM LINE

An experienced user can move through an Access table very quickly by using keyboard keys and keyboard shortcut keys to navigate the data. Access provides several shortcuts that can instantly jump you from your current location to some other location within the table.

You can also use the keyboard to navigate within a table by pressing keys called **shortcut keys** on the keyboard. After you become proficient with the shortcut keys, this approach can sometimes be a faster way to navigate than using the mouse.

The following shortcut keys can be used to navigate within a table:

IMPORTANT

To use shortcut keys such as Shift+Tab or Ctrl+Home, you must hold down the first key while pressing the second key.

Key	Description
Tab	To the next field in the current record.
Enter	To the next field.
Page Up	Up by one screen, selecting a record farther up in the table.
Page Down	Down by one screen, selecting a record farther down in the table.
Right arrow key	To the next field in the current record.
Left arrow key	To the previous field.
Down arrow key	To the next record.
Up arrow key	To the previous record.
Home	To the first field of the current record.
End	To the last field of the current record.
Ctrl+Down arrow	To the last record in the current field.
Ctrl+Up arrow	To the first record in the current field.
Ctrl+Home	To the first field of the first record.
Ctrl+Page Down	To the right by one screen, selecting a field farther right in the table.
Ctrl+Page Up	To the left by one screen, selecting a field farther left in the table.
Ctrl+End	To the last field of the last record.
Shift+Tab	To the previous field.

Use Access shortcut keys

You have seen how you can use the mouse and the navigation buttons to move among records and fields. You can also use the keyboard and keyboard shortcut keys to navigate among the records in the tblGuests table. You will see how easy it is to jump from one record to another specific point in the table.

1 **With the GuestID field in the first record selected, press Tab.**

Access selects the FirstName field in the first record.

2 **Press Enter.**

Access selects the LastName field in the first record.

3 **Press Page Down.**

The table moves down one screen, causing Access to select a record farther down in the table. The record you end up in will vary depending on your display settings and the size of your datasheet window.

> **TIP**
>
> Notice that the same field, LastName, remains the selected field as you press Page Down and then Page Up.

4 **Press Page Up.**

The table moves up one screen, causing Access to select the first record.

5 **Press the Right arrow key.**

Access selects the Address field in the first record.

6 **Press the Left arrow key.**

Access selects the LastName field in the first record.

7 **Press Shift+Tab.**

Access selects the FirstName field in the first record.

8 **Press the Down arrow key.**

Access selects the FirstName field in the second record.

9 **Press the Up arrow key.**

Access selects the FirstName field in the first record.

> **TROUBLESHOOTING**
>
> When a field with a check box is selected, the edges of the check box become notched.

10 **Press End.**

Access selects the MailingList field in the first record.

<div class="sidebar">

CHECK THIS OUT ▼

Relational Databases
Access is a **relational database** application. With relational databases, you can combine data from different tables. A relationship between multiple tables is created by linking a field name in one table with a field name in one or more other tables.

Relational databases have many advantages—such as reducing the time it takes to type the data and reducing the amount of disk space needed—because information can be stored in only one table instead of in multiple tables. Relational databases are also faster to update because outdated or incorrect information needs to be corrected in only one table, instead of in several. You will learn more about relationships in Lesson 3, "Working with Tables."

</div>

11 **Press Home.**

Access selects the GuestID field in the first record.

12 **Press Ctrl+End.**

Access selects the MailingList field in the last record.

13 **Press Ctrl+Home.**

Access selects the GuestID field in the first record.

 14 **Click the Close button in the top-right corner of tblGuests.**

ANOTHER METHOD

You can also close a table by clicking Close on the File menu.

The table closes.

QUICK REFERENCE ▼

Navigate using the keyboard

- Press the keyboard key that will move the insertion point to the field or record you want to access,
- Press and hold the Shift or Ctrl key while simultaneously pressing another keyboard key to perform the desired action.

QUICK CHECK

Q. Which key or key combination would you press to move to the first field of the first record in the database?

A. **To move to the first record of the first field, press and hold down the Ctrl key, and then press the Home key.**

Key Points

✔ *The Access database program can be started from the Start menu, from a file folder, or from the desktop.*

✔ *You can open an existing database from the task pane or the Open dialog box.*

✔ *The Database window Objects bar can be used to select and open a database object.*

✔ *You switch from Design view to Datasheet view, or vice versa, with the click of a button on the toolbar.*

✔ *Access allows you to use the mouse, the navigation buttons, the scroll bars, and the keyboard to navigate through a table in the Database window.*

◆ **If you are continuing to other lessons:**

Close the Adventure Works 01 Database.

Keep Access open for the next lesson.

◆ **If you are not continuing to other lessons:**

Close the Adventure Works 01 Database.

Close Access.

Quick Quiz

True/False

T F **1.** *DBMS* stands for Database Modification System.

T F **2.** When you first start Access, the *database pane* appears on the right side of the Access window.

T F **3.** A table is made up of fields and records that are arranged in rows and columns.

T F **4.** An Access group contains a list of shortcuts to different types of objects in the database.

T F **5.** According to the Leszynski naming convention, the name of a query object should begin with *que*.

Multiple Choice

1. Which term below refers to a window that opens within the main Access window once you have opened an existing database?
    a. Active window
    b. Database window
    c. Current window
    d. Objects window

2. When viewing a table in Datasheet view, the intersection of a row and a column is called a _____.
    a. union
    b. pivot point
    c. cell
    d. link

3. Which of the following terms refers to a row of fields in a database table?
    a. record
    b. cell
    c. object
    d. group

4. The Access view that allows you to define fields and examine and modify field properties is called _____ view.
    a. Datasheet
    b. Design
    c. Properties
    d. Field

5. Which of the following shortcut keys can be used to jump to the last field of the current record?
    a. Ctrl+End
    b. Ctrl+Tab
    c. Shift+Tab
    d. End

Short Answer

1. What feature of the Access Database window would you use to select a type of object that you wish to open?
2. How do you start Access using the Windows XP Start menu?
3. What is the Office Assistant?
4. Why are tables the foundation for all other database objects?
5. Why is it an advantage to be able to link tables in a relational database?
6. Identify at least three ways that you can navigate in a table in Access?
7. How would you view a list of the names of all of the tables defined in an Access database?
8. What are the two available modes for a table in Datasheet view, and how are they different?
9. How do you open a table in Design view?
10. How do you change your view of a table from Design view to Datasheet view?

On Your Own

Exercise 1

On the Objects bar, click Forms, and open frmEmployees in Datasheet view. Switch to Design view, and describe the difference between viewing a table in Design view and seeing a form in Design view.

Exercise 2

On the Objects bar, click Tables, and open tblEmployees. Look at the table in Design view and then in Datasheet view. Using the shortcut keys, navigate to the last field of the last record. Using the Specific Record box, move to the 18th record. Using the shortcut keys, move to the EmployeeID field in the 18th record. Using the navigation buttons, move to the first record, and close the table.

Exercise 3

On the Objects bar, click Tables, and open tblReservations. Look at the table in Design view and then in Datasheet view. After examining the fields defined for this table, can you think of any other fields that would be useful in this table? Do you see any fields that could be removed from this table without impacting the operation of the resort?

One Step Further

Exercise 1

On the Objects bar, click Tables, and open tblReservations. Look at the table in Datasheet view. Press the F11 key to access the Database window, and double-click on the tblSuites table to open it. View this table in Datasheet view. Since Access is a relational database, it is possible to link one table to another. Which field(s) would you use to link the tblSuites table to the tblReservations table to create a relationship between these tables?

Exercise 2

This lesson showed you how toolbars can be turned on or off. Can you think of any reasons why you would ever want to turn off a toolbar that is currently displayed?

Creating Tables

After completing this lesson, you will be able to:

- ✔ *Create a database.*
- ✔ *Create a table using the Table Wizard.*
- ✔ *Create and modify a table in Design view.*
- ✔ *Add fields to tables.*
- ✔ *Add and edit records.*
- ✔ *Print tables.*
- ✔ *Move and delete fields.*
- ✔ *Delete records.*

KEY TERMS

- ■ AutoNumber
- ■ caption
- ■ data type
- ■ hyperlink
- ■ landscape
- ■ portrait

- ■ primary key
- ■ Print Preview
- ■ record selector
- ■ row selector
- ■ Table Wizard
- ■ template

Tables are the foundation of Microsoft Access databases because they store the data used by all other Access objects. The organization of the tables in a database determines how efficient the database is and how easy it is to access the information in the database. Before you create a database, you should consider the information that the database will contain and how the tables in the database will organize that information.

After you've planned the tables that you want to include in your database, you can create them using the **Table Wizard**, which walks you through making a new table, or you can make a more customized table on your own without the help of the wizard.

In this lesson, you'll learn how to create tables and then use Design view to modify them by creating new fields, rearranging existing fields, and deleting unwanted fields. You'll also learn how to add new records, change the information in records, and print a table after you modify it.

IMPORTANT

You will create all the practice files used in this lesson.

Creating a Database

> ## THE BOTTOM LINE
>
> It is very important to carefully plan your database before attempting to create it. A good database design results in better performance and requires fewer system resources and less storage space. Be sure to consult with the people who will be using a database before completing the design. It is important that the design meets the needs of the people who will eventually have to work with the database.

Creating a database requires some preparatory work. Before you even start Access, you should plan how the database will be organized and what tables you will need to create in the database. At a minimum, you should:

- Decide what information you want to store in the database and determine the most logical way to arrange the tables. Typically, you create a table for each general category of information to avoid putting the same information in more than one table.
- Gather all the information that will become part of the database, such as other computer documents, spreadsheets, files, pieces of paper, ledger books, and so on.
- Decide what information you want to store in each table. The different types of information will become the different fields for your table. For example, in a table listing reservation information for Adventure Works, you might want to include information such as the reservation number, the guest identification number, the check-in and check-out dates, the number of guests, the suite that they are staying in, and whether they are eligible for a group discount.
- Interview the people who will use the database. Let them know what tables you plan to create and the fields you plan to put in the tables. The users might have suggestions, such as particular categories of information that they would find useful.

Using these techniques to plan your database will help you figure out the purpose of the database and whether you can use a database **template** to create it. Access has several database templates, which are ready-made databases containing all the formatting required to build a special-use database. For example, if you need a database to track time and billing, you can use the Access database template with features specific to time and billing. Access has database templates for asset tracking, contact management, event management, expenses, inventory control, ledgers, order entry, resource scheduling, service call management, and time and billing.

> ## TIP
>
> When you plan a database, you might find it helpful to sketch out your ideas on paper. Draw boxes to represent the tables, queries, forms, and reports in the database, and draw lines between the boxes to show on which tables the other objects are based. You should also include a list of the fields in each table so that you can be sure that you aren't storing the same information in more than one place.

Creating a database is very similar to opening an existing one. Opening an existing database is discussed in Lesson 1, "Understanding Databases."

When you start Access to begin creating your database, the Getting Started task pane appears by default. However, there is also a New File task pane in Access that gives you various options for creating your database from scratch. If you select one of the Template options, you will select a template to use for your database, and then the Database Wizard will walk you through the creation of your database by asking you a series of questions. Based on your responses, the wizard creates the database objects (such as forms, queries, or reports) that your database needs.

IMPORTANT

In this lesson, you will create a database and two tables without using the Database Wizard.

If you create your database without the help of the wizard, as you do in the following exercise, you need to create each database object yourself.

To create a database by using a template, click one of the options in the Templates section of the task pane. You can view templates on the Microsoft Office Web site by clicking the Templates Home Page option. You can also select from the templates installed on your system by clicking the On My Computer option and selecting the template that you want to use from the Databases tab of the Templates dialog box that appears.

◆ Be sure to start Access before beginning this exercise.

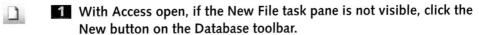

Create a database without using a wizard

In this exercise, you will create a new database named Adventure Works 02.

1 With Access open, if the New File task pane is not visible, click the New button on the Database toolbar.

The New File task pane appears on the right side of the window.

ANOTHER METHOD

You can also display the New File task pane by clicking the File menu, and then clicking the New option on that menu.

2 In the New File task pane, click the Blank Database option in the New section of the task pane.

FIGURE 2-1

The Access window and the New File task pane

New button   Blank Database option   New File task pane

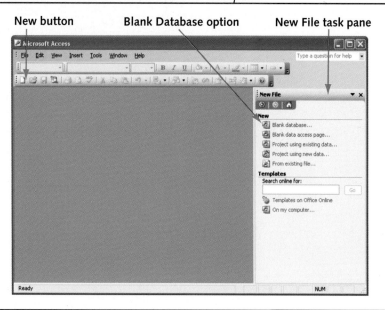

The File New Database dialog box appears.

3 **Click the Save In down arrow, click the icon for your hard disk, and double-click the Access Practice folder.**

Access will save the new database in the Access Practice folder.

4 **In the File Name box, delete the existing text, and type Adventure Works 02.**

FIGURE 2-2

The File New Database dialog box

Folder to save in   Save In down arrow

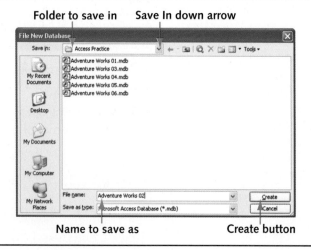

Name to save as   Create button

5 **Click the Create button.**

Access saves the Adventure Works 02 database in the Access Practice folder. The Database window for the Adventure Works 02 database appears with Tables already selected on the Objects bar.

FIGURE 2-3

The Database Window

Tables selected in the Objects bar   Options for creating tables

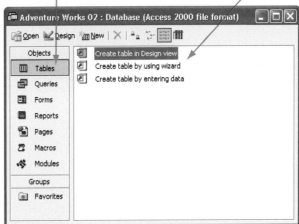

TIP

Naming conventions for an Access database file follow those for Microsoft Windows files. A file name can contain up to 215 characters including spaces, but creating a file name that long is not recommended. File names cannot contain the following characters: \ / : * ? " < > |. The extension for an Access database file is *.mdb*.

◆ **Keep this database open for the next exercise.**

QUICK REFERENCE ▼

Create a database without using a wizard

1 Start Access and display the New File task pane.

2 Click the Blank Database option.

3 Specify a drive and folder to contain the file, name the file, and click Create.

QUICK CHECK

Q. Which toolbar button can you click to open the New File task pane?

A. **You can click the New button to open the New File task pane.**

Creating a Table Using the Table Wizard

THE BOTTOM LINE

The Table Wizard is a fast and convenient way to create new tables for your database. It allows you to choose from a variety of options presented to you in a step-by-step format.

After you've created a database, you'll need to create some tables to hold the data in the database. The easiest way to create a table is to use the Table Wizard, which steps you through the process of creating a table.

The Table Wizard offers two categories of tables: Business and Personal. The Business category contains templates for common tables such as Customers, Employees, and Products. Among the options in the Personal category are Household Inventory, Recipes, Plants, and Exercise Log. Each sample table contains many fields that you can use for the table. For example, in the Addresses table, you can select from fields for first name, last name, postal code, home phone, work phone, and e-mail address. To add a field to your table, you just click the field that you want.

TIP

When you use the Table Wizard to create a table, you can select fields from a number of different sample tables.

The Table Wizard also prompts you to select a **primary key** field for the table. A primary key is a field that uniquely identifies each record in a table. For example, a social security number in an employee database could serve as a primary key because it uniquely identifies each employee; no two employees can have the same social security number.

To understand the value of a primary key, consider the employees at Adventure Works. It is quite possible that the resort could hire two people with exactly the same name, such as Jeff Smith. With a primary key field, each Jeff Smith will have his own employee identification number. One might have employee ID H110 and the other could have employee ID M220. You would then use the employee ID instead of the last name to keep track of data for each Jeff Smith.

Create a table using the wizard

You have just created a new database in the last exercise, but it does not yet contain any objects. You will now create a table called tblSuppliers, which will contain information about the companies that supply materials and services to the Adventure Works resort.

1 In the Database window, double-click Create Table By Using Wizard.

The first Table Wizard dialog box appears. In this dialog box you choose a category of tables, select one or more tables from the list, and select fields to be included for the new table from each selected sample table.

FIGURE 2-4

The first Table Wizard dialog box

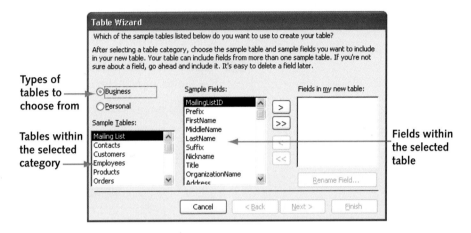

2 In the Sample Tables list, scroll down, and click Suppliers.

The possible fields for the Suppliers table appear in the Sample Fields list, with the SupplierID field already selected.

3 Click the > (Add) button.

The SupplierID field moves to the Fields In My New Table list, and Access selects the SupplierName field, the next field in the list.

FIGURE 2-5

The SupplierID field has been added to the table

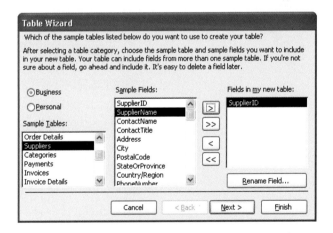

ANOTHER METHOD

Click the >> (Add All) button to add all the fields in the Sample Fields list to the Fields In My New Table list.

4 **Click the > (Add) button.**

The SupplierName field moves to the Fields In My New Table list.

5 **Click the Address field, and click the > (Add) button.**

The Address field moves to the Fields In My New Table list, and Access selects the City field.

6 **Click the > (Add) button.**

The City field moves to the Fields In My New Table list, and Access selects the Postal Code field.

7 **Repeat step 6 to add the PostalCode and StateOrProvince fields to the Fields In My New Table list.**

All fields have now been added for this table.

FIGURE 2-6

All fields for this table have now been selected

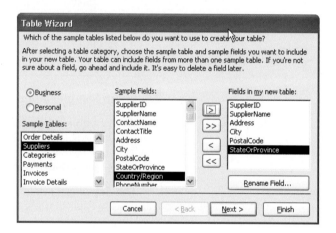

TROUBLESHOOTING

If you want the StateOrProvince field to appear before the PostalCode field in the finished table, add the StateOrProvince field to the Fields in my new table list before adding the PostalCode field.

8 **Click the Next button.**

The next Table Wizard dialog box appears.

FIGURE 2-7

The second Table Wizard dialog box

Enter a table name here

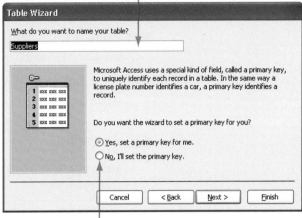

Choose a key option

9 In the What Do You Want To Name Your Table? dialog box, delete the existing text, type tblSuppliers, and then verify that the Yes, Set A Primary Key For Me option is selected.

TROUBLESHOOTING

If you want to manually choose the primary key field for your table, click the No, I'll Set The Primary Key option. The next Table Wizard dialog box that you see will help you choose the primary key.

10 Click Next.

The next Table Wizard dialog box appears. This dialog box lets you choose between opening the table in Design mode or in Datasheet mode, where you can begin entering data records.

FIGURE 2-8

The third Table Wizard dialog box

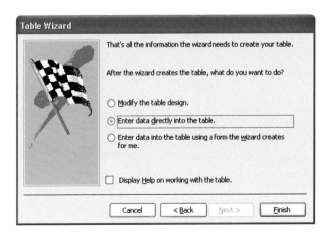

TROUBLESHOOTING

If the Display Help On Working With The Table check box is selected, Access Help will open when the table is created.

11 Verify that the Enter Data Directly Into The Table option is selected and the Display Help On Working With The Table check box is cleared.

Setting these options will cause the table to open in Datasheet view when you click the Finish button, and the Access Help system will not open automatically.

12 Click Finish.

The new table, tblSuppliers, appears in Datasheet view.

FIGURE 2-9

The new tblSuppliers table

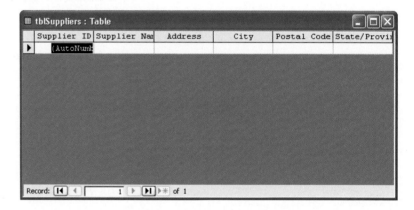

TROUBLESHOOTING

The Supplier ID field is the primary key field that was created by Access. The AutoNumber data type is discussed in the next section of this lesson.

13 On the Table Datasheet toolbar, click the View button.

The table appears in Design view. The field names that appeared from left to right in Datasheet view now appear from top to bottom in the Field Name column.

FIGURE 2-10

The tblSuppliers table in Design view

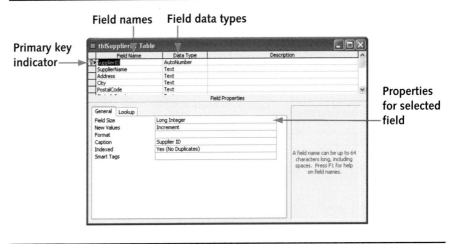

Access places a key icon next to the SupplierID field name to indicate that it is the primary key field.

◆ Close the tblSuppliers table, and keep the database open for the next exercise.

About Spaces in Field Names

In the previous exercise, you might have noticed that in Datasheet view, field names appear with spaces and in Design view, field names do not have spaces. Why is this?

In general, Access allows spaces in field names, but not all database programs do. Therefore, if you might ever need to transfer data from Access to another application, you should avoid spaces in field names. You should also avoid spaces if you plan to use macros, database access programs, or Microsoft Visual Basic with your Access database. Because of these limitations, this book doesn't use spaces in field names.

The reason that you see spaces in the field names in Datasheet view is because each field also has a **caption**, which is used instead of the field name. Fields do not need captions, but if there is a caption, it appears at the top of the field column—instead of the field name—when the table is in Datasheet view. For example, in the figure following Step 13 of the previous exercise, the field name SupplierID doesn't have spaces; however, if you look in the Field Properties section of the Table Design view window, you'll see that the caption for the field is Supplier ID, with a space. When the table appears in Datasheet view, as it does in Step 12, the caption (with a space) appears instead of the field name.

When you create a table by using the Table Wizard, the wizard creates captions that include spaces. When you create a table from scratch, as you will in the next exercise, captions appear only if you create them.

QUICK CHECK

Q. Do you have to add fields to a new table in the same order they are shown in the sample tables?

A. No, you can add the fields to the new table in any order that you want them to be.

QUICK REFERENCE ▼

Create a table using a wizard

1 Double-click the Create Table By Using Wizard option in the Tables section of the Database window.

2 Select the table or tables to be used, select the fields from each selected table that you want to include, and add them to the field list for the new table.

3 Name the table and decide if it should have a primary key.

4 Select the option to enter Design view or Datasheet view and click Finish to create the table.

Creating and Modifying a Table in Design View

THE BOTTOM LINE

It is not always possible to use the Table Wizard to create your tables. You may not find all the fields you want in the sample tables. You can, however, create any table from scratch in Design view. You define the field names, the field data types, and set the properties for each field. You can also modify an existing table at any time by opening it in Design view.

Although the Table Wizard provides a simple way to create a table, you might need to create a table from scratch if the wizard does not provide the fields that you need. For example, to create a table that keeps track of the suites at Adventure Works, you need to build the table from scratch because there isn't a template in the Table Wizard that contains the fields that you will need, such as the type of suite or the suite price. When you create a table from scratch, you determine the field names.

Certain characters are not permitted in field names, as shown in the following table:

Characters not permitted in field names	Description
.	Period
!	Exclamation point
[ ]	Left and right brackets
'	Left single quotation mark

Field names can be up to 64 characters long, but you should avoid using particularly long field names. Long field names are harder for users to read because the entire field name isn't visible without resizing the column. In addition, long field names make the table difficult to fit on one screen when viewed in Datasheet view. They also require some additional storage space for the database file.

You must also give each field a **data type**, which controls the type of data that can be entered into the field and helps to prevent inaccurate entries in a field. For example, if you have a telephone number field and give it the data type *Number,* users will be able to enter only numbers, not letters or symbols, into that field. Some data types automatically format the data in a field. For example, if you give a field the data type *Currency*, Access formats numbers entered into that field as monetary values with two decimal places and a dollar sign.

The data type **AutoNumber** is a special kind of data type that can be used to create a primary key field for a table. The data in an AutoNumber field is generated by Access whenever a new record is added to a table. For example, if you number each resort reservation as it comes in, you could use the AutoNumber field to automatically generate the number for the next reservation.

The following table lists the available data types for each field, the type of data that can be entered into each field, and the number of allowable characters. Text is the default data type for new fields.

Data Type	Allowable Field Values	Character Storage
Text	Alphanumeric characters (letters of the alphabet and numbers)	Up to 255 characters
Memo	Alphanumeric characters (similar to the Text data type, but with more characters)	Up to 64,000 characters
Number	Numeric values	1, 2, 4, or 8 bytes, depending on the numeric format
Date/Time	Numeric values	8 bytes
Currency	Numeric values	8 bytes
AutoNumber	Sequential numbers that Access automatically creates each time a new record is added	4 bytes
Yes/No	Yes/No, True/False On/Off values	1 bit (1/8 byte)
OLE Object	OLE (Object Linking and Embedding) objects that interact with Visual Basic	Up to 1 gigabyte
Hyperlink	Web addresses, Internet addresses, or links to other database objects or applications	Up to 64,000 characters
Lookup	Values from another table or list	Typically 4 bytes

TROUBLESHOOTING

Hyperlinks are discussed later in this lesson. The Lookup Wizard is discussed in Lesson 3, "Working with Tables."

When you create or modify fields, a **row selector** appears to the left of the currently selected, or active, field. If the field is the primary key field for the table, a key symbol appears next to the row selector. To make a field the primary key, you click the Primary Key button on the Table Design toolbar. You can choose only one primary key field per table.

Create a table in Design view

You previously created a table for your supplies using an Access wizard, and that table is now visible in the Tables list in the Database window. You now need to create a table named tblSuites to keep track of the rooms at the resort. You will create this table from scratch using Access Design view.

1 In the Database window, double-click Create Table In Design View.

A blank table appears in Design view, with the insertion point already in the first cell in the Field Name column.

FIGURE 2-11

Design view for a new table

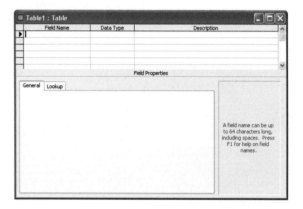

2 Type SuiteID into the Field Name cell.

3 On the Table Design toolbar, click the Primary Key button.

A primary key symbol appears to the left of the SuiteID row, designating SuiteID as the primary key field. Text appears as the default data type.

TIP

To remove the primary key designation from a field, click in the row for the field, and click the Primary Key button on the Table Design toolbar.

4 In the Data Type column, click in the first cell, click the down arrow that appears, and then click AutoNumber.

The numbers in the SuiteID field will be generated by Access. AutoNumber is a serial counter that will add 1 to the last key value currently in the table when a new record is created, and assign the new value as the key of the new record.

5 In the Field Name column, click in the next blank cell, type SuiteType, and then press Tab.

Access selects the next blank cell in the Data Type column, a down arrow appears, and Text appears as the default data type. Text is the correct data type for this field.

6 In the Field Name column, click in the next blank cell, type SuiteRate, and then press Tab.

Access selects the next blank cell in the Data Type column, a down arrow appears, and Text appears as the default data type. You will change this data type.

7 Click the down arrow, and click Currency.

Access will format data entered into the SuiteRate field as currency, with a dollar sign and two decimal places. Your Design view window should look like the following figure.

FIGURE 2-12

Design view with fields defined

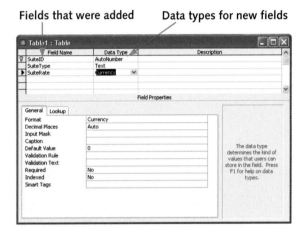

Fields that were added   Data types for new fields

8 On the Table Design toolbar, click the Save button.

The Save As dialog box appears.

FIGURE 2-13

The Save As dialog box

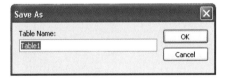

9 Type tblSuites into the text box, and click OK.

Access saves the new table as tblSuites.

10 On the Table Design toolbar, click the View button.

The table appears in Datasheet view. Note that in the blank record, the SuiteRate field is already formatted as a currency value. That is because you applied the Currency data type to it in Design view.

FIGURE 2-14

The tblSuites table in Datasheet view

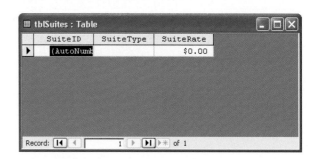

◆ **Keep the table and the database open for the next exercise.**

Adding Hyperlinks to a Table

One of the choices for the data type for a field is a hyperlink. A **hyperlink** lets table fields hold links to sites or Web pages on the Internet or a company intranet. When a user clicks a hyperlink, his or her Web browser starts and displays the page to which the link points. For example, if Adventure Works has a table that keeps track of the vendors that it regularly uses, the table could include a hyperlink to each vendor's Web site.

To place a hyperlink in a field, you must set the field's data type to Hyperlink, and type the Web or intranet address—such as www.microsoft.com—into the table in Datasheet view. To add a hyperlink to a table:

- With the table open in Design view, click in the Data Type cell for the field where you want the hyperlink.
- Click the down arrow that appears, and click Hyperlink.
- On the Table Design toolbar, click the View button to display the table in Datasheet view. When you are prompted to save changes, click Yes.
- Click in the first record for the field defined with the Hyperlink data type.
- Type the Web or intranet address.

TROUBLESHOOTING

When typing the Web or intranet address, you don't have to include http:// at the beginning of the address.

QUICK CHECK

Q. How can you tell if a table has a primary key defined?

A. **When you examine the table in Design view, if a key has been defined the record selector for the key field will contain a key icon.**

QUICK REFERENCE ▼

Create a table in Design view

1 Double-click the Create Table in Design View option in the Database window.

2 Enter field names in the Field Name column and assign a Data Type for each field.

3 Designate a primary key if the table requires a key field.

4 Save the table and switch to Datasheet view to enter data for the table.

Adding Fields to Tables

THE BOTTOM LINE

No matter how well you plan your database design, you will frequently discover that you need to add additional fields to one or more tables after they have been created. This could be due to an oversight in the planning stage, or changing business, academic, or personal needs that require new data. It is very easy to add new fields to any existing Access table using Design view.

After creating tblSuites, which keeps track of the guest suites at Adventure Works, you decide to add three new fields to the table: a Building field (which will designate the name of the building that the suite is in), a #ofOccupants field (which will specify how many people can stay in the suite), and a Notes field (which will hold notes about the suites, such as repairs that need to be made). The process for adding fields to an existing table is similar to the process for adding fields to a new table, which you did in the previous exercise.

Add new fields to existing tables

You just created the tblSuites table in Design view, and defined three fields for the table. You now realize that you need to add additional fields. You will again use Design view to add the three new fields to the existing table.

1 **On the Table Datasheet toolbar, click the View button.**

tblSuites appears in Design view.

TROUBLESHOOTING

If you want to add a field between fields that already exist, click in the row for the field that you want the new field to precede, and click the Insert Rows button on the Table Design toolbar. A new blank row will be inserted before the row you selected.

FIGURE 2-15

The tblSuites table in Design view

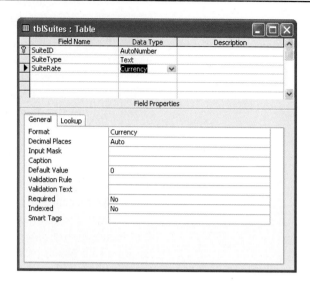

2 In the Field Name column, click in the first blank cell, type **Building**, and press Tab.

Access selects the next blank cell in the Data Type column, a down arrow appears, and Text appears as the default data type. Text is the correct data type for this field.

3 In the Field Name column, click in the next blank cell, type **#ofOccupants**, and press Tab.

Access selects the next blank cell in the Data Type column, a down arrow appears, and Text appears as the default data type. Text is not the correct type for this field so you will change it.

4 Click the down arrow, and click Number.

The #ofOccupants field now has the data type of Number.

5 In the Field Name column, click in the next blank cell, type Notes, and press Tab.

Access selects the next blank cell in the Data Type column, a down arrow appears, and Text appears as the default data type. Text could work for this field, but there is a better data type to use so you will also change this type.

6 Click the down arrow, and click Memo.

TIP

Memo is selected as the data type for this field because Memo fields are not limited to 255 characters, as Text fields are.

The Notes field has the data type of Memo.

FIGURE 2-16

New fields added to tblSuites

New fields and their associated data types

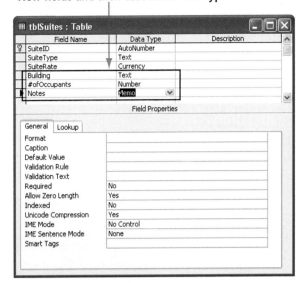

7 On the Table Design toolbar, click the Save button.

Access saves the changes you have made to the tblSuites table.

8 On the Table Design toolbar, click the View button.

The table appears in Datasheet view with the field names SuiteID, SuiteType, SuiteRate, Building, #ofOccupants, and Notes. There is no data in the table yet.

FIGURE 2-17

New fields in Datasheet view

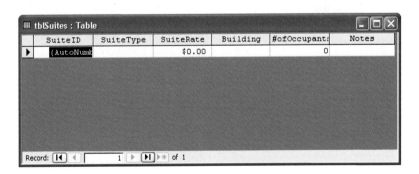

◆ Keep the table open for the next exercise.

QUICK CHECK

Q. How can you insert a new field between two existing fields?

A. **First you click in the row for the field that you want the new field to precede, and then click the Insert Rows button on the Table Design toolbar.**

QUICK REFERENCE ▼

Add new fields to existing tables

1 Open the table in Design view.

2 Click in the first blank Field Name row and enter the name for the new field,

or,

Insert a row between existing fields and enter the new field name.

3 Assign a data type for the field.

4 Save the table when all fields have been entered.

Adding and Editing Records

THE BOTTOM LINE

It is very easy to enter data into an Access table in Datasheet view. You just position the mouse pointer in the first blank record to add a new record, or in the cell containing the data you want to change for an existing record. As soon as you enter the data and exit the record being entered or modified, Access saves the data to disk.

So far in this lesson, you created a database, two tables for that database, and the fields for those tables. Now you need to put some data in the tables that you created. Data is entered into a table in Datasheet view by clicking in the cell where you want the data to go and typing the data into that cell.

To edit existing data in a table, you click in the cell that you want to change, use traditional editing keys such as the Backspace key to delete text to the left of the insertion point and the Delete key to delete text to the right of the insertion point, and then type the new data. You can also select part or all of the entry with the mouse pointer and start typing, which deletes the selected data and replaces it with the new data.

When you select any part of a record to create or change, a **record selector** appears to the left of the record to show the current status of the record.

CHECK THIS OUT ▼

Record Locking
Individual records, instead of entire pages, are locked when another user edits them.

Record Selector	Status
▶	The current record is selected, and the record has been saved as it appears.
▶**	This is a new record, into which you can enter data.
✎	You are editing this record, and changes aren't saved yet.
⊘	This record is locked by another user; you cannot edit it. Records become locked in a multiuser environment (one in which more than one person can use the database at a time) when another person is editing the record.

If the record selector box is empty, it means that no users are currently modifying the record.

Access is different from most other Microsoft Office applications when it comes to saving changes. In most applications, you need to manually save your work as you go along. When entering data in Access objects, however, your work is saved by Access whenever you move to another record. This means that when you close a table, you will not be prompted to save changes because your changes will already have been saved. However, if you create a new object or make structural changes (such as adding new fields) to an existing object, you will need to manually save your work. Access will prompt you to save if you attempt to close an object to which you have done more than enter data. This also applies to formatting changes to a table. If you change column widths or make color or font changes, you will be prompted to save the table if you try to close it before you save it.

Add new records and modify existing data

In the previous exercises, you have created a new table called tblSuites and added several fields to the table. In this exercise, you will add three records to the tblSuites table, and then you will modify the data in one of these records.

1 **In the SuiteType field, click in the first empty record, type 2BR, and then press Tab.**

Access selects the SuiteRate field in the first record.

TIP

Notice that the AutoNumber data type in the SuiteID field automatically gives the first record the Suite ID of 1.

2 **Type 75, and press Tab.**

Access selects the Building field in the first record when you press the Tab key.

TROUBLESHOOTING

Notice that Access automatically formats the data in the SuiteRate field in currency format at $75.00. This is because you defined the field with a Currency data type.

3 **Type Lake View, and press Tab.**

Access selects the #ofOccupants field in the first record.

4 **Type 4, and press Tab.**

Access selects the Notes field in the first record.

5 Type Corner Room.

The first record is complete.

FIGURE 2-18

One record added to tblSuites

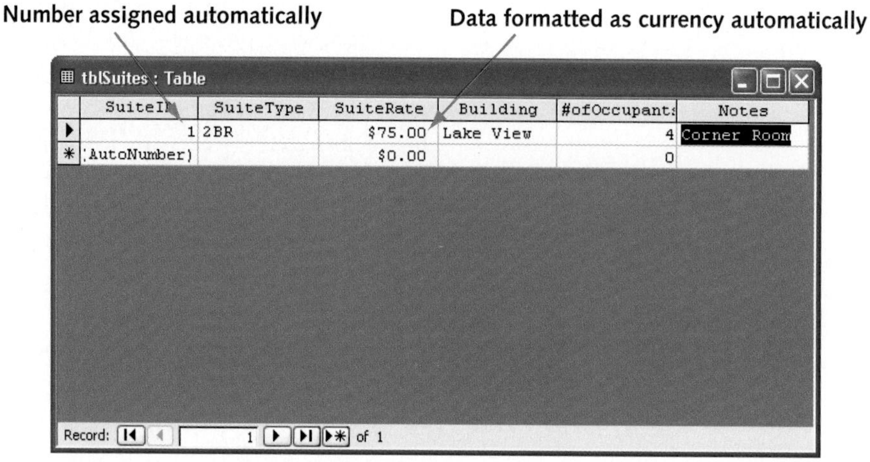

Number assigned automatically   Data formatted as currency automatically

IMPORTANT

Each time you start a new record, the data in the previous record is saved.

6 In the SuiteType field, click in the first blank record, and follow the previous steps to enter the following information into the record:

SuiteType: 3BR
SuiteRate: 99
Building: Lake View
#ofOccupants: 6
Leave the Notes field blank.

7 In the SuiteType field, click in the first blank record, and follow the previous steps to enter the following information into the record:

SuiteType: 3BR
SuiteRate: 99
Building: Mountain View
#ofOccupants: 8
Notes: Has bunk beds in one bedroom

Your datasheet should now contain three records and should look similar to Figure 2-19. In the next step, you will edit the data in one of the records.

TROUBLESHOOTING

You will not be able to see all the text in the Notes field because the column is not wide enough. You will learn how to resize columns in Lesson 3, "Working with Tables."

FIGURE 2-19

New records shown in Datasheet view

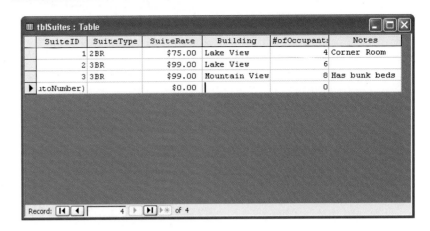

8 In the first record, click in the SuiteType field, delete the existing text, and then type **1BR**, and then press Tab.

Access selects the text on the SuiteRate field.

9 Delete the existing text, and then type **69**.

10 In the first record, click in the #ofOccupants field, delete the existing text, and then type **2**.

Your datasheet should now look similar to Figure 2-20.

FIGURE 2-20

Datasheet with modified data fields

Edited fields

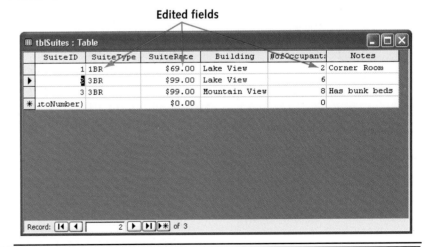

◆ Keep the database open for the next exercise.

QUICK REFERENCE ▼

Add new records to a table

1 Open the table in Datasheet view.

2 Click in the first blank row and enter the data value.

3 Use the Tab key, the mouse, or the arrow keys to move to the next field to be entered.

Modify data in existing records

◆ Select the data in the existing record and modify it as needed.

Printing Tables

THE BOTTOM LINE

You can print the contents of a table simply by clicking the Print button on the toolbar. You can also use the Print Preview feature of Access to preview how the table will look when printed. From Print Preview, you can make changes to the layout using the Page Setup dialog box if you notice any problems in how the data will print, such as page orientation and margins.

After you're finished adding records to a table, you might want to print a copy of the table. To print a table, you click the Print button on the Table Datasheet toolbar or click Print on the File menu.

Depending on how many fields and records there are in your table, the entire table might not fit on one sheet of paper when you print it. To see how your table will appear when printed, you can click the **Print Preview** button on the toolbar, which will show how the table will appear if printed using the default **portrait** orientation, meaning the short edge of the paper is at the top of the page. If your table does not fit on the paper using portrait orientation, you can try **landscape** orientation, in which the long edge of the paper is at the top of the page. Landscape orientation often works better than portrait orientation for printing tables with a lot of fields. To change paper orientation, you click Page Setup on the File menu (or on the Print Preview toolbar) and click the option for the orientation that you want in the Page Setup dialog box.

Preview and print a table

The tblSuites table has been created and now contains several data records. You can now use Print Preview to see how the table will appear when you print it, and then you will print the table data.

 1 On the Table Datasheet toolbar, click the Print Preview button.

The table appears in Print Preview in portrait orientation.

TROUBLESHOOTING

If the table you are printing has multiple pages, you can click the Last Page navigation button in the bottom-left corner of the Print Preview window to see how long the printed document will be.

FIGURE 2-21

A table in Print Preview mode

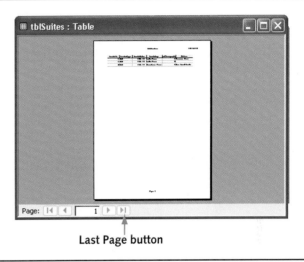

Last Page button

Close

2 On the Print Preview toolbar, click Close.

Print Preview closes.

3 On the Table Datasheet toolbar, click the Print button.

A message box appears, telling you that Access is printing the table.

ANOTHER METHOD

To print a table, you can also click the Print option on the File menu, or, use the Ctrl+P shortcut keys.

◆ Keep the table open for the next exercise.

QUICK REFERENCE ▼

Preview a table before printing it

◆ Click the Print Preview button while the table is open in Datasheet view.

Print a table

- Click the Print button on the toolbar.
- Click the Print option on the File menu.
- Press the Ctrl+P keys on the keyboard.

QUICK CHECK

Q. What is the default paper orientation when printing an Access table?

A. The default paper orientation is portrait.

Moving and Deleting Fields

THE BOTTOM LINE

After creating your table, you may notice that the data does not display in the order that you want to see it. You can very quickly change the order of fields in a table to make it display as you would prefer to see it. You can also remove fields from tables if you find that you just no longer need the data that field contains.

After you start using a table, you might realize that you included some unnecessary fields in the table, or that data entry would be more efficient if the fields were in a different order. Deleting fields, which appear as columns in Datasheet view, is different from deleting individual records, which appear as rows. If you delete a field, you lose all the data in the field for every record in the database.

You can delete or rearrange fields by displaying the table in Design view and then deleting or rearranging the rows. Each row in Design view represents one of the fields that appears as a column in Datasheet view. So, if you delete a row in Design view, you delete a field (or column) in Datasheet view. When you move and delete rows in Design view, you use the row selector to select all the cells in the row.

Rearrange fields and delete a field

Now that you have added data to your table and examined it in Datasheet and Print Preview modes, you notice that you would like to change the appearance and content of the table. In this exercise, you will change the order of the fields in tblSuites and delete the #ofOccupants field.

1 **On the Table Datasheet toolbar, click the View button.**

The table appears in Design view.

2 **In the Field Name column, click in the Building row.**

The row selector appears to the left of the word *Building*.

 3 **Click the row selector for the Building row to select the entire row.**

Access selects the Building row.

4 **Drag the row selector up to just below the primary key symbol that is to the left of the SuiteID row.**

The Building row moves below the SuiteID row.

FIGURE 2-22

Building row moved below the SuiteID row

Building field moved to new location within the table

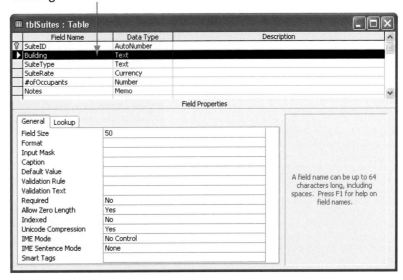

▶ **5** In the Field Name column, click in the #ofOccupants row.

The row selector appears to the left of the word *#ofOccupants*.

6 Click the row selector for the #ofOccupants row to select the entire row.

Access selects the #ofOccupants row.

7 On the Table Design toolbar, click the Delete Rows button.

An alert box appears, asking if you want to permanently delete the field(s). If you have selected the wrong row, or have changed your mind about deleting the field, you can click No and the field will re-main in the table. In this case, you are going to delete the field.

8 Click Yes.

Access deletes the #ofOccupants row from the table.

ANOTHER METHOD

To delete a row, you can also click Delete Rows on the Edit menu or right-click the field name and click Delete Rows on the shortcut menu that appears.

9 On the Table Design toolbar, click the Save button.

Access saves the table.

IMPORTANT

If you try to switch to Datasheet view without saving changes, Access prompts you to save changes.

10 On the Table Design toolbar, click the View button.

The table appears in Datasheet view. Note that the Building field now displays after the Suite ID field, and the #ofOccupants field is no longer present.

FIGURE 2-23

The tblSuites table with changes in Datasheet view

Building now follows Suite ID   #ofOccupants no longer displays at all

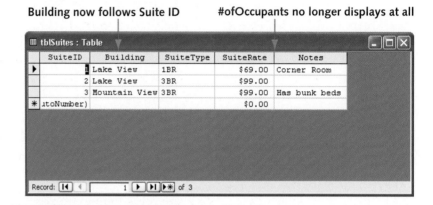

◆ Keep the table open for the next exercise.

Q. What happens to the data for a field that is being deleted from a table?

A. **When the field is deleted, all data for that field is also deleted and is lost forever.**

QUICK REFERENCE ▼

Moving fields in Design view

1 Open the table in Design view.

2 Click in the row for the row to be moved.

3 Drag the row selector to the new location.

4 Save the table.

Delete fields from a table

1 Open the table in Design view.

2 Click in the row for the row to be deleted, and then click the row selector.

3 Click the Delete Rows button on the toolbar.

4 Save the table.

Deleting Records

THE BOTTOM LINE

You can delete an entire record from a table at any time, but great care must be taken when deleting records. Once the record is deleted, it cannot be restored. It is always a good idea to back up your database before deleting records in case you do delete a record by accident. If so, you can restore the database and perform the delete operation again.

Deleting a record, an individual row of data containing information from many fields, is a simple procedure that should be done carefully. Once a record is deleted, it cannot be restored. Therefore, make sure that you are removing the correct records. If you plan to delete several records, it is a good idea to create a backup of the entire database in case you accidentally delete the wrong records. Unlike fields, records are deleted in Datasheet view.

Delete a record from a table

After examining the data in your table, you decide that tblSuites should be limited to records of suites only in the Lake View building. In this exercise, you will delete the record for the suite in the Mountain View building.

TROUBLESHOOTING

You do not have to select an entire record to delete it.

1 Click anywhere in the record for the suite in the Mountain View building.

The record selector appears to the left of the record.

2 On the Table Datasheet toolbar, click the Delete Record button.

An alert box appears, asking you if you want to delete the record(s). You can click No to cancel the operation and retain the record if you have selected the wrong record to be deleted.

ANOTHER METHOD

To delete a record, you can also click Delete Record on the Edit menu or right-click the record and click Delete Record on the shortcut menu that appears.

FIGURE 2-24

The Delete Record warning dialog box

3 Click Yes to confirm the delete and remove the record from the table.

Access deletes the record.

◆ Close tblSuites.

Q. If you are going to be deleting multiple records from a table, what should you do first before you begin to delete the records, and why would you do that?

A. **You should back up the database first, so if you accidentally delete the wrong record, you can restore the database from the backup and start over.**

QUICK REFERENCE ▼

Delete a record from a table

1 Open the table in Datasheet view.

2 Click anywhere in the row to be deleted.

3 Click the Delete Record button on the toolbar.

4 Click Yes to confirm the delete.

◆ **If you are continuing to other lessons:**

Close the Adventure Works 02 Database.

Keep Access open for the next lesson.

◆ **If you are not continuing to other lessons:**

Close the Adventure Works 02 Database.

Close Access.

Key Points

✔ *Access makes it very easy to create a new database.*

✔ *You can create a table using a wizard or create it manually in Design view.*

✔ *You can add fields to tables and modify the layout of tables in Design view.*

✔ *Using Datasheet view, you can add records to tables and edit existing records.*

✔ *It is easy to print a table in Access, and you can also preview how the table will look when printed before you print it.*

✔ *You can delete fields from tables in Design view.*

✔ *You can delete entire records from a table in Datasheet view.*

Quick Quiz

True/False

T F **1.** One of the first steps involved in planning a database is to determine what information you need to store in the database, and the most logical way to arrange the tables.

T F **2.** The Access Table Wizard contains three categories of tables you can choose from, Business, Personal, and Internet Services.

T F **3.** A field name and a caption are one and the same thing.

T F **4.** Once a table has been defined, it cannot be changed so you must plan each table very carefully before creating it.

T F **5.** Access automatically saves table data when it has been updated as soon as you move from the record being updated to another record in the table.

Multiple Choice

1. What is the name of the Access feature that guides you step-by-step through the creation of a database table?
   a. Table Guide
   b. Table Maker
   c. Table Wizard
   d. Table Starter

2. Which Access menu contains the New option that you can click to cause the New File task pane to appear?
   a. Edit
   b. View
   c. Tools
   d. File

3. Which of the following terms refers to the field in a table that uniquely identifies each record in the table?
   a. primary key
   b. sort key
   c. record ID
   d. identifier

4. When a table is displayed in Datasheet view, which of the following is a field property that supplies the label for each field shown at the top of the datasheet columns?
   a. Field Name
   b. Field Label
   c. Caption
   d. Tag

5. Which Access data type would you specify for a field whose values are to be supplied from some other table or list?
   a. OLE Object
   b. Lookup
   c. Memo
   d. AutoFill

Short Answer

1. How do you add a field to a table?
2. How do you delete a record?
3. What techniques might help you plan a database?
4. How do you move a field to a new location within a table?
5. How do you print a table?
6. What is a primary key?
7. What are the two ways to create a table?
8. How do you create a database?
9. How do you enter a record in a table?
10. How do you view a table before printing it?
11. What does the AutoNumber data type do?

On Your Own

Exercise 1

Create a new table in Design view that lists conferences that will be held at Adventure Works. Include the following fields:

1. ConferenceDate with the Date/Time data type
2. OrganizationName with a Text data type
3. #OfDays with the Number data type
4. #OfParticipants with the Number data type
5. #OfRooms with the Number data type

Move the #OfRooms field so that it appears above #OfDays, and delete the #OfParticipants field. Close the table without saving changes.

Exercise 2

Open tblSuppliers in Design view and delete the Address, City, PostalCode, and StateOrProvince fields. Add a field for TypeOfBusiness, save the table, and then enter the following two records:

1. Supplier Name: Party Eternal
   TypeOfBusiness: Entertainment supplies
2. Supplier Name: Ritzy Restaurant Supply
   TypeOfBusiness: Restaurant décor items

Print the table, delete the record for Party Eternal, and then close the table.

Exercise 3

While Adventure Works has many built-in attractions and fine restaurants, the guests frequently would like to know about other restaurants, entertainment, and attractions within a short driving distance of the resort. Add a new table to the Adventure Works 02 database and name it tblAttractions. The table should contain the name of the attraction, the location or address of the attraction, the approximate distance in miles from the resort, a phone number, a link to the attraction's Web site if available, and a short description of what it has to offer. Include any other fields that you think may be useful for this table. When you have finished creating the table, save it and close the database.

One Step Further

Exercise 1

Open the Adventure Works 02 database and open the tblAttractions table that you just created. Switch to Datasheet view if necessary, and enter at least five attractions. Types of attractions that guests would be interested in might include a cinema, a golf course, hot-air balloon rides, historic homes or buildings, or anything else you might think of. Create the data for your five attractions and close the table and the database.

Exercise 2

Create a new database and save it in your practice folder. This database will contain information about your personal music collection. Name the database MYMusic_XXX, where the XXX is replaced with your initials. Create a table to contain the information about your music collection. Include any fields you think are appropriate, but at the very least it should include the name of the artist, the record company, the year it was released, what format it is (CD, mini-CD, MP3, vinyl, etc.), and some rating value to be assigned by you according to how much you like it (one to five stars, for example). When you have created the table, save it and switch to Datasheet view and add at least ten items to the table.

LESSON 3

Working with Tables

After completing this lesson, you will be able to:

✔ *Change the format of a table.*
✔ *Modify field properties.*
✔ *Sort records in a table.*
✔ *Find records in a table.*
✔ *Use filters with a table.*
✔ *Establish relationships between tables.*
✔ *Create subdatasheets.*
✔ *Import records from an external source.*

KEY TERMS

- Caption property
- Default Value property
- exporting
- field properties
- Field Size property
- filter
- Find
- Format property
- import
- input mask
- Lookup field
- Office Clipboard
- one-to-many relationship
- one-to-one relationship
- referential integrity
- sort
- subdatasheet

Microsoft Access provides many ways to change the entry, format, properties, organization, and storage of information in your database tables. As the tables in your database become more efficient, your database becomes more efficient.

To reduce errors during data entry, you can modify individual fields within tables to accept only certain types of data or specific data formats. For example, you can set a Date field to accept only six numbers and have Access automatically insert slashes between those numbers so that all dates in the field will appear in the format *10/27/05*. You can further reduce the amount of time spent typing by importing information from other tables or spreadsheets into Access.

After the data is entered into the table, you can change the organization of the data by performing a **sort** to list information numerically or alphabetically. For example, you could organize a table of employee hiring information by date hired, salary offered, or position. If you want to see only some of the information in a table, you can use a **filter** to restrict the data that appear by specifying which criteria you want to view, such as records for students enrolled in a particular class or who have a GPA greater than 3.0.

When there are many tables in a database, you might find that you spend a lot of time flipping back and forth between tables. You can save time by establishing relationships between tables that contain similar fields and creating subdatasheets, which display the data from one table in another.

Formatting a Table Datasheet

THE BOTTOM LINE

Although the Access default datasheet format is clear and easy to read, you can change the formatting of the datasheet to meet your particular needs. You can increase or decrease the size of the font, add color to the datasheet, and apply special effects to the datasheet cells. For cells with large data fields, you can increase the size of the columns to make all or more of the data visible.

When you create a table, Access automatically formats the table with a 10-point Arial font and silver gridlines. Access uses this default format because it is easy to read on a computer screen. Figure 3-1 shows the default appearance of an Access table datasheet.

FIGURE 3-1

The Access default datasheet appearance

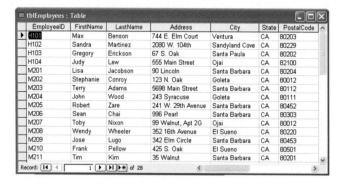

If you do not want to use the default format, however, you can customize the appearance of your tables by changing the font, the font size, and the font properties (such as whether the font is bold or italicized). You can also change the background color, alter the color of the gridlines, or assign a special effect to make cells appear raised or sunken. You can change the height and width of rows and columns, freeze columns, and even hide columns. Figure 3-2 below shows the same table shown above with a sunken cell effect, a blue background, and a 14-point Times New Roman font.

FIGURE 3-2

A table datasheet with nondefault formatting

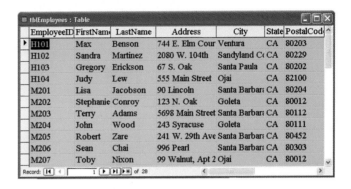

As you can see in the illustration above, some of the data is not completely visible because the columns for the fields are too narrow. By default, Access sets column widths to one inch and does not adjust the column widths if font size and formatting make the text longer than one inch.

The easiest way to make a column wide enough to show all the data is to double-click the line that separates the column from the next column. Access automatically expands the column to the correct size to show all the data. To make a column wider or narrower than this automatic setting, move the mouse pointer over the line between the field names until the pointer changes to a resizing double-headed arrow, and drag the column edge to the left or right.

◆ **Be sure to start Access before beginning this exercise.**

◆ **Before beginning this exercise, open the Adventure Works 03 database file from the Access Practice folder on your hard disk.**

Format the font attributes for a table datasheet

Your test database should be open. You will now open the tblEmployees table in datasheet view and change the appearance of the datasheet. You will change the font used for the table, the size of the font, and the font style.

1 **In the Database window, on the Objects bar, click Tables, if necessary.**

All tables currently defined in the database will be listed in the Database window.

2 **Click tblEmployees, and click Open on the Database window toolbar.**

The table opens in Datasheet view. Notice that the table appears in the default format of 10-point Arial font with silver gridlines.

FIGURE 3-3

The tblEmployees table in default datasheet format

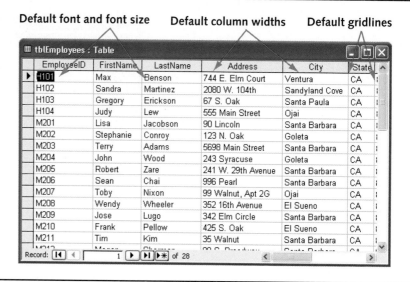

Default font and font size   Default column widths   Default gridlines

3 If the Formatting (Datasheet) toolbar is not visible, click the View menu, point to Toolbars, and click Formatting (Datasheet).

The Formatting toolbar appears.

Times New Roman ▾

4 On the Formatting toolbar, click the Font down arrow, scroll down, and then click Times New Roman.

The font changes to Times New Roman.

B

5 On the Formatting toolbar, click the Bold button.

The font changes to bold.

10pt ▾

6 On the Formatting toolbar, click the Font Size down arrow, and click 12.

The font changes to 12 points.

ANOTHER METHOD

You can also modify the font properties by clicking Font on the Format menu to display the Font dialog box. In the Font dialog box you can apply all of the formatting performed in this exercise.

FIGURE 3-4

The datasheet with the font changes visible

New font, font size, and font style applied

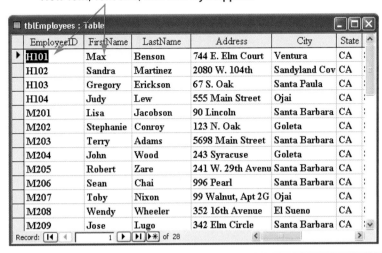

◆ Keep the datasheet open for the next exercise.

Format a datasheet's color, cell appearance, and column sizes

You changed the font appearance of the datasheet in the previous exercise. You will now change the table background to light blue, use a special effect to make the cells appear raised, and then adjust the column widths to accommodate the formatting changes.

 1 On the Formatting toolbar, click the Fill/Back Color down arrow, and click a light blue square.

The table background changes to light blue.

 2 On the Formatting toolbar, click the Special Effect down arrow, and click the Raised (second) option.

The table changes to the raised cell effect. Next, you will change the column widths on some of the columns in order to view all of the data for those fields.

ANOTHER METHOD

You can also modify the Datasheet format by clicking Datasheet on the Format menu to display the Datasheet Formatting dialog box. All of the formatting performed in this exercise can also be specified in that dialog box.

FIGURE 3-5

The datasheet with a colored background and cell effects

New background color and cell effects applied

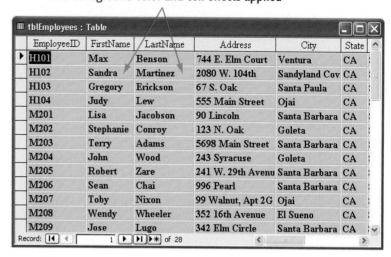

The Raised cell effect is not visible if the table background is white or if the table has colored gridlines.

3 Move the mouse pointer over the line between the Address and City field names until the pointer changes to a resizing double-headed arrow.

When the pointer changes to the double-headed arrow, you can double-click it to automatically adjust the column width, or you can drag it left or right to change the width.

4 Double-click the line.

The column expands so that the widest record in the Address field, 241 W. 29th Avenue, is fully visible.

You can also change column width by clicking in the column that you want to change and clicking Column Width on the Format menu to display the Column Width dialog box. Column widths are measured by the number of characters in the field, so a column with a measurement of 4 holds four characters.

5 Double-click the line between the City and State field names.

The column expands so that the widest record in the City field, Sandyland Cove, is fully visible.

TROUBLESHOOTING

You can return column widths to the default settings by clicking in the column that you want to change, clicking Column Width on the Format menu, and then clicking Standard Widths in the Column Width dialog box. You can change the default column width by clicking Options on the Tools menu, clicking the Datasheet tab in the Options dialog box, and then typing a new value in the Default Column Width text box.

6 Scroll to the right, and double-click the line between the Home Phone and Notes field names.

The column expands so that all the phone numbers are fully visible.

FIGURE 3-6

The datasheet with all formatting changes applied

Columns widened to display all data

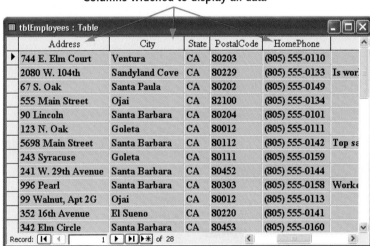

◆ Save the tblEmployees table to save your changes, and then close the table.

◆ Keep the database open for the next exercise.

Saving a Table as a Web Page

Although many people might need to view the data in a database, you might not want everyone who needs the information in the database to use the database to view that information. Allowing too many people to access a database increases the chance that someone will add incorrect data, change existing data, or accidentally delete correct data. To avoid this, you may want to make only certain tables accessible instead of providing access to the whole database itself.

One way to do this is to publish data in HTML. HTML is an acronym for Hypertext Markup Language, which is a language used for defining formatting, links, and other special handling of text, images, and objects on a

Web page. The data can be viewed in a browser, either on the World Wide Web or on internal company Web pages. Others can view the data, but they will not be able to change the data or the database itself. The process of publishing database information in another format is called **exporting**.

When you save a table as a Web page, an HTML page is created with the data formatted approximately as it appeared in the original table. To export a table to HTML:

1. In the Database window, click the table to be saved as a Web page.
2. On the File menu, click Export.
3. The Export Table dialog box appears.
4. Click the Save In down arrow, and navigate to the place where you want to save the new file.
5. Click the Save As Type down arrow, and click HTML Documents (*.html; *.htm).
6. In the File Name box, type the new name of the file, and click Export All.

IMPORTANT

The steps listed above can be followed to export any Access object, not just tables.

QUICK REFERENCE ▼

Adjust font characteristics of a datasheet

1 Open the table in Datasheet view.

2 Select a new font from the Font list.

3 Select a new font size from the Font Size list.

4 Set the font style using the Font Style buttons on the Formatting toolbar.

Adjust the datasheet appearance and cell sizes

1 Open a table in Datasheet view.

2 Click the Fill/Back color button and select a new color for the background.

3 Click the Special Effects button and select a cell effect to be applied to the datasheet.

4 To adjust the column width automatically, double-click the lines between the columns,

or,

To adjust column width manually, position the mouse pointer over the column separator lines and drag it in either direction.

Modifying Field Properties

THE BOTTOM LINE

Every field in an Access table has a set of field properties that can be set and adjusted to make sure your data looks like you expect it to look. The properties available for any given field depend on the Data Type defined for the field. You can modify these properties in Design view by first selecting the field, then accessing the property you want to change in the lower half of the Design view window.

In Access, the data entered into fields and the appearance of that data are controlled by **field properties.** You set and adjust field properties in the Field Properties section of the Table Design view window.

FIGURE 3-7

The Design view window and the Field Properties area

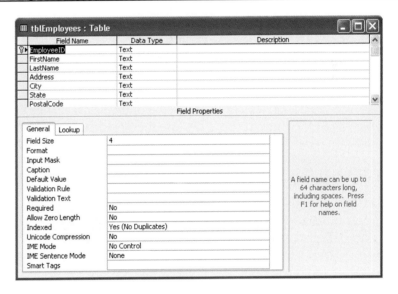

Every field has field properties specific to the data type for the field. However, a few field properties are common to almost all data types:

- The **Field Size property** limits the number of characters contained in text fields and the amount of disk space reserved for number fields. For example, if you have a field that contains state abbreviations (such as NY or CA), you could limit the size of the field to only two characters to reduce the chance for errors. Text fields can be set to hold from one to 255 characters. Number fields have several advanced settings, which are beyond the scope of this course.
- The **Format property** allows you to specify a format for the data in the field. For example, if the field will contain a date, you can choose from several date and time formats such as Short Date (*10/27/05*) or Long Date (*Wednesday, October 27, 2005*).
- The **Caption property** sets a caption for a field, which will appear as the field name—instead of the field name—when the table is in Datasheet view. For example, a field name might be *EmployeeID*

(without spaces), but if the caption is *Employee ID* (with a space), *Employee ID* (with a space) will appear on the datasheet.

■ The **Default Value property** reduces the time spent on data entry by automatically entering a default value in a field every time a new record is added to the table. This is a good feature to use if the data in a certain field is almost always the same. For example, if most of Adventure Works guests are from California, you could enter *CA* as the default value for the State field in a table containing guest addresses. If a guest comes from out of state, you can delete the default value and enter the correct state.

Modify field properties

You have seen in previous exercises that you can change the overall appearance of the datasheet. You can also modify the appearance of individual fields by modifying field properties. You will now add captions to some of the fields, change the date format of the DateHired field, and use the Field Size property to limit the size of the EmployeeID field. You will also specify a default value for the Hours field.

1 **Click tblHumanResourcesData, and click Open on the Database window toolbar.**

The table opens in Datasheet view. Note that the field names appear without spaces in them, dates appear in Short Date format (such as *2/25/98*), and the first blank record already has a default value of *0* entered in the Hours field.

2 **On the Table Datasheet toolbar, click the View button.**

The table appears in Design view, with the Employee ID cell already selected. The properties for the EmployeeID field appear in the Field Properties section of the Table Design view window.

3 In the Field Properties section, click in the Caption box, and type Employee ID (with a space).

The caption of the EmployeeID field changes to *Employee ID*.

TIP

When you click in a box for a property, an explanation of the property appears in the right side of the Field Properties section.

FIGURE 3-8

The new caption has been entered

EmployeeID Caption updated

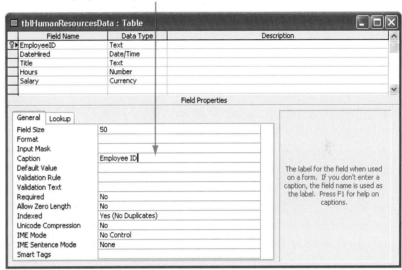

4 In the Field Properties section, click in the Field Size box, delete the existing text, and then type 4.

All employee identification numbers at Adventure Works are four characters long. Access will now limit the Field Size for the EmployeeID field to four characters.

5 In the Field Name column, click in the DateHired cell.

The properties for the DateHired field appear in the Field Properties section of the Table Design view window.

6 In the Field Properties section, click in the Format box, click the down arrow that appears, and then click Medium Date.

The format of the DateHired field changes to Medium Date. The Medium Date format displays dates as *25-Feb-98*.

7 Click in the Caption box, and type Date Hired (with a space).

The caption of the DateHired field changes to *Date Hired*.

FIGURE 3-9

The DateHired Field Properties area

DateHired field selected   Format and Caption properties updated

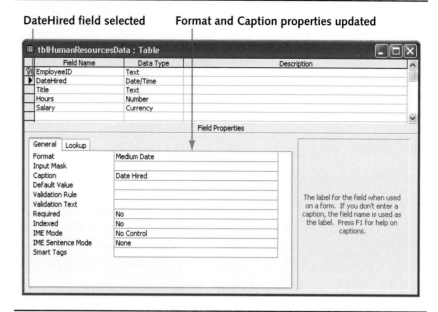

8 **In the Field Name column, click in the Hours cell.**

The properties for the Hours field appear in the Field Properties section of the Table Design view window.

9 **In the Field Properties section, click in the Default Value box, delete the existing text, and then type 40.**

The default value for the Hours field changes to *40*. This value will now appear in the blank record at the end of the current datasheet data.

FIGURE 3-10

The Hours Field Properties area

Hours is the selected field   Default property updated

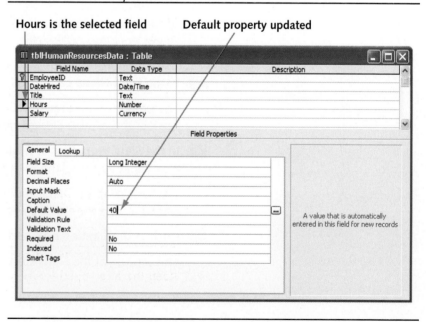

Setting a default value will not change any of the field's existing data.

10 **On the Table Design toolbar, click the Save button.**

An alert box appears, warning that some data might be lost because you changed the Field Size property for one of the fields.

11 **Click Yes.**

Access saves the table with the changes you have made.

12 **On the Table Design toolbar, click the View button.**

The table appears in Datasheet view. Note that the EmployeeID field has the caption *Employee ID* (with a space), the DateHired field has the caption *Date Hired* (with a space), the data in the DateHired field follows the Medium Date format, and the Hours field in the blank record at the bottom of the table displays a default value of *40*.

You might need to scroll down to see the Hours field in the blank record.

FIGURE 3-11

The updated fields shown in Datasheet view

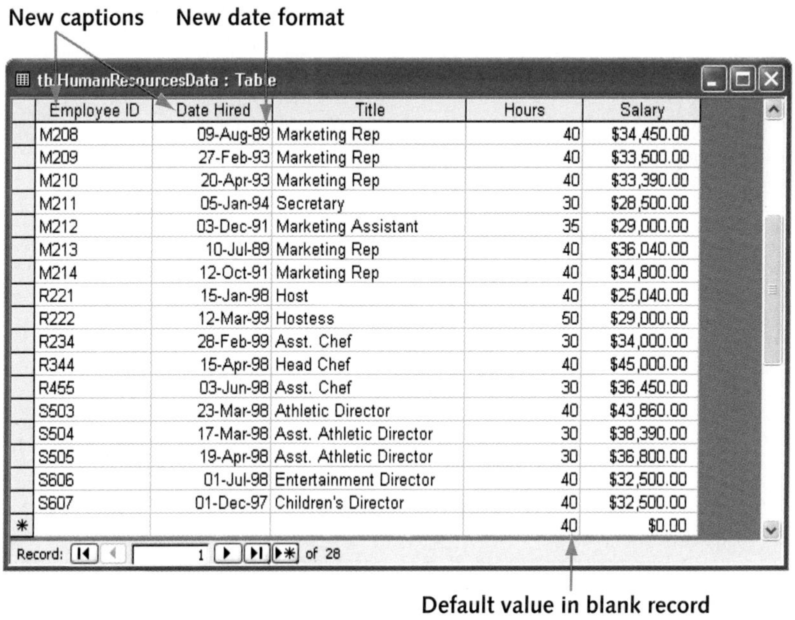

New captions   New date format

Employee ID	Date Hired	Title	Hours	Salary
M208	09-Aug-89	Marketing Rep	40	$34,450.00
M209	27-Feb-93	Marketing Rep	40	$33,500.00
M210	20-Apr-93	Marketing Rep	40	$33,390.00
M211	05-Jan-94	Secretary	30	$28,500.00
M212	03-Dec-91	Marketing Assistant	35	$29,000.00
M213	10-Jul-89	Marketing Rep	40	$36,040.00
M214	12-Oct-91	Marketing Rep	40	$34,800.00
R221	15-Jan-98	Host	40	$25,040.00
R222	12-Mar-99	Hostess	50	$29,000.00
R234	28-Feb-99	Asst. Chef	30	$34,000.00
R344	15-Apr-98	Head Chef	40	$45,000.00
R455	03-Jun-98	Asst. Chef	30	$36,450.00
S503	23-Mar-98	Athletic Director	40	$43,860.00
S504	17-Mar-98	Asst. Athletic Director	30	$38,390.00
S505	19-Apr-98	Asst. Athletic Director	30	$36,800.00
S606	01-Jul-98	Entertainment Director	40	$32,500.00
S607	01-Dec-97	Children's Director	40	$32,500.00
*			40	$0.00

Record: 1 of 28

Default value in blank record

◆ **Keep the table open for the next exercise.**

Reducing Data Entry Errors

It's easy to make mistakes when you enter data—especially a lot of data—into a table. You can simplify data entry by applying an **input mask** or **Lookup field** to fields in your table.

Input masks reduce the chance of mistakes during data entry in several ways. First, input masks limit the number of characters that you can enter. If your student ID numbers are always 6 characters long, for example, you could set the input mask to allow only six characters. Second, input masks can be set to accept only certain data types. For example, if an input mask is set to accept short dates (which use only numbers), you cannot enter alphabetical characters. Third, input masks can also be set to automatically fill in data that appear in every entry. For example, if you set an input mask for a field with a date, you could have the mask automatically enter slash marks between the day, month, and year portions of the field.

You can create an input mask by using the Input Mask Wizard. To start the wizard:

1. In Design view, click in the cell for the field that you want to contain the input mask. The field properties for the field appear in the Field Properties section of the Table Design view window.
2. In the Field Properties section, click in the Input Mask box. The Build button appears next to the box.
3. Click the Build button. The Input Mask Wizard starts.
4. Follow the wizard's instructions.

Another way to reduce mistakes during data entry is to use Lookup fields. A Lookup field reduces the chance for incorrect entries by presenting users with a drop-down list of choices for the field. With only a limited number of choices, the drop-down list reduces the chance that the user will enter an invalid value. The values in the Lookup field can be taken from another field (generally from another table) or created by the person who designs the table.

You can use the Lookup Wizard to help you create a Lookup field. To start the Lookup Wizard:

1. In Design view, click in the Data Type cell for the field that you want to contain the Lookup field, click the down arrow that appears, and click Lookup Wizard.
2. The Lookup Wizard starts.
3. Follow the wizard's instructions.

Smart Tags

Smart tags are a feature that was first introduced in Windows XP, and was available in some of the Office XP applications. In the Microsoft Office System, this feature has now been incorporated into Access. A smart tag can be defined for any field in an Access table, using Design view. The Smart Tag property is shown in the Field Properties area of the Design window.

When a smart tag is applied to a database field, the Smart Tag Action button will appear whenever the pointer is passed over or near the field defined with the tag. Clicking the button will reveal a shortcut menu that has a list of options that can be performed for the field with the tag. This could include sending e-mail to the person if the tag is applied to a name, scheduling a meeting with the person, adding the person to your contacts list, and other options. Smart tags can also be defined to retrieve stock quotes, retrieve a company report from MSN Money Central, or display your personal calendar.

While smart tags are beyond the scope of this lesson, they are a feature that promises to add even more power to an already powerful database system. The smart tags available for Access at this time are somewhat limited, but more are being developed all the time. If you would like to learn more about smart tags, you can visit the www.officesmarttags.com site.

QUICK REFERENCE ▼

Modify table field properties

1 Open the table in Design view.

2 Click in the row for the field you want to modify.

3 Click in any field property for the selected field and enter the new property, or choose a property from a drop-down list or dialog box for the property.

4 Save the table to save your changes.

Sorting Records in a Table

THE BOTTOM LINE

There will be times when you want to find specific data quickly, or view the data in a specific order. Access allows you to sort a table in ascending or descending order using any field in the table as the sort key. All other data for each record still remains associated with the sorted field, the data is just displayed in order by the selected sort field.

Even if you didn't follow a particular order when you first entered data into a table, you can quickly organize the data in a field alphabetically or numerically by performing a sort. There are two types of sorts: ascending and descending. An ascending sort organizes the data in a field from the lowest value to the highest or in alphabetical order starting with A. A descending sort has the opposite effect; it organizes the data in a field from the highest value to the lowest or in reverse alphabetical order starting with Z.

To reorganize data, you click in the field that contains the values that you want to sort and click either the Sort Ascending or Sort Descending button on the Table Datasheet toolbar. For example, Adventure Works has a table that tracks employee data and has fields for employee ID, last name, and first name, among others. To sort the records in the database by employee ID, you click in the EmployeeID field and click the Sort Ascending button. To view the employee data in alphabetical order by last name, you click in the LastName field and click the Sort Ascending button.

Even though you sort using the data in only one field in a record, all the fields in a record move together. This feature keeps related data together during sorts and prevents you from accidentally separating data within records.

Sort table data by a specific field

The tblHumanResourcesData table is open in Datasheet view, and you have modified some of the field properties in a previous exercise. You would like to see the data in descending salary order, so you will sort that field using the Sort Descending button. You then perform another sort so that the employee IDs appear in order, from lowest to highest.

1 Click in any record in the Salary field, and click the Sort Descending button on the Table Datasheet toolbar.

Access reorganizes the table in descending order by salary. The record for the employee who earns the largest salary of $45,200 appears at the top.

FIGURE 3-12

Table data sorted by Salary in descending order

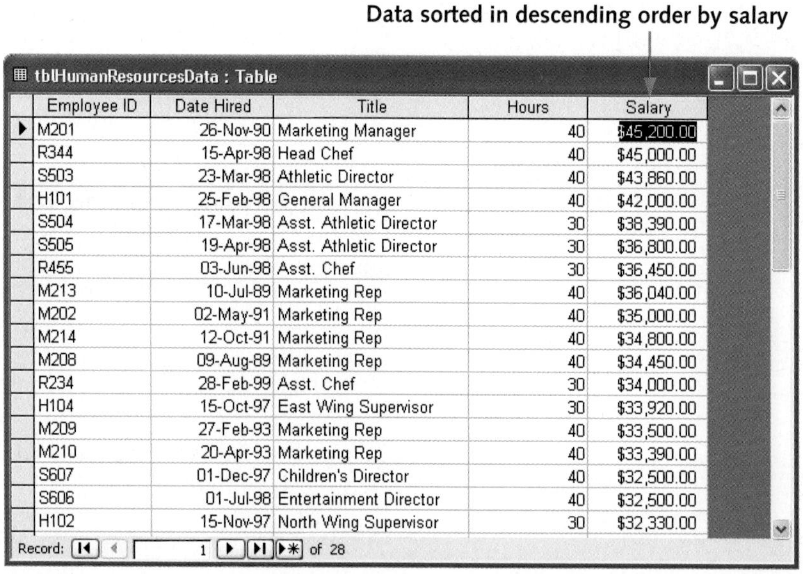

Data sorted in descending order by salary

Employee ID	Date Hired	Title	Hours	Salary
M201	26-Nov-90	Marketing Manager	40	$45,200.00
R344	15-Apr-98	Head Chef	40	$45,000.00
S503	23-Mar-98	Athletic Director	40	$43,860.00
H101	25-Feb-98	General Manager	40	$42,000.00
S504	17-Mar-98	Asst. Athletic Director	30	$38,390.00
S505	19-Apr-98	Asst. Athletic Director	30	$36,800.00
R455	03-Jun-98	Asst. Chef	30	$36,450.00
M213	10-Jul-89	Marketing Rep	40	$36,040.00
M202	02-May-91	Marketing Rep	40	$35,000.00
M214	12-Oct-91	Marketing Rep	40	$34,800.00
M208	09-Aug-89	Marketing Rep	40	$34,450.00
R234	28-Feb-99	Asst. Chef	30	$34,000.00
H104	15-Oct-97	East Wing Supervisor	30	$33,920.00
M209	27-Feb-93	Marketing Rep	40	$33,500.00
M210	20-Apr-93	Marketing Rep	40	$33,390.00
S607	01-Dec-97	Children's Director	40	$32,500.00
S606	01-Jul-98	Entertainment Director	40	$32,500.00
H102	15-Nov-97	North Wing Supervisor	30	$32,330.00

Record: 1 of 28

2 Click in any record in the EmployeeID field, and click the Sort Ascending button on the Table Datasheet toolbar.

Access reorganizes the table in ascending order by employee ID. The record for employee H101, whose employee ID number is first in ascending order, appears at the top.

FIGURE 3-13

Table data sorted by EmployeeID in ascending order

Data sorted in ascending order by Employee ID

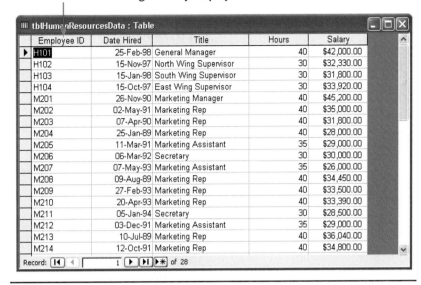

◆ Save the tblHumanResourcesData table.

◆ Keep the database open for the next exercise.

QUICK REFERENCE ▼

Sort table data by field

1 In Datasheet view, click in any record in the field you want to sort.

2 Click the Sort Ascending or the Sort Descending button on the toolbar.

Finding Records in a Table

THE BOTTOM LINE

Access enables you to quickly find specific data or records within your tables using the Find command. You can search using only one field or you can search on the entire table. Access will display only the record or records that contain the data you searched for.

Tables in Access often get very large, and finding certain data can become very time-consuming. To locate specific information in a table, you can use the **Find** command. For example, in a table listing employee names and addresses, you could use Find to locate the record for an employee with a specific last name or to locate all addresses for employees who live in Santa Barbara.

You can use the Find command to search just one field or the entire table. If you are working with a large table, limiting your search to a single field means that the search will run faster than it would if the search had to examine all the information in the table. For example, if you are searching for the employee with the last name of Chai, the search will run faster if you search just the LastName field, instead of the entire table. By default, Access searches the last field you clicked in before beginning the search. If you want to search the entire table, you can select that option in the Find and Replace dialog box.

Find specific data within a table

The tblHumanResourcesData table is still open in Datasheet view, sorted on the EmployeeID field. You will now use the Access Find command to search the table for any employees with a job title of Host.

1 Click in any cell in the Title field.

 2 On the Table Datasheet toolbar, click the Find button.

The Find and Replace dialog box appears, with Title already in the Look In box.

ANOTHER METHOD

You can also open the Find and Replace dialog box by clicking the Find or the Replace options on the Edit menu, or by pressing Ctrl+F (Find) or Ctrl+H (Replace).

IMPORTANT

You can change your search to the entire table, rather than a single field, by clicking the Look In down arrow and selecting the table name.

FIGURE 3-14

The Find and Replace dialog box

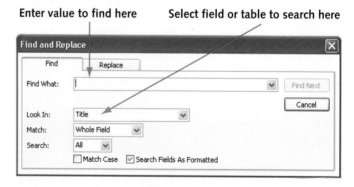

3 In the Find What box, type Host, and click Find Next.

Access selects the record that contains Host in the Title field.

FIGURE 3-15

The record containing Host is selected by the Find command

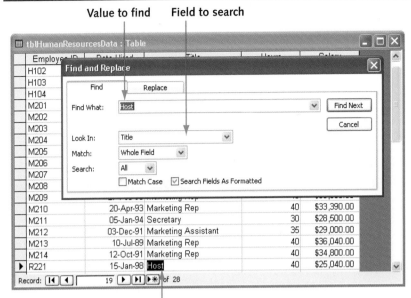

The first record found containing Host

◆ **Close the Find and Replace dialog box.**

◆ **Keep the database table open for the next exercise.**

QUICK REFERENCE ▼

Using the Find command for a specific field

1 In Datasheet view, click in any cell for the field you want to search on.

2 Click the Find button on the toolbar.

3 Enter the data value you want to search for and click Find Next.

Using Filters with a Table

THE BOTTOM LINE

In a large database, it can be difficult to locate records containing data you want to see due to the large amount of data you have to look through to find the data you are searching for. Filters make it much easier to do this. Using filters, you can cause Access to display only the records that meet the filter criteria. The other records are temporarily hidden. You can filter data in two ways. You can filter based on a specific value for a given field, or on the contents of the currently selected field.

By using a filter, you can restrict data so that only records in a table meeting certain criteria are displayed. For example, you can create a filter to view records in tblHumanResourcesData for only employees who earn more than $30,000 a year.

In Access, you can create filters in two different ways. Filter By Form allows you to specify a field and a specific value in that field to use as the filter. Filter By Selection filters based on the contents of the currently selected field.

Filters do not affect the table itself, and they can be turned on and off using the Apply Filter and Remove Filter buttons. These two buttons are actually the same button; the button name changes (although the picture on the button does not) depending on the filter state. After you have created a filter, the Apply Filter button becomes the Remove Filter button. When you click the Remove Filter button, the table reverts to its original display.

Apply and remove Access filters

You previously used the Find command to locate specific data. You can also use the Access Filter commands to find data. You will first use the Filter By Form feature to create a filter that restricts the data in tblHumanResourcesData to employees who work 40 hours each week. You will then use the Filter By Selection feature to create a filter to find only those employees who have the job title of Marketing Rep.

 1 On the Table Datasheet toolbar, click the Filter By Form button.

The Filter By Form window for tblHumanResourcesData appears.

2 Click in the Hours field, click the down arrow that appears, and then click 40.

TROUBLESHOOTING

The values in the drop-down menus are values that exist in at least one record in the table.

FIGURE 3-16

The table with the Filter By Form value set

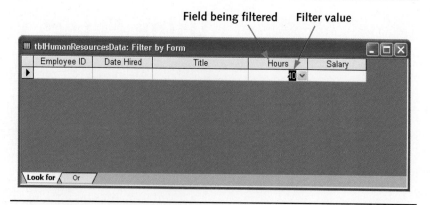

3 On the Filter/Sort toolbar, click the Apply Filter button.

The table appears, showing only records for employees who work 40 hours each week.

FIGURE 3-17

The table with the Filter By Form value applied

All records containing 40 in the Hours field

Employee ID	Date Hired	Title	Hours	Salary
H101	25-Feb-98	General Manager	40	$42,000.00
M201	26-Nov-90	Marketing Manager	40	$45,200.00
M202	02-May-91	Marketing Rep	40	$35,000.00
M203	07-Apr-90	Marketing Rep	40	$31,800.00
M204	25-Jan-89	Marketing Rep	40	$28,000.00
M208	09-Aug-89	Marketing Rep	40	$34,450.00
M209	27-Feb-93	Marketing Rep	40	$33,500.00
M210	20-Apr-93	Marketing Rep	40	$33,390.00
M213	10-Jul-89	Marketing Rep	40	$36,040.00
M214	12-Oct-91	Marketing Rep	40	$34,800.00
R221	15-Jan-98	Host	40	$25,040.00
R344	15-Apr-98	Head Chef	40	$45,000.00
S503	23-Mar-98	Athletic Director	40	$43,860.00
S606	01-Jul-98	Entertainment Director	40	$32,500.00
S607	01-Dec-97	Children's Director	40	$32,500.00
*			40	$0.00

Record: 1 of 15 (Filtered)

Note the (Filtered) status

 4 On the Table Datasheet toolbar, click the Remove Filter button.

The table returns to its original display.

5 In the Title field, click in any record containing Marketing Rep.

 6 On the Table Datasheet toolbar, click the Filter By Selection button.

The table appears, showing only records for employees with the title
Marketing Rep.

FIGURE 3-18

The table with the Filter By Selection value applied

All fields containing Marketing Rep in the Title field

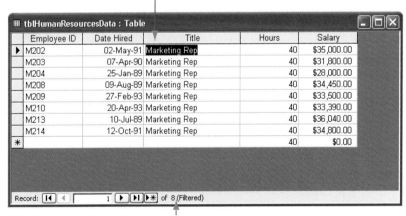

Employee ID	Date Hired	Title	Hours	Salary
M202	02-May-91	Marketing Rep	40	$35,000.00
M203	07-Apr-90	Marketing Rep	40	$31,800.00
M204	25-Jan-89	Marketing Rep	40	$28,000.00
M208	09-Aug-89	Marketing Rep	40	$34,450.00
M209	27-Feb-93	Marketing Rep	40	$33,500.00
M210	20-Apr-93	Marketing Rep	40	$33,390.00
M213	10-Jul-89	Marketing Rep	40	$36,040.00
M214	12-Oct-91	Marketing Rep	40	$34,800.00
*			40	$0.00

Record: 1 of 8 (Filtered)

Note the (Filtered) status

 7 On the Table Datasheet toolbar, click the Remove Filter button.

The table returns to its original display.

◆ Save the tblHumanResourcesData table.

QUICK CHECK

Q. How is the table data affected when either Filter By Form or Filter By Selection is applied?

A. **The table data itself is not affected at all. Data that does not meet the filter criteria is temporarily hidden, but it is restored as soon as the filter is removed.**

◆ **Close the tblHumanResourcesData table.**

◆ **Keep the database open for the next exercise.**

QUICK REFERENCE ▼

Search for data using Filter By Form

1 In Datasheet view, click the Filter By Form button on the toolbar.

2 Click the down arrow for the field or fields you want to filter, and select the filter value for each field you want to use.

3 Click the Apply Filter button to filter the data based on your selected values.

4 Click the Remove Filter button to restore all data.

Search for data using Filter By Selection

1 In Datasheet view, click in any record in any field containing the value you want to filter by.

2 Click the Filter By Selection button to apply the filter.

3 Click the Remove Filter button to restore all data.

Establishing Relationships Between Tables

THE BOTTOM LINE

One of the powerful assets of Access is the fact that it is a relational database. You have the ability to create "relationships" between tables that allow them to share data. This reduces the overall size of the database by eliminating redundant data fields, and enables you to create forms, queries, and reports containing data pulled from multiple tables.

You can establish relationships between tables that contain similar information or fields. There are three types of relationships that you can establish between the fields in tables: one-to-one, one-to-many, and many-to-many. Many-to-many relationships are beyond the scope of this lesson. The field that is used to establish a relationship between two tables is referred to as the join field.

A **one-to-one relationship** exists when two tables have an identical field containing the same information, meaning each record in a table has one matching record in a related table. For example, both tblEmployees and tblHumanResourcesData have an EmployeeID field that contains 28 records listing the employee IDs for the same 28 employees of Adventure Works. The lists are identical, which means that employee H101 has one record in tblEmployees (listing the employee's address and phone number) and one record in tblHumanResourcesData (listing the employee's salary, position, date of hire, and hours worked per week). The relationship between tblEmployees and tblHumanResourcesData is a one-to-one relationship because if there is a record containing H101 in the EmployeeID field of tblEmployees, there is one and only one record containing H101 in tblHumanResourcesData.

A **one-to-many relationship** exists when each record in a table has one or more matching records in the related table. For example, tblVendors lists the vendors that sell products to Adventure Works. Each vendor and its vendor ID appear only once in tblVendors. The products ordered from these vendors are listed in tblProducts, and because each vendor sells more than one product, the VendorID might appear several times in this table. If you established a relationship between tblVendors and tblProducts, the result would be a one-to-many relationship.

> **TIP**
>
> Most database relationships are one-to-many relationships.

An advantage to establishing relationships between tables is that you can enforce **referential integrity**, which helps prevent inaccurate values from being entered into related fields. Referential integrity requires that the record(s) in one table in a relationship have one or more corresponding records in the other table in the relationship. If referential integrity were enforced between tblVendors and tblProducts, for example, you could not enter a product into tblProducts if the vendor was not also listed in tblVendors.

Relationships between tables can be created, modified, and enforced with referential integrity from the Relationships window, which is opened by clicking the Relationships button on the Database toolbar.

> **TIP**
>
> Access 2003 allows you to print a copy of the relationships in your database. You can do this by selecting the Print Relationships option on the File menu.

You can print the relationships as they appear in the Relationships window by clicking the Print Relationships command on the File menu. When you print relationships, a report is created that contains the relationships exactly as they appear in the Relationships window. You can customize this report and even save it as a separate object in the database.

> **TIP**
>
> Reports are discussed in more detail in Lesson 6, "Designing a Report."

Create a relationship between tables

The tblProducts table contains descriptions of products sold by the vendors that Adventure Works buys from. You will now create a relationship between the tblProducts table and the tblVendors table. You will use the VendorID field that exists in both tables to establish the relationship.

1 **On the Database toolbar, click the Relationships button.**

The Relationships window appears.

2 **On the Relationship toolbar, click the Show Table button.**

The Show Table dialog box appears. In this case it lists all of the tables that are defined in the database. You can also create relationships using queries by clicking the Queries tab at the top of the dialog box.

FIGURE 3-19

The Show Table dialog box

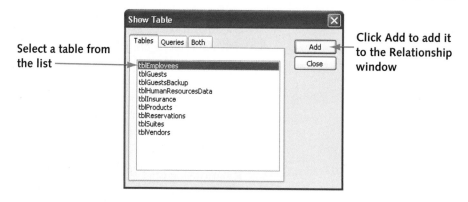

3 **Click tblProducts, and click Add.**

Access adds the field list for tblProducts to the Relationships window.

ANOTHER METHOD

You can also open the Show Table dialog box by clicking Show Table on the Relationships menu.

4 **Click tblVendors, and click Add.**

Access adds the field list for tblVendors to the Relationships window.

5 **Click Close.**

The Show Table dialog box closes, and the Relationships window becomes completely visible. The Relationships toolbar is also visible.

FIGURE 3-20

The Relationships window with tables added

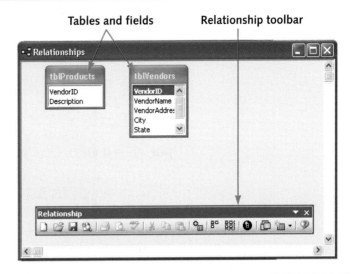

6 **In the tblProducts field list, click VendorID, and drag the field name on top of the VendorID field in the tblVendors field list.**

The Edit Relationships dialog box appears, as shown in the following figure. This dialog box shows you the tables and the fields involved in the relationship. At the bottom of the dialog box it tells you what type of relationship this is.

FIGURE 3-21

The Edit Relationships dialog box

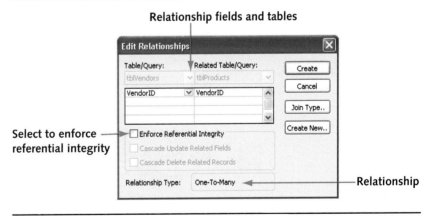

7 **Select the Enforce Referential Integrity check box, and click Create.**

The Edit Relationships dialog box closes, and a line appears between the VendorID fields in the tblProducts and tblVendors field lists, indicating that a relationship exists between these two tables.

TROUBLESHOOTING

The 1 next to tblVendors indicates that it is on the one side of the one-to-many relationship, while the infinity sign (•) next to tblProducts indicates that it is on the many side.

FIGURE 3-22

The Relationships window with a relationship shown

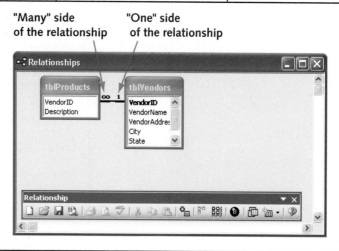

8 **On the Relationship toolbar, click the Save button.**

Access saves the Relationships window.

◆ **Keep the Relationships window open for the next exercise.**

Print the Relationships window

Now that you have established a relationship between two tables, you can print the relationships in the database. You will also attempt to add a record to one of the tables that will test the referential integrity of the relationship.

1 **Click the File menu, and then click Print Relationships.**

The relationships in the database appear as a report in Print Preview.

2 **On the Print Preview toolbar, click the Print button.**

A message box appears, telling you that Access is printing the relationship.

3 **Click the Close button in the top-right corner of the Print Preview window.**

An alert box appears, asking if you want to save changes.

4 **Click No.**

The alert box closes.

5 **Click the Close button in the top-right corner of the Relationships window.**

The Relationships window closes.

6 **In the Database window, click tblProducts to select it and then click Open on the Database window toolbar.**

The table opens in Datasheet view.

7 Click the New Record button at the bottom of the datasheet.

The insertion point is placed in the VendorID field of a blank record.

8 In the VendorID field, type RQ, and press Tab.

The insertion point moves to the Description field.

9 In the Description field, type Pillow Chocolates (1000), and press Enter.

An alert box appears, indicating that you cannot add this record because a related record is required in tblVendors. This is because you set the Enforce Referential Integrity option in the Edit Relationships dialog box.

10 Click OK.

The alert box closes. The record has not been added to the table.

11 Click in the VendorID field, delete the existing text, type WW, and then press Enter.

Access selects the text in the Description field. No alert box appears; WW is an acceptable value. The record has now been added to the table.

TROUBLESHOOTING

WW is the code for Wide World Importers, which *is* a record in tblVendors.

◆ Close the tblProducts table.

◆ Keep the database open for the next exercise.

QUICK REFERENCE ▼

Create a relationship between tables

1 Click the Relationships button on the toolbar to open the Relationships window.

2 Click the Show Table button to display the Show Table dialog box.

3 Click on each table to be added to the window and click Add, then click Close.

4 Drag the field to be used from one table to the corresponding field in the other table.

5 In the Edit Relationships dialog box, select any options you want to use and click Create.

6 Click Save to save the relationship.

Print a relationship

1 Click the File menu, and then click Print Relationships.

2 Click the Print button in the Print Preview window.

Creating Subdatasheets

THE BOTTOM LINE

When two tables are related to each other in a one-to-many relationship, Access allows you to create a subdatasheet, which is basically a table within a table. It allows you to see the data contained in both tables by expanding a record in the "one" table to see the related data contained in the "many" table without opening the second table as a new datasheet.

If you have two tables in a one-to-many relationship, you can create a **subdatasheet** to allow you to see the records from one table while the other table is open. A subdatasheet is a table within a table. For example, if you create a subdatasheet from the one-to-many relationship between tblVendors and tblProducts, you can see the products carried by each vendor listed in tblProducts by expanding the record in tblVendors.

TIP

You can use a subdatasheet to view *and* to edit related records in tables with a one-to-many relationship.

For a subdatasheet to work, there must be at least one identical field in both the table that you are working in and the table that you want to insert as a subdatasheet, and that field must be the primary key for at least one of the tables. For tblVendors and tblProducts, that field is VendorID, the primary key in tblVendors.

Create a subdatasheet for related tables

You have already established a relationship between two tables, using the primary key field from tblVendors as the relationship field. Your database now has the required elements defined to create a sub-datasheet. In this exercise, you create a subdatasheet in tblVendors that contains the related information from tblProducts.

1 **In the Database window, Click tblVendors, and click Open on the Database window toolbar.**

The table opens in Datasheet view.

2 **On the Insert menu, click Subdatasheet.**

The Insert Subdatasheet dialog box appears, with tblProducts already selected.

3 **Click OK.**

The Insert Subdatasheet dialog box closes, and tblVendors appears in Datasheet view, with plus signs (+) to the left of the records, indicating the presence of subdatasheets.

TROUBLESHOOTING

To delete a subdatasheet, point to Subdatasheet on the Format menu, and click Remove.

FIGURE 3-23

The tblVendors datasheet with subdatasheets defined

Plus signs indicate a subdatasheet is present.
Click the plus sign to see the subsheet.

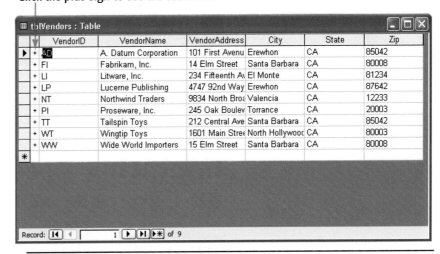

4 Click the plus sign (+) to the left of the first record, for VendorID AD,
A. Datum Corporation.

The subdatasheet of products offered by A. Datum Corporation, taken
from tblProducts, appears.

FIGURE 3-24

The tblVendors datasheet with a subdatasheet visible

Plus sign becomes a minus
sign when clicked   Subdatasheet for vendor

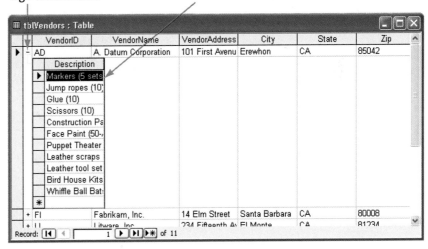

TIP

You can enter new data directly into a subdatasheet by clicking in the
first empty record in the subdatasheet and typing.

◆ Save the tblVendors table.

◆ Close tblVendors.

◆ Keep the database open for the next exercise.

QUICK REFERENCE ▼

Create a subdatasheet and view the subdatasheet

1 Open the table on the "one" side of the relationship in Datasheet view.

2 Select the Subdatasheet option from the Insert menu.

3 Select the table on the "many" side of the relationship, if necessary, and click OK.

4 Click the plus sign next to any record to view the subdatasheet for that record.

QUICK CHECK

Q. What is required for a subdatasheet to work?

A. **For a subdatasheet to work, there must be at least one identical field in each of the two tables involved, and it must be a primary key in one of the tables.**

Importing Records from an External Source

THE BOTTOM LINE

Since a database management system (DBMS) such as Access provides such powerful and flexible methods for working with data, you might want to convert other existing files to a database table. Access can import text data from a word processing file, spreadsheet data, Web pages, or even from other database files and database programs and automatically create Access tables from those files, or add data to existing tables. Some requirements have to be met for this to be successful, but it provides an easy method for putting the power of a database to work on virtually any type of data.

When adding data to tables, you might find that some of the data that you want in your database already exists in a Microsoft Excel worksheet, an HTML file, a text file, or a table from another database program. Although you could print the data and type it in your database, it is easier to **import** the information into Access from the source.

To import data, the field names in the source must be identical to the field names in the table where the data is being copied. Also, the data types in the source must be compatible with the data types in the table where the data is being copied. For example, if a field in the source contains text and you attempt to copy it into a table for which the corresponding field is a number, you'll receive an error message.

◆ **Make sure you have access to the ImportPractice file in the Lesson 03 folder in the Access Prractice folder.**

Import Excel spreadsheet data to an Access table

The Access Practice folder contains an Excel spreadsheet file. You will now import this file from the practice file folder to create a new table within the Adventure Works 03 database.

1 **On the File menu, point to Get External Data, and click Import.**

The Import dialog box appears.

2 **In the Look In box, verify that the Access Practice folder is selected.**

You will see a list of the database files displayed in the file list window. You will not see the ImportPractice file because the Files Of Type box at the bottom of the dialog box is set to look for Access database files.

3 **Click the Files Of Type down arrow, and locate and click on the Microsoft Excel (*.xls) option.**

When you change the file type, the ImportPractice file will become visible in the file list window.

TROUBLESHOOTING

If it takes a long time to import a spreadsheet, an error might have occurred. You can cancel the import process by pressing the Ctrl+Break keys.

4 **Click the ImportPractice file name to select it, and then click Import.**

The first Import Spreadsheet Wizard dialog box appears. When importing Excel data, this dialog box lets you choose to import a worksheet, or a named range.

FIGURE 3-25

The first Import Spreadsheet Wizard dialog box

Show Worksheets option

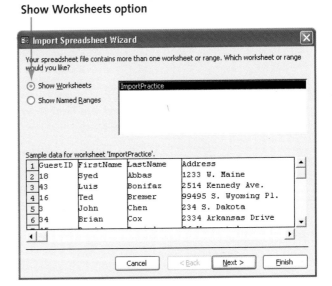

TROUBLESHOOTING

If you encounter problems while importing records, Access will add a row to your table called Import Errors. For a list of the errors, double-click the Import Errors table in the Tables section of the Database window

5 **Verify that the Show Worksheets option is selected, and click Next.**

The next Import Spreadsheet Wizard dialog box appears. This next dialog box allows you to tell the wizard if the data being imported contains field labels, which it does in this case.

TIP

The column headings (field names) for the imported data appear in the row to the right of the number 1.

FIGURE 3-26

The second Import Spreadsheet Wizard dialog box

Select if the first row of the data to be imported contains field names

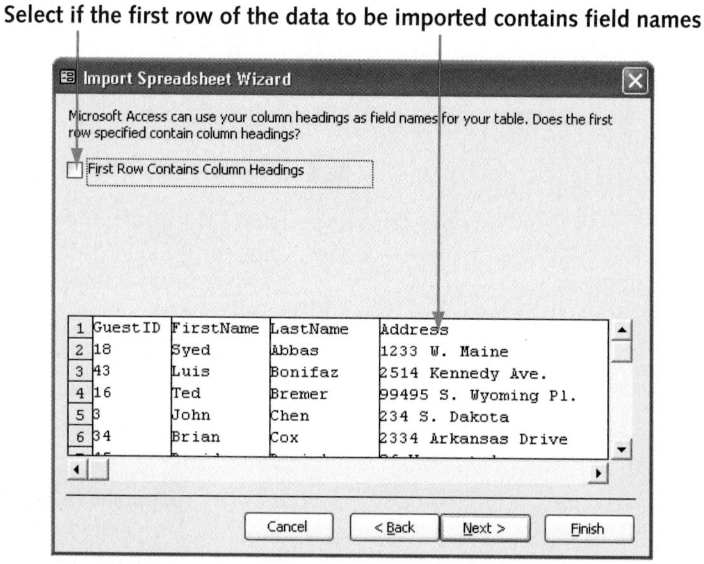

6 **Select the First Row Contains Column Headings check box, and click Next.**

The next Import Spreadsheet Wizard dialog box appears, as shown in the following figure. This dialog box allows you to specify whether you are importing to a new database table or to an existing table.

FIGURE 3-27

The third Import Spreadsheet Wizard dialog box

Import to a new or existing table

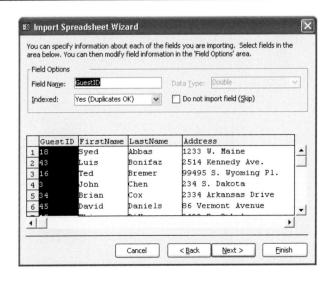

TROUBLESHOOTING

If you choose the In An Existing Table option, you must be sure that the field names and data types of the data that you are importing match those in the existing table.

7 Verify that the In A New Table option is selected, and click Next.

The next Import Spreadsheet Wizard dialog box appears. This dialog box allows you to choose fields in the file being imported that you do not want to import by selecting the Do Not Import Field (Skip) check box.

FIGURE 3-28

The fourth Import Spreadsheet Wizard dialog box

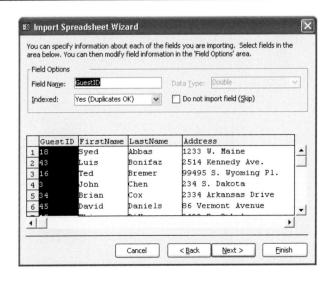

8 Click Next to accept all fields.

The next Import Spreadsheet Wizard dialog box appears. This dialog box allows you to set a primary key yourself, or let the wizard choose a primary key field, or to not set a primary key field at all.

FIGURE 3-29

The fifth Import Spreadsheet Wizard dialog box

Select a primary key option

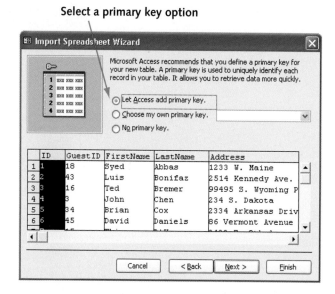

9 Click the Choose My Own Primary Key option, verify that GuestID appears in the box to the right, and then click Next.

GuestID is selected as the primary key, and the next Import Spreadsheet Wizard dialog box appears. This is the final dialog box in the Import process and it allows you to specify the name for the table being created.

IMPORTANT

You can always change or delete the primary key specification in Design view after the table is created.

FIGURE 3-30

The final Import Spreadsheet Wizard dialog box

Specify a name for the table

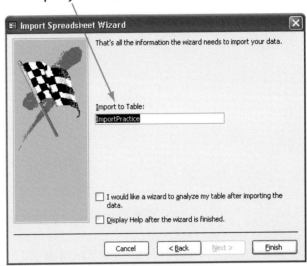

TROUBLESHOOTING

If you do not have the Table Analyzer Wizard installed on your computer, the I Would Like A Wizard To Analyze My Table After Importing The Data check box will not appear.

10 In the Import To Table box, delete the existing text, and type tblImportPractice.

TIP

If you leave the Display Help After Wizard Is Finished check box selected, Access Help will open after you import the table.

---

11 Verify that the I Would Like A Wizard To Analyze My Table After Importing The Data and Display Help After Wizard Is Finished check boxes are cleared, and click Finish.

A message box appears, telling you that Access is finished importing the table.

12 Click OK.

The new table, tblImportPractice, now appears in the list of tables in the Database window.

 13 Click tblImportPractice, if necessary, and click Open on the Database window toolbar.

The table opens in Datasheet view.

FIGURE 3-31

The imported table in Datasheet view

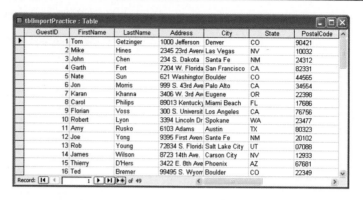

◆ **Close tblImportPractice.**

Copying Records into a Table

If the records that you need for your table already exist in some other database table, these records can be copied from one table to another, even if the other table is in another database. If you want to copy data from one table to another, you have to follow the same rules that you follow when importing data from an external source: The field names in the originating table must be identical to the field names in the table into which the data is being copied, and the data types in the originating table must be compatible with the data types in the table into which data is copied.

To copy data from one table to another, you use the Copy and Paste buttons. After you select the data to be copied and click the Copy button, the data is saved on the **Office Clipboard**. The Office Clipboard is a special file accessible in Microsoft Excel, Word, Access, Outlook, or PowerPoint and can be used to copy and paste data within a file, between files, or between applications.

The Office Clipboard can hold up to twenty-four different items. To choose which saved item will be pasted, to clear the clipboard, or to paste all the items on the clipboard, you display the Office Clipboard from the Edit menu, and then click on any item in the Clipboard that you want to paste into the current database.

QUICK REFERENCE ▼

Import data from an external source to a new table

1 Click the File menu, point to Get External Data, and then click Import.

2 Use the Import dialog box to locate the file to be imported.

3 Follow the steps of the Import Wizard and choose the options in each step that pertain to the file being imported.

4 In the final Import Wizard dialog box, enter a name for the table and click Finish.

5 You can then open the table in Datasheet view to see if the import process worked correctly.

QUICK CHECK

Q. What is required when importing external data into an existing Access table?

A. The field names in the file being imported must match the field names in the table being imported to.

◆ **If you are continuing to other lessons:**

Close the Adventure Works 03 Database.

Keep Access open for the next lesson.

◆ **If you are not continuing to other lessons:**

Close the Adventure Works 03 Database.

Close Access.

Key Points

✔ *Access allows you to quickly and easily change the format of table datasheets.*

✔ *You can open a table in Design view to modify field properties.*

✔ *Tables can be sorted into ascending or descending order on any field in the table.*

✔ *You can use the Find command to locate specific records in a table.*

✔ *Filter By Form and Filter By Selection can be used to reduce the amount of visible data and allow you to focus only on records containing data you want to see.*

✔ *Access allows you to establish relationships among tables that have common fields.*

✔ *When tables have a one-to-many relationship between them, you can create subdatasheets to view the data from both tables.*

✔ *If you have external files that you want to convert to a database, you can import those files into an Access table.*

Quick Quiz

True/False

T F **1.** The default format for an Access table datasheet is 12-point Helvetica, with black gridlines.

T F **2.** You can change the background color of a table datasheet using the Fill/Back Color button on the Formatting toolbar.

T F **3.** The maximum number of characters that a text field can hold is determined by the Max Digits field property.

T F **4.** You can use the Sort Ascending and the Sort Descending buttons to sort data in up to three different fields at one time.

T F **5.** A subdatasheet allows you to view the data from the related table while viewing the datasheet for the primary table in the relationship.

Multiple Choice

1. Which of the following actions can you perform to change the appearance of a table datasheet?
   a. change the font size
   b. apply special effects to cells
   c. change column sizes
   d. All of the above

2. Which of the following would you do to cause a datasheet column to expand so the largest entry in that column is visible?
   a. right-click the column, then click Expand from the pop-up menu
   b. double-click the line between the column to expand and the column to its right
   c. click once on the field name for the column
   d. click the column selector to select it, click the Edit menu, and then click Expand

3. Which property below allows you to specify an initial value to automatically appear in a new table record?
   a. Caption
   b. Format
   c. Default Value
   d. Initial Value

4. Which feature of a relationship do you set to require that a record being entered into the "many" table of a one-to-many relationship must have a corresponding record in the "one" table?
   a. referential integrity
   b. cascade entry
   c. mirror validation
   d. None of the above

5. The process of copying data from some external file into an Access table is referred to as _____.
   a. extrapolation
   b. exporting
   c. importing
   d. data acquisition

Short Answer

1. What is a subdatasheet?
2. What is referential integrity?
3. What are the two types of filters?
4. What is the difference between a one-to-one relationship and a one-to-many relationship?
5. How do you import records?
6. What does the Find command do?
7. What field property can be used to limit the number of characters allowed in a field with a Text data type?
8. What do input masks and Lookup fields do?

9. What are the two types of sorts?

10. What does a filter do?

On Your Own

Exercise 1

Import the Excel worksheet ImportPractice, and name the new table tblGuestList. Change the MailingList field to display either Yes or No. (Hint: Use the Format property for the field.) Sort the table so that the records are arranged alphabetically by last name. Set the text to 12-point Bookman Old Style (choose any other font if that is not available on your system), and make the background of the table yellow. Adjust the column widths so that all the text is visible. Search for the address that includes the word Carter. Use the Filter By Form button to find only records for guests from CA. Save and close the table.

Exercise 2

Set up a one-to-many relationship between tblSuites and tblReservations. Enforce referential integrity so that you cannot accidentally make a reservation for a suite that doesn't exist. Print a copy of the relationships in the database, and do not save the report that Access creates. Save and close the Relationships window.

Exercise 3

Open the tblInsurance table in the Adventure Works 03 database and examine it in Datasheet view. Open the tblHumanResourcesData table in Design view and add a field named PlanID. Set its Data Type and Field Length properties according to the data you see in the tblInsurance table. Create a meaningful Caption for the field, and assign one of the existing plan IDs as a Default value. Save the tblHumanResourcesData table and switch to Datasheet view. Assign one of the existing health plan codes to each employee in the tblHumanResourcesData table. Close the table when finished.

One Step Further

Exercise 1

Open the Adventure Works 03 database and then open the Relationships window. Create a one-to-many relationship between the tblInsurance and the tblHumanResourcesData table, using the PlanID field as the join field. Make sure to enforce referential integrity. Print the relationship. Open the tblHumanResourcesData table and insert a new employee (don't forget to enter the new employee in the tblEmployees table as well). Assign a new ID to the employee and create the other required data. Try to assign a Health Plan code of **F**. Does Access let you assign that code? If not, assign some other valid health plan ID for the record.

Exercise 2

Open the tblHumanResourcesData table in Datasheet view. Sort the table in ascending sequence using the Health Plan data field. Print the sorted table. Sort the table again using the Employee ID field to return it to its original sequence. Use Filter By Selection to select and filter the table on each of the Health Plan ID codes, starting with A, then B, etc. Print the results of each filter before removing the filter. Compare the employees returned for each filter to the list of all employees sorted by health code. Do all of the employees show up in each list for each plan ID? Open the tblInsurance table and insert a subdatasheet, if one is not already present, using the relationship between the insurance and human resources table. Expand the subdatasheet for each health plan ID and compare the list of employees to the results of your filter printouts for each plan ID code.

LESSON 4

Creating and Using Queries

After completing this lesson, you will be able to:

✔ *Create and run a query.*
✔ *Specify criteria in a query.*
✔ *Use comparison operators in a query.*
✔ *Create a calculated field.*
✔ *Create a multiple-table query.*
✔ *Print a query.*

KEY TERMS

- AutoJoin
- calculated field
- comparison operator
- criteria
- expression
- join
- join line
- multiple-table query
- query
- select query
- wildcard

Queries give Microsoft Access the ability to deliver information to people in a virtually unlimited number of ways. A **query** is a database object that allows you to extract fields and records from tables, based on criteria that you provide. Creating a query is like asking Access a question. When you run the query, Access provides the answer.

The most basic type of query in Access is the **select query**, which extracts data from one or more tables and displays the results in a format almost identical to Datasheet view for tables. The select queries that you create are limited only by the data in the database and your own ingenuity. You can create select queries that use fields from more than one table, reorder data in tables, and perform calculations on the data in tables. For example, the employees at the reservation desk of Adventure Works outdoor vacation resort use a query that, when run, extracts records for all rooms occupied during the current month, sorts the records by room number, and calculates the total charges for each room. All the queries created in this lesson are select queries.

At first glance, a query may appear to be nothing more than a filter or a sort mechanism. In Lesson 3, "Working With Tables", you used filters and the Sort Ascending and Sort Descending buttons to view a subset of the overall data in a table, and sort it into a different sequence than it is normally displayed. You will soon discover that queries are much more powerful and versatile than simple filter and sort commands. There are some significant differences between queries and the filter and sort commands, including:

- One advantage to the Filter and Sort commands is that they are easier to apply and can be performed much faster than creating a query.

- One disadvantage to the Filter and Sort commands is that they cannot be saved. When you create a query, it can be saved and instantly re-run any time you need it. With a Filter or Sort, you need to reapply the command each time you want to use it.
- Another disadvantage to the Filter and Sort is that they can only be used on the table that is currently open. A query can be used to extract data from multiple tables or queries, and the tables and queries it accesses do not need to be open when the query is run.

Queries and the tables that they are based on are interactive. If you change the data in the query results datasheet, the data in the table(s) that the query is based on will also be changed. Alternatively, if you change the data in the table(s), the query results will also change.

IMPORTANT

Before you can use the practice files in this lesson, be sure you install them from the book's companion CD to their default location. For additional information on how to find and open files used in this book, see the "Using the CD-ROM" section at the beginning of this book. To complete the procedures in this lesson, you will need to use the Adventure Works 04 database file.

Creating and Running a Query

THE BOTTOM LINE

In essence, a query is a question you ask about your database. It is a means of extracting and viewing data that meets specific conditions, or displaying the data in a different layout or order than the table itself. Although similar to a filter, a query is much more versatile. You can specify selection criteria for the fields used in a query, and Access also provides a set of comparison operators to use when creating queries. In addition, when relationships exist, a query can extract data from multiple tables and display it as one common datasheet.

In Access, you can create a query either in Design view or by using the Simple Query Wizard. If you know the information that you want to extract and want to create the query without using or knowing the conventions for creating a query, the Simple Query Wizard is the easier approach. After you understand how queries are composed and structured, you might find it easier and more powerful to create queries in Design view. A query can be modified in Design view after being created, regardless of how it is created.

After you create a query, you run it by clicking the Run button on the Query Design toolbar. When the data that meets the query specifications has been pulled from the data sources (tables or other queries) Access will display the query results in a datasheet of rows and columns, just like a table.

◆ Be sure to start Access before beginning this exercise.

◆ Before beginning this exercise, open the Adventure Works 04 database file from the Access Practice folder on your hard disk.

Use the Simple Query wizard to create a query

The Simple Query Wizard is an Access feature that allows you to quickly and easily create a select query. You will use the Adventure Works 04 database and the Simple Query to create a query. The query you create here will extract only the FirstName, LastName, and HomePhone fields from the tblEmployees table and display them in datasheet format.

◆ Open the Adventure Works 04 database file from the Access Practice folder on your hard disk.

1 On the Objects bar, click Queries, if necessary.

The options to Create Query In Design View and Create Query By Using Wizard appear. There are currently no queries in the Adventure Works 04 database.

FIGURE 4-1

The Database window with Queries selected

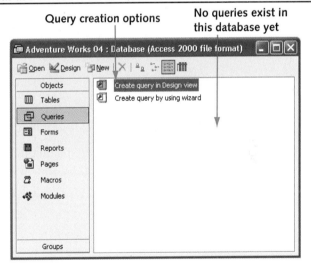

IMPORTANT

When creating queries, in order to select fields from more than one table, the fields in the different tables must first be in a relationship. Multiple-table queries are discussed later in this lesson.

2 Double-click Create Query By Using Wizard.

The first Simple Query Wizard dialog box appears. In this dialog box you select the table or query on which this query is to be based. After selecting the data source, you then select the fields to include from that source.

FIGURE 4-2

The first Simple Query Wizard dialog box

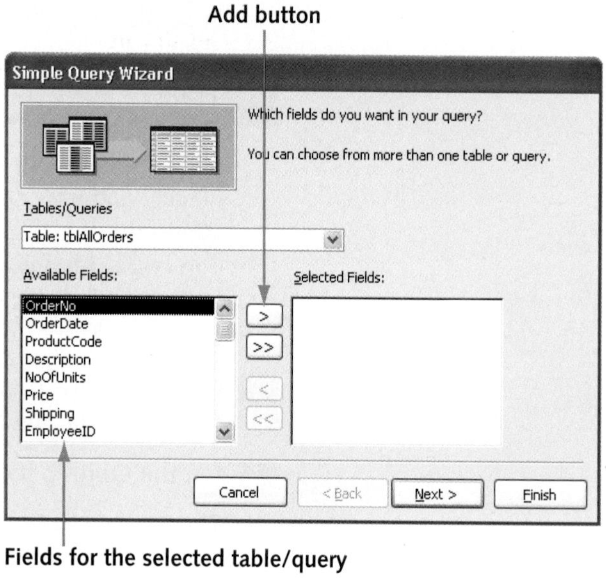

Add button

Fields for the selected table/query

ANOTHER METHOD

You can also start the Simple Query wizard by clicking Create Query By Using Wizard once to select it, and then clicking the Open button or the Design button on the Database Window toolbar.

---

3 **Click the Tables/Queries down arrow, and click Table: tblEmployees.**

The fields in tblEmployees appear in the Available Fields list.

4 **Click FirstName in the Available Fields list, and click the > (Add) button.**

Access adds the FirstName field to the Selected Fields list.

ANOTHER METHOD

You can also double-click the field name to move it to the Selected Fields list. You could also add all fields from this table by clicking the >> (Add All) button.

---

5 **Click LastName in the Available Fields list, and click the > (Add) button.**

Access adds the LastName field to the Selected Fields list.

6 **Click HomePhone in the Available Fields list, and click the > (Add) button.**

Access adds the HomePhone field to the Selected Fields list. You have now selected all of the fields to be used in this query.

7 **Click Next.**

The next, and final, Simple Query Wizard dialog box appears.

FIGURE 4-3

The final Simple Query Wizard dialog box

Name the query here

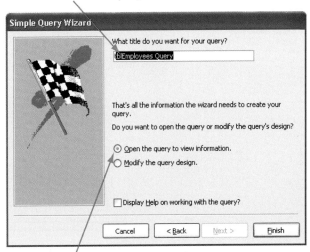

Choose to open in Data view or Design view here

TROUBLESHOOTING

If you click the Modify The Query Design option button, the query
will appear in Design view when you click the Finish button.

---

8 **In the What Title Do You Want For Your Query? box, type
qryEmployeePhoneList, and verify that the Open The Query
To View Information option is selected, and then click Finish.**

The query appears in Datasheet view. Note that only the FirstName,
LastName, and HomePhone fields from tblEmployees appear in
qryEmployeePhoneList. Also note that the query name has the "qry"
prefix, which is the standard used for queries according to the
Leszynski naming convention discussed in Lesson 1.

FIGURE 4-4

The query in Datasheet view

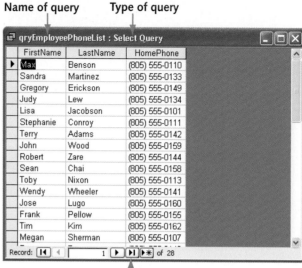

Name of query   Type of query

FirstName	LastName	HomePhone
Max	Benson	(805) 555-0110
Sandra	Martinez	(805) 555-0133
Gregory	Erickson	(805) 555-0149
Judy	Lew	(805) 555-0134
Lisa	Jacobson	(805) 555-0101
Stephanie	Conroy	(805) 555-0111
Terry	Adams	(805) 555-0142
John	Wood	(805) 555-0159
Robert	Zare	(805) 555-0144
Sean	Chai	(805) 555-0158
Toby	Nixon	(805) 555-0113
Wendy	Wheeler	(805) 555-0141
Jose	Lugo	(805) 555-0160
Frank	Pellow	(805) 555-0155
Tim	Kim	(805) 555-0162
Megan	Sherman	(805) 555-0107

Navigation buttons

◆ Close qryEmployeePhoneList.

◆ Keep the database open for the next exercise.

QUICK CHECK

Q. How do I start the Simple Query Wizard?

A. Double-click the Create Query By Using Wizard option in the Queries area of the Database window.

QUICK REFERENCE ▼

Creating a query using the Simple Query Wizard

1 Click Queries on the Objects bar, and then double-click Create Query By Using Wizard.

2 Select the table or query to use from the Tables/Queries list.

3 Select the fields to be used from the Available Fields list and click Next.

4 Type a name for the query.

5 Select an option to open it in Design view or Datasheet view and click Finish.

Specifying Criteria in a Query

THE BOTTOM LINE

One reason for creating and running a query is to limit the amount of data displayed so you can look only at records containing the data that interests you. In a large table, it can be very difficult to spot the records that have the information you are looking for. You can reduce the amount of data displayed in a query by specifying criteria for your query. Only the fields and records that match all of the criteria you specify will be displayed when you run the query.

You can refine query results by setting **criteria** for the query. Query criteria are the rules that the query follows to determine what information to extract. When you set criteria for a query, Access extracts only fields and records that match your criteria.

When a query is displayed in Design view, you will see the Criteria row in the Design grid section.

FIGURE 4-5

The query Design grid and the Criteria row

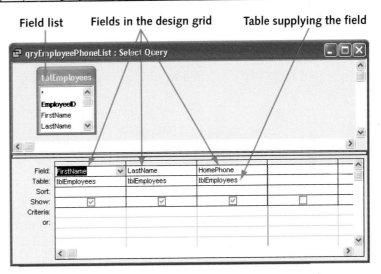

You use the Criteria row to specify criteria that limit query results. An alphabetical phrase, such as LI, is one kind of criterion that you can specify in a query. For example, suppose that you have a table that tracks orders placed by Adventure Works. You want to view all orders placed with the Litware, Inc. vendor, which has the vendor code LI. If you create a query with the letters LI entered in the Criteria row of the Vendor Code column, only orders for Litware, Inc. would appear in the query result.

You can also customize criteria by using a **wildcard**. A wildcard is a character such as an asterisk or question mark that can be used in place of one or more characters in a criterion. The following table shows the wildcards that you can use in the Criteria row to restrict query results.

Wildcards are usually used in fields with a Text data type, but they can also be used with other data types. For example, you could type *2/*/05* to extract records for any date in February 2005.

Wildcard	Usage	Example
*	Matches any one or more character(s).	*wh** finds *what, white,* and *wh2gH.*
?	Matches any one alphabetic character.	*w?ll* finds *wall, will,* and *well.*
[*]	Matches any character(s) within the brackets.	*m[ae]ll* finds *mall* and *mell,* but not *mill.*
[!*]	Matches any character(s) not in the brackets.	*m[!ae]ll* finds *mill* and *mull,* but not *mall* or *mell.*
[*-*]	Matches any character in a range. The range must be in ascending order (A to Z, not Z to A).	*m[a-c]d* finds *mad, mbd,* and *mcd.*

Wildcard	Usage	Example
#	Matches any single numeric character.	*10#* finds *100* and *109.*

Wildcards are a convenient way to extract information that follows a pattern or for which you remember only part of the value. For example, an asterisk instructs Access to find fields with one or more characters in that part of the field. Entering *A** as the criterion for a FirstName field will locate records containing first names that begin with *A*; *Amy, Alice, Alex, Andrew,* and *A* (by itself) all meet the criterion. You can also use an asterisk at the beginning or middle of a criterion statement. For example, to find all first names that contain the letter *a*, you would type **a**.

You can specify criteria for more than one field in a query at a time. If you enter a criterion in more than one column in the Criteria row, the query results will include only records that match both criteria. For example, you can create a query that extracts records from tblEmployees for employees whose last names begin with B *and* who began work in 1996.

◆ **Make sure the Database window is displayed and Queries is selected on the Objects bar.**

Create a query in Design view

You used the Simple Query Wizard in the previous exercise to create a query. You can also create queries in Design view, as you will do now. You will create a query using the tblHumanResourcesData table to extract a list of all employees who have the text Marketing in their job title.

1 **Double-click Create Query In Design View.**

The Query Design view window and the Show Table dialog box appear. The Show Table dialog box lets you add tables (or queries) to the Query Design window.

ANOTHER METHOD

To create a new query in Design view, you can also click the Create Query In Design View option once to select it, and then click the Design button on the Database window toolbar.

2 **In the Show Table dialog box, click tblHumanResourcesData, and click Add.**

A field list displaying the fields in the tblHumanResourcesData table appears at the top of the Query Design view window.

ANOTHER METHOD

You can also double-click the table name to add it to the Query Design view window.

3 **Close the Show Table dialog box by clicking the Close button.**

The Show Table dialog box closes, and the Query Design view window becomes completely visible.

FIGURE 4-6

The Query Design view

Unnamed query

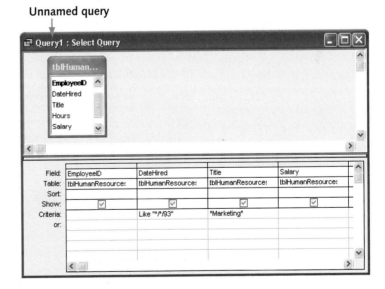

CHECK THIS OUT ▼

Create a Query Quickly
Did you know that you can create a query using all of the fields in a given table by double-clicking the asterisk (*) at the top of the field list for the file? If you do that, Access will place the table name in the first blank Field column in the design grid.

4 **In the tblHumanResourcesData field list, click EmployeeID, and drag the field name to the first blank cell in the Field row in the Design grid.**

Access displays the EmployeeID field name in the Field row, and also note that Access adds the table, or source, name below it.

ANOTHER METHOD

You can also double-click the field name in the field list to add it to the first blank cell in the Field row. You can add all fields to the grid by double-clicking the title bar for the table field list to select all the fields, and then dragging the selected set of field names to the Field Name row.

5 **Repeat step 4 to add the DateHired, Title, and Salary fields to the blank cells in the Field row.**

Your design grid should now contain four fields and should resemble the following figure.

FIGURE 4-7

The query design grid with fields added

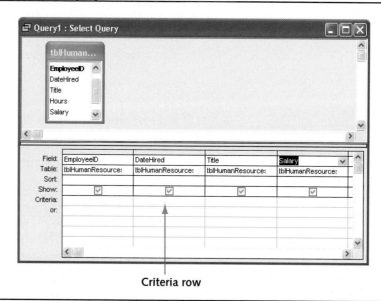

Criteria row

TROUBLESHOOTING

If you don't see another blank cell in the Field row, use the scroll bar at the bottom of the Design grid to scroll to the right.

IMPORTANT

For step 6 to work, set your computer to show two-digit years (05) instead of four-digit years (2005). For additional information on setting the years to two digits or four digits, see the "Using the CD-ROM" section at the beginning of this book.

6 **In the DateHired column, click in the Criteria row, and type ***/*/93**.**

When run, the query will find only records for employees who were hired during 1993.

TROUBLESHOOTING

When you move the insertion point to another cell, the word *Like* and a pair of quotation marks appear in the cell with the criterion. The word *Like* is inserted before any criterion that uses a wildcard, and the quotation marks are placed around the string of characters that Access will use to restrict data.

7 In the Title column, click in the Criteria row, type *Marketing*, and then press Enter.

When run, the query will find only records for employees who were hired during 1993 *and* whose job title includes the word *Marketing*.

FIGURE 4-8

The query design grid with criteria added

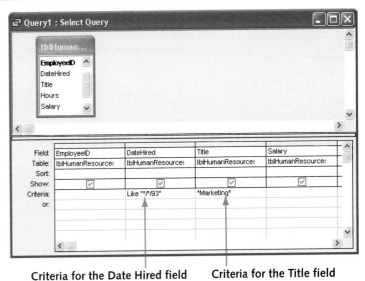

Criteria for the Date Hired field   Criteria for the Title field

8 On the Query Design toolbar, click the Run button.

The query results appear in datasheet format, displaying records for any employee hired during 1993 whose job title includes the word *Marketing*.

FIGURE 4-9

The query in Datasheet view

Only employees hired in 93 appear in the results datasheet.

Only employees with Marketing titles appear in the results datasheet.

	EmployeeID	DateHired	Title	Salary
▶	M207	05/07/93	Marketing Assistant	$26,000.00
	M209	02/27/93	Marketing Rep	$33,500.00
	M210	04/20/93	Marketing Rep	$33,390.00
*				$0.00

Record: 1 of 3

◆ Close the query without saving changes.

◆ Keep the database open for the next exercise.

QUICK REFERENCE ▼

Create a query in Design view and add criteria

1 Double-click the Create Query In Design View option in the Database window.

2 Using the Show Table dialog box, add a table to the Design grid and close the Show Table dialog box.

3 Drag the fields to be included from the table field list to the Field row of the Design grid.

4 Click in the Criteria row for any field and enter the criteria for each field that requires it.

5 Click the Run button to run the query.

Using Comparison Operators in a Query

THE BOTTOM LINE

When a query includes numeric fields, you can use comparison operators to select values based on a range of values. For example, if you were searching a human relations (personnel) database, you could easily create a query to find any employee of the institution or business who is making more than $50,000.00 a year. The comparison operators can be used with great effect when creating queries that are searching for a range of data values.

For fields containing numbers, you can use a **comparison operator** in a criterion to define a range of values for one or more fields, such as data greater than, less than, or equal to a specific value. A comparison operator is a character or series of characters that defines the values that the query should find. For example, if you are modifying a table that tracks orders placed by Adventure Works, you could use a comparison operator in a query to extract all orders for which the price is $500 or more. If you were searching an academic database, you could search for all students with a 4.0 GPA for a specified school term.

TIP

While primarily used for numeric fields, comparison operators can also be used with Date/Time and Text fields. For example, typing >=*Smith* will find all names after and including *Smith* in the alphabet. Typing *Between 10/12/2004 and 10/12/2005* will find all dates between the dates specified.

The following table describes some of the operators that you can use to specify criteria in a query.

Operator	Meaning	Example	Effect
>	Greater than	>50	Displays records with values greater than 50.
<	Less than	<100	Displays records with values less than 100.
>=	Greater than or equal to	>=10	Displays records with values greater than or equal to 10.
<=	Less than or equal to	<=20	Displays records with values less than or equal to 20.
Between... and...	Between two numbers	Between 30 and 40	Displays records with values between 30 and 40, including 30 and 40.
=	Equal to	=30	Displays records with a value of 30.
<>	Not equal to	<>30	Displays records that do not have a value of 30.

As with other types of criteria, comparison operators are also used in the Criteria row in the Query Design view window. To create a query to extract orders with a price of $500 or more, you would type *>=500* in the Criteria row of the Price column.

◆ **Make sure the Database window is displayed and Queries is selected on the Objects bar.**

Create a query using comparison operators

You have created a couple of simple queries so far using two different methods. You will now create a query that uses comparison operators to extract a range of data. You will now create a query based on tblAllOrders that will return a list of orders for which the price per unit was $100 or more. Then you will restrict the query to find only orders for more than one unit.

1 **Double-click Create Query In Design View.**

The Query Design view window and the Show Table dialog box appear; tblAllOrders is already selected in the Show Table dialog box because it is the first table in the database.

2 **In the Show Table dialog box, click Add, and then click Close.**

The Show Table dialog box closes, and the field list for tblAllOrders appears in the top section of the Query Design view window.

3 In the tblAllOrders field list, double-click OrderNo.

The OrderNo field appears in the first blank cell in the Field row in the Design grid.

4 Repeat step 3 for the OrderDate, NoOfUnits, and Price fields.

Your design grid should now contain four fields.

5 In the Price column, click in the Criteria row, and type >=100.

TROUBLESHOOTING

The criteria that you type do not have to be in the same format as the data in the field. For example, in step 5, you could type >=$100.00 instead of >=100.

When run, the query will select and display only records for items with a price equal to or more than $100.

FIGURE 4-10

A comparison operator added to the Price field

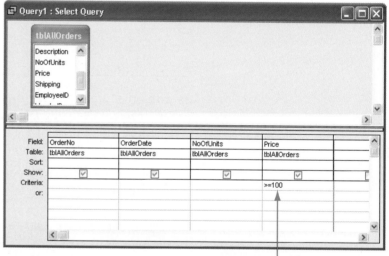

Criteria for the Price field

 6 On the Query Design toolbar, click the Run button.

The query results appear in a datasheet showing all records in the table that have items with a price equal to or more than $100.

FIGURE 4-11

The query results using the comparison operator

Only records with a price of $100.00 or more are returned.

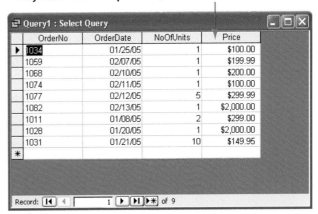

7 **On the Query Datasheet toolbar, click the View button.**

The query appears in Design view.

8 **In the NoOfUnits column, click in the Criteria row, and type >1.**

The query will display records of orders for more than one unit that also have a unit price of more than $100.

FIGURE 4-12

The query Design grid with two comparison operators

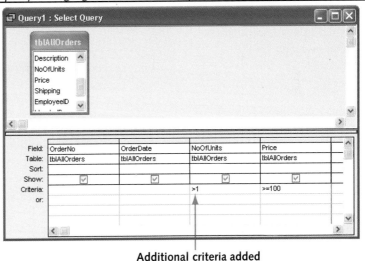

Additional criteria added

IMPORTANT

Remember, if you specify criteria in more than one field, and all in the same Criteria row, only records that match ALL of the criteria will be returned. You will see in Lesson 8, "Creating Custom Queries," how to create queries using multiple Criteria rows to alter the effect of the query.

9 **On the Query Design toolbar, click the Run button.**

The query results appear, showing only records for items with a price equal to or more than $100 and for more than one unit.

FIGURE 4-13

The query results with two comparison operators

The results have changed because of the additional criteria.

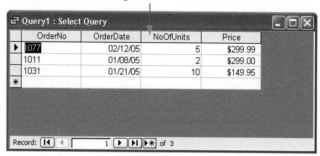

◆ Close the query without saving changes.

◆ Keep the database open for the next exercise.

Sorting Query Results

As with tables, query results can be sorted in ascending or descending order, based on the values in a field. For example, in the previous exercise you might have wanted to sort the results by price.

> **TIP**
>
> Sorting records in a table is discussed in Lesson 3, "Working with Tables."

To sort query results, you use the Sort row in the Design grid, instead of using buttons on the toolbar. To sort query results by the values in a particular field, click in the Sort row of the column for that field, click the down arrow that appears, and then click Ascending or Descending. You can remove a sort order by deleting the text in the Sort row.

QUICK REFERENCE ▼

Using comparison operators in a query

1 Double-click the Create Query In Design View option in the Database window.

2 Using the Show Table dialog box, add a table to the Design grid and close the Show Table dialog box.

3 Drag the fields to be included from the field list to the Field row of the Design grid.

4 Click in the Criteria row for any field and enter the operators and values for each field that requires selection criterion.

5 Click the Run button to run the query.

Creating a Calculated Field

THE BOTTOM LINE

In addition to returning only data that matches your criterion, queries can also create a data field that contains the result of a calculation. This would be useful if you ran a query to calculate the total cost of an order, for instance. Instead of storing the calculated value in the database table, which requires storage space for each record, you can create a query to just calculate the value. When the query is closed, the value disappears and does not require any additional disk space in the table.

In the previous exercise, you created a query that extracts all orders for items with a price more than $100 and for more than one unit. However, the query doesn't tell you the total cost for each order. You can set the query to calculate the total cost by creating a **calculated field**.

Calculated fields combine one or more fields with one or more operators to perform calculations for which you might otherwise use a calculator. This combination of operators and fields is called an **expression** and is used to tell Access what calculations to perform on the data.

TIP

You do not have to include spaces in expressions.

In expressions, all field names are surrounded by square brackets ([]), and the operators used are the same characters used in most mathematical calculations: + (addition), - (subtraction), * (multiplication), and / (division). Expressions follow the same order of operations that you probably learned in high school math.

- Calculations surrounded by parentheses are calculated first. For example, (6 + 3) * 2 will equal 18, not 12.
- Multiplication and division are calculated before addition and subtraction. For example, 3 + 2 * 5 equals 3 + 10, or 13, not 5 * 5, or 25.
- For expressions containing only addition and subtraction or only multiplication and division, Access makes the calculations from left to right. For example, 6 / 3 * 2 equals 2 * 2, or 4, not 6 / 6, or 1.

To create a calculated field, click in the first blank column in the Field row in the Design grid, type the name to be assigned for the new field, and then type the expression for the calculation. For example, to create a calculated field named TotalCost that multiplies the Price and NoOfUnits fields to find the total cost of the order, you would type *TotalCost:[Price]*[NoOfUnits]*.

◆ **Make sure the Database window is displayed and Queries is selected on the Objects bar.**

Create a calculated field in a query

Using calculated fields in a query reduces the amount of data that needs to be saved in a table. You can calculate the value at any time using a query so there is no need to store the value in the record. You will now create a query using a calculated field to determine the hourly wage of the resort's employees. The calculated field will calculate the number of hours that each employee works each year and divide the employee's salary by that number.

1 **Double-click Create Query In Design View.**

The Query Design view window and the Show Table dialog box appear.

2 **In the Show Table dialog box, click tblHumanResourcesData, click Add, and then click Close.**

The Show Table dialog box closes, and a field list displaying the fields in tblHumanResourcesData appears in the top section of the Query Design view window.

3 **In the tblHumanResourcesData field list, double-click EmployeeID.**

The EmployeeID field appears in the first blank cell in the Field row in the Design grid.

ANOTHER METHOD

You can also drag the field from the field list to the Field row of the grid.

4 **Repeat step 3 for the Hours and Salary fields.**

The Design grid should look like the following figure.

FIGURE 4-14

The table fields being used in the query

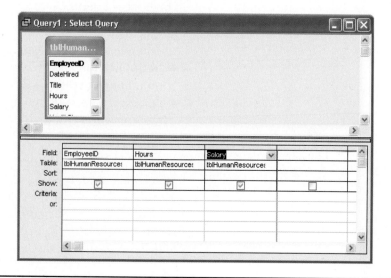

5 In the Field row, click the first blank cell, and type
HourlyWage:[Salary]/([Hours]*52).

The Hours field contains the number of hours worked weekly by employees. The expression in step 5 calculates the number of hours that employees work per year by multiplying the number of hours worked per week by 52. The parentheses around *[Hours]*52* ensures that Access performs that calculation first.

6 In the Show row for the new field, select the check box, if necessary.

A check appears inside the check box.

FIGURE 4-15

The Design grid with the calculated field added

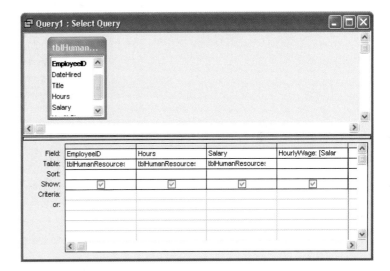

TROUBLESHOOTING

The check box in the Show row determines whether a field is displayed in the query result. If the check box is selected, the field will appear in the query results. If it is not selected, the field will not be visible in the results datasheet.

7 On the Query Design toolbar, click the Run button.

The query results appear, with the results of the calculation in the HourlyWage field.

FIGURE 4-16

The query results showing the calculated value

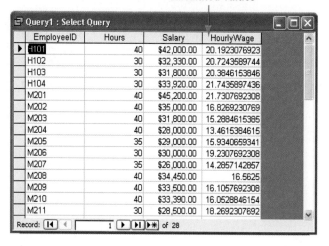

Calculated values

EmployeeID	Hours	Salary	HourlyWage
H101	40	$42,000.00	20.1923076923
H102	30	$32,330.00	20.7243589744
H103	30	$31,800.00	20.3846153846
H104	30	$33,920.00	21.7435897436
M201	40	$45,200.00	21.7307692308
M202	40	$35,000.00	16.8269230769
M203	40	$31,800.00	15.2884615385
M204	40	$28,000.00	13.4615384615
M205	35	$29,000.00	15.9340659341
M206	30	$30,000.00	19.2307692308
M207	35	$26,000.00	14.2857142857
M208	40	$34,450.00	16.5625
M209	40	$33,500.00	16.1057692308
M210	40	$33,390.00	16.0528846154
M211	30	$28,500.00	18.2692307692

Record: ◄ ◄ 1 ► ►I ►* of 28

IMPORTANT

You are not permitted to change the data in the HourlyWage field when the query is in Datasheet view. Access will perform the calculation using the current data in tblHumanResourcesData each time that you run the query.

8 **On the Query Datasheet toolbar, click the View button.**

The query appears in Design view.

9 **In the HourlyWage column, click in the Sort row, click the down arrow that appears, and then click Descending.**

Access will sort the query results in descending order by the values in the HourlyWage field when you run the query.

10 **On the Query Design toolbar, click the Run button.**

The query results appear. The record for the employee making the highest wages per hour appears at the top of the table.

FIGURE 4-17

The query results sorted on the calculated value

Calculated field sorted in descending order

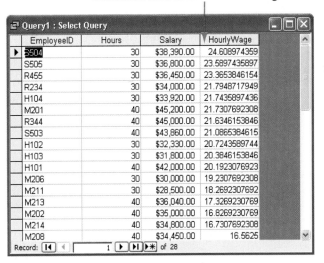

11 **On the Query Datasheet toolbar, click the Save button.**

The Save As dialog box appears. You use this dialog box to assign a name to your query and make it available anytime you want to run it.

12 **Type qryHourlyWage, and click OK.**

Access saves the query as qryHourlyWage.

◆ **Close the query.**

◆ **Keep the database open for the next exercise.**

Q. When you create an expression in Access, which portion of the expression will be evaluated first if present?

A. **Any portions of the expression that are surrounded by parentheses will be evaluated before any other parts of the expression.**

QUICK REFERENCE ▼

Using a calculated field in a query

1 Double-click the Create Query In Design View option in the Database window.

2 Using the Show Table dialog box, add a table to the Design grid and close the Show Table dialog box.

3 Drag the fields to be included in the query from the table's field list to the Field row of the Design grid.

4 Click in the first blank Field column and enter the name of the calculated field, then a colon, and then the expression.

5 Select the Show box, if necessary, to make sure the field displays when the query runs.

6 Click the Run button to run the query.

Creating a Multiple-Table Query

The fact that Access is a relational database enables you to eliminate redundant data when designing your database. That is, you don't have to include a lot of the same information in multiple tables, which saves storage space. But, there will be times when you want to see data from two or more tables combined to provide you with all the information you need to make decisions. With Access, you can create queries that pull data from multiple tables, as long as a relationship has been established between the tables involved, or if a relationship can be established between fields contained in the tables.

The ability to create a **multiple-table query** is one of the more powerful features of Access. With multiple-table queries, you can extract fields from two or more tables, which allows you to combine information that can't be found in any individual table. For example, tblHourly provides data about how much each employee earns per hour, but it does not include the employee's names. Employee names are listed in tblEmployees, which does not include wage information for the employees. You could combine the information found in both of these tables by using a multiple-table query.

TIP

Multiple-table queries can also be used to extract data from two queries or a combination of tables and queries.

To use fields from more than one table, you must first **join**, or create a relationship, between fields in different tables. If the two fields that you want to join contain identical data, and at least one of the fields is a primary key, Access automatically joins the fields, using a setting called **AutoJoin**. For example, tblEmployees and tblHourly have identical EmployeeID fields that can be used to create a query that will show hourly wage information *and* names—data from two separate tables.

TIP

Relationships are discussed in Lesson 3, "Working with Tables."

If one of the fields is not a primary key—even if both fields contain identical data—Access does not automatically join the fields; you have to do it manually. To join the two fields manually, click the field in the first field list and drag it until it is on top of the corresponding field in the second field list. A join line appears.

TIP

Primary keys are discussed in Lesson 2, "Creating Tables."

If you create a query in Design view and add tblEmployees and tblHourly to the Query Design view window, Access automatically joins the EmployeeID fields, and a join line appears between the joined fields. Although a join line looks like the line that appears when two tables are in a relationship, a **join line** indicates that two of the fields in the tables are in a relationship, not that the tables themselves are in a relationship. If you display the Relationships window for the database, two tables with joined fields do not appear unless the tables are also in a relationship. You can see the join line between joined fields only in the Query Design view window.

IMPORTANT

If you do not want Access to automatically join related fields, you can turn off AutoJoin by clicking Options on the Tools menu, clicking the Tables/Queries tab, and clearing the Enable AutoJoin check box.

◆ **Make sure the Database window is displayed and Queries is selected on the Objects bar.**

Create a query using multiple tables

You will now create and run a query that extracts employee names from tblEmployees and employee salary information from tblHourly. The EmployeeID field is the common field between these two tables and the join will use that field to relate the tables.

1 **Double-click Create Query In Design View.**

The Query Design view window and the Show Table dialog box appear.

2 **In the Show Table dialog box, click tblEmployees, and click Add.**

The tblEmployees field list appears in the top section of the Query Design view window.

TROUBLESHOOTING

To use an existing query as a source for a multiple-table query, click the Queries tab or the Both tab in the Show Table dialog box.

3 **In the Show Table dialog box, click tblHourly, and click Add.**

The tblHourly field list appears in the top section of the Query Design view window.

4 **In the Show Table dialog box, click Close.**

The Show Table dialog box closes. The join line between the EmployeeID fields in tblEmployees and tblHourly indicates that the two fields are joined.

TIP

If you discover after closing the Show Table dialog box that you want to add another table to the query, click the Show Table button on the toolbar to reopen it. You can also right-click on any open area in the table field list portion of the query window, and then click Show Table from the pop-up menu that appears.

FIGURE 4-18

The Query Design window showing both tables

The join line for the EmployeeID field

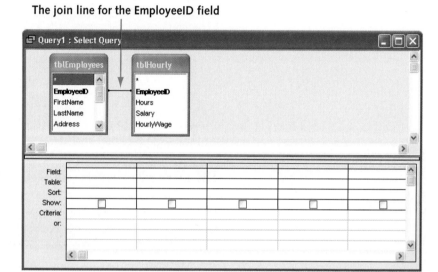

IMPORTANT

Access joined the two fields automatically because both fields contain the same information, and in this case, both of them are the primary key fields for their respective tables.

5 In the tblEmployees field list, double-click the LastName field.

The LastName field appears in the first blank cell in the Field row in the Design grid.

6 Repeat step 5 for the FirstName field in tblEmployees and the Hours, Salary, HourlyWage, and EmployeeID fields in tblHourly.

7 In the HourlyWage column, click in the Sort row, click the down arrow that appears, and then click Descending.

Access will sort the query results in descending order by the values in the HourlyWage field. Your Design grid should now contain six fields, two from the tblEmployees table and the rest from the tblHourly table.

FIGURE 4-19

The completed query showing fields from two tables

Fields added to grid

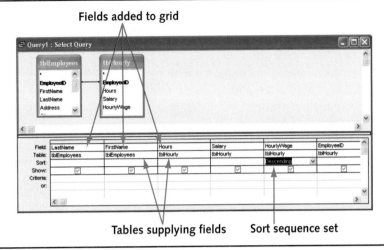

Tables supplying fields   Sort sequence set

TROUBLESHOOTING

The Table row in the design grid displays the source table for the fields in the Field Row.

8 On the Query Design toolbar, click the Run button.

The query results appear, sorted in descending order by hourly wage.

FIGURE 4-20

The query in Datasheet view after being run

Query results, drawing data from two tables, sorted by Salary in descending order

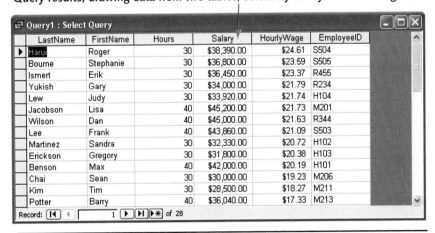

◆ Save the query as qryHourlyWithNames but do not close the query.

◆ Keep the query and the database open for the next exercise.

QUICK CHECK

Q. When two fields are joined by a join line in a multiple-table query, do those fields also show up in the Relationships window?

A. **They will not show up in the Relationships window unless the tables they are contained within are also defined in a relationship.**

QUICK REFERENCE ▼

Create a multiple table query

1 Double-click the Create Query In Design View option in the Database window.

2 Using the Show Table dialog box, add two or more tables to the Design grid.

3 Close the Show Table dialog box and Access will display a join line for the fields in each table that are identical. (If Access cannot join two fields automatically, you will have to do it manually by dragging one field over another.)

4 Drag the fields to be included in the query to the Field row of the Design grid.

5 Enter any selection criteria or sort criteria that are required.

6 Click the Run button to run the query.

Printing a Query

THE BOTTOM LINE

You can print the results of a query the same way you can print a table datasheet. You can also preview the query before printing it, to see if you need to adjust the paper orientation, margin settings, or other print options.

The method for printing a query is essentially the same as the method for printing a datasheet. Because query results often extend several pages, you might want to preview a query first by clicking the Print Preview button on the Query Design or Query Datasheet toolbar. Print Preview shows you what the query will look like and how many pages it will fill after it is printed. You can print a query:

- From Print Preview by clicking the Print button on the Print Preview toolbar.
- From Datasheet view by clicking the Print button on the Query Datasheet toolbar.
- From any view by clicking Print on the File menu.

◆ **Make sure the qryHourlyWithNames query is still open in Datasheet view from the previous exercise.**

Preview and Print a query

You created a query named qryHourlyWithNames in the previous exercise, and it should still be open. In this exercise, you will preview that query in Print Preview and then you will print the query results.

1 **On the Query Datasheet toolbar, click the Print Preview button.**

The query appears in Print Preview. Note that the pointer has turned into a magnifying glass. Click the mouse and Access will "zoom in" to the query results, making them appear larger. Click the mouse again and you will "zoom out" to the size you see in the figure below.

FIGURE 4-21

The query results in Print Preview

How the data will appear when printed

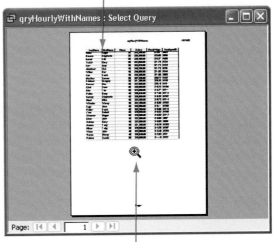

Pointer becomes a magnifying glass

TROUBLESHOOTING

If the query requires more than one page, you can use the navigation buttons in the bottom-left corner of the Print Preview window to view the other pages.

2 **On the Print Preview toolbar, click Close.**

Print Preview closes.

3 **On the Query Datasheet toolbar, click the Print button.**

A message box appears, telling you that qryHourlyWithNames is printing.

QUICK CHECK

Q. How can you determine how many pages will be required to print the results of a query?

A. **Use the navigation buttons in the lower left area of the Print Preview window.**

QUICK REFERENCE ▼

Preview a query before printing it

1 Run the query.

2 Click the Print Preview button on the Query Datasheet toolbar.

Print the results of a query

- Click the Print button on the Print Preview toolbar,
- Click the Print button on the Query Datasheet toolbar,
- Click Print on the File menu.

◆ If you are continuing to other lessons, close the open query, and close the Adventure Works 04 Database. Keep Access open for the next lesson.

◆ If you are not continuing to other lessons, close the open query and the Adventure Works 04 Database. Close Access.

Key Points

✔ *You can create a query using a wizard or create it manually in Design view.*

✔ *To see the results of your query, click the Run button on the Query Design toolbar.*

✔ *Specifying selection criteria for your query limits the data returned to only the records and fields that match the criteria.*

✔ *You can use comparison operators in a query to select a range of data or to eliminate some data.*

✔ *It is possible to create a calculated field within a query.*

✔ *Tables that have common fields can be used to create a multiple-table query.*

✔ *Printing a query is essentially the same as printing a table.*

Quick Quiz

True/False

T   F   **1.** Changing the data displayed in the query results datasheet does not have any effect on the data stored in the table.

T   F   **2.** Access allows you to specify a criteria value for every field contained in the query Design grid.

T   F   **3.** Comparison operators can only be used for numeric fields.

T   F   **4.** When you create a calculated field in a query, the field is added to the end of the table it is based on when the query is saved.

T   F   **5.** You can extract data from a table and from another query when creating a new query, as long as there is a field in one object that can be related to a field in the other object.

Multiple Choice

1. Which of the following is the most basic type of query that you can create in Access?
   a. simple query
   b. select query
   c. table query
   d. object query

2. Which wildcard character below would you use when you want to match any one alphabetic character?
   a. *
   b. !
   c. #
   d. ?

3. Which of the following sets of characters is used to enclose any field name used when creating a calculated field expression?
   a. [ ] (square brackets)
   b. ( ) (parentheses)
   c. ' ' (single quotes)
   d. " " (double quotes)

4. Access is unable to automatically join two fields when creating a multiple-table query if one of the fields is _____.
   a. named the same as the other field
   b. the same data type as the other field
   c. not defined as a primary key
   d. All of the above

5. What comparison operator could you use to select all values from a field that range from 100 to 200, including 100 and 200?
   a. lower... upper...
   b. between... and...
   c. low... high...
   d. None of the above

Short Answer

1. What are the two ways to create a query in Access?

2. What is a multiple-table query?

3. How can you sort query results?

4. What is a wildcard?

5. How do you print a query in Datasheet view?

6. What is a calculated field?

7. What view do you use to modify a query?

8. How do you specify criteria for a query?

9. What are comparison operators?

10. How do you run a query?

On Your Own

Exercise 1

Create a query using the Wizard or in Design view that shows which of the resort's suites were occupied during the months of June, July, and August for the year 2005. List the suite numbers, the check-in and check-out dates, and sort the query on the check-in date field. Save the query as qryCheckInDate.

Exercise 2

Using the Simple Query Wizard, create a query called qryOrderCost based on tblAllOrders that contains the OrderNo, NoOfUnits, Price, and Shipping fields. Add a calculated field called GrandTotal to the query that multiplies the number of items purchased by price and adds the shipping costs. Run the query. Restrict the query results to orders with totals over $250, run the query again, and then print the results. Close and save the query.

Exercise 3

Select the Create Query In Design View option from the Database window. From the Show Table window select the tblEmployees, tblHumanResourcesData, and the tblInsurance table to be included in the query. Access will automatically join the Employee ID fields in the employee and human resources tables. Create a join from the HealthPlan field in tblHumanResourcesData to the PlanID field in the tblInsurance table. Add the EmployeeID, LastName, and FirstName fields from the tblEmployees table, the Title and HealthPlan fields from the tblHumanResourcesData table, and the PlanType and Rate fields from the tblInsurance table. Sort the query on the HealthPlan field. Run the query and save it as qryInsByType.

One Step Further

Exercise 1

Open the MyMusic_XXX (where XXX represents your initials) database that you created in Lesson 2. Open the table you created for your music collection data and switch to Design view if necessary. If your table does not already have a field to describe the category, or genre, of the music (i.e., Rock, Pop, Classical, etc.) add such a field to the table. Switch to Datasheet view and add values for each record in the table that describes what category each entry falls into. Create a query using the wizard or Design view, and use all of the fields in the table. Enter selection criteria to retrieve all entries that are on a CD and are in any category of your choice. Run the query and examine the results. Modify the query to select all records that are *not* on CD but are in the same category you used for the first query. Close the query without saving it, and close the database.

Exercise 2

Create a query using the Simple Query Wizard. Use the tblVendors table as the source for the query, and select all fields. Save the query as qryVendorWildcards, and open the query in Design view. Enter criteria using wildcards to extract the following data from the table. Enter criteria for only one bullet point at a time, run the query to see if the correct data was extracted, switch back to Design view, delete the current criteria, enter the next wildcard, and run the query again. In all you will enter criteria and run the query five separate times.

- Extract all records that have a Vendor Name beginning with the letter "L."

- Extract all records that have a period (.) in the Vendor Name field.

- Extract all records whose address contains a three digit number that begins with a "2."

- Extract all records that have a "T" in the second digit of the Vendor ID field.

- Extract all records that have an "F" in the address field that is followed by the letter "i."

Windows XP

What Is Windows XP?

Microsoft Windows XP is the newest version of the Windows **operating system**. An operating system is a collection of programs that control the way a computer's hardware devices interact with programs, as well as the way the computer responds to your commands. Programs are tools that help you perform certain tasks. Whenever you work with your computer, you are using Windows—either directly or indirectly through another program, such as Microsoft Word.

Logging On to a Windows XP Professional Computer on a Network Domain

Many computers running Windows XP Professional are connected to a **local area network** (LAN) and are configured as part of a **network domain**. Others might be connected to a LAN but not one that uses a domain, or they might be stand-alone computers. This section applies to the first kind of computer.

The process of starting a computer session is called **logging on**. To log on to a network domain, you must have a valid **user account** (a profile that describes the way the computer environment looks and operates for that particular user), and you must know your user account name and password. You must also know the **domain name**. You can get all this information from your network administrator.

When Windows XP is installed on a computer, an account is created with the administrative privileges required to control that particular computer. Someone—usually a network administrator—can use that account to create other accounts on the computer. These accounts are generally for specific people, and they might have more restricted privileges that prevent the account owners from changing some of the settings on the computer.

Logging On to a Windows XP Home Edition Computer

Your computer might be used by only you, or it might be used by several people. If only you use your computer, it needs only one configuration, or user account. If other people use your computer, everyone can use the same account, or you can set up a separate user account for each person. Each account is associated with a **user profile** that describes the way the computer environment looks and operates for that particular user. This information includes such things as the color scheme, desktop background, fonts, and shortcuts, and it can vary from profile to profile.

The process of starting a computer session is called logging on. If only one user account has been set up, Windows XP automatically logs on using that account when you start the computer. If multiple accounts have been set up, Windows XP prompts you to select your user profile and, if your account has been password-protected, to enter your password. Each user has a user account name and a user account picture. Each user can change his or her own account name and account picture; users with administrative privileges can change any user's account name and picture.

Logging On to a Stand-Alone Windows XP Professional Computer

Windows XP Professional is generally used in a networked environment, but you do not have to be connected to a network domain to run it. For example, you might have Windows XP Professional installed on a laptop computer that you use both at the office and at home; or you might travel with your Windows XP Professional computer, work offline, and connect to your network over a remote connection, or you may have set up a home or small business network without domains.

When you log on to a Windows XP Professional computer that has been, but is no longer, connected to a network domain, you log on in the ordinary manner, and your user information is validated against information that was stored on the computer the last time you logged on to the domain. If your Windows XP Professional computer is not currently configured to work on a network, the process of logging on is identical to that of Windows XP Home Edition.

Understanding Windows XP Components

When you start Windows for the first time, your screen should look similar to the illustration that follows. As you install programs and customize Windows to suit the way you work, you will see additions and changes to this screen, but the same basic components will still appear.

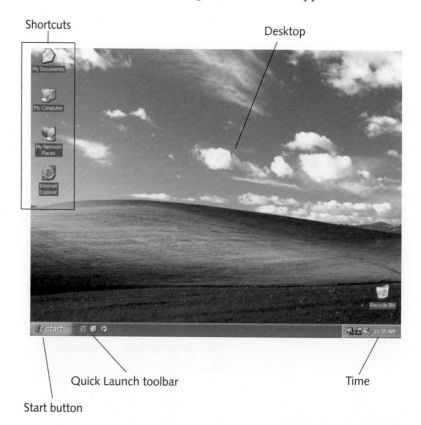

It's helpful to know the correct names of the basic components of Windows and the ways that you can use the mouse to interact with them. The following list describes the basic Windows components.

- **Desktop** The desktop is composed of the contents of your computer screen after Windows has been started. The desktop includes icons for frequently used programs.
- **Quick Launch bar** The Quick Launch bar is an area of the taskbar that contains several buttons that represent programs that are used frequently.
- **Shortcuts** Shortcuts are a type of icon that offers quick access to files, folders, or programs. You double-click shortcuts to open files, folders, or programs. Shortcuts look similar to other icons except each has a curved arrow in its lower-left corner.
- **Start button** The Start button is located on the left edge of the taskbar, and it is the launching point for every program and window on your computer. Click the Start button to open a series of menus for starting programs, finding and opening folders and files, setting options, getting help, adding hardware and software, and shutting down the computer.
- **Taskbar** The taskbar is the strip along the bottom of the screen. It typically shows, from left to right, the Start button, the Quick Launch bar, buttons for certain utilities and programs (such as the volume control for your computer's sound system), and the time. Also, all open programs are displayed as buttons on the taskbar.
- **Time** The time is displayed near the right edge of the taskbar. You can also use this area of the taskbar to display a calendar.
- **Window** A portion of the screen that displays a file, folder, or program. Several windows can be displayed on the screen at one time, either side by side, top to bottom, or overlapping.

Starting Programs

The first time you start Windows XP, the Start menu is displayed until you click something else. Thereafter, you open the Start menu by clicking the Start button at the left end of the taskbar. The Start menu has been significantly redesigned in Windows XP to provide easier access to your programs. When it first opens, it looks something like this:

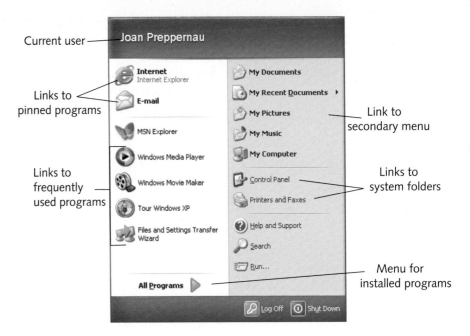

Current user — Joan Preppernau

Links to pinned programs

Internet
Internet Explorer

E-mail

MSN Explorer

Windows Media Player

Links to frequently used programs

Windows Movie Maker

Tour Windows XP

Files and Settings Transfer Wizard

All Programs ▷

My Documents

My Recent Documents ▶

My Pictures

My Music

My Computer

Control Panel

Printers and Faxes

Help and Support

Search

Run...

Log Off   Shut Down

Link to secondary menu

Links to system folders

Menu for installed programs

- You can pin links to your favorite programs to a special area at the top of the left side of the Start menu to make the programs easy to find and start. By default, Microsoft Internet Explorer and Microsoft Outlook Express are pinned to the Start menu. If you change your default Web browser or e-mail program, the pinned area is automatically updated to reflect that change.

Below the first horizontal line on the left side of the Start menu is a list of links to your most frequently used programs. On the right side of the Start menu are links to the locations where you are most likely to store the files you create, a link to a directory of other computers on your network, and links to various tools that you will use while running your computer. The commands you will use to log off of or shut down your computer are located at the bottom of the Start menu. Clicking the All Programs text or arrow will display a menu of all installed programs on your computer.

Moving and Closing Windows

The space on your desktop is limited, so you should manage it carefully. Sometimes that means moving a program's window to another part of the desktop or shrinking it so that it appears as a button on the taskbar. At other times, "managing your desktop" means resizing a program's window so that you can simultaneously view another program or document window on your desktop. The primary components of a window are:

- The *title bar*, in addition to telling you the name of the program and (usually) the name of the document you are working on, can be used to move the program window around on the screen. To move a program window, drag its title bar.
- The *Minimize* button shrinks a window so that it is displayed as a button on the taskbar.
- The *Maximize* button expands the window so that it fills the desktop (except for the taskbar).
- When a window is maximized, the Maximize button is replaced by the *Restore Down* button, which returns the window to its previous size.

- The *Close* button closes a program, removing it from the computer's temporary storage (memory). This button also closes dialog boxes and windows.
- The *resize area* can be used to change the size and shape of a window. Drag the resize area to make the window tall and narrow, short and wide, or any size in between.

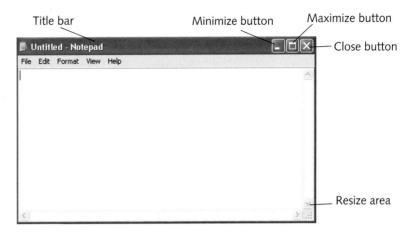

Switching Between Programs

It's common in Windows to have more than one program running at the same time. Each program runs in its own window. Usually, when two windows are on screen at once, the one with the title bar that is blue (the default color) or brightly colored is the **active window**. The inactive window usually has a gray or lightly colored title bar. To switch between windows when you can see more than one of them on screen, just click anywhere in an empty area of the window you want to make active. When working with Windows, you frequently won't be able to see all of the windows you have open. In that case, you can switch from one window to another by clicking a program's button on the taskbar. To quickly display the desktop when it is covered by windows, click the Show Desktop button on the taskbar.

Logging Off of Windows XP

The process of ending a computer session is called **logging off**. Logging off ends the Windows session for your account but leaves the computer turned on. It is important to log off when you leave for the day, or even when you leave your computer for an extended period of time, to safeguard against other people accessing your personal information. For example, if your account has administrative privileges and you go out to lunch without logging off or otherwise protecting your computer against intrusion, someone could create a local user account with administrative privileges for themselves and later use that account to log on to your computer.

Shutting Down a Windows XP Professional Computer

Rather than simply logging off of your computer, you might want to turn it off, or **shut down**, to conserve energy. Shutting down closes all your open applications and files, ends your computing session, and shuts down

Windows so that you can safely turn off the computer's power. This process ensures that your data is safely stored and any external connections are appropriately disconnected.

Other Options

In addition to logging off and shutting down your computer, the Windows XP Professional Shut Down dialog box presents these options:

- Restart ends your session, shuts down Windows, and then starts Windows again without turning off the computer.
- Stand by maintains your session (the programs that are open and any work you are doing in them) and keeps the computer running on low power with your data still in memory. To return to a session that is on stand by, press Ctrl+Alt+Del.
- Hibernate saves your session and turns off your computer. The next time you start the computer, your session is restored to the place where you left off.

NOTE: The Windows XP Home Edition Turn off computer screen provides the Restart and Hibernate options, but not the Stand by option.

Getting Help When You Need It

Microsoft Windows XP Professional offers an extensive help system, which features reference guides, context-sensitive help, interactive troubleshooters, and Web-based support. You can use these resources to find out about virtually anything in Windows, from what the Notepad program does to why your CD-ROM drive isn't working.

Using the Windows Help System

Windows XP takes the concept of the Help file to new heights with the Help and Support Center. As the name implies, the Help and Support Center is the place to go when you're having troubles—you can help yourself, or you can ask other people for help. The help offered includes multimedia product tours targeted at different audiences, general and specific articles, a comprehensive glossary, tutorials and demonstrations, and links to most of the tools that you need to keep your computer running smoothly. You can choose from a list of common topics on the main page of the Help and Support Center, search the database by keyword or phrase using the **Search** box, or look up specific topics arranged in alphabetical order in the **Index** or table of contents. When you're connected to the Internet, you can easily include the Microsoft Knowledge Base in your searches as well.

When you search for information, your search results are divided into three areas:

- The Suggested Topics listing displays topics that are most likely to be of interest to you, cause the search terms you entered match the keywords defined by the topic's author.

- The Full-text Search Matches listing displays all the topics in which the individual words of your search terms appear.
- The Microsoft Knowledge Base listing displays articles that pertain to your search phrase from Microsoft's online database of product support information. This listing is available only when you are online.

You can search the entire support database, and you can conduct a subsequent search within the results of a previous search, thereby narrowing down the search results to define your problem. If you can't solve your problem on your own, you can communicate with other Windows XP users and experts via online newsgroups, consult online with Microsoft support personnel, or request remote assistance from a friend or coworker. Using Remote Assistance, you can allow another person to connect to your computer via the Internet and take control of your computer to figure out what the trouble is.

The Help and Support Center contains links to Web-based information to ensure that it is always up to date. This means that you don't have access to all the features of the Help and Support Center when you are offline.

There are two ways to access the Help and Support Center:

- Click Help and Support on the Start menu.
- Press F1. Depending on what area of Windows you are in, this might open the Help and Support Center to a page that is specific to that area. For example, if you press F1 from within Control Panel, the Help and Support Center opens to the Control Panel topic.

When it starts, the Help and Support Center looks like the following figure.

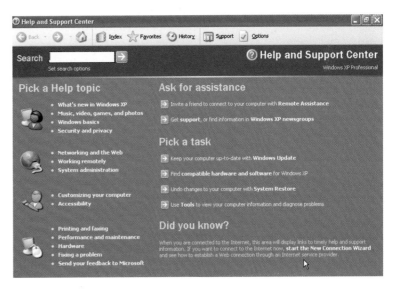

Creating a List of Favorite Help Topics

When you learn a new skill or work on a large project—from studying a foreign language to remodeling a room—it's helpful to keep a "cheat sheet" handy. The notes on it might not mean a lot to anyone else, but they can be invaluable to you. The **Favorites** button in the Windows XP Help and Support Center window is an electronic version of a written reminder. Here, you can store the topics you find most useful as you discover them, and you can quickly retrieve them later. It's like creating your own reference guide, containing only the subjects that interest you and skipping everything else.

Using Interactive Troubleshooters

In an ideal world, your computer would work exactly the way you want it to, all the time. In reality, your computer is a combination of hardware and software with an almost infinite number of variations—and the combinations change as your needs change. You might buy a scanner, switch from one printer to another, add and remove programs, or connect to different networks at different times. In such a complex system, problems can sometimes occur. Fortunately, Windows provides interactive **trouble shooters** to help you diagnose and solve problems. The troubleshooters are part of the help system. They're called interactive because they rely on your answers to a series of questions to solve your particular problem. Based on the information you supply, the troubleshooters provide step-by-step instructions for diagnosing and fixing the problem.

Using the "What's This?" Feature

Context-sensitive help is information that you can display while using a particular feature; you don't have to open the Windows XP help window. One type of context-sensitive help is pop-up descriptions. A pop-up description appears if you point to a Windows element for a few seconds. Pop-up descriptions, although helpful, are necessarily brief. For a more complete description of an element, use the What's This? feature. This button is available in dialog boxes and toolbars throughout Windows. When used, it will display a pop-up window containing a more detailed description of a control or Windows element.

Adding Features Using Windows Update

Imagine that you take your car to a service station and the mechanic recommends an engine tune-up, new tires, and an upgraded alarm system— for free. That's the kind of service Microsoft **Windows Update** provides to help you keep Windows running smoothly. Windows Update links you to specific pages on Microsoft's Web site and lets you add Windows features and upgrades as they become available. The first time you use Windows Update to look for features and upgrades, it adds a small program called a control to your system. The control determines what components of Windows you might want to add or update on your computer. Using that information, Windows Update displays a "shopping list" of files. When you have selected the items you want from the list, click the Review and install link. Windows Update will transfer, or download, the items you selected from the Web site to your computer, and Windows Update installs and sets them up for you.

Managing Files and Folders

Files are some of the most important resources you will use in Microsoft Windows XP. Every document, picture, or sound you work with is a file. Programs (such as Microsoft Word or Microsoft Excel) are actually collections of files. Windows itself is a collection of hundreds of files, each with its own purpose. Files even specify the shape of the mouse pointer and the result of clicking an item.

To keep track of all your files, you need to group them in a logical way. In Windows, you do this by creating folders, which store related files. Think of a folder like a kitchen cabinet. One cabinet might store food, while another stores dishes. In Windows, one folder might store documents you create (such as a memo in Word or a workbook in Excel), while another might store pictures you download from the Internet. You might also divide your kitchen cabinets: a shelf for glassware, another for coffee cups, and so on. If you have lots of glasses, you might divide the shelves, perhaps water goblets on the left and brandy snifters on the right. In Windows, you can have folders within folders to provide additional levels of organization.

When Microsoft Windows XP is installed on a computer, it creates four **system folders:**

- *Documents and Settings*. This folder contains a subfolder for each user profile—each user who has logged on to the computer or who has logged on to a network domain through the computer. Windows XP may create multiple profiles for one person if that person logs on in different ways.
- *Program Files*. This is the folder where most programs install the files they need in order to run.
- *temp*. The operating system and various other programs might store temporary files in this folder.
- *WINDOWS*. Most of the critical operating system files are stored in this folder. Within each profile subfolder in the Documents and Settings folder, Windows XP creates three folders:
- *My Documents*. This folder is a convenient place to store documents, spreadsheets, and other files you want to access quickly.
- *My Pictures*. This subfolder of My Documents has special capabilities for handling picture files.
- *My Music*. This subfolder of My Documents has special capabilities for handling music files.

Viewing and Opening Folders

The two most popular ways to navigate through folders are to use My Computer or **Windows Explorer**. My Computer displays all the available resources on your computer, including icons for disk drives and the network. Windows Explorer displays the files and folders on your computer and network. In Windows, My Computer and Windows Explorer are almost identical. The major difference is that the Folders pane appears by default in Windows Explorer and not in My Computer.

You can open My Computer by double-clicking the My Computer icon on the desktop. You can open Windows Explorer by clicking the Start button, pointing to All Programs, pointing to Accessories, and then clicking Windows Explorer on the Accessories submenu. It's a matter of personal preference whether you use My Computer or Windows Explorer to view files, folders, and other resources.

When Windows Explorer is first opened, the left side of the window displays the Folders pane. The right side of the window displays the contents of the folder that is selected in the Folders pane. By default, the My Documents folder is selected when you open Windows Explorer. To open a folder, double-click it in the Folders pane. When you double-click a folder, its contents appear in the right pane, replacing the contents of the folder you selected previously. If the new folder contains a **subfolder** (a folder within a folder), you can double-click the subfolder and continue navigating through the lower-level folders until you find the file or folder you're looking for. To return to a higher-level folder, click the Up button on the Standard Buttons toolbar. To return to other previously opened folders, click the Back button on the Standard Buttons toolbar.

On the right side of the Windows Explorer window, you can view your files and folders in several different ways. You can view thumbnails or slideshows of graphic files, display file and folder types as tiles or icons, or view a detailed or not-so-detailed file list. The view options for each folder are available on that folder window's toolbar, and they vary depending on the contents of the folder. Available views include the following:

- *Details view* displays a list of files or folders and their properties. The properties shown by default for each file or folder are Name, Size, Type, and Date Modified. For pictures, the defaults also include Date Picture Taken and Dimensions.
- *Filmstrip view* displays the currently selected picture at the top of the window above a single row of smaller versions of all the pictures in the current folder.
- *Icons view* displays the icon and file name for each file or folder in the current folder.
- *List view* displays a list of files and folders in the current folder, with no other information other than the file name and a small icon representing the file type.
- *Thumbnails view* displays up to four miniature representations of the files contained in each folder. These thumbnails are displayed on top of a folder icon that is about an inch and a half square.
- *Tiles view* displays a large file type icon or folder icon, the file or folder name, and up to two additional pieces of information for each file in the current folder. The additional information varies depending on the type of file.

Opening, Editing, and Saving Files

After you have found a file by navigating through the folders in Windows Explorer or My Computer, you can double-click the file to open it, and then you can modify it as desired. For example, you can edit the text in a document or change the colors in a picture. A file is associated with the program that is used to read it, so if you double-click a file that was created in Notepad, the Notepad program starts and displays the file. If Windows can't find the program associated with the file or if you want to use a program other than the associated one, use the Open With command (which is located on the shortcut menu that appears when you right-click a file).

All files have names, and all file names consist of two parts—the name and the extension—separated by a period. The type of file or the program in which it was created is indicated by the extension. The extension is a short (usually three letters, sometimes two or four) abbreviation of the file type.

By default, Windows XP hides file extensions, but you can turn on an option to see them if desired. Files also have icons, which are graphic representations of the file type. Depending on the way you're looking at your files, you might see a large icon, a small icon, or no icon.

Printing a File

You can print a file directly from Windows Explorer without first opening the file. This can be a great timesaver if you have several documents that don't need to be changed—just printed using the default print settings. To print from Windows Explorer, open the folder that contains the file you want to print, right-click the desired file, and then click Print on the shortcut menu. Windows will open the file using the program that created it, print the file, and then close the program and the file.

Sorting Files

As you work with larger numbers of files, you'll need to find the files you want quickly and efficiently. One way to find a file easily is to group folder contents by a certain characteristic, like date. Then if you know the date when you saved the file, you can find the file easily.

There are several ways to view files in Windows Explorer—as icons, in a list of file names, in a list with file details (such as when each file was last modified), or as file names with **thumbnails**. When you sort files, it's a good idea to display them in Details view. Details view lists each file on a line by itself, with columns for the name of the file, the amount of storage space it takes, the type of file it is, and the date when it was last saved. In Details view, you can click a column heading to sort files by that column.

Creating Files and Folders

Folders are easy to create in Windows Explorer, and there is no limit to the number you can have. So it's a good idea to think about the way you want to organize your folders. You might create a folder for each major project, or for each client, or for the months of the year—it depends on how you prefer to organize your storage space.

You can also create files in Windows Explorer. When you create files, you create a placeholder for a particular type of content, like a graphic or text file, by giving it a name. Then you fill in the content later. This process is the opposite of the more typical way to create files, which involves starting a program like Notepad, entering data, and then saving the data as a file. Creating a file in Windows Explorer has certain benefits over creating a file in a program. It's faster because you don't have to run the program, and it creates structure for the file by predetermining its name and the program that will be used to work with it.

Moving, Copying, and Renaming Files and Folders

Just like you occasionally need to reorganize the space in your closets and drawers, you'll find that you need to reorganize your files and folders. You might, for example, want to move files from their current folder to a new folder you've made, or copy a folder so that you have an original version of all its contents and a duplicate to experiment with. You might need to rename a file or folder to better reflect its contents.

You can move and copy files or folders using the Move To Folder and Copy To Folder commands on the Edit menu in Windows Explorer, or you can simply drag a file or folder from one place to another. If you drag a file or folder from place to place on the same disk, Windows moves the item. If you drag a file or folder from one disk to another disk, Windows copies the item. To be able to choose whether to copy or move a file or folder that you drag, right-click to drag it. When you release the mouse button to drop the item, a shortcut menu appears. On the shortcut menu, click either Copy Here or Move Here.

To rename a file or folder, right-click it, and click Rename on the shortcut menu. The name of the file is selected. Type the new name, and press Enter. The file is renamed.

Deleting Files and Folders

Although disk space has become remarkably inexpensive, it's still a finite quantity. Just like any other finite resource, it needs to be conserved by deleting unnecessary files and folders. Deleting a file or folder doesn't erase it from the disk the way an eraser removes pencil marks. It's more like tossing something into a junk drawer. Eventually, the drawer gets full, and you empty it out. Sometimes, things get tossed into the drawer by mistake, and you need to take them out and put them back where they belong.

In Windows, this "junk drawer" is called the Recycle Bin. To send a file or folder to the Recycle Bin, select the item, and press the Delete key on the keyboard. Click Yes to confirm the deletion. You can also send a file or folder to the Recycle Bin by clicking the file or folder to select it, then right-clicking, then clicking the Delete option on the shortcut menu. To view the contents of the Recycle Bin, double-click its icon on the desktop. To remove an item from the Recycle Bin and move it back to its original location on disk, click the item to select it, and then click the Restore this item option in the left side of the Recycle Bin window. To permanently delete an item in the bin, click the item, and then click the Delete option on the File menu. (You can also right-click the item and select Delete from the menu that appears.) Click Yes to confirm the deletion. To permanently delete everything in the bin, click the Empty the Recycle Bin option in the left side of the Recycle Bin window.

Using Windows on a Network

When computers are connected so that they can exchange information, they are networked. A computer network might be composed of hundreds of computers, or just two. The most common type of network is the local area network, or LAN, in which computers in a building or several buildings in close proximity (such as a university campus or an office complex) are connected using cables or phone lines. You can also connect to a network through a dial-up connection. With a dial-up connection, your computer uses phone lines to connect to a second computer, which is connected to the rest of the computers on the network using cables.

Using My Network Places

There are several ways to examine the contents of your network, but the most straightforward approach starts with the My Network Places icon on the desktop. My Network Places is a window that displays all resources—such as computers, hard disks, files, and folders—available to you on the network. When you open My Network Places, you see the Network Tasks pane on the left side of the window, and a list of network places on the right. In the Network Tasks pane you see options to:

- *Add a network place* Click the Add a network place task to start the Add Network Place Wizard. This wizard helps you to create new shortcuts to shared folders and resources on your network, Web, and FTP servers. If you don't have folders on a Web server already, the Add Network Place Wizard will help you create a new folder for storing your files online.
- *View network connections* Clicking this icon displays a list of all the locations connected to your computer on a network.
- *Set up a home or small office network* Clicking this option helps you set up or modify a network so you can share files, folders and devices, such as printers.
- *Computers near me* This option is displayed in My Network Places when your computer is in a **domain**. Click this icon to narrow your search to only those computers, printers, and resources that share a domain with your computer.
- *View workgroup computers* This task is displayed in My Network Places when your computer is in a **workgroup** and not in a domain. Click this icon to narrow your search to only those computers, printers, and resources that share a workgroup with your computer.

After you've clicked an icon, you can navigate between and within the computers and folders that appear, just as if they were on your own computer. However, depending on the access rights your network administrator has assigned to you, you might not be able to delete or change network files and folders as you can on your own computer.

Working with User Accounts in Windows XP Professional

If your computer is part of a network, your network administrator must set up a user account or accounts for the computer to be able to access the network. User accounts can be established during the setup process or at any time from Control Panel.

If you have administrative privileges, you can create **local computer** user accounts that allow other people to access your computer. Even if you aren't connected to a network, you might share a computer with other users. Each user needs a user name and a Windows password. For example, you might want to create a local user account for a friend so that he or she can log on to your computer to check e-mail. Each user account belongs to a **group** with **permissions** to perform certain operations on the computer. The most common groups are:

- *Administrators*, who have unrestricted access to the computer.
- *Power Users*, who have most administrative capabilities but with some restrictions.

- *Users and Guests*, who are restricted from making system-wide changes.
- *Backup Operator*, who can override security restrictions for the purpose of backing up or restoring files.

Other groups are available for support personnel, network administrators, and remote users. There are also special groups that might be created when a computer is upgraded from other versions of Windows to Windows XP Professional. And finally, anyone assigned to the Administrators group can create custom groups.

Working with User Accounts in Windows XP Non-Networked Computers

For computers not connected to a network, Windows XP Professional and Home Edition supports two levels of user privileges: computer administrator and limited. Users with computer administrator accounts have permission to do everything, including:

- Create, change, and delete accounts.
- Make system-wide changes.
- Install and remove programs.
- Access all files.

Users with limited accounts have permission to do things that affect only their own account, including:

- Change or remove their password.
- Change their user account picture.
- Change their theme and desktop settings.
- View files they created and files in the Shared Documents folder.

Each Windows XP Home Edition or non-networked Professional user account is represented on the logon screen by the user account name and also by a user account picture.

Accessing and Browsing the Internet

The Internet is a network made up of thousands of computers all over the world, connected by the same kinds of cables used by telephones and cable TV. The Internet is a technology, not a place or an organization. The Internet is not owned by a government, company, or individual. It continues to exist and evolve because its development is in the mutual best interest of computer users worldwide.

The World Wide Web (or simply the Web) is essentially a multimedia interface to the Internet. In the early days of the Internet, information was exchanged in text format only. Advances in hardware and software technology made it possible to add graphics, sound, and other multimedia capabilities to the Internet. Sites on the Internet that are capable of providing content in this multimedia format are called **Web sites**. Collectively, all of the Web sites around the world are called the Web. You can think of the Web as a multimedia extension of the Internet.

Today, most people access information on the Internet via the Web. As part of the Internet, the Web isn't a place; it's the collection of millions of files stored on Internet servers around the world. You access these Web sites using a Web **browser** such as Microsoft Internet Explorer. Two popular uses of the Internet are to find information on the Web and to exchange messages with other people through e-mail and newsgroups.

Connecting to the Internet

Setting up access to the Internet is easier than ever with Windows XP. The Internet community can be divided into three basic parts: end users (such as yourself), Internet service providers (ISPs), and the Internet backbone. As an end user, you connect to the Internet backbone through a modem, a DSL line, or an organization's network. Most networks connect computers that are in close proximity, such as those in a building or campus of buildings. These networks are called local area networks (LANs).

A modem converts computer signals into audio waves that can travel through phone lines. The waves travel through a phone line or another cable directly to your ISP's computer. This computer is called a server because it serves the requests of many users at a time. An ISP (Internet Service Provider) typically leases fiber-optic cables from a long-distance carrier. These cables can transmit large amounts of data quickly, and they form the Internet backbone. After you've connected to your ISP's server, you have access to all other Internet-connected computers around the world. An ISP can be a commercial service to which you subscribe, just like cable television, or it can be an organization that provides Internet access free to its employees or members over a local area network.

As an individual, you cannot connect your computer directly to the Internet; you must access the Internet through a computer or network of computers that acts as a go-between. To connect your computer to this go-between, you might use a local area network (LAN); a high-speed broadband connection such as cable, ISDN, or DSL; or a dial-up connection. Whichever type of connection you use, the Windows XP New Connection Wizard can help you with the necessary setup work.

Accessing Your Computer Remotely

If you travel a lot or often work at home, you don't necessarily have to take all your files and folders with you. Instead, you can work, via the Internet, on your own computer using **Remote Desktop**, a new Windows XP feature. To use Remote Desktop, both the computer you are currently working on and the one you want to access must be running Windows XP. You must have administrative permissions on the computer you want to be able to access remotely in order to turn on Remote Desktop.

Exploring the Web

A Web site is a collection of related files called **Web pages**, and it is operated by a particular person or organization. Most Web pages can be opened from **hyperlinks** within other pages. When you explore the Web, you can click hyperlinks (or simply links) that display different pages in the same Web site or you can click hyperlinks that take you to other sites on the Web. A hyperlink can be a word, a phrase, or even a picture.

When you connect to the Internet using Internet Explorer, the first page the browser displays is your home page. This page is the starting point for your Web discovery. If you installed software provided by your ISP, your ISP's Web site might be your home page.

From your home page, you display another page either by clicking a link to it or by typing its address. A **Web address** (also called a **URL**, which stands for Uniform Resource Locator) provides a way to locate a particular Web page, just like a street address provides a way to locate a particular house. If you know a Web page's address, you can display the page by typing its address in the Address bar, which is located below the Standard Buttons toolbar in the Internet Explorer window.

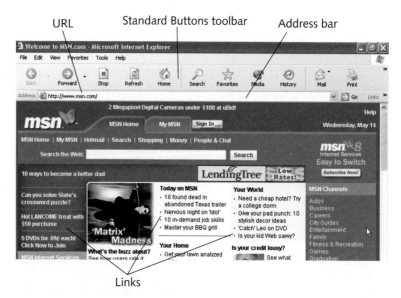

The page that you display probably has links of its own. You can click one of these links or type another address in the Address bar to display yet another page, which probably has its own links. This process of displaying Web page after Web page is called surfing the Web. As you surf, you can go back and forth between the pages you've visited by clicking the Back and Forward buttons on the Standard Buttons toolbar—this is like flipping through pages in a magazine. If you start to feel lost, you can display your home page by clicking the Home button on the Standard Buttons toolbar.

Finding Information on the Web

There might be times when you enjoy surfing the Web for its own sake, but there are probably other times when you want to find specific information on the Web as quickly as possible. If you know the type of information you're looking for but not which pages contain it, you can search for that information on the Web.

One method for finding information on the Web is to use a **search engine**. Search engines are programs that look for information on the Web based on the text that you specify. Although some search engines charge a fee to perform a search, most search engines are free. Many of the free search engines are comparable in quality; however, each engine has a slightly different user interface and provides different features. When you perform a search using Internet Explorer, it uses several search engines at once.

Keeping Track of Web Sites

You will probably find that you want to frequently revisit certain Web pages. Instead of typing a Web address or clicking a series of links each time you want to view a particular Web page, you can use Internet Explorer's Favorites or History lists to go directly to the page. The Favorites list is like the speed dial buttons on a telephone. When you add a Web page to the list, you can return to that page with a single click. The History list is like the redial button on a telephone, except instead of displaying the last page you've visited, it displays a list of all of the pages you've visited recently.

Subscribing to a Newsgroup

A **newsgroup** is like an Internet-based club. Instead of face-to-face meetings, discussions are carried on among members by sending e-mail messages to the group. Everyone else in the group can read and respond to these messages (although the Outlook Express newsreader also lets you respond only to the person who sent a message). Because newsgroups often have thousands of members, there are usually many different discussions, or **threads**, going on at the same time. A thread contains an original newsgroup message followed by all of the replies to that message.

You join a newsgroup by **subscribing** to it. Subscribing identifies you to the newsgroup and tells the newsgroup's administrator that you want to view its messages (also called posts). After you have subscribed, you can read and answer posts sent by other members of the group. If you have a question or topic that is not currently being discussed in the group, you can post a new thread.

Think of a newsgroup as a type of party. Everyone's in the same room, but various people are involved in different conversations. Each conversation comprises comments, replies, and opinions relating to a particular topic. These exchanges are like threads. In the Outlook Express newsreader, threads are marked by plus and minus symbols appearing next to the headers of the original messages. Clicking a plus symbol expands the thread so that you can see all of the replies. When you expand a thread, message replies are indented below the original message. Clicking a minus symbol collapses the thread.

Communicating with Others

Electronic mail (e-mail) is the most popular way to communicate and share information with others via computers. Microsoft Windows XP provides extensive e-mail capabilities, and it includes tools to help you exchange information by phone, by fax, or via the Internet.

You can send, receive, and organize **e-mail messages** in Microsoft Outlook Express. An e-mail message is any message sent from a computer to one or more other computers and transmitted as electronic impulses through a telephone line or other cable. An e-mail message can contain text (such as a memo or a letter), a picture, or a combination of both. E-mail messages can even include recorded sound or video clips. To keep track of your collection of e-mail addresses, telephone numbers, and fax numbers, you use the Address Book in Outlook Express.

Sending and Receiving E-Mail Messages with Outlook Express

E-mail provides people with an alternative to mailing documents through a post office or an overnight courier service. E-mail is inexpensive, it is easily accessible, and messages are received within minutes of being sent.

To send an e-mail message, you must know the recipient's **e-mail address**. An e-mail address is a unique identifier for a person on a network, just as a street address uniquely identifies a building's location in a particular city. If you send messages to others on your organization's network, the addresses follow the rules determined by your organization. When a person is hired, he or she is assigned an e-mail address. One typical approach is to use a person's first name and last initial as an e-mail address, such as *mariannek*.

If you send a message to someone outside of your organization, the message will be routed via the Internet to its destination. Therefore, the address will follow the rules set forth by InterNIC (the Department of Commerce organization that establishes Internet standards), such as *mariannek@example.com*. The example.com part of the address is called a **domain name**, which identifies the particular computer that *Mariannek's* Internet Service Provider (ISP) uses to manage her e-mail service.

Consider a letter that you send to a friend. You drop the letter into the nearest mailbox. From there, the letter is taken to the nearest post office, which in turn sends the letter to the nearest delivery post office. From there, a postal carrier delivers the letter to the recipient. E-mail travels in a similar fashion. An e-mail message must be routed from the sender's computer to his or her ISP's server, which in turn sends it to the recipient's ISP server (identified by *example.com*). The message resides on this server until the recipient (*mariannek*) checks her e-mail. She uses an e-mail program to connect her computer to her ISP's server so that she can retrieve her e-mail messages.

When you launch Outlook Express, the window you see will look something like the following figure. There are folders for your e-mail shown in the upper-left pane of the window, contact information is shown on the lower-left. The headers for the messages currently in the folder selected in the upper-left folders pane are displayed in the upper-right pane, and the text of the currently selected message is shown in the lower-right pane.

Folders list · Messages in selected folder · Unread message · Text of selected message

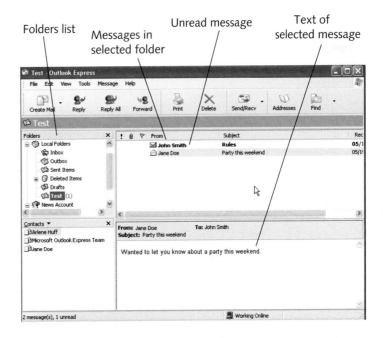

Keeping Track of Contacts

The **Address Book** in Outlook Express stores important information about your contacts. If you store e-mail addresses in the Address Book, you can insert them from the Address Book when creating messages, instead of having to type them manually. You can also store information in the Address Book that can be used by other programs. For example, a fax number you type in the Address Book can be used in the Send Fax Wizard.

Organizing Your Messages

When you receive mail that is delivered by the post office, you probably sort through it. Some of it you throw away, and the rest you might organize into categories: bills, catalogs, and personal letters, for instance. You can arrange your e-mail messages in Outlook Express in the same way.

In fact, Outlook Express can organize your incoming mail for you, if you set up **message rules**, which let you tell Outlook Express what to do with certain types of messages. You can use the message rules feature to automatically move all incoming messages from specific contacts into any folder located in the Outlook Express Folders List. You can organize the following types of messages in Outlook Express:

- From a sender or account you specify.
- With a subject line or message body that contains words you specify.
- To a recipient or recipients you specify.
- Marked with a priority level you specify.
- Bigger than, smaller than, or equal to a size you specify.
- With an attachment.
- With security features.

For any of the types of messages above, you can select the following actions for your rule:

- Move or copy the message to a folder you specify.
- Delete the message.
- Forward the message to a recipient or recipients you specify.
- Reply to the message.
- Highlight the message with color or a flag.
- Using the Message menu, mark the message as read, a watched conversation, or an ignored conversation.

If you specify Watch Conversation on the Message menu, Outlook Express marks this message with an eyeglass icon, and the message headers for all responses to this message appear in red. The recipients of a watched message will also see the text *This message is being Watched* near the top of the message window. If you specify Ignore Conversation, Outlook Express hides all responses to the message.

Searching for Files and Folders

Your computer uses and stores two types of files: **program files** and **document files**. A program file is used by a program, such as Microsoft Word or Microsoft Excel, to aid in performing a task; in most cases, you can't open or edit these files. A document file contains information that you can view and edit by using a program such as Word or Excel. Whenever you create a document, such as a letter, a memo, or a report, you're creating a document file. You also create document files when you create worksheets, databases, or other types of files. A document file, then, contains information that you or somebody else has compiled.

When you first install and use Microsoft Windows XP, hundreds of program files are copied to the hard disk so that you can use all of the features of Windows. Most of these files are dedicated to running Windows features, so they're not files that you open and edit. Over time, you might create dozens or perhaps hundreds of document files that you can open and edit. If you have installed Windows XP over a previous version of Windows, you might already have hundreds of document files stored in various folders on your hard disk. On a network, you could have access to thousands of document files created by others.

In any case, the more document files that are available to you, the more difficult it can become to find the file that you want to view or edit at any given time. If you're careful about organizing your files within folders, you can often find a file by opening a folder and looking through the list of file names in that folder. As the number of files and folders on your hard disk increases, however, so can the chance that you will forget in which folder or under what name you stored a particular file. Finding a file without knowing its name can be as tough as trying to find a building without knowing its address. If you're searching for a file on a network, you'll have even more difficulty unless you have a map, that is, unless you're familiar with other people's computers and the folder structures they have created.

You can search for all types of objects, including files, printers, and computers, using a new feature of Windows XP called **Search Companion**. You can search for files on your own computer, on other computers on your network, or even on the entire Internet. You can search for computers on your organization's network, and you can also search for people on your network or on the Internet.

Search Companion is user friendly and comes equipped with a guide, in the form of an animated screen character. The default character is Rover the dog, but you can change the character to Merlin the wizard, Courtney the tour guide, or Earl the surfer. If you want, you can remove the character entirely.

Included in Search Companion is **Indexing Service**, which indexes the files on your computer while your computer is idle, improving search speed. (Indexing creates a database of file names and contents so that Search Companion can search the database instead of having to search the files themselves.)

The Search Companion provides several ways to locate files. For instance, you can find a file even if you know only part of a file name or a few unique words that are in the file. You can also search for folders on your hard disk or on the network.

Searching for Files and Folders by Name

Sorting the contents of a folder can help you find a file in a folder that contains many other files. All you need to know is which folder contains the file you want and a distinguishing characteristic of the file, perhaps part of the file's name. However, if you know only a distinguishing characteristic but not which folder the file is in, you're better off using the Windows Search Companion. That way, you can easily search your entire hard disk and possibly the network to which your computer might be connected.

To display the Search Companion, open Windows Explorer or My Computer, and click the Search button on the Standard Buttons toolbar. The Search Companion appears in a pane in the left side of the window.

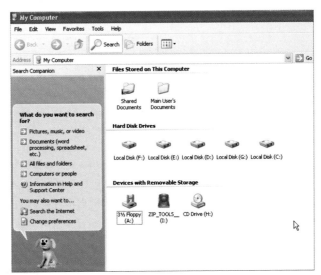

You can use the Search Companion to enter the name, or a partial name of a file that you want to find. You can instruct the Search Companion to search all drives, or a specific drive, or a folder and subfolders contained on some drive.

Searching for Files That Contain Specific Text

If you don't remember the name of a file that you want to locate, but you know that it contains certain identifying words, you can instruct the Search Companion to locate only those files that contain specific text. For instance, you might know that the file you want to locate contains the words *tennis lessons*, even though you can't remember the name of the file. In this case, you can use the Search Companion to search for all files that contain the text *tennis lessons* anywhere within the file's contents.

Searching for Files Using Other Criteria

You can also use the Search Companion to search for files that have certain **attributes**, which are identifiers that Windows stores as part of the properties for a file. Attributes include the date on which a file was created or last modified and the program in which the file was created.

For instance, you can search for all files that were created between September 1, 2004, and September 15, 2004, or you can search for all files that were created using Word. The Search Companion has several search options available. Clicking the arrows associated with each search option will display the sub-options that you can choose from to execute the search. The following figure shows the three specialized search options available in the Search Companion task pane, and the sub-options that you can choose from by clicking the arrow associated with the option.

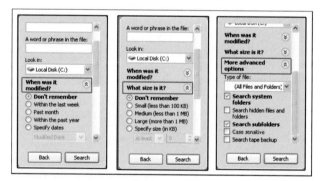

A few of the available search options include:

- The *When was it modified* category lets you search for files that were created or modified on a certain date or within a range of dates.
- The *What size is it* category lets you search for files of a particular size.
- The *More advanced options* category lets you search for files that were created using a specific program. Click the list arrow on the Type of file box and select the file type you want to find.

The *More advanced options* category displays additional options for refining your search. These options include letting you search for hidden files or folders, search sub-folders and search system folders. You can also perform searches that are case-sensitive, that is, you can specify which letters in the text you're looking for must be uppercase. In addition, you can search for files on a backup tape if desired.

Select the desired check boxes to display the options you want. By combining options, you can perform more sophisticated searches. For example, you could search for e-mail messages created in the last month that include the word *BUDGET* in uppercase letters.

Using the Indexing Service

When searching, the Search Companion searches all folders on the specified drive in alphabetical order by folder name and then by file name. You can speed up your searches by enabling the Indexing Service. If you enable this feature, Windows creates an index file that lists all files on all available resources. The index file stores the names and attributes of each file and folder.

After you perform a search, when the search results are shown in the right-hand side of the window, the Search Companion will display information about the search and additional options on the left side of the window. Clicking the Yes but make future searches faster link in the task pane on the left will cause a pane to appear on the right side of the window giving you the option of turning on the Indexing Service. If you do turn it on, you will not notice any obvious change at that moment, but from that point on, Indexing Service will be running on your computer.

If you have a large hard disk or a network connection, it might take an hour or longer to create the index. However, Windows will create the index only when your computer is not carrying out other requests. So creating the index will not slow down your computer when you are performing other tasks. After the index file is created, the Search Companion will use this file whenever you perform a search, rather than searching hard disks and other resources folder by folder. Searching the index file can be much faster than searching by folder, so enabling the Indexing Service is a good idea.

Accessing Your Entire Network

Windows Explorer gives you access not only to drives and resources on your own computer, but also to drives and resources across your entire network and the Internet through the My Network Places folder. To browse to another computer or resource on your network, open Windows Explorer in either Tasks view or Folders view, and click My Network Places.

If you want to access a particular network drive or resource on a regular basis—for example, if you regularly connect to a specific server—you can map the drive in Windows Explorer to make it more easily available. When you map a drive, you assign it a local drive letter so you can easily browse to it. You can also instruct Windows to reconnect to that drive every time you log on.

Customizing Your Desktop

As you use Microsoft Windows XP more and more, you will probably develop personal preferences for the way in which your desktop is set up, and the way in which some Windows features function. You might want your desktop icons to be arranged in a particular way, for instance, or you might want certain options to appear on the Start menu. You might want to change the way your mouse works. You can even make the Windows environment more comfortable and attractive by changing the appearance and functionality of the desktop, the taskbar, the Start menu, and the mouse.

Creating Shortcut Icons on the Desktop

As you continue to work with Windows, you'll find yourself using certain programs, folders, devices, or documents over and over again. Accessing these items can become time-consuming if you constantly have to navigate through multiple menus or folders to reach them. Customizing the Start menu addresses this problem to a certain extent by hiding menu items you rarely use and "pinning" programs you use frequently. However, the fastest and easiest way to access a program, folder, file, or device is to create a shortcut icon to it on the desktop.

A shortcut icon represents a folder, file, or program; double-clicking a shortcut icon opens a window for that folder, file, or program. Shortcut icons can be placed in any folder on your hard disk, but the most common place you find shortcut icons is on your desktop. In fact, when Windows is installed, it adds several shortcut icons to your desktop so that you can easily start programs by double-clicking the shortcut icons. You can add shortcut icons to the desktop yourself, and you can use shortcut icons to help new Windows users feel less intimidated.

Arranging Icons on the Desktop

In Windows XP, you can right-click a blank area on the desktop to display a shortcut menu that includes ways to organize icons. Once you have used Windows for awhile and added several more icons to the desktop, you might want to do more than align them; for instance, you might want to reorganize the desktop. You can use the options on the Arrange Icons menu to reorganize your desktop icons.

If you no longer need a particular shortcut icon, simply drag it to the Recycle Bin. This procedure deletes the shortcut icon from the desktop; it does not delete the file, folder, program, or device that the icon represented.

Changing the Appearance of the Desktop

You can customize the desktop in many ways besides arranging the icons on it. For example, you can change the color scheme of the Windows components, and you can select a background picture (also called wallpaper) to appear on the desktop. Changing the color scheme sometimes has a purpose beyond simply making the screen more attractive. Color schemes labeled *high contrast*, *large*, and *extra large* can make the display easier to see for people with visual impairments.

Applying a Screen Saver

Originally, screen savers prevented a problem with monitors called burn-in. Burn-in is the "ghost" of an image that has appeared on a screen for too long. In effect, the image became permanently etched into the phosphor of the computer screen. The result was like trying to look "through" one image in order to see another—making the monitor ineffective. A **screen saver** solves the burn-in problem by displaying an animated image on the screen after the computer has remained idle for a specified interval. Modern manufacturing has eliminated the possibility of burn-in for most monitors, but screen savers continue to be popular.

Cleaning Up Your Desktop

A new feature in Windows XP is the **Desktop Cleanup Wizard**. The Desktop Cleanup Wizard helps you clean up your desktop by moving rarely used shortcuts to a desktop folder called *Unused Desktop Shortcuts*. The **Unused Desktop Shortcuts** folder is a temporary holding area for the shortcuts you are not using. You can restore shortcuts from this folder to your desktop, or you can delete the entire folder.

Changing Mouse Properties

A computer mouse is like a car: all models have the same basic functions, but each is designed differently, and it takes a little time to get accustomed to a new one. Unlike a car, though, you can enhance a mouse's performance easily—and without getting any grease on your hands! To customize a mouse, use the Mouse Properties dialog box, which you can open from the Control Panel.

Working with the Start Menu

The Start menu is a list of options that is your central link to all the programs installed on your computer, as well as to all the tasks you can carry out with Windows XP. The first time you start Windows XP, the Start menu is displayed until you click something else. Thereafter, you open the Start menu by clicking the Start button at the left end of the taskbar.

The Start menu has been significantly redesigned in Windows XP to provide easier access to your programs. You can pin links to your favorite programs to a special area at the top of the left side of the Start menu to make the programs easy to find and start. You can rearrange the pinned programs by dragging them into whatever order you want. By default, Microsoft Internet Explorer and Microsoft Outlook Express are pinned to the Start menu. If you change your default Web browser or e-mail program, the pinned area is automatically updated to reflect that change.

Below the first horizontal line on the left side of the Start menu is a list of links to your most frequently used programs, which includes the last six programs you started. (You can adjust that number if you want.) On the right side of the Start menu are links to the locations where you are most likely to store the files you create, a link to a directory of other computers on your network, and links to various tools that you will use while running your computer. The commands you will use to log off of or shut down your computer are located at the bottom of the Start menu.

Customizing and Using the Taskbar

The **taskbar** is your link to current information about what is happening on your Windows XP computer. In addition to the Start button, the taskbar displays a button for each open program. You click a taskbar button to activate the window of the program it represents. The taskbar buttons are resized depending on the number of programs that are currently open, and they disappear when you close the programs they represent.

If you start the same program more than once so that several instances of the program are open at the same time (for example, three instances of Internet Explorer, or two Microsoft Word documents), and the taskbar is becoming crowded, similar windows are grouped onto one button that is labeled with the name of the program. A number following the program icon on the button indicates the number of open windows represented by the button. You can click the button to display a pop-up list of the open windows and then click the one you want to activate. This new feature makes it easier to work with your open windows.

By default, the taskbar displays one row of buttons and is docked at the bottom of the desktop, but you can control its size and position:

- You can dock the taskbar at the top, bottom, or on either side of the desktop.
- When the taskbar is docked at the top or bottom, you can expand the taskbar to be up to half the height of your screen by dragging its border up or down.
- When the taskbar is docked on the left or right, you can adjust its width from nothing (only the border is visible) to up to half the width of your screen.
- You can stipulate that the taskbar should be hidden when you're not using it, or that it should always stay on top of other windows so that it is not accidentally hidden.
- You can lock the taskbar to prevent it from being changed.

Windows XP taskbar buttons change size so that they fit on the taskbar as programs are opened and closed. The maximum number of buttons that can fit on the taskbar varies based on your monitor and display settings. When you exceed the maximum, Windows either tiles the buttons or displays a scroll bar, depending on the current taskbar configuration.

The notification area is located at the right end of the horizontal taskbar or at the bottom of the vertical taskbar. By default, the notification area displays the current time. Icons appear temporarily in the notification area when activities such as the following take place:

- The printer icon appears when you send a document to the printer.
- A message icon appears when you receive new e-mail messages.
- The Windows Automatic Update icon appears to remind you to look online for updates to the operating system.

- Information icons appear to give you information about various program features.
- Network connections and Microsoft Windows Messenger icons appear when those features are in use. (Inactive connections are indicated by the presence of a red X on the icon.)

In addition to the items that are visible by default, the taskbar can also display its own set of toolbars. The most frequently used of these is the **Quick Launch toolbar,** which displays single-click links to programs and commands. (This toolbar is hidden by default.) Windows XP installs links to Microsoft Internet Explorer, Microsoft Windows Media Player, and the Show Desktop command on the Quick Launch toolbar. You can add more program shortcuts to the Quick Launch toolbar at any time by dragging a program or shortcut icon onto it.

Index

A

A3 Paper, A4 Paper, B4 Paper, B5 Paper, 649
Absolute reference, 397-398
Access
    introduction to, 773-774
    moving around in, 778-783
    starting, 774-777
    See also Databases
Access form, 780
Access user interface, 775
Accounting format, 261
Active cell, 234
Add to Contacts button, 497
Add To Dictionary button, 133
Addition, 390
Address Book
    to send document, 506
    to send e-mail, 496-499
Address Cards view, 466, 482
Align Right button, 703
Alignment, 105
    cell contents, 269-272
    in document, 60-62
    on slides, 701-703
    vertical, 103
    in WordArt, 180
Alphabetic order, sorting by, 849
Animation
    chart objects, 760-762
    Motion Paths, 755, 758, 760
    Office Assistant, 430-432
    slide objects, 758-760
    slides, 752-762
Animation effects, custom, applying, to text, 755-758
Animation Order list, 758-760
Animation Scheme, applying, 753-755
Apply Filter button, 852
Appointment(s)
    deleting, 530-531
    editing, 528-530
    recurring, 523-525
    scheduling, 518-523
    versus events, 523
    versus meeting, 512

Appointment(s), organizing
    by arrangements, 533-536
    by categories, 531-533
Appointment Area, 513
Area chart, 193, 362
Argument list, 400
Arrangements
    for viewing e-mail messages, 448-450
    organizing appointments by, 533-536
Arrow keys, 34
Arrows
    adding, to charts, 379-382
    as scroll tools, 36
Ascending order, 353
Ask a Question box, 22-23
    Excel, 234
    Word, 8, 22-23
Assign Task button, 571-572
Asterisk (*), as wildcard, 880, 884
Attachments
    opening, from Reading pane, 452-453
    sending message with, 443-446
Attachments arrangement, 449-450
Attribute, 54, 311, 313
Auto Fill, 397
AutoComplete, 411
AutoContent Wizard, 593-595
AutoCorrect, 153-158, 707-710, 712
AutoCorrect button, for spelling check, 133
AutoCorrect dialog box, 154, 708
AutoCorrect Exceptions dialog box, 155, 157
AutoFilter, 355-357
AutoFilter dialog box, Top 10, 357
AutoFit, 707, 709-710
AutoFormat, 309-311
AutoFormat dialog box, 310
AutoJoin, 894
AutoNumber, 811-812
AutoNumbering, 698
AutoPreview, 448
AutoRecover, 608
AutoShape, 167, 185-190

U

ADDENDUM TO THE END USER LICENSE AGREEMENT FOR MICROSOFT SOFTWARE

MICROSOFT OFFICE PROFESSIONAL EDITION 2003 AND MICROSOFT OFFICE ACCESS 2003

This Addendum to the End User License Agreement ("EULA") for Microsoft Software ("Amendment") amends and supplements the terms of the EULA for Microsoft Office Professional Edition 2003 and Microsoft Office Access 2003 software (the "software"), and is between Microsoft Corporation (or based on where you live, one of its affiliates) and you. This Addendum applies to each validly licensed copy of the software.

By using any portion of the software, you accept these terms. If you do not accept them, do not use the software and return it for a full refund, if applicable.

The following describes additional terms for use of the software. If there is a conflict with the terms of the EULA, these additional terms supersede the terms of the EULA to the extent of any inconsistency:

NO SEPARATION OF SOFTWARE. In order to be validly licensed to use the software and otherwise exercise your rights under Section 1 of the EULA you must install all discs contained in this package or that accompany this Addendum. If you do not install all such discs, you are not licensed to use the software and may not install or use any portion of the software.

Part number: X12-07708

System Requirements

Your computer system must meet the following minimum requirements for you to install the practice files from the CD-ROM included with this book and to run Microsoft Office 2003.

- A personal computer running Microsoft Office 2003 on a Pentium 233-megahertz (MHz) or higher processor.
- Microsoft Windows® 2000 with Service Pack 3 (SP3), Windows XP, or later.
- 128 MB of RAM or greater.
- At least 2 MB of available disk space (after installing Microsoft Office 2003).
- A CD-ROM or DVD drive.
- A monitor with Super VGA (800 X 600) or higher resolution with 256 colors.
- A Microsoft mouse, a Microsoft IntelliMouse, or other compatible pointing device.